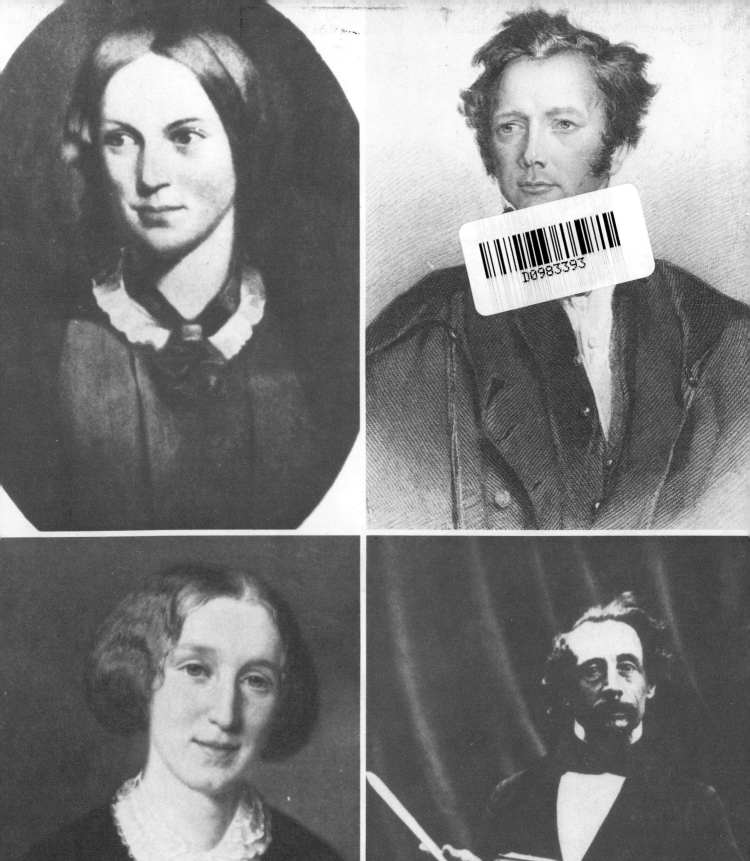

154255

Dictionary of Literary Biography • Volume Twenty-one

Victorian Novelists
Before 1885

Dictionary of Literary Biography

1: *The American Renaissance in New England,* edited by Joel Myerson (1978)

2: *American Novelists Since World War II,* edited by Jeffrey Helterman and Richard Layman (1978)

3: *Antebellum Writers in New York and the South,* edited by Joel Myerson (1979)

4: *American Writers in Paris, 1920-1939,* edited by Karen Lane Rood (1980)

5: *American Poets Since World War II,* 2 volumes, edited by Donald J. Greiner (1980)

6: *American Novelists Since World War II,* Second Series, edited by James E. Kibler, Jr. (1980)

7: *Twentieth-Century American Dramatists,* 2 volumes, edited by John MacNicholas (1981)

8: *Twentieth-Century American Science-Fiction Writers,* 2 volumes, edited by David Cowart and Thomas L. Wymer (1981)

9: *American Novelists, 1910-1945,* 3 volumes, edited by James J. Martine (1981)

10: *Modern British Dramatists, 1900-1945,* 2 volumes, edited by Stanley Weintraub (1982)

11: *American Humorists, 1800-1950,* 2 volumes, edited by Stanley Trachtenberg (1982)

12: *American Realists and Naturalists,* edited by Donald Pizer and Earl N. Harbert (1982)

13: *British Dramatists Since World War II,* 2 volumes, edited by Stanley Weintraub (1982)

14: *British Novelists Since 1960,* 2 volumes, edited by Jay L. Halio (1983)

15: *British Novelists, 1930-1959,* 2 volumes, edited by Bernard Oldsey (1983)

16: *The Beats: Literary Bohemians in Postwar America,* 2 volumes, edited by Ann Charters (1983)

17: *Twentieth-Century American Historians,* edited by Clyde N. Wilson (1983)

18: *Victorian Novelists After 1885,* edited by Ira B. Nadel and William E. Fredeman (1983)

19: *British Poets, 1880-1914,* edited by Donald E. Stanford (1983)

20: *British Poets, 1914-1945,* edited by Donald E. Stanford (1983)

21: *Victorian Novelists Before 1885,* edited by Ira B. Nadel and William E. Fredeman (1983)

Yearbook: 1980, edited by Karen L. Rood, Jean W. Ross, and Richard Ziegfeld (1981)

Yearbook: 1981, edited by Karen L. Rood, Jean W. Ross, and Richard Ziegfeld (1982)

Yearbook: 1982, edited by Richard Ziegfeld; associate editors: Jean W. Ross and Lynne C. Zeigler (1983)

Documentary Series, volume 1, edited by Margaret A. Van Antwerp (1982)

Documentary Series, volume 2, edited by Margaret A. Van Antwerp (1982)

Documentary Series, volume 3, edited by Mary Bruccoli (1983)

Dictionary of Literary Biography • Volume Twenty-one

Victorian Novelists
Before 1885

Edited by
Ira B. Nadel
University of British Columbia
and
William E. Fredeman
University of British Columbia

A Bruccoli Clark Book
Gale Research Company • Book Tower • Detroit, Michigan 48226
1983

Advisory Board for
DICTIONARY OF LITERARY BIOGRAPHY

Louis S. Auchincloss
John Baker
D. Philip Baker
A. Walton Litz, Jr.
Peter S. Prescott
Lola L. Szladits
William Targ

Matthew J. Bruccoli and Richard Layman, *Editorial Directors*
C. E. Frazer Clark, Jr., *Managing Editor*

Manufactured by Edwards Brothers, Inc.
Ann Arbor, Michigan
Printed in the United States of America

Copyright © 1983
GALE RESEARCH COMPANY

Library of Congress Cataloging in Publication Data
Main entry under title:

Victorian novelists before 1885.

(Dictionary of literary biography; v. 21)
"A Bruccoli Clark book."
Includes index.
1. English fiction—19th century—Bio-bibliography.
2. English fiction—19th century—History and criticism.
3. Novelists, English—19th century—Biography.
I. Fredeman, William E. (William Evan), 1928-
II. Nadel, Ira Bruce. III. Series.
PR871.V55   1983   823'.8'09 [B]   83-8848
ISBN 0-8103-1701-X

Contents

Contents

Foreword

The popularity of the Victorian novel, paralleling the emergence of a new readership, a new form of reading, and a recognition of the social value of fiction, is amply evident in the thirty entries in this volume devoted to the Victorian novelists before 1885. A survey of such a wide and varied group of writers, from major figures such as Dickens and Thackeray to lesser novelists such as Mrs. Ewing and G. W. M. Reynolds, underscores the presence of several common themes. Perhaps the most important of these is the increasing concern with literacy in the Victorian period, which in turn created a larger audience for fiction.

From the outset, public education prominently emphasized the teaching of reading as an absolute essential in an age of commerce and industry. While major support for universal education would not come until well into the 1870s, Parliament, in the first Reform Bill of 1832, allocated limited funds for public education; and, although few children spent more than one or two years in school, the teaching of reading dominated the curriculum in the early classrooms. By 1867, with the second Reform Bill, a new urgency to improve the literacy of the nation developed along with a determination to go beyond the Bible as the principal reading text. Although Matthew Arnold, as late as 1860, was highly critical in his school inspector's reports of the methods employed in the teaching of reading, eleven years later English literature was introduced into the curriculum, and by 1880 it had become one of the most popular school subjects. Despite a highly suspect 1851 census figure revealing a literacy rate of sixty percent for men and fifty-five percent for women, by 1870 the literacy rate had risen dramatically, creating an audience eager for popular works of fiction.

Accompanying this growth in literacy, and to satisfy the popular demand for fiction, the circulating libraries, in concert with publishers, evolved that quintessential form of the Victorian novel, the triple-decker—a three-volume edition, usually in postoctavo format, with approximately 325 pages per volume, selling at the fixed (and exorbitant) price of thirty-one shillings and six pence—a sum well beyond the means of the average novel reader. Mudie's Select Library, located first in Southampton Row and later in New Oxford Street, was the largest and most influential of the circulating libraries. For a subscription of a guinea a year, members could borrow an unrestricted number of titles, one volume at a time; often families would have multiple subscriptions to enable them to take out several volumes simultaneously. These libraries gave readers access to an incredibly rich collection of materials, for Mudie's, in its heyday, purchased annually more than 120,000 volumes. To encourage maximum profits, Mudie favored the triple-decker and worked closely with publishers to insure a steady flow of three-volume novels: from Richard Bentley alone, Mudie often acquired as many as 120 new titles a year. Inevitably, Mudie and his principal competitor, W. H. Smith, by the works they agreed to stock, subtly shaped the literary taste of Victorian readers, imposing middle-class values on both the composition and reception of popular fiction. Their domination of the field led to de facto censorship and to controversies with publishers, who could suffer enormous losses if their titles were excluded by the lending libraries. Some excellent works doubtless never reached print owing to the pressures put on publishers by Mudie and Smith, and there are many documented instances of publishers' readers forcing a new novelist to tailor his work to a formula that would be acceptable. A case in point is Oliver Madox Brown's "The Black Swan," which at the urging of William Smith Williams, the reader for Smith, Elder, was so radically revised that the published version, *Gabriel Denver* (1873), is no more than an anemic parody of the author's original work. However, the triple-decker did not go wholly unchallenged: part-publications, cheap reprints, and magazine serializations all competed for a significant share of the large potential readership.

While the publishing of novels in parts provided perhaps the most serious threat to the triple-decker, it also played the major role in the emergence of another important innovation in Victorian fiction: the advent of the illustrated novel, in which *The Pickwick Papers* (1836-1837) plays so prestigious a role. Intended from its inception to be published in illustrated monthly parts selling for a shilling, which would later be consolidated and published as a separate volume, *The Pickwick Papers* was the brainchild of the illustrator Robert Seymour. Seymour's publisher, Chapman and Hall, after approaching several writers who declined the assignment, commissioned Dickens, then known only by his pseudonym of "Boz," to provide a modest letterpress as a companion to the four drawings which Seymour would provide for each number. The suicide of the artist after the appearance of the first number on 31 March 1836 proved to be one of the most fortuitous events in the history of Victorian fiction. Not only did the tragedy eventuate in Dickens's producing an enlarged prose narrative which became the springboard for his brilliant career and in the long and fruitful collaboration between the novelist and the illustrator Hablôt Knight Browne ("Phiz"), it also established a fashion for illustrated fiction that would persist throughout the century.

A number of recent studies—by John H. Harvey, N. John Hall, and John Buchanan-Brown—have examined illustrations for the Victorian novel, and the illustrators of the 1860s, when new technologies revolutionized the whole art of illustration, have been thoroughly surveyed in the classic monographs of Gleeson White and Forrest Reid. Notice should be taken here, however, of the impact that the fashion for illustrated fiction, following on the tradition launched by *The Pickwick Papers*, had on the novelists themselves. Two points are of singular importance: first, that illustrations had a palpable effect on the form of fiction, involving both the format of publication, especially in serialization, and the aesthetics of the novel as artifact; and, second, that the close liaisons that developed between individual novelists and particular illustrators—Dickens and Browne, Trollope and John Everett Millais, George MacDonald and Arthur Hughes (Thackeray is sui generis in having illustrated his own novels)—amounted in many cases to virtual collaboration, in which author and artist sought to meld text and image, at their best intensifying the reciprocal verbal and visual meanings of both the novel and the illustrations: a phenomenon which has textual as well as critical implications. But the illustrated novel also had commercial and cultural appeal. Readers not only more readily purchased illustrated fiction, thereby increasing sales and profits; they appear also to have sought in the visual interpretations of the illustrations confirmation of their own reading experiences.

Publishing in monthly parts had several advantages for both publishers and writers. The former could substantially reduce the risks of publication since they could vary the number printed in relation to sales, generate income from more advertisers and thereby spread their costs, and increase public interest through the device of suspended action; authors benefited by receiving on-going payment for their work while it was still in progress. By the 1860s magazine serialization began seriously to undermine publication in parts, since readers, for the same outlay, could obtain their monthly illustrated installment of the novel and at the same time enjoy the diversified contents of the periodical. As popular as these two alternative methods of publication were, however, they did not, until much later, offer serious competition to the triple-decker, which retained its popularity due to the demand for fiction in book-length and complete form. But by 1885, the supremacy of both the triple-decker and the lending libraries would be openly challenged: by authors seeking to undermine the high price and limited sales of the triple-decker and the monopolistic interference of the proprietors of the lending libraries; by publishers eager to escape the yoke of Mudie and his competitors and to regain their business autonomy; and by readers demanding access to cheap copies of their favorite novelists. (See the Foreword to *DLB 18, Victorian Novelists After 1885*.)

How and by whom fiction was read naturally influenced the growth and development of the novel during the Victorian period. But, equally, what may be called the politics of the novel was a determining force in shaping the genre and making it suitable for "prime time" entertainment, appropriate for consumption in the family environment. Publishers tended to seek out and be attracted to writers who could and would meet the prescriptions of the triple-decker (or one of the serialized formats) and the proscriptions of the lending libraries; and often writers were encouraged by significant financial incentives to shape their work to the demands of the medium—to expand it, say, from two to three volumes; to alter or elaborate a scene or an ending to give the work wider appeal; perhaps even to extend the role of a character who had won favor with the reading public.

Concomitant with these technological, aesthetic, moral, and commercial forces that were shaping the novel was a social one that gave new significance and value to the reading of fiction. Perhaps not quite by mid-century, but certainly within the next two decades, the novel had become respectable; no longer was it considered frivolous, harmful, or distracting because it encouraged the fancy. Because its subject matter dealt increasingly, and more realistically, with social and political issues and with characters from everyday life, the novel assumed a seriousness that it had not enjoyed during the period of the Silver Fork School, whose novelists—Frances Trollope, Lady Blessington, and the early Bulwer-Lytton—explored the lives and manners of fashionable and sophisticated men and women removed from the realities of familiar life. Problematic contemporary issues started to become commonplace: education in Dickens's *Hard Times* (1854); social reform in Disraeli's *Sybil* (1845); the condition of the working classes in Mrs. Gaskell's *Mary Barton* (1848); the status of institutions such as the church in Trollope's *Barchester Towers* (1857); the nature of science and medicine in George Eliot's *Middlemarch* (1871-1872). Marriage and love tended to replace romance and sentiment. A new realism, social in origin and individual in focus, began—not, it should be noted, without protest—to characterize Victorian fiction; and with it came a new social consciousness on the part of the novelist. Dickens describes the situation in the preface to *Oliver Twist* (1838): "What manner of life is that which is described in these pages, as the everyday existence of a Thief? What charms has it for the young and ill-disposed, what allurements for the most jolter-headed of juveniles? Here are no canterings on moonlit heaths, no merry-makings in the snuggest of all possible caverns, none of the attractions of dress, no embroidery, no lace, no jack-boots, no crimson coat and ruffles, none of the dash and freedom with which 'the road' has been, time out of mind, invested. The cold, wet, shelterless midnight streets of London; the foul and frowsy dens, where vice is closely packed and lacks the room to turn; the haunts of hunger and disease, the shabby rags that scarcely hold together; where are the attractions of these things? Have they no lesson, and do they not whisper something beyond the little-regarded warning of an abstract moral precept?"

This is the "Condition of the People," as Disraeli labels it in his advertisement to *Sybil: or, The Two Nations*, a subject that dominates so much later Victorian fiction. To many readers, these accounts of the other nation of the poor were as alien as reports from travelers to the strange and unexplored wildernesses of darkest Africa. Instead of a fiction providing the reading public with glimpses of a genteel world that confirmed the social fantasies of romantic illusion, novelists such as Dickens became the moral spokesmen against urban decay, social injustice, and political abuse. Could a heroine from Birmingham become involved with a surgeon?, Harriet Martineau asked when reviewing the history of her novel *Deerbrook* (1839) in her *Autobiography* (1877). Readers in 1839 had difficulty accepting such a match, but, slowly, that too changed.

Satire and the handling of setting and time

also gradually began to expand the experiential world of the novel. Thackeray's *Vanity Fair* (1847-1848), with its critique of the aristocracy, its use of multiple settings in Brussels, London, and Paris, and its preoccupation with historical events, offers an early example. But other novelists and novels explored equally unfamiliar terrains and topics: radical politics in Charles Kingsley's *Alton Locke* (1850); the world of Parliament in Trollope's Palliser series; the life of the Victorian dandy in Laurence Oliphant's *Picadilly* (1870). Unlike the romantic fiction of the past, the Victorian novel provided not a distraction from the world it encompassed but an engagement with it that was at once exact and adventurous, original and realistic . . . and, perhaps most significant of all, characterized by that same prodigality that identifies most things Victorian.

Although the matter is covered in the foreword to *Victorian Novelists After 1885*, some explanation should be given in this volume of the editorial decision to distribute the entries on the Victorian novelists between two volumes, an expedient necessitated by the sheer quantity of the material. A simple alphabetical division was initially proposed, but it would have created a practical and critically unacceptable imbalance in the volumes. Other possibilities were explored, but there proved to be no single event during the period and no individual publication that was sufficiently pivotal to provide an adequate rationale for dividing the novelists included; neither was there any critical landmark, such as Buchanan's *The Fleshly School of Poetry* (1872) might be for the poetry, that could be construed as a fork in the chronological highway of Victorian fiction. Publishing history did, however, offer one useful, if admittedly somewhat arbitrary, demarcation, in the year 1885, which, with the publication of George Moore's *Literature at Nurse* (printed in the Appendix to *Victorian Novelists After 1885*) marks a distinct transition between the traditional three-volume and the modern one-volume format of the Victorian novel. This volume, thus, contains biographical entries on Victorian novelists who published most of their work in triple-deckers and who died before the year 1885; the companion volume includes writers who lived past this date and who saw one or more of their novels appear as single volumes. Obviously, there are exceptions, such as Oliver Madox Brown, who died in 1874 and whose sole novel was published in one volume; but in these cases, the date of death takes precedence in assigning the novelist to one or the other volume. Regardless of its form of publication, and as important as that aspect of the novel during the period has been shown to be, what ultimately remains remarkable about the fiction of the Victorian age is its variety, its extensiveness, and its extraordinary and continued appeal to modern readers. As Trollope triumphantly remarked, by 1870 the English had become "a novel-reading people from the Prime Minister down to the last appointed scullery-maid."

These volumes on the Victorian novelists before and after 1885 offer biographical access to the leading figures in what amounts to the last major revolution in reading in English literary history.

The editors would like to extend their thanks to all of the contributors and to the editorial staff of the *DLB* for their combined efforts in bringing this project to fruition.

–Ira B. Nadel and
William E. Fredeman

Acknowledgments

This book was produced by BC Research. Karen L. Rood is senior editor for the *Dictionary of Literary Biography* series. Philip B. Dematteis was the in-house editor.

The production coordinator is Lynne C. Zeigler. Art supervisor is Robin A. Sumner. Cynthia D. Lybrand is typesetting supervisor. The production staff included Angela Bardin, Mary Betts, Patricia Coate, Lynn Felder, Joyce Fowler, Nancy H. Lindsay, Laura Ingram, Sharon K. Kirkland, Alice A. Parsons, Walter W. Ross, Joycelyn R. Smith, Debra D. Straw, and Meredith Walker. Joseph Caldwell is photography editor. Jean W. Ross is permissions editor. Mary Bruccoli and Charles L. Wentworth did the photographic copy work.

Valuable assistance was given by the staff at the Thomas Cooper Library of the University of South Carolina: Michael Freeman, Gary Geer, Alexander M. Gilchrist, W. Michael Havener, David Lincove, Roger Mortimer, Donna Nance, Harriet B. Oglesbee, Elizabeth Pugh, Jean Rhyne, Paula Swope, Jane Thesing, and Ellen Tillett.

Professor Daniel Schwarz wishes to express his gratitude to the American Philosophical Society, whose grant enabled him to travel to England to investigate a recently discovered pseudonymous work by Disraeli.

Dictionary of Literary Biography • Volume Twenty-one

Victorian Novelists Before 1885

Dictionary of Literary Biography

William Harrison Ainsworth
(4 February 1805-3 January 1882)

Patrick Kelly
University of Saskatchewan

SELECTED BOOKS: *Poems by Cheviot Tichburn* (London: Arliss, 1822);

December Tales (London: Whittaker, 1823);

Letters from Cockney Lands, as Will Brown (London: Ebers, 1826);

Sir John Chiverton: A Romance, anonymous, by Ainsworth and J. P. Aston (London: Ebers, 1826);

Rookwood: A Romance (3 volumes, London: Bentley, 1834; 2 volumes, Philadelphia: Carey, Lea & Blanchard, 1834);

Crichton (3 volumes, London: Bentley, 1837; 2 volumes, New York: Harper, 1837);

Jack Sheppard: A Romance (3 volumes, London: Bentley, 1839; 2 volumes, Philadelphia: Lea & Blanchard, 1839);

The Tower of London: A Historical Romance (13 monthly parts, London: Bentley, 1840; 1 volume, Philadelphia: Lea & Blanchard, 1841);

Guy Fawkes; or, the Gunpowder Treason: An Historical Romance (3 volumes, London: Bentley, 1841; 1 volume, Philadelphia: Lea & Blanchard, 1841);

Old Saint Paul's: A Tale of the Plague and the Fire (12 monthly parts, London: Cunningham, 1841);

The Miser's Daughter: A Tale (3 volumes, London: Cunningham & Mortimer, 1842);

Windsor Castle: An Historical Romance (3 volumes, London: Colburn, 1843);

Saint James's; or, the Court of Queen Anne: An Historical Romance (3 volumes, London: Mortimer, 1844; 1 volume, New York: Colyer, 1844);

James the Second; or, the Revolution of 1688: An Historical Romance (3 volumes, London: Colburn, 1848);

(portrait by Daniel Maclise)

3

The Lancashire Witches: A Romance of Pendle Forest (3 volumes, London: Colburn, 1849; 1 volume, New York: Stringer & Townsend, 1849);

The Life and Adventures of Mervyn Clitheroe (Parts 1-4, London: Chapman & Hall, 1851-1852; parts 5-12, London: Routledge, 1857-1858; 1 volume, London & New York: Routledge, 1858);

The Star Chamber: An Historical Romance (2 volumes, London: Routledge, 1854; 1 volume, New York: Routledge, 1873);

The Flitch of Bacon; or, The Custom of Dunmow (London & New York: Routledge, 1854);

Ballads: Romantic, Fantastical and Humorous (London & New York: Routledge, 1855);

The Spendthrift: A Tale (London & New York: Routledge, 1857);

The Combat of the Thirty, from a Breton Lay of the Fourteenth Century (London: Chapman & Hall, 1859);

Ovingdean Grange: A Tale of the South Downs (London: Routledge, 1860);

The Constable of the Tower: An Historical Romance (3 volumes, London: Chapman & Hall, 1861);

The Lord Mayor of London; or, City Life in the Last Century (3 volumes, London: Chapman & Hall, 1862);

Cardinal Pole; or, the Days of Philip and Mary: An Historical Romance (3 volumes, London: Chapman & Hall, 1863);

John Law the Projector (3 volumes, London: Chapman & Hall, 1864);

The Spanish Match; or, Charles Stuart at Madrid (3 volumes, London: Chapman & Hall, 1865);

Auriol; or, The Elixir of Life (London: Routledge, 1865);

The Constable de Bourbon (3 volumes, London: Chapman & Hall, 1866);

Old Court: A Novel (3 volumes, London: Chapman & Hall, 1867);

Myddleton Pomfret: A Novel (3 volumes, London: Chapman & Hall, 1868);

Hilary St. Ives: A Novel (3 volumes, London: Chapman & Hall, 1870);

Talbot Harland (London: Dicks, 1871);

Boscobel; or, the Royal Oak: A Tale of the Year 1651 (3 volumes, London: Tinsley, 1872);

The Good Old Times: The Story of the Manchester Rebels of '45 (3 volumes, London: Tinsley, 1873);

Merry England; or, Nobles and Serfs (3 volumes, London: Tinsley, 1874);

The Goldsmith's Wife: A Tale (3 volumes, London: Tinsley, 1875);

Preston Fight; or, the Insurrection of 1715; A Tale (3 volumes, London: Tinsley, 1875);

Chetwynd Calverley: A Tale (3 volumes, London: Tinsley, 1876);

The Leaguer of Lathom: A Tale of the Civil War in Lancashire (3 volumes, London: Tinsley, 1876);

The Fall of Somerset (3 volumes, London: Tinsley, 1877);

Beatrice Tyldesley (3 volumes, London: Tinsley, 1878);

Beau Nash; or, Bath in the Eighteenth Century (3 volumes, London & New York: Routledge, 1879);

Stanley Brereton (3 volumes, London & New York: Routledge, 1881).

COLLECTIONS: *Historical Romances* (20 volumes, Philadelphia: Barrie, 1898-1901);

The Novels of William Harrison Ainsworth (20 volumes, London: Gibbings/ Philadelphia: Lippincott, 1901-1902).

The student of Victorian literature is more likely to know of William Harrison Ainsworth as an influential editor and a famous dandy than to have read his novels. Ainsworth's conspicuous place in the social world of literary London in the 1830s and 1840s is no doubt part of his importance, for his life impinged upon the lives of many authors of his time, both minor and major. Yet several of his novels still deserve attention. In the brief but remarkable vogue for criminal romance or "Newgate novels," *Rookwood* (1834) and *Jack Sheppard* (1839) remain central works. And Ainsworth's early historical novels, despite the archaic style and the often wooden characterization, show by their vivid depiction of life in a turbulent past the salutary influence of Sir Walter Scott.

Born on 4 February 1805 in Manchester, the city he was later to celebrate in the partially autobiographical novel *The Life and Adventures of Mervyn Clitheroe* (1851-1852, 1857-1858) and in the historical romance *The Good Old Times* (1873), Ainsworth early showed an enthusiasm for the romantic subjects that were to mark the forty-one novels of his long career. Although on the surface he appeared to be following in his father's footsteps toward the law, young William's true bent found expression in the Gothic melodramas that he wrote during adolescence. His imagination received ample sustenance through his reading of Mrs. Radcliffe and through the influence of his father and his father's young clerk, James Crossley. Thomas Ainsworth, though not a literary man, is credited in the preface to *Rookwood* with inspiring

Age twenty-one; miniature by Freeman

Age twenty-nine; sketch by Daniel Maclise

Age about sixty

Age seventy-six

William Harrison Ainsworth

his son's "strange passion for highwaymen" by often recounting their exploits to him. Perhaps more significant is the influence of Crossley, who, sharing the author's antiquarian fascination for history, was to become his lifelong friend and literary adviser.

After his father's death in 1824, Ainsworth left for London to continue his studies in the law. In 1826 he published in collaboration with J. P. Aston his first novel, *Sir John Chiverton*. Although the novel was read and enjoyed by Scott, it offers essentially the same stew of Gothic and melodramatic effects that are found in the juvenilia. In the same year Ainsworth married Fanny Ebers, the daughter of his first publisher. After first working in his father-in-law John Ebers's firm, Ainsworth set out on his own as a publisher. He continued in this profession for a year and a half and, though not financially successful, he began to forge connections in the literary world. In the early 1830s, after his venture into publishing, Ainsworth practiced law intermittently. But his more vital life was lived at the meetings of the Fraserians, the group that had founded *Fraser's Magazine* in 1830 and counted among its number William Makepeace Thackeray and Thomas Carlyle. At the same time he began the careful planning of *Rookwood*, the novel that was to make him one of the literary lions of London.

When it appeared in 1834, *Rookwood* was immediately categorized by reviewers as a novel of the Newgate class—the school of fiction that Edward Bulwer-Lytton had inadvertently founded in writing *Paul Clifford* (1830) and *Eugene Aram* (1832), novels which deal sympathetically with criminal heroes. Ainsworth certainly offers an engaging portrait of the highwayman Dick Turpin, but there is none of Bulwer-Lytton's dissective analysis of motives. Turpin's role in the novel is actually almost peripheral, for his adventures comprise essentially a subplot. Yet it was Ainsworth's account of Turpin's ride from London to York (the police all the while in close pursuit) and his description of the pathetic death of Turpin's mare, Black Bess, after the feat was accomplished, that earned the author the most praise in his own day.

The basic plot of the novel concerns the conflict of two brothers, Ranulph and Luke Rookwood, over their father's estate. The apparently illegitimate Luke learns that his father was secretly married to Susan Bradley, Luke's mother. Therefore, he is legitimate and, because he is the elder brother, also the rightful heir. He is driven by the fanatical sexton, Peter Bradley (really Alan Rookwood, the wronged brother of Luke's grandfather), to try to win both the estate and Eleanor Mowbray, heiress to the grandfather's fortune. In pursuit of these goals, he abandons his first love, the Gypsy Sybil Lovel, and is murdered for his unfaithfulness by the Gypsy queen. The novel ends with Ranulph and Eleanor

1834 drawing by Daniel Maclise depicting a meeting of the Fraserians

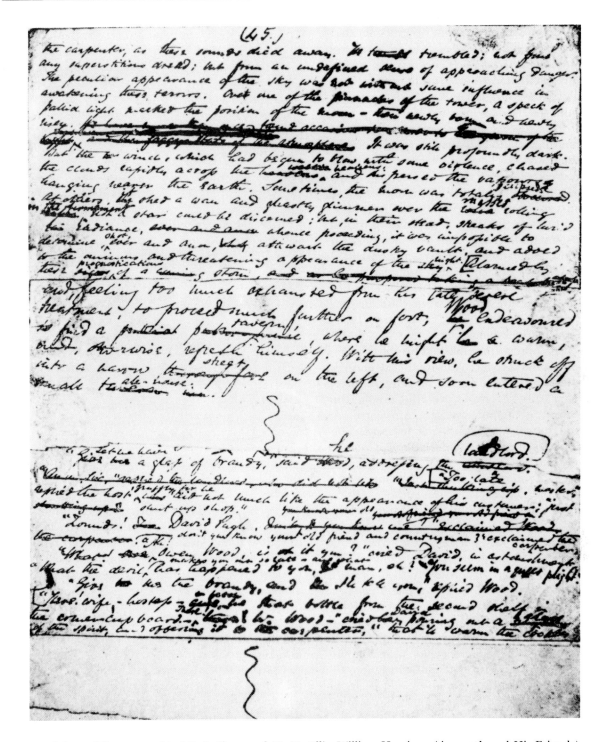

A page of the manuscript of Jack Sheppard *(S. M. Ellis,* William Harrison Ainsworth and His Friends*)*

married and the Rookwood family curse at an end.

In his revealing preface, Ainsworth claimed that his purpose was to transplant "the bygone style of Mrs. Radcliffe" to English settings and characters. But the novel does not display any of that skillful application of Gothic elements to psychological and social mysteries that is found, for instance, in the novels of Charles Dickens and the Brontë sisters. On the whole, *Rookwood* is a curious blend of the complicated Gothic plot of confused inheritance with the heroic and romantic adventures of a highwayman. It is not insignificant that the novel is interspersed with ballads, for one feels that Turpin belongs properly to the ballad tradition. Consequently, Ainsworth's famous description of Turpin's ride, good as it is, clashes with the Gothic atmosphere of Rookwood Place.

With the success of *Rookwood*, Ainsworth no longer had to court the literary world of which he was so enamored, for he was immediately accepted into the great salons of the day. Reports of the author at this time emphasize his dandified looks and compare him to the great lights of masculine fashion, the Count d'Orsay and Benjamin Disraeli. After his separation from his wife in 1835 for reasons that remain obscure, Ainsworth himself became famous as a host in his new home at Kensal Lodge. It was through Ainsworth that Dickens was introduced to his future biographer, John Forster, and the future illustrator of *Oliver Twist* (1837-1839), George Cruikshank.

In 1837 Ainsworth published his third novel, *Crichton*. This work, concerned with the adventures of a Scottish hero in France in the sixteenth century, was his first truly historical novel. But despite the book's critical and popular success, Ainsworth returned to criminal romance in *Jack Sheppard*. The structure of this novel is built on the parallel careers of a good apprentice, Thames Darrell, and a bad apprentice, Jack Sheppard. Ainsworth's emphasis is not a moral one, however, for the author seeks to win sympathy for his criminal hero by depicting vividly his several hairbreadth escapes from prison and by painting his pursuer, the thieftaker Jonathan Wild, in the most hideous colors. The novel is much more realistic than *Rookwood*: Ainsworth's Gothic horrors are now the same ones found in *Oliver Twist*, the rookeries and slums of the London underworld. *Jack Sheppard* not only outsold *Oliver Twist* when the two appeared in volume form; it also inspired a remarkable series of stage adaptations. Yet the novel was castigated for its immorality, especially by Thackeray, who viewed it along with Bulwer's novels as epitomizing the potential for dangerous influence in Newgate fiction.

While *Jack Sheppard* and *Oliver Twist* were appearing concurrently as serials in *Bentley's Miscellany* in 1839, Ainsworth agreed to take over the editorship of the periodical from Dickens, who had quarreled bitterly with Richard Bentley. Ainsworth, who had briefly edited a periodical when he was barely nineteen, was, like Dickens, to combine editing and novel-writing during a large part of his career. His editorship of *Bentley's Miscellany* was held only for

The real Jack Sheppard, painted by Sir James Thornhill at Newgate Prison shortly before his execution on 16 November 1724

the brief period between March 1839 and December 1841, but it was followed by his founding of *Ainsworth's Magazine* in February 1842 and his purchasing the *New Monthly Magazine* in June 1845. At the same time, Ainsworth had begun to mine the genre of historical romance—the form which, but for a few isolated attempts at contemporary themes and settings, characterizes the rest of his career as a novelist. It was in the early 1840s that Ainsworth wrote some of his best historical works: *The Tower of London* (1840), *Guy Fawkes* (1841), *Old Saint Paul's* (1841), and *Windsor Castle* (1843).

Ainsworth's historical novels testify to the influence of Scott on almost every page. Like Scott, he was an antiquarian (especially of English history in the sixteenth and seventeenth centuries) and delighted in displaying the fruits of his research in footnotes, notes at the back of the text, and even in scholarly digressions on historical events or buildings within the novel proper. He attempts to provide a kind of historical local color and to capture the spirit of the times. *The Tower of London* and *Old Saint Paul's*, probably his two most effective historical novels, are typical in this respect. Both works take their titles from famous structures and both

*Arundel Terrace in Brighton, Ainsworth's home
from 1853 to 1867*

deal with brief but eventful times in English history. In *The Tower of London*, the tower becomes a Gothic castle of history wherein are enacted the conspiracies of 1553 and 1554, first on behalf of, and then against, Mary Tudor. In *Old Saint Paul's*, London's plague and the great fire of 1666 are played out against the imposing backdrop of the cathedral. In both novels the author attempts, not to comprehend the meaning of historical events, but to capture the flavor of life at a precise and significant time in the past.

During the rest of his life, Ainsworth continued to combine the onerous tasks of editing with writing historical novels. Although he put an end to *Ainsworth's Magazine* in 1854, he continued to edit the *New Monthly Magazine* and bought control of *Bentley's Miscellany*. But his move from London to Brighton in 1853, apparently for financial reasons, meant that he could no longer take a significant part in London social life. Even though he continued to write novels at an even greater pace than before and retained *Bentley's Miscellany* until 1868 and the *New Monthly Magazine* until 1870, he gradually sank into obscurity to both friends and readers. He married again in 1878, but no account exists of his second wife. Nevertheless, the people of Manchester had not forgotten him, for they held a banquet in his honor on 5 September 1881. Ainsworth died shortly thereafter, on 3 January 1882.

Although Keith Hollingsworth's evaluation of Ainsworth's Newgate fiction as essentially entertainment and of Ainsworth himself as a clever craftsman and shrewd judge of the popular taste for criminal romance has remained largely unchallenged, there has been some reappraisal of the historical novels in the last decade. Ainsworth is still placed in the tradition of Scott, but the case is made that he is more than a servile imitator. Like Tennyson and Arnold, he shares the Victorian preoccupation with finding in the past some clarification of a bewildering present.

Ultimately, Ainsworth's life and his fiction seem to be of a piece, for just as his early works and the frantic pace of his social life reveal his genius for capturing the fashions of the time, so his later works and almost reclusive life suggest an inability to modify and adapt his talents to suit new readers and a new world. But because of his passionate affair with the literary scene and the exuberance with which he pursued his early career as both a novelist and an editor, Ainsworth continues to be an important figure for the student or scholar who seeks to appreciate the literary culture of the 1830s and the 1840s.

References:

S. M. Ellis, *William Harrison Ainsworth and His Friends* (2 volumes, London: John Lane, 1911);

Keith Hollingsworth, *The Newgate Novel* (Detroit: Wayne State University Press, 1963);

Llewellyn Ligocki, "Ainsworth's Tudor Novels: History as Theme," *Studies in the Novel*, 4 (Fall 1972): 364-377;

George J. Worth, *William Harrison Ainsworth* (New York: Twayne, 1972).

George Borrow

(5 July 1803-? August 1881)

Michael Collie
York University

SELECTED BOOKS: *The Zincali; or, An Account of the Gypsies of Spain* (2 volumes, London: Murray, 1841; 1 volume, New York: Wylie & Putnam, 1842);

The Bible in Spain; or, The Journeys, Adventures, and Imprisonments of an Englishman, in an Attempt to Circulate the Scriptures in the Peninsula (3 volumes, London: Murray, 1843; 1 volume, New York: Winchester, 1843);

Lavengro: The Scholar, the Gypsy, the Priest (3 volumes, London: Murray, 1851; 1 volume, New York: Putnam's, 1851);

The Romany Rye: A Sequel to Lavengro (2 volumes, London: Murray, 1857; 1 volume, New York: Harper, 1857);

Wild Wales: Its People, Language, and Scenery (3 volumes, London: Murray, 1862; 1 volume, New York: Putnam's, 1868);

Romano Lavo-Lil: Word-Book of the Romany, or English Gypsy Language (London: Murray, 1874; New York: Putnam's, 1905);

Celtic Bards, Chiefs, and Kings, edited by H. G. Wright (London: Murray, 1928).

COLLECTION: *The Works of George Borrow: Norwich Edition*, edited by C. K. Shorter, 16 volumes (London: Constable, 1923-1924; New York: Wells, 1923-1924).

George Borrow achieved instant literary fame when John Murray published his *The Bible in Spain* (1843). The four editions of this three-volume work in the year of publication, followed in 1846 by a single-volume edition (the first title in Murray's Colonial & Home Library), ensured that this mid-century best-seller was widely known in England; pirated editions in the United States were similarly popular. The book that so pleased the reading public was the turning point in a long life and a remarkable career.

That the obscurity of his origins affected George Borrow deeply became apparent when he wrote the autobiographical books that made him famous. His father, Thomas Borrow (1758-1824), who had left his family home in Cornwall when his apprenticeship to a Liskeard maltster terminated, served first in the Coldstream Guards and later in the West Norfolk Militia, initially as the sergeant and later as the officer in charge of the regiment's recruiting team. Borrow's mother, Ann (1772-1858), was the daughter of Samuel Parfrement, a tenant farmer on the outskirts of East Dereham in Norfolk. The Borrows had two children, John Thomas, born in 1800 or 1801, and George Henry, who said he was born on 5 July 1803 in East Dereham. John Borrow, whose date of birth is uncertain because its registration has yet to be found, played only a small part in the life of his famous brother; he briefly held a commission in the West Norfolk Militia, studied art in Norwich, London, and Paris, and then emigrated to Mexico to work for a number of mining companies, dying there in 1832. Because the West Norfolk Militia was constantly on the move between 1803 and 1816, Borrow to the age of thirteen had little formal education: indeed it amounted to no more than a few months at a school in Huddersfield, a year at Edinburgh High School, and a short spell of less than a year at a Protestant academy in Clonmel, Ireland. When the war was over and his parents had settled in Norwich, Borrow attended Norwich School for three years beginning in 1816, after which he was articled for five years to Simpson and Rackham, a well-established firm of solicitors in Norwich.

Borrow was exceptional in a number of ways. At six feet three inches he was unusually tall for that period. He was athletic both in the water and on land. Throughout his life he engaged in long-distance pedestrian journeys, including trips of several hundreds of miles through Cornwall, Wales, Ireland, Scotland, and, overseas, to Constantinople and back. To his already striking appearance his prematurely gray hair added a note of strangeness, and throughout his life he had fits that temporarily incapacitated him. This giant of a man found early in life that he had an affinity with Gypsies. He

Borrow as a young man, painted by his brother, John
(National Portrait Gallery)

learned their language, Romany; studied varieties of the same language when he encountered it overseas; lived and traveled with them; shared their profound knowledge of horses; and acquired their skills and a deep insight into their distinctive culture that affected the quality of his own life. He also found early that he had the gift of tongues. He learned Latin from a tutor; Greek and French at school; Welsh from a groom in Norwich; Irish in exchange for a pack of cards in Clonmel; Italian from an émigré priest in Norwich; German from William Taylor; Hebrew from the Jew he named Mousha in *Lavengro: The Scholar, the Gypsy, the Priest* (1851); and other languages, including Danish and Dutch, by means of a self-help system in which he compared a book in a familiar language with one in an unfamiliar language, sentence by sentence, until he had a knowledge of the words and a sense of the grammar of the unfamiliar one. While still at home Borrow offered instruction in "all" European languages; by 1817 William Taylor said that he had a mastery of twelve; and by 1823 he could translate "with facility and elegance" twenty. A recent study shows that in his middle years he had a working knowledge of more than fifty languages. Though often criticized for doing so, he persisted in calling himself a "philologist," which, however, he thought less important than knowing about horses.

Borrow's literary career falls into two parts. Throughout his life he devoted much time and energy to translation, mostly but not exclusively verse translation, from a great variety of foreign literatures; and in his middle years he wrote those distinctively English prose works that made him famous. He wished to be a great translator and by accident became a great writer of prose.

The termination of his period of articling coinciding with the death of his father in 1824, Borrow gathered up his already immense pile of verse translations and went immediately to London to earn his living with his pen. He abandoned the law, he said, because he preferred to use the English language precisely. Although he chose to conceal much of what he did between 1824 and 1833, thus creating the "veiled period" which so puzzled early biographers and critics, energetic periods of hard work were evidently interspersed with those journeys overseas to which he referred cryptically in later life. What Borrow, in an autobiographical note, called the hackwork of his first period in London (1824-1826) included contributions of articles and reviews to the *Universal Review* and the *New Monthly Magazine*; the compilation of the six-volume *Celebrated Trials and Remarkable Cases of Criminal*

Sir Richard Phillips, the London publisher for whom Borrow did a great deal of hackwork for low pay between 1824 and 1826 (National Portrait Gallery)

Jurisprudence, from the Earliest Records to the year 1825 for Sir Richard Phillips; the translation of *Faustus: His Life, Death, and Descent into Hell*, a novel in the grotesque mode by Friedrich Maximilian von Klinger (which translation was banned almost immediately by libraries both because of its sensational character and because Borrow had interpolated an attack on the citizens of Norwich); *The Life and Adventures of the Famous Colonel Blood* (which Borrow disguised in *Lavengro* under the fictitious title, *Life and Adventures of Joseph Sell, the Great Traveller*); and those as yet unidentified pieces which Borrow in a biographical note about himself subsumed within the phrase "doing common work for booksellers," work that may well have included a number of stories and plays for children. In 1826 Borrow published by subscription in Norwich his *Romantic Ballads, Translated from the Danish* (some copies of which were subsequently issued with two different title pages in London). Although a few years later his attempt to publish further verse translations in collaboration with John Bowring fell through, Borrow never abandoned this early body of work. Throughout his life he continued to revise it and seek out opportunities for publication.

Library and other records show that after the period on the open road that is described in *Lavengro* (six months or so in 1826), Borrow spent much

of his time in Norwich, but what he did precisely and how he earned his living between 1826 and 1832 have never been determined. No doubt chiefly on account of his flair for language, Borrow in 1833 was introduced to the officers of the British and Foreign Bible Society, for which organization he worked for the next seven years, first in Russia (1833-1835) and then in Spain (1835-1840). In Saint Petersburg he assisted with the translation of the New Testament into Manchurian, which, despite immense practical difficulties, he then manufactured as an eight-volume, leather-bound edition, supposedly for distribution in China from the society's London headquarters. In Spain he attempted to distribute on the society's behalf a new translation of the New Testament which he had manufactured in Madrid and which lacked those commentaries prescribed by Catholic authority. This attempt involved hazardous journeys through a bandit-infested Spain that was rent by civil war, as

Borrow in 1848

First page of the manuscript of Borrow's autobiographical novel, Lavengro *(1851)*

Borrow's house at Oulton Broad

well as constant disputes with officials, and on three occasions brief periods of imprisonment for continuing to distribute New Testaments when ordered not to. During his period with the Bible Society, however, Borrow never abandoned the life of literature. In Saint Petersburg, he published two small collections of his verse translations, *Targum* (1835) and *The Talisman* (1835). In Spain, he published his translation of the Gospel according to St. Luke into Spanish Romany (1837), while during his last year in Spain, when Mrs. Mary Clarke and her daughter Henrietta lived with him in Seville, he began to collect material for a book about the Gypsies which he had had in mind at least since he visited a Gypsy encampment in Badajoz in 1835. Back in England in 1840 he married Mrs. Clarke, the widow of Lt. Henry Clarke who had died in 1818, settled down on his wife's estate at Oulton Broad, and wrote *The Zincali* (1841), an anthology consisting of historical accounts of Gypsy life, Borrow's own descriptions of Gypsies in the countries where he had encountered them, a Gypsy vocabulary, and translations of various poems. This was quickly followed by an extremely lively, idiosyncratic account of Borrow's Spanish years based on his

letters to the Bible Society, which told less than the whole truth but which was immensely successful when it appeared in 1843 as *The Bible in Spain*.

Borrow devoted the rest of his long life to autobiography, translation, and travel. As to the first, he perplexed his readers by restricting his account of his own life to the twenty-five years covered by his masterpiece *Lavengro* and its sequel, *The Romany Rye* (1857). *Lavengro* is a Gypsy term meaning "expert with words," as opposed to *sapengro*, "expert with snakes," which Borrow also was. *Romany Rye* means "man of the Gypsies." Though brilliant fabrications in the romantic mode, those two books expressed a characteristic Victorian unwillingness to face the truth about self, and as such were recognized and enjoyed as classics of the art of evasion, Borrow's racy style and graphic power compensating for what he chose not to reveal. The three volumes of *Lavengro* and the first volume of *The Romany Rye* consist of a colorful, visually arresting but essentially selective and episodic account of the narrator's early adventures in London and in various parts of rural England. Taken together they constitute one of the classics of nineteenth-century autobiography. This, at least, is the reputation they enjoyed at the end of the century, after the initially hostile response to both books had abated. Early readers were disappointed with *Lavengro* because it was not the full autobiography they had expected and with *The Romany Rye* because Borrow attached to it the notorious "Appendix," a forcefully written but vitriolic attack on his critics. At the same time, he continued to work at his verse translations, published *The Sleeping Bard* in 1860, formed those grandiose publication plans announced at the end of *The Romany Rye*, had that final excursion into philology that is represented by *Romano Lavo-Lil* (1874), but to the end of his life failed to come to terms with the fact that his feel for language was not matched by the poetic ability that would have allowed him to be a good translator. From his pedestrian excursions, however, came the last of his principal works, *Wild Wales* (1862), a book that is still in print and is still widely read.

Because early writers on Borrow found it difficult to determine what he had written and published, a few words need to be said about the titles which gave people difficulty. Borrow did not write parts of *Celebrated Trials*, as Clement Shorter maintained he did; he did not write a book called *Tales of the Wild and the Wonderful*; and he did not translate all or part of the New Testament into Basque or Mexican dialects. Notwithstanding the doubts raised by Carter and Pollard, he did translate *The Death of Balder* (1889). Similarly, though there is a question about *when* Borrow translated the work he called *The Turkish Jester* (1884), his correspondence and manuscripts show the translation to be definitely his. Of the eleven books Borrow listed in an advertisement in the first edition of *The Romany Rye* as being "ready for the press," only *Wild Wales* was published during Borrow's lifetime, but several attempts were made to reconstitute the volumes Borrow had said he wanted published, notably in *Ballads of All Nations* (1927), edited by R. B. Johnson, and *Celtic Bards, Chiefs, and Kings* (1928), edited by Herbert Wright. The Norwich edition of Borrow's works is too unreliable to be recommended, though it contains a certain amount of material not published elsewhere.

Borrow died at Oulton in 1881 and was buried in Brompton cemetery.

Translations:
Friedrich Maximilian von Klinger, *Faustus: His Life,*

Borrow's grave in Brompton Cemetery

Death, and Descent into Hell, translated by Borrow (London: Simpkin & Marshall, 1825);

Romantic Ballads, Translated from the Danish (Norwich: S. Wilkin, 1826);

Targum; or, Metrical Translations From Thirty Languages and Dialects (St. Petersburg: Schulz & Beneze, 1835);

Alexander Pushkin, *The Talisman,* translated by Borrow (St. Petersburg: Schulz & Beneze, 1835);

Embéo e Majaró Lucas, Saint Luke's Gospel translated into Spanish Gypsy by Borrow (Madrid: n.p., 1837);

Ellis Wynn, *The Sleeping Bard; or, Visions of The World, Death, and Hell,* translated from the Welsh by Borrow (London: John Murray, 1860);

The Turkish Jester (Ipswich: W. Webber, 1884);

The Death of Balder from the Danish of Johannes Ewald (London: Jarrold, 1889);

Ballads of All Nations, edited by R. B. Johnson (London: Alston Rivers, 1927).

Letters:

T. H. Darlow, ed., *Letters of George Borrow to the British and Foreign Bible Society* (London: Hodder & Stoughton, 1911).

Biographies:

W. I. Knapp, *The Life, Writings, and Correspondence of George Borrow* (2 volumes, London: Murray, 1899);

Herbert Jenkins, *The Life of George Borrow* (London: Murray, 1912);

C. K. Shorter, *George Borrow and His Circle* (London: Hodder & Stoughton, 1913);

René Fréchet, *George Borrow (1803-1881): Vagabond polyglotte–Agent biblique–Ecrivain* (Paris: Didier, 1956);

Michael Collie, *George Borrow: Eccentric* (Cambridge: Cambridge University Press, 1982);

David Williams, *A World of His Own: The Double Life of George Borrow* (Oxford: Oxford University Press, 1982).

Reference:

John Carter and Graham Pollard, *An Enquiry into the Nature of Certain Nineteenth Century Pamphlets* (London: Constable, 1934).

Papers:

Borrow's papers are widely scattered. The more substantial collections are in the Huntington Library in San Marino, California; the Berg Collection in the New York Public Library; the Humanities Research Center, the University of Texas at Austin; the Symington Collection, Rutgers University; the Brotherton Collection, the University of Leeds; the Scott Library, York University, Toronto; the Fales Library, New York University at Washington Square; and the British Library, notably in the Ashley Collection. Borrow's letters and reports to the British and Foreign Bible Society are in the Library of the Bible House in London. His letters to John Hasfeld are in the P. N. Tikhanov Collection, M. E. Saltykov-Shchedrin State Public Library, Leningrad. A few important autograph manuscripts, as well as a large collection of Borroviana, are in the Norfolk Record Office in Norwich. Other important, though less substantial, Borrow holdings are to be found in some twenty libraries in England, Australia, Canada, and the United States.

Anne Brontë

(17 January 1820-28 May 1849)

John Merritt

BOOKS: *Poems by Currer, Ellis and Acton Bell*, by
Charlotte, Emily, and Anne Brontë (London:
Aylott & Jones, 1846; Philadelphia: Lea &
Blanchard, 1848);
Agnes Grey, as Acton Bell (London: Newby, 1847;
Philadelphia: Peterson, 1850);
The Tenant of Wildfell Hall, as Acton Bell (3 volumes,
London: Newby, 1848; 1 volume, New York:
Harper, 1848).

COLLECTIONS: *The Life and Works of Charlotte
Brontë and Her Sisters*, Haworth Edition, edited
by Mrs. Humphry Ward and C. K. Shorter (7
volumes, London: Smith, Elder, 1899-1900);
The Shakespeare Head Brontë, edited by T. J. Wise and
J. A. Symington (19 volumes, Oxford: Black-
well, 1931-1938);
The Clarendon Edition of the Novels of the Brontës, I. P.
Jack, general editor (3 volumes, Oxford:
Clarendon Press, 1969-).

In *Conversations in Ebury Street* (1924), George
Moore declared that "if Anne Brontë had lived ten
years longer, she would have taken a place beside
Jane Austen, perhaps even a higher place"; in addition, he described her first novel, *Agnes Grey* (1847),
as "the most perfect prose narrative in English literature."

If Moore's estimation of Brontë's work and
potential was somewhat inflated, his claims for her
served as an overdue and refreshing corrective to
the trend—long established by biographers and
critics—of either damning her with faint praise or
making her the subject of frankly disparaging remarks. Typical of the latter were May Sinclair's dismissal of her as "the weak and ineffectual Anne"
and George Saintsbury's pronouncement that "the
third sister Anne is but a pale reflection of her
elders." The cumulative effect made Brontë appear
a nebulous figure in the history of English letters;
and led to the widely accepted concept of her as an
artist and a woman of no importance.

The source of this misleading image of Anne
Brontë was her older sister Charlotte, who became,
in effect, her first biographer and critic. Since
Anne's life is not well documented (only a handful

(Brontë Society)

of her letters and papers are extant), there has been
an inevitable tendency to rely too much on information about her from reported and written statements by Charlotte. Many of these—particularly
her lukewarm assessments of Anne's literary
abilities and her frequent references to Anne's pen-
siveness, docility, and religious morbidity—were accepted for decades as absolute; now they are being
weighed more carefully as Charlotte's objectivity as
a witness and impartiality as a judge are cross-
examined.

Some of the undisputed facts about Anne
Brontë are that she was the youngest daughter of
the Reverend Patrick and Maria Branwell Brontë;
that she was born in the northeastern county of
Yorkshire, England; and that she spent her childhood and formative years in the Brontës' family
home—the parsonage on the outskirts of the re-

Sketch of a church drawn by Anne Brontë at the age of eight (Brontë Parsonage Museum)

mote village of Haworth. She received her formal education between 1835 and 1837 at Miss Margaret Wooler's boarding school. During Anne's attendance there, the school was relocated from Roe Head to Dewsbury Moor, near Leeds.

Straitened family finances compelled Anne to search for employment, and between April and the latter part of 1839 she worked as a governess in the home of Mr. and Mrs. Joshua Ingham of Blake Hall. She occupied her second post as a governess to the three daughters of the Reverend and Mrs. Edmund Robinson of Thorp Green Hall, near York, for five years, beginning her duties in May 1840. Her brother, Branwell, joined her there in January 1843, when he was hired as tutor to the Robinsons' only son, Edmund. The significance of this period of Anne Brontë's life and the vital importance which it played in her education, her maturation, and her growing understanding of mankind should be neither overlooked nor underestimated. The Robinsons were wealthy and privileged and were related to people of importance (including a marquis and a member of Parliament); the social milieu in which they moved was wide and varied. It can be fairly assumed that Anne Brontë, as a part of the Robinson household, came into contact with many

of her employers' relations and friends; she would have had ample opportunity to observe their behavior at close quarters, thus gaining insights into the ways of the world which would have eluded her had she remained in the relatively narrow confines of Haworth Parsonage. Unfortunately, Anne's main extant direct reference to Thorp Green Hall is extremely brief, tantalizingly pregnant with meaning, but frustratingly cryptic; it concludes with the enigmatic words: ". . . during my stay I have had some very unpleasant and undreamt-of experience of human nature." After resigning in June 1845, she spent her few remaining years at Haworth with her father; her sisters, Charlotte and Emily; and her brother, Branwell; Emily and Branwell predeceased her in 1848.

From an early age, and until at least 1845, Anne and Emily (who were described as being "like twins, inseparable companions in the very closest sympathy") collaborated in writing the saga of a fictitious island named Gondal. Although none of their Gondal prose has survived, a number of their Gondal poems do exist.

A book of poems by Charlotte, Emily, and Anne, who used the pseudonyms of Currer, Ellis, and Acton Bell respectively, appeared in 1846.

Anne's first novel, *Agnes Grey*, was published in one of three volumes—the other two contained Emily's *Wuthering Heights*—in December 1847. Her second and last novel, *The Tenant of Wildfell Hall*, was published in June 1848.

Anne Brontë's books are primarily concerned with morality; she is preoccupied with the ethical principles which, for good or ill, govern human behavior. Her two novels present a closely observed, occasionally satirical, rarely humorous, and often melancholy view of what she regards as a profoundly imperfect world. Her prose frequently achieves elegance through its simplicity; her direct and didactic manner is tempered with a disarming sincerity, so that it succeeds in persuading rather than alienating the reader. The philosophy guiding her intent as a writer is that "the end of Religion is not to teach us how to die, but how to live; and the earlier you become wise and good, the more of happiness you secure." Nevertheless, as the critic Terry Eagleton has observed, "for such a resolutely moral writer, Anne Brontë is remarkably unsmug."

Agnes Grey is the novel in which, according to Mrs. Gaskell, Charlotte's "sister Anne pretty literally describes her own experience as a governess." This remark, which seems as much an oversimplification as saying that *Villette* (1853) is the novel in which Charlotte pretty literally describes *her* own experience as a teacher in Brussels, has resulted in *Agnes Grey* being interpreted as a mere autobiography or diary—an estimation which does great disservice to Brontë's abilities as an artificer. This erroneous view of the book is also due, in part, to a frequent misunderstanding of the mode in which it is written. Purporting to be a "true history," it is in the tradition of the fictitious memoir which dates back to the eighteenth century and such novels as *Robinson Crusoe* (1719) and *Moll Flanders* (1721). Indeed, the influence of Defoe and other writers of that period on Brontë has been noted frequently. *Moll Flanders* claims to be a true history and, like *Agnes Grey*, contains many references to its truthfulness and moral purpose. Moll's avowal that "publishing this account of my life is for the sake of the just moral of every part of it, and for instruction, caution, warning, and improvement to every reader" is closely echoed by Agnes Grey's claim that "my design, in writing the last few pages, was not to amuse, but to benefit those whom it might concern," and by the phrase which begins the novel: "All true histories contain instruction."

Brontë's publicly declared purpose as a writer (stated in her preface—dated 22 July 1848—to the second edition of *The Tenant of Wildfell Hall*) was "to

Anne, Emily, and Charlotte Brontë as painted by their brother, Branwell, about 1835. Branwell apparently painted over his self-portrait in the space between Emily and Charlotte (National Portrait Gallery)

tell the truth, for truth always conveys its own moral to those who are able to receive it . . . and if I can gain the public ear at all, I would rather whisper a few wholesome truths therein than much soft nonsense." Clearly, she intended to instruct, and she shrewdly chose the most appropriate form to achieve her goal; Inga-Stina Ewbank points out that "for the purposes of instruction, truth is more impressive than fiction—hence her [Brontë's] insistence on *Agnes Grey* being a genuine autobiography."

Brontë does not analyze the workings of the human mind; rather, she writes in what F. R. Leavis has described, in another context, as "the tradition coming down from the eighteenth century that demanded a plane-mirror reflection of the surface of 'real' life." Consequently, she makes the reader form opinions of her fictional people by their actions rather than by the psychological forces which motivate those actions. She reveals the nature of her characters not so much by what they think as by what they say and do. The resulting effect bears a resemblance to a morality play—a world of black and white, right and wrong, in which only very occasionally is the conscience of a character torn between the polarities of good and evil.

In *Agnes Grey*, goodness is equated with adherence to a set of values which takes for granted the supreme importance of love and compassion for one's fellow man as stated in the tenets of Christianity; but such goodness is represented by only a tiny minority of characters in the book. Among them are Agnes herself; her father, an impoverished clergyman; her mother, who, by marrying Mr. Grey for love against the wishes of her wealthy parents, has cheerfully sacrificed a handsome inheritance and thus rejected materialism; and by Agnes's elder sister, Mary.

It is of great import that all the characters in the story for whom Agnes feels true affinity and respect are members of the poor and working classes; one of these is Edward Weston, a conscientious, underpaid curate of firm faith and ardent piety, whom Agnes marries in the final chapter. Through her sympathetic presentation of such people, juxtaposed with her unflattering and often satirical depiction of the hollow values of the bourgeoisie and the aristocracy, Brontë makes an unmistakable equation between wealth and moral bankruptcy. In its indictment of the conduct of the financially privileged members of Victorian England, *Agnes Grey* qualifies as a novel of sociological as well as moral significance. It is also a novel about failure—a subtly cynical portrayal of the triumph of mediocrity over excellence.

Agnes begins her career as a governess at the age of eighteen, with eager, almost naive anticipation: "how charming to be entrusted with the care and education of children . . . to train the tender plants, and watch their buds unfolding day by day!" But chapter two (which has the splendidly ironic title "First Lessons in the Art of Instruction") marks the beginning of Agnes's disillusionment; soon after initial contact with her first pupils, she becomes conscious of "a vicious tendency in the bud." The rest of the story depicts her varied, valiant, but futile attempts to combat the callousness, selfishness, vanity, greed, cruelty, and indifference of her employers and her young charges.

The human failings (and their unhappy consequences) which Agnes so clearly deplores are most effectively demonstrated in the career of her oldest pupil, Rosalie Murray. Agnes's evaluation of her is clear-sighted but compassionate: "her faults . . . I would fain persuade myself, were rather the effect of her education than her disposition: she had never been perfectly taught the distinction between right and wrong." With the connivance of her unscrupulous and ambitious mother, Rosalie exchanges her idle career as a heartless coquette for a

marriage of convenience to a wealthy, aristocratic, but debauched man, Sir Thomas Ashby. In her eagerness to become the mistress of Ashby Park, Rosalie rationalizes that "reformed rakes make the best husbands, *everybody* knows." Agnes Grey knows better!

Agnes's own marriage to Edward Weston serves as a modest rather than triumphant conclusion to the novel; he is a vaguely sketched, particularly one-dimensional character, and her union with him seems to be Brontë's nod in the direction of the traditional happy ending. In dramatic terms, the event is anticlimactic and at variance with the powerful sense of disillusionment which pervades two chapters near the end of the novel, when Agnes pays her final visit to Rosalie. Having confided to Agnes that she now despises her rich, dissipated husband, Rosalie is reluctant to let her former governess go. The following excerpt from chapter twenty-three demonstrates, in style, the clarity of Brontë's prose; in content, it testifies to the author's tacit acknowledgment of the predominantly melancholy nature of the human condition: "it was with a heavy heart that I bade adieu to poor Lady Ashby, and left her in her princely home. It was no slight additional proof of her unhappiness, that she should so cling to the consolation of my presence, and earnestly desire the company of one whose general tastes and ideas were so little congenial to her own—whom she had completely forgotten in her hours of prosperity, and whose presence would be rather a nuisance than a pleasure, if she could but have half her heart's desire." The supreme irony of this often ironic novel is that it is Agnes—a teacher by instinct and profession—who learns how to come to terms with life. *She* is the pupil who says "I had been seasoned by adversity, and tutored by experience," and who, as a result, formulates the simple but sound philosophy that "the best way to enjoy yourself is to do what is right and hate nobody." Her ultimate defeat is that she has failed to educate others to share that philosophy. Why the author allowed this defeat is better understood if one recalls that elsewhere Brontë qualified her contention that "truth always conveys its own moral" by adding the artfully sardonic phrase: "to those who are able to receive it."

Agnes Grey was received quite warmly when it appeared in 1847, but being published as part of a "three-decker" with *Wuthering Heights* was definitely not to its advantage. Emily's novel had a mixed reception: it was generally misunderstood and considered "coarse"—as, indeed, were all the early Brontë novels when they were first presented to the

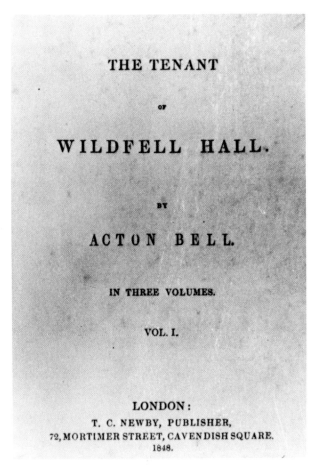

THE TENANT

OF

WILDFELL HALL.

BY

ACTON BELL.

IN THREE VOLUMES.

VOL. I.

LONDON:
T. C. NEWBY, PUBLISHER,
72, MORTIMER STREET, CAVENDISH SQUARE.
1848.

Title page of Brontë's second novel

public—but its strangeness and eccentricities made good copy. Consequently, it got the attention, if not necessarily the praise, of the critics. The inevitable comparisons were made, and *Agnes Grey*—by its very nature—appeared "less powerful."

The major preoccupation of Brontë's other novel, *The Tenant of Wildfell Hall* (1848), is very much the same as that of *Agnes Grey*, but the war between good and evil is waged on a considerably larger battleground. *The Tenant of Wildfell Hall* is much longer than its predecessor, and more complex in structure, scope, and the number of characters it contains.

It has been suggested that *Agnes Grey* influenced the composition of *Jane Eyre*, and close examination shows that they contain a considerable number of similarities in "cast of thought, incident and language." For example, Agnes's "marked features," "pale hollow cheek," and "ordinary dark brown hair" anticipate Jane Eyre's unprepossessing physical appearance. (Traditionally, it is Charlotte,

not Anne, who has been credited with the introduction of the irreversibly plain heroine to English fiction.)

Also, there are indications that *Wuthering Heights* influenced the subsequent composition of *The Tenant of Wildfell Hall*. The two books have a number of similarities, including an unusual degree of passionate intensity (in *The Tenant of Wildfell Hall*, this is particularly evident in the vehemence of which Gilbert Markham is capable). George Moore commented that Anne Brontë "could write with heat, one of the rarest qualities"—but it is a quality conspicuous by its absence in *Agnes Grey*. *Wuthering Heights* and *The Tenant of Wildfell Hall* also show similarities in construction, such as the device of employing double narrators—Mr. Lockwood and Ellen Dean in *Wuthering Heights*; in *The Tenant of Wildfell Hall*, Gilbert Markham and Helen Huntingdon.

Gilbert—a gentleman farmer—falls in love with Helen, the enigmatic tenant of Wildfell Hall, who is presumed to be a widow. She is, in fact, the estranged wife of the alcoholic and lecherous Arthur Huntingdon. Gilbert's narrative, in the early chapters, skillfully maintains the air of mystery which surrounds Helen and demonstrates his growing attachment to her. This narrative, which begins and ends the novel, is contained in a series of letters (the form bears some resemblance to Mary Shelley's *Frankenstein* [1818]). Gilbert's letters provide the framework for a transcript of Helen's diary, which she has given to Gilbert to help him understand the trials of her past life. This diary, containing a graphic account of her optimistic entry into marriage with Huntingdon and of the gradual disintegration of that marriage brought about by his debauchery, occupies the central and major part of the novel.

Arthur Huntingdon and his cronies are forcefully portrayed; the depths of depravity to which they are capable of sinking is demonstrated in some remarkably vivid and lurid scenes, and there has been some speculation that Brontë's inspiration for such incidents could have come from her years at Thorp Green Hall. Charlotte Brontë claimed that Anne "had, in the course of her life, been called on to contemplate, near at hand, and for a long time, the terrible effects of talents misused and faculties abused." The reference is to their brother, Branwell's, refuge in alcohol and drugs following his abrupt dismissal from his post as tutor at Thorp Green Hall. To the end of his life, Branwell adhered to his assertion that the cause of that dismissal was the discovery by his employer, the Reverend Edmund Robinson, of a clandestine love affair between Branwell and Robinson's wife, Lydia. The suggestion that Anne may have been an unwilling witness to this liaison is interesting but refutable; what is beyond dispute is that she closely observed the ravaging effects that gin and laudanum had on the mind and body of her brother.

Helen Huntingdon's diary effectively demonstrates her gradual metamorphosis from an optimistic, eager young girl—convinced that she can reform her rakish, irresponsible husband—into a mature, somewhat cynical, worldly-wise woman. It depicts her long, arduous struggle to persuade the man she loves to heed the principles of Christianity in order to overcome his many weaknesses and to live a life that will lead to salvation, not degradation. Helen, like Agnes Grey, is highly principled and deeply religious; also like Agnes, she is a teacher by instinct. Helen firmly believes that "it is our duty to admonish our neighbours of their transgressions"; and when speaking of her son, Helen states that "the child's education was the only pleasure and business of my life." Plainly, she is adamant that the son will not emulate the behavior of the father, and that he will be "perfectly taught the distinction between right and wrong."

Unlike Agnes, she is not a teacher by profession; she is, in fact, a member of the privileged classes. Consequently, compared with Agnes, she is much more openly self-assured and composed. Brontë succeeds admirably in convincing the reader of the air of elegance in Helen's demeanor and the element of self-reliance in her conduct (which strongly hints of feminism). In the words addressed by Helen to her enemies (including her husband's shallow mistress, Annabella Wilmot), Brontë employs a grand style of language which is reminiscent in its imperious tone of the prose in wrathful letters of the first Queen Elizabeth.

Although *The Tenant of Wildfell Hall*, like *Agnes Grey*, has a conventional happy ending (Huntingdon dies as the result of his excesses, and after a respectable lapse of time, Helen marries Gilbert), it, too, is a novel about defeat. Ultimately, the significance of the marriages of Helen and Agnes to men who love them pales beside the facts that Helen has failed to save Arthur Huntingdon and that Agnes has failed to save Rosalie Murray. Both books have overtones of despair, reflecting Brontë's bleak but realistic and unflinching view of the world.

The reviews of *The Tenant of Wildfell Hall* in the summer of 1848 were varied; an accusation that the author had "a morbid love for the coarse, not to say the brutal" was echoed in several quarters, but the book was recommended by the *Athenaeum* as "the most interesting novel we have read for a month past." A flurry of public interest led to a hurried printing of a second edition in August with a preface by the author—the final words she wrote specifically for publication. Brontë was bold and defiant in her response to a critic who had suggested that if *The Tenant of Wildfell Hall* had been written by a woman, that fact would make it even more unpalatable to him: "in my own mind, I am satisfied that if a book is a good one, it is so whatever the sex of the author may be. All novels are or should be written for both men and women to read, and I am at a loss to conceive how a man should permit himself to write anything that would be really disgraceful to a woman, or why a woman should be censured for writing anything that would be proper and becoming for a man."

Charlotte Brontë was disturbed by *The Tenant of Wildfell Hall* and made no secret of her distaste for the book. In her "Biographical Notice of Ellis and Acton Bell" (1850), she referred to the fact that Anne's second novel had had a predominantly unfavorable reception: "At this I cannot wonder. The choice of subject was an entire mistake. Nothing less congruous with the writer's nature could be conceived. The motives which dictated this choice were pure, but, I think, slightly morbid." Thus, in September 1850, in her influential position as one of the most lionized writers of her time, Charlotte Brontë helped to quell interest in *The Tenant of Wildfell Hall* by publicly condemning it. Privately, during the same month, she sealed the fate of Anne's second novel by declining Smith, Elder's offer to issue a reprint edition, saying, "*Wildfell Hall* it hardly appears to me desireable to preserve." Less than seven years later, in her *Life of Charlotte Brontë*, Mrs. Gaskell's brief reference to *The Tenant of Wildfell Hall* included this telling phrase: "it is little known."

During her brief and seemingly circumscribed life, Anne Brontë only once ventured outside her home county of Yorkshire; the occasion was a fleeting visit to London with Charlotte in July 1848, an incident now renowned in the annals of English literature—it has even found a niche in the *Oxford Book of Literary Anecdotes*! The purpose of this urgent, hurried journey was to disprove the rumors then rampant (and unscrupulously fueled by Anne's and Emily's publisher T. C. Newby in order to capitalize on the astonishing current success of Charlotte's *Jane Eyre*) that Currer, Ellis, and Acton Bell were not three authors but one. Determined to disassociate themselves from this falsehood, Anne

Anne Brontë's grave at Scarborough

and Charlotte gained entry to the Cornhill office of Charlotte's publisher George Smith, who had no knowledge of the Bells' true identities or of their gender; there, Charlotte startled him with the dramatic declaration, "We are three sisters."

Many years later, George Smith recorded his impressions of Anne, based on that very brief meeting with her; he said, "She was a gentle, quiet, rather subdued person, by no means pretty, yet of a pleasing appearance. Her manner was curiously expressive of a wish for protection and encouragement, a kind of constant appeal which invited sympathy." Although "of a pleasing appearance," Anne had no serious suitors during her lifetime; however, it has been suggested by some biographers—and avowed by others—that she was in love with William Weightman, an attractive, exuberant young man who served as the Reverend Patrick Brontë's curate from August 1839 until his death from cholera in September 1842. The evidence to support this theory is flimsy and is based primarily on a remark in a letter written by Charlotte: "He [Weightman] sits opposite to Anne at Church sighing softly and looking out of the corners of his eyes to win her attention—and Anne is so quiet, her looks so downcast—they are a picture." The significance of

this statement is severely undermined by observations about Weightman made by Charlotte in other letters, which clearly demonstrate her opinion of him as an inveterate flirt; she says, among other things, "I'm afraid he is very fickle" and "He would fain persuade every woman under thirty whom he sees that he is desperately in love with her." It appears that Weightman did not feel strongly about Anne; the conjecture that she felt strongly about *him* is based on several of her poems, written after September 1842—including *A Reminiscence* (1844) and *Severed and Gone* (1847)—which lament the death of a loved one and which *may* be autobiographical in nature. No other romantic connections are alleged for Anne; she received no recorded offers of marriage, and she died a spinster at the age of twenty-nine. Her death, from tuberculosis, took place at the coastal resort of Scarborough.

Eighty years separated Anne's death from W. T. Hale's *Anne Brontë: Her Life and Writings* (1929), the first publication to treat her as more than a peripheral player in the Brontë story and to challenge some of the myths which had surrounded "dear, gentle Anne." In his sympathetic, often astute monograph, Hale firmly states: "The truth about her is that her gentleness was not weakness.

Childlike and unsophisticated in many ways she was, but she had a power of will and a strength of character that always carried out the dictates of her sense of duty." Professor Hale's point of view was innovative; and by choosing to focus his attention on Anne, he created a precedent. Since then, a number of prominent critics have deemed Anne Brontë and her work to be worthy of serious consideration. The result of this re-evaluation has been a growing conviction that she is a minor but worthwhile nineteenth-century novelist who, although admittedly less gifted than her sisters, demonstrates a considerable degree of individuality, originality, and even daring in her modest but far from negligible output.

F. B. Pinion's contention that "there can be little doubt that, had *The Tenant of Wildfell Hall* received more critical attention, its merits would be more widely recognised," can be applied with equal validity to *Agnes Grey*. The 1979 publication of a carefully edited edition of *The Tenant of Wildfell Hall* in the Penguin English Library and the appearance in the same year of *The Poems of Anne Brontë: A New Text and Commentary* by Edward Chitham are encouraging signs that there is indeed a growing trend to regard Anne's work in a fresh and positive light. There can be no doubt that as her books are more widely read—with care and attention—there will be a commensurate acknowledgment and appreciation for what she achieved during her brief but productive life.

Other:

Preface to *The Tenant of Wildfell Hall*, 2nd edition (London: Newby, 1848).

Biographies:

W. T. Hale, *Anne Brontë: Her Life and Writings* (Bloomington: Indiana University, 1929);

Winifred Gérin, *Anne Brontë* (London: Nelson, 1959);

Ada Harrison and Derek Stanford, *Anne Brontë: Her Life and Work* (London: Methuen, 1959).

References:

Miriam Allott, ed., *The Brontës: The Critical Heritage* (London: Routledge & Kegan Paul, 1974);

Phyllis Bentley, *The Brontës* (London: Home & Van Thal, 1947);

Charlotte Brontë, "Biographical Notice of Ellis and Acton Bell," prefixed to *Wuthering Heights and Agnes Gray* (London: Smith, Elder, 1850);

Edward Chitham, ed., *The Poems of Anne Brontë: A New Text and Commentary* (London: Macmillan, 1979);

W. A. Craik, *The Brontë Novels* (London: Methuen, 1968);

Terry Eagleton, *Myths of Power: A Marxist Study of the Brontës* (London: Macmillan, 1975);

Barbara Evans and Gareth Lloyd Evans, *Everyman's Companion to the Brontës* (London: Dent, 1982);

Inga-Stina Ewbank, *Their Proper Sphere–A Study of the Brontë Sisters as Early Victorian Novelists* (London: Edward Arnold, 1966);

Elizabeth Gaskell, *The Life of Charlotte Brontë* (2 volumes, London: Smith, Elder, 1857);

George Moore, *Conversations in Ebury Street* (London: Heinemann, 1924), chapter 17;

F. B. Pinion, *A Brontë Companion* (London: Macmillan, 1975);

W. S. Stevenson, *Emily and Anne Brontë* (London: Routledge & Kegan Paul, 1968);

Tom Winnifrith, *The Brontës* (London: Macmillan, 1977);

Winnifrith, *The Brontës and Their Background* (London: Macmillan, 1973).

Papers:

Locations of significant holdings include the Brontë Parsonage Museum, Haworth (three of Anne's four extant letters, manuscripts of some poems, drawings, illustrations, etc.); the Ashley Library, British Museum (Anne's fourth extant letter, manuscripts of some poems); the Berg Collection, New York Public Library (manuscripts of some poems); and the Bonnell Collection, J. Pierpont Morgan Library, New York (manuscripts of some poems).

Charlotte Brontë

Herbert J. Rosengarten
University of British Columbia

BIRTH: Thornton, Yorkshire, 21 April 1816, to Patrick and Maria Branwell Brontë.

MARRIAGE: 29 June 1854 to Arthur Bell Nicholls.

DEATH: Haworth, Yorkshire, 31 March 1855.

BOOKS: *Poems by Currer, Ellis and Acton Bell*, by Charlotte, Emily, and Anne Brontë (London: Aylott & Jones, 1846; Philadelphia: Lea & Blanchard, 1848);
Jane Eyre: An Autobiography, "edited by Currer Bell" (3 volumes, London: Smith, Elder, 1847; 1 volume, New York: Harper, 1847);
Shirley: A Tale, as Currer Bell (3 volumes, London: Smith, Elder, 1849; 1 volume, New York: Harper, 1850);
Villette, as Currer Bell (3 volumes, London: Smith, Elder, 1853; 1 volume, New York: Harper, 1853);
The Professor: A Tale, as Currer Bell (2 volumes, London: Smith, Elder, 1857; 1 volume, New York: Harper, 1857);
The Twelve Adventurers and Other Stories, edited by C. K. Shorter and C. W. Hatfield (London: Hodder & Stoughton, 1925);
Legends of Angria: Compiled from the Early Writings of Charlotte Brontë, edited by Fannie E. Ratchford and William Clyde De Vane (New Haven: Yale University Press, 1933);
Five Novelettes, edited by Winifred Gerin (London: Folio Press, 1971).
COLLECTIONS: *The Life and Works of Charlotte Brontë and Her Sisters*, Haworth Edition, edited by Mrs. Humphry Ward and C. K. Shorter (7 volumes, London: Smith, Elder, 1899-1900);
The Shakespeare Head Brontë, edited by T. J. Wise and J. A. Symington (19 volumes, Oxford: Blackwell, 1931-1938);
The Clarendon Edition of the Novels of the Brontës, I. R. Jack, general editor (3 volumes, Oxford: Clarendon Press, 1969-   ).

Charlotte Brontë's fame and influence rest on a very slender canon of published works: only four novels and some contributions to a volume of

(National Portrait Gallery)

poetry. Her reputation may be explained in part by the astounding success of her first novel, *Jane Eyre* (1847); it owes much also to the romantic appeal of her personal history, given prominence soon after her death by Elizabeth Cleghorn Gaskell's excellent biography, a work preeminent in its genre. Of greater importance, perhaps, is the recognition by historians of fiction that Charlotte Brontë's work made a significant contribution to the development of the novel; her explorations of emotional repression and the feminine psyche introduced a new depth and intensity to the study of character and motive in fiction, anticipating in some respects the work of such writers as George Eliot and D. H. Lawrence.

25

Her strength as a novelist lies in her ability to portray in moving detail the inner struggles of women who are endowed with a powerful capacity for feeling, yet whose social circumstances deny them the opportunity for intellectual or emotional fulfillment. Charlotte Brontë was not in any formal sense a proponent of women's rights, but in her writing she speaks out strongly against the injustices suffered by women in a society that restricts their freedom of action and exploits their dependent status. Her protests grew out of her own experience, which provided much of the material for her fiction; though she once insisted that "we only suffer reality to *suggest*, never to *dictate*," her novels include many characters and incidents recognizably drawn from her life, and her heroines have much in common with their creator.

Charlotte Brontë was born on 21 April 1816 at Thornton in the West Riding of Yorkshire. Her father, Patrick Brontë (1777-1861), a native of County Down in Ireland, had risen above the poverty of his family to become an undergraduate at St. John's College, Cambridge, and in 1807 was ordained a priest in the Church of England. In 1812 he met, courted, and married Maria Branwell (1783-1821), a pious and educated young woman from Cornwall. Their life together was tragically brief; Maria bore six children in seven years (Maria in 1813; Elizabeth, 1815; Charlotte; Patrick Branwell, 1817; Emily Jane, 1818; Anne, 1820), then died of cancer in 1821 at the age of thirty-eight. Her death may have been hastened by the family's move in 1820 from Thornton to Haworth, where Mr. Brontë had been appointed perpetual curate. Beautiful as the landscape might be around Haworth, physical conditions in this rugged little mill town must have been harsh and unpleasant for the parson's delicate wife. The Brontës' new home was a stone-flagged parsonage, standing exposed to the elements at the top of a steep hill and on the edge of the open moors. Its situation was rendered even more unhealthy by its proximity to the overcrowded cemetery of St. Michael's Church. Sanitation in Haworth was primitive: as late as 1850 a government inspector found open sewers and overflowing cesspits on the main street, next to outlets for drinking water. It is hardly surprising that infant mortality rates in Haworth were high or that there were frequent outbreaks of cholera and typhoid. Throughout her life, Charlotte Brontë was to suffer from fevers, colds, and bilious attacks undoubtedly attributable to this most inhospitable environment.

Nor was there much consolation to be found in the society of Haworth. Its inhabitants, even thirty years later, struck Mrs. Gaskell as a "wild, rough

The Reverend Patrick Brontë

Maria Brontë (Brontë Parsonage Museum)

population" among whom there was "little display of any of the amenities of life." Mr. Brontë won the respect of his parishioners, but there was little social contact between the townsfolk and the family at the parsonage; the Brontë children thus turned to one another for companionship and entertainment. This interdependence was intensified after the death of Mrs. Brontë. The early loss of their mother had a lasting effect on the children, particularly Charlotte; all her published novels are concerned in one way or another with young women who must lead a lonely path through life without the warmth and security of parental love. Not that the young Brontës were uncared for: after Maria's death, her sister Elizabeth Branwell came to live at the parsonage and supervised the household until her own death in 1842. Aunt Branwell was a rather stern, formal woman, however, with rigid and somewhat ascetic religious views; "the children respected her," notes Mrs. Gaskell, "and had that sort of affection for her which is generated by esteem; but I do not think they ever freely loved her." Yet the children were happy enough: they played and roamed the moors together; they read widely under the vigorous tutelage of their father, discussed social and political issues of the day, and developed those qualities of intellect and inventiveness that were to flower in the works of their maturity.

In August 1824 Mr. Brontë sent Charlotte to join Maria and Elizabeth at the recently opened Clergy Daughters' School at Cowan Bridge, near Tunstall in Lancashire. This was a charitable institution, where the daughters of poor clergymen might receive an education suited to their station and be prepared for future employment as governesses. Its founder was William Carus Wilson, a well-intentioned but overzealous clergyman who appears to have given little thought to the physical needs of the children in his charge; he imposed a stern regime of ascetic piety and self-denial which, in combination with inadequate attention to proper diet and the unhealthy situation of the school buildings, produced a succession of illnesses among the pupils and an outbreak of typhoid in April 1825. Charlotte Brontë would later give a vivid portrait in *Jane Eyre* of the school and its director; though colored by personal bitterness, her account of "Lowood Institution" is in essentials an accurate depiction of the harshness of life at Cowan Bridge. Writing to a friend in 1848 concerning the advisability of sending children to the Clergy Daughters' School (then removed to Casterton), Brontë speaks in very matter-of-fact tones of the school's "rickety infancy": "Typhus fever decimated the school

periodically, and consumption and scrofula in every variety of form, [which] bad air and water, and bad, insufficient diet can generate, preyed on the ill-fated pupils." Her own sisters were among the victims of such conditions: first Maria, then Elizabeth, contracted consumption, were removed from the school, and died at home, Maria on 6 May 1825 and her sister on 15 June 1825. The death of Maria was especially painful to Charlotte; her eldest sister had become a guide and mentor, and Charlotte would later eulogize her patient virtue and premature wisdom in *Jane Eyre* in the portrait of Helen Burns.

After this tragic loss, Mr. Brontë decided to educate his children himself, and for the next six years they lived at home under the watchful eyes of Aunt Branwell and Tabitha Ackroyd, the parsonage servant. More than ever they were thrown upon their own resources; yet, despite their lack of social contact, they were never bored or unoccupied. Mr. Brontë encouraged them to read—and they read voraciously: Shakespeare, Milton, Bunyan, Dryden, Scott, Wordsworth, Byron; the *Arabian Nights Entertainments*; Whig and Tory newspapers; monthly magazines, notably *Blackwood's Edinburgh Magazine*; illustrated annuals like the *Keepsake*. Though their own collection was small, the Brontës had access to the library of the Keighley Mechanics' Institute, less than four miles away, which Mr. Brontë had joined soon after its foundation in 1825. The breadth of their reading attests to their father's liberality of mind; it also helps to explain the curious variety of subjects and techniques displayed in the children's own early writings.

Their apprenticeship to literature had begun before the deaths of Maria and Elizabeth with the composition and performance of little plays under Maria's direction. After the return from Cowan Bridge, Charlotte and Branwell assumed the leadership in devising imaginary worlds populated by romantic figures from myth, history, and high society, whose doings they chronicled in a series of interwoven tales. The first of the series, the "Young Men's Play," originated with Mr. Brontë's gift to Branwell in June 1826 of a set of twelve toy soldiers; each of the children took one, naming it after a particular hero (Charlotte called hers after the Duke of Wellington), and made up stories, eventually in written form, about the exploits of the "Twelves." That a group of imaginative children should collaborate in the creation of a fantasy world is by no means unusual; what sets the storymaking of the youthful Brontës apart is that it occupied them all well into adulthood—Emily and Anne were still devising plots for their world of Gondal in

Haworth Parsonage, next to the cemetery that may have contributed to the Brontë sisters' poor health and early deaths

1845—and came dangerously close to an unhealthy obsession from which Charlotte had to free herself in 1839 by a conscious and explicit act of rejection.

The bulk of Charlotte's juvenile writings is concerned with the history of Angria, a kingdom that grew out of her extended collaboration with Branwell. It began as a confederacy of the "Twelves," located in Africa, whose capital was called "Glass Town" and whose rulers were four genii: Tallii (Charlotte), Brannii, Emmii, and Annii. The geography of this new land, first described in Charlotte's tale "The Twelve Adventurers" (manuscript dated 15 April 1829), was inspired in part by the Reverend J. Goldsmith's *Grammar of General Geography* (1803) and articles in *Blackwood's Edinburgh Magazine*; its supernatural inhabitants were unmistakably related to their counterparts in the *Arabian Nights* and Ridley's *Tales of the Genii* (1764); its cities borrowed features from those depicted in the extravagant pictures of John Martin, whose work was often reproduced in contemporary annuals; its populace came from the society columns of newspapers or magazines, from portraits of the aristocracy which the young Brontës copied from books, and from the political controversies of the day which they keenly followed and eagerly discussed. This mixture of fantasy and reality is well exemplified by Charlotte's "Tales of the Islanders" (June 1829-June 1830), an extended narrative set in a fairy-tale world in which her characters debate the political and religious issues of contemporary England, especially the Catholic Emancipation Act of April 1829 and the storm surrounding the Duke of Wellington. In this story Charlotte also introduced the Duke's sons, the Marquis of Douro and Lord Charles Wellesley, who were to take over from their father as leading personages in the world of Glass Town.

As the early "plays" gradually merged into the history of the Glass Town Confederacy and the actions of its great notables, the children collaborated in a systematic charting of events and relationships. In January 1829 Branwell began *Branwells Blackwoods Magazine* (subsequently to be called *Blackwoods Young Mens Magazine*), an imitation of the children's favorite periodical reproduced in miniature form, presumably to correspond to the size of their original soldier heroes. Charlotte took over the editorship in August, and under the pseudonym of Captain Tree, or in the characters of Douro or Lord Charles, wrote poems and stories about Glass Town society, frequently alluding to characters or incidents developed in Branwell's manuscripts. The narratives became more complex; Glass Town acquired greater sophistication and became Verreopolis, then Verdopolis; Branwell began to chronicle the military and political upheavals that were to become the focus of his interest in the emerging kingdom of Angria, while Charlotte gave more and more of her attention to the personalities and domestic relations of Verdopolitan celebrities. Her tale of "Albion and Marina" (October 1830) introduced the theme of passionate romantic love that was to dominate her subsequent contributions to the joint saga.

Charlotte's participation in Verdopolitan affairs came to a temporary halt in January 1831 when, with the financial support of her godparents, the Atkinsons, she was sent to Roe Head, a small private school near Mirfield under the direction of Miss Margaret Wooler and her sisters. Here she stayed for a year and a half in much happier circumstances than at Cowan Bridge; indeed, Miss Wooler was to become a lifelong friend, and Brontë would return to Roe Head in 1835 as an assistant teacher. Here also she met the two girls whose enduring friendship was to lift her out of her social isolation at Haworth and to sustain her often in

Elizabeth Branwell ("Aunt Branwell"), who raised the Brontë children after their mother died in 1821

times of emotional duress. Ellen Nussey was a quiet, timid, pious girl whose family lived at Rydings, a big house in Birstall that would later lend some of its features to Thornfield Hall in *Jane Eyre*. Stolid, unimaginative, conservative, Ellen yet possessed a ready fund of sympathy and affection that quickly won a response from Charlotte. Her other new-found friend, Mary Taylor, offered a startling contrast of personality. Mary's father, a cloth manufacturer and banker at Gomersal, had suffered bankruptcy in 1825 and spent the rest of his life working to pay off his debts. From him Mary inherited strong Radical views, a blunt outspokenness, and an independence of spirit that would lead her to immigrate to New Zealand. Ellen and Mary became integral parts of Charlotte's life; the three corresponded regularly for over twenty years, exchanging news about themselves and their families, and Charlotte's visits to their homes provided her with a wealth of impressions which she was to draw on when she came to write her great novels. *Shirley* (1849) is especially indebted to Brontë's memories of the Taylors, who are presented there as the Yorke family; Mary herself appears as young Rose Yorke, as well as lends some of her ideas about society to the novel's eponymous heroine. Ellen's shy and retiring nature contributes something to the depiction of Caroline Helstone; and Shirley's residence, "Fieldhead," is based on Oakwell Hall, an Elizabethan house near Birstall owned by relatives of the Nussey family. When Mrs. Gaskell came to write the biography of Charlotte Brontë, Ellen Nussey and Mary Taylor provided her with lengthy reminiscences, and Nussey was able to supply her with over 300 letters by Brontë which she had kept over the years.

At Roe Head, Charlotte worked hard to make up for the deficiencies in her formal education; Ellen Nussey later recalled that she "always seemed to feel that a deep responsibility rested upon her; that she was an object of expense to those at home, and that she must use every moment to attain the purpose for which she was sent to school, i.e., to fit herself for governess life. . . ." On her return to Haworth in May 1832 Charlotte continued her studies and tutored her younger sisters; but though much of her time was thus occupied, she had not lost interest in the story of Verdopolitan society and renewed her contributions to the saga. In "The Bridal" (August 1832) she enlarged upon the relationship between the Marquis of Douro and his first great love, Marian Hume, filling out the Byronic lineaments of her hero's character and developing the themes of temptation and betrayal,

The Reverend William Carus Wilson, the model for Mr. Brocklehurst in Jane Eyre *(Brontë Society)*

duty and desire, that were to recur throughout her juvenilia.

Branwell's writing at this time was mainly concerned with the history and politics of the Confederacy, and his pedantically detailed narratives make dull reading beside Charlotte's lively and melodramatic accounts of romantic intrigue and rival lovers. The children still worked together on the intricate elaboration of their world, and Charlotte's stories assume a knowledge on the reader's part of events described elsewhere by Branwell; but after her return from Roe Head, Charlotte's writing shows a distinct advance in descriptive power and depth of character portrayal. Arthur Wellesley, Marquis of Douro, now Duke of Zamorna, becomes the dominant figure in most of the prose narratives produced by Charlotte after 1832. A compound of moody grandeur, dashing bravery, and sadistic heartlessness, Zamorna wears a mantle woven from Milton and Byron: "O Zamorna! what eyes those are glancing under the deep shadow of that raven crest! They bode no good. . . . Satan gave them their glory to deepen the midnight gloom that always follows where their lustre has fallen most lovingly. . . . All here is passion and fire unquenchable. Impetuous

sin, stormy pride, diving and soaring enthusiasm, war and poetry, are kindling their fires in all his veins, and his wild blood boils from his heart and back again like a torrent of new-sprung lava. Young duke? Young demon!" ("A Peep into a Picture Book," May 1834). While Branwell explores Zamorna's political fortunes in the newly created kingdom of Angria (established in the narratives of 1834), Charlotte follows the twists and turns of his unpredictable nature as he torments a succession of beautiful, heartsick women, whose Griselda-like meekness in suffering serves only to arouse his scorn or anger.

The Angrian stories of this period also see the development of a subject touched on in Charlotte's earliest narratives, the antagonism between two brothers. This first appeared in the form of Lord Charles Wellesley's hostility toward his older brother Arthur; their rivalry gives way to the deeper rift between Edward and William Percy, the sons of Zamorna's archenemy Alexander Percy, earl of Northangerland. The young Percys are first described in Branwell's story "The Wool is Rising" (June 1834); cast off by their father, they establish themselves in the wool trade, but Edward's cold ambition soon leads him to a harsh assertion of mastery over William. Charlotte picked up this theme in several stories ("The Spell," June-July 1834; "My Angria and the Angrians," October 1834; "The Duke of Zamorna," July 1838; "The Ashworths," 1839-1840); ultimately it would find its way into the first of her adult novels, *The Professor* (1857), in the relationship between Edward and William Crimsworth.

Charlotte's absorption in the Angrian world was interrupted in July 1835 when, at the invitation of Miss Wooler, she returned to Roe Head as a teacher. She was accompanied by Emily, who was to receive free tuition as part of the arrangement, but Emily's unhappiness at her exile from Haworth soon led to her replacement by Anne. Despite Miss Wooler's kindness, Charlotte found her duties tedious and distasteful; separated from her creative partner Branwell and allowed little free time, she became increasingly frustrated by the fetters placed on her imagination. A series of diary jottings from this period known as the "Roe Head Journals" show the extent to which the demands of daily routine clashed with powerful inner yearnings. "All this day," she wrote on 11 August 1836, "I have been in a dream half-miserable & half ecstatic miserable because I could not follow it out uninterruptedly, ecstatic because it shewed almost in the vivid light of reality the ongoings of the infernal world. . . . The thought came over me am I to spend all the best part of my life in this wretched bondage forcibly suppressing my rage at the idleness the apathy & the hyperbolical & most asinine stupidity of those fat-headed oafs & on compulsion assuming an air of kindness patience & assiduity?" She recorded waking visions of Angrian scenes which presented themselves to her with frightening vividness; her attempts to repress such imaginings produced feelings of guilt and melancholy. "If you knew my thoughts," she wrote to Ellen Nussey on 10 May 1836, "the dreams that absorb me; and the fiery imagination that at times eats me up and makes me feel Society as it is, wretchedly insipid, you would pity and I dare say despise me."

School vacations brought some relief and allowed Brontë to continue her Angrian narratives. "Passing Events" (April 1836), "Julia" (June 1837), and "Four Years Ago" (July 1837) all develop aspects of the political drama worked out by Branwell, but focus on scene and character rather than on plot. The "infernal world" still exerted its power over her; but Brontë—now past her twentieth year—was moving away from the colorful excitement of simple melodrama toward a maturer exploration of feeling, especially the suffering of women in love. The later Angrian romances reflect this new maturity in their treatment as well as in subject matter. "Mina Laury" (January 1838), in its depiction of Zamorna's heartlessness and Mina's selfless devotion, displays greater unity and coherence than Brontë's earlier stories, and Byronic excess in characterization now gives way to more realistic analysis of character and motive. Setting, too, in these later stories is less exotic, more suggestive of the writer's own environment; in "Stancliff's Hotel" (June 1838) and "Henry Hastings" (February-March 1839) the cloud-capped palaces of Angria are replaced by country houses in a recognizably English landscape. "Henry Hastings" also gives prominence to characters and situations that reemerge in Brontë's adult fiction. The female protagonist, Elizabeth Hastings, is reserved and self-effacing, but her calm exterior conceals intense emotion. Like her yet-distant successor Jane Eyre she is faced with a conflict between duty and desire and is saved from a surrender to feeling by her concern for self-respect. There is an element of autobiography in Brontë's depiction of Elizabeth as "the little dignified Governess" who dresses plainly, values her independence, and loves her degenerate and reckless brother despite his public dishonor. Branwell had written several stories in the persona of Henry Hastings; through the story of Elizabeth's

Charlotte Brontë's watercolor of Glass Town, the capital city of the imaginary African confederacy created by the Brontë children (Brontë Parsonage Museum)

loyalty to her reprobate brother, Brontë might express her feelings toward Branwell, whose conduct was already giving evidence of that weakness of character that would lead him to alcoholism and drugs.

Anne's departure from Miss Wooler's school (now relocated at Dewsbury Moor) in December 1837, and her own increasingly depressed spirits, led Charlotte to give up her post and return to Haworth in May 1838. Her respite was brief, however; the family's precarious financial circumstances, made more difficult by Branwell's failure to establish himself as a painter in Bradford, led Charlotte Brontë to seek employment once again, and in May 1839 she became governess to the children of the Sidgwick family of Stonegappe, near Lothersdale. The experience was an unhappy one: the Sidgwicks treated Brontë with what seemed to

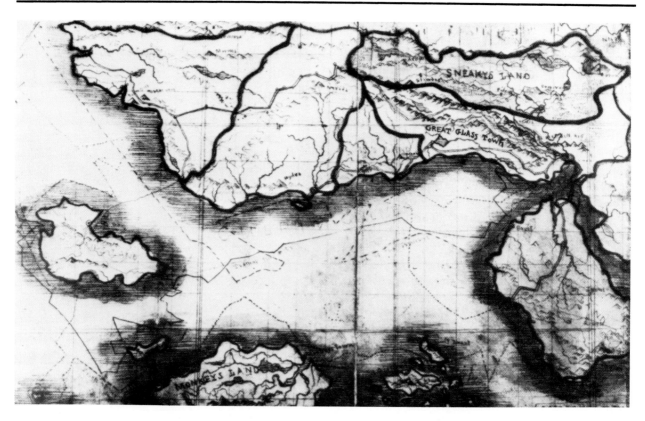

Branwell's map of the Glass Town Confederacy (British Museum)

her to be undue coldness and condescension; the children tormented her by their rudeness and lack of discipline; and after less than three months she was back at home, telling Ellen Nussey that "I never was so glad to get out of a house in my life." Relieved of this burden, Brontë returned to her writing with new vigor and produced "Caroline Vernon" (July-December 1839), the last of her Angrian tales. The account of a young girl's infatuation with her guardian, the Duke of Zamorna, "Caroline Vernon" shows another advance in Brontë's analysis of feminine psychology. Romantic passion is here treated with critical detachment and seen as a destructive force; Brontë does not identify with her heroine, presenting her instead as an inexperienced and undisciplined adolescent, "raw, flighty & romantic."

Sheltered though her own life was in comparison to that of her heroines, Charlotte Brontë discovered to her surprise that she herself was capable of arousing admiration: twice in the same year she received proposals of marriage. The first came from Henry Nussey, Ellen's brother, a curate in Sussex, who wrote in March 1839 to offer Brontë

his hand, since "in due time he should want a wife to take care of his pupils." She had no difficulty in turning down this cool suitor, telling Ellen that she could not feel "that intense attachment which would make me willing to die for him; and, if ever I marry, it must be in that light of adoration that I will regard my husband." Her second proposal, the following August, came from another clergyman, an impetuous young Irish curate who was smitten after only one meeting with her; him, too, she refused. The prospects of her finding a man she could truly love seemed remote; "I'm certainly doomed to be an old maid," she wrote to Ellen Nussey; "I can't expect another chance—never mind I made up my mind to that fate ever since I was twelve years old."

The sober awareness that her dreams of passionate love would never be matched by reality may have contributed to her decision to abandon Angria after "Caroline Vernon." In an undated manuscript placed by most scholars at the end of 1839, Brontë announces her desire "to quit for awhile that burning clime where we have sojourned too long—its skies flame—the glow of sunset is always upon it— the mind would cease from excitement and turn now to a cooler region where the dawn breaks grey and sober, and the coming day for a time at least is subdued by clouds." In penning these lines, Brontë was probably thinking about her first venture into realistic prose fiction, which took form in the winter of 1839-1840, and in a revised version of early 1841 culminated in the unfinished story known as "Ashworth." In part, this is a return to old subjects; the central figure, a Yorkshire industrialist named Alexander Ashworth, owes much in character and personal history to Alexander Percy, the Northangerland of Branwell's narratives. Percy's sons Edward and William, already depicted as rivals in the Angrian cycle, reappear as Edward and William Ashworth, and like their earlier namesakes are cast out by their father to make their own way in the world. However, when the story shifts from the Ashworths to a picture of life in a girls' school, focusing on the lonely figure of an orphaned child, the narrative gains new life and interest, and Brontë can be seen moving in the direction of a favorite theme in her later novels. That she regarded "Ashworth" as a serious venture into adult fiction is apparent from her request for an opinion from Hartley Coleridge (son of the poet S. T. Coleridge), to whom she sent a portion of the manuscript in December 1840, describing her story as a "demi-semi novelette." Coleridge's verdict evidently was unfavorable, since in her reply Brontë promised to commit her protagonists to oblivion. This was not the first time that she had sought advice from a

well-known writer; in 1837 she had corresponded with the poet laureate Robert Southey, who had been similarly discouraging, warning her that "literature cannot be the business of a woman's life, and it ought not to be. The more she is engaged in her proper duties, the less leisure will she have for it. . . ."

Under the pressure of "proper duties," Brontë left home once again in March 1841 to become a governess in the White family at Rawdon, near Bradford. The Whites proved to be more amiable employers than the Sidgwicks; but Brontë left them in December to set in motion a plan the family had discussed for six months. This was for the three sisters to open their own school, with financial support from Aunt Branwell; as a preliminary step to strengthen their qualifications for such a venture, Charlotte and Emily wanted to spend a half-year in school on the Continent, where they might improve their grasp of foreign languages. Belgium was fixed upon, since there the cost of living was low; also, Mary and Martha Taylor were at school in Brussels and spoke favorably of their experience.

After a short time spent sight-seeing in London (Charlotte Brontë would recall the excitement of this first visit to the capital in both *The Professor* and *Villette*, 1853), Charlotte and Emily, accompanied by Mr. Brontë, arrived at the Pensionnat Heger in Brussels on 15 February 1842, there to recommence the lives of schoolgirls at the ages of twenty-five and twenty-three respectively. The

Some of the miniature books and magazines produced by the Brontë children. The coin shown is about the size of a U.S. half-dollar. (Brontë Parsonage Museum)

Ellen Nussey, who became Charlotte Brontë's lifelong friend
(Brontë Society)

school's owner and directress was Claire Zoé Parent Heger, who was thirty-seven years old at the time of the Brontës' arrival in the rue d'Isabelle. In 1836 she had married Constantin Heger, a widower five years her junior, who taught at the Athénée Royal de Bruxelles; after their marriage, M. Heger retained his post at the Athénée, but also assisted his wife in the operation of her school and gave classes there in literature. He was something of a romantic figure, having fought at the barricades during the Belgian revolution of 1830, and displaying a moody impetuousness that undoubtedly had a special appeal for one whose imaginary heroes had been similarly governed by violence of feeling. From the outset, the Hegers showed great kindness to the two strange little Englishwomen. Their lessons in French literature and composition were supervised by M. Heger, who assigned readings in the great French writers and corrected their exercises with comments aimed at sharpening their perception of style. Under Heger's guidance, Charlotte Brontë encountered the works of such authors as Chateaubriand, Hugo, and Lamartine and copied out extracts from their writings; she also wrote a variety of devoirs on such topics as "La Justice Humaine," "Le Palais de la Mort," "La Chute des

Feuilles," and "La Mort de Napoléon," which, despite the inevitable stiffness of academic set pieces, show commendable fluency and precision. Charlotte Brontë's adult writings in English, characterized by a poetic quality often derived from syntactic inversions, antitheses, and repetitions, would owe much to these exercises performed under the demanding tutelage of Constantin Heger; and her study of French romanticism taught her how to make language convey heightened states of feeling normally expressed in poetic form.

The sisters made few friends at the pensionnat, partly because of their natural shyness and diffidence, partly because of their Protestant suspicion of all things Catholic and their belief in the superiority of all things British. Charlotte Brontë was especially scathing in her comments on the Hegers' Belgian pupils, whose character she described to Ellen Nussey as "cold, selfish, animal and inferior" and whose principles she regarded as "rotten to the core." Nevertheless, Brontë's first year in Belgium was busy and enjoyable; in addition to her own schoolwork, she gave English lessons, visited the Taylor sisters and their cousins, the Dixons, explored art galleries and museums, and saw an exhibition of paintings at the Brussels Salon of 1842 which she was later to recall in an episode in *Villette*. Above all, she found herself drawn more and more strongly to Constantin Heger, an attraction carefully omitted by Mrs. Gaskell from her biography. Heger's dominant personality, his acute intelligence, his position as mentor and friend, all combined to arouse in Brontë an admiration for one

Miss Wooler's school at Roe Head, where Charlotte Brontë spent
a miserable three years as a teacher

The Duke of Zamorna and Alexander Percy, two of the characters in the Brontës' Angrian stories, as sketched by Branwell (Brontë Parsonage Museum)

whom she could regard as her master. Had she been younger, her feelings might have taken the form of a schoolgirl infatuation, quickly roused and quickly quenched; but at twenty-six she had deeper yearnings, desires which possibly she did not understand herself.

Toward the end of 1842 life in Brussels took on a darker shade. First, in September, came news of the death of William Weightman, Mr. Brontë's attractive young curate since 1839, with whom all the sisters had playfully flirted. An even greater shock was the sudden death of Martha Taylor, who died of cholera in October and was buried at the Protestant Cemetery outside Brussels; the tragedy impressed itself deeply in Charlotte Brontë's mind and would later be alluded to directly in *Shirley*, where Martha appears as Jessie Yorke. A final somber note was struck at the end of October by the death of Aunt Branwell. Charlotte and Emily immediately left for Haworth, taking with them a letter of condolence for Mr. Brontë from Constantin Heger, who expressed the hope that one of the girls, if not both, might be allowed to return.

Charlotte did return, at the end of January 1843; this time, however, she traveled alone (Emily had decided to stay in Haworth), experiencing difficulties much like those she later bestowed on Lucy Snowe, who makes a similar journey in *Villette*. Her second year in Brussels began well; she was warmly received by the Hegers and promoted to the position of salaried teacher. She gave English lessons to M. Heger and his brother-in-law and continued her own studies in German; she paid frequent visits to her English acquaintances, the Dixons and the Wheelwrights. But without Emily's companionship, and in the absence of Mary Taylor (now in Germany), Charlotte felt increasingly isolated. Her relations with Mme Heger were deteriorating; to Emily she complained of Madame's aversion to her and expressed the belief that she was being spied upon. Allowing for an element of exaggeration in Brontë's complaints, there is little doubt that Mme Heger had become more guarded in her exchanges with the little English teacher; though Brontë never made any avowal of an attachment to Constantin Heger, her feelings must have been quite apparent to the shrewd directress of the pensionnat, who probably sought ways of reducing Brontë's opportunities for social contact with her husband. Brontë found herself in an increasingly "Robinson-Crusoe-like condition," lamenting that M. Heger had "in a great measure withdrawn the light of his countenance." Thrown more and more upon her own resources, Charlotte Brontë withdrew into the childhood world of her imagination; to Branwell, the former partner of her fantasies, she spoke of recurring "as fanatically as ever to the old ideas, the old faces, and the old scenes in the world below." When the school holidays came in mid-August, the Hegers left on their vacation, the teachers and pupils went home, and Brontë was abandoned to her own devices until school resumed at the end of September. Her solitude bore heavily upon her, and she entered a state of nervous depression. The feelings of bitter frustration, loneliness, and possibly guilt were too much for her; on 1 September she took the extraordinary step of confessing to a Catholic priest in Sainte Gudule, the collegiate church close to the rue d'Isabelle. Writing to Emily the next day, Charlotte described the incident in full and finally dismissed it as a "freak"; but its details

Charlotte Brontë about 1838, as painted by J. H. Thompson of Bradford (Brontë Society)

remained clearly impressed upon her memory and provided her with an important scene in *Villette* ten years later.

By the end of the year her loneliness and homesickness had become too much for her, and on 1 January 1844 Brontë left Brussels for the last time. The strength of her feelings for M. Heger, however, was undiminished; the pain she suffered at parting from him was to last for the next two years, as she sought to maintain his friendship by correspondence. Some of her letters to Heger have survived; they were evidently torn up by the recipient, then reassembled by Madame, and now maintain a patchwork existence under glass at the British Library. They reflect a rising desperation in Brontë; in no sense are they love letters, yet they are unmistakably passionate in their pleas for some acknowledgment, some signal of recognition and regard. What Heger thought of all this is not known; there is no evidence that he felt anything but a kindly affection and concern for an apt and hardworking young pupil-teacher. In Brontë's eyes, however, Heger constituted an ideal: cultured, energetic, masterful (she addresses him in one letter as "mon maître"), and there is something of Heger in the heroes of all her mature novels, especially in the figure of Paul Emanuel in *Villette*.

At their parting, Heger had given Brontë a diploma attesting to her experience and qualifications; once back in Haworth, she hoped to make use of this in realizing the sisters' original plan of opening their own school. She set about seeking pupils and in July 1844 sent Ellen Nussey copies of a prospectus she had drawn up, describing "The Misses Brontë's Establishment for the Board and Education of a limited number of Young Ladies." She also wrote to a number of acquaintances to announce her intentions, on one occasion enclosing the diploma she had received from Heger. Her efforts proved fruitless; not one prospective pupil applied, and by the close of the year the plan had been abandoned.

With the failure of the school project, Charlotte Brontë's life seemed to have reached a point of stagnation. She no longer heard anything from Constantin Heger, although she continued writing to him until November 1845. Mary Taylor, her principal source of intellectual stimulation outside her own family, left for New Zealand in March 1845. Ellen Nussey remained always ready to offer friendship and comfort, but she was too limited and unimaginative to provide Brontë with an outlet for her deeper needs and concerns. To make matters worse, in July 1845 Branwell was dismissed from his

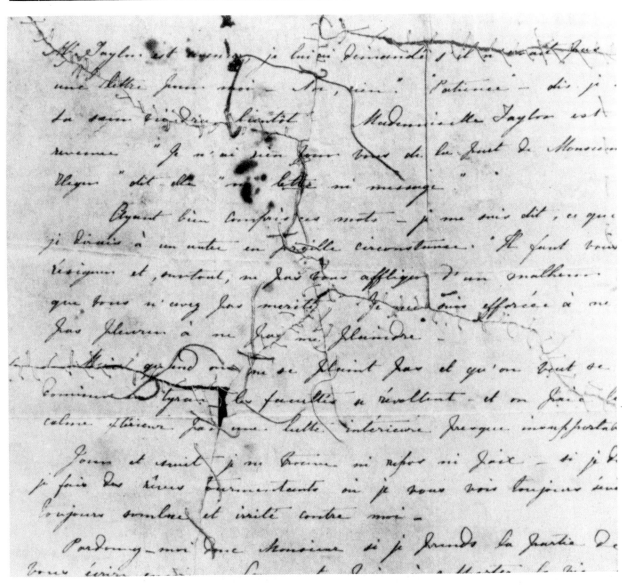

An 1845 letter from Charlotte Brontë to M. Heger, torn up by him and sewn back together by his wife (British Museum)

post as tutor in the Robinson family of Thorp Green, accused of improper conduct toward his employer's wife, and came home to plague the family with his increasingly drunken and irrational behavior. Charlotte, once his closest companion, became bitterly critical of his "frantic folly" and dissipation; her disgust at his moral depravity would shortly find expression in *The Professor*, where her narrator William Crimsworth reflects on the spectacle of "a mind degraded by the practice of mean subterfuge, by the habit of perfidious deception, and a body depraved by the infectious influence of the vice-polluted soul."

Driven closer together by Branwell's progres-

sive deterioration, Charlotte and her sisters now entered a phase of literary production from which their brother was excluded. Its beginnings are chronicled in Charlotte's "Biographical Notice of Ellis and Acton Bell," prefixed to the 1850 edition of *Wuthering Heights and Agnes Grey*. In the autumn of 1845, Charlotte "accidentally lighted on a MS volume of verse" in Emily's handwriting and was immediately convinced that the poems merited publication. After Emily's initial reluctance had been overcome, the Brontë sisters set out to realize their long-cherished dream of authorship. They made a small selection of their poems; then, with some of the small legacy left to each of them by Aunt

The prospectus for the Brontë sisters' proposed school, which failed to attract even one application (Brontë Parsonage Museum)

Branwell, they paid the London firm of Aylott and Jones thirty-six pounds, ten shillings to meet the expenses of paper, printing, and advertising. The Brontës became the Bells: Currer (Charlotte), Ellis (Emily), and Acton (Anne). Male-sounding pseudonyms were preferred, as Charlotte explained in her "Biographical Notice," because "we had a vague impression that authoresses are liable to be looked on with prejudice; we had noticed how critics sometimes use for their chastisement the weapon of personality, and for their reward, a flattery, which is not true praise." *Poems by Currer, Ellis and Acton Bell* appeared in one volume at four shillings in May 1846; it received several

friendly notices, but by June 1847 only two copies had been sold.

Lack of success in their first venture into print did not deter the sisters, however; even before the appearance of the *Poems*, they had already decided to try their hand at publishable fiction. In this they were doubtless encouraged by the enormous popularity of novels with the Victorian public. Thanks to such developments as part publication, cheap one-volume reprints, and subscription circulating libraries, a successful writer might now command a huge audience. The Brontë sisters were certainly impelled by the honorable motive of seeking critical applause, but undoubtedly they also hoped to turn their love of writing to good account and make some money by their pens. To this end each wrote a short novel: *Wuthering Heights* by Emily, *Agnes Grey* by Anne, and *The Professor* by Charlotte. Their intention was to have them published together as a three-volume work, the format imposed on most new fiction by the needs of the circulating libraries. Fair copies of the manuscripts were completed by the end of June 1846 (that of *The Professor* is dated 27 June) and sent to Henry Colburn on 4 July. However, finding an interested publisher proved much more difficult than had been the case with the *Poems*, since the sisters could not meet the costs of production themselves; over the next twelve months, the manuscripts suffered half a dozen rejections. Finally, in July 1847 the London firm of Thomas Cautley Newby agreed to publish *Wuthering Heights* and *Agnes Grey*, provided that the authors contributed fifty pounds toward the cost of production; but Newby flatly refused to include *The Professor*. The sisters accepted these harsh terms, and Charlotte was left to find a separate publisher for her own novel; her search proved fruitless, for though it was instrumental in leading her to the firm that would swiftly accept and publish *Jane Eyre*, *The Professor* never reached print during her lifetime.

The novel's lack of appeal for prospective publishers is partly attributable to its prosaic subject matter and lack of sensational incident; indeed, it was the publisher's objections on this score that led Brontë in her next work (*Jane Eyre*) to the mode of romantic melodrama. *The Professor* suffers also from awkwardness in construction and in the handling of plot: the clumsy opening in epistolary form (a stratagem dropped after the first chapter), the loose arrangement of episodes, the lack of any real suspense, and the anticlimactic ending all make the story seem flat and unexciting. Nevertheless, the book does have real power in its delineation of character and in its exploration of the individual's struggle to find emotional fulfillment despite socially repressive circumstances.

The Professor's effectiveness in depicting strong emotions derives largely from its autobiographical origins; in her portrayal of the love between teacher and pupil in a Belgian girls' school, Brontë drew heavily on her recent experiences in Brussels. She sought to disguise this personal element by making her narrator-protagonist a man, a device she had frequently employed in her Angrian tales; and she revived the Angrian motif of enmity between two brothers, the elder, hardheaded and ambitious, the younger, cultured and sensitive. Like most Brontë

A silhouette of Branwell Brontë, whose degenerate behavior grieved and disgusted his sisters (Brontë Society)

protagonists, William Crimsworth is an orphan, in this case the ward of an aristocratic family. He begins his career by rejecting the status of dependent and chooses to enter a voluntary servitude as clerk to his elder brother Edward, a blunt and morose mill owner. William's independent nature cannot bear the yoke of his brother's tyranny, however, and he strikes out afresh, becoming a teacher in a boys' school in Brussels. This first part of the narrative is an uneasy mixture of social comedy and melodrama, the tone strained and uncertain; but Brontë succeeds in establishing William as a quirky yet intelligent character, chafing under his bondage to inferior minds and eager to assert his individuality. A related concern is the connection between sexual power and social identity, a theme explored in all of Brontë's subsequent novels; Crimsworth is made

JANE EYRE.

An Autobiography.

EDITED BY

CURRER BELL

IN THREE VOLUMES.

VOL. I.

LONDON:
SMITH, ELDER, AND CO., CORNHILL.
——
1847.

Title page of Charlotte Brontë's first published novel, which was successful with the public and with most of the critics

painfully conscious that as "a dependant amongst wealthy strangers" he is unattractive to the band of young women who cluster around his prosperous brother. Though there is a self-pitying tone to William's reflections, his emotional vulnerability and sense of failure at this stage are necessary elements in his development; as the novel progresses, he acquires greater confidence and maturity in his relationships with women, until he is ready to take on the dominant role as a lover.

A factor in William's growth is his friendship with the radical and outspoken manufacturer Hunsden Yorke Hunsden, a precursor of Hiram Yorke in *Shirley*. Hunsden, who encourages William to rebel against Edward, embodies the force of instinctual feeling; this makes him both attractive and dangerous. His association with potentially anarchic impulses is signified by recurring allusions to a demonic element in his nature, and at the end of the novel the mature Crimsworth sees Hunsden's influence as a threat to his son Victor's moral education.

The portrait of Hunsden creates some unresolved ambiguities: he is both a capitalist and a critic of capitalism, a cynic and a sentimentalist. He is a friend to Crimsworth, yet subtly undermines the latter's sense of security and self-esteem. Potentially Hunsden is an interestingly complex character, but he lacks the development necessary to make his idiosyncrasies seem wholly credible.

Once the narrative shifts from England to Belgium, Charlotte Brontë demonstrates much firmer control of her material. The vague industrial setting of a Yorkshire mill town is replaced by the precise topography of Brussels; the melodramatic stereotypes of the early chapters give way to characters with a depth and vividness owing much to real life. Zoraïde Reuter, the manipulative directress of the girls' school where Crimsworth is eventually hired to give English lessons, is partly modeled on Mme Heger in her cool efficiency. Through her, and through his encounters with some of her pupils, Crimsworth discovers the superficiality and duplicity of the Catholic system of education. Although Brontë sometimes invites the reader to laugh at her narrator's pompousness or mild vanity, Crimsworth is generally the mouthpiece for her own views; and nowhere is this more evident than in his contemptuous accounts of "Romish wizardcraft" and its victims, the Belgian schoolgirls, who are deceitful, shallow, and "mentally depraved." In making her hero such a bluff proponent of British Protestantism, Brontë intended no irony; she herself had spoken critically of Roman "mummeries" in letters from Brussels in 1842-1843. Nor would her readers have taken exception to such denunciations; despite the political freedom enjoyed by English Catholics since the Catholic Emancipation Act of 1829, Victorian Englishmen regarded Catholics with an undiminished suspicion that was intensified by the Tractarian controversies of the 1830s and 1840s which threatened the hegemony of the Anglican church.

Related to the theme of Catholic treachery is Mlle Reuter's role as seductress and temptress in a struggle with Crimsworth for sexual dominance. Though she is engaged to M. Pelet (Crimsworth's employer at the boys' school) she flirts with the young Englishman, who is saved from imminent folly only by accidentally overhearing her in conversation with Pelet. Henceforth he treats her with a haughty disdain worthy of a Zamorna, which paradoxically serves to make him seem more fascinating in the directress's eyes. This curious turn in their relationship is seen by Crimsworth as further evidence of the degeneration fostered by a despotic

Norton Conyers at Swarcliffe, a mansion in which a madwoman had been kept locked in an attic room in the eighteenth century. Brontë visited here in 1839, and probably based some aspects of Thornfield on the house.

religious system; because Zoraide herself lives by the values of a spiritual tyranny, she respects the manifestation of authority in others. Her new submissiveness arouses Crimsworth to a pleasurable sense of his own power; once he has won recognition of his masculine strength, however, he turns his back on such "low gratification" in favor of the higher charms offered by his Anglo-Swiss pupil Frances Henri.

The comedy of Crimsworth's entanglement with Zoraide Reuter now gives way to a much more earnest study of a relationship based on intellectual as well as emotional compatibility. There are obvious parallels between Crimsworth's situation in England and Frances's sufferings at the Brussels pensionnat, emphasizing the link between inferior social status and the enforced repression of feeling. Orphaned, poor, and (after her aunt's death) utterly alone, Frances draws Crimsworth's interest by her meekly deferential manner, behind which he perceives flashes of warmth and proud defiance. It is hard to avoid the conclusion that, in her depiction

of this relationship, Charlotte Brontë was expressing some of her fantasies about Constantin Heger, her "maître" in Brussels. Through Frances Henri's suffering, and her eventual triumph over the schemes of Mlle Reuter, Brontë could play out a dream of what might have been; here, true merit might defeat hypocrisy, and the professor clasp his pupil in a warm embrace. Brontë's immersion in the hopes and longings of her principal characters gives conviction to her portrayal of their feelings, but the focus on romantic love costs the novel much of its earlier bite. Through Frances, Brontë adumbrates some of her concerns about the plight of women without money or connections; however, as an idealized embodiment of the author's own yearnings, Frances lacks the depth and complexity needed to carry the burden of such concerns effectively.

Several years after the composition of *The Professor*, when she had won fame as the author of *Jane Eyre* and *Shirley*, Charlotte Brontë again sought its publication and wrote a preface outlining her original intentions. She had sought to create a hero who "should work his way through life as I had seen living men work theirs—that he should never get a shilling he had not earned—that no sudden turns should lift him in a moment to wealth and high station. . . . As Adam's son he should share Adam's doom, and drain throughout life a mixed and moderate cup of enjoyment." That *The Professor* is sometimes slow, even dull, is perhaps the inevitable consequence of the author's rejection of the sensational in fiction; but her attempt to view life as unromantically as possible, and to focus on the pains and pleasures of a recognizably ordinary life, places Charlotte Brontë at the forefront of developments in modern literary realism.

Even while *The Professor* was going its fruitless round of the publishers, Charlotte was occupied with her next story. In August 1846 she accompanied her father to Manchester, where he underwent an operation for cataracts; and during his convalescence she began *Jane Eyre*. The work continued in Haworth, sometimes with great intensity (as when she wrote the chapters on Thornfield), and aided by critical counsel from Emily and Anne. The book was in its final stages when, on 15 July 1847, the manuscript of *The Professor*, now divorced from its former companions, arrived at the firm of Smith, Elder in London. It was seen by the firm's reader, William Smith Williams, a sensitive and literate man who was to become a close friend of Brontë's. Williams recognized the book's power, but doubted its success as a publication; after consulting with George Smith, he wrote to Brontë, declining *The Professor* but inviting the author to submit a work that might be published in three volumes. Maintaining her pseudonym of Currer Bell, Brontë sent off the manuscript of *Jane Eyre* on 24 August, five days after completing the fair copy. The book was accepted at once; within a month Brontë was correcting proofs; and on 19 October 1847, *Jane Eyre: An Autobiography*, "edited by Currer Bell," was published in three volumes at thirty-one shillings, sixpence.

The book won immediate and widespread acclaim. The *Times* called it "a remarkable production," a tale that "stand[s] boldly out from the mass." The *Edinburgh Review* saw it as "a book of singular fascination," and *Fraser's Magazine* urged its readers to "lose not a day in sending for it." Within three months the novel went into a second edition, and a third appeared in April 1848: no small achievement for a three-volume novel by a wholly unknown author. One of its first readers was the novelist Thackeray, who had been sent a copy by William Smith

Williams; "exceedingly moved & pleased" by the novel, Thackeray asked Williams to convey his thanks to the author. Touched by this response, Brontë dedicated the second edition to Thackeray and added a preface expressing her admiration for the author of *Vanity Fair* (1848), "the first social regenerator of the day."

In this chorus of praise, there were some discordant notes. The *Christian Remembrancer* for April 1848 commented unfavorably on the "extravagant panegyric" of the preface to the second edition, denounced the novel's "moral Jacobinism," and expressed displeasure at the author's attacks on Christian practice. Even more condemnatory was the unsigned notice in the *Quarterly Review* for December 1848, written by Elizabeth Rigby (soon to become Lady Eastlake). Jane Eyre is here described as "the personification of an unregenerate and undisciplined spirit," exerting the moral strength of "a mere heathen mind which is a law unto itself." The novel is accused of being "pre-eminently an anti-Christian composition," guilty of "a murmuring against the comforts of the rich and against the privations of the poor, which, as far as each individual is concerned, is a murmuring against God's appointment." The prevailing tone, one of "ungodly discontent," allies the novel in the reviewer's opinion to the cast of mind and thought "which has overthrown authority and violated every code human and divine abroad, and fostered Chartism and rebellion at home. . . ."

The plot of *Jane Eyre* might well disturb those to whom the divisions of social rank were sacred, since it follows the progress of a poor orphan from a loveless and humiliating dependence to happiness and wealth as an heiress and the wife of her former employer. Jane is an outcast, a rebel who triumphs over the forces of social convention expressed through caste, religion, and sexual tradition. Victorian readers were disturbed by the novel's suggestion that women need not always be passive or submissive, and by its treatment of love, which, by contemporary standards, seemed coarse and offensive. The supremacy of romantic love is an ancient theme in literature, but in *Jane Eyre* it was presented with a frankness and intensity new to English fiction. That intensity is made possible by Brontë's choice of a first-person narrator. Jane Eyre dominates her world, which exists only as it impinges on her consciousness; every action is filtered through the medium of her sensibility, every character lives only as an actor in the drama of her life. An outline of the plot might suggest that Brontë's novel is little more than a creaky melodrama peopled by crude carica-

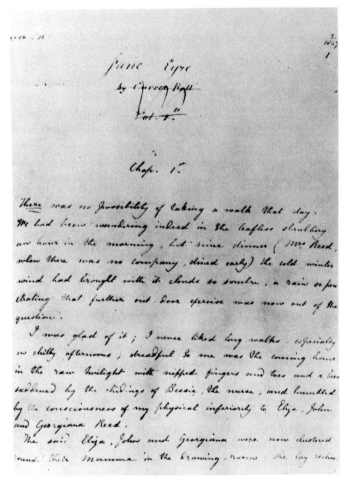

First page of manuscript of Jane Eyre *(British Museum)*

tures, but such is the authority, the conviction with which Jane tells her story that the reader is swept along by the narrative, undisturbed by improbabilities of character or plot.

One version of the novel's origin, related by Mrs. Gaskell, is that during a discussion with her sisters about the qualities necessary in a protagonist, Charlotte Brontë declared that she would show them "a heroine as plain and as small as myself, who shall be as interesting as any of yours." Such an intention is evident in the introductory chapters of *Jane Eyre*, where the ten-year-old Jane is seen as a prickly and unappealing child. She is an outsider, excluded by her Aunt Reed from the domestic circle around the hearth (a recurring image in the novel), and markedly different from her handsome but unpleasant cousins. She lacks their external attractiveness and confident air and is looked on with contempt even by the servants; only the solitary world of books and the imagination offers her any

comfort, while her yearning for love must satisfy itself with an old doll. Yet the reader is soon made conscious of Jane's inner strength; her fierce assertion of self against the Reeds' cruelty and injustice intimidates even her aunt. Charlotte Brontë conveys very powerfully the child's sense of alienation, helplessness, and anger in the face of adult oppression. Jane's rebellion at Gateshead against the tyranny of the Reeds is the first step in her progress toward spiritual freedom; at the same time, the wretchedness she feels after her violent outburst against Mrs. Reed reveals the danger of giving "uncontrolled play" to passionate feelings. The destructive potential of passion, imaged in chapter four as a fiery heath left "black and blasted," is to become a major theme in the Thornfield section of the novel.

In depicting Jane's search for the warmth and security of familial love, Charlotte Brontë undoubtedly endowed her heroine with some of her own

The publisher George Smith, to whom Charlotte and Anne Brontë revealed their identities in July 1848 (Brontë Parsonage Museum)

yearnings; and the autobiographical strain is even more evident in the chapters of *Jane Eyre* describing Lowood Institution, a thinly veiled reminiscence of life at the Clergy Daughters' School at Cowan Bridge. Mr. Brocklehurst, the "black marble clergyman," conveys the tone of William Carus Wilson's evangelical fervor in his speech, but the element of hypocrisy in Brocklehurst's sermonizing probably owes more to Charlotte Brontë's sense of justice than to the truth about Carus Wilson. Unlike his fictional counterpart, Carus Wilson had the welfare of his pupils at heart, but he lacked administrative experience, and his school was plagued in its early days by financial difficulties. Mrs. Gaskell's description of the Clergy Daughters' School and its director, in the first editon of *The Life of Charlotte Brontë*, seems to confirm the picture given in *Jane Eyre*; but it should be remembered that she had obtained much of her information from Brontë herself, before the latter's death. Under the threat of legal proceedings by Carus Wilson's family (as well as by Branwell's former employer, Mrs. Robinson, now Lady Scott), Mrs. Gaskell made extensive revisions for the third edition of the biography and presented Carus Wilson in a less unfavorable light.

Mrs. Gaskell did not, however, soften her account of the cruel treatment suffered by Charlotte's eldest sister, Maria, at the hands of one of Carus Wilson's teachers. Maria was Brontë's model for the character of Helen Burns, Jane Eyre's first friend at Lowood, who achieves almost saintly stature by her meekness and patient endurance of hardship, and who teaches Jane the importance of Christian love and humility. Charlotte Brontë obviously intended to pay tribute to the qualities of her dead sister, but she was artist enough not to be satisfied with a simple portrait from life; Helen Burns teaches Jane the virtues of patience and forgiveness, but her spiritual ardor and otherworldly faith are too intense for one like Jane, whose needs and desires are firmly rooted in this world, and who recoils from the "unfathomed gulf" of heaven and hell.

At eighteen, Jane leaves Lowood for "a new servitude," to become a governess at Thornfield Hall. Here the novel enters the realm of romance; the realism of character and setting which marks the descriptions of life at Gateshead and Lowood gives way to the mode and materials of Gothic melodrama, a vein that Charlotte and Branwell had mined in their Angrian chronicles. Social concerns are not wholly absent from Thornfield; in her account of Rochester's house party, Charlotte Brontë treats the empty pretensions of the English upper class with the same brand of bitter satire that she directs against Mr. Brocklehurst's religious hypocrisy. For the most part, however, the narrative moves on to a plane where dreams, visions, and presentiments have the force of waking reality: the world of cruel teachers and burned breakfasts gives way to one of mystery, terror, and sudden violence. The master of Thornfield is Edward Fairfax Rochester; like his predecessor, Zamorna, he is a compound of the Gothic villain and the Byronic hero: moody, passionate, overpoweringly attractive to women, burdened by a guilty past. Thornfield itself, with its crenellated front, its dark corridors, its hidden secret on the third story, becomes an English version of the Gothic castle, ruled by a tyrant and haunted by specters. What saves this section of *Jane Eyre* from descending to the level of adolescent fantasy and sensational melodrama is Brontë's concentration on the intensity of Jane's feelings and her use of such conventional materials to reflect and underscore her heroine's emotional turmoil. In the dark confines of Thornfield, Jane's troubled and passionate nature can find a release denied her in the "real" world; Rochester's brooding sexuality offers her the possibility of realizing desires normally forbidden expression. The danger that Jane runs in giving way to such feelings is expressed in language heavily charged with romantic symbolism; images of darkness, storm, and ruin counterpoint the description of the lovers' rising passions, and when Jane accepts Rochester's proposal, Nature herself protests, reminding the reader of the groans and "signs of woe" with which Nature greets the fall of mankind in Milton's *Paradise Lost* (1667). When Jane finally discovers Rochester's secret, the insane wife he has kept hidden at Thornfield for ten years, she is confronted by a frightening projection of one extreme of her own nature; Bertha Rochester is what Jane might have become: a creature governed by unbridled, irrational passions, stripped of human identity.

The visionary and nightmare qualities of these chapters, strongly suggestive to post-Freudian readers of a disturbed libido, give way to more conventional moral concerns, as Jane rejects Rochester's plea that she live with him as his mistress and flees Thornfield in obedience to the dictates of conscience and self-respect. Here—despite the accusations of the *Quarterly Review*—the novel takes on a distinctly Christian quality, albeit in a somewhat unorthodox mingling of traditional Protestant values and romantic supernaturalism. Jane is seen as a suffering sinner who, like Christian in Bunyan's *Pilgrim's Progress* (1678), must struggle through the world beset by trials and temptations in search of grace. At moments of intense spiritual crisis she is guided by a benevolent Providence, first manifested in the vision of her mother which tells her to "flee temptation," then sensed as "the might and strength of God" that comes to her rescue in her deepest despair and leads her through the marsh to her cousins' house. Though modern critics, often eager to see in Jane a prototype of the modern liberated woman, rightly emphasize her spirit of independence and self-reliance, it should also be recognized that in her quest for earthly happiness Jane is guided by a simple faith that gives her the inner strength to continue her search. Conviction of the validity of her own feelings is made possible by an unwavering belief in God—not the Calvinistic deity of Mr. Brocklehurst but a loving God expressed in and through nature.

The pattern of trial, temptation, and providential intervention established in the Thornfield episode and echoed in Jane's account of her subsequent wandering on the moors is repeated in the course of her relationship with her cousin, St. John Rivers. Rochester had threatened to destroy Jane's moral nature; St. John, whose powerful will and spiritual ambition almost overwhelm Jane's sense of self, poses an equally serious threat to the passions that give her life. Modeled in part upon Henry Martyn, the devout missionary whom Mr. Brontë had known at Cambridge and who had done much work in India, St. John displays an ardent and eloquent Evangelicalism that is unmistakably sincere. Yet in his pride and ambition he is less than perfect; and the struggle between his sensual nature and his spiritual zeal gives him enough humanity to make him more than just a mechanical foil to Rochester.

Jane is saved from surrendering her will to St. John's only by another providential intervention, this time in the form of Rochester's voice calling to her from afar. Her return to Rochester and their subsequent marriage (made possible by Bertha's fiery demise) is a satisfying conclusion to the story of their troubled love; yet there is a subdued, even anticlimactic quality about the novel's final chapters, perhaps because both Jane and Rochester have lost the spirit of willful defiance that is the basis of their appeal. So much of *Jane Eyre* is pervaded by the language and ideas of romanticism, especially in its emphasis on spiritual rebellion against a corrupt society, that Rochester's retributive maiming and his belated submission to divine law may seem a rather weak surrender to conventional morality. That Jane should now settle into a life of quiet middle-class domesticity also seems a renunciation of the passionate idealism that has hitherto marked her nature. Such an ending, however, reflects a sober recognition that life cannot always be lived at fever pitch. Only those who are prepared to turn their backs on the claims of nature can devote their lives to the unswerving pursuit of an ideal; and significantly the novel's closing paragraphs are concerned with the missionary achievements of St. John Rivers, doomed, like his real-life counterpart Henry Martyn, to an early death in the service of his God.

For *Jane Eyre*, Charlotte Brontë received £ 500: for a first novel, a princely amount indeed, especially in comparison to the terms obtained from T. C. Newby by Emily and Anne, whose advance of £ 50 toward the cost of production was never refunded. Anne's next novel, *The Tenant of Wildfell Hall*, was also published by Newby; at its appearance in June 1848, Newby sought to profit from the success of *Jane Eyre* by suggesting to an American publisher that *The Tenant of Wildfell Hall* was written by the same author as *Jane Eyre*—that in fact Currer, Ellis, and Acton Bell were the pseudonyms of a single author. This alarmed Smith, Elder, who had already promised Currer Bell's next work to the New York firm of Harper, and who now asked for assurances that Currer Bell was not acting in bad faith. Accordingly, on a wet evening in July 1848, Charlotte and Anne walked across the moors to

Keighley, caught the night train to Leeds, and presented themselves next morning in London to an astonished George Smith, dispelling any doubts the publisher might have had about their separate identities.

Thus began a relationship that was to last until Charlotte Brontë's death seven years later. When they first met, George Smith was twenty-four years old, eight years Brontë's junior, an attractive and energetic young businessman with an open and generous disposition. He and his widowed mother formed a strong attachment to Brontë; they shepherded her around London during her several visits to the capital, introduced her to the literary lions of the day, and on one occasion took her on a brief tour of Scotland. That there was a kind of playful flirtation between them is clear from the tone of Brontë's letters to Smith over the years: there is a lightheartedness, a vivaciousness not apparent in her other correspondence. But Brontë was under no illusion that their friendship might ripen into something deeper: as she told Ellen Nussey in June 1850, "I believe that George and I understand each other very well, and respect each other very sincerely. We both know the wide breach time has made between us; we do not embarrass each other, or very rarely, my six or eight years of seniority, to say nothing of lack of all pretension to beauty, etc., are a perfect safeguard." George Smith was later to tell Mrs. Humphry Ward that he "never could have loved any woman who had not some charm or grace of person, and Charlotte Brontë had none. . . . But I believe that my mother was at one time rather alarmed. . . ."

George Smith was anxious to follow up the success of *Jane Eyre* with another work by Currer Bell, and in December 1847 W. S. Williams suggested that Brontë write a novel for serial publication. She rejected this proposal but revealed that she was already planning a new three-volume novel based on a reworking of the materials she had used in *The Professor*. She made several attempts to begin this new work; one such commencement survives in the undated and untitled manuscript fragment known as "John Henry" or "The Moores," which describes the relationship between an overbearing mill owner and his intelligent, sensitive younger brother. The characters and framework of this story are strongly reminiscent of *The Professor*, but other elements, such as the characters' names and the younger brother's disdain for superiority based on rank or wealth, point toward *Shirley*. That novel began to take shape early in 1848, and Brontë made such steady progress that the first volume and part

of the second were completed before the end of September. Then came a series of tragedies which ended all joy in composition and might well have destroyed the creative impulse in one less strong than Charlotte Brontë.

First, on 24 September 1848, came the death of Branwell. Though he had been declining for a long time, his death still came as a heavy blow to his family. Charlotte, who had been the most angry and embittered at his degenerate conduct, was the one who felt his loss the most deeply, and for several weeks after the funeral she was prostrated by grief and illness. This was succeeded by an even severer shock: Emily fell prey to consumption, and after a brief but heroic struggle, she died on 19 December 1848. More anguish was to follow; even before Emily's death, Anne's health had begun to deteriorate, and now she too suffered a rapid decline. In May 1849 Charlotte and Ellen Nussey took her to Scarborough in the hope that fresh sea air might bring some improvement, but she died there on 28 May, three days after their arrival.

Now, at thirty-three, Charlotte was the sole survivor of the six Brontë children. Grief and solitude weighed heavily upon her, but she pressed on with *Shirley*, finding in work an anodyne for her suffering; as she told William Smith Williams after the novel's completion, "the occupation of writing it has been a boon to me. It took me out of dark and desolate reality into an unreal but happier region." The manuscript of *Shirley* was finished by the end of August 1849. Before sending it off to Smith, Elder, Brontë prepared a lengthy preface in which Currer Bell took to task the hostile reviewer of *Jane Eyre* in the *Quarterly Review*. The peevish tone and somewhat laborious ironies of the intended preface did not please George Smith, and when *Shirley: A Tale* was published in three volumes on 26 October 1849, no preface was included. However, Brontë's angry scorn of the *Quarterly Review* had already found release in the text itself: in Mrs. Pryor's account of her employment as a governess in the Hardman family, the unpleasant Hardmans are made to condemn themselves in words taken verbatim from Elizabeth Rigby's attack on *Jane Eyre*.

In that novel, Brontë had focused on the personal history and emotional experience of an individual; in *Shirley*, she sought to diffuse the interest among a number of characters and to bring them into contact with the public world of politics and social conflict. The novel is set in the West Riding of Yorkshire during the troubled years of 1811-1812, when the economic hardships ensuing from the war with France, complicated by an embargo on trade with America and the introduction of new machinery, led to massive unemployment and widespread rioting in the wool-producing districts. Much of the novel's action centers on Robert Moore, a local mill owner who is threatened on one hand by bankruptcy and on the other by Luddite machine-breakers. With the help of the militia, he routs a force of workers who had set out to destroy his mill; subsequently, however, he is shot by a religious fanatic and seriously wounded. Alongside this plot of industrial conflict is developed the story of Caroline Helstone, Moore's cousin, and her friendship with Shirley Keeldar, a spirited young heiress and landowner. Caroline, who lives with her guardian, a stern Tory clergyman, falls in love with Moore, but, believing that she has lost him to Shirley, enters into a dangerous decline. She is saved from death by the care of Mrs. Pryor, Shirley's elderly companion, who reveals herself to be Caroline's long-lost mother. Shirley herself is in love with Louis Moore, Robert's brother and her former tutor; despite opposition from class-conscious relatives, Shirley encourages Louis's attentions, and at the novel's conclusion they are married. Caroline and Robert are also united, the latter having recovered from his wound and acknowledged his love for his devoted cousin.

Brontë's choice of a subject so different from that of *Jane Eyre* was governed in part by her response to criticism of that novel's romantic excesses. G. H. Lewes in particular, writing in *Fraser's Magazine*, had mingled praise for the novel's strength of characterization and narrative power with an admonition about the dangers of melodrama. The opening of *Shirley*, with its warning to the reader that he should expect, not romance, but "something unromantic as Monday morning" is clearly an answer to that charge and a declaration of solemn intent, though couched in such ironic terms as to make it clear that the author is also mocking her critics. There is certainly a homely realism in much of the first volume, notably in the portraits of the three curates and of the house-proud Hortense Moore, characters drawn with a comic touch that is rare in Brontë's adult fiction. There is no comedy, however, in her description of the hardships of the Yorkshire unemployed, or in her accounts of the bitter confrontations of master and men. Her choice of this grim subject may have been inspired by the Chartist agitation that had troubled England for a decade, reaching its climax with a massive demonstration in London in April 1848. That Brontë should have turned to a historical parallel, the Luddite disturbances, to explore the "Condition of England" question reflects her natural reluctance to become involved in contemporary political controversy; as she told Williams in April 1848, "political partizanship is what I would ever wish to avoid as much as religious bigotry."

Charlotte Brontë took pains to present an accurate picture of the Luddite uprisings in the West Riding. She doubtless recalled stories about this period of Yorkshire history told by Miss Wooler at Roe Head, and by her father, who had known some of the principal antagonists during the time of his curacy at Hartshead-cum-Clifton. To supplement such anecdotal sources, Brontë studied the files of the Leeds *Mercury* for 1811-1813, making copies of some of its reports on Luddite activities. The result in *Shirley* is an authentic recreation of the period in which local events are merged with issues of national policy, and fiction is expertly blended with historical fact. The climax of the novel's industrial theme, the attack on Robert Moore's mill, is a reworking of a famous incident in April 1812, when a band of Luddites stormed William Cartwright's mill at Rawfolds, near Hartshead, and suffered a heavy defeat; the assault and its consequences were prominently reported in the Leeds *Mercury*. *Shirley* is not simply fictionalized history, however; Brontë's interest lies primarily in her characters and their relationships, and she adapts or changes historical detail to suit the needs of her narrative. Her treatment of history is also colored to some extent by her Tory partialities: she presents the plight of the workers sympathetically, but it is plain that she regards their cause as mistaken, their leaders as rabble-rousers and troublemakers. At the same time, she is critical of the callousness and narrow self-interest of the manufacturers, who exploit the poor with little regard for their misery. The plot of *Shirley* deals in part with the reeducation and rehabilitation of the mill owner Robert Moore, whose contact with the suffering he has helped to create teaches him to value men more than machines. In this respect the novel offers an oblique comment on the need for more tolerant attitudes on the part of the governing class in the England of 1848.

The theme of industrial conflict is interwoven with the stories of Caroline and Shirley, through whom Brontë explores another important social issue: the failure of Victorian society to give women the kinds of opportunities afforded to men to develop their abilities, realize their potential, and exercise some control over their lives. Not unlike the factory workers, women are exploited, their needs ignored, their roles strictly defined by male authority. Shirley, by virtue of her wealth and social station, can successfully challenge this domination, much to the anger and frustration of most of the men she encounters; Caroline, however, poor and unconnected, has few choices: the role of genteel spinster (a forbidding fate, as reflected in the lives of Miss Mann and Miss Ainley), or the servitude of the governess-trade described with bitter restraint by Mrs. Pryor. Rescue ultimately comes in the only form possible for a woman in Caroline's position: marriage. Yet as Brontë makes clear in a long (and somewhat uncharacteristic) reflection by Caroline in volume two, chapter eleven, such salvation does not come to all; and the struggle for success in an overstocked "matrimonial market" all too often leads women into degrading and humiliating competition, making them objects of scorn and ridicule to men. The solution is to give single women "better chances of interesting and profitable occupation than they possess now" and to cultivate girls' minds, not keep them "narrow and fettered." Brontë's feminism lacks the political dimension that marked the growth of the women's movement later in the century, but her call for women's emancipation from domestic slavery puts her at the forefront of that movement and gives *Shirley* added force and interest.

Few of the book's early reviewers, however, found much to praise in Brontë's attempt to branch out into realms of social comment. Only Eugène Forcade, writing in the *Revue des deux mondes* (15 November 1849), voiced approval of the novel's assertion of "moral liberty, the spirit of rebelliousness, the impulses of revolt against certain social conventions," noting that its subtitle might well have been "On the Condition of Women in the English Middle Class." For the most part, critical responses reflected disappointment that *Shirley* was not cast in the same mold as *Jane Eyre*. Reviewers were bored by the characters' lengthy conversations, or offended by the aggressive and unwomanly conduct of the eponymous heroine. While acknowledging the author's descriptive powers, they found the plot slow-moving, the chief male characters unconvincing. There is some basis for such complaints. The narrative lacks focus and unity, in large part because of the almost equal emphasis given to the two heroines and the course of their respective love affairs. The belated introduction of Shirley, who does not appear until the eleventh chapter, gives an awkward wrench to the plot, which has hitherto centered on the relationship between Caroline and Robert. The character of Shirley herself is drawn with mixed success: though she has an appealing liveliness and intellectual vigor, her attractions seem

somewhat brittle, and her love for the wooden and uninteresting figure of Louis Moore belies all the positive aspects of her nature. From the account given by Mrs. Gaskell, it is known that Brontë intended, through Shirley, to portray her sister Emily as she might have been had she lived. Undoubtedly Shirley has some of Emily's characteristics—her love of nature, her stoicism, her almost mystical apprehension of experience; but Emily did not have Shirley's dazzling beauty, her aggressive wit and charm, or her ability to dominate all around her. It is likely, rather, that some aspects of Emily's character were grafted onto the portrait of Shirley as the novel was being written; the first volume had been completed before Emily's death in December 1848, and it is possible that when she returned to the novel's composition, Charlotte modified her original conception to include Emily's qualities in the portrayal of Shirley as a kind of posthumous tribute. *Shirley* was an extremely ambitious effort by a young novelist eager to win recognition as a serious writer. It may lack the concentration, the driving force of a single vision that gives *Jane Eyre* its power; but in its treatment of complex social issues and its panoramic study of a turbulent period of English history, *Shirley* ranks with novels like Disraeli's *Sybil* (1845), Mrs. Gaskell's *Mary Barton* (1848), or Dickens's *Hard Times* (1854) as a significant contribution to the Victorian debate about the goals and values of industrial capitalism.

Between the publication of *Shirley* in October 1849 and the appearance of *Villette* in January 1853, Charlotte Brontë's life was marked by loneliness, depression, and recurring illness. She occupied herself with household affairs and the care of her father, but the sense of loss weighed heavily upon her, renewed daily by all the associations of the parsonage and the surrounding moors. She found some relief, and an outlet for her creative energies, in editing her sisters' literary remains. At Smith, Elder's suggestion she prepared an edition of *Wuthering Heights* and *Agnes Grey*, together with selections from her sisters' poems. The book was published in one volume at six shillings in December 1850, with a "Biographical Notice" and other prefatory materials by Charlotte which gave the reading public its first glimpse into the lives of the Brontës, as well as dispelling the still-current notion that all their works had been the production of one person. Brontë also emended the text of *Wuthering Heights*, correcting the many errors introduced by its first publisher, T. C. Newby, softening the harsh and incomprehensible dialect of Joseph, and altering the staccato paragraphing to create a greater smoothness of effect. Modern critics have taken her to task for these textual changes; but her introductory comments about Emily's character and about *Wuthering Heights* itself are perceptive and intelligent.

Brontë's widening circle of acquaintances, the result of her literary fame, afforded another source of distraction from her grief. She paid several visits to the Smiths in London and found herself, much to her dislike, the center of eager curiosity and attention. She met Thackeray, for whom her earlier admiration was cooled somewhat by his worldliness and evident enjoyment of fashionable society. She was introduced to G. H. Lewes, with whom she had corresponded since the publication of *Jane Eyre*, and was taken by his remarkable likeness in features to her sister Emily. She also struck up a friendship with Harriet Martineau and became her guest at Ambleside in December 1850; in Miss Martineau's company she met Matthew Arnold, who displeased her by his affected manner and "seeming foppery." In August 1850, staying at Windermere with Sir James Kay-Shuttleworth and his wife, Brontë met her future biographer, Elizabeth Cleghorn Gaskell, and was at once drawn to this warmhearted and sympathetic woman, telling her much that was subsequently to be incorporated into *The Life of Charlotte Brontë*. The most eventful of Brontë's excursions from Haworth was her trip to London at the end of May 1851. Staying as usual at the Smiths', she was taken on numerous outings. She attended four of Thackeray's six lectures on the English humorists; met Richard Monckton Milnes (the future biographer of Keats) and the eminent Scottish scientist Sir David Brewster; breakfasted with the poet Samuel Rogers; and paid five visits to the Crystal Palace, home of the Great Exhibition which had opened on 1 May 1851. In George Smith's company, she attended two performances by the great French tragedienne Rachel, whose acting made her "shudder to the marrow of my bones: in her some fiend has certainly taken up an incarnate home." Smith also indulged her taste for phrenology, the pseudoscience of determining character by examining the conformation of the skull, to which Brontë makes frequent reference in her novels: they visited a Dr. J. P. Browne, whose phrenological study of "Miss Fraser" (her pseudonym on this occasion) resulted in a surprisingly accurate picture of Brontë's character.

Soon after her return to Haworth, Brontë began work on her new novel. The task proved difficult, partly because she could not free herself from the depression that grew out of her solitude.

Now thirty-five years old, she saw no prospect of an end to her spinsterhood. For a short time she had received the attentions of James Taylor, George Smith's manager in Cornhill; but he struck her as lacking in intellect and good breeding, and any possibility of a union between them evaporated when Taylor left England in May 1851 to act as Smith's agent in India. Despite the blank prospect that opened before her, Brontë struggled on with her writing; and by the spring of 1852 her creative powers had returned with much of their old strength. After preparing a list of changes and corrections for the new one-volume edition of *Shirley* in March, she worked steadily on *Villette*, sending Smith the last volume in November. A temporary difficulty had been created by her father's wish that the book end happily; Mrs. Gaskell relates that Mr. Brontë "disliked novels which left a melancholy impression upon the mind." Charlotte would not alter her plan of having Paul Emanuel drown at sea; however, notes Mrs. Gaskell, she sought "so to veil the fate in oracular words, as to leave it to the character and discernment of her readers to interpret her meaning." Of greater concern to Brontë was the book's reception by her publisher, not least because she feared that George Smith might take offense at the use she had made of him and his mother in her depiction of the Brettons. She was conscious, too, that the book lacked "public interest" and touched on nothing topical or exciting. Her anxieties were increased by Smith's criticism of the shift in interest from John Graham Bretton to Paul Emanuel in the third volume. Smith seemed reluctant to proceed with the novel's printing; so, unable to bear any further delays or uncertainties, Brontë went up to London to see him. Her visit had the desired effect: whatever objections Smith might have had were overcome, the printing went ahead, and on 28 January 1853 *Villette*, by Currer Bell, made its appearance in the familiar three-volume format at thirty-one shillings, sixpence.

With *Villette* Brontë returned to the autobiographical mode which had given *Jane Eyre* such coherence and conviction despite the implausibility of its plot. This time, however, she avoided an uncritical identification with her heroine: Lucy Snowe embodies much of Brontë's own experience and outlook, and in many respects is a projection of her creator's inner self, but the novel is not simply a fictionalized expression of personal feelings or the enactment of Brontë's secret dreams and fantasies. Despite its obvious connection with the writer's life in Brussels, *Villette* is imbued with a critical irony from which even its narrator is not exempt.

VILLETTE.

By CURRER BELL,

AUTHOR OF "JANE EYRE," "SHIRLEY," ETC.

IN THREE VOLUMES.

VOL. I.

LONDON:
SMITH, ELDER & CO., 65, CORNHILL.
SMITH, TAYLOR & CO., BOMBAY.
——
1853.
The Author of this work reserves the right of translating it.

Title page of the last novel published during Brontë's lifetime

An outline of the plot can scarcely convey the complexity or intensity of the emotional struggles it dramatizes. The reader first meets the heroine, Lucy Snowe, as a fourteen-year-old girl in the household of her godmother, Louisa Bretton, a widow with a sixteen-year-old son, John Graham Bretton. Lucy is joined by little Paulina Home, whose mother has recently died and whose father is going abroad to secure his business affairs. The elfin Polly attaches herself to John Graham, who treats her with an appropriately adolescent mixture of amusement and indifference. Forced by circumstances to support herself, Lucy takes employment as companion to a elderly invalid, Miss Marchmont, whose history of a love frustrated by fate prefigures Lucy's own subsequent experience. At Miss Marchmont's death, Lucy travels to Villette, capital of Labassecour ("little town" and "the farmyard": Brontë's ironic names for Brussels and Belgium); here she becomes a teacher at the Pensionnat de Demoiselles owned by Mme Beck. In Villette

Lucy meets the Brettons again; John Graham, now ten years older, is a practicing physician for whom the scheming Mme Beck is evidently setting her cap. He seems to encourage Madame's advances, while in reality he is paying court to one of her pupils, the flighty Ginevra Fanshawe. For a time Lucy is herself drawn into "Dr. John's" sphere; however, any chance of his giving her serious attention is ended by the reappearance of Paulina Home, whose father has become the Count de Bassompierre, and who quickly becomes the focus of Dr. John's interest. Lucy herself finds an admirer in Paul Emanuel, Mme Beck's cousin, who teaches literature at the pensionnat; despite his stormy nature and Madame's attempted interference, Paul wins Lucy's love, establishes her in her own little school in Villette, and departs for the West Indies to manage some family affairs. Lucy remains faithful to him during the three years of his absence, but during his return home he perishes in a shipwreck.

In plot and setting, *Villette* has obvious similarities to *The Professor*, but it is not merely a refashioning of the materials used in the earlier work. It is colored even more highly than *The Professor* by Brontë's recollections of her two years at the Pensionnat Heger. The Hegers' school, with its cluster of classrooms and dormitories, its sheltered garden and *"allée défendue,"* is recreated in careful detail. The Hegers themselves are unmistakably the models for Mme Beck, the school's calculating directress, and Paul Emanuel, the fiery teacher whose unpredictable temper alternately delights and terrifies his pupils. Even the girls and teachers at Mme Beck's school can be identified with real-life originals Brontë had met in Brussels. Many other aspects of *Villette* are clearly autobiographical; such events as Lucy's journey through London and across the Channel, her visit to an art exhibition and a concert, her attendance at a performance by "Vashti" (Rachel), all are drawn from the writer's own experiences in Brussels and London. Lucy's relationship with the Brettons adumbrates elements of Brontë's friendship with George Smith and his mother. Lucy herself has recognizable similarities to Brontë, from her contemptuous dislike of Belgians and her distrust of Catholicism to her consciousness of physical inferiority and her susceptibility to depression.

Despite the temptation to regard *Villette* as autobiographical, however, the question of Lucy's likeness to her creator must be treated with caution, for Brontë distances herself from her narrator in a number of ways. Though Lucy speaks with the most authority, she is not always honest with herself or with her reader, and sometimes her interpretation of character or event betrays the biases of a mind warped to some extent by a sense of failure, frustration, and inadequacy. Lucy describes herself as a "looker-on" at life and dreads the revelation of her own feelings; thence springs the agony she feels when asked by M. Paul to take a part in the school play. From her vantage point of seemingly detached observer, she passes caustic comment on the weaknesses or pretensions of those around her. Even as a girl, her determination to avoid emotional involvement is evident in her almost clinical scrutiny of little Polly's suffering at the temporary separation from her father. Writing to George Smith shortly before completing the manuscript, Brontë explained her choice of the heroine's name (she had wavered between "Frost" and "Snowe"): "A *cold* name she must have; partly, perhaps, on the '*lucus a non lucendo*' principle—partly on that of the 'fitness of things,' for she has about her an external coldness." Convinced that fate has decreed that her life be deprived of warmth or love, Lucy is determined to protect herself from rebuff, from the pain that self-exposure might entail; for this reason, she at first conceals from Dr. John (and from the reader) the fact of their earlier acquaintance. She takes a masochistic satisfaction in the contrast between the beauty of her empty-headed young friend Ginevra and her own plainness. Her crusty manner leads Ginevra to call her "Diogenes" or "Timon," nicknames that Lucy enjoys, since they confirm her preferred posture of cynical coldness and spiritual independence.

Yet Lucy is a creature of strong feelings; and inevitably those feelings seek an outlet, first in the morbid depression that leads her to make a confession to a Catholic priest, then in an imagined attachment to Dr. John, who treats her kindly during her illness. This last episode and the subsequent shift of interest to Paul Emanuel have been seen as a structural weakness in the novel; but Lucy's fantasies about Dr. John are a necessary prelude to the real love that awakens in her later. The young Englishman is a kind of conventional novel hero; with his good looks, charming manner, and gentlemanly breeding he presents Lucy with a model of the masculine virtues that, in her longing for love, she can hardly resist. Not until she has buried this romantic illusion (a literal interment, with the burial of Dr. John's letters) can she recognize that love is possible in less conventional, but also less superficial terms in the hitherto comic form of Paul Emanuel.

The irascible schoolteacher takes Lucy into the last stages of her emotional growth, liberates her from her neurotic repressions, and enables her to find expression for her natural yearnings. From the first he perceives the powerful feelings that Lucy tries to deny, and like Rochester with Jane Eyre, he teases those feelings to the surface by a mixture of insult and kindness. Paul is perhaps the most credible (and likable) of Brontë's male characters: she does not minimize his faults—his jealous pride, his overbearing manner, his pettiness; yet it is he who assumes the role of hero in *Villette*, not the more glamorous John Graham Bretton. He is the "natural" man, incapable of disguise or deceit, whose very weaknesses make him more human and accessible than the polished (and rather superficial) doctor. In the claustrophobic world of the pensionnat, Paul is a breath of fresh air and gives Lucy for the first time in her life a hope of happiness. Like Greatheart in *Pilgrim's Progress*, he becomes her champion, battling for her soul with Apollyon, the redoubtable Mme Beck.

Though cast in the same mold as Zoraïde Reuter of *The Professor*, Modeste Maria Beck is a far more formidable character. The argument as to whether or not she is a just representation of her original, Mme Heger, is irrelevant; her function is to be Lucy's crafty, passionless antagonist, a proponent of spiritual tyranny and Romanist subversion, and for this she is endowed with qualities of intellect and perceptiveness that make her a worthy enemy. Lucy acknowledges her powers and even voices her admiration for her ability to manipulate others. In some respects they are similar in temperament: both are secretive, both conceal their true feelings and assume a persona appropriate to the occasion; but while Mme Beck plays roles systematically as a means of maintaining her power, Lucy does so out of necessity, for fear of giving herself away and losing the mastery over self that protects her from pain.

Punctuating the story of Lucy's struggle with Mme Beck and her own feelings is the recurring motif of the ghostly nun, a Gothic device that turns out to have a somewhat bathetic explanation, but that is nevertheless effective as a means of projecting the turbulence of Lucy's emotions and suggesting the illusory nature of her grasp on reality. The nun in the garden, like the figure of Justine Marie who seems to stand between Lucy and M. Paul, is real enough, yet also a creation of her heated imagination; when she returns from her almost hallucinatory expedition to the park where she has seen Paul with her imagined rival Justine Marie, Lucy finds the ghostly nun lying on her bed—nothing more than a bolster covered in a black stole.

The discovery is a fittingly ironic comment on Lucy's capacity for self-deception and misconstruction.

Distorted though her vision may be at times, Lucy Snowe's painful circumstances are not imaginary. In *The Professor* and *Jane Eyre*, Brontë had already examined the plight of a young woman of feeling and intelligence cast into the world and forced to make her own way. Her own experience had shown her that society placed no premium on inner worth; that happiness was doubtful for those who must earn their own bread; that love, sexual fulfillment, even domestic comfort were achieved by few women. Lucy Snowe tries to detach herself from life out of a conviction that any kind of emotional commitment must bring suffering and humiliation. Even though she wins love in the end, it is a very limited happiness that she is granted, since Paul is snatched away from her at the last moment by a cruel and arbitrary fate. Lucy may have gained maturity of vision and freedom from her neurotic fears of inadequacy, but her creator's pessimism denies her the final reward of romantic reunion: the return to an Edenic garden, permitted to Jane Eyre, is no longer possible.

Villette's intensity of feeling, its concentration on the heroine's yearning and frustration, its veiled and enigmatic ending did not sit well with early readers. Reviewers praised the novel's detailed portrait of school life and found much to applaud in the freshness and vitality of "Currer Bell's" eccentric schoolmaster hero, but there was some dissatisfaction with the novel's emphasis on Lucy's suffering: the *Spectator* felt that Lucy "took a savage delight in refusing to be comforted," and Harriet Martineau protested in the *Daily News* at the "amount of subjective misery," the "atmosphere of pain" that hung about the novel. Readers familiar with the details of the author's life treated *Villette* as a personal revelation; Thackeray saw it as little more than the expression of Brontë's own yearnings for love, while Matthew Arnold declared the novel "disagreeable" because "the writer's mind contains nothing but hunger, rebellion and rage. . . ." Such dismissive judgments, ignoring the book's narrative art and structural ironies, were less than just, yet they reflect an ineluctable truth: the source of the novel's strength, its power to arouse and disturb, does lie in the author's painful attempt to reconcile the conflict between her desires and her sense of inadequacy. *Villette* strikes the modern reader as a successful book because Brontë was able to transform her own "hunger, rebellion and rage" into a dramatic study of a tormented female sensi-

bility, revealing its distortions and excesses as well as its nobility in suffering.

Even before the publication of this, her final work, Brontë's life had entered a new phase that was to bring her, however briefly, the happiness she had sought for so long. On 13 December 1852 she received a proposal of marriage from Arthur Bell Nicholls (1818-1906), her father's dour Irish curate since 1845. She had long suspected his interest in her, but the strength of his feeling took her by surprise. Though his evident suffering and abrupt dismissal by an enraged Mr. Brontë aroused her sympathy, she was not attracted to him, and discouraged his suit. Nicholls persisted in his addresses, however; he and Charlotte entered into a clandestine correspondence, and in April 1854, with Mr. Brontë's reluctant consent, they became engaged. Charlotte's feelings for Nicholls had ripened into respect, but she had no illusions about the brilliance of her prospects, telling Ellen Nussey that "what I taste of happiness is of the soberest order." Fifteen years earlier, she had refused Henry Nussey because he did not inspire in her "that intense attachment which would make me willing to die for him"; experience had cured her of such romantic idealism, and she was now ready to take refuge in the comfort of a relationship promising at least affection and security.

Brontë's increasing preoccupation with domestic affairs and a growing coolness in her relations with George Smith made it difficult for her to apply herself seriously to the task of writing a new novel. She did make several attempts, beginnings which survive in the manuscript fragments "The Story of Willie Ellin" and "Emma." The former, written in the early summer of 1853, represents a return to the theme of two rival brothers which Brontë had first explored in her juvenile stories. Like their many predecessors, the brothers bear the names Edward and William; the elder, Edward Ellin, is a cruel guardian to his ten-year-old brother, whom he intends to apprentice to trade. Willie seeks refuge in the former family house, Ellin Balcony, but is recaptured and whipped for his recalcitrance. The fragments show Charlotte Brontë experimenting with alternative plot lines, introducing different characters to act as Willie's protectors. One short part presents an unusual narrative point of view: the speaker appears to be a disembodied spirit that haunts the Ellins' ancestral home. The other fragment, "Emma," begun on 27 November 1853, is a more conventional account about a young girl called Matilda Fitzgibbon, who is left by her father as a boarder at a girls' school. At first presumed to

The Reverend Arthur Bell Nicholls (Brontë Parsonage Museum)

be an heiress, she is treated with great partiality; but when the discovery is made that her father had given a fictitious name and address, and that he has disappeared, "Matilda" is confronted by her irate schoolteacher and collapses. The fragment is interesting chiefly for its satirical portrait of Miss Wilcox, the eldest of the sisters who run the school; the chief male character, who takes the rejected Matilda under his wing at the end of the fragment, is called Mr. Ellin. "Emma" was published posthumously in the fourth number of the *Cornhill Magazine* (April 1860), with a laudatory introduction by Thackeray.

With her marriage to Arthur Bell Nicholls on 29 June 1854, Charlotte Brontë's literary activity came to an end. The couple honeymooned in Wales and Ireland, returning at the beginning of August to Haworth (Charlotte could not be prevailed upon to leave her ailing father for long), where Nicholls resumed his duties as Mr. Brontë's curate. For the first time since the deaths of Emily and Anne, Charlotte Brontë found life at the parsonage congenial and satisfying; her new role as a wife kept her active and occupied, and her husband, now reconciled with her father, daily revealed qualities which won her respect and increased her attachment to him. But the pleasures of this domesticity were

short-lived. In January 1855 she discovered she was pregnant; she soon began to suffer from extreme nausea and vomiting, a condition which her delicate constitution was unable to bear. Worn out by the struggle, she died on 31 March 1855. Once more the house fell silent. Mr. Brontë remained there until his own death in 1861; Nicholls watched over him in his last years, then returned to his native Ireland, where he remarried in 1864.

Two further publications of importance maintained Brontë's prominence in the literary world after her death. One was Smith, Elder's publication in March 1857 of Mrs. Gaskell's controversial biography, *The Life of Charlotte Brontë*; this proved so successful that a second edition was required in April, but under the threat of legal action by the families of William Carus Wilson and Lady Scott (formerly Mrs. Edmund Robinson of Thorp Green), Mrs. Gaskell was obliged to make extensive revisions for the third edition, published in September. In her desire to present Brontë as an almost saintly heroine, Mrs. Gaskell had perhaps allowed herself to believe too readily in some of the more exaggerated accounts of the Brontë family's adversities. The same motive doubtless led her to omit any reference to Charlotte's infatuation for Constantin Heger, although she was aware of the letters that Charlotte had written to Heger after her final departure from Brussels. Not until 1913 would the letters and the circumstances surrounding them come into public view, when they were reproduced in the *Times* by Marion H. Spielmann.

During her researches in preparation for the writing of the *The Life of Charlotte Brontë*, Mrs. Gaskell accompanied Sir James Kay-Shuttleworth on a visit to Haworth. They succeeded in persuading Nicholls to lend them a large number of unpublished manuscripts, including that of *The Professor*. Though Mrs. Gaskell did not think the latter would add to Brontë's reputation, she bowed to Sir James's insistence that the book be published and returned the manuscript to Nicholls with the suggestion that he revise the work for publication. Nicholls did so, making some small changes to remove what Mrs. Gaskell had called the novel's "coarseness and profanity in quoting texts of scripture," and adding a brief prefatory note dated 22 September 1856. *The Professor* was finally published by Smith, Elder in two volumes in June 1857 and was given a muted reception by its first readers. In his introductory note, Nicholls maintained that *The Professor* and *Villette* were "in most respects unlike," but the reviewers fastened on the obvious similarities and treated the earlier work as little more than a crude sketch of its successor. They regarded it as a literary curiosity; its interest lay in its connection with the career so movingly described by Mrs. Gaskell, rather than in any claims it might have to serious critical attention. *The Professor* would find its defenders: Peter Bayne praises its vivid character portrayals, thinks the story "full of life," and compares the novel favorably to *Villette*. Even Bayne, however, is forced to acknowledge that it is "by no means a wonderful book." Modern criticism has not sought to reverse that judgment.

In the course of his study, Bayne accords Charlotte pride of place among the Brontë sisters because she had "ten times more power" than Anne and a nature with more geniality and culture than Emily's. Later critics have moved in a different direction, finding Emily to be the greater writer. The stark and mythopoeic qualities of *Wuthering Heights* undeniably reflect a genius and a vision beyond Charlotte's capacities. Yet Emily's enigmatic romance, unique of its kind, was a dead end in English fiction, whereas the painful realism of Charlotte's studies of the human heart gave a fresh impetus and a new direction to the genre of the novel.

Bibliographies:

Thomas J. Wise, *A Bibliography of the Writings in Prose and Verse of the Members of the Brontë Family* (London: Clay, 1917);

G. Anthony Yablon and John R. Turner, *A Brontë Bibliography* (London: Hodgkins, 1978; Westport, Conn.: Meckler, 1978);

R.W. Crump, *Charlotte and Emily Brontë, 1846-1915: A Reference Guide* (Boston: Hall, 1982).

Biographies:

Elizabeth Cleghorn Gaskell, *The Life of Charlotte Brontë*, third edition, revised (2 volumes, London: Smith, Elder, 1857);

Thomas J. Wise and John A. Symington, eds., *The Brontës: Their Lives, Friendships and Correspondence* (4 volumes, Oxford: Blackwell, 1932);

Winifred Gerin, *Charlotte Brontë: The Evolution of Genius* (Oxford: Clarendon Press, 1967).

References:

Christine Alexander, *The Early Writings of Charlotte Brontë* (Oxford: Blackwell, 1983);

Miriam Allott, ed., *The Brontës: The Critical Heritage*

(London: Routledge & Kegan Paul, 1974);

Peter Bayne, *Two Great Englishwomen: Mrs. Browning and Charlotte Brontë* (London: Clarke, 1881);

Asa Briggs, "Private and Social Themes in *Shirley*," *Brontë Society Transactions*, 13, part 68 (1958): 203-219;

"Charlotte Brontë's Tragedy: The Lost Letters," *Times* (London), 29-30 July 1913, p. 9;

Mildred G. Christian, "The Brontës," in *Victorian Fiction: A Guide to Research*, edited by Lionel Stevenson (Cambridge, Mass.: Harvard University Press, 1964), pp. 214-244;

Robert A. Colby, "*Villette* and the Life of the Mind," *PMLA*, 75 (1960): 410-419;

Enid L. Duthie, *The Foreign Vision of Charlotte Brontë* (London: Macmillan, 1975);

Robert B. Heilman, "Charlotte Brontë's 'New' Gothic," in *From Jane Austen to Joseph Conrad: Essays Collected in Memory of James T. Hillhouse*, edited by Robert C. Rathburn and Martin Steinmann, Jr. (Minneapolis: University of Minnesota Press, 1958), pp. 118-132;

Jacob Korg, "The Problem of Unity in *Shirley*," *Nineteenth Century Fiction*, 12 (1957): 125-136;

David Lodge, *Language of Fiction: Essays in Criticism and Verbal Analysis of the English Novel* (London: Routledge & Kegan Paul, 1966), pp. 114-143;

Robert B. Martin, *The Accents of Persuasion: Charlotte Brontë's Novels* (London: Faber, 1966);

Fannie E. Ratchford, *The Brontës' Web of Childhood* (New York: Columbia University Press, 1941);

Herbert J. Rosengarten, "The Brontës," in *Victorian Fiction: A Second Guide to Research*, edited by George H. Ford (New York: MLA, 1978), pp. 172-203;

Kathleen Tillotson, *Novels of the Eighteen-Forties* (Oxford: Clarendon Press, 1954), pp. 257-313;

Tom Winnifrith, *The Brontës and Their Background: Romance and Reality* (London: Macmillan, 1973).

Papers:

Important manuscript holdings of Charlotte Brontë's prose writings are to be found at: the British Library; the Brontë Parsonage Museum, Haworth; Harvard College Library; Humanities Research Center, University of Texas; Huntington Library; New York Public Library; Princeton University Library; Pierpont Morgan Library.

Emily Brontë

Tom Winnifrith
University of Warwick

BIRTH: Thornton, Yorkshire, 30 July 1818, to Patrick and Maria Branwell Brontë.

DEATH: Haworth, Yorkshire, 19 December 1848.

BOOKS: *Poems by Currer, Ellis and Acton Bell*, by Charlotte, Emily, and Anne Brontë (London: Aylott & Jones, 1846; Philadelphia: Lea & Blanchard, 1848);
Wuthering Heights, as Ellis Bell (2 volumes, London: T. C. Newby, 1847; 1 volume, Boston: Coolidge & Wiley, 1848).

COLLECTIONS: *The Life and Works of Charlotte Brontë and Her Sisters*, Haworth Edition, edited by Mrs. Humphry Ward and C. K. Shorter (7 volumes, London: Smith, Elder, 1899-1900);
The Complete Poems of Emily Jane Brontë, edited by Shorter (New York: Hodder & Stoughton, 1908; London: Hodder & Stoughton, 1910);
The Shakespeare Head Brontë, edited by T. J. Wise and J. A. Symington (19 volumes, Oxford: Blackwell, 1931-1938);
The Clarendon Edition of the Novels of the Brontës, I. R. Jack, general editor (3 volumes, Oxford: Clarendon Press, 1969-   ).

The biographer of Emily Brontë faces considerable problems. Her slender output of one great novel and some impressive but baffling poems does not give one a great deal upon which to build. Unlike her sister Charlotte, whose works do have an autobiographical streak, Emily did not seem to draw upon her own rather humdrum experiences in creating her masterpiece. Attempts to find a real-life Heathcliff in Emily Brontë's Irish forebears or Yorkshire neighbors seem highly speculative. Because Charlotte Brontë won instant fame while she was still alive, far more is known about her life than about Emily's; and it is largely through Charlotte's eyes that Emily is seen: either in incidental references among her correspondence to Ellen Nussey when Emily was alive, or in pious memories when she was dead. Emily Brontë's surviving correspondence is limited to a handful of brief notes, the diary papers she wrote at four-year intervals with her

(National Portrait Gallery)

sister Anne, and some exercises she wrote in French in Brussels.

This pathetic paucity of primary evidence has left biographers free to indulge in wild speculation. The temptation to fill the drab life of a genteel English spinster with the wild power of *Wuthering Heights* (1847) is certainly great, but the unadorned facts, insofar as they can be ascertained, may serve to make her imaginative achievement more impressive. Emily Jane Brontë was the fifth child and fourth daughter of the Reverend Patrick Brontë, who moved in April 1820 to the village of Haworth eight miles from Thornton, her birthplace. Emily's mother, who had given birth to her youngest daughter, Anne, on 17 January 1820, died in November 1821, having been ill for several months. Like all the Brontë novels, *Wuthering Heights* has more than its fair share of children who have lost one or both parents.

Faced with the care of six motherless children, Mr. Brontë made efforts to marry again, but soon invited his wife's sister, Elizabeth Branwell, to keep house for him. In July 1824 he sent his two elder daughters, Maria and Elizabeth, to Clergy Daughters' School at Cowan Bridge, Charlotte following in August and Emily in November. In the spring of 1825 there was an epidemic at the school, Maria and Elizabeth died, and Emily and Charlotte were removed from Cowan Bridge. It is difficult to know whether the portrait of Lowood in *Jane Eyre* (1847) is an accurate picture of Cowan Bridge, and although Charlotte clearly was unhappy there, it cannot be known how Emily felt at the age of six. Her subsequent departures from Haworth were brief, and she was not happy away from home.

Emily was indeed at Haworth for the next ten years. In 1826 Mr. Brontë brought home some wooden soldiers, and the precocious children began writing stories about them. With Charlotte and their brother, Branwell, as the main instigators, an imaginary realm in Africa, called Angria, was invented; but at a fairly early stage Emily and Anne broke away and invented their own realm of Gondal, set in the Pacific Ocean. The first of their diary notes, written in November 1834, gives the first mention of Gondal. They continued writing prose and poems about Gondal until the end of their lives. None of the prose has survived, and the poetry, the earliest of which dates to 1836, is difficult to interpret. Various efforts have been made to fit the poems into a coherent saga, but these efforts are probably misguided. Some poems appear not to be about Gondal at all, but rather to reflect Emily's own feelings.

Charlotte had been sent away in 1831 for a year and a half to a school in East Yorkshire run by Miss Wooler. This school was far more pleasant than Cowan Bridge, and Charlotte made some friends there. In July 1835, Charlotte returned to the school as a teacher, taking Emily with her as a pupil; but this economical arrangement was not a success, and Anne replaced Emily. Emily returned to Haworth and found Branwell there. He had made an equally unsuccessful foray in London in an attempt to earn a living as a painter. With Anne and Charlotte away at Miss Wooler's, Emily and Branwell were thrown into each other's company; and although some of Branwell's influence can be detected in Emily's prose and poetry, the theory that he was the real author of *Wuthering Heights* can probably be discounted.

In spite of her previous failure, Emily made another attempt to leave home, going as an assistant teacher to Law Hill, a school run by Miss Patchett near Halifax. Charlotte wrote a letter complaining of the harsh conditions under which Emily worked. Her lack of formal education (virtually all her lessons having been taken at home), her shy temperament, and her homesickness would seem to have made Emily far from an ideal teacher, but the slighting nature of Charlotte's remarks made Miss Patchett reluctant to discuss her eccentric but distinguished assistant with subsequent biographers. The date and duration of Emily's stay at Law Hill are still in doubt. The recent discovery that Charlotte's letter, dated by most biographers 2 October 1837, is clearly postmarked 2 October 1838, would seem to fix Emily's stay in the winter of 1838 to 1839. Law Hill is regarded as important for *Wuthering Heights* because a house nearby, High Sunderland Hall, is assumed to be the model for the house known as Wuthering Heights, and it has even been suggested that the germ of the story of Heathcliff was to be found in recollections of a local Halifax character, Jack Sharp. The parallels are not exact, and the other main claimant to being the model of Wuthering Heights, Top Withens, near Haworth, certainly has a situation similar to the lonely house of Emily's novel, although Top Withens itself is too humble to be equated with Wuthering Heights.

Returning to Haworth in 1839 at the age of twenty, Emily continued to write poetry. Her sisters made brief and unsuccessful efforts to become governesses, but Emily remained at home, either because she was the most domesticated of the sisters or because she was the least suited to become a teacher. Her July 1841 birthday note is, however, full of enthusiasm for a project that the Brontës should run their own school at Haworth. In order to achieve this the sisters would need foreign languages, and so in February 1842 Emily and Charlotte set out to Brussels; Anne had obtained a post as a governess for the Robinson family at Thorp Green.

The position of the Brontës at the Pensionnat Heger in Brussels was halfway between those of pupils and teachers. Some reminiscences exist of Emily as a teacher, and not surprisingly her forbid-

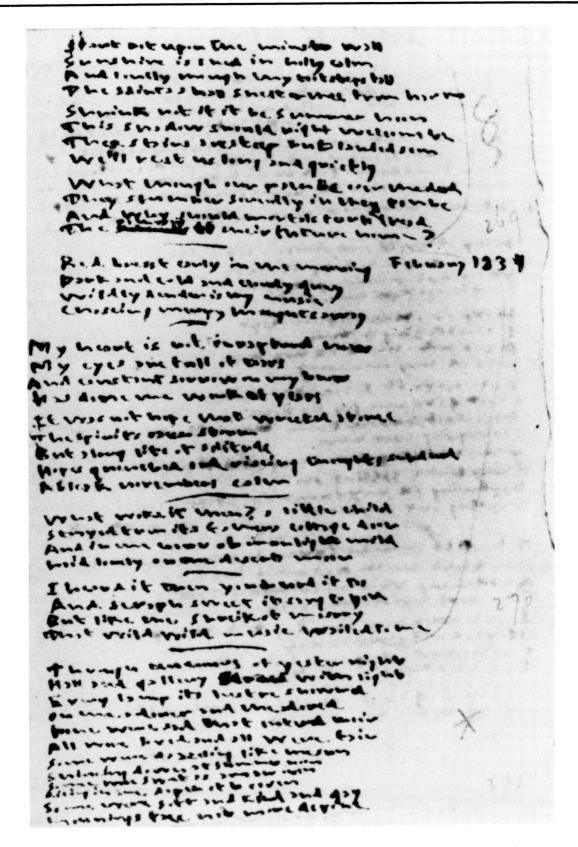

Manuscript of three of Brontë's poems–"Stand not upon the minster wall," "Redbreast, early in the morning," and "Through the hours of yesternight"–written between 1837 and 1839 (John Howell Books, 1982 Anniversary Catalogue)

ding reserve did not attract her pupils to her. On the other hand, M. Heger spoke highly of her intellectual gifts as a student, and her surviving exercises show high imaginative power as well as a good command of French. It is not certain how much German Emily learned; critics have perhaps in too facile a fashion seen the influence of German romanticism behind *Wuthering Heights*.

In November 1842, the Brontës were forced to return home by the death of their aunt. They had previously been shocked by the death of their father's curate, William Weightman, in September, and by the death of their friend Martha Taylor in Brussels. Charlotte returned to Belgium, where she endured much loneliness and the pangs of unrequited love for M. Heger, but Emily remained at home. Their aunt had left the three girls some money, and there are reports of Emily considering the best way of investing it. For most of 1843 Emily was alone with her father, since Branwell had joined Anne at Thorp Green and Charlotte was still in Brussels, from which she returned at the beginning of 1844. In February 1844 Emily copied her poetry down into two notebooks, one of which she entitled "Gondal Poems." The other notebook would seem to have contained poetry of a subjective nature.

Emily continued to write poetry in 1844 and 1845, and in a diary note in July 1845 refers enthusiastically to Gondal, although Anne is less sanguine. Branwell Brontë returned home in July 1845 (after being dismissed from his post at the Robinsons for some reason too disgraceful for Victorian prudery to make explicit), and for the rest of his life he was a source of constant anxiety to his family. Mr. Brontë's health was also giving cause for concern. The plan to start a school had foundered in 1844 through lack of interest, and both Charlotte, who wrote letters to M. Heger which he refused to answer, and Anne, who had been badly shocked by her experiences at Thorp Green, were in low spirits. It was in these unpromising circumstances that Emily wrote some of her greatest poetry and *Wuthering Heights*.

The chronology of the poems and the novel is confusing. Emily continued to write new poems in 1844 and 1845 in both Gondal and non-Gondal notebooks. In the former category can be placed "Remembrance" and "The Prisoner," an extract from a long Gondal poem; and in the latter category belong "The Philosopher" and "Stars." These poems are generally considered to be Emily's finest apart from "No Coward Soul is Mine," written in January 1846. In the autumn of 1845, Charlotte discovered a notebook of Emily's containing poetry

Law Hill School near Halifax, where Brontë taught in 1838-1839 (Brontë Parsonage Museum)

which she thought was very impressive. Emily was, however, extremely annoyed by the discovery; it took hours to reconcile her to it, and days to persuade her that the poems should be published. But published they were in May 1846, together with a selection of Charlotte's and Anne's poetry. Gondal references were largely eliminated from the printed selection, which contained both Gondal and non-Gondal poems, including the four famous ones but not "No Coward Soul is Mine," which was presumably written too late for publication. After this Emily wrote only one more poem, in September 1846, which she began to revise in May 1848. Her abandoning of poetry has been variously explained. It has been argued that the fact of publication killed the poetry in her; more prosaically it has been suggested that she was busy with *Wuthering Heights*.

But this explanation has its own difficulties. It is known from a letter of Charlotte's in April 1846 to Aylott and Jones, the publishers of the Brontës' poetry, that the three sisters were well on their way to completing three separate works of fiction, and they had completed these by July 1846. Thus *Wuthering Heights* was finished two years before Emily died, and it is difficult to see what Emily was doing in these two years, when both Anne and Charlotte were busy with second novels. It has been suggested that Emily was also writing a second novel; a more original idea is that she extended *Wuthering Heights* from one-volume length to two volumes when it was decided that Charlotte's novel *The Professor* should try its own fortunes. Eventually the not very reputable firm of Thomas Newby agreed to publish *Wuthering Heights* in two volumes and Anne's *Agnes Grey* in one volume. Newby was dilatory in producing the books, and the terms he offered were not favorable, but the two novels were eventually published in December 1847.

Unlike Charlotte's *Jane Eyre*, which was an immediate success when it was published by Smith, Elder at about the same time, *Wuthering Heights* was received with bewilderment. Reviewers were baffled and shocked by the story, though some paid tribute to its strange power. Perhaps the poor reception of *Wuthering Heights* prevented Emily from embarking on another novel. A letter from Newby, fitting an envelope addressed to Ellis Bell, her pseudonym, and referring to another novel in progress, has been found; but Newby confused all three sisters, and the novel in question may be Anne's *The Tenant of Wildfell Hall*. This novel was published in June 1848, and, though some modern critics have seen it as Anne's answer to Emily's heterodox views, contemporary reviewers saw *The Tenant of Wildfell Hall* as further evidence of the Brontës' coarseness and immorality.

Meanwhile all was not well with the Brontës' health. Branwell had degenerated badly since 1845, and he died on 24 September 1848. His physical and spiritual welfare must have caused anxiety for all three sisters, and there are stories of Emily, the tallest of the three, bearing the brunt of looking after him and carrying him about. Anne's health had also been worrying Charlotte, but on 9 October Emily was reported as having a cough and a cold. She struggled through her normal household tasks until almost the day of her death, refusing, according to the popular legend, all medical aid. Her death came very suddenly on 19 December 1848, and she was buried three days later at Haworth.

It is difficult to get any clear impression of Emily's personality or even her personal appearance from the scanty evidence available. Contemporary portraits, not very well authenticated, show Emily in different guises; a certain amount of romanticizing must be allowed for in these pictures. Contemporary accounts suggest that she made no effort to present herself in an attractive fashion. Charlotte Brontë remarked rather oddly that her sister resembled G. H. Lewes, the husband in all but name of George Eliot, although portraits of Emily and Lewes do not seem to bring out the resemblance. Charlotte's memories of her sister, and in particular her remark that the portrait of Shirley in her 1849 novel of the same name was based upon Emily, are likely to have been influenced by a pious

wish to speak well of the dead. Emily's originality is borne out by her novel, but tributes to her strength of character ignore the fact that she seemed almost unable to survive outside Haworth. A certain amount of sentimentality must also be allowed for in the picture of Emily working closely in harmony with her two sisters: this picture would seem to be contradicted by the anger of Emily at the discovery of her poems, and by the fact that Anne Brontë, both in her poetry and her second novel, appears to be trying to refute Emily's views. Charlotte's desire to speak highly of her dead sister is of course both understandable and creditable; less creditable has been the refusal of many modern biographers to abandon the hushed superlatives and to admit that Emily, like many great artists, would appear to have had a rather difficult personality.

Her poetry is also difficult to evaluate and to interpret. It was not written for publication, and though she did revise much of her early work in 1844, some of what has been preserved can be discounted as immature early drafts. Gondal is a barrier to the proper appreciation of the poetry. In spite of misguided attempts, notably by Miss Fannie Ratchford in *Gondal's Queen: A Novel in Verse* (1955), to make a coherent pattern of the Gondal saga, the details of the history of this imaginary land cannot be known. Clearly Gondal is a land dominated by dynamic, cruel people prompted by the same violent emotions of love and hate which rule *Wuthering Heights*. One of these characters is called sometimes

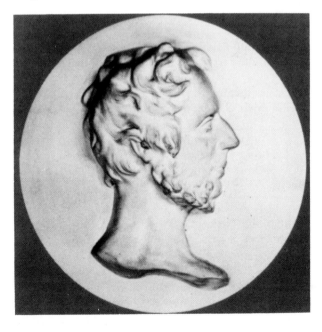

A medallion of Branwell Brontë, who died three months before his sister Emily (Brontë Parsonage Museum)

by her initials A.G.A., and it is tempting, but not necessarily correct, to say that other female characters in the poems who behave in the same Heathcliff-like fashion are A.G.A under a different name. Possibly, as in *Wuthering Heights*, more than one generation is involved; it is also possible that Brontë changed the story as she went along. The idea that all poems are Gondal poems seems mistaken in view of Brontë's division of her work into two notebooks. There is also a subjective element in some Gondal poems: in the poem variously entitled "The Prisoner" and "The Visionary," a dreary Gondal tale full of chains that clank and jailers who growl, Brontë appears to have a sudden moment of inspiration and describes the prisoner's vision of release in an impassioned outburst quite unlike anything else in English poetry. This outburst is generally printed in selections from Brontë without its Gondal trappings, and this may be some encouragement to those wishing to appreciate the poems without a knowledge of Gondal.

Much of Brontë's poetry is monotonous and humdrum, achieving its simple effects through narrative force and a clear rhythm. Words like "drear" and "dark" are too frequent, but even in these poems Emily rises above the level of her sisters by occasionally inserting an unexpected, often a prosaic, word. Her thought, moreover, is clearly highly original. It is in "No Coward Soul is Mine" that one sees best her unorthodoxy as well as her command of sound effects in lines like:

> Vain are the thousand creeds
> That move men's hearts, unutterably vain
> Worthless as withered weeds
> Or idlest froth amidst the boundless main.

But it is possible to see traces of this brilliance in earlier poems like "The Old Stoic," written in 1841:

> Riches I hold in light esteem
> And Love I laugh to scorn
> And lust of Fame was but a dream
> That vanished with the morn.

Some poems are—like *Wuthering Heights*—difficult to interpret because the context is not known; nor, as the manuscript of such poems is sometimes missing, is it always known for certain how to punctuate them. "The Philosopher" is such a poem. Brontë makes one of the speakers talk about three gods warring within his breast, and there is a baffling allusion to three rivers, but it is difficult to see who is speaking to whom, or to what the tripartite division refers. The imagery may be biblical, and is clearly powerful, but it is hard to see where it is leading. It would seem that in her later and finer poems Emily Brontë was slowly working her way to a mystical vision of a universe compared to which all of life's pains and joys were meaningless.

Some sort of commentary on the poems of Emily is provided by Anne's poetry and by *Wuthering Heights*. It would seem that Anne was trying, not very successfully, to counter her sister's philosophy in poems like "The Three Guides"; in the same way that *The Tenant of Wildfell Hall* has superficial resemblances to *Wuthering Heights*, but a fundamentally different message, so "The Three Guides" would appear to reprimand the unorthodoxy of "The Philosopher." The relationship of the poems to *Wuthering Heights* is a little more difficult to determine. Some work has gone into tracing forerunners of Heathcliff and Cathy in the wild, reckless, amoral inhabitants of Gondal. The rugged landscape in which many of the poems are set resembles the moors in *Wuthering Heights*, both being close to the barren beauty of the countryside near the Brontës' home. In some of the later poems, Brontë seems to be trying to solve some of the metaphysical problems which she raises in her novel. And yet it is a disservice to both the highly practical novel and the deeply philosophical poetry to try to interpret them in the same fashion.

Wuthering Heights begins with the reflections of the narrator, Lockwood, who has come to stay at Thrushcross Grange, but goes to visit his landlord, Heathcliff, at Wuthering Heights. Lockwood, whose name suggests a closed mind, is clearly a fool and makes all kinds of mistakes: he thinks Heathcliff a capital fellow; he suggests that a pile of dead rabbits are domestic pets; and he cannot understand the relationship of Heathcliff to a girl he meets at Wuthering Heights called Catherine Heathcliff, who turns out to be the wife of Heathcliff's dead son. Other inhabitants of Wuthering Heights are a very rough servant, Joseph, and a fairly rough youth, Hareton. Lockwood is forced to stay the night at Wuthering Heights because of bad weather, and he has two bad dreams. One of these involves an almost comic episode in which Lockwood is denounced for yawning at a sermon divided into 491 parts delivered by the Reverend Jahez Branderham. This would seem to be an attack on the folly of conventional moral standards. In the other dream, a child called Catherine Linton is struggling to get in at the window while Lockwood tries to prevent her. This dream has reverberations throughout the novel; Lockwood's cruelty shows

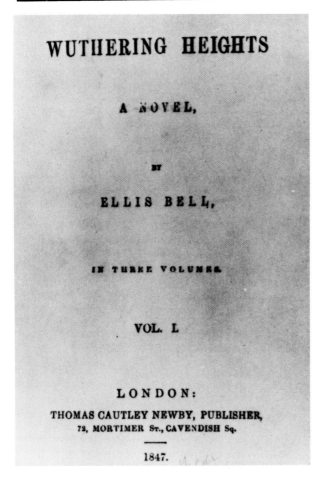

Title page of Brontë's only novel

be so conveniently present at several crises in the novel, and the reader does find himself passing judgment on her. These judgments have, like most pronouncements on *Wuthering Heights*, been very variable, one critic even finding that Nelly is the villain of the novel. A more balanced view would suggest that Nelly stands for conventional morality, and that her failure to stem or even to understand the tragic passions involved in the story she tells is a further indictment of conventional goodness.

The story Nelly tells is certainly a tragic one. Some thirty years before Lockwood visited Wuthering Heights, Mr. Earnshaw had left the house, inhabited by his wife, son Hindley, daughter Cathy, manservant Joseph, and maidservant Nelly Dean, on a long journey to Liverpool. (Brontë's chronology is very exact, and every event can be dated accurately with no inconsistencies.) On his return Mr. Earnshaw brings not the fiddle his daughter had asked for, nor the whip Hindley had requested, but a dark Gypsylike waif he had found abandoned in the streets of Liverpool. His motives for this act of charity do not seem clear; some have suggested that the boy was his illegitimate son, but there is little evidence for this, although the Earnshaws do call him Heathcliff, the name of a son they had lost in infancy. Heathcliff soon gains the affection of Cathy, but Hindley is always hostile to him. One day Mr. Earnshaw presents the boys with two colts, and on finding that his is lame, Heathcliff demands that Hindley make an exchange with him, threatening to report his bullying to Mr. Earnshaw if Hindley refuses.

Mrs. Earnshaw, always a shadowy figure, has died earlier, and shortly after the incident of the colts Hindley is sent away to college. Mr. Earnshaw grows old and dies, much to the grief of Cathy and Heathcliff, who comfort each other with thoughts of heaven. At this stage, Nelly, who is impressed by the children's piety, is definitely on their side, and the reader is inclined to share her sympathy. Hindley returns home after his father's death with a wife, Frances, and Heathcliff is relegated to a menial position. Frances dies after giving birth to a son, Hareton, whom Lockwood has seen at Wuthering Heights, and Hindley takes to drink, maintaining his savage hostility to Heathcliff—who is, however, allowed to run wild together with Cathy.

Cathy and Heathcliff are surprised on an uninvited visit to Thrushcross Grange, home of the Linton family. Cathy hurts her leg in trying to escape and is kept at Thrushcross Grange. The Linton children, Edgar and Isabella, visit Wuthering Heights, and Heathcliff throws a tureen of apple

that his mind is still closed to the power and pathos of Wuthering Heights in the same way that he tries to keep the window closed.

Heathcliff is awakened by Lockwood's cries after his second dream, and, although considerably disturbed by the episode and by Lockwood's blundering explanations, Heathcliff manages to remain polite to Lockwood. This superficial politeness attracts Lockwood's and the reader's curiosity and sympathy toward Heathcliff, although the reader's judgments will later have to be revised. Lockwood falls ill on his return to Thrushcross Grange and whiles away his convalescence by asking his housekeeper, Nelly Dean, about the previous history of the inhabitants of Wuthering Heights.

Nelly Dean is a more interesting narrator than Lockwood. One obvious reason the story is told at second hand by her rather than by one of the characters principally involved is that the events would seem too violent and melodramatic if narrated directly. It is slightly awkward that Nelly Dean, in spite of her humble status, should have to

Shibden Hall, near Halifax, the probable model for Thrushcross Grange in Wuthering Heights

sauce in Edgar Linton's face. Heathcliff is jealous of the attention Cathy gives to Edgar, and Nelly, still vaguely sympathetic to Heathcliff, gives him kindly advice, as she does Cathy, who tells her that Edgar has asked her to marry him. Heathcliff overhears this conversation; and when he hears Cathy say that it would degrade her to marry Heathcliff since Hindley had brought him so low, he leaves—thus not waiting for the end of an impressive speech from Cathy, stressing her total unity with Heathcliff, and including the famous words "Nelly, I am Heathcliff."

Heathcliff in fact leaves Wuthering Heights for over three years. Cathy rushes desperately onto the moors, becomes severely ill, and is taken in by the Lintons. The Linton parents die, and after an interval of three years, Cathy marries Edgar Linton. Nelly Dean breaks off her narrative at this point, and Lockwood temporarily resumes his. This break does not allow the reader to explore interesting questions such as why Cathy takes so long to make up her mind. It also glides over a subtle change in Nelly Dean's loyalties: hitherto she has been more friendly to the Earnshaws than to the Lintons, and

this loyalty has embraced Heathcliff, who seems preferable to the spoiled and cowardly Edgar Linton; on Cathy's marriage, Nelly comes to live with her at Thrushcross Grange, and Edgar begins to appear in a better light. He and his sister are very kind to Cathy, who seems conventionally happy until the point at which Nelly resumes her narrative some six months after the marriage.

The conventional idyll is broken by the return of Heathcliff, who in his absence has contrived to acquire wealth and the manners of a gentleman. It is not clear *how* he has done this; the reason *why* he has done it should be clear when one remembers Cathy's unlucky speech which had impelled him to leave. He uses his wealth to gain a hold over Hindley by gambling with him at Wuthering Heights, and uses his gentlemanly manners to charm Isabella Linton into falling in love with him. No doubt he had intended to become rich to win Cathy, who is at first overjoyed to see him, but becomes distressed when Edgar raises objections and Isabella further complicates matters. Edgar is naturally and conventionally jealous, but it would be a mistake to think of Cathy as being jealous of Isabella. Her distress is not caused by normal sexual possessiveness, as she knows Heathcliff cares nothing for Isabella, but because she is aware that she and Heathcliff, who is intent on his revenge, have lost that fundamental sympathy with each other that they had had in childhood. Cathy's distress leads to mad ravings even before Heathcliff elopes with Isabella, brutally attempting to kill her spaniel beforehand.

Heathcliff and Isabella are away for over two months. During this time Cathy experiences a complete breakdown, but is gently nursed back to partial health by her husband. She is pregnant, having conceived a child at about the time of Heathcliff's initial return. It is uncertain what the implications of this are, or even if Brontë was aware of them. Certainly the love of Cathy and Heathcliff appears to transcend ordinary sexual love, which is much better represented by the feelings of Edgar. In addition, Cathy's daughter when she is born appears to have some Linton characteristics. The latter point is not a very strong one, since Isabella and Heathcliff also have a child who owes nothing to his father. The wedding night of Heathcliff and Isabella is not, and could not be described, but there are glimpses of its horror when Isabella writes a letter describing her return to Wuthering Heights. She paints a dark picture of the inhumanity of Heathcliff and the squalor of the house. The old servant, Joseph, mocks at Isabella's ladylike airs, and one feels in spite of her misfortunes that Isabella is a little spoiled. Isabella's letter is the nearest approach to a first-person narrative by someone directly involved in the action, and, since it has a melodramatic air about it, is perhaps a sign of how wise Brontë was to tell her strange story through Nelly Dean and Lockwood. Nelly visits Wuthering Heights and finds Isabella looking like a slattern, but Heathcliff flourishing. He is affable to Nelly, but demands with threats that she should carry a letter to Cathy arranging a meeting. As the story reaches its climax, Nelly again pauses in her narrative, and the focus reverts to Lockwood, who foolishly imagines a possible affair between himself and Catherine.

From light comedy, the resumption of Nelly's narrative returns the reader to high tragedy: three days after Nelly's visit to Wuthering Heights Heathcliff and Cathy meet at Thrushcross Grange while Edgar is at church. They realize that she is near death, and mingle recrimination, anguish, and ecstasy. Although Edgar is just about to return, Heathcliff embraces her passionately. He releases her unconscious as Edgar enters the room, and she dies giving birth to a puny premature daughter, Catherine, without regaining consciousness. Edgar is exhausted, but Heathcliff stays awake in the garden of Thrushcross Grange, savagely dashing his head against the trunk of a tree. After the funeral, Isabella visits her old home to announce that she is leaving for London. With typical violence, she crushes her wedding ring with a poker. She tells of frightening quarrels between Hindley and Heathcliff. Hindley, now a confirmed drunkard, does not outlive his sister very long; on his death it is discovered that he has gambled away all his rights to Wuthering Heights, and Heathcliff now becomes the owner of the house and the guardian of Hindley's son, Hareton. Meanwhile Isabella has given birth to a son, whom, understandably but confusingly, she calls Linton Heathcliff.

Top Withens, near Haworth, believed to have suggested the locale of Wuthering Heights (Yorkshire Post)

Thirteen years pass, in which young Catherine grows up, lovingly cared for by Nelly Dean and Edgar Linton (who does not, however, play a very active part in the rest of the novel). Isabella dies in London, asking Edgar to look after her son. While Edgar is away, Catherine contrives to visit Wuthering Heights and discovers that Hareton is her cousin. Edgar returns with the sickly Linton, but Heathcliff demands his rights, and insists that the boy come to him.

On her sixteenth birthday, Catherine and Nelly meet Heathcliff and Hareton on the moors, and against Nelly's wishes go to Wuthering Heights. Edgar is feeble and Hareton is uncouth. Heathcliff now begins to plot a grotesque parody of the triangular relationship that had existed between him, Edgar, and Cathy, with the added advantage that if Linton marries Catherine and then dies, he will gain the ownership of both houses. A correspondence between Linton and Catherine is nipped in the bud by Nelly; but the next winter, when Nelly and Edgar are both ill, Catherine visits Linton several times. Encouraged by Heathcliff, the cousins appear to get on well together, although the fundamental difference between them appears when Catherine describes their different ideas of a perfect day, Catherine preferring activity and Linton calm. This passage is sometimes mistakenly linked with the distinction between Wuthering Heights and Thrushcross Grange, seen as representing the forces of storm and calm. In fact, the active landscape Catherine describes is more like that of Thrushcross Grange, and Linton talks of the moors.

When Nelly and Edgar discover what has been happening, they forbid communication between Linton and Catherine. All these events happen in the winter previous to Nelly's narrative, and the past now begins to catch up with the present. A pathetic letter from Linton ensures further meetings with Catherine. Both Edgar and Linton are now dying, and Heathcliff is engaged in a bitter race with death. This he wins by kidnapping Nelly and Catherine and blackmailing Catherine into marrying Linton, forestalling Edgar's efforts to change his will by bribing his lawyer. The feebleness of all the other characters to control their destiny against Heathcliff's wicked designs may seem slightly improbable; but faced with Heathcliff's dynamic energy, the reader, like the other characters, accepts the inevitable.

Linton dies, leaving Catherine's rights as heiress of Wuthering Heights to his father. Modern readers may be shocked that a woman's rights could be bypassed so easily: a contemporary reviewer on the contrary remarked that the book proved that Satan was master of the law of entail. Zillah, the maidservant, acts as temporary narrator at this point, explaining the circumstances which Lockwood found on his visit to Wuthering Heights. Catherine Heathcliff is imprisoned in the house under Heathcliff's control, while her other cousin, Hareton, disgusts her by his boorish ways. Lockwood sees this when he visits Wuthering Heights bearing a letter from Nelly to Catherine. Catherine cannot answer as she has no paper, and accuses Hareton of stealing her books in his efforts to learn to read. Hearing their quarrel, Heathcliff checks his wrath on noticing the strange resemblance of Hareton to Cathy, his aunt. Lockwood departs for London, having tired of Thrushcross Grange, still imagining a possible romance between himself and Catherine.

He returns a year later to hear the end of the story. Nobody is at home at Thrushcross Grange, so he walks up to Wuthering Heights. Here he overhears Catherine and Hareton reading together. Spring is in the air and flowers are growing in the yard. Nelly Dean tells him the rest of the story. Catherine, after initially rebuffing Hareton, relents, teaches him to read, and falls in love with him. Heathcliff sees this, but seems unable to thwart the destruction of his plans. He is reminded of Cathy and his youth when he sees the pair together, and seems aware that his death is imminent, although he is still vigorous and in early middle age. His death is very sudden. Catherine and Hareton plan to move to Thrushcross Grange, leaving Wuthering Heights to Joseph and the ghosts of the previous generation. These ghosts are still active, as Lockwood realizes when he hears a small boy blubbering that he has seen Heathcliff walking the moors with a woman, although as Lockwood passes the graves of Edgar, Cathy, and Heathcliff, he piously reflects that he cannot imagine unquiet slumbers for anyone under that quiet earth.

Typically, the novel ends with an ambiguity: it is not clear whether Lockwood is any wiser than at the beginning, and whether the reader is meant to believe that Heathcliff has achieved peace or that he roams with Cathy as a ghost over the moors. Perhaps he does both. Nor is it clear whether the marriage of Catherine and Hareton and their plan to move to Thrushcross Grange represent a defeat for Heathcliff and a rejection of all he stands for, including the wild, stormy atmosphere of Wuthering Heights; or whether Catherine and Hareton are a pale imitation of Cathy and Heathcliff, and their earthly joys are a model of the unearthly ecstasy of

Heathcliff once he is united with Cathy.

Heathcliff dominates the novel, and the reader is not really interested in Catherine and Hareton. Catherine does remind one of her mother, and indeed the names "Cathy" and "Catherine" are almost interchangeable in the novel. This confusion (which has been avoided here by arbitrarily calling the elder "Cathy" and the younger "Catherine") is presumably deliberate. When Lockwood visits Wuthering Heights for the first time he finds the signatures of Catherine Earnshaw, Catherine Linton, and Catherine Heathcliff; both heroines have a share in all three names. In spite of these links and in spite of the fact that Catherine is at first sight more admirable than her petulant and selfish mother, the reader seems to be meant to see Catherine mainly as an instrument in Heathcliff's monstrous plan of revenge. Likewise, Hareton's wooing of Catherine by learning to read is not especially exciting, and even slightly ridiculous; what is interesting about Hareton is that he seems oddly fond of Heathcliff, and even, as Charlotte Brontë noted, strikes some sparks of affection in return.

These slight marks of affection for Hareton were said by Charlotte to be Heathcliff's one redeeming feature. Other critics have been kinder, and certainly Heathcliff's ferocious energy has exercised a strange fascination over most readers. Unlike Milton's Satan or the Byronic hero or even the heroes of German romantic novels, all of which have been seen as possible models for him, Heathcliff is curiously mean and calculating in his villainy. The episode of the exchange of horses shows him in a bad light at an early stage in the novel, and sentimentality about his proletarian origins cannot disguise the fact that in the latter part he behaves like the worst kind of grasping capitalist landlord. Nor can his romantic desire for revenge on Cathy and Hindley and Edgar excuse the deliberate way he warps the lives of Catherine and Hareton and Linton by forcing them to enact a grotesque imitation of the lives of their predecessors. Isabella's treatment is perhaps more excusable, as she brought disaster on her own head, and her shoddy and shallow romanticism deserves to be shown up.

Heathcliff tells the truth even if in rather a savage fashion; this is part of his attraction, and it is also a trait he shares with his creator insofar as one can ascertain anything about Emily Brontë. Like Cathy, Heathcliff has an immense wealth of unexpected violent—almost Shakespearean—imagery at his command; indeed, rich images, especially those concerned with the weather and the animal kingdom, are a strength of the whole book. Comparison with *King Lear* is inevitable.

Like *King Lear*, *Wuthering Heights* is set in a wild landscape, and it is part of Heathcliff's attraction that he is associated with the landscape and with Wuthering Heights. The opposition between the two houses is an important theme in the book. It is dangerous to see Wuthering Heights through Isabella's eyes as rough and rude in comparison to the civilized luxury of Thrushcross Grange; people do not seem very happy at Thrushcross Grange, which has a cold, formal air about it in contrast to the organic warmth of Wuthering Heights. Lockwood is at pains to stress that Wuthering Heights, both inside and outside, has a certain amount of refinement. Yet one must not be sentimental about Wuthering Heights: it has a fire in summer not just to show organic warmth, but to show that it is cold; the trees outside are warped in the same way as Heathcliff warps the lives of other people; and the name "Wuthering" is a local dialect term for the roaring of the wind—attractive to hear at a safe distance, but both frightening and depressing to experience at close quarters.

An attempt has been made to link the two houses and the two generations into some immense cosmic scheme, whereby the two elements of storm and calm are present discordantly in the first generation, but are somehow fused harmoniously with the marriage of Catherine and Hareton. This attempt by Lord David Cecil in *Early Victorian Novelists* (1934) has been very influential, but it is far too schematic. Linton Heathcliff has a stormy father, but it is difficult to see anything but a rather deadly calm in his character; and he is proof, if proof is needed, that in a certain sense storm is better than calm. Thus Cecil's contention that *Wuthering Heights* is an amoral book, refusing to pass judgment on either side in any controversy, seems to fall to the ground if, in spite of all conventional values and the conventional views of Nelly Dean shaping the narrative, the reader still feels drawn to Heathcliff and his turbulent environment.

Few would doubt Cecil's third point, that through the story of Heathcliff and Cathy, Brontë is trying to state some fundamental metaphysical truth. It is the breadth of this ambition which raises *Wuthering Heights* above the level of the poems, which seem to have a narrower scope. In an important article, "The Rejection of Heathcliff?" in *Essays in Criticism*, 8 (1958), Miriam Allott tries to show that Brontë is somehow on Heathcliff's side and believes in what he stands for, but Allott sees the death of Heathcliff and the move to Thrushcross Grange as an elegiac statement of regret at the passing of an impossible dream. More recently there have been more narrowly sociological interpretations of the end of the book by Mrs. Q. D. Leavis in *Lectures in America* (1969) and T. Eagleton in *Myths of Power* (1975). These have seen the triumph of Hareton and Catherine as the triumph of nineteenth-century capitalism over eighteenth-century yeomanry. All these interpretations, although they provide valuable insights, seem to ignore the fact that the end of the novel is a great deal more enigmatic than they make out.

Other modern critical articles on *Wuthering Heights* tend to be eccentric or to deal with only a very small section of the book. Two modern full-length studies of Emily Brontë, by John Hewish and Winifred Gerin, correct the earlier biographical errors of amateur works such as those by Spark and Stanford, Simpson, and Robinson, but do not quite clear up the mystery of Emily Brontë's enigmatic

personality or offer a definitive interpretation of her famous book. The publication of the Clarendon *Wuthering Heights* (1976) supplies a definite text, but adds little in its introduction apart from some useful information about Newby's imperfections as an editor. Recent critical interest in Charlotte Brontë, an author so much easier to tie down to a definite meaning than Emily, has meant that Emily has slightly lost ground at her sister's expense, although *Wuthering Heights* remains the most popular and the most typical Brontë novel in both academic and popular circles. It is worth remembering that it was only in 1899 with the publication of the Haworth edition of the Brontë novels that Emily was finally established as a novelist superior to Charlotte in the introductions of Mrs. Humphry Ward, which remain some of the best prose written on the Brontës.

Emily Brontë remains enigmatic because so little is known about her, and what is known is contradictory. Her life seems one of dreary con-

High Sunderland Hall, near Halifax, on which Brontë based many of the features of the house called Wuthering Heights

formity; her book seems designed to outrage and shock. Even the modern reader, whose susceptibility to shock must be less than that of his Victorian counterpart, is still outraged not so much by the violence of word, deed, and atmosphere as by the sudden surprise to his sensibilities when he finds characters appealing to him in spite of what they do. Perhaps the only certain message of *Wuthering Heights* is that nothing is certain. Brontë's defiance of rigid categories and her refusal to divide people into saints and sinners, gentry and servants, good and bad is very un-Victorian, but does not seem out of keeping with what is known of her temperament.

Heathcliff's cruelty and Cathy's selfishness do not prevent them from being attractive. The Lintons are spoiled and weak, but Isabella's and her son's sufferings and Edgar's devotion to his wife win them sympathy. Hindley is profligate and cruel, neglecting even Hareton in a shocking fashion; but Nelly Dean, who is Hindley's foster sister and has an old retainer's loyalty, finds a mournful pathos about his fall and inspires the reader to do the same. Joseph, the servant at Wuthering Heights, is hypocritical, pharisaical, a believer in hell fire and predestination. Brontë would appear to have believed in truth, tolerance, and universal salvation. Yet it is one of the oddest features of the novel that one feels that Joseph, who is always present at Wuthering Heights, is somehow akin to Brontë in his savage contempt for almost everything and his belief that gloom is good for the soul.

Heathcliff himself, at first sight so straight an unredeemed villain or Byronic hero, acts at times in a surprising fashion. One can never quite make out the significance of the episodes in which he catches Hareton when Hindley drunkenly drops him over the banisters, or in which—spitting and cursing—he prevents Hindley from bleeding to death, although he has threatened to kill Hindley and Hindley has just tried to kill him. It is odd, too, to find Heathcliff offering to make a cup of tea for Nelly Dean and Catherine at a time when he is acting villainously toward both of them. These touches of humanity prevent Heathcliff and *Wuthering Heights* from lapsing into unrealistic melodrama; one is reminded of the sudden unexpected words in Brontë's poetry, and homely glimpses of the authoress of *Wuthering Heights* baking the bread.

Heathcliff stands unredeemed, says Charlotte Brontë in her introduction to the second edition, but qualifies her remark by saying that his affection for Hareton partially redeems him. She then gives a surprising hint about the origins of Heathcliff's name. Most readers will think of a heath as an arid waste as in *King Lear*, and there are plenty of barren wastes on the moors near Wuthering Heights and in Heathcliff's heart. But there is also a small flower named a heath, and it is to this that Charlotte links the mighty and rugged cliff that stands for *Wuthering Heights*. Emily Brontë would appear to be a wilting flower who created a mighty rock.

Biographies:

A. Mary F. Robinson, *Emily Brontë* (London: Allen, 1883);

Charles Simpson, *Emily Brontë* (London: Countrylife, 1929);

Muriel Spark and Derek Stanford, *Emily Brontë* (London: Owen, 1953);

J. Hewish, *Emily Brontë* (London: Macmillan, 1969);

Winifred Gérin, *Emily Brontë* (Oxford: Oxford University Press, 1971).

References:

Miriam Allott, "*Wuthering Heights*: The Rejection of Heathcliff?," in *Essays in Criticism*, 8 (1958): 27-47;

Jacques Blondel, *Emily Brontë: Experience spirituelle et creation poetique* (Clermont-Ferrand: Presses Universitaires de France, 1956);

David Cecil, *Early Victorian Novelists* (London: Constable, 1934);

E. Chitham, "Almost like Twins," *Brontë Society Transactions*, 85 (1975): 365-373;

C. W. Davies, "A Reading of *Wuthering Heights*," *Essays in Criticism*, 19 (1969): 254-273;

T. Eagleton, *Myths of Power* (London: Macmillan, 1975);

F. R. Leavis and Q. D. Leavis, *Lectures in America* (London: Chatto & Windus, 1969);

W. D. Paden, *An Investigation of Gondal* (New York: Bookman, 1958);

J. F. Petit, ed., *Emily Brontë* (Harmondsworth, U.K.: Penguin, 1973);

Fannie E. Ratchford, *Gondal's Queen: A Novel in Verse* (Austin: University of Texas Press, 1955);

C. P. Sanger, *The Structure of "Wuthering Heights"* (London: Hogarth Press, 1926);

Mary Visick, *The Genesis of "Wuthering Heights"* (Hong Kong: Hong Kong University Press, 1958);

Irene Cooper Willis, *The Authorship of "Wuthering Heights"* (London: Hogarth Press, 1936);

Tom Winnifrith, *The Brontës* (London: Macmillan, 1977);

Winnifrith, *The Brontës and Their Background* (London: Macmillan, 1973).

Oliver Madox Brown

(20 January 1855-5 November 1874)

William E. Fredeman
University of British Columbia

BOOKS: *Gabriel Denver* (London: Smith, Elder, 1873);

The Dwale Bluth, Hebditch's Legacy, and Other Literary Remains of Oliver Madox-Brown, edited by William M. Rossetti and F. Hueffer (2 volumes, London: Tinsley, 1876).

Oliver Madox Brown (known as Nolly to his friends and family) was born at Grove Villas, Finchley, on 20 January 1855 and died on 5 November 1874, the first anniversary of the publication of his single novel, *Gabriel Denver*. The middle child of the painter Ford Madox Brown and his second wife, Emma Hill, Oliver was the brother of Catherine Madox Brown, who married the music critic Franz Hueffer, and the uncle of Ford Madox Hueffer (later Ford). His half sister, Lucy Madox Brown—whose mother was Ford Madox Brown's first wife, Elizabeth Bromley—married, in the year of Oliver's death, William Michael Rossetti. Brown's connections thus link him on both sides with figures prominent in literature and art.

Most of what is known about his early life consists of anecdotes exemplifying his precocity. What Westland Martson states perfunctorily in the *Dictionary of National Biography*, that "from early boyhood he showed remarkable capacity, both in painting and literature," John H. Ingram in his biography dramatizes unnecessarily: "Reared in so rare a forcing-ground as was his parents' home, little Oliver speedily displayed signs of hereditary genius, and many are the significant anecdotes and remarks related by his relatives in proof of his innate cleverness." All three of Ford Madox Brown's children gave early indication of artistic talent, but it was chiefly Nolly who proved a surprise to his father. "He seems to be turning out a perfect genius," Ford Madox Brown wrote to Frederic Shields in 1868, bragging of Oliver's talents in fusing design and picturesqueness, "that only belongs to the higher class of men"; "you will think I am mad to talk so," he confessed, "but I truly believe it."

The uncritical enthusiasm of the domestic environment in which Oliver spent his youth was probably intensified by the death of a baby brother,

Oliver Madox-Brown

Arthur Gabriel, in 1857. If it tended to cause the boy to overestimate his own abilities and to indulge himself emotionally through expressive outlets, at least it provided a sympathetic atmosphere in which his natural talents could develop. Oliver's general and artistic education were superintended by his father, though he had brief periods of formal instruction. He spent two years in the junior classes of University College under Mr. Case in 1863-1865, where he was "chiefly distinguished among his schoolfellows for his idleness" and where he was regarded as "the dirtiest boy in the school." In 1871, he attended life classes in the atelier of M. Barthe in Chelsea, where he received a prize of a month's free instruction in a drawing competition judged by G. F. Watts. The most influential outside force on his education seems to have been Jules Andrieu, later the French consul at Jersey, who, during the last four years of Brown's life, instructed him in French and Latin. (Andrieu provided the motto for the title page of *Gabriel Denver*: "Le bonheur vient souvent bien tard,—après la mort de toutes nos espérances. Aussi faut-il aux malheureux beaucoup d'esprit pour le reconnaître, et de force pour l'arrêter au passage.")

Under his father's tutelage, Oliver produced his first watercolor, *Centaurs Hunting*, at the age of eight; what may be called his first finished work, *Queen Margaret and the Robbers*, was done three years later. Dante Gabriel Rossetti, to whom Oliver presented the painting, assured the young boy that "I consider it very beautiful both in design and colour, and a first effort of which you need never be ashamed, however much you may advance as an artist." He saw in the work a high promise; James McNeil Whistler, to whom Rossetti showed the painting, also "admired it very much indeed": "Hard study and application are not to be dispensed with by any one entering on Art; but it is something to make such a beginning as this, and so feel sure that, though without labour no perfection can ever be attained, still there is no doubt of your labour to become a complete artist being really worth your while and not a mistaken course in life as it is with many." From this point, it seemed certain that Oliver was destined for a career in art. In style and technique, Oliver's works are markedly imitative of his father, who, as Dante Gabriel reported to William Rossetti (perhaps remembering his own stultifying apprenticeship with Brown), "makes his Son work on the strict Praeraphaelite system."

Between 1868 and 1872, Oliver continued his painting, almost exclusively in watercolor, exhibiting *The Infant Jason Delivered to the Centaur* at the Dudley Gallery in 1869. The picture illustrates, with exact fidelity to detail, the episode in William Morris's poem *The Life and Death of Jason* (1867). In the next four years, Oliver exhibited five pictures; his last, generally regarded as his best, was *A Scene from Silas Marner*, shown at the Society of French Artists in Bond Street in 1872. Interestingly, none of the reviewers of Ingram's biography had anything to say about Oliver's paintings, and over the years they have seldom been exhibited. He never appeared in an exhibition devoted to the Pre-Raphaelites until the Herron-Huntington Hartford exhibit in 1964, when *The Infant Jason* was shown. Oliver's single experiment with book illustration was for W. M. Rossetti's edition of *The Poetical Works of Byron* in the Moxon Popular Poets series (1870). He collaborated with his father in illustrating this volume, providing two of the drawings—*Mazeppa* and *The Deformed Transformed*; an oil version of the *Mazeppa* was exhibited at the British Institution in

1871, and he commenced, but never completed, an oil version of *The Deformed Transformed*.

Although he continued to paint and to be interested in art until his death, Oliver began to turn his attention to literature around 1869. During this year, when he was fourteen, Oliver "produced some sonnets, six or seven in number," which he destroyed "in a fit of morbid irritability of bashfulness caused by their being shown to a few friends." Two of these early sonnets have survived, however: one was adopted as the motto and printed in gilt on the frame of a picture by Marie Stillman, a student of Ford Madox Brown, and was included in *The Dwale Bluth, Hebditch's Legacy, and Other Literary Remains of Oliver Madox-Brown* (1876); the second, on a chameleon, written about the same time, was first printed by Ingram.

It was during his fifteenth year, according to the memoir in the *Literary Remains*, that Oliver first "thought out his narrative" for his one completed novel, projecting it initially in verse, a scheme from which "he was diverted by reflecting that, among the authors belonging to, or highly prized in, his own social circle, there were various writers of poetry, but few or none who produced prose fiction." It would appear, then, that in composing *The Black Swan* over the winter of 1871-1872, Brown

Drawing of Oliver Madox Brown at the age of five, by his father, Ford Madox Brown

was committing himself to becoming the novelist among the Pre-Raphaelite group, with whom he was closely affiliated. Having previously flirted with and certainly not mastered the twin arts of Pre-Raphaelitism, poetry and painting, he saw in fiction possibilities that so far had gone unsounded.

By the summer of 1872, Brown had finished *The Black Swan* and was hoping to attract a publisher. He had also commenced (probably in June) the writing of his second novel, *The Dwale Bluth*. By September, when Brown embarked on a walking tour of Sussex and Kent, *The Black Swan* had been submitted to William Smith Williams, the reader for Smith, Elder who had been so largely responsible for promoting the publication of Charlotte Brontë's *Jane Eyre* (1847). The source of the contact is uncertain, though Ingram attributes it to "female intervention," explaining that it was Lowes Dickinson's wife, Williams's daughter, who, struck by the "power and originality" of the book, succeeded in getting her father to read it.

The negotiations for the publication of the novel—for what was to prove to be the transformation of *The Black Swan* into *Gabriel Denver*—occupied several months. From Williams's first letter, they must have been a devastating disappointment to the young author. Although sufficiently impressed by the book to encourage Brown in revising it, Williams insisted from the outset on changes—in tone, plot, motivation, even in title—that necessitated a total restructuring of the book and considerable rewriting. Williams's scruple was in large part on moral (that is to say, commercial) grounds: the novel had to be made acceptable to the conservative circulating libraries. Though Brown was reluctant to mutilate his story, expedience clearly loomed larger than integrity, and a patchwork novel seemed more attractive than honest anonymity. (Nor was Brown advised by his family to stand too insistently on his artistic prerogative.) There followed a long correspondence between Brown and Williams in which, point by point, Brown made the required concessions and agreed to the dilution of *The Black Swan*, renamed *Gabriel*

Watercolor of a scene from Silas Marner, *exhibited by Brown at the Society of French Artists in 1872*

Denver, to make it acceptable to the publishers. He spent the fall and winter of 1872-1873 "completely rewrit[ing] the whole story page by page." By 10 March 1873 he had completed his revisions, which included four new chapters and a new conclusion. At last Williams was satisfied, and he wrote at once to tell Brown that he was submitting *Gabriel Denver* to Leslie Stephen, the editor of the *Cornhill* magazine. Stephen ultimately rejected the novel, but Smith, Elder decided to publish it in book form, agreeing to purchase *Gabriel Denver* outright for £ 50. "It will make only one volume of the usual novel size," Williams wrote to Brown, "and though your name is not yet known to the public as a writer, I hope that your first book will make so strong an impression on the novel readers as to establish your popularity as a writer of romance." Brown had to endure further frustrations when Smith, Elder decided to delay publication until the fall.

Published on Guy Fawkes Day, 5 November 1873, a year to the day before Oliver Madox Brown's death, *Gabriel Denver* narrates the effect of passion on personality. Gabriel Denver, traveling on the ship *Black Swan* with his cousin-fiancée Deborah (his wife Dorothy in the earlier *Black Swan*), betrays her for Laura, an old acquaintance also on board. (In the original version, Laura and the unhappily-married Denver meet for the first time on the ship and fall in love.) Deborah sets fire to the ship for revenge upon the reunited lovers and then commits suicide. The ship nearly founders in a storm following Deborah's burial at sea and, in his delirium, Denver sees Deborah inviting him to join her in death in the ocean; but at the last moment, Laura saves him. (In the original, the *Black Swan* is destroyed in the fire, and the only survivors— Denver, Dorothy, and Laura—are set adrift in a lifeboat. Dorothy goes mad after drinking sea-water, confesses in her delirium that it was she who set the fire, and dies. Denver and Laura are picked up by a passing ship, but Laura dies from exposure. At the end, Denver leaps into the sea with her body in his arms.) In *The Black Swan,* the compulsiveness of Denver's love for Laura is set against the hatefulness of his marriage to his wife, but in *Gabriel Denver* the evil of the fiancée is intensified. The destruction of the lovers in *The Black Swan* is tragic but appropriate; in *Gabriel Denver* their being saved deflates the intensity of fatalism surrounding them. The decorative cover of the novel by Ford Madox Brown of a burning ship and small boat with a large cloud of billowing smoke provided a striking illustration paralleling the powerful story. The novel received mixed reviews, although it was strongly praised by

Dante Gabriel, Christina, and William Michael Rossetti among others.

After finishing *The Black Swan,* Brown had started writing a new novel set in Devonshire; this would become *The Dwale Bluth.* He was diverted from this work for two months while transforming *The Black Swan* into *Gabriel Denver*; then, instead of going back to it, he began *Hebditch's Legacy,* a sensation-type novel set in London involving hidden wills and other contrivances. The novel, which was left unfinished, does contain some vivid descriptions of characters and of London street scenes. During the course of writing this work, Brown tried to do some legal research in the British Museum reading room but was denied an admission card because he was not yet twenty-one.

Brown returned to his Devonshire novel in July 1874 and sent the first several chapters to Williams, who transmitted them to the editor of the *Cornhill.* After being held for some time, the manuscript was returned to Brown without comment. This seems to have discouraged Brown, who left the novel unfinished. *The Dwale Bluth*—the title is the Devonshire name for the deadly nightshade or belladonna plant—begins with an often comical account of the misfortunes of several generations of the Serpleton family, which is under a curse due to having been connected with the murder of Thomas à Becket. The latest heir to the estate, Jeffrey Serpleton, returns from his wanderings married to a Spanish gypsy; the wife gives birth to a daughter, Helen. Soon after, parents and baby depart, leaving the estate in the care of Jeffrey's brother, the eccentric Reverend Oliver Serpleton, and his sharp-tongued housekeeper, Margery. Six years later Jeffrey, whose wife has died, returns and leaves Helen in Oliver's charge. Oliver, also a widower, raises Helen with his own daughter, Leah.

One day the two girls, while playing, discover a strange plant; they take it to Oliver, who tells them it is the poisonous deadly nightshade or Dwale Bluth and confiscates it. But the plant winds up being carelessly thrown into the garden, where it takes root. Later Helen finds it and eats the berries, and almost dies; after her recovery, she is believed to have some sort of occult powers.

The novel breaks off with Helen still a girl; when it resumes (Brown never wrote the transitional episodes), she has grown up to become the widowed Mrs. Thurlstone and is in love with a blind poet, Arthur Haenton. One evening, while they sit embracing on a cliff overlooking the sea, Thurlstone—who was not drowned after all, as had been believed—appears. He forces Helen to return

*Cover of the only novel published by Brown during his lifetime.
The cover was illustrated by his father.*

home with him by threatening to throw the blind man off the cliff. Brown's manuscript breaks off at this point, but the editors of the *Literary Remains* supplied the ending he was believed to have intended: Helen, constantly watched by the husband she never loved, develops brain fever; in a fit, she strangles on her own hair. The blind poet, meeting her funeral procession, is informed of her death. After wandering grief stricken around the countryside for three days, Haenton stumbles into the churchyard and finds her fresh grave. Starving, he eats the berries of the plant which has been placed on the grave—the Dwale Bluth—and dies.

Thus *The Dwale Bluth*, like *The Black Swan*, is ultimately a story of unhappy marriage, illicit love, and the deaths of the lovers. But the earlier chapters sparkle with humor; the characterizations of Oliver Serpleton and Margery are memorable; and the depiction of the children, Helen and Leah, shows a good grasp of child psychology. Ingram calls *The Dwale Bluth* Brown's "masterpiece."

In person, Oliver Madox Brown was noted for his somewhat cynical wit and was apparently able to hold his own in conversations with his father's artistic friends. He was also given to humorous exaggeration, as is shown in letters to his friend, the poet Philip Bourke Marston (several of these are reproduced in Ingram's memoir). He carried a large ebony walking stick inlaid with ivory that had been given to him by William Rossetti; he also carried a gold watch which, for some reason, he refused to wind and which finally became totally useless from neglect. He loved animals, particularly cats, and kept a menagerie which included white rats, frogs, a toad, chameleons, and salamanders; while still quite young, he bought a duck from some older boys to keep them from abusing it. His descriptions of animals—rats leaving the burning ship in *The Black Swan*, Helen's pet toad in *The Dwale Bluth*—have been praised for their accuracy.

During the last year or so of his life, Brown was frequently subject to severe headaches, which interfered with his ability to write. In spite of this, he continued work on *Hebditch's Legacy* and *The Dwale Bluth* and started two short stories: "The Yeth-Hounds" is a Devonshire ghost story; "Dismal Jenny" is the first of a projected series of tales of London life. In September 1874 he suffered an attack of gout, which was followed by hectic fever and blood poisoning. He spent five weeks in bed at his parents' house at 37 Fitzroy Square; too weak to hold a pen, he dictated a final fragment to his mother and William Rossetti. Given the title "The Last Story," this was an account of poor children in a London slum as seen through their eyes. He also read (or had read to him) Blackmore's *Lorna Doone* (1869) and the first few chapters of Thomas Hardy's *Far from the Madding Crowd* (1874), then being serialized in the *Cornhill*. According to Ingram, when he came to the chapter where Gabriel Oak cares for the lambs through the winter night, he exclaimed: "No wonder they did not want *my* writing!" He finally became delirious and died on 5 November.

Although he did not begin his career as a writer until 1871—only three years before he died at the age of nineteen—Oliver Madox Brown achieved a notable success as a minor writer of promise and power. The publication of his *Literary Remains* in 1876, including *The Black Swan* plus *The Dwale Bluth* and *Hebditch's Legacy*, renewed the praise for his work. In his ability to evoke natural description with an emphasis on detail, in his development of forceful themes, and in his use of symbols to display the elements of good and evil in addition to his belief in the reciprocal interchange between painting and literature, Oliver Madox Brown remains perhaps the most important novelist of literary Pre-Raphaelitism.

Biographies:

John H. Ingram, *Oliver Madox Brown: A Biographical Sketch, 1855-1874* (London: Stock, 1883);

Ford Madox Hueffer, *Ford Madox Brown: A Record of His Life and Work* (London: Longmans, 1896).

References:

Anonymous [Edward Bulwer-Lytton?], Review of *Gabriel Denver*, *Athenaeum* (22 November 1873);

Anonymous, Review of *Gabriel Denver*, *Saturday Review* (23 May 1874);

Anonymous, Review of *Gabriel Denver*, *Spectator* (28 March 1874);

Anonymous, Review of *Literary Remains*, *Athenaeum* (19 February 1876): 261;

J. Arthur Blaikie, "Oliver Madox Brown," in *The Poets and the Poetry of the Century*, edited by A. H. Miles, volume 8 (London: Hutchinson, 1891-1897);

Blaikie, Review of Ingram's biography, *Academy*, no. 585 (21 July 1883): 39;

James Darmesteter, "Oliver Madox Brown," in his *English Studies*, translated by Mary Darmesteter (London: Fisher Unwin, 1896);

William E. Fredeman, "Oliver Madox Brown," in his *Pre-Raphaelitism: A Bibliocritical Study* (Cambridge: Harvard University Press, 1965);

Fredeman, "Pre-Raphaelite Novelist Manqué," *Bulletin of the John Rylands Library*, 51 (Autumn 1968): 27-72;

Ford Madox Hueffer, "The Younger Madox Browns: Lucy, Catherine, Oliver," *Artist*, 19 (February 1897): 49-56;

Philip Bourke Marston, "Oliver Madox Brown," *Scribner's Magazine*, 12 (July 1876): 425-428;

Justin McCarthy, "Oliver Madox Brown," *Gentleman's Magazine*, 16 (February 1876): 161-165;

G. A. Simcox, Review of *Gabriel Denver*, *Academy* (22 November 1873);

T[heodore] W[atts]-[Dunton], "Oliver Madox Brown's Literary Remains," *Examiner* (29 January 1876): 129;

Robert Lee Wolff, *Strange Stories and Other Explorations in Victorian Fiction* (Boston: Gambit, 1971), pp. 37-43, 66.

Edward Bulwer-Lytton

Allan C. Christensen

BIRTH: London, 25 May 1803, to General William Earle Bulwer of Heydon Hall, Norfolk, and Elizabeth Barbara Lytton Bulwer.

EDUCATION: B.A., Cambridge University, 1825; M.A., Cambridge, 1833.

MARRIAGE: 29 August 1827 to Rosina Doyle Wheeler; children: Emily, Robert.

AWARDS AND HONORS: Chancellor's Medal, Cambridge University, 1825; created a baronet, 1838; Honorary Doctor of Laws degree, Cambridge University, 1864; raised to peerage as first Baron Lytton of Knebworth, 1866.

DEATH: Torquay, Devonshire, 18 January 1873.

BOOKS: *Ismael: An Oriental Tale, with Other Poems* (London: Hatchard, 1820);

Delmour; or, The Tale of Sylphid, and Other Poems, anonymous (London: Carpenter, 1823);

Sculpture: A Poem Which Obtained the Chancellor's Medal, July, 1825 (Cambridge: N.p., 1825; New York: Peabody, 1831);

Falkland (London: Colburn, 1827; New York: Harper, 1830);

O'Neill; or, The Rebel (London: Colburn, 1827);

Pelham; or, The Adventures of a Gentleman (3 volumes, London: Colburn, 1828; 2 volumes, New York: Harper, 1828);

The Disowned (4 volumes, London: Colburn, 1828; 2 volumes, New York: Harper, 1829);

Devereux: A Tale (3 volumes, London: Colburn, 1829; 2 volumes, New York: Harper, 1829);

Paul Clifford (3 volumes, London: Colburn, 1830; 2 volumes, New York: Harper, 1830);

The Siamese Twins: A Satirical Tale of the Times (London: Colburn & Bentley, 1831; New York: Harper, 1831);

Eugene Aram: A Tale (3 volumes, London: Colburn & Bentley, 1832; 2 volumes, New York: Harper, 1832);

Asmodeus at Large (Philadelphia: Carey, Lea & Blanchard, 1833);

England and the English, 2 volumes (London: Bentley, 1833; New York: Harper, 1833);

Godolphin: A Novel (3 volumes, London: Bentley, 1833; 2 volumes, Philadelphia: Carey, Lea & Blanchard, 1833);

A Letter to a Late Cabinet Minister on the Present Crisis (London: Saunders & Otley, 1834);

The Last Days of Pompeii (3 volumes, London: Bentley, 1834; 2 volumes, New York: Harper, 1834);

The Pilgrims of the Rhine (London: Saunders & Otley, 1834; New York: Harper, 1834);

Rienzi, the Last of the Roman Tribunes (3 volumes, London: Saunders & Otley, 1835; 2 volumes, New York: Harper, 1836);

The Student: A Series of Papers (2 volumes, London: Saunders & Otley, 1835; 1 volume, New York: Harper, 1836);

The Duchess de la Vallière (London: Saunders & Otley, 1836; New York: Harper, 1837);

Athens: Its Rise and Fall, 2 volumes (London: Saunders & Otley, 1837; New York: Harper, 1837);

Ernest Maltravers (3 volumes, London: Saunders & Otley, 1837; 2 volumes, New York: Harper, 1837);

Leila; or, The Siege of Granada (Berlin: Asher, 1837; London: Longmans, 1838; New York: Harper, 1838);

Alice; or, The Mysteries: A Sequel to "Ernest Maltravers" (3 volumes, London: Saunders & Otley, 1838; 2 volumes, New York: Harper, 1838);

Richelieu: or, The Conspiracy (London: Saunders & Otley, 1839; New York: Harper, 1839);

The Sea Captain; or, The Birthright: A Drama (London: Saunders & Otley, 1839; New York: Harper, 1839);

Money: A Comedy (London: Saunders & Otley, 1840; New York: Taylor, 1845);

Night and Morning (3 volumes, London: Saunders & Otley, 1841; 2 volumes, New York: Harper, 1841);

Eva, The Ill-Omened Marriage, and Other Poems (London: Saunders & Otley, 1842);

Zanoni (3 volumes, London: Saunders & Otley, 1842; 1 volume, New York: Harper, 1842);

The Last of the Barons (3 volumes, London: Saunders & Otley, 1843; 1 volume, New York: Harper, 1843);

Confessions of a Water Patient, in a Letter to W. Harrison Ainsworth (London: Colburn, 1846);

Lucretia; or, The Children of Night (3 volumes, London: Saunders & Otley, 1846; 1 volume, New York: Harper, 1846);

The New Timon (London: Colburn, 1846; Philadelphia: Carey & Hart, 1846);

A Word to the Public (London: Saunders & Otley, 1847);

Harold, the Last of the Saxon Kings (3 volumes, London: Bentley, 1848; 1 volume, New York: Harper, 1848);

King Arthur: An Epic Poem, 2 volumes (London: Colburn, 1849; Philadelphia: Hogan & Thompson, 1851);

The Caxtons: A Family Picture (3 volumes, London: Blackwood, 1849; 1 volume, New York: Hurst, 1849);

Letters to John Bull Esquire (London: Chapman & Hall, 1851);

Not so Bad as We Seem; or, Many Sides to a Character: A Comedy (London: Chapman & Hall, 1851; New York: Harper, 1851);

"My Novel," by Pisistratus Caxton: or, Varieties in English Life (New York: Harper, 1852; 4 volumes, Edinburgh & London: Blackwood, 1853);

Address to the Associated Societies of the University of Edinburgh on His Installation as Their Honorary President and His Speech at the Public Dinner, January 20th 1854 (Edinburgh & London: Blackwood, 1854);

Speech Delivered at the Leeds Mechanics' Institution (London: Routledge, 1854);

What Will He Do With It? by Pisistratus Caxton (4 volumes, London: Blackwood, 1858; 1 volume, New York: Harper, 1859);

Speech on the Representation of the People Bill, Delivered in the House of Commons, March 22nd 1859 (London: Blackwood, 1859);

The Haunted and the Haunters (London: Blackwood, 1859; Chicago: Rajput Press, 1911);

St. Stephen's: A Poem (London: Blackwood, 1860);

The New Reform Bill: Speech Delivered in the House of Commons, Revised and Corrected by the Author (London: Saunders & Otley, 1860);

A Strange Story (2 volumes, London: Low, Marston, 1862; New York: Harper, 1862);

Caxtoniana: A Series of Essays on Life, Literature and Manners (2 volumes, London: Blackwood, 1863; 1 volume, New York: Harper, 1863);

The Boatman, by Pisistratus Caxton (London: Blackwood, 1864);

Lost Tales of Miletus (London: Murray, 1866; New York: Harper, 1866);

The Rightful Heir (London: Murray, 1868; New York: Harper, 1868);

Miscellaneous Prose Works (3 volumes, London: Bentley, 1868);

Walpole; or, Every Man Has His Price (London: Blackwood, 1869; New York: De Witt, 1875);

The Coming Race (London: Blackwood, 1871; New York: Felt, 1871);

The Parisians (4 volumes, London: Blackwood, 1873; 1 volume, New York: Harper, 1874);

Kenelm Chillingly: His Adventures and Opinions (3 volumes, London: Blackwood, 1873; 1 volume, New York: Harper, 1873);

Pamphlets and Sketches (London: Routledge, 1875);

Quarterly Essays (London: Routledge, 1875);

Pausanias the Spartan (London: Routledge, 1876; New York: Harper, 1876).

COLLECTION: *Works*, Knebworth Edition (37 volumes, London: Routledge, 1873-1877).

In his own day, Bulwer's position among the most unquestionably popular and the most critically esteemed novelists seemed firmly established. As with so many Victorian writers, though, his fortunes declined drastically after his death, and not until fairly recently has the trend been reversed and a new awareness of his positive achievement become possible. Readers now seem willing to forgive his stylistic flaws—notably a certain bombast and straining aftereffects—in order to appreciate the intellectual vigor and emotional earnestness of his admittedly imperfect fictional works. Though he belonged to an age of intense formal experimentation, his restless efforts to expand the boundaries of the fictional form impress many modern readers as especially personal, ambitious, and in some respects prophetic. Indeed he was, as it now appears, as unorthodox in his own way as any of his great contemporaries. His version of artistic unorthodoxy inspired him to withstand the contemporary tendency toward realism in fiction and to seek to interest his readers in an invisible region of ideal forms and psychic events. To an even greater extent than the other "metaphysical" novelists, he was apparently struggling to translate into prose fiction the sort of idealist and mythic vision that is associated with the major romantic poets. These struggles, as he thought of them, to save his and his readers' souls from the currently destructive, materialistic view of reality involved him, moreover, in a highly self-conscious and reflective kind of artistry. He wrote voluminously about the principles of his craft, so that he has come to be significant not only as a novelist but also as the chief theorist among the Victorian practitioners of fiction.

His serious loyalty to a conception of his ideal self and of his mission began to manifest itself in youth. The youngest and most interestingly precocious of three surviving sons, Edward Bulwer was the favorite of his independently rich mother, who encouraged him to believe he must become worthy of her aristocratic Lytton forebears. She taught him to dislike his irascible father, General Bulwer, who had failed to gain the peerage for which he had intrigued and who died when his youngest son was only four. Protected thereafter from any threats to his self-confidence, Edward was educated somewhat erratically at small schools; it was decided not to expose him to the rigors of a public school like Eton because of his weak health and sensitive character. He was able to live and to dream, as he came to think of it, in the serenity of his inner or

ideal world, until at the age of sixteen he fell inno-
cently and utterly in love with a girl whose identity
remains unknown. They met daily for a few weeks
on the banks of the Brent near Ealing, where he was
being schooled, and their relationship became impressed on his memory as the only perfect one of his
life. She was the ideally sympathetic partner of his
soul, an inhabitant of his own inner world, and he
would never meet such a being again in reality. The
girl's father took steps to separate the young lovers
and to force her into a marriage which, as she predicted to Bulwer in a last letter a few years later,
shortly caused her early death; and she summoned
him at least to visit her grave in the Lake District. He
obeyed in the summer of 1824, when he was also in
sentimental despair because of the death of his
literary hero, Byron. His twenty-first year thus
began with the tragic conviction that he must
hereafter live primarily as the survivor and faithful
mourner of an irrecoverably lost ideal splendor.

That ideal loyalty was not yet, however, so
entirely tragic. As a healthy and talented undergraduate at Trinity College, Cambridge, who had
already received some pleasant recognition for
certain poetic endeavors (and who would receive
the Chancellor's Medal for his poem *Sculpture* in
1825), he clearly hoped to impress his contemporaries with the value of his sensibility and his
insights. He imagined himself as an ambassador to
his own and to future generations from the eternal
and ideal world, which he associated with his ancestral past and with his peculiarly intense inner life.
But he also became aware of the potential dilemma
of divided loyalties: the claims of the figures and
landscapes of his inner world conflicted with his
ambition to be appreciated and acclaimed as their
representative in external reality. The conflict became apparent, perhaps, when he found himself
pursued by the dangerous Lady Caroline Lamb,
who first seemed to force him to reenact the role of
their belovedly antisocial and anarchic Byron. Yet,
after a stormy affair, she threw him in the direction
of her social-climbing Irish protégée, Rosina
Wheeler, to whom he became engaged. For Rosina's
sake he suffered his mother's rejection and the
temporary cutting off of his allowance and began to
devote his considerable literary talents and capacity
for self-discipline to the task of earning money and
social success. As Rosina's husband, he seems even
to have become rather intoxicated by the notion of
cutting a dashing figure on the London social, literary, and political stages. While successfully playing
the demanding role of the dandy, he entered Parliament as a Radical in 1831 and salved his idealist

*Lady Caroline Lamb, with whom Bulwer had a stormy
affair in his youth*

conscience with his conviction that he was devoted
to the noble cause of the people.

The protagonists of his first two completed
novels are, respectively, a gloomy misanthrope and
a glitteringly sociable dandy, and they show Bulwer
already trying to base his fiction on the idea of
"metaphysical" conflicts. Largely epistolary in form,
Falkland (1827) may even seem *too* metaphysical or
mythical in its disdain for ordinary realism in fiction. The self-indulgent, rambling letters of the
protagonist locate the action primarily in the mind
or soul, where the reader loses a firm grasp of
chronology and sometimes of what is really supposed to be happening externally. Yet Bulwer has
thus managed to give an interestingly personal imprint to material derived from Byron as well as from
Goethe, Wordsworth, Chateaubriand, and other
romantic sources. The story of the cynical but self-
tormented and half-unwilling seducer, Erasmus
Falkland, and the virtuous young wife, Lady Emily
Mandeville, becomes a sort of allegory that quite
transcends ethical categories. Using the imagery of
his settings and the dreams of his characters to help

convey the point, Bulwer makes Falkland typify the anarchic energy of a personality and Lady Emily the demands of an individual's social role. These two sides of a human identity cannot, it seems, coexist peacefully, and so the lovers are destroyed: Lady Emily hemorrhaging from a burst blood vessel; Falkland, some time later dying while fighting with the Constitutionalists in Spain. In light of the allegorical intention, the moral criticism of Bulwer's mother and others—that he had dealt too leniently with adultery—seems irrelevant.

Falkland did not achieve popular or critical favor, and in recognizing its weaknesses, Bulwer decided that it had, like Goethe's *Sorrows of Young Werther* (1774), been useful chiefly as a way of purging his bosom of "perilous stuff." His need for money as well as his desire to support the claims of the social and moral aspects of life led him to devise *Pelham* (1828) as an antidote to *Falkland*. Taking his hint from the recently popular novels of fashion, the so-called "Silver-Fork" school, he created an attractive dandy hero whose adventures could comically expose the foibles of man in society. *Pelham* was an immensely successful novel, to the extent that its protagonist's adoption of black as the color of his evening dress revolutionized European men's fashion. To Carlyle's compiler of a clothes philosophy, Diogenes Teufelsdröckh in *Sartor Resartus* (1833-1834), the novel seemed the major example of its genre. Yet as more careful readers saw, *Pelham* was also a satire of the genre, for its protagonist only pretended to be flippantly trivial, and so the novel conveyed an impression of the absurdity of fashionable dandyism. On this level, the racy comedy of Henry Pelham's adventures and the amusing outrageousness of many remarks in the book can continue to charm and delight.

Again, however, a still deeper allegorical or metaphysical level threatens at moments to undermine the comfortable solidity of the novel's realistic social settings. The main characters begin to function as the protagonist's alter egos, as he realizes that under the surface they too are searching desperately for a true identity. These alter egos are Lord Vincent, whose political activities slowly corrupt him; the lonely Lady Roseville, who gradually finds it impossible to enact her elegant social role and retires abroad; and Sir Reginald Glanville, who, like Falkland in the earlier novel, has an anarchic and disastrous influence upon all who come in contact with him. Glanville, especially, threatens the comic surfaces; and when, on his behalf, Pelham must descend to the criminal underworld, the novel takes on a more seriously epic dimension. Pelham thereby proves his true heroism, and in marrying Glanville's sister Ellen, he at last attains a symbolic self-integration. But he too must retire at the end from the artificial social scene where he has not yet discovered the way to enact a truly useful role. Despite all his secret study of Bentham, Mill, and Ricardo, and his supposedly sincere desire to help his fellow man, the conflicting claims of his lonely individual ego must finally force him into isolation.

In the five most hectic years of his life, though, Bulwer continued in reality to live anything but a life of isolation. He helped his wife make their drawing room in Hertford Street into one of the most fashionable (as his friend Disraeli and others have testified) in London. Associated at the same time with Lord Durham and other Radicals, he worked vigorously in Parliament on behalf of the Reform Bill, and as editor of the *New Monthly Magazine* he conscientiously composed innumerable articles and maintained decent literary standards. While generously supporting other deserving young writers (though notoriously unfair to Tennyson), he also revealed considerable acumen and skill in his analyses of the contemporary cultural and intellectual climate. In this regard his *England and the English* (1833) remains one of the most stimulating and convincing anatomies of the English character. In the book Bulwer argues that "we live in an age of visible transition—an age of disquietude and doubt—of the removal of time-worn landmarks." He criticizes the confusion and uncertainty in the country but perceives a solution in the philosophy of Jeremy Bentham. Less a systematic analysis than an anecdotal, factual, but at times impressionistic account, *England and the English* nonetheless provides an important inquiry into the state of the English society and politics at the beginning of the Victorian era. Like J. S. Mill, who wrote an appendix for early editions of this work, Bulwer was particularly fascinated by the exciting new philosophy of utilitarianism, with which he hoped somehow to reconcile his own romantic idealism.

During these years, he found the time to do the necessary scholarly research and to compose the four novels set in the eighteenth century that succeeded *Pelham*. Of these, *Paul Clifford* (1830) and *Eugene Aram* (1832) have probably seemed, as the initiators of the so-called Newgate school, the most interesting to subsequent generations. Based on Godwin's sentimental theory that penal legislation should recognize the fundamental core of goodness or perfectibility even in criminals, *Paul Clifford* has been considered the first *Tendenzroman* (novel with a purpose) in English. *Eugene Aram* then enlarged upon these ethical speculations in its treatment of a historical figure who had committed murder in the service of the noblest human ideals. As the works of a thoughtful legislator in a Parliament concerned with reform of the penal code, these novels naturally aroused some controversy, which probably increased their commercial success. Indeed, Bulwer had encouraged the controversy in the case of *Paul Clifford* by implicitly developing extended parallels between eighteenth-century highwaymen and nineteenth-century politicians whose plausible manners concealed a real moral corruption.

All four novels nevertheless continued to demonstrate their author's underlying alienation from social and political concerns. The structure of each involves a division between realistic plot and allegorical subplot, in which the latter contains the fundamental truth that finally overwhelms the significance of the main story line. In every case the protagonist is led through the three stages of exile, efforts to construct a new identity, and return to the lost and ruined Eden. There he discovers at last the crucial secret about his identity that has been unfolding all along in connection with the allegorical figures—his alter egos—of the subplot.

While suggestive enough in *The Disowned* (1828), the title of which implies Bulwer's own situation at the time of his marriage, and in the two Newgate novels, the allegorical scheme may be worked out most successfully in *Devereux* (1829). In this intriguing work, the purported autobiography of an early eighteenth-century English Catholic, the initial exile results from the intrigues of an unknown enemy who murders Devereux's adored Isora and causes him to be disinherited. Devereux then gains "experience" for many long years as a Continental soldier of fortune, until circumstances lead him to discover that his enemy has been his beloved but tormented, jealous, and supposedly dead brother, Aubrey. There has been, he comes to understand, a metaphysical necessity about the murder of Isora, for which he too must bear the guilt. For the love between him and Isora has typified (like Bulwer's juvenile affair at Ealing) a perfect integration with his anima, the very idea of himself, and such an integration cannot exist for long in reality. To avoid corruption or symbolic destruction, then, Isora had to be physically killed so that her ideal purity could remain intact. At the end, Devereux comes to embrace the Wordsworthian conviction that events or persons take on their truest value only in retrospect. He is thus content to become the survivor of his passionate self and the storehouse of memories of what literally exists no longer, and he commits his memories, as his lasting and authentic identity, to the ages yet unborn. So too does Bulwer seem almost pleased to imply a discrepancy between his own noble idea of himself and his frenetic but irrelevant public career.

As he confessed, in fact, to Disraeli but to few others, he was longing to give up that career in which to friendly eyes he cut such a brilliantly promising figure and to hostile eyes such an irritatingly arrogant one. The strain of work, politics, and social life caused him to neglect his family—by 1831 he had both a daughter and a son—and with other factors was leading to a definitive estrangement from Rosina. A breakdown in his health in 1833 provided the necessary impetus for his effective retirement from the public stage, although he remained somewhat quietly in Parliament until 1841. A long trip to Italy (thereafter one of his favorite parts of the Continent) ended unhappily with the failure of his and Rosina's last attempt at a reconciliation, and he retreated to a relatively quiet and scholarly solitude. He did not, however, discover much serenity of spirit, for to his evident disappointment the world within himself no longer seemed so rich and vital as it had in his youth. That idea of himself, which he had wanted to protect over the years, now appeared almost barren, and in his desperate anxiety to escape that awareness he kept his mind as busily occupied as ever. His intellectual occupations were aesthetically fruitful ones, which, despite the sad desperation motivating them, prompted some of his most original and best work. In particular, he studied all the great German writers of the last few generations and prepared a translation of Schiller's lyric poetry. An interest in Italian art led him to speculate extensively about the aesthetics he believed common to both Italian painting and the literature of German idealism.

Three especially ambitious fictional works derived from the aesthetic theories of what might be called his middle phase: *Godolphin* (1833), *Ernest Maltravers* (1837) with its sequel *Alice* (1838), and *Zanoni* (1842). While they are supposedly impersonal artifacts rather than semiautobiographical efforts at communication, they have impressed critics as the works in which Bulwer is most originally and characteristically himself. Aloof and unconcerned about any reading public, he has also found the leisure to work out his intentions most thoughtfully and painstakingly in these creations. He would later become aware of certain flaws—particularly with respect to the catastrophe at the end of *Godolphin*—but more fully than in any of his earlier works, save possibly *Devereux*, the "execution" seems

Knebworth, Bulwer-Lytton's estate in Hertfordshire

in these novels to have corresponded with his original "design."

One result is an increased control of the tendency toward abstraction in plotting and characterization. The reader appreciates, for example, the neatness with which the characters and careers of the hero and heroine of *Godolphin* are contrasted and balanced against each other. Although not specifically modeled on Goethe's *Elective Affinities* (1809), their story possesses the formal clarity of that work as Percy Godolphin and Constance Vernon each becomes involved with a new partner. Then exactly halfway through the story their reunion implies the fusion of two nearly opposite attitudes toward life and art, each of which has remained sterile in itself. But before their union can become creative, their past finally overtakes them, just as the long-threatening storm of the Reform Bill controversy breaks over an imperfectly integrated and sterile British society. (The catastrophe is the symbolic equivalent of the volcanic eruption at the end of *The Last Days of Pompeii*, 1834.) While the main patterns of *Godolphin* thus remain clear and orderly, the novel implies a number of parallels between psychological, aesthetic, and political developments that become increasingly complex. In

Ernest Maltravers and *Alice*, on the other hand, the complexity threatens to obscure the clarity of the form, but here too the governing idea finally prevails over a wealth of detail. The story follows the pattern of the Künstlerroman (artist's apprenticeship novel), as the protagonist pursues various incarnations of the *Ewig-Weibliche* (eternal female) who are always shadowed by the demonic figures typifying his dangerous and creative energies.

The most formally and intellectually fascinating of Bulwer's works is *Zanoni*, for it manages to fuse more daringly suggestive and disparate elements into a whole than any of the others. To some extent an allegory of Science versus Art, it presents the immortal beings Mejnour and Zanoni, who resemble Blake's Urizen and Los as personifications of eternal tendencies within the human identity. These immortal beings interact plausibly enough with the ordinary mortals in the story, who are once more various kinds of artists. Like the previous works, *Zanoni* can thus be analyzed as a Künstlerroman, in which many events are focused around Clarence Glyndon's growth as an imaginative painter. In addition, the work contains historical figures and is set in late eighteenth-century Italy and France. It deals with the sterility of the so-called

"Age of Reason" and culminates in the Paris of the "Reign of Terror"—making the point that the latter results naturally from the former. In an individual or a society, the civilized effort to impose rational limits and controls on life will, if pressed too far, unleash the terrifying, revolutionary energy of the irrational subconscious (characterized on the individual level as the appalling Dweller of the Threshold). Above all else, *Zanoni* may be seen as a hymn to the imagination, which the earlier works have also discussed, and in its own complexity the novel symbolizes the imagination at work. In *Zanoni*, Bulwer has dramatized in Coleridgean terms a number of attempts to reconcile and fuse opposites and so to destroy in order to recreate. As Zanoni, the type of Art, gives up his immortality and sacrifices himself on the guillotine to redeem Viola and their child, he becomes similar to Prometheus, Brünnhilde, and Jesus, who sacrificed themselves on behalf of a dubiously worthy humanity. As a great symbol for the creative process, *Zanoni* employs, in the manner of *Sartor Resartus*, the motif of a translator-editor; but like other works that deal self-reflexively with their own creation, it remains unique.

The series of symbolic, creative actions in *Zanoni* emphasizes especially the self-sacrificing aspect of the imaginative process. And indeed the other aesthetic novels too had finally preached the Victorian virtues of benevolence, resignation, and self-annihilation as the only way to action and creativity. The artist must give up his aesthetic detachment and his concern with his own identity and artistic purity in order to involve himself ever more fully in the ordinary and impure human condition. Bulwer seems thus to have used these most aesthetic of his vehicles to condemn the very attitude that produced them, thereby expressing a continuing self-division. But whereas in his earlier novels the socially and politically engaged author had confessed a wish to escape from his engagement, the aloof author now revealed his secret need to renounce his aloofness.

The temperamental inability to do just that may have been partially responsible for Bulwer's chronic bouts of depression and for his periods of painfully uncreative dryness. Yet the other novels of this middle phase show that the *idea* of his plight and his awareness of other conflicts underlying human life could still stimulate his creativity in a variety of ways. In the historical novels, for example, he was able to suggest both the necessity and the futility of social and political engagement, as observed in the careers of certain Hegelian world-historical figures. Although such figures served

authentically liberating causes, which must be kept alive, they were inevitably defeated in their own day because the fickle populace was always unworthy of the vision of freedom. In *Rienzi* (1835), the hero fails because the degenerate Romans of his age respect physical force more than they respect the humane ideal of intellectual freedom. The Saxons in *Harold* (1848) also prove unworthy, in their baffling superstitiousness, of their enlightened last king; in this case, though, some of the tragedy derives from the fact that in committing himself to a noble political cause, the idealist has had to lose his freedom. And the same inevitable loss of personal integrity seems manifested in the career of Warwick the Kingmaker in *The Last of the Barons* (1843). His original ideal of a Lancastrian alliance between peasants and aristocracy would have brought out the true nobility of England (anticipating the Young England idea of Bulwer's day). But political realism leads him at last to favor a Yorkist restoration based on mercenary values and the support of a burgeoning middle class. The novel ends almost cynically, hailing the corrupt Edward IV as the expression of the zeitgeist and a necessary stage in the progressive realization of the idea of freedom.

As in the case of *The Last Days of Pompeii*, Bulwer was most assiduous in his historical research for these novels and was proud of the discoveries and insights that he could document. He used his imagination too, he said, not to romanticize in the manner of Sir Walter Scott, but to discover new truth and to reconstruct a historical atmosphere faithfully. Yet his principal interest, it is clear, lay less in the accuracy of his numerous details than in the conflicting historical ideas or tendencies these details were supposed to illustrate. To some extent these ideas applied with particular relevance to the historical forces at work in Bulwer's own day—the "hungry forties"—and *The Last of the Barons* certainly contains allusions to such phenomena as Chartism and Young England. While avoiding the romantic escapism of Scott, however, Bulwer has also in large part avoided writing tracts specifically for his own day. These novels therefore remain interesting primarily as philosophical speculations about history and human destiny. Often in rather ingenious ways, they develop the ideas about zeitgeists and the working out of national and racial identities that Bulwer has derived from Hegel, Herder, Kant, and Goethe. Even *The Last Days of Pompeii*, which lacks the intellectual depth and complexity of the other novels, is a treatment of the drama of human life that is the same, in its fundamental terms, in all ages and places.

The remaining two novels of this middle period are *Night and Morning* (1841) and *Lucretia* (1846), and they may seem more precisely anchored in the historical realities of the nineteenth century. Set in France and England, they specifically treat the fragmented and anarchic national identities that have resulted, according to Bulwer, from the failure of the French Revolution and other revolutionary attempts. He perceives within each country something like the mutually hostile "Two Nations" of Disraeli, and to help describe them, he coins in *Lucretia* the terms *haves* and *have-nots*. Although the ruling-class *haves* seem the guiltier party, both nations are made up of craftily selfish and unscrupulous predators. In a universe that seems empty of all other values, men have turned rather desperately to monstrous forms of egoism in their need to dedicate their vital energies to some purpose. Individuals thus struggle for wealth and social position in the vicious intrigues of *Night and Morning*, which in its characters, atmosphere, and milieu often reminds one strikingly of Balzac's "Human Comedy." (One of its plausibly saintly hypocrites, Robert Beaufort, was also a probable prototype for Pecksniff in Dickens's *Martin Chuzzlewit*, 1842-1844, and from this point on Bulwer and Dickens would exercise considerable influence on each other.) As *Lucretia* makes clear, however, these egoistic exploiters are only apparently rational in their devotion to material goals. On the most fundamental psychological level they desire mainly to feel assured of the power of their own egos, as they encounter and destroy other egos. This desire to struggle and destroy for its own sake particularly characterizes Olivier Dalibard, one of Bulwer's most frightening confidence artists. One follows with a certain awe the stages of Dalibard's campaign against his beautiful pupil Lucretia Clavering. He successfully seduces, corrupts, and comes nearly to control her, but their relationship as collaborators in evil proves unstable. The logic of things forces each to begin plotting the other's death, and after a long, silent war, in which they are aware of each other's intentions, Lucretia emerges the murderous victor.

These criminal figures are, in fact, the most fully developed embodiments hitherto of a type that has appeared in each of Bulwer's novels. As represented most notably by the Jesuit Abbé Montreuil in *Devereux* and Lumley Ferrers in *Ernest Maltravers* and *Alice*, these ruthless egoists possess an almost uncanny ability to beguile, fascinate, and control lesser personalities. Animally magnetic and diabolically clever, they are also heroes of willpower who can seemingly gain whatever they decide to concentrate their energies upon. Evidently they also have some relationship to Bulwer's conception of himself, for ever since his "Byronic" days, he had occasionally expressed pride in his own superior psychic and volitional energies. Yet an odd pathos also attaches to his portrayals of these outlaw figures: they are lonely in their cynicism and their inability to experience holier human feelings.

On the conscious level, though, Bulwer had designed these novels not as self-revelations but as dispassionate reflections upon the eternal mystery of evil. Cruelty, violence, and other forms of evil existed, according to a meditative passage in *Lucretia*, as necessary elements in the fabric of life itself, and so one must learn to contemplate them calmly without demanding "poetic justice." In fact, one might even perceive aspects of the beauty of the presumably divine scheme in them—as a sort of Blakean "fearful symmetry," perhaps. And, as in the other works of his aesthetic phase, Bulwer appealed again to the example of Goethe, whose true Olympian serenity permitted him to handle good and evil with a sublimely nonpartisan amorality. There was, moreover, a noble literary tradition stretching back to Shakespeare and the ancient Greek dramatists that justified an aesthetic interest in crime and the criminal mentality. Bulwer thus believed that his latest work existed in good company, and many of his admirers shared his conviction of the special artistic grandeur of *Lucretia*. It reminded Macaulay, for example, of "some fine Martyrdoms which I have seen in Italy"—specifically of certain paintings by Poussin and Salvator Rosa at which "it is real suffering to look, and yet we cannot avert our eyes."

Bulwer possessed a great many important admirers at this stage—including the once uncomprehending Carlyle. In his own incompletely Olympian detachment, he was in touch with many of them and even still rather involved in the literary intrigues of the day. One of his most interesting literary relationships at this point was with the actor William Charles Macready, for whom he had written a handful of successful plays during the past decade. Yet it is a sign of his essential aloofness that he did not realize the strength of his enemies and the nature of the really extraordinary storm of protest that the publication of *Lucretia* was to provoke. The enmity to Bulwer had begun in the early 1830s in circles associated with *Fraser's Magazine*—notably including Thackeray. In curiously bitter attacks, these critics had expressed irritation with Bulwer's personality, his dandy mannerisms, and the pompous seriousness with which he took his

Part. VIII.

The Caxtons

There entered in the first drawing room in my Father House in Russell St — an Elf !!! clad in white, — white — small, delicate — with curls of jet over her shoulders, with eyes so large, & so lustrous that they shone thro' the room, as no *merely human* eyes could possibly shine; — the Elf approached — & stood facing us. —

The sight was so unexpected & the apparition so strange — that we remained for some moments gazing at it in startled silence —

At length my Father, the bolder, & wiser man of the two, & more fitted to deal with the eirie things, of an other world had the audacity to step close up to the little creature — & bending down to examine its face said, — "What do you want my pretty child !"

Page from the manuscript for the first of Bulwer-Lytton's novels about the Caxton family (The Earl of Lytton,
The Life of Edward Bulwer, First Lord Lytton)

literary vocation. Now they concentrated on the vulgar sensationalism, moral degeneracy, and dangerous sympathy with evil that they discerned in *Lucretia* and its vicious Newgate predecessors. The venomousness of the attacks unnerved Bulwer to the point of shattering his self-confidence, and in a moment of rashness he announced in print the abandonment of his career as novelist. Although he could not maintain that abandonment for long, he looked with more desperation than ever for a way to escape his detached and guilty loneliness.

The third phase of his career developed as the result of a conscious decision to change his way of living and thinking. Wishing to feel himself a vitally engaged and working member of the human community, he turned his attention to activities like farming that figured, as he fancied, among the chief absorbing interests of ordinary Englishmen. He had inherited his mother's property, Knebworth in Hertfordshire, in 1843 and had extensively renovated and architecturally embellished the house to make it a more fitting symbol of his ancestral heritage; he also at this time changed his name to Bulwer-Lytton. Now he began to concentrate on the agricultural aspects of his heritage—the condition of the lands and the welfare of his tenants—as he came indeed to associate the soul of any Englishman with the agricultural roots of English society. For in these years of controversy over repeal of the Corn Laws and of the revolutionary events of 1848-1849 throughout Europe, Bulwer-Lytton's social and political theories were undergoing an interesting development: he was renouncing the Radicalism that had associated him with the utilitarians and reforming Whigs of the 1830s and was embracing a philosophy similar to that of Disraeli's Tory Democracy. Giving up, as he conceived it, a loyalty to some abstract idea of the people, he wanted to serve the concrete welfare of the real country by uniting the various classes in a common purpose. The longing to sense himself a part of that national enterprise also carried him back into active politics. He returned to Parliament in 1852 as a Conservative member for his county, worked busily for his party in and out of the House of Commons, and became colonial secretary in Lord Derby's government of 1858.

The three Caxton novels that belong to this period resulted from a correspondingly conscious decision to appeal to a new popular audience. Resigning his "intellectual" or aesthetic efforts to communicate with the elite of all ages, he decided for the first time to attempt serial publication and so to feel his monthly contact with a real and ordinary public. He tried specifically to stir the middle-class readers of *Blackwood's Magazine* with healthy sentiments rather than with abstract ideas. By conveying his own good-humored sympathy for ordinary mortals, despite their flaws and absurdities, he hoped to elicit and strengthen the latent humanity and tolerance of his readers and so to do his part to cement social bonds. These comical Caxton novels are thus precisely intended to counteract Marxist and other doctrines that were breeding class hatreds and to heal the fragmentation that the earlier novels had delineated tragically. To this end, Bulwer-Lytton has also organized each novel around a symbol that helps to focus his vision of a healthy community in which the organic, integrating elements triumph over the threats of disintegration. There is, for example, the symbolic Caxton family itself in *The Caxtons* (1849). The relationship between its generations is made explicitly relevant to that between Britain and her colonies when some of the characters immigrate to Australia, for Bulwer-Lytton, the future colonial secretary, already had theories about colonialism. And in *"My Novel," by Pisistratus Caxton* (1852), which is in part about its own creation, the image of composing a novel similarly functions as a symbol for the ongoing life of an organic society. The work is also incidentally interesting in its election episodes as a commentary on British politics at the time of the first Reform Bill; and in its treatment of Italian exiles, it comments as well upon the early period of the Risorgimento.

With these works Bulwer-Lytton achieved his greatest popular and critical success, and close friends—such as Dickens, Forster, and Macaulay—assured him that he had never written anything so good. He may thus have felt satisfied with the validity of his new theories. From a modern point of view, though, the value of the theories may lie less in their intrinsic worth than simply in their ability to fascinate Bulwer-Lytton and rouse him again to creativity. For once his creativity had been engaged, he finished by composing works that revealed him as essentially the same idealist as ever. The Caxton novels are not, after all, as genially easygoing and loose in structure as Bulwer-Lytton believed; they contain many of the carefully controlled patterns and tendencies toward abstraction that characterized the earlier novels. In Randal Leslie of *"My Novel,"* Bulwer-Lytton has created one of his most formidable heroes of ruthless, egoistic willpower, whose cynical world view indeed threatens the moral realities of the novel as a whole. Bulwer-Lytton was, therefore, an "idealist," as

Henry James would later remark of George Eliot, who had "commissioned [him]self to be real, . . . and the intellectual result is a very fertilizing mixture."

The last of the Caxton novels, *What Will He Do With It?* (1859), is one of Bulwer-Lytton's most impressive works and so is something of a case apart. It followed upon four years of literary sterility—the longest and most agonizing such period of Bulwer-Lytton's life—in which, despite the apparent success of his public career, he was again living in a personal hell. For one thing, his estranged and now deranged wife, Rosina, seemed to haunt him day and night like the ghost of his guilty past, and she did all she could to torment him and to destroy his career. (In 1851, Bulwer-Lytton and Dickens had tried to set up a Guild of Literature and Art to subsidize struggling writers and artists; when the play Bulwer-Lytton had written to benefit the guild was being premiered before the queen at Devonshire House, the duke had to employ detectives to prevent the disguised Rosina's avenging arrival.) For this and other personal reasons, Bulwer-Lytton believed that his Caxtonian vein and all other veins of inspiration had, as he told his son, quite "dried up." As something of an act of grace, then, he suddenly found that it was possible to give aesthetic coherence to his various anxieties, hopes, and theories within a new fictional framework. In the central character of Guy Darrell, for example, he portrays his own anguished guilt and sense of futility. In the idyllic episodes of the young lovers, Lionel and Sophy, with their sad aftermath, he expresses the nostalgia for an innocent past that still operated so powerfully and self-defeatingly in his own situation. The guilt of the past, on the other hand, also looms inescapably as another of the major motifs of the story, as character after character discovers himself haunted and blackmailed for his sins. English society as a whole, in fact, is paralyzed by its guilt and by the suffocating selfishness of a moribund ruling class. Typified by the House of Vipont, that class functions under the token aegis of its imbecile head, the marquess of Montfort, precisely as the Barnacles do in Dickens's *Little Dorrit* (1855-1857). Both Dickens and Bulwer-Lytton were reacting with extreme anger to the scandalous exposures of ruling-class ineptitude during the Crimean War.

Amid powerful evocations of the Victorian wasteland, however, Bulwer-Lytton has also placed the remarkable actor William Waife, called "the Comedian," who serves as a humble antithesis and alter ego to the haughty Darrell. In his conception of this confidence artist, at once so radically innocent and so marked by guilt, lies the principal imaginative achievement of the novel. Because he could conceive of such a character, Bulwer-Lytton was able to imagine—albeit barely and after some anguished soul-searching—the redemption of Darrell and his world; so this novel, in which Bulwer-Lytton shows his fullest sympathy for human frailty and a genuine sense of his unity with humanity, manages to end happily. It is the last time, though, that he could nerve himself to imagine a triumph of the humbling and humanizing Comic Spirit.

For unlike George Meredith, Bulwer did not in his deepest heart wish to be reconciled through the Comic Spirit to the absurdities and limitations of life in this world. As his last four novels therefore make abundantly clear, he had remained the idealist who had only very temporarily commissioned himself to be an accepter of realities. These novels maintain, nevertheless, a clear relevance to the realities and burning intellectual issues of the second half of the nineteenth century. Indeed they are specifically designed to treat the implications of Marxist and Darwinian theories as well as of other allegedly materialist and scientific influences upon contemporary "Culture." Bulwer-Lytton was even ready to admit that such unfortunate influences were increasing in strength and—sadly enough—probably had history on their side. He thus conceived of *The Parisians* (1873) as another epic depiction of modern society, like *The Caxtons*, but in the last money-mad years of the Second Empire he discerned an epic of decay. In fact, the spectacle of the Commune depressed him to the point that he was unable to complete the novel. As he had already intuited in his utopian satire, *The Coming Race* (1871), the new race was going to be peacefully but appallingly materialistic in its successful classlessness and its harmonious integration with the physical environment. In this context he fancied that sensitive and thoughtful individuals must, like the young protagonist of *Kenelm Chillingly* (1873), lose the "motive-power" necessary to life. Only the least noble elements of humanity would reveal themselves as the fittest to survive, and typical of these was the radiantly and eternally youthful Margrave of *A Strange Story* (1862). A prototype of Wilde's Dorian Gray, Margrave had managed to divide himself from his soul and conscience and so had discovered an ability to survive through the centuries.

While expressing disaffection from the conditions of life in the present period, these experimental late novels also convey Bulwer-Lytton's loyalty to the identifying principle of the individual soul. More patently allegorical than the Caxton novels, they trace a process whereby the protagonist rejects three "material" aspects of his identity in order to demonstrate his loyalty to the figure of the *anima*. He rejects the figures that typify his amoral physical being, his civilized and ethically disciplined social identity, and his rational, intellectual self. In this way he remains true to the chaste woman, connected with the very idea of himself, who has generally gone before him to heaven. As one gathers from Bulwer-Lytton's letters and other writings, this saintly female typifies a capacity that one can never fully know or realize in this life and for which there is no scientific evidence. But Bulwer-Lytton intuited that such a soul had to exist in order to make life comprehensible, and he adduced ingenious proofs for his irrational Victorian faith.

As a considered and lucid treatment of the matter, *A Strange Story* is in fact a particularly valuable work. First serialized in Dickens's *All the Year Round* and benefiting from Dickens's suggestions, the story is the autobiography of Dr. Allen Fenwick, who has written an important medical treatise entitled "The Vital Principle; Its Waste and Supply." (The "principle" that he devotes his life to investigating evidently resembles that called "Vril" in *The Coming Race*; related to man's own volitional power, it is the basic energy of the physical universe and when liberated operates in ways strikingly similar to nuclear power.) While continuing his research, Fenwick encounters the puzzling Margrave—who would seem to possess more of the vital principle than anyone—and his experiences begin to lead Fenwick farther and farther from the regions of science. He loses his initial rationalist and determinist mentality, enters strange, mystical realms, and finally cultivates religious modes of thought. Having given up his orthodox medical research, he writes the present work in which he identifies the vital principle as a spiritual rather than biological phenomenon. The novel is also of great interest, incidentally, for the figure of the perpetually knitting Mrs. Poyntz, one of Bulwer-Lytton's most unusual and convincing representations of the strong matrons who live by social rules and typify society.

While Mrs. Poyntz remains a credible female, Bulwer-Lytton also uses such figures to symbolize the occult energies operating everywhere. In these late novels, especially, he charts the regions that also fascinated symbolist poets, and indeed these works strongly influenced some of them. As he contemplated the approach of death in his relatively

Bulwer-Lytton in 1850, as painted by Daniel Maclise

peaceful last years, his conception of these regions became somewhat more Christian. He devoted great attention to the church fathers and read widely in traditional and orthodox works about prayer, the soul, and the hereafter. Still, he remained a Rosicrucian, with a somewhat unorthodox fascination for spiritualist manifestations. The most significant source of his faith in the ideal world, however, must always have been his youthful, Wordsworthian intimations of immortality—particularly his recollections of the idyllic romance at Ealing. Treated or referred to over and over again in his works, that memory came to haunt him increasingly toward the close of his life. His last novel, *Kenelm Chillingly*, gives the story its fullest treatment and so recreates the atmosphere of his ideal regions with special poignance in the Moleswich episodes that were composed a few weeks before his death. He died at the winter home he had maintained at Torquay since 1864, on 18 January 1873. He was buried in Westminster Abbey.

Repeatedly and with a great variety of means, Bulwer-Lytton attempted to convey his "metaphysical" vision in fiction. The ideas and conceptions that lie behind each novel may seem even more interesting and impressive with the passage of time, as their daringly prophetic qualities are discerned: the influence of scientific research, the power of women in society, the need for legal reforms—all of these have come to be recognized. His reach exceeded his grasp, to be sure, and he knew that his execution hardly ever did full justice to his conception. Criticism leveled until recently at Bulwer-Lytton has unfortunately insisted, however, not only on the admitted weakness of his execution but also on the wrong-headedness of his conceptions. Even as late as the 1950s, critics attacked him for not being a realistic novelist and for not building up "a world in which there is [a] 'servile copy of particulars.' " But recent critics, such as Jack Lindsay, Joseph I. Fradin, Robert Lee Wolff, Allan C. Christensen, and Edwin M. Eigner, analyze the work of Bulwer-Lytton in terms of narrative form, archetypal patterns, and theories of the novel suggesting new areas of exploration. The notion that a novel should offer a realistic copy of the surfaces of life is surely a prejudice that fails to take account of the enormous potentialities of the form. In an age that was becoming increasingly aware of those potentialities, Bulwer-Lytton may have been one of the most restlessly original and stimulating of talents.

Other:
The Poems and Ballads of Schiller, translated by Bulwer-Lytton (2 volumes, London: Blackwood, 1844);
The Works of Laman Blanchard: Sketches from Life, memoir by Bulwer-Lytton (3 volumes, London: Colburn, 1846);
The Odes and Epodes of Horace: A Metrical Translation into English, translated by Bulwer-Lytton (London: Blackwood, 1869; New York: Harper, 1870).

Periodical Publication:
"On Art in Fiction," *The Monthly Chronicle*, 1 (March 1838): 42-50; (April 1838): 138-149.

Letters:
Robert, First Earl of Lytton, *The Life, Letters, and*

Literary Remains of Edward Bulwer, Lord Lytton, by His Son (2 volumes, London: Kegan Paul, Trench, 1883);
Malcolm Orthell Usrey, ed., "The Letters of Sir Edward Bulwer-Lytton to the Editors of *Blackwood's Magazine*, 1840-1873, in the National Library of Scotland," Ph.D. dissertation, Texas Technical College, 1963.

Biographies:
Victor Alexander, Second Earl of Lytton, *The Life of Edward Bulwer, First Lord Lytton, by His Grandson* (2 volumes, London: Macmillan, 1913);
Michael Sadleir, *Bulwer: A Panorama: Edward and Rosina, 1803-1836* (Boston: Little, Brown, 1931);
Sibylla Jane Flower, *Bulwer-Lytton: An Illustrated Life of the First Baron Lytton, 1803-1873* (Aylesbury, U.K.: Shire, 1973).

References:
Allan Conrad Christensen, *Edward Bulwer-Lytton: The Fiction of New Regions* (Athens: University of Georgia Press, 1976);
Curtis Dahl, "Edward Bulwer-Lytton," in *Victorian Fiction: A Second Guide to Research*, edited by George H. Ford (New York: MLA, 1978), pp. 28-33;
Edwin M. Eigner, *The Metaphysical Novel in England and America: Dickens, Bulwer, Melville, and Hawthorne* (Berkeley: University of California Press, 1978);
Eigner, "Raphael in Oxford Street: Bulwer's Accommodation to the Realists," in *The Nineteenth-Century Writer and His Audience*, edited by Harold Orel and George J. Worth (Lawrence: University of Kansas Humanistic Studies, no. 40, 1969), pp. 61-74;
Joseph I. Fradin, " 'The Absorbing Tyranny of Every-day Life': Bulwer-Lytton's *A Strange Story*," *Nineteenth-Century Fiction*, 16 (1961): 1-16;
Keith Hollingsworth, *The Newgate Novel, 1830-1847: Bulwer, Ainsworth, Dickens, and Thackeray* (Detroit: Wayne State University Press, 1963);
Park Honan, Introduction to *Falkland*, edited by Herbert Van Thal (London: Cassell, 1967);
B. G. Knepper, "Shaw's Debt to *The Coming Race*," *Journal of Modern Literature*, 1 (1971): 339-353;
Coral Lansbury, *Arcady in Australia: The Evocation of Australia in Nineteenth-Century English Literature* (Calton, Australia: Melbourne University Press, 1970);
Jack Lindsay, *Charles Dickens: A Biographical and Critical Study* (London: Dakers, 1950);

Michael Lloyd, "Bulwer-Lytton and the Idealising Principle," *English Miscellany*, 7 (1956): 25-39;

Jerome J. McGann, Introduction to *Pelham; or, The Adventures of a Gentleman*, edited by McGann (Lincoln: University of Nebraska Press, 1972);

Matthew Whiting Rosa, *The Silver Fork School: Novels of Fashion Preceding "Vanity Fair"* (New York: Columbia University Press, 1936);

Charles H. Shattuck, ed., *Bulwer and Macready: A Chronicle of the Early Victorian Theatre* (Urbana: University of Illinois Press, 1958);

Robert Lee Wolff, "Devoted Disciple: The Letters of Mary Elizabeth Braddon to Sir Edward Bulwer-Lytton, 1862-1873," *Harvard Library Bulletin*, 22 (1974): 5-35, 129-161;

Wolff, *Strange Stories, and Other Explorations in Victorian Fiction* (Boston: Gambit, 1971);

Richard A. Zipser, *Edward Bulwer-Lytton and Germany* (Berne: Herbert Lang/ Frankfurt: Peter Lang, 1974).

Papers:
Most of Bulwer-Lytton's papers are deposited in the Hertford County Records Office. There are also important collections in the National Library of Scotland; in the Pierpont Morgan Library, New York; in the Parrish Collection at Princeton University Library; and in other university libraries. The number of extant papers is vast, and they are, for the most part, not yet catalogued.

Mortimer Collins
(29 June 1827-28 July 1876)

Norman Page
University of Alberta

BOOKS: *Idyls and Rhymes* (Dublin: McGlashan, 1855);

Summer Songs (London: Saunders & Otley, 1860);

Who Is the Heir? A Novel (3 volumes, London: Maxwell, 1865);

Sweet Anne Page (3 volumes, London: Hurst & Blackett, 1868);

The Ivory Gate (2 volumes, London: Hurst & Blackett, 1869);

A Letter to the Right Honourable Benjamin Disraeli MP (London: Hotten, 1869);

The Vivian Romance (3 volumes, London: Hurst & Blackett, 1870; 1 volume, New York: Harper, 1870);

Marquis and Merchant (3 volumes, London: Hurst & Blackett, 1871; 1 volume, New York: Appleton, 1871);

The Inn of Strange Meetings and Other Poems (London: King, 1871);

The Secret of Long Life (London: King, 1871);

The British Birds: A Communication from the Ghost of Aristophanes (London: The Publishing Co., 1872);

The Princess Clarice: A Story of 1871 (2 volumes, London: King, 1872);

Two Plunges for a Pearl (3 volumes, London: Tinsley, 1872; 1 volume, New York: Appleton, 1872);

Squire Silchester's Whim (3 volumes, London: King, 1873);

Miranda: A Midsummer Madness (3 volumes, London: King, 1873);

Mr. Carington: A Tale of Love and Constancy, as Robert Turner Cotton (3 volumes, London: King, 1873);

Transmigration (3 volumes, London: Hurst & Blackett, 1874);

Frances (3 volumes, London: Hurst & Blackett, 1874);

Sweet and Twenty (3 volumes, London: Hurst & Blackett, 1875);

Blacksmith and Scholar and From Midnight to Midnight (3 volumes, London: Hurst & Blackett, 1876);

A Fight with Fortune (3 volumes, London: Hurst & Blackett, 1876);

You Play Me False: A Novel, with Frances Collins (3 volumes, London: Bentley, 1878);

The Village Comedy, with Frances Collins (3 volumes, London: Hurst & Blackett, 1878);

Pen Sketches from a Vanished Hand, from the Papers of the Late Mortimer Collins, edited by Tom Taylor, with notes by the editor and Mrs. Mortimer Collins (2 volumes, London: Bentley, 1879);

Thoughts in My Garden, edited by Edmund Yates,

Mortimer Collins

London, he lived from 1862 until his death at Knowl Hill in Berkshire. Collins was married around 1849 to Susannah Hubbard Crump, who died in 1867; in 1868, he married Frances Cotton.

His wide interests included athletics, natural history, mathematics, chess, and classical literature, especially the plays of Aristophanes. Numerous literary friendships included R. D. Blackmore, R. H. Horne, and Frederick Locker-Lampson. Collins's most successful book was a volume of essays, *The Secret of Long Life* (1871), which ran into five editions. He was also well known for his skill at composing light verse.

He published the novels *Who Is the Heir?* (1865), *Sweet Anne Page* (1868), *The Ivory Gate* (1869), *The Vivian Romance* (1870), *Marquis and Merchant* (1871), *The Princess Clarice* (1872), *Two Plunges for a Pearl* (1872), *Squire Silchester's Whim* (1873), *Miranda* (1873), *Transmigration* (1874), *Frances* (1874), *Sweet and Twenty* (1875), *Blacksmith and Scholar and From Midnight to Midnight* (1876), *A Fight with Fortune* (1876), *You Play Me False* (1878), and *The Village Comedy* (1878). The last two of these were written in collaboration with his second wife. Collins also published *Mr. Carington* (1873) under the pseudonym of Robert Turner Cotton.

Although now forgotten, Collins's novels were reviewed at length by the leading critical journals, though not always favorably. The influential *Saturday Review*, for instance, published on 30 September 1865 a damning criticism of his first novel: it found the author "in the darkest ignorance about human nature and character" and "utterly innocent of any knack either of constructing a plot or even of executing decent detached sketches." Five years later the same journal remarked of *The Vivian Romance* that "he has written a very foolish book." Although his work did not always satisfy the critics, however, the fact that his books found publishers over a long period suggests that he enjoyed a steady following among subscribers to the circulating libraries. Collins was prone to using thinly-disguised living personalities in his novels—for instance, Swinburne appears as "Swynfen" in *Two Plunges for a Pearl*, and the *Athenaeum* reviewer deplored this "reprehensible sketch of an epicene poetaster." The largely autobiographical novel *Sweet Anne Page* embroiled him in a controversy of a similar kind and was withdrawn from the circulating libraries. His fiction shows the influence of the "sensation novel" popularized by Wilkie Collins (no relation), and his debut as a novelist belongs to the same decade as *The Woman in White* (1860) and *The Moonstone* (1868). Mortimer Collins's eccentrically digressive style and

with notes by the editor and Mrs. Mortimer Collins (2 volumes, London: Bentley, 1880); *Selections from the Poetical Works*, edited by F. P. Cotton (London: Bentley, 1886).

In his energy, his practice of many genres, and the eclecticism of his tastes, Mortimer Collins is a very good example of the kind of Victorian writer who, without achieving any large-scale success, contrived to make a profession of literature and who, in spite of the demands of Grub Street, succeeded in remaining a man of broad general culture. Edward James Mortimer Collins was born in Plymouth, the son of Francis Collins, a solicitor who had published a volume of verse. He became first a private tutor and then a schoolmaster in Guernsey (Channel Islands), but quit the teaching profession in 1856 to devote himself to literature. His earliest publications were poems, including the collection *Idyls and Rhymes* (1855). For the rest of his life he lived by journalism (as a contributor to *Punch*, *Temple Bar*, *Tinsley's Magazine*, and other periodicals), by editing various papers, and by producing nearly twenty novels, most of them published in the conventional three-volume form. After a period in

lack of skill in plotting disqualify him, however, from being considered a serious rival of his namesake. Mortimer Collins, writing in 1868, ranked himself as a poet, "below Browning in insight, above him in lyrical powers, and a trifle above Tennyson in both," and as a novelist, "far superior to your Trollopes and Wilkie Collinses"; but posterity has not endorsed this self-estimate.

Letters:

Frances Collins, ed., *Mortimer Collins: His Letters and Friendships, with Some Account of His Life* (London: Low, 1877).

Reference:

Stewart M. Ellis, ed., *Wilkie Collins, Le Fanu, and Others* (London: Constable, 1931).

Charles Dickens

George H. Ford
University of Rochester

BIRTH: Portsmouth, Hampshire, 7 February 1812, to John and Elizabeth Barrow Dickens.

MARRIAGE: 2 April 1836 to Catherine Hogarth; children: Charles, Mary, Kate, Walter Landor, Francis Jeffrey, Alfred Tennyson, Sydney Smith Haldemand, Henry Fielding, Dora Annie, Edward Bulwer-Lytton.

DEATH: Rochester, Kent, 9 June 1870.

BOOKS: *Sketches by Boz, Illustrative of Every-Day Life and Every-Day People* (first series, 2 volumes, London: Macrone, 1836; second series, London: Macrone, 1837); republished as *Watkins Tottle and Other Sketches Illustrative of Every Day Life and Every Day People* (2 volumes, Philadelphia: Carey, Lea & Blanchard, 1837) and *The Tuggses at Ramsgate and Other Sketches Illustrative of Every Day Life and Every Day People* (Philadelphia: Carey, Lea & Blanchard, 1837);
The Village Coquettes: A Comic Opera in Two Acts, as "Boz," with music by John Hullah (London: Bentley, 1836);
The Posthumous Papers of the Pickwick Club, Edited by "Boz" (20 monthly parts, London: Chapman & Hall, 1836-1837; 5 volumes, Philadelphia: Carey, Lea & Blanchard, 1838);
The Strange Gentleman: A Comic Burletta, in Two Acts, as "Boz" (London: Chapman & Hall, 1837);
The Life and Adventures of Nicholas Nickleby (20 monthly parts, London: Chapman & Hall, 1837-1839; 1 volume, New York: Turney, 1839);
Sketches of Young Gentlemen, Dedicated to the Young

Ladies (London: Chapman & Hall, 1838);
Memoirs of Joseph Grimaldi, Edited by "Boz," 2 volumes (London: Bentley, 1838; Philadelphia:

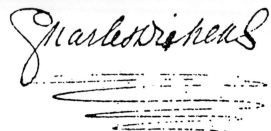

Carey, Lea & Blanchard, 1838);

Oliver Twist; or, The Parish Boy's Progress, by "Boz" (3 volumes, London: Bentley, 1838; 2 volumes, Philadelphia: Carey, Lea & Blanchard, 1839);

Sketches of Young Couples, with an Urgent Remonstrance to the Gentlemen of England (Being Bachelors or Widowers), on the Present Alarming Crisis (London: Chapman & Hall, 1840);

The Old Curiosity Shop (2 volumes, London: Chapman & Hall, 1841; 1 volume, Philadelphia: Lea & Blanchard, 1841);

Barnaby Rudge: A Tale of the Riots of 'Eighty (London: Chapman & Hall, 1841; Philadelphia: Lea & Blanchard, 1841);

American Notes for General Circulation (2 volumes, London: Chapman & Hall, 1842; 1 volume, New York: Wilson, 1842);

The Life and Adventures of Martin Chuzzlewit (20 monthly parts, London: Chapman & Hall, 1842-1844);

A Christmas Carol, in Prose: Being a Ghost Story of Christmas (London: Chapman & Hall, 1843; Philadelphia: Carey & Hart, 1844);

The Chimes: A Goblin Story of Some Bells That Rang an Old Year Out and a New Year In (London: Chapman & Hall, 1845; Philadelphia: Lea & Blanchard, 1845);

Pictures from Italy (London: Bradbury & Evans, 1846); republished as *Travelling Letters Written on the Road* (New York: Wiley & Putnam, 1846);

The Cricket on the Hearth: A Fairy Tale of Home (London: Bradbury & Evans, 1846; Boston: Redding, 1846);

The Battle of Life: A Love Story (London: Bradbury & Evans, 1846; Boston: Redding, 1847);

Dombey and Son (20 monthly parts, London: Bradbury & Evans, 1846-1848; 1 volume, New York: Burgess, Stringer, 1847);

The Haunted Man and the Ghost's Bargain: A Fancy for Christmas Time (London: Bradbury & Evans, 1848; Philadelphia: Althemus, 1848);

The Personal History of David Copperfield (20 monthly parts, London: Bradbury & Evans, 1849-1850; 2 volumes, New York: Harper, 1852);

A Child's History of England (3 volumes, London: Bradbury & Evans, 1852-1854; 1 volume, Boston: Jenks, Hickling & Swan, 1854);

Bleak House (20 monthly parts, London: Bradbury & Evans, 1852-1853; 1 volume, New York: Harper, 1853);

Hard Times: For These Times (London: Bradbury & Evans, 1854; New York: McElrath, 1854);

Little Dorrit (20 monthly parts, London: Bradbury & Evans, 1855-1857; 1 volume, Philadelphia: Peterson, 1857);

A Tale of Two Cities (London: Chapman & Hall, 1859; Philadelphia: Peterson, 1859);

Great Expectations (3 volumes, London: Chapman & Hall, 1861; 2 volumes, New York: Harper, 1861);

The Uncommercial Traveller (London: Chapman & Hall, 1861; New York: Sheldon, 1865);

Our Mutual Friend (20 monthly parts, London: Chapman & Hall, 1864-1865; 1 volume, New York: Harper, 1865);

Hunted Down: A Story, with Some Account of Thomas Griffiths Wainewright, The Poisoner (London: Hotten, 1870; Philadelphia: Peterson, 1870);

The Mystery of Edwin Drood (6 monthly parts, London: Chapman & Hall, 1870; 1 volume, Boston: Fields, Osgood, 1870);

A Child's Dream of a Star (Boston: Fields, Osgood, 1871);

Is She His Wife? Or, Something Singular: A Comic Burletta in One Act (Boston: Osgood, 1877);

The Life of Our Lord (New York: Simon & Schuster, 1934);

The Speeches of Charles Dickens, edited by K. J. Fielding (Oxford: Clarendon Press, 1960).

COLLECTIONS: *Cheap Edition of the Works of Mr. Charles Dickens* (12 volumes, London: Chapman & Hall, 1847-1852; 3 volumes, London: Bradbury & Evans, 1858);

The Charles Dickens Edition (21 volumes, London: Chapman & Hall, 1867-1875);

The Works of Charles Dickens (21 volumes, London: Macmillan, 1892-1925);

The Works of Charles Dickens, Gadshill Edition, 36 volumes (London: Chapman & Hall/New York: Scribners, 1897-1908);

The Nonesuch Edition, edited by Arthur Waugh et al. (23 volumes, London: Nonesuch Press, 1937-1938);

The New Oxford Illustrated Dickens (21 volumes, Oxford: Oxford University Press, 1947-1958);

The Clarendon Dickens, edited by Kathleen Tillotson et al. (5 volumes published, Oxford: Clarendon Press, 1966-   ).

The life story of Charles Dickens is, from several perspectives, a success story. Generally regarded today as one of the greatest novelists in the English language, Dickens had the unusual good fortune to have been recognized by his contemporaries as well as by posterity. He was not one of the neglected artists such as Keats, doomed to wait for later generations to discover his stature. Instead, Dickens's *The Posthumous Papers of the Pickwick Club* (1836-1837), which began publication when he was twenty-four years old, was a phenomenally popular success on both sides of the Atlantic. Before he was thirty, when he had already produced five vastly scaled novels, he came to America for a visit and was accorded the most triumphant reception ever staged for a foreign visitor. As the newspapers said, even the enthusiastic reception of General Lafayette in 1824 did not equal the way Dickens was received. His success was also reflected in his earnings: in the 1850s Dickens was making as much as £ 11,000 for one of his novels, a figure to be contrasted with the mere £ 600 earned in a year by his eminent contemporary and fellow novelist Thackeray. After his death the success story continued. During the over 110-year period since then there have been times, of course, when his status among critical readers declined markedly, as during the decades following his death and during the early years of the twentieth century. Since 1950, however, the curve of his reputation has shot upward so high that recently there has been more written about Dickens each year than about any other author in the English language except Shakespeare.

In the history of novel writing, Dickens's early start stands out as especially unusual. Poets and musicians often create significant compositions in their youth. Novelists, contrariwise (at least major

novelists), are generally late starters, perhaps because novel writing calls for perspectives of a special sort. The explanation for Dickens's early start is provided by the all-purpose word *genius*, with which the young man was evidently abundantly endowed. But genius in novel writing needs experiences to work with, painful experiences as well as pleasant ones. It was Dickens's fortune to have encountered both sorts while still a youth. Dickens's ancestry included a mixture of servants and office workers. His paternal grandfather, who died before Dickens was born, had been a steward in an aristocratic estate where Dickens's grandmother (who died when the boy was twelve) had been the housekeeper. One of her two sons, John Dickens (1785-1851), who had grown up on this country estate, obtained employment in London at the pay office of the British navy, a position that necessitated his moving to other localities from time to time. John Dickens was to be immortalized many years later by his son's portrait of him as Mr. Micawber. He reputedly resembled Micawber in loquaciousness and in pseudoelegance of manner, as well as in his fondness for libations—all of which make him sound like the father of another literary genius, James Joyce. In 1809 John Dickens married Elizabeth Barrow (1789-1863), whose father also worked in the pay office. Years later, she, too, would be the model for one of her son's characters, the fast-chattering Mrs. Nickleby. With two such talkers for parents, the son

Charles Dickens's parents, Elizabeth Barrow Dickens and John Dickens (Dickens Fellowship)

was to have a more than adequate early exposure to the spoken voice.

Eight children were born to John and Elizabeth, the first, Frances (Fanny), in 1810, and the second, Charles, over a year later. His birthplace was a house in Portsmouth, a town to which his father had been transferred some time previously. Except for a short stay in London, Dickens's boyhood was passed in towns on the south coast of England, especially in the twin towns of Rochester and Chatham, where the family settled when he was five. This pocket of preindustrial England had a powerful impact on Dickens's attitudes. He is conventionally thought of as the novelist of the big city, which he was; but it is noteworthy that during the last ten years of his life he chose to live not in London but near the town of Rochester, in Kent, in the region where he had spent his boyhood. Here in the town of Chatham he had attended a good school; discovered his favorite novelists, such as Smollett; and generally enjoyed himself. He did suffer from bouts of ill health; and sometimes he was afraid to go to bed after listening to the hair-raising bedtime stories inflicted on him by the nurse, especially a story called "Captain Murderer." Nevertheless, these first eleven years were happy ones.

This idyll was shattered after his family moved to London, where his father's casual mismanagement of his income finally led to his imprisonment for debt and to his twelve-year-old son's being sent to work in a blacking warehouse. The boy's job consisted of pasting labels on bottles of black shoe polish, this menial job being performed near a window within sight of passersby in the street. Living alone in cheap lodgings and nearly starving, Charles was overwhelmed with a sense of having been willfully abandoned by his parents and sentenced to remain in a rat hole for life. That his novels would be full of characters who are orphans is not surprising. The blacking warehouse experience lasted in reality only a few months, but to the boy, and to the grown man in retrospect, the time seemed endless. As he wrote in his autobiography more than twenty years later: "I never had the courage to go back to the place where my servitude began. . . . My old way home by the borough made me cry, after my eldest child could speak." Eventually he was rescued by his father, who had acquired some funds, and was sent to a school in London from the ages of twelve to fifteen. His mother, strangely unaware of her son's feelings, wanted him to stay at work rather than resume school, and Dickens never forgave her for her failure to provide the love and understanding he most desperately needed. A further twist of the knife had occurred

Old Hungerford Stairs, near the blacking warehouse where Dickens spent several miserable months of his boyhood

before the ordeal was over. His older sister, Frances, had been fortunate enough to be enrolled in the Royal Academy of Music before her father was imprisoned and to continue her studies there while Charles worked in the warehouse. In June 1824, she was awarded a silver medal for her excellent playing and singing. Her young brother was present at the awards ceremony, and, as he later wrote, he "felt as if my heart were rent. I prayed . . . that night, to be lifted out of the humiliation and neglect in which I was."

The importance of these unhappy experiences, especially in a career so seemingly happy and successful, cannot be exaggerated; it set up in Dickens's mind a specter of insecurity that was never to disappear. These experiences may also have contributed to his zealous resolution to excel and to his almost ruthless energy in all his pursuits, in particular his writing. As he noted in a letter of 1855: "Whoever is devoted to an art must be content to deliver himself wholly up to it, and to find his recompense in it." Dickens has often been characterized as the great recorder of life in the Victorian age, or as one of its major critics, but he was also, in his energetic pursuit of his goals, the embodiment of his age, the archetypal Victorian.

With the dark world behind him, Dickens began attending school at Wellington Academy in London. It was not as good a school as the one he had attended in Chatham, but it served his purposes, and at the end of his three years there he was head of his class and the winner of a prize for Latin. At fifteen he had finished his formal education and begun a lifetime of work. The possibility that he might go on to a university was apparently never considered by anyone. One of Dickens's sons, Henry, would attend Cambridge, but he himself was to acquire learning on his own; his college was the great library of the British Museum in London, where he was admitted as a reader on his eighteenth birthday. Here he soaked himself in works of history and literature (especially Shakespeare) that would make up a storehouse of knowledge to draw upon during the busy years ahead. In sum, Dickens's education, formal and informal, did not equip him to edit a learned journal such as the *Westminster Review* (of which George Eliot, the most erudite of novelists, would be an editor), but it did equip him to write novels. Perhaps a more extensive exposure to learning would have enabled him to write a better version of his embarrassingly crude potboiler *A Child's History of England* (1852-1854), but it is doubtful that it would have enabled him to write a better novel than the one he was writing at the same time, his great masterpiece *Bleak House* (1852-1853).

During the seven years after leaving school, the young Dickens lived at home with his family (although he was sometimes absent on trips). His experience during this apprentice period included exposure to the worlds of law, politics, journalism, and the theater. For the first two years he was a clerk in a law office, and it is remarkable how often in his novels he sets up scenes, usually comic ones, portraying the antics of junior clerks in lawyers' offices. For the next four years his employment involved the preparation of shorthand reports for lawyers who worked in Doctors' Commons. He had learned shorthand from one of his uncles, John Henry Barrow, an experienced reporter, who eventually obtained for Dickens a position as shorthand reporter in Parliament. Dickens's mastery of shorthand gained him some notoriety both for his speed and his accuracy, and these skills continued to be of use to him in his next position, that of a news reporter on the staff of the *Morning Chronicle*, which he joined in 1834. In this new role, he was frequently sent on journeys to report on election speeches in distant places. From his two years as a reporter of political events as well as from his years covering Parliament, Dickens acquired an extraordinary amount of information about the political life of his country during a crucial period following the passing of the Reform Bill of 1832. He also acquired from these experiences a realization that political oratory is often absurdly empty. During the rest of his life he was appalled at times by the ineptitude of some political leaders, but his more typical response was to find them funny, especially in their public speeches (of which he had listened to thousands). In an early sketch, "The House," he likened the House of Commons to a pantomime that was "strong in clowns." The members of Parliament, he comments, "twist and tumble about, till two, three and four o'clock in the morning; playing the strangest antics, and giving each other the funniest slaps on the face that can possibly be imagined, without evincing the smallest tokens of fatigue." The members, he adds, are "all talking, laughing, lounging, coughing, oh-ing, questioning, or groaning; presenting a conglomeration of noise and confusion, to be met with in no other place in existence, not even excepting Smithfield [the cattle market] on a market-day, or a cock-pit in its glory."

This awareness of political absurdities appears very early in Dickens's writings. In his first month as a news reporter, he had been sent to Edinburgh to report on a banquet being given in honor of Earl Grey, the retiring prime minister. Dickens's

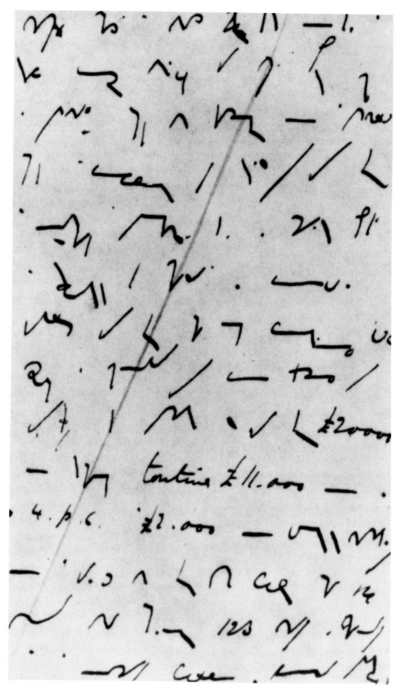

A page of notes by Dickens in the shorthand he learned from his uncle and used in his reporting jobs (Dickens Fellowship)

amusement on this occasion was prompted not by Grey's address but by the behavior of the dinner guests, who had become impatient because the guest of honor had not arrived on schedule. One of these guests, he reports, was so impressed by the fare available at the banquet, the "cold fowls, roast beef, lobster, and other tempting delicacies (for the dinner was a cold one)," that he decided "the best thing he could possibly do, would be to eat his dinner, while there was anything to eat. He accordingly laid about him with right good-will, the example was contagious, and the clatter of knives and forks became general. Hereupon, several gentlemen, who were not hungry, cried out 'Shame!' and looked very indignant; and several gentlemen who were hungry cried 'Shame!' too, eating, nevertheless, all the while, as fast as they possibly could. In this dilemma, one of the stewards mounted a bench and feelingly represented to the delinquents the enormity of their conduct, imploring them for decency's sake, to defer the process of mastication until the arrival of Earl Grey. This address was loudly cheered, but totally unheeded; and this is, perhaps, one of the few instances on record of a dinner having been virtually concluded before it began." Dickens was only twenty-two years old when he composed this report from Edinburgh, but already developed are some of the characteristic earmarks of his mature prose style, especially the imperturbable jocularity of tone with which the absurd episode is suffused—a jocularity enhanced when, as here, the episode involves man as a political animal.

In addition to his experiences as journalist during this period between leaving school and becoming a creative writer, the young Dickens was also deeply involved with the theater, both as a spectator and as a potential actor. If in the daytime he were committed to the law or to journalism, it was to the world of the footlights that he was committed at night. At the age of twenty, in fact, he decided to become an actor and wrote a letter to the manager of Covent Garden Theatre recommending himself as endowed with "a natural power of reproducing in his own person what he observed in others." The letter led to his being invited for an audition to offer a sample of his histrionic talents. When the day came, however, Dickens was stricken with a cold so severe that he had to excuse himself, proposing that he would reapply the following season. He never did reapply. Nevertheless, this incident of the audition usually prompts any admirer of Dickens's writings to a moment of reflection. Suppose the stagestruck young man had not been ill that day? Suppose that he had made a triumphant appearance? Might he have been lost to literature? As he himself remarked in a letter: "See how near I may have been to another life." And in his novel *Great Expectations* (1861) almost thirty years later, there is a passage about how one day in our lives can make changes lasting a lifetime. His protagonist Pip reflects about having spent his first day with the beautiful girl Estella: "That was a memorable day to me, for it made great changes in me. But it is the same with any life. Imagine one selected day struck out of it, and think how different its course would have been." Happily, the young man was, of course, not lost to literature; in fact, it was only a few months after that memorable day of the nonaudition that he was to send his first literary effort to a publisher.

In 1830, Dickens was introduced into the household of George Beadnell, a prosperous banker, and his wife and their three daughters. The youngest daughter, Maria, was twenty years old, and with her the eighteen-year-old Dickens fell overwhelmingly in love. Writing to her three years later, Dickens still affirmed: "I never have loved and I never can love any human creature breathing but yourself." The relationship developed happily for some time, and at the outset, Maria was apparently encouraging with her teenaged suitor. But by 1832, her parents began to discourage his attentions, perhaps having heard reports about his father's unreliability, or perhaps on the grounds that Dickens himself did not seem to have suitable prospects. In any event, Maria was sent abroad to a finishing school in Paris, and after her return, her interest in Dickens had cooled altogether. In March 1833, he returned all the letters she had written to him, lamenting his fate and reminding her, with a flourish, that she had been "the object of my first, and my last love." The infatuation lasted four years, and the frustrations of the relationship were even more painful for Dickens to look back upon than were his experiences in the blacking warehouse. His best friend and biographer, John Forster, at first found this story of Dickens's adolescent love to be incredible, especially incredible being the importance that the mature Dickens ascribed to it in his development. Only gradually did Forster come to realize how hurt his friend had been by a sense of social inferiority in this thwarted early love affair. The depth and long-lasting quality of these feelings are evident in the fact that while Dickens decided to share with Forster the autobiographical fragment he had written about his blacking warehouse experiences, he could not bring himself to share what he had written about the Maria Beadnell episode; and a few years later, he simply burned it.

One of the lasting effects of the thwarting was its influence on his desire to succeed and to become financially secure, just as David Copperfield, in his novel, would be impelled to strenuous efforts to succeed. As Dickens explained to Forster: "I went at it with a determination to overcome all the difficulties, which fairly lifted me up into that newspaper life, and floated me away over a hundred men's heads." When at last Dickens tried his hand at literature, the same driving energies persisted: with his pen he would show those unseeing banking Beadnells (by heaven!) what a paragon they had missed being allied to. But first he had to pass through his literary apprenticeship as he had passed through his earlier apprenticeships to law, journalism, and the stage. During the three years before launching his first full-length novel, Dickens was learning the craft of literature by writing occasional short pieces which he called sketches. Some of these pieces tell a story; others are simply descriptions of London localities such as Newgate Prison or Monmouth Street (the shopping center for secondhand clothing); and others offer portraits of picturesque characters such as a cabdriver or a circus clown.

The first sketch, "A Dinner at Poplar Walk," was submitted for publication in late 1833, when Dickens was twenty-one, and appeared in the *Monthly Magazine* in January 1834. Later in life he looked back upon the excitement he had felt on those occasions. This first sketch, he recalled, had been "dropped stealthily one evening at twilight, with fear and trembling, into a dark letter-box, in a dark office, up a dark court in Fleet Street." Some weeks later, when he bought a copy of the magazine and saw his sketch "in all the glory of print," he was overcome with emotion. "I walked down to Westminster Hall, and turned into it for half-an-hour, because my eyes were so dimmed with joy and pride, that they could not bear the street, and were not fit to be seen there." The emotional satisfaction of seeing his sketch in print was the only reward Dickens received for this publication; indeed, he received no payments whatever for the first nine of his sketches, which were all published in the *Monthly Magazine*. Thereafter, having established his literary credentials, he was able to require payments for his efforts when they appeared in magazines or newspapers and receive further payments when the sketches were collected and published in volumes in 1836. There were some sixty sketches in all, making up two volumes entitled *Sketches by Boz*. The pen name of Boz, used for this first publication, continued to be used to refer to Dickens by affectionate readers throughout his lifetime, even though the true identity of Boz had been established by the summer of 1836. The name was borrowed from the nickname that Dickens devised for his youngest brother, Augustus, calling him "Moses" after one of the Primrose children in Goldsmith's *Vicar of Wakefield* (1766). Augustus mispronounced this name as "Boses," which was shortened to "Bose" and eventually to "Boz" (which is pronounced as rhyming with "laws" rather than with "foes").

Sketches by Boz was well received by reviewers and had an encouraging sale. The favorable reception was partly attributable to the witty illustrations provided by George Cruikshank (1792-1878), the most popular illustrator of the period and an artist whose established reputation was especially helpful

An illustration of a London pawnshop by George Cruikshank for
Sketches by Boz

for a hitherto unknown writer. Many years later the two men became estranged, but in this earlier period they were good friends. Cruikshank was also Dickens's illustrator for *Oliver Twist* (1838) and *Memoirs of Joseph Grimaldi* (1838). In any event, the initial collaboration worked well, and the *Sketches by Boz* caught the eye of several well-pleased reviewers. One of the first of these recommended it in particular to American readers because the volume would "save them the trouble of reading some hundred dull-written tomes on England, as it is a perfect picture of the morals, manners, habits of a great portion of English society." He added: "It is hardly possible to conceive of a more pleasantly reading book." Another reviewer noted that although parts of the book picture the "wretchedness" of London's slums, the writer's disposition "leads him to look on the bright and sunny side of things." Most acutely, this reviewer described Dickens as "a close and acute observer of character and manners, with a strong sense of the ridiculous."

This review, appearing in the *Morning Chronicle* on 11 February 1836, gave Dickens a special degree of pleasure because of its having been written by George Hogarth, his prospective father-in-law. Hogarth (1783-1870) was a cultivated man of many talents. After working some years as a lawyer in Edinburgh, where he had connections with Sir Walter Scott, he gave up law for journalism and moved to England as a newspaper editor. He was also an accomplished musician and the author of books and articles about music. In 1834, he and Dickens came to know each other at the offices of the *Morning Chronicle*, and Dickens was soon a frequent visitor at Hogarth's house, where he met the eldest daughter, Catherine (1815-1879), who was called Kate. George Hogarth was an admirer of the *Sketches by Boz* (as his review indicated), knowing them "by heart," as Dickens remarked. Dickens, in turn, became an admirer of Hogarth's pretty daughter. Early in 1835 he became engaged to her, and in April 1836, they were married. Kate's appearance at this time was described by a woman who had known her: she was "plump and fresh-coloured; with . . . large, heavy-lidded blue eyes." Her mouth was "small, round and red-lipped, with a genial smiling expression of countenance, notwithstanding the sleepy look of the slow-moving eyes." During the year of their engagement, however, there were many occasions when Kate's expression must have been no longer genial and smiling, for her hardworking fiancé was frequently too busy to visit her. The curious letters he wrote to

Catherine (Kate) Dickens, drawn by Daniel Maclise shortly after her marriage to Dickens (Dickens Fellowship)

her during this period almost always involve his reporting that in order to meet some publisher's deadline, he must defer the pleasure of a visit; and if she complained of such neglect, she was likely to receive an admonishing lecture in Dickens's next letter urging her to change her ways. One such admonishment concluded by his sounding rather like his own Mr. Pecksniff: "You may rest satisfied that I love you dearly—far too well to feel hurt by what in any one else would have annoyed me greatly." These letters to Kate are sometimes affectionate and playful, but are clearly different in tone from the passionate infatuation that Dickens had expressed during his earlier courtship of Maria Beadnell. In defense of Dickens, it may be added that his repeated references to overwork during his courtship seem altogether justifiable. To obtain and furnish suitable living quarters demanded strenuous efforts from Dickens in his various employments. By Christmas 1835, he was able to rent a suite of three rooms in Furnival's Inn, where the young couple resided for their first year of marriage. Here at Furnival's Inn, his first child was born some nine months after his honeymoon; and here, too, he completed writing his first novel, which had been taking shape during the last months of his courtship.

Dickens's shift from being a writer of sketches to a writer of novels was effected in a remarkably haphazard way. A few days after his twenty-fourth birthday in 1836, he received a proposal from Chapman and Hall, who were planning to bring out a book of illustrations by a well-known comic artist, Robert Seymour (1798-1836). What the publishers wanted from Dickens was a series of comic stories and sketches that could provide materials for Seymour to illustrate. The series would eventually appear as a book, but its first appearance would be in twenty monthly installments. Dickens at once set to work, and by late March, within a day of his marriage to Catherine Hogarth, the first installment appeared of *The Posthumous Papers of the Pickwick Club*, later to be known simply as *The Pickwick Papers*.

Seymour's guiding idea was to portray the inept antics of a group of Londoners who had organized a hunting and fishing club, a "Nimrod Club," as he called it. Dickens tried to adapt his text to Seymour's idea by including some sporting transactions in the early installments—as when one of the Pickwickians, Mr. Winkle, is ignominiously unseated by a rented horse or when he goes shooting at a country estate and bungles his handling of his gun. Such episodes were what Seymour wanted for

A page of manuscript for The Pickwick Papers. *The chapter should be numbered XXXVII; the error appeared in the serial publication but was subsequently corrected (Sotheby, 23 November 1971).*

his illustrations; but there were not to be many of them, for as Dickens had forewarned his publishers, he "was no great sportsman" even though he had been "born and partly bred in the country." As publication got under way, it became evident that the novelist and the illustrator were in disagreement not only about how much emphasis was to be on the comedy of country sports. Dickens gradually began taking over as manager of the whole Pickwick project, with the twenty-four-year-old novelist, not the thirty-eight-year-old illustrator, calling the shots. Otherwise, as Dickens saw it, the tail would be wagging the dog. For Seymour, who was in a state of

depression, the relationship with Dickens was intolerably galling, and in April, he shot himself. One of the illustrators who applied to be Seymour's replacement was William Makepeace Thackeray, later to be Dickens's rival as leading novelist of the age, but Thackeray was passed over in favor of Hablôt Browne (1815-1882). Browne was even younger than Dickens, and there was never any question from this time on that the novelist was fully in charge of the production.

One important legacy of his having started working with Seymour was the distinctive method of publication in monthly numbers that they had adopted. As a way of publishing novels, this was an innovation, and one that gradually came to be looked upon with favor by the early Victorian reading public. All of Dickens's novels were to be published in installments; and for thirty-five years or so after *The Pickwick Papers*, other novelists, such as Thackeray, would also publish in monthly numbers. An interesting feature of serial publication was its enabling the novelist to get an early impression of how the work was being received by the public. *The Pickwick Papers* looked at first like a loser: the opening chapters failed to attract attention, and only 500 copies of the second installment were printed. Some months later, the publishers were frantically trying to print enough copies to meet the demands of thousands of *Pickwick Papers* enthusiasts. Of the final number (October 1837) some 40,000 copies were printed. What was the reason for this turnaround? Most of Dickens's contemporaries traced the change to the fourth number, in which he had

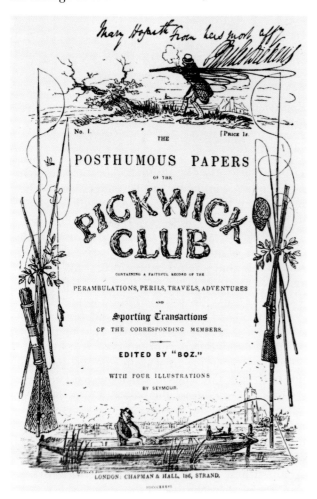

Cover of the first monthly part of Dickens's comic masterpiece, with an inscription by Dickens to his sister-in-law (Dickens Fellowship)

introduced two strikingly colorful Cockney characters: Sam Weller and his father, Tony, the fat coachman. Sam's mixture of impudence and warmheartedness, and his worldly-wise anecdotes purveyed in a lively Cockney accent, made him an ideal foil for Mr. Pickwick's innocent and well-intentioned benevolence. By having Sam become Mr. Pickwick's servant, Dickens had recreated an endearing pair like Sancho Panza and Don Quixote, and his readers greeted the combination with a level of enthusiasm rarely to be matched in the history of literature. *The Pickwick Papers* ended up as the most sensational triumph in nineteenth-century publishing. For a full-scale account of this triumph, the opening chapter of *Dickens and His Readers*, by George Ford, may be consulted. As Ford shows, one of the most striking aspects of the popularity of *The Pickwick Papers* was that it appealed to all classes of readers, the highly educated as well as the ill educated. In June 1837, one early reader, Mary Russell Mitford, recommended *The Pickwick Papers* to a friend in a letter: "It is fun—London Life—but without anything unpleasant: a lady might read it all *aloud*. . . . All the boys and girls talk his fun . . . and yet they who are of the highest taste like it the most." As an example of high taste, Miss Mitford cited a judge, Lord Denman, who "studies *Pickwick* on the bench while the jury are deliberating." This letter provides several clues to account for the success of Dickens's first novel. That it could be read aloud, as she noted, without offensive references to sexual exploits, was an important element of Dickens's recipe. *The Pickwick Papers* was still being published in the year Victoria became queen, and its appearance coincided with a change of attitudes toward the laxity and lewdness that had been such prominent features of life and literature in the 1820s. There is plenty of hearty drinking and eating in *The Pickwick Papers*: in one scene even the saintly Mr. Pickwick imbibes so much cold punch that he passes out and awakes to find himself on exhibition in a village pound. But there are no comparable bedroom incidents in this rollicking tale, and in general the benevolence and warmheartedness of the protagonist tone down the rough horseplay of some of the scenes which resemble the so-called "novel of high spirits" written by Dickens's immediate predecessors, such as Pierce Egan (1772-1849).

Miss Mitford's mentioning of how the lord chief justice enjoyed *The Pickwick Papers* is a reminder of one of the many triumphs of this novel: its presentation of the lawyers and judges encountered by Mr. Pickwick on the occasion of his being sued for breach of promise by his landlady, Mrs.

Illustrations for The Pickwick Papers *by the original artist for the series, Robert Seymour,
and by his replacement, Hablôt Browne ("Phiz")*

Bardell, a widow. The funniest of many funny scenes in the novel is the trial scene of *Bardell* v. *Pickwick*, featuring Mrs. Bardell's lawyer, Serjeant Buzfuz, whose ludicrously eloquent speech for the plaintiff is a magnificent parody of legalese and of courtroom tactics. After Mr. Pickwick loses the case he chooses to go to prison rather than pay the settlement, and in the scenes of life behind bars there is, of course, much less opportunity for comedy. In this part of the novel there is a sad seriousness that anticipates the prison scenes of some of the later novels such as *Little Dorrit* (1855-1857). In fact, some solemn readers misread *The Pickwick Papers* by arguing that the prison episode is the key to the whole book and that the funny parts are finally subordinate. To reinforce their argument, they point to some of the strangely melodramatic short stories interspersed throughout the novel, such as "A Madman's Manuscript," as further examples of seriousness unmixed with comedy. Such arguments may provide a useful corrective, but a fair-minded rereading of the whole novel would suggest its limitations. Humor is the chief quality of Dickens's first novel, as his own contemporaries recognized.

In his later life, after his vision had become a much more somber one, many of his readers wished he would return to the vein of pure comedy in which they believed *The Pickwick Papers* to have been written. Despite the successes he was to achieve with other kinds of novels, it was this early sunshine-studded tale that was probably his best-liked book among Victorian readers. In the second half of the twentieth century this evaluation no longer holds. Most admirers of Dickens now would not recommend newcomers to his work to try their teeth first on *The Pickwick Papers*; instead they would urge postponing a reading of it until one has enjoyed some of the later writings in which the artist is more surefooted. *The Pickwick Papers* was a kind of slapdash production, and the result, as even Miss Mitford remarked, was "rather fragmentary." The artful construction evident in such a novel as *Bleak House* is not yet developed. What is already fully developed and abundantly present in dozens of episodes is a brilliant prose style—or styles, rather—and a command of dialogue, which variously combine for delightful comic effects unsurpassed by other novelists and even by Dickens himself. "The Inimitable," as he sometimes referred to himself in fun, had earned the right to his title at the early age of twenty-four.

Also at the age of twenty-four, Dickens began to earn enough from his writing of fiction so as to be able to give up working for the *Morning Chronicle*, which he did in November 1836. It was well that he could do so, for at this time he was absurdly over-committed to a long list of literary projects and deadlines. Sparked by the dizzying success of *The Pickwick Papers* and by a youthful faith that his energy was unfathomable, and also aware of his new responsibilities as husband and father-to-be, Dickens had signed one agreement after another with three different publishers during 1836. The *Sketches by Boz* would be completed, fortunately, in December, but *The Pickwick Papers* was only halfway complete at this date, and an installment had to be written for every month until November 1837. Dickens had also made a loose agreement with another publisher that he would have completed a novel, "Gabriel Vardon," by November 1836! Of this novel there was no sign at this date. Indeed, it did not surface until four and a half years later, in 1841, and then with a different publisher and different title (*Barnaby Rudge*). With Richard Bentley, another publisher, he had made even more extensive commitments late in 1836: he had contracted to write two novels and also to take on the role of editor of a new magazine, *Bentley's Miscellany*—a position he held until January 1839. In late 1836, he had also tried his hand at writing the libretto for a comic opera, *The Village Coquettes*, which was performed in December and was well received for a few weeks.

One review of the opera reported that the first-night audience insisted that Boz appear on-stage at the end of the performance, and there was much astonishment among those who were seeing him for the first time. They seem to have expected that he would look like one of the Pickwickians or even like Tony Weller! Instead, they saw a thin young man, of medium height, modest in manner, but with long, wavy dark hair and wearing a flamboyantly colorful dandy-style vest. His expression was one of amiability and good humor. What the audience saw that night was the Dickens still visible today in the fine portrait painted three years later by his friend Daniel Maclise (1806-1870).

The following year, 1837, was a little less frantic. It opened with the publication of the first of the twenty-four monthly installments of his second novel, *Oliver Twist*. Unlike *The Pickwick Papers* and most of Dickens's other novels, which appeared first in separate numbers with each number having its own cover, the installments of *Oliver Twist* were part of a magazine, *Bentley's Miscellany*. Although there were four more installments than had been used for *The Pickwick Papers*, each installment was considerably shorter; so the whole novel, although appearing over a period of more than two years, was also considerably shorter than *The Pickwick Papers*. But there were more significant differences between the two novels than the differences in their forms of serialization. For readers who had grown fondly accustomed to the fun and frolics of successive numbers of *The Pickwick Papers*, this new novel by Boz must have prompted a sense of shock. Most of the adventures of the young protagonist consist of a succession of encounters with the worlds of brutality and crime. The story opens with the death of Oliver's mother in a dark, cold workhouse where she has given birth to him, and the child is raised in this bleak environment under the stern management of Mr. Bumble, the beadle. As a young boy Oliver escapes to London, where he is initiated into a gang of criminals headed by Fagin, a Jew, who has organized a number of boys into a team of pickpockets, the most expert of whom is the Artful Dodger. Fagin also receives other kinds of stolen property provided by the housebreaker and robber Bill Sikes, who lives with Nancy, a prostitute. Fagin's gang seeks to make Oliver work for them, but the boy escapes and eventually obtains protection in kindly households in the country. The novel ends

George Cruikshank's illustration of Oliver Twist asking for more porridge

with the gruesome death of Sikes after his brutal murder of his mistress and a scene of Fagin in his condemned cell in Newgate prison following his capture by the police. *Oliver Twist* thus exposes its readers to a world of crime and meanness, a dog-eat-dog world that is altogether different from the jolly world of *The Pickwick Papers*. To emphasize the difference further, this dark and sordid world is presented by Dickens from the perspective of an orphan, a lost child whose sense of bewilderment and fright reminds one of how the twelve-year-old Dickens had himself responded to the soul-crushing experiences of the blacking warehouse.

Dickens's decision to write in a mode so different from one that had already proven in his hands to be triumphantly successful must have taken a lot of nerve, for the expectation of a reading public is for the novelist to repeat. On this point there is a sympathetic comment by another successful and popular novelist, Angus Wilson, in his 1966 introductory essay on *Oliver Twist*. An "anxious question which would have pressed upon Dickens," Wilson notes, was "would his second novel maintain the fantastic popularity of *Pickwick Papers*? Every novel is a hurdle for the popular novelist, but certainly the second is the most alarming."

Dickens, however, seems to have had some good reasons for being less alarmed than might have been expected. He had chosen to write a kind of novel that had already become established as highly popular in the hands of his immediate predecessors, the so-called Newgate novel, such stories of crime and punishment as Edward Bulwer-Lytton's *Paul Clifford* (1830) or Harrison Ainsworth's *Rookwood* (1834). Indeed, it was this school of fiction that seems to have attracted him for models before he became immersed in the world of Mr. .Pickwick. When he was only twenty-one, he spoke in a letter of "my proposed novel." One scholar, Kathleen Tillotson, argues persuasively that what Dickens was referring to at that date was not *The Pickwick Papers* but an incipient *Oliver Twist*, and that his second novel was, in effect, his first.

In any event the gamble paid off, by and large. Inevitably, he did lose some readers who found the whole criminal scene to be "painful and revolting," as one of them said. Another, Lady Carlisle, commented loftily: "I know there are such unfortunate beings as pick-pockets and street walkers . . . but I own I do not much wish to hear what they say to one another." A different kind of reader was put off by the prominence of the social criticism in the opening chapters, in which Dickens exposes the cruel inadequacies of workhouse life as organized by the New Poor Law of 1834. This law had been the brainchild of the Utilitarians, and anyone attacking it would call down the ire of such Utilitarian readers as Harriet Martineau. After these exceptions are granted, however, there can be no doubt that this second novel was another extraordinary success. Its greatness was different from that of *The Pickwick Papers*, but it was still incontestably greatness. In the twentieth century it has remained one of Dickens's most popular and best-known novels; as Angus Wilson said of it; "perhaps more than any other it has a combination of sensationalism and sentiment that fixes it as one of the masterpieces of pop art." As proof of this comment, one may cite the remarkable popular success of Lionel Bart's musical comedy version, *Oliver!* First staged in 1960, this work established a London record for its more than six years of performances. The film version of *Oliver!* was seen by vaster audiences, although how much the status of Dickens benefited from the film is difficult to assess inasmuch as the only reference to *Oliver Twist* occurs in the long list of credits with which the film opens. There, in the midst of the names of technicians, costume designers, and suchlike is a line in small letters announcing that the production has been freely adapted from a novel by Charles Dickens! Nevertheless, the film does have a virtue in reminding one that in the midst of the nightmare of Dickens's story there is also a good deal of comedy. In chapter seventeen of *Oliver Twist*, Dickens himself comments with amusement about the combination: "It is the custom on the stage, in all good murderous melodramas, to present the tragic and the comic scenes, in as regular alternation, as the layers of red and white in a side of streaky bacon." Although his comment is only half serious, it is evident that he follows the streaky-bacon recipe in this novel by its effective appeal to both the reader's sense of humor and his sense of fear. The beadle, Mr. Bumble, for example, is on one level the despicable petty tyrant in uniform who flourished in Hitler's Germany and still flourishes in other countries. He is like the nameless master of the workhouse from whom Oliver asks for "more," and who (according to Arnold Kettle, a Marxist critic) "is not anyone in particular but every agent of an oppressive system everywhere." But as Dickens presents Bumble, he is not only frightening but also a figure of fun, as in the scene of his proposing marriage to Mrs. Corney—a hilarious incident. In the later parts of the novel, Mr. Bumble becomes the stock comic figure of the henpecked husband with the domineering wife. When told that "the law supposes that your wife acts under your direction,"

Mr. Bumble comments: "If the law supposes that, the law is a ass—a idiot." An even more distinctly sustained comic scene is of the Artful Dodger in court demanding his "priwileges" as an Englishman and admonishing his judges that "this ain't the shop for justice." The humor in the presentation of Fagin is more complex, at least for later readers, in view of the repeated references to him as "the Jew." Responding to accusations of anti-Semitism, Dickens pointed out that at the time of the action of *Oliver Twist* all of the fences in London were Jewish, and, more important, that the most villainous characters in his novel are Sikes and Monks, rather than Fagin. In any event, the memorable early scenes of the Merry Old Gentleman, with his toasting fork and handkerchief tricks, are funny as well as vivid.

The successful launching of *Oliver Twist* inspired Dickens in the spring of 1837 to rent a terrace house at 48 Doughty Street in Bloomsbury, where he lived for the next two and a half years before moving to a larger house on Devonshire Place. Of the three houses in London in which he lived, only the Doughty Street one has survived (although the bomb damage it suffered in World War II required considerable restoration). In 1925 it was bought as a museum by the Dickens Fellowship, and, especially recently, has become one of the most successful literary museums in London, attracting every year thousands of visitors for a tour of its twelve small rooms, including a little back room displaying the desk on which *Oliver Twist* and *Nicholas Nickleby* were written.

The Doughty Street household consisted not only of Dickens and Kate and their child but of Kate's younger sister, Mary Hogarth, who had sometimes stayed with them earlier at Furnival's Inn to help her sister during pregnancy and to be a companion for her brother-in-law—a not unusual arrangement in nineteenth-century families. What was unusual was the intensity of Dickens's feelings about this seventeen-year-old girl, whose animated company he had come to depend upon, and whose sweet innocence represented an ideal spirit, a shining lamp in a world of darkness. On 7 May 1837, the lamp was suddenly put out forever. After attending an evening showing of *The Village Coquettes*, the two sisters and Dickens had returned in high spirits to Doughty Street, where Mary was suddenly stricken with some unidentified illness, and the next day she died in his arms. After the funeral, he and Kate went to a country retreat for some weeks, and the numbers of both *The Pickwick Papers* and *Oliver Twist* were suspended from publication for a month.

The shock of Mary's death had profound ef-

Portrait by Hablôt Browne of Mary Hogarth, Dickens's sister-in-law, whose death at age seventeen shattered Dickens. She was the inspiration for Little Nell in The Old Curiosity Shop *(Dickens Fellowship).*

fects on Dickens as a man and as a novelist. Until the day of his own death he wore the ring she had been wearing when she died. It was his wish that, like Heathcliff in Emily Brontë's *Wuthering Heights* (1847), he would be buried beside her (which proved to be impossible). And for ten months he dreamed of her every night, the dreams ceasing only after a visit to Yorkshire during which he wrote to Kate about them. According to a Freudian critic, Steven Marcus, the extraordinary cessation of these nightly visions may have been prompted not merely by his reporting the phenomenon to his wife but by an experience he had in Yorkshire at this same time, of his coming across the gravestone of a boy "eighteen long years old" who, Dickens said, had "died at that wretched place. I think his ghost put Smike into my head upon the spot." Thoughts of Smike, the boy who was to die in his projected novel *The Life and Adventures of Nicholas Nickleby* (1837-1839), may thus have affected thoughts of Mary and purged the vision. For the novel following *Nicholas Nickleby*, there can be no doubt how Dickens's feelings about the life and death of Mary Hogarth shaped Little

Nell's portrait and the story of her dying. As he tried to write her death scene in *The Old Curiosity Shop* (1841), he confessed in a letter: "I shan't recover from it for a long time. . . . Old wounds bleed afresh when I only think of the way of doing it. . . . Dear Mary died yesterday, when I think of this sad story." In later novels there are other young women characters who seem to be modeled on Mary Hogarth, even though they do not die. Of these women, several of whom are seventeen—Mary's age when she died—it was remarked by John Greaves, usually a most indulgent reader of Dickens, that they are "perhaps rather colourless creations."

Dickens was soon back at his desk, completing *The Pickwick Papers* late in 1837 and *Oliver Twist* in spring 1839; and then, before he was thirty, he published three more full-length novels: *Nicholas Nickleby*, *The Old Curiosity Shop*, and *Barnaby Rudge*. It was an extraordinary performance, and all of these novels were (*Barnaby Rudge* less so) popular and critical successes.

The main plot of *Nicholas Nickleby* involves some stock characters, heroes, and villains in stock situations of fortunes lost and found. The chief villain is a miserly businessman, Ralph Nickleby, who schemes to frustrate the career of his young nephew, Nicholas, who has come to London to seek his fortune after the death of his father. Ralph hates Nicholas and arranges for him to take a low-paying job as a teacher in Yorkshire, a job which the young man eventually quits after exposing corruption at the school. For a time Nicholas makes a living with a troupe of traveling actors headed by Mr. Vincent Crummles. On his travels Nicholas is accompanied by a crippled youth, Smike, whom he had defended at school. Later, Nicholas gets a good job in London in the office of two benevolent businessmen, the Cheeryble brothers; they introduce him to a wealthy heiress whom he finally marries. On various occasions, Nicholas prevents his uncle from carrying out wicked schemes—as, for example, his attempt to sell Kate, Nicholas's sister, to her aristocratic admirer, Lord Verisopht. Wicked Uncle Ralph finally loses his fortune and is driven to hang himself after he discovers that Smike, the unfortunate youth whom he had tried to persecute, was his own son.

In one of the best critical essays on this novel, Michael Slater admitted in 1978 that this main plot "is largely a lifeless bore" featuring some "crashing melodramatic clichés." A similar complaint was made by Dickens's best friend, John Forster, who, in reviewing the novel in 1839, contrasted its clumsy plot with Fielding's *Tom Jones* (1749): "A want of

Tombstone of George Taylor in Yorkshire, which gave Dickens the idea for the character of Smike in Nicholas Nickleby

plan is apparent in it from the first, an absence of design. The plot seems to have grown as the book appeared by numbers, instead of having been mapped out beforehand." Both critics have put their fingers on the weakest aspect of Dickens's early novels, one that continues to be evident even in *The Life and Adventures of Martin Chuzzlewit* (1842-1844). In his later novels, fortunately, Dickens would toil to correct his clumsy construction and to shape and plan his narratives. Yet it is misleading to cite Slater and Forster on Dickens's plot without remarking that almost everything else they have to say about *Nicholas Nickleby* is enthusiastic. What sustains this novel, as they and other critics have found, is its gallery of colorful characters whose vitality charges it with energy. The best known of these was and is Wackford Squeers, the semiliterate proprietor and master of a school in Yorkshire. As with *Oliver Twist*, part of the appeal of *Nicholas Nickleby* was its exposure of some contemporary corrupt institution. Dotheboys Hall, as Mr. Squeers's school is aptly called, was modeled in part on schools visited by Dickens in preparation for

Page from the manuscript for Nicholas Nickleby (Sotheby, 23 November 1971)

writing his novel. Also memorable is Nicholas's mother, said to have been modeled in part on Dickens's own mother. Mrs. Nickleby's loquacious monologues are full of most delightful absurdities, as are the speech and actions of some of the members of the theater troupe. Overall, *Nicholas Nickleby* is Dickens's most theatrical novel, and the theatricality is not limited to the scenes onstage. Perhaps its staginess may account for its having received "little attention from modern criticism," as Slater's essay notes. Perhaps the same quality might account for the remarkably successful stage version of *Nicholas*

Nickleby put on in London and New York in 1980-1981, each two-part performance lasting a total of eight hours! Critics were astonished by how effective this awesome experiment turned out to be.

The statement about little attention being paid to *Nicholas Nickleby* in modern criticism is equally applicable to *The Old Curiosity Shop*, and, in this instance, stage or screen treatment does not modify the situation. (The 1970s film musical *Quilp* was an embarrassment.) Much of the discussion of this novel has been historical, such as George Ford's chapter "Little Nell: The Limits of Explanatory

Dickens at the height of his fame in 1839, as painted by Maclise. An engraving from this portrait was used as the frontispiece to Nicholas Nickleby *(National Portrait Gallery).*

Criticism," which deals with the striking contrast between how Dickens's contemporaries responded to the life and death of Nell and how later generations have rejected that story as an absurdity. Her impact on early readers was simply overwhelming, and her death sent thousands of households into a state of mourning. Francis Jeffrey, a sophisticated and sometimes severe literary critic, was so moved by the story that he likened the young novelist to Shakespeare as a writer of great tragedy. There had been "nothing so good as Nell since Cordelia," Jeffrey affirmed. Sales figures—soaring to an unprecedented 100,000 copies—indicate what a hit Dickens had made. Little Nell became Dickens's trademark, a household word in England and America and also in the Russia of Dostoevski. In the late Victorian period there occurred a distinct shift of taste whereby Nell was no longer appreciated. Even Swinburne, who idolized Dickens's writings, asserted that Nell was about as real as a child with two heads; and Oscar Wilde capped the reaction by observing that one must have a heart of stone to read the death of little Nell without laughing. In the

twentieth century it has been Wilde's verdict on Nell rather than Francis Jeffrey's that has prevailed.

A once-familiar formula for achieving success with novel readers was: "Make 'em laugh; make 'em shudder; make 'em cry." Dickens's first novel fitted the first category, and his second fitted the second. *The Old Curiosity Shop*, his fourth novel, is best known for fitting the "cry" category, and because of what seems today to be an ineffective use of pathos in this early novel, its other qualities have tended to be overlooked. This neglect is to be regretted, for Little Nell is not the only character in *The Old Curiosity Shop*. Indeed, Nell's situation leads to her being connected with some of the most colorful characters ever created by Dickens. At the age of fourteen, she discovers that her grandfather, keeper of the Old Curiosity Shop in London, has become a maniacal gambler. In order to get him away from the moneylenders who have him in their power, the girl persuades the old man to join her on a journey on foot through the English countryside. Such a journey, as in *Nicholas Nickleby*, leads to encounters with all sorts of characters on the road, such as Mrs. Jarley, the owner of a traveling waxworks show. Nell works for Mrs. Jarley for a time before becoming ill and dying in a remote hamlet, where her repentant grandfather soon follows her into his own grave. Even more memorable than the characters encountered on the road are the persons associated with Nell and her grandfather back in London. The chief moneylender, Daniel Quilp, is a dwarf with the head of a giant, a combination of prankster and villain, a creature who participates in some haunting scenes of terror and fun. Quilp's gouging of his victims is aided by the legal research of his lawyer, Sampson Brass, and Sampson's awesome sister, Sally—these three make a striking trio of gargoyles. In a different vein, there is the song-singing Dick Swiveller, a law clerk who works in the offices of the Brasses. Dick and his illiterate companion, a servant girl he calls "The Marchioness," provide a combination of fun with tender affection. The endearing scenes between these two outcasts show how beautifully Dickens can handle tender relations when he avoids the heavy mawkishness that mars his accounts of the affectionate nature of Little Nell.

His fifth novel, *Barnaby Rudge*, again demonstrates his versatility. In it he tries his hand at a historical novel (his other venture in this vein would be *A Tale of Two Cities* almost twenty years later). *Barnaby Rudge* is also a murder mystery, the murderer being a former servant named Rudge, who had been employed at an estate in the country. His son, Barnaby, is a picturesque half-wit, devoted to his mother and to a pet raven named Grip. During the Gordon Riots of 1780, a central incident in the novel, Barnaby is induced to join one of the mobs in London which burned and pillaged the houses and property of Roman Catholic citizens. For his part in the rioting Barnaby is sentenced to death, although he is finally granted a reprieve. This story of civic anarchy had a special appeal for Dickens's contemporaries because of its relevance to political and economic conditions in England during the 1840s. A severe economic depression during the "Hungry Forties," together with the spread of the radical Chartist movement, inspired among the ruling classes a dread of violent rioting. *Barnaby Rudge* was thus a topical novel and fared well. In recent decades it has not continued to do so. In 1970, for example, a survey was made of publishers in the United States and England to discover the sales figures for Dickens's novels: *Barnaby Rudge* was at the bottom of the list of fifteen novels in both countries. Nevertheless, a few critics have made high claims for it: Angus Wilson's opinion is that it represents "the turning point in Dickens's growth from an extraordinary to a great novelist." Wilson's comment also dates from 1970, and perhaps this novel will be treated to fresh reappraisals in future decades.

Mention needs to be made of the distinctive way in which *Barnaby Rudge* was published. Like *The Old Curiosity Shop*, it appeared in weekly installments in *Master Humphrey's Clock*, a special kind of periodical that Dickens had launched in April 1840. Early in the previous year he had given up being editor of *Bentley's Miscellany*, but the urge to run a periodical remained with him and, if done successfully, would—he hoped—enable him to take a rest from writing novels. The rest, however, was very short-lived. His original aim with *Master Humphrey's Clock* had been to feature assorted sketches, essays, and episodes, rather than to provide another full-length novel; it was to be somewhat in the vein of Addison's *Spectator* papers—much beloved by Dickens. But the scheme did not find favor with the public, and Dickens found himself back at his novelist's desk. His hoped-for rest from the labors of novel writing had to be postponed until January 1842, when he and Kate sailed to America, leaving their children with friends. For the next five months, the only writings he would turn out were letters home to friends and family.

After his tour of America, Dickens claimed that he had traveled some 10,000 miles. The exaggeration was pardonable, for he and Kate did cover a lot of territory. After landing in Boston, they spent considerable time on the eastern seaboard in New York, Philadelphia, and Washington, followed by a brief excursion into the slave states ending at Richmond, Virginia. More adventurously, they traveled west by riverboat from Pittsburgh to Saint Louis, where they saw a prairie. The return route included crossing Ohio by coach, a visit to Toronto and Montreal, and back to New York via Lake Champlain. What Dickens was seeking was a rest from novel writing and also, presumably, some materials for a travel book to be written at a later date. He did not come to America to lecture or, as he did in 1868, to offer paid public readings. In 1842 he spoke at only a few banquets, and such performances were not for pay. On this first visit he came simply to see and to be seen.

TABLEAUX VIVANS.

BOZ BALL.

February 14th, 1842.

ORDER OF THE DANCES AND TABLEAUX VIVANS.

1.—GRAND MARCH.

2.—TABLEAU VIVANT—"Mrs. Leo Hunter's dress *déjeûné*."

" ' Is it possible that I have really the gratification of beholding Mr. Pickwick himself?' ejaculated Mrs. Leo Hunter. 'No other, ma'am,' replied Mr. Pickwick, bowing very low. 'Permit me to introduce my friends—Mr. Tupman—Mr. Winkle—Mr. Snodgrass—to the authoress of the 'expiring frog.'"—*Pickwick Papers.*

3.—AMELIE QUADRILLE.

4.—TABLEAU VIVANT—" The middle-aged lady in the double-bedded room."

"The only way in which Mr. Pickwick could catch a glimpse of his mysterious visiter, with the least danger of being seen himself, was by creeping on to a bed, and peeping out from between the curtains on the opposite side. To this manœuvre he accordingly resorted.— Keeping the curtains carefully closed with his hand, so that nothing more of him could be seen than his face and night-cap, and putting on his spectacles, he mustered up courage, and looked out.— Mr. Pickwick almost fainted with horror and dismay. Standing before the dressing-glass, was a middle-aged lady in yellow curl-papers, busily engaged in brushing what ladies call their 'back hair.' It was quite clear that she contemplated remaining there for the night; for she brought a rush-light and shade with her, which, with praiseworthy precaution against fire, she had stationed in a basin on the floor, where it was glimmering away, like a gigantic lighthouse in a particularly small piece of water.'

5.—QUADRILLE WALTZ—selections.

6.—TABLEAU VIVANT—" Mrs. Bardell faints in Mr. Pickwick's arms."

" ' Oh, you kind, good, playful dear,' said Mrs. Bardell, and without more ado she rose from her chair and flung her arms round Mr. Pickwick's neck, with a cataract of tears and a chorus of sobs. 'Bless my soul !' cried the astonished Mr. Pickwick. 'Mrs. Bardell, my good woman—dear me—what a situation—pray, consider.—Mrs. Bardell, don't—if any body should come !—' —' Oh! let them come,' exclaimed Mrs. Bardell, frantically ; 'I'll never leave you— dear, kind, good soul.' And with these words, Mrs. Bardell clung the tighter. 'Mercy upon me,' said Mr. Pickwick, struggling violently ; ' I hear somebody coming up the stairs. Don't—don't, there's a good creature don't !' But entreaty and remonstrance were alike unavailing ; for Mrs. Bardell had fainted in Mr. Pickwick's arms ; and before he could gain time to deposit her in a chair, Master Bardell entered the room, ushering in Mr. Tupman, Mr. Winkle and Mr. Snodgrass."

Part of the program for the Boz Ball given in Dickens's honor in New York during his first visit to America (Humanities Research Center, University of Texas)

His reactions to the American scene changed dramatically during these five months. In January and February he was as enthusiastic about America as Americans were enthusiastic about him. By June he was almost totally disillusioned. Because his two books about America were written after disillusionment had set in, they do not give a reliable account of the change in his opinions. The most effective way of following what happened is to read Dickens's letters and to watch a love match gradually turning sour. When he arrived in Boston he was an ardent pro-American, full of great expectations. Politically, Dickens is always hard to categorize, but at this stage he could be described as a Liberal-Radical, impatient with the whole English establishment of aristocratic privilege. In a letter he speaks of the "swine-headed" obstinacy of George III and notes how lucky Americans are to live in a "kingless country freed from the shackles of class rule." A self-made man, Dickens rejoiced to be in a country in which the self-made man seemed to be king. The New York *Herald* responded by asserting: "Dickens's mind is American—his soul is republican—his heart is democratic." But within two months the honeymoon was over, and Dickens's letters are full of laments about the failure of the American experiment. Slavery appalled him, and so did Congress: Washington, he said, is where one encounters "slavery, spittoons, and senators." Above all, American newspapers appalled him. In an early speech, he had ventured to make a reasonable plea for international copyright, whereupon many newspapers set about attacking him viciously. Upon reading such "unmanly" attacks Dickens commented: "I have never in my life been so shocked and disgusted." Despite his enjoyment of hospitality and many friendly encounters (his closest friendship was with Cornelius Felton, a professor of classics at Harvard), Dickens's overall response to America was one of keen disappointment. On the ship from New York back to England he encountered some steerage passengers who had tried living in America and had found the environment hostile. "They had gone out to New York," Dickens says, "expecting to find its streets paved with gold; and had found them paved with very hard and very real stones." Metaphorically at least, Dickens's own experience during his five-month visit resembled the experiences of these returning immigrants.

Dickens landed in England on 29 June 1842. After six months of vacation he was eager to resume his writing schedule. Following a happy reunion with children and friends in London, the family moved to Broadstairs for the summer. This "little fishing town on the sea coast," as Dickens described it in a letter, had become since 1837 a favorite summer locality in which to rent a house for himself and his family. Ideal working conditions were combined at Broadstairs with the relaxations of long walks and sea bathing. Here he began work on his two-volume travel book *American Notes for General Circulation*, which he completed in a burst of speed and published in October 1842. The book sold well and was usually reviewed with approval. Thomas Hood observed that the work would please any readers who could be "content with good sense, good feeling, good fun, and good writing." Nothing in the book, he said, had been "set down in malice." This verdict might be generally shared by later readers. Knowing from his letters how critical he had eventually become about America, one can watch his efforts to tone down his disappointment and to be fair. About the American newspapers, however, there was no pulling of punches, and with good cause. On 11 August there appeared on the front page of a New York paper a forged letter purportedly written by Dickens consisting of diatribes against his American hosts, and many Americans were taken in by it. The effect of this scurrilous trick was to give edge to Dickens's attacks on American journalism in the *American Notes*. The press in America responded predictably to Dickens's criticisms, as did some private individuals. Most of Dickens's American admirers, however, accepted the book as a fair sketch, although many of them would not accept what he was to say about America in his next novel, *The Life and Adventures of Martin Chuzzlewit*.

Martin Chuzzlewit is the first novel by Dickens that is unified by a theme, although this unification is only loosely sustained. Its theme is selfishness. As originally conceived, the novel would confine its examples of selfishness to the English scene. The young protagonist, Martin, suffers from a mild infection of selfishness, but he is finally cured of it and thereby reaps his reward by becoming heir to his Grandfather Chuzzlewit's fortune. Other characters infected with selfishness are represented as incurable. The most striking of these are Seth Pecksniff and Jonas Chuzzlewit. Pecksniff professes to be a teacher of architecture (Martin is one of his students for a time), but in this role, as in all others, he is a colorful and eloquent fraud, the arch-embodiment of the hypocrite—and also, it must be added, a great comic creation. Jonas Chuzzlewit is much less a comic figure. A greedy man of business who murders his father, Jonas has as his motto: "Do other men, for they would do you." Less clearly

Maclise's sketch of Dickens reading The Chimes *to his friends at John Forster's house in London, December 1844 (Dickens Fellowship)*

allied to the theme is a gin-drinking nurse, the immortal Mrs. Gamp, who fulfills her need for praise by inventing an imaginary spokesman, Mrs. Harris, whom she quotes with pleasurable relish. Her praises are also voiced by the undertaker, Mr. Mould, who observes that Mrs. Gamp is the sort of woman one would bury for nothing, and do it neatly, too.

Although Mrs. Gamp and Pecksniff are two of Dickens's most memorable creations, the novel in which they appear was not well received. Some years earlier a reviewer had said of the author of *The Pickwick Papers* that "he has risen like a rocket, and will come down like the stick." Not until this sixth novel, however, did the prediction seem to come true. Sales of the early installments were alarmingly poor, and reviews were alarmingly hostile. In an effort to give his failing novel a turnaround with his public, Dickens hit upon a scheme to have his protagonist seek his fortune in America, where further exhibits of selfishness would be abundantly available. The American scenes in *Martin Chuzzlewit* are open-stopped satire, beginning with Martin's arrival in America and encounter with the shouting newsboys: "Here's this morning's New York Sewer! Here's this morning's New York Stabber! . . . Here's the New York Keyhole Reporter!" The scenes of Martin in the swampy land development called Eden bring to mind Gulliver among the

Yahoos. But however powerful as satire, even these American episodes did not generate satisfaction with the work on the part of the English reading public; and in America, as Carlyle said in his picturesque vein: "All Yankee-Doodle-Dum blew up like one universal soda-bottle."

In the midst of these discouragements in 1843, Dickens found a way to restore his sagging self-confidence. Instead of beginning another novel, he tried his hand at a short fable also dealing, like *Martin Chuzzlewit*, with the theme of selfishness. It was the first and best of his Christmas books, *A Christmas Carol*, which caught on at once and has become his most widely known piece of writing. It illustrates most effectively his theory that a Christmas fable should exhibit what he called "fancy" in ways that would be inappropriate in the more realistic world of a long novel. These fanciful ways include the three memorable ghosts who show Scrooge the past, present, and future.

Despite the reassurance provided by the reception of his *Christmas Carol*, Dickens was ill at ease about his finances. To increase his income, he shifted to a new firm, Bradbury and Evans, who promised him more profitable contracts. But more drastic measures were required to enable him to make up for the various drains upon his earnings. One of these drains involved looking after his parents: his father, an inveterate sponger, had run up heavy debts while Dickens was in America. One of John Dickens's letters seeking a loan from Charles's bankers at this time glitters with Micawber-like flourishes: "Contemporaneous events place me in a difficulty which without some anticipatory pecuniary effort I cannot extricate myself from." The extricating was later to be performed, of course, by his son. More significant expenditures were called for by Dickens's household of wife and five children, a household recently enlarged by the addition of Kate's sixteen-year-old sister, Georgina Hogarth (1827-1917). At times Georgina reminded him strongly of Mary Hogarth, then dead for seven years—"her spirit shines out in this sister," he wrote. But Georgina was not to suffer Mary's fate; she was a member of his household and his intimate companion until his death. "Aunt Georgy," as she was called by the children, who adored her, soon became a crucially important member of the family, reliable and energetic in ways her indolent (and frequently pregnant) sister Kate seemed unable to manage. But she, like all members of the household, needed to be provided for, and one efficient way of doing so, in Dickens's view, was to sublet his London house and to move his "whole menagerie" to the

Continent for a year's residence, where living expenses would be less than half what they were in England. In July 1844, they settled in Genoa, traveling there via Paris and Marseilles. This year in Italy was devoted primarily to sight-seeing and traveling. Eventually, it would provide materials for his second book of travel, *Pictures from Italy*, published in May 1846. On the whole, it was a period of rest for Dickens. His only significant writing was his second Christmas book, *The Chimes* (1845), a short fable relating to the "Condition of England Question" with emphasis upon the inhumanity of Utilitarian theories of social and economic relationships. In November, he returned by himself to London in order to try out the story by reading it aloud to a group of his friends, who were overwhelmed by his performance.

In July 1845, the whole family returned to England. During the next eleven months, Dickens continued to abstain from writing novels; instead, he completed his Italian travel book and also his third Christmas story, *The Cricket on the Hearth* (1846). Much of his time was taken up with other pursuits. In October he accepted the editorship of a newly founded liberal newspaper, the *Daily News*.

*Tavistock House, Bloomsbury, Dickens's home
from 1851 until 1858*

An illustration by "Phiz" for Bleak House

Hardly had the paper begun publication in January 1846 when Dickens resigned from the editorship, having discovered that he was temperamentally unsuited for the position. Much more successful were his ventures into amateur acting. In 1845 he and a group of friends successfully produced Ben Jonson's *Every Man in his Humour* with Dickens playing Bobadil, as well as being director and stage manager. Dickens reveled in this chance to act before an audience, and for the rest of his life he welcomed opportunities to throw himself into performing in farces and tragedies.

In the summer of 1846, Dickens again moved his whole family to the Continent, this time to Switzerland. One of the worst of his Christmas stories, *The Battle of Life* (1846), was written during this period, and also one of his better novels, *Dombey and Son* (1846-1848). There is a noteworthy gap of four years between his launching of this novel and the start of his previous novel, *Martin Chuzzlewit*. His pace of writing was thus strikingly different from the sprawling productivity of his earlier years, and this restraint affected the quality of his art as a novelist. Philip Collins notes that there is today a "critical consensus" that *Dombey and Son* is Dickens's

"first mature masterpiece." It is also the first of his novels in which the action occurs at about the same date as when it was published, rather than being set in earlier decades: in *Dombey and Son* the characters travel by railroad rather than by stagecoach. Indeed, as Steven Marcus states in his brilliant chapter on this novel, the railroad is one of the two "massive images" around which the story is organized, the other being the sea. Both images are associated with change—overall change in social and economic life, and, in particular, change in the life of a family, "a single and rather small family as it persists through time." The head of this family, Mr. Dombey, is a proud man of business and the widowed father of two children. The younger child, Paul, is doted upon by his father; the older child, Florence, who herself dotes on her father, is strangely resented by him and treated with an icy coldness that chills the whole household. Mr. Dombey suffers a terrible blow when little Paul dies shortly after beginning school, and a further blow when his second wife, Edith, runs away from home to have an affair with one of his employees. Finally, his family business, the House of Dombey, collapses into bankruptcy. At the end, having his eyes opened by such adversities,

Dombey learns the real value of his daughter's steady devotion to him; with her and her husband, Walter Gay, he will spend the rest of his days. Perhaps the title might more appropriately have been "Dombey and Daughter," for it is the complex relationship between Florence Dombey and her father that is the central concern of this mature novel.

The generally high regard in which the story of Mr. Dombey and his children is held by modern criticism was anticipated by its reception among its first readers. After the relative failure of *Martin Chuzzlewit*, the response to *Dombey and Son* was reassuring to Dickens. The critical reaction was generally enthusiastic, and the sales were like earlier days. In fact, after this novel, the gnawing anxieties about financial survival which had plagued him in the early 1840s were no longer a serious issue. From this time forward, to all intents and purposes, he was secure.

In April 1847, in the midst of writing *Dombey and Son*, he had again returned to England from the Continent but this time was disinclined to write his expected Christmas story (which he postponed until 1848, when it would appear under the title *The Haunted Man and the Ghost's Bargain*, the last of these stories). Much of his energy was expended in 1847 upon a charitable project fostered by Baroness Burdett-Coutts, a wealthy heiress. The project aimed to provide a friendly shelter for prostitutes seeking rehabilitation. Urania Cottage, as the shelter was named by Dickens, also served as a refuge for other women in distress. Urania Cottage was but one of several good works participated in by Dickens in his role as responsible citizen. He was also concerned with such problems as water pollution, as in his speeches before the Metropolitan Sanitary Association in the 1850s, and with popular education, as advocated in his speeches to working-class audiences. He served as a trustee of a fund to assist retired actors, and he was a founder of the Guild of Literature and Art. Some of these causes called for unobtrusively working behind the scenes; others called for more conspicuous performances as a public speaker, and all reports indicate that Dickens was a superb speaker and an extraordinarily effective advocate. (The collection of his speeches edited by K. J. Fielding in 1960 gives some idea of his powers of persuasion.)

Despite these diversions, his principal efforts during the two remaining decades of his life were expended on the writing of novels. Following the final number of *Dombey and Son* there was a rest period of about a year before the fresh and delight-

Mrs. Maria Winter, the former Maria Beadnell, Dickens's first love and the model for Flora Finching in Little Dorrit *(Dickens Fellowship)*

ful opening number of *The Personal History of David Copperfield* was published in May 1849. It was an immediate hit, and after seven months, Dickens could report in a letter: "I think it is better liked than any of my other books." According to Edgar Johnson, it is still today "the best-loved of all Dickens' novels" and it was Dickens's own "favourite child." Part of its appeal depends on its use of the first person, an innovation in the Dickens canon, which is handled with consummate skill, especially in the scenes of David's childhood. George Orwell reports that when he first began reading this novel at the age of nine, its mental atmosphere was "so immediately intelligible" that he thought it must have been written "by a child." Also innovative, for Dickens, is that here is a true Bildungsroman; the protagonist changes and develops and learns, as contrasted with the static character of Oliver Twist. Perhaps most skillful of all is how Dickens combines personal history with imagined characters and events. The core of the novel is the autobiographical fragment about his experiences in the blacking warehouse, and in those blacking scenes of *David Copperfield* it could be said that David *is* the boy Charles. But most of the novel is not based on historical correspondence. Even in the character of the protagonist there are marked differences from that of his creator: combined with his demonstrated tenderness there was in Dickens a hard, almost ruthless streak which is omitted entirely from the character of his consistently gentle hero. This difference in character results, in turn, in a different attitude toward the exposure of the wrongs of social institutions. There is hence less crusading in this work than in most of Dickens's novels—except, perhaps, *Great Expectations*, his other first-person Bildungsroman, which also features a gentle protagonist as narrator.

David Copperfield is one of Dickens's novels that is commonly read in childhood. Among other qualities it has the virtues of a children's classic: it is memorable because of the special kind of fears it arouses, as in the scenes with Mr. Murdstone or Mr. Creakle, or even the gargoylelike menacings of Uriah Heep; it is memorable, too, for its fun. But *David Copperfield* is also a classic for adults; and while continuing to respond to its frightening parts and its wonderful humor, one may find, as George Ford suggests in an essay, upon rereading it as a grownup, that this is a sadder book than one had remembered it to be. "Dickens himself recognized its predominant tone when in later years he was looking back over his own life from the lonely pinnacle of the monumentally successful man, and asked: 'Why is it, that as with poor David, a sense comes always crushing on me now, when I fall into low spirits, as of one happiness that I have missed in life, and one friend and companion I have never made?' All the steam that rises from Mr. Micawber's delectable hot rum punch cannot obscure the nostalgic impression, in almost every chapter, of roads not taken and of doors that never opened."

If satirical exposures of institutional inadequacies were kept to the minimum in *David Copperfield*, Dickens seems to have decided to make up for his restraint when he began writing his next novel, *Bleak House*. This work seethes with discontents sometimes expressed in fiery invectives, discontents which are also prominent in others of his novels of the 1850s and 1860s: *Hard Times* (1854), *Little Dorrit*, and *Our Mutual Friend* (1864-1865). This group, anticipated by *Dombey and Son*, was labeled by Lionel Stevenson as Dickens's "Dark Period" novels, and the term seems apt. What is strange about the chronology, however, is that the 1850s and 1860s, economically and in other areas, were not a dark period, but rather a rare bright one. These were decades when the English seemed at last to have solved some of the big problems that had looked to be insoluble in the 1830s and 1840s. As the historian G. M. Young has said: "Of all the decades in our history, a wise man would choose the eighteen-fifties to be young in."

Dickens evidently would not have agreed with Young's cheerful report; he preferred to write as an angry outsider, critical of the shortcomings (as he saw them) of mid-Victorian values. Predictably, these Dark Period novels cost him some readers who felt that the attacks on institutions were misguided, unfair, and finally, tiresome. Such a reader was Fitzjames Stephen, whose irritated response to Dickens's account of the Circumlocution Office (in *Little Dorrit*) led to his writing the nastiest review of a Dickens novel ever to appear in England during Dickens's lifetime. According to Stephen, Dickens's literary fare was simply "puppy pie and stewed cat." More temperate and representative was an article of 1857 entitled "Remonstrance with Dickens," lamenting all the Dark Period novels. "We admit that Mr. Dickens has a mission," writes this critic, "but it is to make the world grin, not to recreate and rehabilitate society." Citing in particular what he calls the "wilderness" of *Little Dorrit*, he adds: "We sit down and weep when we remember thee, O *Pickwick*!" Obviously not all of Dickens's contemporaries felt likewise, for among the reading public, from *Bleak House* onward, the Dark Period novels fared well, as they have continued to do in the second half of the twentieth century. In fact, these are the novels that have been chiefly responsible for the remarkable "Dickens boom," as Hillis Miller called it, of the 1960s and after. Among this group it is *Bleak House* that seems to have been most highly regarded by modern criticism.

During the thirteen-month interval between the final number of *David Copperfield* and the great opener of *Bleak House*, Dickens had been engaged in various other activities. Most important was his effort to make a success as editor of a new weekly magazine—a success that had hitherto eluded him. This time, as both owner and editor, he made it, and handsomely. *Household Words*, founded in January 1850, flourished exceedingly, with an average sale of 40,000 copies a week. Its title page announced that it was "conducted" by Charles Dickens. What this meant was that all contributions would appear anonymously, no matter how eminent the contributor, including those by Dickens himself. "Conducted" also meant the assurance for readers that Dickens had approved the contribution, whether it was a sketch, an installment of a novel, or some journalistic report on current issues such as sewage disposal or juvenile illiteracy or the role of detectives in the expanding metropolis. In his role as citizen, as well as editor, Dickens became increasingly involved with such issues during the 1850s. In

Dickens (on the ground) acting in Wilkie Collins's play, The Frozen Deep, *as depicted in the* Illustrated London News, *17 January 1857*

1852, in fact, he was asked to run for Parliament but decided that he could do more good for the world by sticking to his journalism in *Household Words* and to his craft as a novelist in *Bleak House*. Also during this thirteen-month interval, he moved his family into a larger residence, Tavistock House, where the tenth and last of his children was born (his infant daughter, Dora, had died a few months earlier).

The narrative technique of *Bleak House* is much more experimental than that of *David Copperfield* and involves the use of two narrators. Half the book is told in the first person and is again, like *David Copperfield*, the story of one character's growing up and self-discovery—in this case the story of a girl, Esther Summerson, an illegitimate child. The other half of the novel, told in the third person, deals with lives and institutions which variously relate to Esther's story, such as what happens to her mother, Lady Dedlock, and how legal delays, enacted in the fogbound Court of Chancery, cripple the spirits and empty the pockets of generations of litigants who have been involved with the "mighty maze" of a law case known as "Jarndyce and Jarndyce." As G. K. Chesterton observes (alluding to *Hamlet*): "The whole theme is what another En-

glishman as jovial as Dickens defined shortly and finally as the law's delay. The fog of the first chapter never lifts." But *Bleak House* is not only a novel of social criticism; it is also a detective novel, perhaps the first detective novel in English. The shooting death of Mr. Tulkinghorn, a lawyer, leads to a relentless hunt for the murderer directed by a colorful detective, Inspector Bucket. Among Bucket's suspects is Esther's mother, Lady Dedlock, who, although innocent of the murder, dies from exposure and exhaustion during the pursuit and finds her resting place at the grave of her former lover, Captain Hawdon. Meanwhile, Inspector Bucket tracks down the true murderer, Hortense, a Frenchwoman who had been Lady Dedlock's maid. Esther is thereafter free to marry Alan Woodcourt, a surgeon, and to reside with him in a house that is, despite its name—"Bleak House"—a generally cheerful and happy home for her and for her family.

The closing number of *Bleak House* was written in France at a house near Boulogne that Dickens had rented for the summer. In the autumn he took a two-month vacation trip to Italy and returned to Tavistock House in time for Christmas. His plan had been not to think about writing another novel until the next summer, but special circumstances once again put him back to work at an earlier date. Late in 1853, it was noticed that the circulation of *Household Words* was for the first time slipping, and Bradbury and Evans proposed to Dickens that a rescue operation might be effected if he would bring out a new novel to appear in its pages as a weekly serial. In January he reluctantly started writing, and on 1 April 1854 the first chapter of *Hard Times* was published. Although the rescue operation worked, with the circulation of *Household Words* doubling after the novel began appearing, Dickens found that the task of writing short weekly installments was formidably difficult. He felt hemmed in; the lack of adequate space was, as he said in a letter, "crushing." As a result of this mode of publication, *Hard Times* is Dickens's shortest novel (117,000 words as compared with the 350,000 words of *Bleak House*). Its shortness may account for its having some resemblances to Dickens's fables, such as *A Christmas Carol*, in its making prominent an anti-Utilitarian moral, and even in the names of some of the characters, such as the bullying factory owner, Mr. Bounderby, or the fact-crammed school teacher, Mr. M'Choakumchild. The central drama in *Hard Times* is the conflict between the world of Mr. Gradgrind, a hardware merchant who believes in the exclusive values of fact and rational calculation, and the world of affection and imagination. The latter includes the enjoyment of poetry (which Gradgrind despises) but is more prosaically represented by the entertainments of Mr. Sleary's circus and its horse riders. Such an account unduly emphasizes the abstract aspects of *Hard Times*, for despite the prominence of its fable, its core is distinctly realistic, as was illustrated in the excellent television version of 1977 (which was shown on national networks in the United States as well as in Great Britain). This vivid and sensitive interpretation was filmed in an industrial area of the English Midlands like the town of Preston, near Manchester, which Dickens had visited to report on a strike in January 1854, and which served as the model for Coketown in his novel.

Because of its hard-hitting social criticism, *Hard Times* was a favorite for such readers as George Bernard Shaw and John Ruskin; others, such as George Gissing, found its bleakness so harsh as to make the book unreadable. A similar harshness marks Dickens's next novel, *Little Dorrit*, although the effect of it is different because of a difference in length. Dickens was forty-three years old when he began *Little Dorrit*, about the same age as his pro-

tagonist, Arthur Clennam, whose unhappiness seems to reflect his creator's unhappiness at this time. The action takes place almost thirty years earlier, but significantly the principal setting of this novel is a debtors' prison, the Marshalsea, where Dickens as a boy used to visit his imprisoned father during the blacking warehouse period of his life. That had been in 1824; the novel opens in 1826. As John Holloway said of the characters in this book, "the present is imprisoned in the past"; his statement also seems applicable to Dickens himself in 1855. For in *Little Dorrit* Dickens was looking back not only to the shameful memories of the Marshalsea days but also to the painful memories of his frustrated love for Maria Beadnell. In February 1855, Maria had written to her former admirer, and a meeting was arranged by him with the now forty-four-year-old wife and mother. Dickens was crushed with disappointment when they met, an experience which he drew upon almost literally when he described Arthur Clennam's reunion with Flora Finching, "his old passion." Not only had Flora changed physically (once a "lily" and now a "peony"), she had become a bore; everything she said was "diffuse and silly." The coyness in her manner that had allured him when she was twenty was still there but was now intolerable to him. So Clennam's "old passion," like Dickens's, "shivered and broke to pieces." For these and other reasons, *Little Dorrit* is the saddest of Dickens's novels, a quality which did not prevent its being admired by its early readers (it sold more copies than *Bleak House*) and by later critics. Two important appreciations are Lionel Trilling's classic essay and a chapter by F. R. Leavis, who discovered Dickens's greatness late in life and came to the conclusion that *Little Dorrit* is "his greatest book."

The financial rewards from *Little Dorrit* and from *Household Words* enabled Dickens, as he was finishing the novel, to realize a dream of his early boyhood. Gad's Hill Place, a beautiful eighteenth-century brick house on a hill outside of Rochester, which he had admired during walks with his father, came up for sale, and he bought it. (The owner had been one of his contributors for *Household Words*, Mrs. Lynn Linton.) It had plenty of room for guests (it is today a boarding school for girls), attractive gardens, and a surrounding landscape ideal for walks. Dickens lived there for the final ten years of his life (he sold Tavistock House in 1860). This happy realization of a boyhood dream coincided with an opposite kind of development: the gradual breaking up of his marriage, culminating in a legal separation from Kate in May 1858.

Ellen Ternan, the actress who became Dickens's mistress, around the time of their first meeting in 1857 (Enthoven Collection, Victoria and Albert Museum)

Hints of his growing dissatisfaction as a husband can be detected in his letters of the early 1850s in references to his "miserable" marriage, and in his report to Forster: "Poor Catherine and I are not made for each other, and there is no help for it." But the formal break did not occur until Dickens had met an attractive eighteen-year-old actress, Ellen Ternan, who eventually became his mistress. They first came to know each other in 1856-1857 when Dickens had once again thrown himself into amateur theatricals in order to raise funds for charities. In a new play, *The Frozen Deep*, written by his young friend Wilkie Collins, Dickens made a hit playing the leading role. This production led to Dickens's making acquaintance with a professional acting family consisting of Mrs. Ternan, a widow, and her three daughters, of whom Ellen was the youngest. Although some twenty-seven years younger than Dickens, Ellen fascinated him from the outset, and this infatuation confirmed his resolve to set Kate up in a separate establishment with Charlie, their eldest child. The rest of the children, and also Georgina Hogarth, remained with him at

Gad's Hill. According to accounts of his relationship with Ellen published during the past fifty years, Dickens was also responsible in the 1860s for a third household, having bought a residence for the Ternans in London and later at Peckham. This arrangement put more than financial strains upon Dickens, for he knew that it would be disastrous to his reputation as a writer, especially as a proponent of family and home and editor of *Household Words*, if his relationship became public knowledge. During his lifetime there were rumors, of course; at the time of the separation there was an abundance of gossip. At the Garrick Club some members were overheard by Thackeray airing a story that Dickens was having an affair with his sister-in-law. Thackeray corrected them by affirming, instead, that the affair was with an actress! Dickens became so enraged by such talk that he wrote letters to the newspapers denying all whispered reports of any amorous relations with "a young lady for whom I have great attachment and regard." His gesture of protest was certainly misguided but fortunately did not lead to any disclosures in the press. However, he came dangerously close to public exposure in the summer of 1865: returning from visiting France with Ellen and her mother, Dickens was sharing a

Kate Dickens at the time of her separation from Dickens in 1858 (Gernsheim Collection)

Gad's Hill Place, Dickens's final home, and the chalet there where he did much of his writing after 1865

train compartment with them when a serious wreck occurred, one extensively reported in the news. Afterward, the possibility of publicity must have haunted Dickens, like Banquo's ghost, for anxious months. But for the most part, this skeleton in his closet remained hidden from his public while he was alive and also for more than sixty years after his death. In the 1920s, his daughter Kate Perugini decided that the truth about her father ought to be known and reported the Ellen Ternan story that appeared in *Dickens and Daughter* by Gladys Storey in 1939. In some quarters the disclosures were dismissed as scandalmongering, but further evidence kept surfacing that seemed to substantiate them. There was even a story that Dickens had had a son by Ellen Ternan, a story most emphatically denied by dedicated Dickensians. Yet in some newly discovered papers left after her death by Gladys Storey, and published in 1980 in the *Dickensian*, there is fresh evidence that the story was probably true.

At the earlier stage, in 1858, incidents involving the Ellen Ternan story led to a quarrel between Dickens and his publishers Bradbury and Evans and to his starting a new periodical to replace

Dickens giving a reading from one of his works
(Dickens Fellowship)

Household Words. Published by Chapman and Hall, *All the Year Round* was another success with the reading public, reaching a circulation of 100,000 in the 1860s. Part of its success is attributable to Dickens's publishing in its pages two of his best-known novels: *A Tale of Two Cities* (1859) and *Great Expectations* (1861). The first of these has been one of his most popular novels, especially in the United States, where, in 1970, more copies were sold than of any other novel by Dickens. Philip Collins suggests that its popularity may be due to its shortness and to its having been "dramatized with notable success." This explanation is helpful, but it should be remarked that the popularity of *A Tale of Two Cities* may also derive simply from its being an exceptionally lively story, full of fast-paced action. Like *Barnaby Rudge* it is a historical novel set in the 1770s and 1780s in a period of riot and violence, this time the French Revolution. It was a period that had always fascinated Dickens; he once remarked that he had read Carlyle's *The French Revolution: A History* (1837) "five hundred times." In his *Tale of Two Cities*, London and Paris are linked through a relatively small cast of characters, in particular through Sydney Carton, a London lawyer who falls in love with a young Frenchwoman, Lucie Manette. Carton's love is a hopeless one, for, although talented, he is a confirmed drunkard and knows he is unworthy of his beloved. Instead she marries his look-alike, Charles Darnay, a former French aristocrat who immigrated to London before the revolution. Back in France, Darnay's family members are doomed to be guillotined if captured. Darnay nevertheless takes the risk of returning to France on a mission. As might have been predicted, he is captured there and would most certainly have suffered the fate prescribed for his family had he not been rescued by Carton, who substitutes himself for Darnay and gives up his life in order to save the husband of the woman he loves. Confronting death, Carton affirms his credo: "It is a far, far better thing that I do, than I have ever done."

Despite its popularity, *A Tale of Two Cities* has never received much serious attention from critics. On the other hand, his next novel, *Great Expectations*, has been both popular and a favorite topic for critical discussions. Many of his Victorian readers welcomed this novel for its humor; after the Dark Period novels, *Great Expectations* seemed to them a return to the good-hearted vein of *The Pickwick Papers*. Consonant with this seemingly cheerful vein was Pip's growth from "ugly duckling" into a "proud swan." As Barry Westburg noted in 1977, "The mode of consciousness that defines Pip is

A READING.   39

It was a ghastly figure to look upon. The
murderer staggering backward to the wall, and
shutting out the sight with his hand, seized
a heavy club, and struck her down. *!*   *Action*

The bright sun burst upon the crowded
city in clear and radiant glory. Through
costly-coloured glass and paper-mended window,
through cathedral dome and rotten crevice, it   *Mystery*
shed its equal ray. It lighted up the room
where the murdered woman lay. It did. He
tried to shut it out, but it would stream in.
If the sight had been a ghastly one in the
dull morning, what was it, now, in all that
brilliant light *!!!*   / *Terror to the End* /

He had not moved; he had been afraid
to stir. There had been a moan and motion
of the hand; and, with terror added to rage,
he had struck and struck again. Once he

Page of the prompt copy of one of Dickens's readings, Nicholas Nickleby at the Yorkshire School *(1868),*
with stage directions written in by Dickens (Suzannet Collection)

'expectation'—his mind is typically directed toward the future rather than toward the past"—as contrasted with David Copperfield, for example. Most critical discussions since 1950 argue that the Victorians were misled by some of its great comic scenes such as Mr. Wopsle's playing Hamlet, and also by Pip's career (the alternate endings not affecting the point). Unlike the Victorians, modern critics see *Great Expectations* as a brilliant study of guilt, another very sad book—another Dark Period novel, that is—and one of Dickens's finest in any vein. David Lean's successful screen version, first shown in 1946 and many times revived, has no doubt added to the popularity of this novel, but its critical status is so firmly based as not to require any reinforcements from the camera.

At the time of Dickens's changing his publishers, his career underwent another and more important change: in April 1858, he finally decided, after much hesitation, to start a tour during which he would do readings from his own writings, such as *A Christmas Carol* and the trial scene in *The Pickwick Papers*. At this date he was already an experienced and highly successful reader, but heretofore his performances had been to raise money for charities. Now, instead, he was starred as a professional, raising money for himself. Yet it is evident that he took

Cover of American edition of one of Dickens's readings
(Dickens House Museum)

Dickens on his second American tour in 1868
(Dickens Fellowship)

on this new career not just to earn money; he needed the direct contact with vast audiences of his readers in order to compensate for a sense of loneliness and dissatisfaction which afflicted him powerfully in these late years. The readings exhausted him (his first tour called for eighty-seven performances), but they also exhilarated him. Another result of his readings was one that Forster had predicted when he had urged Dickens not to engage in them—his productivity as novelist inevitably suffered. After finishing *Great Expectations* in the summer of 1861, he was soon launched on another season of readings, and it was three years before he started another novel, the last that he would live to complete: *Our Mutual Friend* (1864-1865). About this novel, there would be no mistaking the tone, as Victorian readers had done with the previous one. *Our Mutual Friend* is grim and bleak, with an air of darkness even more oppressive than that of *Bleak House*. What humor there is is predominantly in a satirical vein, as in the memorable dinner-party scenes at the homes of Mr. and Mrs. Podsnap and of Mr. and Mrs. Veneering. Many readers, from Dickens's generation onward, find that the creaky plot—involving the presumed death by drowning of the hero, John Harmon, and an elaborate sequence of deceptions about his hidden inheritance—makes the book hard to read. Such readers might even agree with a review by the young Henry James, who called it "the poorest of Mr. Dickens's works.... And it is poor with the poverty not of momentary embarrassment, but of permanent exhaustion." James's insights were shrewd, for it is now known that Dickens *was* exhausted while writing this novel; but a writer's state of exhaustion does not necessarily lead to a failure of his art. In fact, some critics today, who have given *Our Mutual Friend* a serious and close reading, find it to be his most impressive creation, praising it for its unified presentation of the theme of money and for its brilliant use of recurring images of dust and foul water to evoke a sense of death in modern life.

After completing *Our Mutual Friend* in November 1865, Dickens resumed his reading tours and occasionally wrote some short fictions, such as "Mrs. Lirriper's Lodgings." It was four years before he tried his hand again at a novel—the longest break between novels in his career and a marked contrast to his pace in the 1830s. Not that he was idle during the interval. In late 1867, he sailed to America for a scheduled tour of eighty readings, which netted him a vast sum of money and a further chance to bask in the warm receptions of enthusiastic audiences in New York, Boston, Baltimore, and Buffalo. (On this visit he limited his travels almost entirely to the eastern seaboard.) On 22 April 1868, he sailed for home. It had been a triumphant visit, and the bad feelings of the *Martin Chuzzlewit* phase of his relations with America had been erased after the passing of twenty-six eventful years. The triumph had, however, been a costly one. Most of the readings had been performed when Dickens was ill with colds and an assortment of other ailments. His determination to continue to meet his engagements, instead of retiring to a sickbed, impressed those of his friends who knew what he was going through but also impressed others that his behavior was suicidal. Back in England, he continued to drive himself. In October he began a projected series of a hundred readings, of which he had completed eighty-six by April 1869. In this series he introduced for the first time the scene of Nancy's

Dickens reading to his daughters Mary and Kate at Gad's Hill (Dickens Fellowship)

murder in *Oliver Twist*. His final series of readings, early in 1870, ended in March with a brief farewell: "From these garish lights I vanish now for evermore."

Some months earlier he had started writing *The Mystery of Edwin Drood*, which was scheduled to be published in twelve monthly numbers, of which he completed six. The early numbers, starting in April 1870, had a sale of 50,000 copies, "outstripping," as he was pleased to note, "every one of its predecessors." Not much significant criticism has been written about *The Mystery of Edwin Drood*: as Philip Collins noted wittily in 1978, "Recent Dickens critics seem to have worn out their brains by the time they arrive at 1870." This is not to say that little has been written about this tantalizing fragment: there are shelfloads of books with *The Mystery of Edwin Drood* as their subject, but they are not critical studies; instead, they are attempts to solve the mystery by conjecture or by simply inventing six more books of the story as Dickens might have written them. (One of the more successful attempts in the latter mode was by Leon Garfield in 1981.) Like Keats's urn, the mystery of Drood doth tease us out

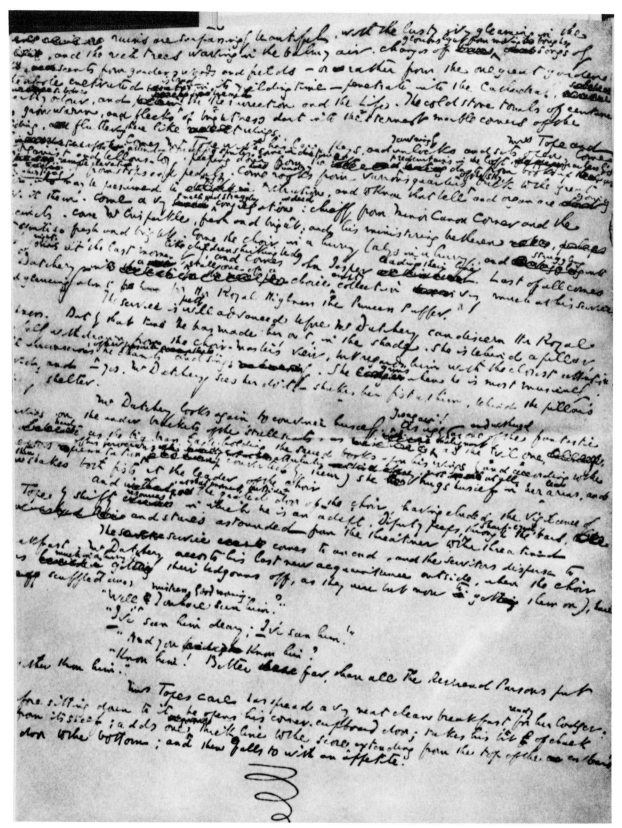

Page from the manuscript for The Mystery of Edwin Drood, *the last page Dickens ever wrote*
(Forster Collection, Victoria and Albert Museum)

of thought, for what is involved is not just the mystery of what happened to Edwin Drood and his uncle but the mystery of how the ailing novelist achieved in this book some of the most extraordinary stylistic feats of his whole career. Graham Greene spoke once of Dickens's "secret prose" with its "music of memory" in *David Copperfield*, and when Dickens writes of time passing and the crumbling cathedral of Cloisterham in *The Mystery of Edwin Drood*, he most tellingly illustrates Greene's comments about his stylistic wizardry.

The last completed page of *The Mystery of Edwin Drood* was written at Gad's Hill on the afternoon of 8 June 1870. That evening Dickens was stricken with an aneurysm in the brain and died the following day without regaining consciousness. Even though he had wanted to be buried in the Rochester area which was so deeply associated with both his lost childhood and with recent triumphs and losses, his wish had to be overruled in favor of Westminster Abbey. On 14 June, in a private ceremony, he was buried in Poet's Corner, which the *Times* described on this occasion as "the peculiar resting place of English literary genius."

Letters:

The Letters of Charles Dickens, Pilgrim Edition, edited by Madeline House, Graham Storey, and Kathleen Tillotson (12 volumes projected, Oxford: Clarendon Press, 1965-   ).

Biographies:

John Forster, *The Life of Dickens* (2 volumes, New York: Scribners, 1905);

Edgar Johnson, *Dickens: His Tragedy and Triumph* (2 volumes, New York: Simon & Schuster, 1952; 1 volume, revised and abridged, New York: Viking, 1977);

Norman MacKenzie and Jeanne MacKenzie, *Dickens: A Life* (New York: Oxford University Press, 1979).

References:

Arthur Clayborough, *The Grotesque in English Literature* (Oxford: Clarendon Press, 1965);

Philip Collins, "Charles Dickens," in *Victorian Fiction: A Second Guide to Research*, edited by George H. Ford (New York: Modern Language Association, 1978), pp. 34-114;

Collins, ed., *Charles Dickens: The Public Readings* (Oxford: Clarendon Press, 1975);

Collins, ed., *Dickens: The Critical Heritage* (London: Routledge & Kegan Paul, 1971);

H. M. Daleski, *Dickens and the Art of Analogy* (New

York: Schocken, 1971);

K. J. Fielding, *Charles Dickens* (London: Longmans, Green, 1963);

George H. Ford, *Dickens and His Readers* (Princeton, N.J.: Princeton University Press, 1955);

Ford and Lauriat Lane, Jr., eds., *The Dickens Critics* (Ithaca, N.Y.: Cornell University Press, 1961);

Leon Garfield, *The Mystery of Edwin Drood* (New York: Pantheon, 1981);

John Greaves, *Dickens at Doughty Street* (London: Hamish Hamilton, 1975);

John Gross and Gabriel Pearson, eds., *Dickens and the Twentieth Century* (London: Routledge & Kegan Paul, 1962);

Alfred Harbage, *A Kind of Power: The Dickens-Shakespeare Analogy* (Philadelphia: American Philosophical Society, 1975);

Barbara Hardy, *The Moral Art of Dickens* (New York: Oxford University Press, 1970);

Humphry House, *The Dickens World* (London: Oxford University Press, 1941);

James R. Kincaid, *Dickens and The Rhetoric of Laughter* (Oxford: Clarendon Press, 1972);

Mark Lambert, *Dickens and the Suspended Quotation* (New Haven: Yale University Press, 1981);

F. R. Leavis and Q. D. Leavis, *Dickens the Novelist* (London: Chatto & Windus, 1970);

Steven Marcus, *Dickens from Pickwick to Dombey* (New York: Simon & Schuster, 1965);

Sylvère Monod, *Dickens the Novelist* (Norman: University of Oklahoma Press, 1967);

Harland S. Nelson, *Charles Dickens* (Boston: Twayne, 1981);

Ada Nisbet, "Charles Dickens," in *Victorian Fiction: A Guide to Research*, edited by Lionel Stevenson (Cambridge: Harvard University Press, 1964), pp. 44-153;

Nisbet and Blake Nevins, eds., *Dickens Centennial Essays* (Berkeley: University of California Press, 1971);

Robert Patten, *Dickens and His Publishers* (Oxford: Clarendon Press, 1979);

Michael Slater, *Dickens and Women* (London: Dent, 1983);

Slater, ed., *Dickens 1970* (London: Chapman & Hall, 1970);

Taylor Stoehr, *Dickens: The Dreamer's Stance* (Ithaca, N.Y.: Cornell University Press, 1965);

Harry Stone, *Dickens and the Invisible World* (Bloomington: Indiana University Press, 1979);

Lionel Trilling, *The Opposing Self: Nine Essays in Criticism* (New York: Viking, 1955), pp. 50-65;

Alexander Welsh, *The City of Dickens* (Oxford:

Clarendon Press, 1971);

Barry Westburg, *The Confessional Fictions of Charles Dickens* (DeKalb: Northern Illinois University Press, 1977);

Angus Wilson, *The World of Charles Dickens* (New York: Viking, 1970).

Papers:

Most of the surviving manuscripts of Dickens's novels are in the Forster Collection at the Victoria and Albert Museum, London. In the Pierpont Morgan Library in New York are the manuscripts of *Our Mutual Friend* and of several of the Christmas books as well as some 1,360 autograph letters by Dickens.

The Dickens House (48 Doughty Street, London) also has a valuable collection of letters which was augmented in 1971 by assorted manuscripts from the great collection of the Comte de Suzannet. The Berg Collection of the New York Public Library has 500 letters and several important manuscripts, including a notebook used by Dickens when planning his novels. Manuscripts of Dickens's sketches and essays are included in collections at Yale University Library, the Huntington Library (San Marino, California), and the Free Library of Philadelphia (which also has a collection of more than a thousand of Dickens's letters).

Benjamin Disraeli

Daniel R. Schwarz
Cornell University

BIRTH: London, 21 December 1804, to Isaac and Maria Basevi D'Israeli.

MARRIAGE: 28 August 1838 to Mary Anne Wyndham Lewis.

AWARDS AND HONORS: Honorary Doctorate of Civil Law, Oxford University, 1853; created earl of Beaconsfield, 1876; made Knight of the Order of the Garter, 1878.

DEATH: London, 19 April 1881.

SELECTED BOOKS: *An Inquiry into the Plans, Progress, and Policy of American Mining Companies* (London: Murray, 1825);

Lawyers and Legislators; or, Notes on the American Mining Companies (London: Murray, 1825);

Vivian Grey (5 volumes, London: Colburn, 1826-1827; 1 volume, New York: Collins & Hannay, Duyckinck, 1826);

The Voyage of Captain Popanilla, by the Author of "Vivian Grey" (London: Colburn, 1828; Philadelphia: Carey, Lea & Carey, 1828);

The Young Duke (3 volumes, London: Colburn & Bentley, 1831; New York: Harper, 1831);

Contarini Fleming: A Psychological Autobiography (4 volumes, London: Murray, 1832; 2 volumes, New York: Harper, 1832);

The Wondrous Tale of Alroy and the Rise of Iskander (3 volumes, London: Saunders & Otley, 1832; 2 volumes, Philadelphia: Carey, Lea & Blanchard, 1833);

England and France; or, A Cure for the Ministerial Gallomania (London: Murray, 1832);

What Is He? (London: Ridgway, 1833);

The Revolutionary Epick (2 volumes, London: Moxon, 1834);

A Year at Hartlebury; or, The Election, by Disraeli and Sarah D'Israeli as Cherry and Fair Star (London: Saunders & Otley, 1834);

The Crisis Examined (London: Saunders & Otley, 1834);

Vindication of the English Constitution in a Letter to a Noble and Learned Lord (London: Saunders & Otley, 1835);

The Letters of Runnymede, The Spirit of Whiggism (London: Macrone, 1836);

Henrietta Temple: A Love Story (3 volumes, London: Colburn, 1836; 1 volume, Philadelphia: Carey & Hart, 1837);

Venetia; or, The Poet's Daughter (3 volumes, London: Colburn, 1837; 2 volumes, Philadelphia: Carey & Hart, 1837);

The Tragedy of Count Alarcos, by the Author of "Vivian Grey" (London: Colburn, 1839);

(Royal Archives)

Coningsby; or, The New Generation (3 volumes, London: Colburn, 1844; 1 volume, New York: Colyer, 1844);

Sybil; or, The Two Nations (3 volumes, London: Colburn, 1845; 1 volume, Philadelphia: Carey & Hart, 1845);

The Speech of Mr. Disraeli in the House of Commons, Friday, 15th May, 1846 (London: Olliver, 1846);

Tancred; or, The New Crusade (3 volumes, London: Colburn, 1847; 1 volume, Philadelphia: Carey & Hart, 1847);

England and Denmark: Speech in the House of Commons 19 April 1848 (London: Ridgway, 1848);

The Parliament and the Government: Speech on the Labours of the Session, August 30 1848 (London: Painter, 1848);

The New Parliamentary Reform: Speech in the House of Commons, Tuesday June 20 1848 (London: Painter, 1848);

Financial Policy: Speech in the House of Commons, June 30 1851 (London: Lewis, 1851);

Lord George Bentinck: A Political Biography (London: Colburn, 1851; New York: Routledge, 1858);

Parliamentary Reform, House of Commons 25 March 1852 (London: Olliver, 1852);

Ixion in Heaven; The Infernal Marriage; Popanilla; Count Alarcos (London: Bryce, 1853; New York: Seaside Library, 1881);

Parliamentary Reform, House of Commons February 28 1859 (London: Routledge, Warne & Routledge, 1859);

Public Expenditure: Speech in the House of Commons June 3 1862 (London: Hardwicke, 1862);

Mr. Gladstone's Finance 1853-62 (London: Saunders & Otley, 1862);

Church Policy: Speech to the Oxford Diocesan Society, October 30 1862 (London: Rivingtons, 1862);

Speech at a Public Meeting of the Oxford Diocesan Society for the Augmentation of Small Livings in the Sheldonian Theatre November 25 1864 (London: Rivingtons, 1864);

"Church and Queen": Five Speeches 1860-4, Edited with a Preface by a Member of the University of Oxford (London: Palmer, 1865);

Two Speeches in the City of Edinburgh on 29 and 30 October 1867 (Edinburgh & London: Blackwood, 1867);

Speeches on Parliamentary Reform 1848-1866, edited by M. Corry (London: Longmans, 1867);

The Prime Minister on Church and State: Speech at the Hall of the Merchant Taylors Company, June 17 1868 (London: Hunt, 1868);

Speeches on the Conservative Policy of the Last Thirty Years, edited by J. F. Bulley (London: Hotten, 1870);

Lothair (3 volumes, London: Longmans, Green, 1870; 1 volume, New York: Appleton, 1870);

Mr. Osborne Morgan's Burials Bill: Speech by Disraeli Moving the Rejection, House of Commons, March 26 1873 (London: Church Defence Institution, 1873);

Inaugural Address Delivered to the University of Glasgow, November 19 1873 (London: Longmans, Green, 1873);

Speech at Aylesbury, 20 September 1876 (London: Holmes Library, 1876);

Endymion, by the Author of "Lothair" (3 volumes, London: Longmans, Green, 1880; 1 volume, New York: Appleton, 1880);

Selected Speeches, edited by T. E. Kebbel (2 volumes, London: Longmans, Green, 1882);

Tales and Sketches, edited by J. L. Robertson (London: Paterson, 1891);

Rumpal Stilts Kin: A Dramatic Spectacle, by "B. D." and "W. G. M.," by Disraeli and W. G. Meredith, edited by M. Sadleir (Glasgow: Maclehose, 1952).

COLLECTIONS: *Hughenden Edition of the Novels and Tales* (11 volumes, London: Longmans, Green, 1881);

The Works of Benjamin Disraeli, Earl of Beaconsfield, Embracing Novels, Romances, Plays, Poems, Biography, Short Stories, and Great Speeches, edited by E. Gosse (20 volumes, London: Dunne, 1904-1905);

The Bradenham Edition of the Novels and Tales of Benjamin Disraeli, 1st Earl of Beaconsfield, edited by P. Guedella, 12 volumes (London: Davies, 1926-1927; New York: Knopf, 1927).

Disraeli's novels merit renewed attention not only because of their wit, insight, breadth, and vision but because they present strikingly original imagined worlds. Like the other major Victorian novelists, Disraeli is a deft psychologist and a student of the manners and mores of his time; moreover, his political career gives his last five novels a unique perspective. Taken as a whole, Disraeli's novels are a considerable artistic achievement and, if quality, originality, and output are all taken into account, need only yield to the works of Austen, Dickens, Thackeray, Eliot, Trollope, Hardy, and maybe Scott among nineteenth-century novelists.

Disraeli's literary career spans over a half century, from 1826 to 1880. He published the first volumes of *Vivian Grey* (1826-1827) when Scott, Blake, Wordsworth, and Coleridge were still alive and before any of the major Victorians, except Carlyle, were published. He concluded his career in 1880, a year when Dickens and Thackeray were dead and George Eliot was to die; Hardy had already published *Far From the Madding Crowd* (1874) and *The Return of the Native* (1878). Disraeli reveals something about the history of taste in the nineteenth century. His early novels—such as *Vivian Grey*—met the middle-class desire for revelations of aristocratic life, for romances about bizarre characters in strange lands, and for extreme behavior on the part of willful egoists posing as latter-day Byrons. As an outsider, as a man who savored his own feelings and sought unusual sensations, the youthful Disraeli saw himself as an heir to Byron and Shelley. But in the later 1830s, Disraeli, like Dickens, responded to audiences who wanted sentiment and sweetness; in *Henrietta Temple* (1837) Disraeli wrote about love between virginal young women and idealistic young men whose motives are temporarily misunderstood because of circum-

stances beyond their control. Even when he wrote of Byron and Shelley in *Venetia* (1837), he threw the mantle of Victorian respectability over them in spite of his empathy with their unconventionality. In the 1840s, the Young England trilogy—*Coningsby* (1844), *Sybil* (1845), and *Tancred* (1847)—met the demand for serious novels that addressed major moral and political ideas. In *Lothair* (1870) he drew upon the public's fascination—rekindled by the conversion of the marquess of Bute—with the journey from Anglicanism to Roman Catholicism, while in *Endymion* (1880) he responded to the interest in character psychology created by Browning, Eliot, and Hardy, which was part of an inward turning and questioning as the Victorian era passed its high tide of confidence. Throughout his career his fiction fulfilled the nineteenth-century fascination with heroic men; this fascination reflected a need for larger-than-life personalities in an age of uncertainty.

In all his novels Disraeli reveled in the infinite variety of human personality and enjoyed setting major and minor characters in motion in a dramatic situation for the sheer joy of hypothesizing how they would behave. He particularly admired independent people who, like himself, had dashing, dynamic, and idiosyncratic personalities. He wished to experience every conceivable emotion and play every possible role. Thus, just as he tested and discarded a number of political positions as he sought his public role, so as an artist he experimented with a variety of styles and wrote in a multitude of genres. Even when he was not entirely successful, as in the union of prose and poetry in *The Wondrous Tale of Alroy* (1832), one is not sorry he made the attempt. He wrote Silver-Fork or "society" novels (*Vivian Grey*, *The Young Duke*, 1831); Bildungsromane, or novels of individual development (*Coningsby* and *Lothair*); a satiric imaginary voyage (*The Voyage of Captain Popanilla*, 1828); a Künstlerroman, or novel about the development of an artist (*Contarini Fleming: A Psychological Autobiography*, 1832); a novel of purpose (*Sybil*, 1845); a historical romance (*Alroy*); and a historical reminiscence (*Endymion*). In *Coningsby* and *Sybil*, he virtually invented the genre of the political novel in English.

Benjamin Disraeli was born on 21 December 1804 in London to a Sephardic Jewish family. He was one of five children, four of whom survived. His father was a successful if historically minor literary figure whose *Curiosities of Literature* (1791-1834), a collection of anecdotes and character sketches in six volumes, is his best-known work. Benjamin's father had him baptized in the Church of England in 1817.

Disraeli's parents, Isaac and Maria D'Israeli

At that point, Disraeli went to a middle-class secondary school, and his unhappy experience there formed some of the background and subject matter of *Vivian Grey*. After about a year of private education under the auspices of his father, he became a clerk in a law firm with which he remained until 1825. In that year, Disraeli suffered a severe financial setback due to speculations that turned out badly, and it was not until very late in his life that he was able to put recurring financial embarrassments behind him.

Disraeli's novels played a crucial role in creating his character and personality. This is especially true of his first four—*Vivian Grey*, *The Young Duke*, *Contarini Fleming*, and *The Wondrous Tale of Alroy*. An 1833 entry in Disraeli's diary shows that the novels compensate for his failure to excel even as they protest against accepted English conventions and manners: "The world calls me 'conceited'—The world is in error. I trace all the blunders of my life to sacrificing my own opinion to that of others. When I was considered very conceited *indeed*, I was nervous, and had self-confidence only by fits. I intend in future to act entirely from my own impulse. I have an unerring instinct. I can read characters at a glance; few men can deceive me. My mind is a continental mind. It is a revolutionary mind. I am only truly great in action. If ever I am placed in a truly eminent position I shall prove this. I could rule the House of Commons, although there would be a great prejudice against me at first. It is the most jealous assembly in the world. The fine character of our English society, the consequences of our aristocratic institutions renders a *career* difficult." The subsequent passage in the diary makes clear that literature is a compensation for the frustration he feels at not being given the opportunity to play a major role in public events: "Poetry is the safety valve of my passions—but I wish to *act* what I *write*. My works are the embodification of my feelings. In *Vivian Grey* I have portrayed my active and real ambition: In *Alroy* my ideal ambition: [*Contarini Fleming: A Psychological Autobiography*] is a development of my poetic character. This trilogy is the secret history of my feelings—I shall write no more about myself."

Vivian Grey is composed of three sections: the rise and fall of Vivian as a political figure, which occupies the first four books; an abortive love affair in book five; and three travel books, six through eight, where he is more an observer of manners than an involved, three-dimensional character. After the first four books, except for the aforementioned love affairs, Vivian's emotional life is a secondary concern.

Published anonymously when Disraeli was twenty-one, the first four books—which purported to expose incompetent and scandalous behavior—were a sensation, and keys were published matching the characters to the supposed real-life models. Disraeli wrote the four additional books in 1827 to capitalize on the interest aroused by the original four. If these last four books have been patronized far more than they deserve, that is in part because the 1853 edition, the text that most readers know, expurgates some of the liveliest passages from the original 1826-1827 edition. Vivian has now renounced ambition, and in book five, Violet Fane, the woman he loves, dies. The rest of the sequel is a travelogue in which Vivian is used as a means of exposing the follies of Continental cus-

Disraeli's sister Sarah, with whom he collaborated on
A Year at Hartlebury *in 1834*

toms and, implicitly, of showing England in a far gentler light than in the original four books.

In the earlier edition, Disraeli's sympathies are with his alter ego Vivian, even when the latter is morally obtuse or has disgraced himself; in the later edition, he is less tolerant of Vivian. The 1853 edition plays down Vivian's impudence and unscrupulousness as well as the narrator's irreverent and playful attitude toward his early machinations. As a political figure, it behooved Disraeli to omit passages that might have helped win the reader's sympathy for Vivian, sympathy that reflected Disraeli's original ambivalence toward his young picaro. The introduction to the 1853 edition is an apology for reprinting the novel at all and exhibits unaccustomed humility.

In both editions the first four books are the most successful. They demonstrate the precocious and ambitious title character's efforts to attain political influence through Machiavellian maneuvers that ultimately fail. Vivian's sensational and erratic school career has striking parallels to Disraeli's; and Vivian's dependence on the cooperation of others reflects Disraeli's own view, in 1826, that a man without wealth, family, and power required help to rise to a position of responsibility. Despite his father's cultivation and tolerance, Vivian becomes an arrogant, condescending, proud, and at times violent young man. Convinced that he is adept at managing and manipulating people for his own ends, Vivian urges the disappointed and sulking former minister, the marquess of Carabas, to form a political party. The proposed party requires a leader, and Vivian, the ever-resourceful master of *Realpolitik*, decides that the one man who would give the project respectability is the marquess's enemy, John Cleveland. Vivian's mission to win Cleveland mirrors Disraeli's own efforts to convince John Gibson Lockhart, Sir Walter Scott's son-in-law, to manage a daily paper, the *Representative*, that he was founding. Just as the *Representative* collapsed, so does the political project. But Vivian is betrayed by the friends upon whom he depends, principally Mrs. Felix Lorraine, the sister-in-law of the marquess. Cleveland holds Vivian responsible for the collapse and challenges him to a duel with pistols. Vivian kills Cleveland, and after an illness attributable to a stricken conscience, he finally leaves England. (It is characteristic of the relationship between fiction and life in Disraeli's career that as soon as the original four volumes were completed in 1826, he began a grand tour.) For all his energy and intelligence, it is hard to imagine what Vivian could have done to arrest his headlong rush to destruction once he committed himself to political intrigue.

While *Vivian Grey* is often thought of as a Silver-Fork novel in the tradition of Plumber Ward's *Tremaine* (1825) and Bulwer's *Pelham* (1828), it is more accurate to say that it is a parody of that kind of novel. *Vivian Grey* is a direct heir of Sterne's *Tristram Shandy* (1759-1767) and Byron's *Don Juan* (1819-1824) in its playful self-consciousness. It is a parody both of the Bildungsroman and of novel writing itself. Disraeli's style and tone are as much the subject as the history of Vivian Grey. As Vivian carries Mrs. Felix Lorraine to her bedchambers after she has fainted, the narrator opens the next chapter by ostentatiously stepping back from the couple in the bedroom: "What is this chapter to be about? Come, I am inclined to be courteous! You shall choose the subject of it. What shall it be, sentiment or scandal? a love scene or a lay-sermon? You shall not choose? Then we must open the note which Vivian, in the morning, found on his pillow.... In some future book, probably the twentieth or twenty-fifth, when the plot begins to wear threadbare, and we can afford a digression, I may give a chapter on Domestic Tactics." Such passages deliberately dispel the illusion that the narrator is someone who exists within the narrative world and call attention to the conventions on which fiction depends. Disraeli is good-naturedly chiding the reader for participating in a farcical relationship in which the author's whims determine what the reader will know.

In the imaginary-voyage tradition, *The Voyage of Captain Popanilla* is certainly indebted to Swift's *Gulliver's Travels* (1726) and *The Tale of a Tub* (1704) and probably also to Johnson's *Rasselas* (1759) and Voltaire's *Candide* (1759) and *Zadig* (1748). In this short work, Disraeli discovered that he could use fiction to express his political and philosophic views. This prepared him for writing the Young England trilogy of the 1840s, in which ideas and principles are paramount. In this early example of political fiction, he avoided character analysis and a coherent, unified plot and relied upon loosely related and implausible episodes and one-dimensional caricatures in the service of ideas. But in the trilogy there would be ample room for character exploration and for Disraeli's increasingly sophisticated narrative technique.

In *The Voyage of Captain Popanilla*, Disraeli voices his suspicion of all systems and dogma and mocks the exclusive reliance on reason. The novel begins by satirizing utilitarianism, but soon moves on to satirize many of the fundamental assumptions on which early nineteenth-century British eco-

nomic and political life was based. Although later Disraeli became an advocate of some of the particular institutions that he ridicules in *The Voyage of Captain Popanilla*, such as the Corn Laws and the colonial system, this early novella foreshadows many of Young England's values, especially its dislike of materialism and expedience: the Young England trilogy develops *Popanilla*'s disdain for a culture that reduces man to a machine and that glorifies reason and logic at the expense of mystery and imagination. Prior to discovering the books of Useful Knowledge, Popanilla seemed to be in a paradise; but man's zeal to improve himself is his curse. After he becomes captivated by his own wisdom and becomes something of a nuisance, he is sent away by the king. He journeys to Vraibleusia—Disraeli's ironic version of England—where he has a series of adventures which reveal the limitations of some English social and political assumptions.

Disraeli probably wrote *The Young Duke* during the winter of 1829-1830, when he had lost money in the stock market and may even have landed in debtor's prison. In any case, he surely needed money for his 1831 trip to the Middle East, a trip which he undoubtedly hoped would be inspiration to help him finish *The Wondrous Tale of Alroy*. But Disraeli felt that in succumbing to the temptation of Colburn, the publisher of *Vivian Grey* who paid him the rather handsome fee of £500 for *The Young Duke*, he was prostituting his talents when he should have been writing serious works.

The Young Duke, like *Vivian Grey*, is a tale of moral degeneration followed by moral redemption. *The Young Duke*'s subject is the dissipation and eventual enlightenment of George Augustus Frederick, duke of St. James, who upon reaching his twenty-first birthday becomes one of the wealthiest men in Europe. But the duke is morally unequipped for the fashionable world into which he is catapulted, or for the wealth that he suddenly has at his disposal. The duke gradually chooses the example of the upstanding Dacres, the Catholics who "lived as proscribed in the realm [England] which they had created," and rejects the amoral aristocrats, epitomized by Sir Lucious and Mrs. Dallington Vere, a twenty-three-year-old widow who lacks standards or scruples. Finally the generous affection, natural grace, and manners of the Dacres, particularly of the daughter, have a significant influence on his ethical development.

In *The Young Duke* can be seen the first seeds of Disraeli's concept—so prominent in the Young England novels—that England must have a politically conscientious aristocracy. Frederick's progress into a responsible member of res publica illustrates a cornerstone of Disraeli's political philosophy: he believed that a self-indulgent aristocracy had abnegated its responsibilities as moral leaders of the nation. That the duke gives his first speech on the subject of Catholic emancipation demonstrates Disraeli's commitment to this cause and the cause it represented for him: the opening of the political process to outsiders and minorities, including Jews. Throughout his career he supported extending the suffrage; he maintained that "the wider the popular suffrage the more powerful would be the natural aristocracy"—the aristocracy of ability. Although a convert, Disraeli was nevertheless pursuing his self-interest, for he understood that any intrinsic barriers would have affected his chances for election to Parliament and higher office. The duke overcomes despair, revives his own soul by discovering another to complete himself, and commits himself to political life; thus he fulfills Disraeli's public and private fantasies.

That Disraeli was something of a dandy in the 1830s is not as great an aberration as it would have been in the later Victorian years. Unconventional behavior, such as wearing ostentatious and bizarre clothes, and the posture of rebellion against traditions and convention were more acceptable in the 1830s than later, just as they were more acceptable in the United States in the late 1960s and early 1970s than in the 1950s. Disraeli was influenced by the unconventional social and moral behavior of Count d'Orsay, to whom he dedicated *Henrietta Temple*; he was also influenced by his close friend Bulwer, a member of Parliament and a dandy who cut a flamboyant, eccentric figure while enjoying public attention and flouting middle-class standards. On the one hand, Disraeli disregarded the manners and morals of the middle class and the staid aristocrats who dominated the Tories, and viewed them from an iconoclastic perspective. On the other hand, he wished to enter Parliament, albeit at first as a Radical; but he lost two elections at High Wycombe in 1832 and another in 1834.

Disraeli's third full-length novel was published in 1832. Like *Vivian Grey, Contarini Fleming: A Psychological Autobiography* is about its title character's ambitious quest for public recognition. But Contarini cannot make up his mind whether to devote his energies to literature or to politics. Nor could Disraeli: at the same time as he adopted the pose of a dandy indifferent to the opinions and judgments of society, he wished to make a mark within the world whose values he flouted. Contarini is the imaginative man who responds to impulses,

passions, and unacknowledged psychic needs; Contarini's father, Baron Fleming, is the pragmatic, rational man who commits himself to public affairs despite his cynical view of mankind—a benevolent Machiavellian. While one aspect of Contarini demands the intensity and solitude of the life of poetry, the other offers the excitement and ego-gratification of a life of action. Alternately, and sometimes simultaneously, Contarini expresses these contradictory selves. No sooner does he make a decision in one direction than he rebukes himself for the life he is leading. Because of Baron Fleming's antipathy to the imaginative life, Contarini turns to Winter, the artist, as a surrogate father. Winter is one of Disraeli's recurring wisdom figures (the most notable is Sidonia in *Coningsby* and *Tancred*) whose role it is to counsel the protagonist.

The novel is built upon the premise that is voiced to Contarini by the oracular Winter: "Never apologize for showing feeling . . . when you do so you apologize for truth." Disraeli may have set the novel in Europe to place it in the tradition of European novels, including Goethe's *The Sorrows of Young Werther* (1787) and *Wilhelm Meister's Apprenticeship* (1795-1796) and the works of Chateaubriand and Sénancour, where feeling is the avenue to truth. Disraeli implies that each man has the capacity to discover his own truth by means of experience, if he is aided by an active imagination. Speaking through Contarini, Disraeli reaffirms the romantic view that a major source of knowledge is an individual's experience; truth is not in the world outside, but within the self: "When I search into my own breast, and trace the development of my own intellect, and the formation of my own character, all is light and order. The luminous succeeds to the obscure, the certain to the doubtful, the intelligent to the illogical, the practical to the impossible, and I experience all that refined and ennobling satisfaction that we derive from the discovery of truth, and the contemplation of nature." Contarini's therapeutic and expressive theory of art shows a rare but acute recognition on Disraeli's part of the reasons he wrote fiction.

The Wondrous Tale of Alroy is Disraeli's ultimate heroic fantasy. He uses the figure of the twelfth-century Jewish prince, David Alroy, as the basis for a tale of Jewish conquest and empire. The historic Alroy was a self-appointed messiah in Kurdistan during a period of severe tribulation and unusual suffering for the Jews, but Disraeli extends Alroy's power and prowess and introduces supernatural machinery and ersatz cabalistic lore and ritual. Undoubtedly the tale of a Jew becoming the most powerful man in an alien land appealed to Disraeli, who at the age of twenty-eight had not yet made his political or artistic reputation. In Alroy's hyperbolic self-dramatization is the thinly disguised voice of the young, frustrated Disraeli who has not yet begun to fulfill the "ideal ambition" of which he wrote in his diary.

The Wondrous Tale of Alroy indicates Disraeli's commitment to his Jewish heritage. His surrogate, the narrator, glories in the Jewish victories and in the triumph of the Prince of Captivity over his oppressors and regrets his fall due to pride and worldliness. Disraeli's footnotes show his knowledge of Jewish customs as well as his wide reading in Jewish studies. Disraeli found the medieval world in which Alroy lived an apt model for some of his own values: he saw in that world an emphasis on imagination, emotion, and tradition; respect for political and social hierarchies; and a vital spiritual life. *The Wondrous Tale of Alroy* anticipates Disraeli's attraction to the Middle Ages in the Young England movement. Writing of the flowering of medieval Jewry under Alroy enabled him to express his opposition to rationalism and utilitarianism.

Recently it has been discovered that in 1834 Disraeli wrote *A Year at Hartlebury; or, The Election* with his sister Sarah. Published under the pseudonyms Cherry and Fair Star, it is based on Disraeli's two unsuccessful 1832 election campaigns. On a first reading, the major character, Aubrey Bohun, is very much an autobiographical figure: he is something of a mysterious outsider, although he comes from a distinguished family; he is egotistical and suspected by others of insincerity and ambition. (At one point the narrator proclaims, "That he was ambitious there is no doubt, and who but fools are not ambitious?") His political positions, particularly his antagonism to the Whigs and his belief that the common people want and need strong leaders, are those of his creator. So is his dream of forming a new conservative party, a dream which is an early version of Young England: "He was desirous of seeing a new party formed, which while it granted those alterations in our domestic policy which the spirit of the age required, should maintain and prosecute the ancient external policy by which the empire had been founded; of this party he wished to place himself at the head." Bohun's brilliant maiden speech, his victory against odds, his ability to captivate able women, and his conviction that he is a great man show how the novel—or at least the political tale which seems to be mostly by Disraeli—expresses Disraeli's "ideal ambition."

Bohun's successful election campaign depends on the activity of Helen Molesworth, the heroine of the novel and the woman whom he loves, and she has characteristics, including living her ambitions vicariously through a man, that resemble Sarah's qualities. At every stage of Disraeli's career he was to feel the presence of a strong female figure—Sarah, Mrs. Austen (who helped Disraeli publish his first novel), his wife, and Lady Bradford (with whom he had a romance in the 1870s after his wife's death). But he did not conceive the female in the background as the traditional Victorian figure who comforts her male. Disraeli believed in the power of refined women to cultivate and soften the aggressive impulses of men into socially acceptable channels. Disraeli's women have vigorous, independent minds and act on their own. Often they have emotional range and sensibility that his men lack.

But the novel has a darker side which may explain why Disraeli published it pseudonymously. Bohun has been married in the past and has wooed Helen under false pretenses. He becomes increasingly unattractive in the last chapters, because the reader understands that Bohun's trifling with her feelings reveals a tremendous failure of character. Bohun's deviousness and unscrupulousness undermine his stature and make his political success seem rather shallow. Disraeli, who knew he would be trying for Parliament again, could not risk being identified with Bohun, who seems willing to enter into an adulterous if not bigamous relationship with Helen. Perhaps the murder of Bohun by a man who had been both his jealous rival and political aide indicates Disraeli's fear of betrayal; or it may be that Disraeli or Sarah or both identified Helen's support of Bohun with their own relationship, making Bohun's marrying Helen seem incestuous, and thus they had to kill him off.

Disappointed with the reception accorded his full-length novels and his satire, *The Voyage of Captain Popanilla*, Disraeli turned to poetry and began to write what he believed would be the major epic poem for his age, *The Revolutionary Epick* (1834). He thought that this poem would reflect the intellectual and cultural texture of his time in the way that Vergil's *Aeneid* and Milton's *Paradise Lost* (1667) reflected the Augustan Age and the Reformation. Because of its chilly reception he abandoned it after the third book. In 1835, he ran for Parliament for a fourth time and lost. In that year he published the most significant of his nonfiction writings, *Vindication of the English Constitution*, an open letter of 200 pages in which he not only defends the House of Lords but introduces his Tory theory of history and politics; he then returned to novel writing and produced *Henrietta Temple* and *Venetia* at a time when he required an outlet for his passions and frustrations.

He also needed money.

The essential focus of these two novels is the way a child relates to his family history. They were written during and subsequent to his affairs with older women, most notably Henrietta Sykes, the wife of Sir Francis Sykes. At this time, he was anxious to wrench himself free from financial dependence upon his father. Until he married in 1838, his father provided him with a center of stability at crucial periods in his life, although neither his father nor his wife seems to have been a strong, dominating figure. In *Henrietta Temple* and *Venetia* Disraeli is more interested than he once was not only in the subtleties of private lives and the way that the child is father to the man but also in complex psychological problems. In contrast to his early novels, he no longer is preoccupied with projecting his own radically vacillating emotions onto his protagonists. In *Henrietta Temple* and *Venetia*, the central characters do mime some *aspects* of Disraeli's life, but they are not larger-than-life depictions of his personal activities, as in *Vivian Grey*, or of his fantasies, as in *Contarini Fleming*. Although these are his only two novels that have women as the title figures, the male characters are the ones who embody Disraeli's values, experiences, and goals.

In the middle 1830s he had begun to achieve a little of the recognition and success that he craved, although he was a long way from fulfilling his insatiable ambition. On the threshold of election to Parliament from a safe Tory district, he knew that he needed to modify his public image as a dandy and eccentric in order to woo his constituency and to succeed once he entered the House of Commons. More conventional artistic control and more consistent point of view are achieved at the sacrifice of the double focus upon the teller as well as the tale that was so prominent a feature of the early novels. The influence of Byron, particularly *Don Juan* with its undisciplined and extravagant speaker and impulsive and uninhibited energy, virtually disappears (although that influence had played a much lesser role in *Contarini Fleming* and *The Wondrous Tale of Alroy* than in *Vivian Grey* and *The Young Duke*). In these middle novels Disraeli wanted his narrator to assume the stance of worldliness and urbanity that he now thought appropriate for tales of aristocratic manners and passions.

As *Henrietta Temple* opens, Ferdinand Armine is the only child of parents whose family fortune is in decline. He has been educated by the family priest, Glastonbury, who obtains a commission for him in Malta. As the favorite of his maternal grandfather, he expects to be heir to a considerable estate and lives extravagantly; but his grandfather leaves his fortune to his granddaughter, Katherine Grandison. To redeem the family fortune, Ferdinand becomes engaged to Katherine; but after he returns home, he discovers the beautiful and gifted Henrietta Temple, with whom he falls in love at first sight. Ferdinand asks her to keep their love a secret until he informs his parents, who are at Bath; Henrietta reluctantly agrees not to tell her father of their engagement until he returns. Of course, Ferdinand does not tell her that he is already engaged to another woman. After three weeks, the Temples learn that Ferdinand has betrayed their trust and is engaged to Katherine.

Upon learning of Ferdinand's duplicity, Henrietta has a nervous collapse and goes to Italy to recover. There she meets and eventually becomes engaged to Lord Mountfort, whose decorum and tact are in striking contrast to Ferdinand's passion. Ferdinand is befriended by Count Mirabel (based on Count d'Orsay), who helps him woo and win Henrietta. Mirabel consoles Ferdinand when he suffers the ignominy of a spunging-house (debtors' prison)—and even raises the necessary funds to pay Ferdinand's debts, although by then Katherine has already learned of his plight and paid for his release. When Mountfort and Katherine discover their temperamental compatability, the obstacles to the marriage of Henrietta and Ferdinand dissolve. The novel concludes with both couples happily married.

The two crucial biographical sources for *Henrietta Temple* are Disraeli's relationship with Henrietta Sykes and his debts. While Ferdinand Armine embodies crucial aspects of Disraeli's experience, he is not simply another of Disraeli's masks. Like Ferdinand, Disraeli was hounded by debts; in fact, he was deeply in debt throughout his life. (As late as 1857, he was faced with a member of the Bentinck family calling in a large loan that he had never expected to have to repay.) Disraeli knew how financial difficulty could haunt a person's psyche and dominate his thoughts.

In the part of *Henrietta Temple* written before his final break with Henrietta Sykes, Disraeli is quite ambivalent about the passionate love between Henrietta and Ferdinand which causes them to abandon their personal and family responsibilities. If Henrietta's ardor for Ferdinand celebrates the "all for love" philosophy that dominated Disraeli's dalliance with Henrietta Sykes, the marriage of Katherine and Mountfort anticipates his practical and economically intelligent marriage to an older widow who adored him and always placed his interest first.

Even the complications that Ferdinand must overcome before marriage to Henrietta reflect Disraeli's maturing vision of sexual love and his understanding that passion is not enough for a lasting adult relationship.

Disraeli was in desperate financial straits when he wrote *Venetia*, in part because *Henrietta Temple*, although his most successful novel since *Vivian Grey*, did not produce anything like the revenue he required to pay his debts. Disraeli chose for his subjects England's most unconventional recent poetic geniuses, Shelley and Byron, because they gave him an opportunity to embody in fiction his pique that major artists like himself were unappreciated, if not ostracized. Disraeli saw himself as heir to the tradition of genius which those figures represented to him. Because Shelley and Byron were both regarded as disreputable and immoral geniuses by the early Victorian establishment, his choice of subject was both a ploy to attract a voyeuristic audience and a statement about the kind of imaginative and personal life that intrigued him. His major figures, Lord Cadurcis and Marmion Herbert, are modeled respectively on Byron and Shelley. (In the novel Herbert is a generation older than Cadurcis, although Shelley was actually three years younger than Byron.) The novel fuses the melodrama of the Gothic plot with Disraeli's intensifying interest in the inner workings of the psyche.

Deserted by her husband and living in self-imposed seclusion in Cherbury, Lady Annabel Herbert (modeled on Byron's wife, who was called Annabelle) devotes her life to her child, Venetia. Cadurcis and his mother come to live at the nearby abbey; because his mother is emotionally erratic if not mentally ill, Cadurcis becomes increasingly dependent on the affection of Lady Annabel and Venetia. When his mother abuses him without provocation, he runs away; during his flight, his mother dies of heart failure. Subsequently Cadurcis leaves the abbey to continue his education. Only the local vicar, Dr. Masham, knows the secret of Venetia's paternity or the reasons for her mother's seclusion. One day Venetia discovers that a closed-off room contains her father's portrait and his poems, which she reads. In true Gothic fashion, she becomes ill; while delirious, she reveals to her mother what she has seen.

After a long absence and years without correspondence, Cadurcis returns and, after renewing his acquaintance with Venetia, proclaims his love. But Venetia refuses, because she feels Cadurcis is not the equal of her father, whom she has apotheosized.

Cadurcis begins to emulate the career of her father as a social rebel and as a poet. He becomes famous and is lionized by London society. He woos Venetia by praising her father in a poem, but Lady Annabel, fearing that her daughter will also be deserted by a poet who has become a public figure, now opposes the relationship. After Cadurcis fights a duel over another man's wife, he becomes a notorious character and leaves England. The scene shifts to Europe, where not only Venetia and Cadurcis but Marmion Herbert and Lady Annabel are reunited. After a short period of bliss, Herbert and Cadurcis drown in a boating accident. Venetia returns to Cherbury but eventually rejects the celibate existence of her mother and marries Cadurcis's loyal if unexciting cousin, George.

In the guises of Herbert and Cadurcis, Disraeli presents Shelley and Byron as sympathetic figures and extenuates their unconventional conduct. Of course, by giving them other names, Disraeli could have it both ways: Herbert and Cadurcis do not parallel Shelley and Byron except in the broad outlines of their careers. While it adds a dimension to the novel, it is doubtful whether a modern reader requires the identification to find the story interesting. While Herbert is nominally Shelley after he finally emerges late in the novel, his energies are rather reduced. He becomes the typical Disraeli wisdom figure and the surrogate father who fulfills the emotional needs of Cadurcis. Cadurcis may be based on Byron, but he is also a recognizable successor to the tempestuous, impulsive, passionate heroes of the previous novels, the men whose energies are never fully controlled and threaten to undermine their possessors: Contarini, Alroy, Vivian Grey, and even Ferdinand. Shelley and Byron provided Disraeli with models of the rebellious overreacher to whom he was attracted, without exposing him to possible criticism for creating dissatisfied social misfits at a time when he was receiving increasing political recognition and knew that he was finally close to gaining the seat in Parliament that he had so frequently sought. Both Herbert as a young man and Lord Cadurcis prior to meeting Herbert represent the self that Disraeli, rather reluctantly but quite consciously, was in the process of putting behind him; their lives are ways that Disraeli tests the premise articulated by Annabel's sister-in-law: "Everything is allowed, you know, to a genius!" Herbert after he matures represents an idealized version of the philosophic, mature man that Disraeli was trying to become; after the most tumultuous, unconventional life, Herbert discovers that human happiness resides in family ties.

Disraeli was easily elected to a safe seat in Parliament in 1837, but his maiden speech on the validity of the election for some Irish seats was a rather reckless and unsuccessful debut. He married a wealthy widow, Mary Anne Wyndham Lewis, in 1838. He tried to ingratiate himself with Sir Robert Peel, the Tory prime minister, and gain a position in the cabinet, but Peel passed him over in 1841. Disraeli's disappointment may have been a factor in his forming Young England.

Young England was a nostalgic movement in the early 1840s which despised utilitarianism, middle-class liberalism, and centralized government and sought to return England to the feudal and monarchal antecedents of its national youth. Among the leaders of the movement, Disraeli was the central figure; then close to forty, he for the first time had some political importance. George Smythe was a man of great gifts but uncertain judgment, who was at least in part the model for Coningsby. Lord John Manners lacked Smythe's extraordinary potential and scintillating intellect but was a kindly, high-principled man who epitomized the integrity

Mary Anne Wyndham Lewis, the wealthy widow whom Disraeli married in 1838

and idealism of Young England; Manners was the model for Lord Henry Sidney in *Coningsby*. Alexander Baille-Cochrane, the next most prominent figure after Disraeli, Smythe, and Manners, was a Scotsman of Disraeli's age and the model for Buckhurst in *Coningsby*. Although Disraeli called himself "the leader of a party chiefly of the youth and new members," Young England was never a numerical factor, only including about a dozen members at best; even Disraeli, Smythe, Manners, and Baille-Cochrane, the four central figures, did not always agree on major issues, and Young England never became more than a small group of like-minded Tories who, as Disraeli put it in the 1870 preface to the collected edition of his fictional works, "living much together, without combination . . . acted together." Although some of Peel's supporters voted with them on certain issues, Young England never achieved a specific legislative program. For example, Young England stood firmly for the Corn Laws, even after Peel had begun to waver. Typical of the kind of community for which Young England longed and of the romantic nostalgia that formed the basis of their political program are the following lines by Manners:

> Each knew his place—king, peasant, peer,
>   or priest—
> The greater owned connexion with the least;
> From rank to rank the generous feeling ran
> And linked society as man to man.

Young England argued that the poor should be cared for by conscientious aristocrats and a responsive church rather than administrative structures created by Poor Laws. They idealized the role of the pre-Reformation Catholic church in creating community ties and in fulfilling community responsibilities.

For Disraeli, Young England was a political program that provided not only an alternative to utilitarianism and Chartism (the Chartists wished to extend the vote to working-class men; in protest against the restricted franchise by which Parliament was selected, they sought to elect a truly representative forum of their own to a convention in London) but also a practical way of advancing his position. For the first time since he began his parliamentary career in 1837, he returned to fiction because he understood the potential of presenting his ideas in an imaginative framework. *Coningsby* reflects the mixture of idealism, fantasy, and escapism that informed Disraeli's dream that a coterie of youth would revive England. But in *Sybil* Disraeli comes to grips with the economic deprivation experienced by the rural and urban poor and seems to be ambivalent about the notion that one heroic man can make a substantive difference.

By the time Disraeli wrote *Tancred* in 1846, Young England had virtually disintegrated following the controversy over funding the Maynooth Seminary in late 1845. Disraeli sharply disagreed with Peel's proposal to increase the government grant to Maynooth, whose purpose was the education of Catholic priests. Influenced by the Oxford Movement and their family ties to Ireland, Smythe and Manners supported Peel. Disraeli used the debate as the occasion for a devastating attack on Peel, whom he had never forgiven for passing him over for office in 1841 and whose conduct and politics he attacked in *Coningsby* and *Sybil*. Those novels, and to an extent *Tancred*, are a response to what he felt was Whig propaganda disguised as history. Disraeli believed that the so-called Glorious Revolution of 1688 had been the occasion for the Whigs' installing an oligarchical political system which he called the "Venetian Constitution." By this he meant that consultation among a group of self-interested aristocrats had replaced the monarchy in substance if not form, reducing the power of the throne until the king was no more than a "doge." For Disraeli, Charles I is a martyr from whom the throne was seized by a party of selfish aristocrats, and the Glorious Revolution is "The Dutch Invasion of 1688" which resulted because "the resources of Holland, however considerable, were inadequate to sustain him [William III] in his internecine rivalry with the great sovereign of France." Those who deposed James II in the name of civil and religious liberty were the very Whig families who formed the "Venetian party" and who "in one century plundered the church to gain the property of the people and in another century changed the dynasty to gain the power of the crown." With the continuing decline of the monarchy and the accelerating abnegation of responsibility on the part of the aristocracy who once cared for those living on their land, the common people, Disraeli felt, had no one to champion their cause. The established Anglican church did not provide for the common people either spiritual solace or the hospitality and charity that the Catholic church had before Henry VIII seized the abbeys and monasteries.

In each novel of the trilogy, Disraeli's persona speaks not as a member of Parliament, which Disraeli had been since 1837, but as an enlightened and perceptive aristocrat. One implicit premise of the trilogy is that a prophetic voice could arouse the sensibilities of his fellow aristocrats to the spiritual and economic plight of the people and to the need for restoring the monarchy and the church to their former dignity. Disraeli also believed in the possibility of great men transforming the imagination of the common people. The myth of the political messiah, which also appealed to Carlyle, recurs in each of the Young England novels. Disraeli's narrator is one of those "primordial and creative mind[s] . . . [that could] say to his fellows: Behold, God has given me thought; I have discoverd truth; and you shall believe!" The comprehensive political consciousness of the speaker is the intellectual and moral position toward which the hero of each volume of the trilogy finally develops. The narrator empathetically traces the quest of the hero (Egremont, Coningsby, and Tancred) to discover the appropriate values by which he can order his own life and fulfill the prominent public role that he feels himself obliged to play. (The complete absence of irony toward the protagonist occasionally has the negative effect of neutralizing Disraeli's wit and vivacity.)

Each of the protagonists overcomes doubt and anxiety because he convinces himself that he possesses the unique intellectual and moral potential to shape not merely his own life but the very fabric of the historical process. Each protagonist's quest is conceived as a heroic attempt to discover the values essential for a new breed of political leaders who will recognize the supremacy of the monarchy and the importance of serving the common people. Coningsby's ambition and self-confidence, Egremont's compassion and consciousness of the miseries of others, and Tancred's spiritual faith and willingness to act on behalf of his beliefs are the ideals to which others (Disraeli's aristocratic audience and hence potential political leaders) must strive. The quest for values takes place against the background of a satire of both a decadent aristocracy lacking in vitality and a sense of responsibility, and of a parliamentary system that seems divorced from the people for whom it is responsible.

Disraeli used three different genres of fiction in his trilogy. *Coningsby* is a Bildungsroman concerned with the intellectual and moral development of the potential leader. *Sybil* is a polemical novel that focuses on the socioeconomic conditions that need to be remedied. And *Tancred*, like Disraeli's neglected *Voyage of Captain Popanilla*, is an imaginary voyage in the tradition of *Gulliver's Travels* and Defoe's *Robinson Crusoe* (1719-1720).

Coningsby opens against the background of political turmoil that existed prior to the debate on the Reform Bill of 1832. Coningsby is the grandson of the arrogant megalomaniac Lord Monmouth, who, like Lord Steyne of Thackeray's *Vanity Fair* (1847-1848), is based upon Lord Hertford. Monmouth has undertaken to educate his orphaned grandson, although he had broken all ties with the boy's father, his youngest son, because he disapproved of his marriage. Coningsby is a young man of enormous potential; as he matures it is clear that he combines the necessary ability, ambition, intellect, judgment, and imagination to become a political leader. Coningsby learns from his travels in England to reject the examples of parasites and social climbers such as Rigby and dissolute aristocrats such as Prince Colonna. Sidonia, a sophisticated and wise Jew of great wealth and vast learning, becomes his mentor and instills in Coningsby the belief that a young man can be a great leader and that heroism and greatness are possibilities for him.

As Coningsby is about to leave Eton, he is uncertain of his future, in part because he lacks both a sure economic base and family ties. He takes a roundabout journey to visit his grandfather. On a visit to his friend Lord Henry Sidney at Beaumanoir, he sees an example of benevolent aristocracy. He visits Eustace Lyle and sees how monastic and Catholic customs have been revived to enrich the spiritual lives and increase the well-being of the common people. Next he visits his friend Oswald Millbank, whose father is a Manchester manufacturer. He learns that a factory at its best resembles the feudal system in its hierarchical organization, clearly defined responsibilities, and concern for the welfare of the workers. Finally, Coningsby arrives at his family home, Coningsby Castle, where Monmouth rules without concern for his neighbors or the common people and without the warmth and grace that Coningsby found at Beaumanoir.

Back at Eton, Coningsby and his friends form a group dedicated to a conservatism that wishes to revive the church and monarchy and to restore the aristocracy's sense of responsibility. On a visit to Monmouth in Paris he meets Edith Millbank, his friend's sister. When Monmouth wants to contest his hated rival, the senior Millbank, in an election, he asks his grandson to be his candidate. But Coningsby refuses, not only because he does not want to offend the Millbank family but also because he could not in good conscience vote with the present Conservatives. When Coningsby refuses to run, Monmouth vows to cut him off from the family as he had cut off Coningsby's father. Monmouth soon dies and leaves Coningsby a very small legacy. But at

the urging of his son, the elder Millbank withdraws his candidate and allows Coningsby to run in his place. He also approves his marriage to Edith, which gives Coningsby the economic base he needs, even before he inherits—as he soon does—most of Monmouth's estate upon the death of the latter's illegitimate daughter.

The effectiveness of *Coningsby* as a work of art depends upon Disraeli's establishing a relationship between the private theme—the development of Coningsby's abilities as a potential leader—and the public theme—the need for revivifying England's political institutions. The insipid political gossip and private debauchery of the aristocracy and their myrmidons give convincing support to Millbank's call for a natural aristocracy of virtue, talent, and property. As a comparative newcomer to wealth, the senior Millbank may be a bit unpolished and prone to anger, but how preferable is his integrity to the amorality and cynicism of Monmouth and his followers! Such dramatic interest as there is depends upon whether Coningsby will develop into an exceptional man, not upon whether he will become simply a moral and capable one. Sidonia, Millbank, and Lyle provide significant *examples* of alternative life-styles to those espoused by Monmouth and his followers. Part of the dramatic potential of *Coningsby* is lost because the rather priggish protagonist's "tempters" hold no appeal for him: the reader does not feel that Coningsby requires the influence of Lyle, the elder Millbank, and especially Sidonia to reject the duplicity of Rigby, the self-centeredness of Monmouth, and the cynicism and decadence of irresponsible aristocrats.

In terms of his career, *Coningsby* may have been the most important novel that Disraeli wrote. He not only defined his political philosophy at a crucial time in his career, but he created in Coningsby and Sidonia two important fictional models for himself. Coningsby, the man who is elected to Parliament in his early twenties and who seems destined for leadership, overcomes apparent loss of wealth and position by means of diligence, self-confidence, and extraordinary ability. It is true that this fantasy figure did not have the burdens of Disraeli's past notoriety, his Jewish ancestry, and his debts, and that at forty it was no longer possible for Disraeli to achieve preeminence at a precocious age. Nevertheless, imagining that merit was acknowledged and setbacks overcome played an essential if indeterminate role in fortifying his self-confidence. But if Disraeli the man of action imagined himself as Coningsby, Disraeli the artist viewed himself as Sidonia, the perspicacious and insightful Jewish polymath. If *Coningsby* embodies the romance of youthful political success, Sidonia is the romance of the Jewish outsider who, despite having no position in government, is one of the most important, sophisticated, and knowledgeable figures in all Europe.

Disraeli wanted the ideas of Young England to have impact upon the governing class. He wished to use *Sybil*, the middle volume of the trilogy, not only to explain but to justify his political philosophy; to do this, he needed to expose the condition of England. He believed that as a potential leader he had to be identified with clearly defined theoretical positions. "My conception of a great statesman is of one who represents a great idea—an idea which may lead him to power; an idea with which he might identify himself; an idea he may develop; an idea which he may and can impress upon the nation." In the 1849 preface to the fifth edition of *Coningsby*, he recalled his realization that he could "adopt the form of fiction as the instrument to scatter his suggestions . . . [and] avail himself of a method which, in the temper of the times, offered the best chance of influencing opinion." Published in 1845, *Sybil; or, The Two Nations* was one of the most inclusive novels of English life since Fielding's *Tom Jones* (1749). *Sybil's* space is coextensive with England, its time is England's history, and its subject is the political and social circumstances of English life.

Sybil's status as a neglected masterpiece depends in part on its brilliant insight into the social and economic circumstances in England between 1832 and 1844 and on its compelling presentation of the life of the common people. (Disraeli drew upon the official government reports, or Blue Books.) In no other Disraeli novel are character and event so subordinated to theme. The plot of *Sybil* is organized around Charles Egremont's gradual development, but no recapitulation of the plot can do justice to the novel's cross section of English life. The opening chapters show bored aristocrats living a dissipated, idle life; Egremont, a younger son of a family that had gradually risen in prominence subsequent to Henry VIII's seizure of the monasteries, is one of these bored aristocrats. He is a warm, generous, and impulsive character, but lacks intense ambition. Yet he is a man of enormous potential, highly intelligent and observant. His widowed mother persuades him to run for Parliament. On the understanding that he has the financial support of his brother Lord Marney, he makes the race and wins. But Marney, an example of the benighted, selfish aristocracy which is oblivious to the needs of the common people and which has no sense of an organic community, refuses to help Egremont pay his election debts. After courting a woman who ultimately marries his brother because Charles lacks an appropriate fortune, Egremont is disgusted with the "arrogant and frigid" aristocratic life which his brother exemplifies for him.

Walking near the ruins of Marney Abbey, Egremont discovers Stephen Morley and Walter Gerard and Gerard's daughter, Sybil, who is planning to become a nun. The Gerards, an old Catholic family, have a legitimate claim to the Mowbray estate. But Gerard is also a worker who identifies with the people, and he becomes one of the leaders of the Chartist movement until he is arrested. Morley, a journalist and later a Chartist theoretician, is attracted to Sybil and thinks of Egremont as a rival for her; he helps Gerard recover his estates by discovering a man who is expert in such affairs. Under the identity of Franklin, Egremont goes to live near the Gerards and becomes close friends with them. After Sybil and her father go to London and lobby on behalf of the Chartist petition, she learns that Egremont is an aristocrat and becomes temporarily disaffected until he arranges for her release after she and her father are seized. Gradually Egremont learns that the people of England are divided into those who are materially comfortable and those who are not. As Egremont is educated about the real condition of England, he learns about the rural poor on his brother's estates and the urban poor created by the Industrial Revolution. He comes to understand that aristocratic and political life ignores the needs of a discontented and miserable population, and he upholds the rights of labor in Parliament. Gerard intervenes during the riotous national strike to save the Trafford factory, which has been presented as a model of the benevolent community that industry can create; this represents to Disraeli the possibility of a union between people and property. Morley uses these riots as an occasion to locate the document sustaining Gerard's claim. Marney and Morley conveniently die in riots, and Egremont becomes heir to Marney's estate and marries Sybil.

It is a curiosity of *Sybil* that the basic theme, the division between the wealthy and the poor, is articulated by Morley—Egremont's amoral, agnostic, and paranoid rival: "Two nations; between whom there is no intercourse and no sympathy; who are as ignorant of each other's habits, thoughts, and feelings, as if they were dwellers in different zones, or inhabitants of different planets; who are formed by a different breeding, are fed by a different food, are ordered by different manners, and are not governed by the same laws." But it is part of the novel's subtlety to show that perspicacity is not the province of the well-meaning characters alone. If at first Morley seems to be Disraeli's spokesman, it should be remembered that his rational analysis provides no solution; he lacks imagination, sympathy, and manners; his abstractions are often not sustained by the action; his disregard for the past is contradictory to Disraeli's beliefs; and Morley's attempt to murder his rival and implicitly to barter her father's safety for Sybil's declaration of love for him completely discredits him. Ultimately, by showing the possibilities of bridging the schism between rich and poor by the merger of Sybil and Egremont, Disraeli refutes Morley's view that the division could not be breached. (Yet how much more effective the novel's resolution would have been—and how shocking to Disraeli's Victorian audience—if Sybil had not had an aristocratic heritage!)

In *Sybil*, Disraeli uses the novel form to discover the potential within extant institutions and to posit their revival as a conservative alternative not only to the present condition of the church, the monarchy, and the political parties, but to the anarchy and disruption of Chartism, which flirted with armed rebellion and roused fears of an English version of the French Revolution.

A major flaw in Disraeli's previous fiction had been his unintentional bathetic change in voice, which has the effect of trivializing both the thrust of his satire and the reader's engagement with the intellectual and emotional lives of his characters. But in *Sybil* rapid changes in tone are often rhetorically effective; they accompany shifts in place and contribute to the contrast between the neglected and the overindulged—and within the latter group, between those like Egremont who recognize their responsibility to the deprived and those like his brother and the residents of Mowbray Castle who do not. By presenting a panorama of people from every class and rapidly sweeping across the geography of England, Disraeli creates an elaborate canvas where the meaning of each episode depends upon its relation to the whole. Disraeli's principal mode of rhetorical argument is the rapid juxtaposition of contrasting scenes not only from chapter to chapter, but even from paragraph to paragraph within a chapter. An example of the latter takes place in the second chapter of book two: after establishing the beautiful landscape that might be seen as one approaches the rural town of Marney, the narrator readjusts the perspective and discovers a scene of deprivation and filth.

In *Sybil*, Disraeli successfully renders the

Disraeli in the 1850s

minor characters as the inevitable results of social and economic conditions that have to be changed, while simultaneously dramatizing the vitality, the individuality, and the essential humanity of what he regarded as England's neglected resource—the downtrodden common people. At times in his fiction Disraeli does tend to associate complacent vulgarity and insolence with the quality of life led by the working class, as if this were prima facie evidence for placing faith in the leadership of a revived aristocracy. But in *Sybil*, the working-class characters such as "Bishop" Hatton, Dandy Mick, and Devilsdust have the kind of energy, intelligence, and resourcefulness that are associated with the minor personae of Shakespeare and Dickens.

The novel's narrator continually argues for the possibility of the heroic mind, demonstrating the effects such minds can have on their followers and indicating the preferability of leadership by extraordinary men to more representative forms of government. The narrator speaks as if his consciousness is identical with the nation's collective conscience. The historical chapters convey the personal urgency of a man who identifies his own well-being with the health of his nation, which is presently undermined by "a mortgaged aristocracy, a gambling foreign commerce, a home trade founded on a morbid competition." The speaker is motivated by the desire to contribute to the welfare of the British people by showing them that their true interest lies neither with the Whigs nor with the present Tories, who under Peel's leadership have departed from the great Tory principles and tradition. Within his consciousness is a historical perspective stretching back to the Norman invasion.

Like Dickens's *Bleak House* (1852-1853), *Sybil* does not constrain or ameliorate the malevolent social forces that blight the quality of English life. Even more than *Bleak House*, *Sybil* opens up the dark side of Victorian England, the side revealed in the Blue Books. Whereas in Dickens's novel the omniscient narrator's panorama of disease, injustice, and grinding poverty alternates with Esther's private journal of personal development and fulfillment, in *Sybil* the historical and sociological perspective pushes relentlessly forward as it satirizes aristocratic pretensions and exposes the discrepancy between those who labor to survive and those who live an idle, luxurious life. Disraeli the novelist is more honest than Disraeli the theoretician of Young England. Hence the novel ends with a tentative conclusion rather than rhetorical optimism. Disturbing facts of economic life and troubling aspects of aristocratic life are not resolved by Egremont's marriage to Sybil. That marriage—after seemingly impossible obstacles are overcome by an unlikely plot—is not the apocalypse that Disraeli seems to have intended, because the lives of Egremont and Sybil remain peripheral to and are transcended by Disraeli's moving presentation of the exploitation in the mines, the degradation of the squalid anarchical outpost, Wodgate, and the recurring threat of rural and urban deprivation. On the last pages, Disraeli emphasizes that while narrating the plot of *Sybil*, he has corrected and reinterpreted Whig historiography: "In an age of political infidelity, of mean passions, and petty thoughts, I would have impressed upon the rising race not to despair, but to seek in a right understanding of the history of their country and in the energies of heroic youth, the elements of national welfare. . . . The written history of our country for the last ten reigns has been a mere phantasma; giving to the origin and consequence of public transactions a character and colour in every respect dissimilar to their natural form and hue. In this mighty mystery all thoughts and things

have assumed an aspect and title contrary to their real quality and style: Oligarchy has been called Liberty; an exclusive Priesthood has been christened a National Church; Sovereignty has been the title of something that has had no dominion, while absolute power has been wielded by those who profess themselves the servants of the People."

Despite some continuity with its predecessors, *Tancred* does not fulfill its function as the climactic volume of the political trilogy. Originally conceived as a novel about reviving the sacred position of the Anglican church by rediscovering its spiritual principles, *Tancred* becomes, whether Disraeli intended it or not, a kind of clumsy metaphor for the discovery of the divine within oneself. It is a fictional version of the Victorian spiritual autobiography epitomized by Carlyle's *Sartor Resartus* (1836), Tennyson's *In Memoriam* (1850), and Newman's *Apologia pro Vita Sua* (1864). Along with *Tancred*, several examples of the genre were published within a few years, including James Anthony Froude's *Shadows of the Clouds* (1847), Newman's *Loss and Gain* (1848), and Charles Kingsley's *Yeast* (1851). *Tancred* reflects Disraeli's continued admiration for romance plots. Like Byron's heroes, Childe Harold and Don Juan, or Scott's heroes in his historical romances, Tancred inhabits an imagined world where day-to-day details rarely intrude into his quest. An imaginary voyage, *Tancred* is loosely held together by the hero's journey, which introduces him to incredible people and fantastic places. The novel begins in the present in England, but Tancred's crusade is virtually a journey backward in time; he discovers remote cultures with religious beliefs and political customs that are now regarded condescendingly by Christian England: Judaism, pagan worship of the Greek gods, and feudalism.

Tancred develops some of the social and political themes begun in *Coningsby* and *Sybil*. Tancred journeys to Jerusalem after convincing himself of the superficiality of contemporary English civilization and the futility of its politics. The political world of the Mideast parodies the intrigues of English politics; the major difference is that weapons rather than votes are the method of settling political disagreements. Syria's "history" parodies England's—civil war followed the deposition of a strong monarch and, when the feudal (or territorial) system was endangered, monarchist sentiments were revived. In the Lebanese mountains Tancred discovers the mirror of Young England's dreams: "a proud, feudal aristocracy; a conventual establishment . . . a free and armed peasantry . . . [and] bishops worthy of the Apostles." Predictably, the Young Syria Movement appeared in 1844 to "profess nationality as their object" and to plead for the restoration of a strong monarchy.

Tancred, begun as an effort to reinvigorate spiritual values in England, really demonstrates Disraeli's disillusionment with Young England as a political movement. The hope voiced in *Coningsby* and *Sybil* has not been fulfilled, for *Tancred* shows that the new generation of leaders is not yet governing. It is very significant that Disraeli has Tancred renounce a parliamentary career when he meets Lord Marney (Egremont) and Coningsby, the heroes of the preceding volumes, who have predicated their hopes on rejuvenating England's political system.

That Tancred becomes a fanatic, alternating between moments of meditation and spasms of frenetic activity when he is ready to sacrifice human life for his vague dreams, reflects Disraeli's disappointment with the demise of Young England and his frustration with his failure to obtain political power. Disraeli was not able to dramatize the enduring spiritual principles on which a revived church could be based and knew that *Tancred* did not provide an alternative to utilitarianism, rationality, and objectivity. As the trilogy's final novel oscillates erratically from its political moorings to its concern with faith, subjectivity, and imagination, it destroys the expectations raised by *Coningsby* and *Sybil* of a major political statement based on a deft analysis of the past, a sustained indictment of the present, and a prophetic vision of the future.

In 1852, Disraeli published *Lord George Bentinck*, a very favorable portrait of one of his Tory political mentors. (The financial assistance of the Bentinck family had enabled Disraeli to purchase his Hughenden estate in 1848.) Lord Derby, although somewhat displeased with his own diminished role in the book, nevertheless gave Disraeli the position of chancellor of the Exchequer in his cabinet in 1852. This was not surprising, since Disraeli's stature as party leader had gradually increased. After the Tory government fell, Disraeli spent 1852-1856 in opposition again. He regained office for a short time in 1858, but in spring 1859 Parliament was dissolved. Serving as chancellor of the Exchequer under Derby, he helped push through the Second Reform Bill of 1867 and became Derby's successor as Tory party leader. In 1868, he became prime minister for a brief time, only to lose to Gladstone in the election of that year and become leader of the minority. It should be noted that in Disraeli's forty-four years in Parliament, the Conservatives had a majority for only eleven.

Lothair (1870) is Disraeli's last effort to cope with the pluralism and dubiety which was becoming so much a part of Victorian life in the late 1860s. The insurrection and brutal suppression in Jamaica in 1865 and the subsequent trial of the British governor of that colony, the financial crisis of 1866, the Reform Bill of 1867 with its extension of the franchise, the Hyde Park demonstrations in favor of the extension, the controversy over disestablishment of the Anglican church in Ireland, and the concomitant disturbances about Irish matters, all made the 1860s a particularly turbulent period.

Disraeli addresses many of the same contemporary intellectual issues raised by Newman's *Apologia* and Arnold's *Culture and Anarchy* (1869): the position of the Anglican church in England; the respective roles of individual conscience, authority, and faith in determining one's religious views; and the moral and spiritual responsibilities of English aristocracy.

While *Lothair* covers the period from August 1866 to August 1868, it ostentatiously omits reference to the Reform Bill and to political activity during that period when Disraeli played such a prominent role. The title character is a kind of educated Everyman testing major nineteenth-century moral, religious, and political positions. He is at the center of a morality play in which characters espousing Roman Catholicism, Anglicanism, Hellenism, and Republicanism try to woo him to their positions. *Lothair* is Disraeli's ideological *Pilgrim's Progress*, even if it does not conclusively dramatize the goal of the title character's quest as he oscillates from position to position.

Lothair is an orphan who succeeds to a huge inheritance at his twenty-first birthday. His father had appointed as his guardians his Scottish Presbyterian uncle, Lord Cullodan, and Cardinal Grandison, who wishes to convert Lothair to Catholicism. The book opens at Brentham, where Lothair is captivated by the gracious, if somewhat idle, life of the duke and his family; he is also enchanted with the duke's daughter, Lady Corisande, to whom he would have proposed had the duchess permitted it. The duke and his family are Anglicans. The cardinal introduces Lothair to the St. Jerome family, including the beautiful Clare Arundel (who, like Sybil, plans on becoming a nun), because he knows that the intense spiritual life at Vauxe will be more appealing if accompanied by sexual attraction. At Vauxe, Lothair is exposed to the ritual and ceremony of Catholicism as well as to the subtle arguments of the priests until Grandison arrives to declare that were Lothair to convert he would become the spokesman and defender of "Divine Truth" and the most important man of the century.

But Lothair also becomes acquainted with Theodora, who is not only indifferent to religion but has been the inspiration for the revolutionary Mary Anne societies and is active in revolutionary movements throughout Europe. Phoebus, one member of Theodora's bohemian circle, is a painter and dandy who considers beauty the primary value in life, while regarding books as useless. Lothair is physically attracted to Theodora. With his loyalties divided among three women and three distinct sets of values, he celebrates his coming of age with a lavish party at his Muriel estate, where Corisande helps foil the plot to convert him to Catholicism. But Theodora wins his loyalty, and he vows to devote his life to her. (Lothair's devotion to the person who inspired the Mary Anne societies is a touching tribute that Disraeli pays to his wife, Mary Anne, and to their mutual romantic love which he believed had sustained him throughout his political career.) He goes to Europe and enlists in battle beside Theodora and her colleague General Bruges in opposition to the forces sponsored by the pope. In the fight, she is killed and Lothair is seriously wounded. He is nursed to health by Roman Catholics in Rome at the St. Jerome Palace under the direction of Clare Arundel. He agrees to take part in a Catholic service at which she gives thanks for his restored health, but he discovers that this service is part of a scheme to win him to the church.

He eventually reaches Syria, where he meets Paraclete, another of Disraeli's wisdom figures, who, after espousing Disraeli's view that God shapes history by assigning genius to particular races, assures him that despite what the Catholics imply, there is more than one true faith: "In my Father's house are many mansions." Eventually Lothair returns to England, marries Corisande, and embraces the Anglican church. But the very circularity of form in which Lothair returns to his starting point, Brentham, to claim his original beloved, Corisande, undercuts the idea that he has progressed. No one, including Lothair, appears ready to give the rudderless ship of state real direction.

Disraeli means to serve up more than an intellectual smorgasbord in which the reader is exposed to various positions: *Lothair* discriminates the wheat from the chaff within each doctrine. Although the novel goes to great length to expose Catholic guile,

Disraeli still admires the religious intensity of Catholic ceremonies and rituals. While the Anglican church seems more moderate in its religious commitment and more concerned with this world than the next, it is a national church which has and may continue to unite England. It may be a virtue that it does not overwhelm the lives of its devotees and seems to make rather gentle demands upon them. It allows even its most devoted followers to love passionately. If Theodora and the Mary Anne societies ask that one give one's life to their cause, they nevertheless offer solace—no different from that offered by traditional religion—to people to whom the wealthy and powerful, and perhaps the organized churches, do not give their full attention. Although Lothair is too submissive and too emotionally captivated to withstand Theodora's influence, he intellectually understands the problem of apotheosizing one's conscience: "Your conscience may be divine . . . and I believe it is; but the consciences of other persons are not divine, and what is to guide them, and what is to prevent or to mitigate the evil they would perpetuate?" The novel dramatizes the implications of Lothair's remark: each major position, including the cardinal's and Phoebus's, reflects someone's acting on his or her own conscience.

By 1870, Disraeli is far more a relativist than in the Young England novels. He is tolerant of the different value systems but critical of duplicity and self-indulgence. Those are the grounds on which, respectively, Catholicism and Phoebus's paganism are criticized. Yet, while Disraeli is not unsympathetic with Theodora's view that a man's conscience is his church, a view that reflects his own youthful attitude, he now understands the necessity of a national church not only as a political institution but because it is desirable that the people of a nation believe in a controlling deity to which they are morally responsible. The Disraeli of the 1870s also knows the danger of each man's acting according to his own conscience.

Lothair's popularity can be attributed not only to Disraeli's status as a former prime minister but to its anti-Catholicism. Contemporary readers would have recognized his references to the conversion of the marquess of Bute, which intensified the pervasive anxiety that the Anglican church would be rent by an exodus to Catholicism. Disraeli feared that one of the pillars of the English social and political system was variously threatened by Catholicism, popular political movements, and atheism. He had convinced himself that Irish disestablishment was a

Disraeli's desk in his office at Number 10, Downing Street

threat to England's national church. It was not the dogma of the Anglican church with which he was concerned, but the substantial contribution that a national church with allegiance only to the crown and to the people made to England's political health. That the England depicted by Disraeli in *Lothair* is torn by religious dissension and is lacking in political direction reflects some bitterness over his last tumultuous months as prime minister in 1868. Disraeli had lost office in the 1868 election because Gladstone had come out clearly for the disestablishment of the Anglican church in Ireland and was supported in that position by Disraeli's ally, Archbishop Manning, who abandoned Disraeli as soon as he saw that the liberals under Gladstone would do better for the Catholics. Disraeli's disillusionment with Roman Catholicism had been intensified in 1868 because he not only felt that he had been betrayed by Manning (the model for Cardinal Grandison), whose support he had for a Catholic University subsidy before Gladstone won the archbishop's favor by sponsoring Irish disestablishment, but he also probably resented the Catholics for causing the difficulties in Ireland which led to his downfall.

Disraeli's wife died in 1872, and he began a romance with Lady Bradford the following year. In 1874, the Tories won a clear victory, and he began his second term as prime minister. His foreign policy was responsible for consolidating the empire and asserting British power in Europe; he bought the Suez Canal and helped establish Britain's position as a world power. In 1876, Queen Victoria raised him to the peerage as the first (and only) earl of Beaconsfield, and he moved over to the House of Lords. By the time he finished *Endymion* in 1880, he was seventy-six and had presided over England's destiny for six years. He was no longer the outsider looking in, but the insider looking out. His interest in defining past social forces and political tensions took a back seat to his interest in demonstrating the fundamentally civilized basis of the English sociopolitical system. Because the focus is on Endymion's ascent more than on the political history of the 1820s through the late 1850s, Disraeli omits most of the social turmoil in the years covered by *Sybil*, as well as the intellectual issues raised in *Lothair*. In *Endymion*, the views a man holds are far less important than the character of that man. Finally, *Endymion* is a bourgeois novel about succeeding in an aristocratic world. Here, Disraeli's satire is more social than political; his target is the aristocracy's hypocrisy and moral sloth. That Endymion is a sympathetic figure as a member of the Whig party which Disraeli spent his political life fighting illustrates the aging statesman's philosophic and political detachment; in 1880 he saw himself in the role of elder statesman.

While *Endymion* parallels *Coningsby* as a Bildungsroman about the growth of a political leader, Endymion's character is less affected by the political and historical events whirling around him than by family and intimate friends. Like Coningsby, Endymion is exposed to a number of positive and negative examples and must choose among them. After his father's career is blunted by financial crises, Endymion does not have a promising future. But partly through his twin sister Myra's marriage to Lord Roehampton, he gradually makes the crucial political and personal ties that enable him to succeed in politics. As the novel closes, Endymion is called to the prime ministry.

A minor work, *Endymion* is about the art—the choreography, the tempo, the style, and the technique—of creating a career, and Disraeli's narrator is a pervasive and anxious presence as the director of this performance. Yet the essential lack of creativity, imagination, and passion on the part of the title character is in striking contrast to the inventiveness of the speaker's mind. Disraeli wanted to show that the movement from obscurity to prominence—the movement of his own career—could be accomplished without guile or excessive ambition. Therefore he transfers the morally ambiguous activity necessary to climb the greasy pole to Myra and, to an extent, to Lady Montfort, who for a time uses Endymion as a plaything to compensate for her own failed marriage. Because of the frustrations of her apparently asexual marriage to a man who ignores her, she funnels her sublimated libidinous energy into political machinations that aid Endymion's career. The intensity, determination, and ruthlessness of Lady Montfort and Myra undermine Endymion's stature within the novel. When he succeeds to the prime ministry, Endymion is a man lacking in real intellectual ability whose fate is controlled by his sister and Lady Montfort. In contrast to the activities of Myra, Lady Montfort, and his wealthy friend Adriana Neuchatel on his behalf, his memories of his parents' misfortunes virtually paralyze Endymion with fears of his own political downfall.

The romance of Endymion regaining the family position appealed to Disraeli, who believed that he himself belonged to a family and a race which was more than the equal of the English nobility and that he was a kind of paradigm illustrating that England was a land of opportunity. In this last novel, Disraeli is more intrigued by the process by which power is obtained than by the goals of power. Endymion's ascent, rather than the quality of his mind or his capacity for leadership, is the subject. Because people are always doing things for him, he lacks the energy, ambition, and dash of the typical Disraeli hero.

Looking back with delight upon his own ascent, despite his position as an outsider and despite his having been patronized as an eccentric and a dandy, Disraeli dramatized the social and political ascent of a host of characters who, by a combination of strong will and good luck, overcome personal and family adversity. After *Sybil*, the second novel of the Young England trilogy, Disraeli's major characters really do not discover essential principles with which to lead the community, but rather search for something beyond politics to compensate for a lack they feel within themselves. Tancred seeks religious truth; Lothair seeks both religion and another person who will fulfill him; Endymion seeks personal relationships. Unlike Tancred or Alroy, Lothair has no religious awakening; unlike Coningsby or Egremont, Endymion does not discover political principles. In these novels, particularly *Endymion*, pliability and flexibility become values in themselves: a man must learn how to make the political and social structure work for him. In the political trilogy, men had the opportunity to shape history; in these novels, history (the concatenation of circumstances in which a man lives) shapes men. Rather than present relentless judgment of a social system that desperately needs changing as in *Sybil*, Disraeli's last novels perceive the social and political order as a benign self-regulating system which corrects its own errors and which is fundamentally untouched by hypocrisy, sloth, or vindictiveness. In *Lothair* and *Endymion*, despite St. Barbe's envy and spite, despite the cardinal's massive duplicity, despite Fenian rallies and European revolution, England's essential health survives.

Disraeli lost the election of 1880 to Gladstone and died in 1881. He deserves to be read and reread. His early novels move one by their teeming life, their exuberance, and their understanding of the ambitious, idealistic heroes. The later novels provide a panoramic vision of Victorian life from the unique perspective of a man who sat in Parliament and held high office. In all his novels Disraeli was an astute observer of manners and morals. Reading them, one has a sense of the changing mores of nineteenth-century social and political life

Disraeli's grave on his Hughenden estate. He chose to be buried here rather than at Westminster Abbey.

from 1826 to 1880. From no other Victorian novelist can so much be learned about the Oxford Movement, the position of Catholics in England, and the human consequences of bad harvests and exploitative landlords.

While Disraeli is read to supplement one's view of the nineteenth century, he is also read because he is a splendid artist. His cosmopolitan, lively, often ironic voice engages attention whether he is presenting the aspirations of potential heroes or the failures of political and religious institutions. The sheer joy in telling is Disraeli's most marvelous asset and delights the reader even if the plot wobbles—as it does on occasion, particularly in the early *Vivian Grey* and *The Young Duke*. He was a brilliant satirist throughout his career, as the caricatures of Phoebus and Lord Monmouth demonstrate. Disraeli knew how to select carefully and to exaggerate details in order to transform a character into a grotesque, but he also knew how to develop meticulously a character by showing him or her in diverse situations. Disraeli was a profound psychologist, and his understanding of human behavior became more and more complex and subtle. The infinite variety of his novels reflects his exuber-

ant enjoyment of the variety he found in life. His great dramatic scenes—the young duke in his gambling den, Ferdinand in the spunging-house, Sybil's search for her father through London, the tommy shop in the mining district—remain among the great moments in English fiction.

Biographies:
J. A. Froude, *The Earl of Beaconsfield* (London: Low, Marston, 1890);

Wilfrid Meynell, *Benjamin Disraeli: An Unconventional Biography* (2 volumes, London: Hutchinson, 1903);

W. F. Moneypenny and G. E. Buckle, *The Life of Benjamin Disraeli* (6 volumes, London: Murray, 1910-1920);

Cecil Roth, *Benjamin Disraeli* (New York: Philosophical Library, 1952);

B. R. Jerman, *The Young Disraeli* (Princeton, N.J.: Princeton University Press, 1960);

Robert Blake, *Disraeli* (London: Eyre & Spottiswoode, 1966);

Christopher Hibbert, *Disraeli and His World* (London: Thames & Hudson, 1978).

References:

Sir Isaiah Berlin, "Benjamin Disraeli, Karl Marx, and the Search for Identity," in *Transactions of the Jewish Historical Society*, 22 (1968-1969);

Stephen R. Graubard, *Burke, Disraeli and Churchill* (Cambridge, Mass.: Harvard University Press, 1961);

John Holloway, *The Victorian Sage* (New York: Macmillan, 1953);

Richard Levine, *Benjamin Disraeli* (New York: Twayne, 1968);

Daniel R. Schwarz, *Disraeli's Fiction* (London: Macmillan, 1979; New York: Barnes & Noble, 1979);

Morris Edmund Speare, *The Political Novel* (New York: Oxford University Press, 1924).

Papers:

The Disraeli papers, known as the Hughenden papers because they were until recently located at Hughenden Manor, Disraeli's home, are at the Bodleian Library, Oxford University.

George Eliot
(Mary Ann Evans)

Joseph Wiesenfarth
University of Wisconsin

BIRTH: South Farm, Arbury, Warwickshire, 22 November 1819, to Robert and Christiana Pearson Evans.

MARRIAGE: 6 May 1880 to John Walter Cross.

DEATH: London, 22 December 1880.

BOOKS: *Scenes of Clerical Life* (2 volumes, Edinburgh & London: Blackwood, 1858; 1 volume, New York: Harper, 1858);

Adam Bede (3 volumes, Edinburgh & London: Blackwood, 1859; 1 volume, New York: Harper, 1859);

The Mill on the Floss (3 volumes, Edinburgh & London: Blackwood, 1860; 1 volume, New York: Harper, 1860);

Silas Marner: The Weaver of Raveloe (2 volumes, Edinburgh & London: Blackwood, 1861; 1 volume, New York: Harper, 1861);

Romola (3 volumes, London: Smith, Elder, 1863; 1 volume, New York: Harper, 1863);

Felix Holt, The Radical (3 volumes, Edinburgh & London: Blackwood, 1866; 1 volume, New York: Harper, 1866);

The Spanish Gypsy: A Poem (Edinburgh & London: Blackwood, 1868; Boston: Ticknor & Fields, 1868);

George Eliot in 1860, drawn by Samuel Laurence

How Lisa Loved the King (Boston: Fields, Osgood, 1869);

Middlemarch: A Study of Provincial Life (8 parts, Edinburgh & London: Blackwood, 1871-1872; 2 volumes, New York: Harper, 1872-1873);

The Legend of Jubal and Other Poems (Edinburgh & London: Blackwood, 1874; Boston: Osgood, 1874);

Daniel Deronda (8 parts, Edinburgh & London: Blackwood, 1876; 2 volumes, New York: Harper, 1876);

Impressions of Theophrastus Such (Edinburgh & London: Blackwood, 1879; New York: Harper, 1879);

Quarry for Middlemarch, edited by Anna T. Kitchel (Berkeley: University of California Press, 1950);

Essays of George Eliot, edited by Thomas Pinney (New York: Columbia University Press, 1963; London: Routledge & Kegan Paul, 1963);

Some George Eliot Notebooks: An Edition of the Carl H. Pforzheimer Library's George Eliot Holograph Notebooks, Mss. 707, 708, 709, 710, 711 [the *Daniel Deronda* notebooks] edited by William Baker (Salzburg: Universitat Salzburg, 1976);

George Eliot's Middlemarch Notebooks: A Transcription, edited by John Clark Pratt and Victor A. Neufeldt (Berkeley: University of California Press, 1979);

A Writer's Notebook, 1854-1879, and Uncollected Writings, edited by Joseph Wiesenfarth (Charlottesville: University of Virginia Press, 1981).

COLLECTION: *The Works of George Eliot*, Cabinet Edition (24 volumes, Edinburgh & London: Blackwood, 1878-1885).

The most learned and respected novelist of the later Victorian period, George Eliot suffered a decline in reputation after her death and into the early twentieth century because the biography stitched together by her widower, John Walter Cross, left out the most interesting parts of her life. "It is not a Life at all," said Gladstone. "It is a Reticence in three volumes." Although her contemporaries Anthony Trollope and Henry James saw her as the first psychological realist in the English tradition, readers of *George Eliot's Life as Related in Her Letters and Journals* (1885) saw her as the sibyl of a dying age. A revival of interest in George Eliot's novels began on the centenary of her birth with an essay in the *Times Literary Supplement* by Virginia

South Farm, Arbury, George Eliot's birthplace

Woolf, and crystallized with the publication of F. R. Leavis's *The Great Tradition* in 1949. Since then she has been at the center of literary study, and *Middlemarch (1871-1872)* is now regarded as one of the outstanding masterpieces of nineteenth-century fiction.

George Eliot was born Mary Ann Evans at five o'clock in the morning of St. Cecilia's Day, 22 November 1819, at South Farm, Arbury, Warwickshire. Her father was Robert Evans (b. 1773) and her mother was his second wife, Christiana Pearson (b. ca. 1788), whom he had married in 1813. Mary Ann had a half brother, Robert (b. 1802); a half sister, Frances (b. 1805), called Fanny; a sister, Christiana (b. 1814), called Chrissey; and a brother, Isaac (b. 1816), who was to be the most important sibling in her life. George Eliot described her father as a man who "raised himself from being an artisan to be a man whose extensive knowledge in very varied practical departments made his services valued through several counties. He had a large knowledge of buildings, of mines, of plantations, of various branches of valuation and measurement—of all that is essential to the management of large estates." These varied activities are telescoped in the word "business" which Caleb Garth, an idealized version of Robert Evans, uses to describe his work in *Middlemarch*. The Pearson family was considered socially superior to the Evans family, and Robert was thought to have done well in marrying Christiana four years after the death of his first wife, Harriet Poynton, in 1809. After the birth of Mary Ann, however, Christiana—the sharp-tongued model of the invalid Mrs. Poyser of *Adam Bede* (1859)—was not in good health; indeed, she lost sickly ten-day-old twin boys in 1818. Consequently she sent her children to school when they were quite young. When Mary Ann was four months old, the family moved to "a charming red-brick ivy-covered house on the Arbury estate" of Sir Francis Parker-Newdigate, which Robert Evans managed. Griff House was the place George Eliot was most attached to: "my old, old home," she later affectionately called it. There Mary Ann saw her father manage the Newdigate property much in the manner that Adam Bede did the Donnithorne woods. There she came to hear the clucking of the relentlessly respectable Pearson sisters, her maternal aunts, whom she later immortalized as the rich and righteous Dodson sisters of *The Mill on the Floss* (1860). The neat and trim Chrissey was the apple of their aunts' eye and the disheveled Mary Ann the bane of their existence. Mary Ann was, however, her father's favorite child, while her mother preferred Isaac to her daughters. It was Robert Evans who gave Mary Ann *The Linnet's Life*, her first book, which she kept until her death.

When she was sent to join Chrissey as a boarder at Miss Lathom's school at Attleborough, Mary Ann was separated from Isaac, who had hitherto been her constant companion. Perforce she turned from fishing, marbles, and top spinning to reading and was deeply immersed in the imaginative world of Scott's *Waverley* (1814) by the time she was eight years old. In 1828, the sisters transferred to Miss Wallington's school in Nuneaton, where Maria Lewis, the chief governess, became Mary Ann's intimate friend. It was under Miss Lewis's tutelage that the child became an ardent Evangelical, although her parents were traditional Anglicans. Having learned French and become adept at music, Mary Ann, age thirteen, exhausted the accomplishments offered by Miss Wallington's school and transferred to the Misses Franklin's school in Coventry. Daughters of a Baptist minister, the Misses Franklin sharpened the dogmatic tendencies of Mary Ann's mind, giving a Calvinist tint to its Evangelical shade. The girl dressed so severely that one visitor mistook her for a schoolmistress. At Nuneaton, nonetheless, Mary Ann learned to excel as a pianist under the guidance of a local church organist. With a year of Parisian experience, Rebecca Franklin—a prototype of Esther Lyon in *Felix Holt, The Radical* (1866)—brought Mary Ann to proficiency in French, and she won Pascal's *Pensees* (1844) as a prize for excellence in the language during her first year at school. Under Miss Franklin's guidance she also lost her provincial pronunciation and learned to speak English faultlessly in a strikingly modulated voice that was to become a marked characteristic of George Eliot as well as of her principle heroine, Dorothea Brooke, whose voice was like that "of a soul that had once lived in an Aeolian harp." Immersion in historical romances combined with a gift for composition led Mary Ann to write a story in imitation of G. P. R. James: the hero is "an outcast from society, an alien from his family, a deserter, and a regicide." "Edward Neville" is the title Gordon S. Haight has given to this first extant fragment of fiction from the pen of George Eliot.

Mary Ann left the Coventry school at the end of 1835; her mother died the following February. After Chrissey married in May 1837, Mary Ann became mistress of Griff. In addition to attending to the housekeeping and caring for her father, she continued her intellectual pursuits. She studied German and Italian with a tutor and made progress

Griff House, George Eliot's favorite home during her childhood

in Latin and Greek. She published her first poem in the *Christian Observer* in January 1840; untitled, though beginning with a quotation from 2 Peter 1: 16, the poem's first stanzas are indicative of its religious fervor:

> As o'er the fields by evening's light I stray,
> I hear a still, small whisper—"Come away!
> Thou must to this bright, lovely world soon say
>   Farewell!"
>
> The mandate I'd obey, my lamp prepare,
> Gird up my garments, give my soul to pray'r,
> And say to earth and all that breathe earth's air
>   Farewell!

As her religious commitment intensified, she proposed composing a chart of ecclesiastical history from the birth of Christ to the Reformation. She was given unlimited use of the Arbury Hall library and read widely in scriptural commentary, the Oxford *Tracts for the Times*, church history, and the edifying biographies of eminent Christians. When, after her "deconversion," the Birmingham theologian Francis Watts visited her in 1842 with the hope of bringing her back to the faith, he could not. Commenting on her extensive reading on religious subjects, he said quite simply, "She had gone into the question."

Robert Evans retired as manager of the Newdigate estate in 1841 and in March moved with his daughter to Bird Grove, a large house on the Foleshill Road, just outside of Coventry. There, in November, Mary Ann found in Charles and Caroline Bray and Caroline's sister and brother, Sara and Charles Christian Hennell, friendship and an intellectual community far different from any she had known previously. Bray was a ribbon manufacturer by trade but a philanthropist and freethinking philosopher by preference. Hennell was the author of *An Inquiry Concerning the Origin of Christianity* (1838), a copy of which Evans bought and read. Hennell had written the *Inquiry* at Caroline's request to substantiate—contrary to her husband's contention—that Christianity was a divinely revealed religion. After a thorough study of the gospels, Hennell concluded that truth of feeling, not divine revelation, shows itself in the "beautiful fictions" at the origin of Christianity. He affirmed that the New Testament account of Jesus' life could not pass the test of history and that the gospels were a compilation of myths expressing man's deepest thoughts and feelings. Evans met the Brays and Hennells, as Charles Bray later remarked, at a point in her life when she was "turning towards greater freedom of thought in religious opinion." Consequently Hennell's treatise acted as a catalyst in a mind prepared for change by reading in Wordsworth, Scott, Carlyle, and their contemporaries in literature and science. On 13 November 1841, eleven days after meeting the Brays at their Rosehill home, Evans wrote to Maria Lewis: "My whole soul has been engrossed in the most interesting of all enquiries for the last few days, and to what result my thoughts may lead I know not—possibly to one that will startle you, but my only desire is to know the truth, my only fear to cling to error."

Shortly thereafter she abandoned her Evangelical faith, denied divine revelation, affirmed the truth of feeling, and cast off taboos associated with fundamentalist belief. For her as for Hennell, Christianity changed from a divinely revealed religion to one of human origin which leads to "the finer thoughts and feelings of mankind" that "find a vent in fiction." In January 1842 Mary Ann refused to attend church, and her outraged father threatened to put her out, sell Bird Grove, and live elsewhere by himself. Only the timely intervention of Fanny, Isaac, Chrissey, and family friends prevented a complete rupture. Mary Ann finally agreed to accompany her father to church as long as she could think as she pleased while she was there: "I have nothing to say this morning, my soul as barren as the desert; but I generally manage to sink some little well at church, by dint of making myself deaf and looking up at the roof and arches." She

lived on with her father at Foleshill—"I and father go on living and loving together as usual, and it is my chief source of happiness to know that I form one item of his"—and she came to regret her failure to tolerate his intolerance during the crisis in their lives, because for her "*truth of feeling*" was, finally, "the only universal bond of union." The large tolerance that would become characteristic of George Eliot's narrative voice first finds expression in those words addressed to Sara Hennell in 1843. The novelist who was later to say that her realistic fiction was meant "to call forth tolerant judgment, pity, and sympathy" found that she had allowed intellectual conviction to run roughshod over filial feeling. George Eliot found in the "Holy War" with her father the *truth of feeling* that would be the hallmark of her fiction.

Through the Brays, Evans met Rufa Brabant, who, when she became Charles Hennell's fiancée, abandoned the project of translating David Friedrich Strauss's *Das Leben Jesu* (1835), having completed only two chapters. Evans assumed the task. Strauss's book argued that Christian myth represented the truth of feelings and aspirations which were an expression of the *idea*, in the Hegelian sense of the word, that divinity and humanity are eventually to be reunited. "Proved to be an idea of reason, the unity of divine and human nature must also have an historical existence." The Jesus of the Gospels is seen as the product of his disciples' idea that he was the heaven-sent Messiah promised in the Old Testament. Jesus, however, was only the *symbolic* anticipation of a Divine Humanity, which is the *real* goal toward which all creation actually strives. Evans was immersed in the translation of this relentlessly

Charles and Caroline Bray and Sara Hennell, three of George Eliot's closest friends (Coventry City Library)

Robert Evans, George Eliot's father, around the time of their disagreement over religion in 1842

picture-restorer in March 1845, she had changed her mind and sent him away: "I did meditate an engagement," she wrote Martha Jackson, "but I have determined, whether wisely or not I cannot tell, to defer it, at least for the present." Shortly she was to become involved more compromisingly with the publisher John Chapman, and more desperately with the philosopher Herbert Spencer.

In her last years in Robert Evans's house, Mary Ann had worked on a translation of Spinoza's *Tractatus Theologico-Politicus* (1670) at the suggestion of Chapman, who had published the *Life of Jesus*. Although her admiration for Spinoza amounted to adulation—Spinoza "says from his own soul what all the world is saying by rote"—she did not complete the translation. From December 1846 to February 1847 she published five essays under the rubric "Poetry and Prose, From the Notebook of an Eccentric" in the Coventry *Herald and Observer*, a newspaper which Charles Bray had bought in June 1846. The most notable of three known reviews from that period was one she wrote of James Anthony Froude's *The Nemesis of Faith* (1849) for the *Herald*. Froude's novel had been publicly burned at Exeter College, Oxford, where he was a fellow; nevertheless, Evans praised his book as one that makes us feel "in companionship with a spirit who is transfusing himself into our souls and so vitalizing them by his superior energy, that life, both outward and inward, presents itself to us in higher relief, in

analytical book from January 1844 to June 1846. Toward the end of her task, she told Caroline Bray that she was "Strauss-sick" because "it made her ill dissecting the beautiful story of the crucifixion, and only the sight of her Christ-image and picture made her endure it." While this work of translation sapped her energy, she also cared for her aging father, whose health began to fail in 1846. He died after a prolonged illness on 1 May 1849. "What shall I be without my Father?" she asked the Brays. "It will seem as if a part of my moral nature were gone. I had a horrid vision of myself last night becoming earthly sensual and devilish for want of that purifying restraining influence." Something of that fear was undoubtedly grounded in the attraction she had felt to Rufa's father, Dr. Robert Brabant, who had toyed with her affections to the extent that his wife, though blind, had seen enough to order Mary Ann out of her house in November 1843. A similar lack of emotional stability had manifested itself in what she called "my unfortunate 'affaire.' " Having accepted the suit of an engaging young

Portrait of George Eliot by François D'Albert-Durade, 1849 (National Portrait Gallery)

colours brightened and deepened." Exhausted by her father's illness and devastated by his death, she could, however, do no further intellectual work. With a legacy of £ 100 in her pocket and an annuity of approximately £ 90 to support her, she set out with the Brays for the Continent, taking the route of the grand tour.

When they arrived in Geneva in July 1849, Evans decided on a protracted stay in the city of Rousseau, whose *Confessions* (1781, 1788), she had told Ralph Waldo Emerson at Rosehill in July 1848, "first wakened her to deep reflection." She lived for a time in a pension, the Compagne Plongeon, where a Piedmontese noblewoman insisted that she change her hairstyle: "The Marquise . . . has abolished all my curls and made two things stick out on each side of my head like those on the head of the Sphinx." She moved in October to the house of the Francois D'Albert-Durades: "I like these dear people better and better—everything is so in harmony with one's moral feeling that I really can almost say I never enjoyed a more complete bien-être in my life than during the last fortnight." She came quickly to call Madame "Maman," and she loved Monsieur "as if he were father and brother both." He was "not more than 4 feet high with a deformed spine," but he was an accomplished painter. With an excellent singing voice as well, D'Albert-Durade was the model of Philip Wakem, the hunchbacked musician-painter of *The Mill on the Floss*. Whether—like Philip—he loved a Maggie in "Minnie," as he called Evans, remains an unanswered question. A salon was held each Monday evening, and Evans mixed with a cultivated Genevese society that admired the plain-looking young lady from England. She sat for a portrait by D'Albert-Durade which she carried back to England, where he escorted her in March 1850. Finding her family uncongenial companions, Marian, as she now called herself, settled with the Brays at Rosehill until January 1851, when she went to London to make her career in journalism and took up residence at John Chapman's house.

The ground floor of 142 Strand housed the offices of Chapman's bookselling and publishing business, and the rest of the building was home for his wife; his two children; and his mistress, Elizabeth Tilley, who was ostensibly the children's governess. The house was large enough to accommodate boarders. Having first met Chapman in 1846, Evans had seen him again at Rosehill in October 1850, when he discussed with Charles Bray his intention to buy the *Westminster Review*. She had just written an excellent notice of R. W. Mackay's *The*

The philosopher Herbert Spencer, object of George Eliot's unrequited love

Progress of the Intellect (1850) for that periodical when she arrived in London. It was not long before she aroused the ire of Elizabeth Tilley, who saw Chapman trying to ensnare Evans in his far-flung amorous net. Evans left London in late March and stayed at Rosehill until May, when Chapman, soon to purchase the *Westminster Review*, invited Evans to edit it; she returned to 142 Strand on 29 September 1851, Chapman having convinced his wife and mistress that her presence was required for business reasons. She served as editor of the *Westminster Review* from January 1852 to July 1854, living at Chapman's until 17 October 1853.

During her years at the Chapman house, Marian Evans met many of the eminent intellectuals of the day who passed through the offices of the *Westminster Review*. The two who became most important to her were Herbert Spencer, to whom she proposed marriage; and George Henry Lewes, who made her his lifelong companion. Evans and Spencer enjoyed each other's companionship in conversation, on walks, and at the theater and opera until she fell very much in love with this handsome confirmed bachelor: "I want to know if you can assure me that you will not forsake me, that you will always be with me as much as you can and share your thoughts and feelings with me. If you become attached to someone else, then I must die, but until then I could gather courage to work and make life valuable, if only I had you near me. I do not ask you to sacrifice anything—I would be very good and cheerful and never annoy you. But I find it impossible to contemplate life under any other conditions," Evans wrote Spencer in July 1852. Although, as she said, "all the world is setting us down as engaged," Spencer found it impossible to return her affection: "Physical beauty is a *sine qua non* with me," Spencer wrote in his *Autobiography* (1904), "as was once unhappily proved where the intellectual traits and the emotional traits were of the highest." George Henry Lewes was a friend of Spencer's, and Evans had been introduced to him by John Chapman at Jeff's bookshop in the Burlington Arcade on 6 October 1851. At first Evans did not like Lewes's manner and thought him very ugly as well. But he became a regular visitor at 142 Strand; and one day, visiting there with Spencer, he stayed behind with Evans after his friend left. By 28 March 1853, she found Lewes "as always, genial and amusing. He has won my liking, in spite of myself." As the dramatic critic of the *Leader*—Lewes wrote his column under the name of Vivian—he had entree to the theaters and began taking Evans there with him. In addition, one contribution or another of Lewes's appeared in almost every edition of the *Westminster Review* that she edited. They were frequently together; and on 17 October 1853, when Marian moved from the Strand to 21 Cambridge Street, Hyde Park, they may have begun to live together as well. Their intimacy almost certainly dates from this time.

During this period Evans was translating Ludwig Feuerbach's *Das Wesen des Christentums* (*The Essence of Christianity*) (1841). Her love for Lewes and Feuerbach's deification of love intersected at precisely the right moment for her. Lewes was a married man whose wife had been notoriously unfaithful to him by the time he met Evans. Agnes Jervis Lewes had borne Thornton Leigh Hunt two children by then, would bear another before Evans and Lewes left for Germany, and yet another after that. Lewes had registered the first child as his own, thus legally condoning the adultery and making it practically impossible to get a divorce under English law. When the second bastard was born, Lewes considered his marriage terminated morally, if not le-

gally. Marian Evans endorsed this interpretation, and Feuerbach gave her the theoretical ground for doing so. He argued that Christian dogma was the symbolic expression of man's conscious and unconscious needs; thus man has "no other definition of God than this; God is pure, unlimited, free Feeling." Man must become conscious of God as "a loving, tender, even subjective human being." Only love enables him to attain that consciousness. "Love is the middle term, the substantial bond, the principle of reconciliation between the perfect and the imperfect, the sinless and the sinful being, the universal and individual, the divine and the human. Love is God himself, and apart from it there is no God." Consequently, "that alone is a religious marriage which is a true marriage, which corresponds to the essence of marriage—of love." In April 1854, Evans wrote Sara Hennell—who was proofreading this translation as she had the Strauss—"With the ideas of Feuerbach I everwhere agree"; in June she corrected the last proof and inserted her name, Marian Evans, on the title page; and in July she left for the Continent with Lewes, representing herself as his wife. In marked contrast to Maggie Tulliver in *The Mill on the Floss*, she did not turn back.

Isaac Pearson Evans, who was so outraged by his sister's relationship with Lewes that he did not speak or write to her for twenty-three years

The Leweses, as they became known, went to Weimar to follow the tracks of Goethe, whose biography Lewes was writing. Evans wrote the first of a series of articles for the *Westminster Review*. She also wrote to Chapman telling him of the joy she had found in her union with Lewes: "Affection, respect, and intellectual sympathy deepen, and for the first time in my life I can say to the moments, 'Verweilen sie, sie sind so schön.'" Meanwhile Charles Bray was defending her character back in England, where spicy gossip garnished delicious rumor: "She must be allowed to satisfy her own conscience. . . . I have known her for years and should always feel that she was better by far than 99/100 of the people I have ever known." Very few felt that way, and the Lewes-Evans liaison was roundly condemned. After a sojourn in Berlin, where Evans worked on a translation of Spinoza's *Ethics* (1677) while Lewes continued with *The Life and Works of Goethe* (1855), they returned to England in March 1855, eventually taking up residence in Richmond. From July 1855 to January 1857 Evans wrote the "Belles Lettres" section of the *Westminster Review* in addition to a series of often brilliant essays that marked her path to fiction. Her article "Evangelical Teaching: Dr. Cumming" convinced Lewes of her genius, and her review "The Natural History of German Life" outlined her theory of realism in art: "Art is the nearest thing to life; it is a mode of amplifying experiences and extending our contact with our fellow-men beyond the bounds of our personal lot. All the more sacred is the task of the artist when he undertakes to paint the life of the People. Falsification here is far more pernicious than in the more artificial aspects of life. . . . The thing for mankind to know is, not what are the motives and influences which the moralist thinks *ought* to act on the labourer or the artisan, but what are the motives and influences which *do* act on him." This is the beginning of a credo on art that is enacted in George Eliot's fiction beginning with "The Sad Fortunes of the Reverend Amos Barton," which she started to write on 23 September 1856.

In "How I Came To Write Fiction" (1857), Marian Evans says that Lewes urged her to try her hand at a novel, certain of her ability in every way but the writing of dialogue and dramatic scenes. Once he had read what she had written, his enthusiasm and encouragement never waned. He sent the manuscript of "Amos Barton" to William Blackwood and Sons, Edinburgh, saying only that the author, whose work was unsigned, was a friend of his. John Blackwood accepted the story and sent fifty guineas as payment. *Scenes of Clerical Life* was now established, with "Amos Barton" making its way into print and "Mr. Gilfil's Love-Story" being written. "Janet's Repentance" was meant to be the penultimate story, but Blackwood's dislike of the first two parts of it discouraged the author, and the series was concluded. The first installment of "Amos Barton" appeared in *Blackwood's Magazine* in January 1857 and the last part in the February issue. Responding to John Blackwood's cover letter for the second installment, Marian Evans signed her name "George Eliot" as "a tub to throw to the whale in case of curious inquiries." She later said that she took this name because "George was Mr. Lewes's Christian name, and Eliot was a good mouth-filling, easily pronounced word." Since Marian Evans was a name held in scorn because of her liaison with Lewes, she was forced to find a pen name that would give her fiction a fair hearing. "George Eliot" was born of scandal to live in honor. The last two stories of *Scenes of Clerical Life* appeared in the next nine issues of *Blackwood's Magazine*, and all three were published as a book in two volumes under the pseudonym "George Eliot" on 5 January 1858.

Scenes of Clerical Life is written out of George Eliot's recollections of the Midlands. People in Warwickshire began immediately to relate fact to fiction: the Reverend John Gwyther of Chilvers Coton Parish Church to the Reverend Amos Barton of Shepperton, his wife Emma to Milly Barton, Christiana Evans to the sharp-tongued Mrs. Hackit, and the Newdigate family to the Oldinports. Further identifications were made not only in "Amos Barton" but in each of the stories to follow. George Eliot was forced to protest that "no portrait was intended" and that "the details have been filled in from my imagination." But these first stories showed how close to the quick her imagination cut. They were also evidence of a realism that transcended local color to express the tragedy, pathos, and humor of life generally.

The sad fortunes of Amos Barton stem from selfishness and misunderstanding, and George Eliot is keen on purging her readers of such faults by letting them see these qualities in others. The two most misunderstood people in the town of Milby are Amos and the Countess Czerlaski. They are both persons whom their neighbors want to misunderstand: Amos is so commonplace that they do not want to believe that anyone could possibly be so dull; the countess is so beautiful that they do not want to believe that she could possibly be good. When Amos gives a home to the uncommonplace countess, Milby makes her his mistress. Two unlikely lovebirds are thus killed with one unpleasant

John Blackwood, publisher of most of George Eliot's books, in 1857

either life or art presents it to him. "Amos Barton" stands forth as a story about the dangers of failing to apprehend the truth of life and about the need for sympathetic understanding to get at that truth.

George Eliot defends her choice of an old gin-sipping parson as the hero of a romance in "Mr. Gilfil's Love-Story": "Dear ladies, allow me to plead that gin-and-water, like obesity, or baldness, or the gout, does not exclude a vast amount of antecedent romance." Just as in "Amos Barton," an unlikely hero is here justified in terms of life as the reader knows it. Gilfil is the remnant of a highly intelligent and sensitive man who, through the lack of these qualities in others, has lost the one woman he passionately loved. Maynard Gilfil, who loves Caterina Sarti, can marry her only after she has been physically and emotionally weakened by her passion for Captain Anthony Wybrow. Sir Christopher Cheverel (whose beautifully restored manor house George Eliot modeled on the Newdigates' Arbury Hall) knows nothing of his nephew Anthony's flirtation and tries to force him into the arms of an heiress and Maynard into the arms of Caterina. All this eventually proves too much for Caterina, who dies in childbirth as Gilfil's wife: "the delicate plant had been too deeply bruised, and in the struggle to put forth a blossom it died." Something in the sensitive and stalwart Gilfil dies with Caterina: "Tina died, and Maynard Gilfil's love went with her into deep silence for evermore." The gin-sipping parson survives into old age—just, generous, sympathetic as well as loved and respected—but only as the gnarled trunk of what had promised to be a splendid tree. "Mr. Gilfil's Love-Story" is a study of the effect of the loss of love on human growth at the same time that it is a study of the selfishness that surrounds Gilfil and Tina and takes life and love from them. In the dramatization of Anthony Wybrow as a Narcissus who lets his lover turn into an Echo and finally loves himself to death, and in the presentation of Maynard Gilfil as an Orpheus who cannot bring his Eurydice back from death, George Eliot tells her story of selfishness and self-lessness, giving mythical resonance to the love story of an ordinary-looking clergyman who likes his dogs and his drink. In this second of the *Scenes of Clerical Life* George Eliot begins to give extraordinary dimension to ordinary lives.

This continues in "Janet's Repentance," where a Christlike clergyman, Edgar Tryan, struggles with a diabolical drunken lawyer, Robert Dempster, for the soul of Dempster's wife Janet, who is herself an alcoholic. Janet is presented as the lost sheep that the Good Shepherd must find and save. Mythically,

fiction. And so is Amos's loving wife Milly, who, isolated from her friends and worn out by children and childbirth, dies—redeeming her husband in his parishoners' eyes: could anyone who grieved as deeply as Amos have ever loved anyone but his lovely, lamented wife?

George Eliot shows her readers how the town's dislike of Amos and the countess has led it to invent reasons for its scorn by creating damaging fictions about them. The townspeople enjoy their own fiction more than the truth they refuse to admit: "the simple truth . . . would have seemed extremely flat to the gossips of Milby, who had made up their minds to something much more exciting." George Eliot is hinting here that readers of her story who object to its being about commonplace people—"But my dear madam, it is so very large a majority of your fellow-countrymen that are of this insignificant stamp"—are like the gossips of Milby who would rather have excitement than truth. If the reader recognizes his own lack of sympathy with the truth in Milby's lack of sympathy with it, he has a better chance to accept the truth the next time in Dempster and Tryan, Christ faces Satan; psychologically, the spoiled child faces the self-possessed man. The story centers on Janet, the action being her repentance. It portrays her moving out of an atmosphere of negativity and hate, centered in Dempster, and into one of affirmation and love, centered in Tryan. It shows how her life is changed by substituting the gospel which Tryan preaches, one emphasizing the efficacy of sorrow, for the one she early espouses: "That is the best Gospel that makes everybody happy and comfortable." This change leads to the "recognition of something to be lived for beyond the mere satisfaction of self, which is to the moral life what . . . a great central ganglion is to animal life." The conversion concerns the town, "a dead an' dark place," as well as Janet. Milby turns from the narrow, self-satisfied way which Dempster's bullying drunkenness exemplifies to the way of self-surrender which is Tryan's Christian message. The narrator penetrates the mystique of heroism by entering minutely into the character of Tryan to understand him by

A rare photograph of George Eliot, taken by John Edwin Mayall in 1858 (Mansell Collection)

feeling with him: "I am on the level and in the press with him, as he struggles his way along the stony road through the crowd of unloving fellow-men." What George Eliot said of Julia Kavanaugh's *Rachel Gray* (1856) can aptly be said of "Janet's Repentance": "It undertakes to impress us with the every-day sorrows of our commonplace fellow-men, and so to widen our sympathies."

Reflecting on *Scenes of Clerical Life*, Mathilde Blind fixed on its realistic portrayal of the commonplace by speaking of George Eliot's "power of rendering the idiom and manners of peasants, artisans, and paupers, of calling up before us the very gestures and phrases of parsons, country practitioners, and other varieties of inhabitants of provincial towns and rural districts." This homely domestic realism, combined with psychological penetration of character, added up to a new kind of fiction. Shortly before the publication of *Scenes of Clerical Life*, George Eliot lamented that Dickens could only give "with the utmost power . . . the external traits of our town population"; she went on to say, "if he could give us their psychological character—their conceptions of life, and their emotions—with the same truth as their idiom and manners, his books would be the greatest contribution Art has ever made to the awakening of social sympathies." What Dickens could not do George Eliot began doing in *Scenes of Clerical Life*. Adapting a program of realism from Ruskin's *Modern Painters* (1843-1856), George Eliot insisted that art had the moral purpose of widening man's sympathy with his fellowman and that this could only be achieved by presenting a true picture of life. "The truth of infinite value" that Ruskin teaches, she says, "is *realism*—the doctrine that all truth and beauty are to be attained by a humble and faithful study of nature, and not by substituting vague forms, bred by imagination on the mists of feeling, in place of definite, substantial reality." By the "thorough acceptance of this doctrine" George Eliot began to remold the English novel.

"There can be no mistake about *Adam Bede*," wrote the reviewer for the *Times*. "It is a first-rate novel, and its author takes rank at once among the masters of the art." George Eliot began writing *Adam Bede* on 22 October 1857 and completed it on 16 November 1858. It was published in three volumes on 1 February 1859. A year later it had gone through four editions with four printings of the last edition; had been translated into French, German, Dutch, and Hungarian; had spawned a sequel; and had brought forward a Warwickshire eccentric named Joseph Liggins who claimed to be George

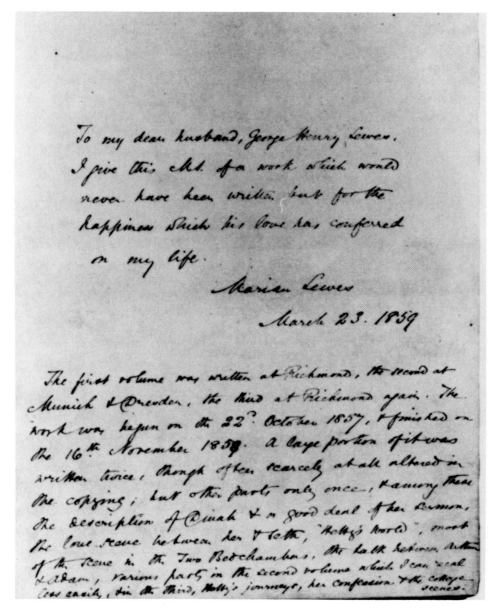

The first page of the manuscript of Adam Bede, *inscribed to G. H. Lewes (British Museum)*

Eliot. *Adam Bede* sold 16,000 copies in a year and earned George Eliot £1,705 in 1859. "In its influence," Lewes wrote to his son Charles, "and in obtaining the suffrages of the highest and wisest as well as of the ordinary novel reader, nothing equals *Adam Bede*."

"The germ of 'Adam Bede,'" George Eliot wrote in her journal, "was an anecdote told me by my Methodist Aunt Samuel (the wife of my Father's younger brother): an anecdote from her own experience. . . . It occurred to her to tell me how she had visited a condemned criminal, a very ignorant girl who had murdered her child and refused to confess—how she had stayed with her praying, through the night and how the poor creature at last broke out into tears, and confessed her crime." George Eliot turned the condemned criminal into Hetty Sorrel, while "the character of Dinah grew out of my recollections of my aunt," and "the character of Adam, and one or two incidents connected with him were suggested by my Father's early life; but Adam is not my father any more than Dinah is my aunt." They are "the suggestions of experience wrought up into new combinations."

Adam Bede presents two levels of society as one century gives way to another in 1799. The gentry are represented by Arthur Donnithorne and the workers by Adam Bede. Their lives intersect in various ways, but especially at the Hall Farm on the Donnithorne estate, which is in the capable hands of the Poyser family. Mrs. Poyser's two nieces live with her. Hetty Sorrel catches the attention of both Arthur and Adam, while Dinah Morris is courted ineffectually by Adam's brother Seth. The more Adam finds himself in love with Hetty, the more Hetty finds herself in love with Arthur, who seduces her in a wood that is under Adam's management. She becomes pregnant, runs away, bears a child, and so neglects it that it dies. Imprisoned for murder, Hetty is visited by Dinah, who brings her to confession and repentance. Adam, who has been sorely tried by the death of his father, now finds himself broken by the infidelity of the woman he loved and the friend he admired. Only the very gradual realization of his love for Dinah and her willingness to marry him allows him to grow whole again.

In these bare details of its plot, *Adam Bede* seems not to be realistic or subtly psychological. It is for this very reason that George Eliot refused to give an outline of the story to John Blackwood, who asked for one after reading the first volume of manuscript. "I refused to tell my story before," she wrote, "on the ground that I would not have it judged apart from my *treatment*, which alone determines the moral quality of art." *Adam Bede* develops in a tragicomic pattern. The tragic element is the idea that a man cannot escape the results of his actions: "Consequences are unpitying," says Mr. Irwine, the novel's excellent clergyman. "You can never do what's wrong without breeding sin and trouble more than you can see," Adam tells Arthur, to no avail. The happier side is the gospel of love that Dinah Morris preaches, with Jesus as her model. As for Jesus, so for Adam: the man of sorrows becomes the loving man. The process requires the self-righteous Adam to get his heartstrings bound around erring creatures—his father, Arthur, and Hetty—all of whom seriously disappoint his expectations. This involves him in suffering and leads him into fellow feeling with these sinners. It also eventually leads him to Dinah, whose attachment to him deepens her own fellow feeling and allows her to accept the common lot of woman as her own.

Adam Bede dramatizes the idea that life is a struggle in which a man succeeds by practicing virtue and working hard. Adam's devotion to work is the touchstone of his success, just as Arthur's emancipation from work leads to his ruin. The life of Adam and the Poysers is a struggle against the ig-

norance, carelessness, vice, and arbitrary ways of their neighbors. The Poysers carry out the struggle against their hired hands, against Hetty, and against old Squire Donnithorne; Adam carries it out against the workmen in the carpenter's shop he manages, against his alcoholic father, and against Arthur. The fistfight he has with Arthur is more than a quarrel between two men over a woman: the new ethic of duty, work, and struggle represented by Adam meets an older ethic of leisure, privilege, and heredity represented by Arthur. The ultimate success of the new over the old is suggested in the return of Arthur in the epilogue, where Dinah likens him to Esau and Adam to Jacob. *Adam Bede* is the mirror of a century that saw the rise of the middle class and the decline in importance of the aristocracy. Set at the turn of the century, it seemed prophetic of things to come. The immediate success of the novel, however, was ascribed to its accurate rendering of country characters and events. Mrs. Poyser was the runaway favorite of readers and critics alike, and her sharp, witty comments on life seemed too true to be the work of a mere novelist—an opinion which led George Eliot to protest: "I have no stock of proverbs in my memory, and there is not one thing put into Mrs. Poyser's mouth that is not fresh from my own mint." Mrs. Poyser's popularity reached its climax when Charles Buxton quoted her in parliamentary debate in the House of Commons on 8 March 1859: dressing down an opponent, he remarked that no doubt the Earl of Malmesbury "would wish that his conduct, as the farmer's wife said in *Adam Bede*, could be 'hatched over again and hatched different.' " Astute critics, like Henry James, found Hetty Sorrel more completely original: "Mrs. Poyser is *too* epigrammatic; her wisdom smells of the lamp." But Hetty Sorrel "I accept . . . with all my heart. Of all George Eliot's female figures she is the least ambitious, and on the whole, I think, the most successful." The discontent of other readers with Hetty, who embodied "the startling horrors of rustic reality," was, however, a prelude to the reception of Maggie in *The Mill on the Floss*.

By the time *The Mill on the Floss* was published on 4 April 1860, it was common knowledge that the pseudonym "George Eliot" belonged to Marian Evans Lewes; that the moral novelist was an immoral woman. The claim of Joseph Liggins to be the author of *Scenes of Clerical Life* and *Adam Bede* became too disruptive for George Eliot to ignore, and she was forced to remove the incognito. The price was high. *The Mill on the Floss* was subjected to scathing criticism: Maggie is not of "the smallest

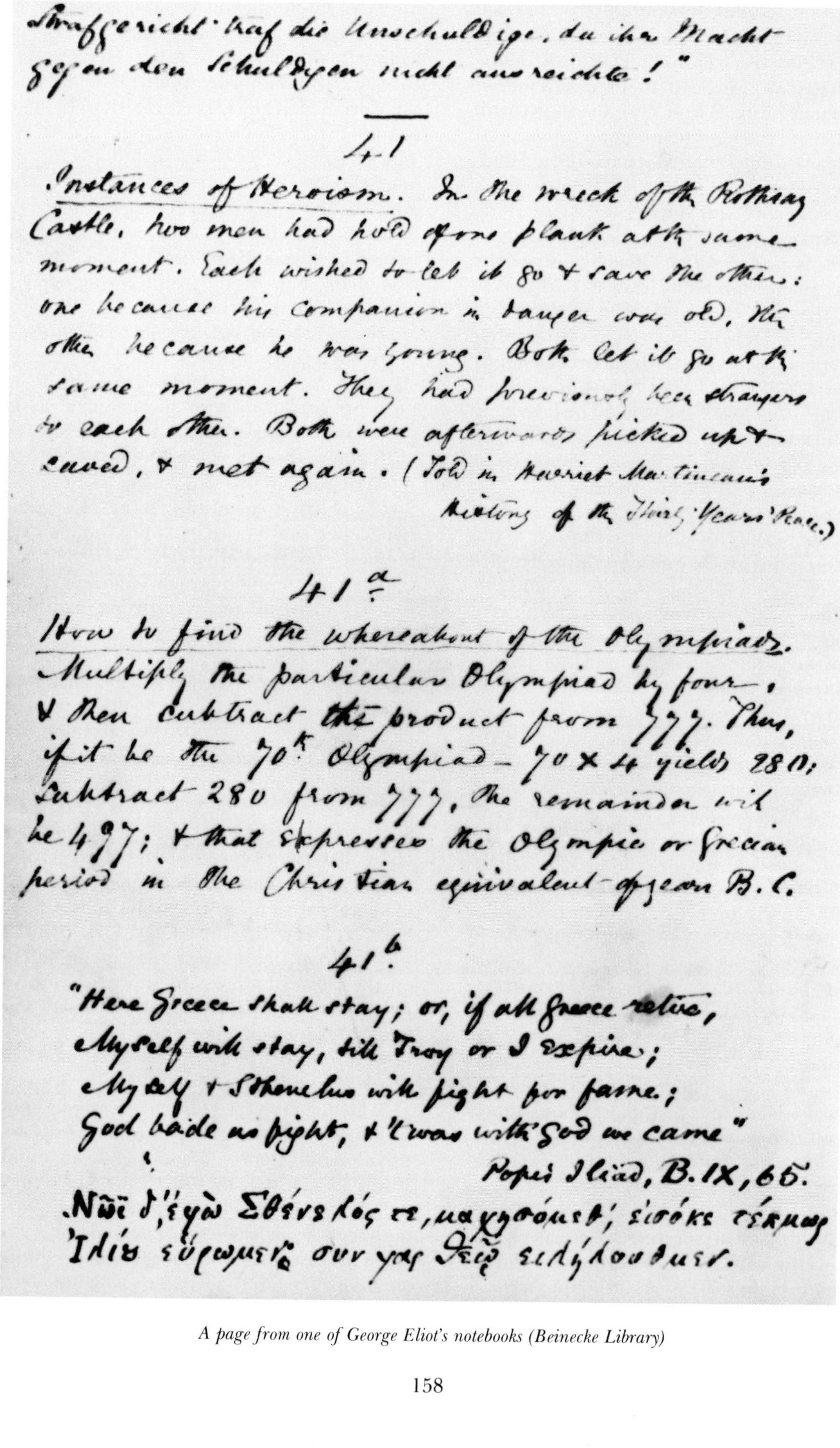

Strafgericht ließ die Unschuldige, da ihre Macht
gegen den Schuldigen nicht ausreichte!"

41

Instances of Heroism. In the wreck of the Rothsay
Castle, two men had hold of one plank at the same
moment. Each wished to let it go & save the other:
one because his companion in danger was old, the
other because he was young. Both let it go at the
same moment. They had previously been strangers
to each other. Both were afterwards picked up &
saved, & met again. (Told in Harriet Martineau's

History of the Thirty Years' Peace.)

41ᵃ

How to find the whereabout of the Olympiads.
Multiply the particular Olympiad by four,
& then subtract the product from 777. Thus,
if it be the 70ᵗʰ Olympiad — 70 × 4 yields 280;
subtract 280 from 777, the remainder will
be 497; & that expresses the Olympic or Grecian
period in the Christian equivalent of years B.C.

41ᵇ

"Here Greece shall stay; or, if all Greece retire,
Myself will stay, till Troy or I expire;
Myself & Sthenelus will fight for fame;
God bade us fight, & 'twas with God we came"

Pope's Iliad, B. IX, 66.

Νῶι δ', ἐγὼ Σθένελός τε, μαχησόμεθ' εἰσόκε τέκμωρ
Ἰλίου εὕρωμεν· σὺν γὰρ Θεῷ εἰλήλουθμεν.

A page from one of George Eliot's notebooks (Beinecke Library)

importance to anybody in the world" but herself, said Ruskin; Tom is "a clumsy and cruel lout"; and "the rest of the characters are simply the sweepings out of a Pentonville omnibus." The great critic whom George Eliot admired but whose wife divorced him because he was unable to consummate their marriage could not abide a novel whose plot, he said, "hinged mainly on the young people's 'forgetting themselves in a boat.'" Ruskin's reaction was symptomatic of that of most critics of the novel: somehow *The Mill on the Floss* affected them where they were weakest. In reading it they followed Maggie's adventures, not "the interaction of the human organism and its environment." They felt that Maggie's free will was unfairly overcome in a moment of crisis. Their simple categories of right and wrong were undermined by a "complex web of heredity, physiology, and environment." Consequently, as David Carroll remarks, "The Victorian reader's sympathies have been turned against his moral judgment and he feels aggrieved."

The Victorian reader who was most aggrieved was undoubtedly Isaac Evans. He was to Marian what Tom Tulliver was to Maggie—a brother whom she loved from her childhood, who early became estranged from her, and who only lately had rejected her altogether. Marian had not told her family of her life with Lewes until nearly three years after she boarded the Channel streamer *Ravensbourne* to go abroad with him. In May 1857 she had written to Isaac to inform him that she now had "someone to take care of me in the world." She had referred to Lewes as "my husband," and Isaac had asked for more details. When she supplied them, he broke off all communication with her except by way of his lawyer. (He was not personally to write to his sister until her marriage in 1880.) The childhood love of sister for brother that had been strained by their different ways of thinking and acting seemed to Marian Evans in 1857 to be irreparably ended. Past and present then came together powerfully in the story of Maggie and Tom in *The Mill on the Floss.*

The novel's long beginning recounts the fortunes of the Dodson sisters and their families. The Tullivers stand apart from the Gleggs and the Pullets and are the center of the story. They have two children whose temperaments reflect Tulliver impetuousness and Dodson respectability. Maggie, like her father, is affectionate, headstrong, and rebellious. Tom, like his mother and aunts, is self-righteous and self-satisfied. More intelligent than her brother, Maggie is interested in many things that mean nothing to him. She is befriended by

George Henry Lewes, George Eliot's "husband," in 1859. The pug dog was given to them by John Blackwood after the successful publication of Adam Bede.

Philip Wakem, whose father has exacerbated Mr. Tulliver's ruin; but Tom banishes Philip from Maggie's life. Along with Philip goes an interest in art, music, and literature that she shared with the one soul that had been completely sympathetic with her own. Maggie turns to religion in an attempt to stupefy her faculties and to banish all wishing from her life, while Tom works off the debts that have resulted from his father's bankruptcy and death. When Maggie realizes, as Philip says, that "we can never give up longing and wishing while we are thoroughly alive," her conduct takes another turn in opening itself up to life. She becomes attached to Stephen Guest, her cousin's fiancé, and, caught up in the tide of her emotions, she drifts away with him in a boat until it becomes too late for them to return home the same day. When, against his pleas, she returns as soon as she can, Tom, now the model of a successful St. Ogg's businessman, repudiates her as a lost woman: "You shall find no home with me. . . .

You have disgraced us all." Only in the end does Tom have a change of heart, but by then it is too late to be effectual. When the river Floss floods and Tom is trapped at the mill, Maggie rows out to save him. In the boat with his sister, Tom in the moment before his death revalues her life: "They sat mutely gazing at each other: Maggie with eyes of intense life looking out from a weary, beaten face—Tom with a certain awe and humiliation." In an instant their boat is swamped: "brother and sister had gone down in an embrace never to be parted."

The power of the book lies in an evocation of childhood that was unequaled when *The Mill on the Floss* was published and in the onrush of the catastrophe toward the novel's end. The flood that kills Tom and Maggie has often been complained of, but it was the ending that George Eliot had intended from the beginning. It enabled her to tie the body of the novel to the history of the place where it is set. St. Ogg's has two legends associated with it: the legend of the flood speaks of a river that grows angry when the Tullivers' Dorlcote Mill changes hands. The legend of St. Ogg tells of a tenderhearted boatman who shows human sympathy in the midst of nature's anger. One legend ties natural effect to human cause and suggests a way to control the river by controlling the working of the mill. The other shows that human kindness enables man to survive nature's ravages. The legend of the flood is one of anger and retribution, and the legend of the patron saint is one of sympathy and love. The flooding of the Floss is closely associated with Tom's anger in the novel, and his attempted rescue is closely associated with Maggie's love. The legends associated with the origin of St. Ogg's are transformed into the characters and events whose story is told as *The Mill on the Floss*.

Having finished the novel, George Eliot left with Lewes for Italy. In Florence he suggested to her the possibility of writing a novel centered on the life of Savonarola, and she began preliminary research for it. All of George Eliot's novels are the product of research—"Whatever she has done, she has studied for," said Emily Davies—even though the earlier ones are principally indebted to recollections of her Warwickshire days. *Romola* (1863), however, was worked up from scratch, and the reading and note taking it required so entered into the author's life that she said of it, "I began it a young woman,—I finished it an old woman." On their return from Italy the Leweses stopped in Switzerland to see Charles, Thornton, and Herbert, Lewes's sons by Agnes. Charles returned home with them after they stopped in Geneva to see the D'Albert-Durades. George Eliot gave the right of translating *Adam Bede* into French to M. D'Albert, who would eventually also translate *The Mill on the Floss* (1863), *Silas Marner* (1863), *Romola* (1878) and *Scenes of Clerical Life* (1884). They returned in June to a house they had taken the year before in Wandsworth, with George Eliot thinking about her Italian novel. But having just acquired three children herself, she wrote instead a novel about a child who comes suddenly into a man's life. The labors of *Romola* were delayed and *Silas Marner* was written. George Eliot began the novel on 30 September 1860 and finished it on 10 March 1861. It was published by Blackwood on 2 April 1861.

Silas Marner is a tale of alienation that is perched on the edge of tragedy but manages to be a comedy of the kind Demetrius called "tragedy in the disguise of mirth." Silas, a weaver, belongs to a Dissenting sect in the northern manufacturing town of Lantern-Yard. He believes in God, is engaged to a woman named Sarah, and trusts his friend William Dane completely. Dane, however, also loves Sarah and betrays Silas's trust by arranging a theft while Silas is incapacitated with catalepsy. The money is cached in Silas's dwelling, and he is accused of the crime. Silas leaves town, goes south, and settles in Raveloe. He lives there without a friend, without a woman to love, and without a God to believe in. Year in and year out he works at his loom, amassing a hoard of gold that becomes his only love until that too is taken from him by the wastrel scion of Red House, Dunstan Cass. Silas reports the theft at the Rainbow, a tavern, and the worthies who are gathered there seriously discuss the crime over their beer pots. During the Christmas season of Silas's fifteenth year in Raveloe, he awakes from a cataleptic seizure to find that a golden-haired child has crawled to his hearth. Eppie replaces his gold as something to love and live for, and he rears her as his daughter with the help of Dolly Winthrop. Having kept secret his first marriage to an opium addict who is now long dead, Godfrey Cass decides to claim the child after the skeleton of his brother, identified by a whip, is found in a drained pit alongside Silas's gold. To prevent a similarly startling revelation of his own guilt, Godfrey confesses to his wife, and they go together to Silas's house to claim Godfrey's daughter. But Eppie refuses to recognize any father except the one who has loved and cared for her. Eventually she marries Aaron Winthrop, and the couple live with Silas. The Rainbow society looks on in the person of its chief elder, Mr. Macey, and approves the happy outcome.

Chap 1   Outside Dorlcote Mill

A wide plain, where the broadening Floss
hurries on between its green banks to the
Northern Sea, & the loving tide, rushing to meet it,
checks its passage with an impetuous embrace.
On this mighty tide the black ships — laden
with the fresh-scented fir-planks, with round sacks
of oil-bearing seed, or with the dark glittering
of coal — are borne along to the town of St Ogg's,
which shows its aged, fluted red roofs & the broad
gables of its wharves between the green banks
& the river brink, tinging the water with a soft
purple hue under the transient glance of this
February sun. Far away, on each hand, stretch
the rich pastures, & the patches of dark earth
made ready for the seed of broad-leaved green
crops, or touched already with the tint of the
tender-bladed autumn sown corn. There is
a remnant still of the last year's golden
clusters of bee-hive ricks rising at intervals
beyond the hedgerows; & everywhere the hedgerows are studded with trees; the distant ships
seem to be lifting their masts & stretching their
red-brown sails close among the branches of
the spreading ash. Just by the red-roofed

First page of the manuscript for The Mill on the Floss (*British Museum*)

Silas in the end gets both the child and the gold; he wins at precisely those points where the Cass brothers lose. He wins because he has learned to love and to act responsibly; they lose because they act irresponsibly. Trusting in chance, Dunstan robs Silas; trusting in chance, Godfrey refuses to acknowledge Eppie until it is too late. But their moments of trust in chance are precisely those that release Silas from its grip. Because his money is taken from him, human feeling is stirred in Silas: he is, as Mr. Macey says, "mushed." Because Eppie comes to him, the stirrings of feeling burgeon into love and responsibility. The moral and emotional hardness that has encased Silas from the time Dane betrayed him is chipped away until a human being is revealed. Silas is redeemed during the Christmas season by the coming of a child for whom he makes himself responsible and whom he learns to love. A father replaces a miser when a child replaces a gold hoard. Eppie then leads Silas back to the community of his fellow men. The novel that began so darkly thus ends brightly. *Silas Marner* finally declares itself a comedy that does not avoid tragedies but contains them: Silas loses all to find all and dies that he might live.

George Eliot had for a third time written a novel about ordinary people. She had once again done for fiction what Wordsworth had done for poetry by showing what was extraordinary in the lives of ordinary men and women. Appropriately, *Silas Marner* begins with lines from Wordsworth—George Eliot's favorite poet:

> A child, more than all other gifts
> That earth can offer to declining man,
> Brings hope with it, and forward-looking
> thoughts.

The novel was received as a relief from the moral complexities of *The Mill on the Floss*, though some reviewers complained again of its low-life realism, like that of the Dutch painters George Eliot had extolled in chapter seventeen of *Adam Bede*. The novel gradually gained wide popularity, surviving in schoolrooms when George Eliot's other novels went unread. *Silas Marner* was mistaken for a simple moral fable that had a "tender religious charm" to it, when in fact it was a version of secular redemption through human love. Its disappearance from reading lists in secondary schools allowed it to find a more critical readership on its own and thereby regain its place as a classic for mature readers.

When *Silas Marner* was reprinted in the Cabinet Edition of *The Works of George Eliot* (1878-1885), it appeared with two stories that had been previously published anonymously. "The Lifted Veil" had appeared in *Blackwood's Magazine* in July 1859, and "Brother Jacob," which was written in August 1860, had appeared in the *Cornhill* magazine in July 1864. These two stories round out the early fiction of George Eliot. "The Lifted Veil," the more important of the two, inverts the action of *Silas Marner*: its protagonist portrays what Silas would have become if he had kept his gold and not found Eppie. Silas dramatizes Carlyle's "Everlasting Yea" and Latimer his "Everlasting No." Latimer can form no bond of fellow feeling with anyone he meets because he cannot accept the mixture of good and evil in human nature. He is blessed with an artist's sensibility but cursed by his inability to create. He is the projection of what George Eliot could have become if she had not sympathetically accepted man as he is: "the only effect I ardently long to produce by my writings is," she says, "that those who read them should be able to *imagine* and to *feel* the pains and joys of those who differ from themselves in everything but the broad fact of being struggling, erring, human creatures." Latimer cannot create because he cannot feel with his fellow man. He is the opposite then of both George Eliot and the best readers of her fiction.

The early phase of George Eliot's career ends with *Silas Marner*, a novel that is generally considered to be the most rounded and balanced of her works. From "Amos Barton" to *Silas Marner*, she gathers together her powers to explore the tragedy and comedy of life as it is lived in carefully delimited rural communities. Beginning with *Romola*, her perspective widens, and she deals with the complexities of human nature as men find themselves living through turning points in the history of Western civilization. She focuses on a period of reformation in Florence in the 1490s in *Romola*; she brings alive the era of Reform in England from 1829 to 1833 in *Felix Holt, The Radical* and *Middlemarch*; and she projects an 1860s Zionist vision of a new Israel in *Daniel Deronda* (1876). George Eliot's last four novels engaged her in a great deal of historical research. "When you see her," Lewes wrote to John Blackwood concerning *Romola*, "mind your care is to discountenance the idea of a Romance being the product of an Encyclopaedia." *Romola* is so filled with learning that Henry James called it "a splendid mausoleum" in which George Eliot's "simplicity . . . lies buried." There was certainly nothing simple about the conception and writing of it. The idea for a novel about Savonarola

147

justify his insincerity by manifesting its prudence.
And ~~illustrious examples every the condend that does~~
~~it god perfect villain immense impact tremendous~~
~~nevertheless~~ in this point of trusting to some throw
of fortune's dice, Godfrey can hardly be called specially
old-fashioned. Favourable chance, I fancy, is
the god of all men who follow their own devices instead of obeying a law they believe in.
Let even a polished man of these days ~~beggetten~~
be set into a position he is ashamed to avow, &
his mind will be bent on all the possible issues that
may deliver him from the calculable results of that
position; let him live outside his income or on think
the resolute honest work that brings wages & he
will presently find himself dreaming of a possible
benefactor, a possible simpleton who may be cajoled
into being his interest, a possible state of mind in
some possible person not yet forth coming. Let
him neglect the responsibilities of his office, & he
will inevitably anchor himself on the chance that
the thing left undone may turn out not to be of
the supposed importance; let him betray his friend's
confidence & he will adore that, same cunning ~~beneath~~

Manuscript for the end of chapter nine of Silas Marner *(British Museum)*

had been presented to George Eliot in Florence in May 1860. After writing *Silas Marner*, she went again to Florence in May 1861 for further research. When she returned to England, reading and note taking continued. On 7 October 1861 she began writing *Romola* but by the end of the month was "utterly desponding" about it. On 1 January 1862 she began writing again and finished it on 9 June 1863, having deserted Blackwood as her publisher—which she later admitted may have been a mistake—to be paid £ 7,000 by Smith, Elder to publish it in fourteen installments in the *Cornhill* magazine before its appearance as a three-volume novel. The encyclopedic research, the delay caused by *Silas Marner*, the false start, the change of publisher, and the serial publication altogether wore George Eliot out and made her, as she said, "an old woman."

Romola is the story of a faithful woman who marries a faithless man. Romola is faithful to her blind, scholarly father, Bardo; to her beloved godfather, Bernardo, a Medicean politician; to Savonarola, the democratic reformer of Florence; and to Florence itself. Her husband, Tito, is unfaithful to these men, to their city, and to Romola. His treachery costs the men their lives, and with nothing to live for, Romola herself wants to die. But she does not: seeking death she finds life. *Romola* is consequently a novel about renaissance. It asks how a woman can be born again once those whom she loves are dead and once personal love itself dies within her. The question is asked in a tragic form that gives universal meaning to a unique period of history, and it is answered in a coda that points away from future tragedy. *Romola* takes up where *The Mill on the Floss* left off: *The Mill on the Floss* ends with a flood, a modern deluge that wrecks a civilization; *Romola* begins in the Renaissance, the rebirth of civilization. The historical time of *Romola* coordinates perfectly with its theme of rebirth. It suggests the intimate relationship between the individual and his civilization while both are in the process of renewing themselves. Thus Savonarola presents to Romola the same ideal that he presents to Florence. Because she is less compromising than he in living out that ideal, she is renewed and Florence is not; she lives and he dies. Romola is reborn from water when her boat is washed ashore, and Savonarola dies by fire when he is burned at the stake. But in his death he is purified, and his principles live on for others to follow. Renaissance is made personal; only when a sufficient number of people embrace it personally can there be a public renewal.

If the Renaissance meant the cultural rebirth

of a civilization and the liberation of the individual, it did not necessarily mean the spiritual rebirth of either. A completely liberated Renaissance man like Tito therefore dies because of selfishness, and late quattrocento Florence falls into anarchy and succumbs to tyranny because it repudiates Savonarola's reform. *Romola* is consequently centrally concerned with the birth of a spiritual ideal in one woman who endures the loss of everyone and everything she loves and survives the license of a civilization that executes the man who gave it an ideal.

At the end of *Romola*—in the coda that George Eliot said belonged to her "earliest vision of the story"—her moral belief in fellow feeling as man's chief saving virtue achieves a new status. Bereft, betrayed, unloved, Romola wants to die, but she must live; others need her. Neither personal pleasure nor personal pain is allowed to be an adequate guide for moral action. Each man, though unique, shares with other men a common humanity that binds him to life when for personal reasons he might choose not to live. Fellow feeling is therefore a universal ethical principle that governs both life and death, and *Romola* puts it to the test. Humanity in the novel is very often deplorable, showing itself in pedantic and vengeful learned men, in faithless and treacherous lovers, in fanatical zealots, and in the bestial rich and the depraved poor. George Eliot shows in the novel that life is painful because of other human beings, but that Romola must affirm life at just that point because the very pain others cause her shows their dire need for her.

When the critics protested against the erotic attraction between Maggie and Stephen in *The Mill on the Floss*, George Eliot replied: "If the ethics of art do not admit the truthful presentation of character . . . *then*, it seems to me, the ethics of art are too narrow, and must be widened!" When the critics set up "a universal howl of discontent" over her departure in *Romola* from "the breath of cows and the scent of hay" that made *Adam Bede* so popular, George Eliot anticipated them in a letter to Sara Hennell: "If one is to have freedom to write out one's own varying unfolding self, and not be a machine always grinding out the same material or spinning the same sort of web, one cannot always write for the same public." In acting like an artist, George Eliot lost some of her audience. The complaint was that the setting was too remote, the evocation of time and place too learned, the "instructive antiquarianism" too lifeless. Whereas Robert Browning called *Romola* "the noblest and most heroic prose poem" that he had ever read and a small coterie came to refer to George Eliot as "the

[handwritten marginalia: Mill ends w/ death & regret; Romola = rebirth, new striving for meaning]

author of *Romola*," the more general reaction to the novel was given in the *Saturday Review*: "No reader of *Romola* will lay it down without admiration, and few without regret."

The publication of *Romola* changed the way that George Eliot was generally viewed by the Victorian public. Although she was still an outsider because of her irregular union with Lewes, she came to be looked upon as a great moral teacher all the same. A new permanent residence (The Priory, 21 North Bank, Regent's Park) and Sunday afternoon receptions added a sense of ritual to her life that enhanced her image as a Victorian sage. The Leweses had The Priory entirely to themselves because Lewes's sons had begun to strike out on their own: Charles, who had a position at the post office, married; Thornton and Herbert went to South Africa to farm a three-thousand acre tract of land on the Orange River (both, however, were to die young, Thornie in 1869 and Bertie in 1875). After another trip to Italy George Eliot settled at The Priory to attempt something altogether new for her in a drama called "The Spanish Gypsy." The first try at writing was a failure, and Lewes took the manuscript away from her when physical and emotional afflictions over her inability to write became gravely debilitating. A month later, on 29 March 1865, she began work on *Felix Holt, The Radical*, which was finished on 31 May 1866. Lewes offered the manuscript to Smith, Elder for £ 5,000; his price was not met because the firm had lost a considerable sum of money on *Romola*. *Felix Holt* was then offered to John Blackwood, who, finding it "a perfect marvel," paid what was asked, and the novel was published on 15 June 1866.

Felix Holt divides its interest between the working class as represented by Felix and the gentry of Transome Court, especially Harold Transome and his aging mother. They are linked together by Esther Lyon, who is courted by both Harold and Felix and who, though reared by the Dissenting clergyman Rufus Lyon, turns out to be the heiress to Transome Court. Felix figures in the novel as a moral catalyst for Esther. Through him she learns what she really wants to do with her life. Set in 1833 at the time of the first election following the passage of the Reform Bill of 1832, the novel presents Felix as a political Radical who accidently kills a man in the midst of a rioting mob. From the courtroom and the jail he wins Esther's conscience and then her heart; at the same time, the elegant Mrs. Transome tries to win Esther as her daughter because Harold had repudiated his mother when he discovered that he is illegitimate. Torn between Felix and poverty

on the one side and Harold and wealth on the other, Esther chooses the former, having briefly experienced the emptiness and sorrow of the latter in a stay at Transome Court.

Felix Holt is not so much Felix's novel as it is Esther's: it is the drama of her moral development. Felix leads Esther to examine the meaning of the goals that she has set for herself: riches, finery, and leisure. Felix forces Esther to confront her erotic impulses and to ask herself whether life is better with love or luxury if one must choose between the two. Felix is indispensable to Esther's ethical and erotic life insofar as she comes to realize that without loving him she cannot be moral: "the man she loved was her hero," and "her woman's passion and her reverence for rarest goodness rushed together in an undivided current." Because of Felix she realizes that Transome Court is a "silken bondage" and "nothing better than a well-cushioned despair."

One of the problems that critics have found with the novel is that there is so much in it that Esther's moving back and forth between two levels of society is not a sufficient dramatic action to unify it. This is especially the case because the characterization of Mrs. Transome is so splendid an achievement that the reader tends to forget the eponymous

The Priory, George Eliot's home from 1863 until her marriage to John Cross

hero, while the speech and movements of this pathetically tragic old woman linger powerfully in the memory. Mrs. Transome is so poignantly drawn that it seems inadequate to think of her as simply an instance of what Esther could become if she turned her back on Felix and took Harold's hand in marriage. The felt life in the novel comes together in Mrs. Transome while its moral intention is focused on the more forgettable Felix. As in Dickens's *Great Expectations* (1861), which anticipates a great deal that is in *Felix Holt*, Mrs. Transome, like Miss Havisham before her, draws out her creator's imaginative genius so completely that no other character is her equal.

[handwritten margin note: Mrs Transome similar to Dickens's Miss Havisham]

With *Felix Holt* finished, George Eliot took up *The Spanish Gypsy* again, but she no longer thought of it as a drama to be staged; it would be a narrative poem with significant dramatic sequences in it. After a trip to Spain in the winter of 1866-1867, she was able to work more comfortably at the poem, and it was completed on 29 April 1868. After its publication, she wrote a series of poems—"Agatha," "How Lisa Loved the King," and the "Brother and Sister" sonnets—before turning her mind once more to a novel. In August 1869 she began work on a novel called "Middlemarch," which in its original conception was only part of the novel that is known by that name today. It was to have focused on Lydgate and the Vincys and to have been set in the middle-class society of the town. Work on this novel was interrupted at the end of 1870 by the writing of two more poems—"The Legend of Jubal" and "Armgart"—and by a peremptory idea for another novel called "Miss Brooke," which would focus on Dorothea and the life of the gentry surrounding a town like Middlemarch. Early in 1871 George Eliot began to amalgamate the Lydgate and Dorothea stories into the one novel under the title *Middlemarch: A Study of Provincial Life*, which Lewes persuaded Blackwood to publish in eight parts, the first part appearing in December 1871 and the last in December 1872. *Middlemarch* was also issued as a four-volume novel in late 1872. "It treats marriage, medical progress, religious idealism, the abstruse researches of mythological Biblical scholarship, recalling Strauss and his peers, the coming of railways into agricultural communities, Reform, conservation, sex, changing fashions in art, and the eternal themes of painful discovery of truth as opposed to romantic, or conventional fantasy," says A. S. Byatt. "It is a novel, above all, about *intelligence* and its triumphs, failures, distractions, fallings-short, compromises and doggedness." The greatness of *Middlemarch* was immediately acknowledged; the

novel was a classic in its own time. Not that it did not raise complaints similar to those that greeted *The Mill on the Floss* where complexity compounded perplexed the critics: it caused confusion because it was even more complex morally and aesthetically than its predecessor. In *The Mill on the Floss* George Eliot had written a tragedy; in *Middlemarch* she wrote an epic. "If we write novels so," asked Henry James, "how shall we write History?"—a question that he answered tellingly in the same review: *Middlemarch* "sets a limit . . . to the development of the old-fashioned English novel." After it, fiction must dare to be difficult. *Middlemarch* could be given too much praise, said Geoffrey Tollotson, only "by saying that it was easily the best of the half-dozen best novels in the world."

Middlemarch: A Study of Provincial Life spreads so wide a canvas that it is frequently compared with *War and Peace*. In it George Eliot weaves together four stories to make one novel. That of Dorothea Brooke shows her making a marriage on idealistic grounds to a scholarly clergyman, Edward Casaubon, who is at least twice her age. She marries him to be his helpmate but turns out to be his critic. Their marriage is a purgatory to each until Casaubon's timely death. A second story, that of Lydgate, is similar to the first. As a gentleman he seems an ideal catch to the daughter of the mayor of Middlemarch, Rosamond Vincy, whose middle-class upbringing requires her to marry into gentility. Her respectability destroys his scientific vocation and leads him to an undistinguished career and an early grave. A third story is that of Nicholas Bulstrode, a banker with a passion for preaching religion and making his favor in God's eyes felt by all—until his past reveals him to have done a dire deed of a kind that he repeats in the present. Linking these three stories together is Will Ladislaw, who learns that Bulstrode is his stepgrandfather, who is mistakenly thought to be Rosamond's lover, and who actually becomes Dorothea's second husband. Ladislaw's love for Dorothea is paralleled by Fred Vincy's for Mary Garth in a fourth story that also introduces the figures of Caleb Garth and Peter Featherstone as original instances of integrity and indulgence, respectively.

A singular note in this novel is the intelligence of the narrator and his sympathy with the human condition. There are no caricatures among the major characters. Each is known so thoroughly that whatever is reprehensible, or indeed even at times criminal, in him is understood in terms of a complex of human desires not very different from those of the reader himself. "With George Eliot, to understand is to pity," says Gordon S. Haight, "—as far as possible, to forgive." In a novel that has no epigraph of its own, one that could serve for the whole novel comes at the head of chapter forty-two, in which the reader is made thoroughly to understand the character of Edward Casaubon: "How much methinks, I could despise this man, / Were I not bound in charity against it!"

Middlemarch begins with a sixteenth-century prelude that presents the life of St. Theresa of Avila as an exemplum of the meeting of individual aspiration and epical opportunity: the time was right for her to become a heroine because Spain had just come to national unity by joining the kingdoms of Aragon and Castile, had just emancipated itself from the Moors at the battle of Granada, and had just begun to produce a literature that would issue in a Golden Age. The one thing it lacked was a spiritual ideal and that was what Theresa gave it by reforming the Carmelite order, founding twenty-six convents and sixteen monasteries. She gave Spain spiritual direction by renewing its religious life. *Middlemarch* goes on to present a series of stories in which individual aspiration does not find an era of epos but only a time of confusion. England in the Reform era is separated into factions either to support or to oppose a new organization of society. This is a period characterized more by pettiness than by magnanimity. The individual aspiring to greatness in such a society finds no sure guidelines and becomes a victim of his lofty aspirations. *Middlemarch*, then, is a novel about individual aspiration coming face to face with social limitation and the unhappy consequences of their meeting. In *Middlemarch* men and women undergo the "varying experiments of Time" from 1829 to 1832; those who emerge as heroes and heroines become in some small way part of the larger historical movement for reform. Caleb Garth insists on reform in the management of estates; Will Ladislaw enters politics on the side of the Reform Bill and becomes a member of Parliament; and Dorothea Brooke promotes the work and ideals of each. Characterized by personal integrity, fellow feeling, and a sense of their place in history, these three characters become instances of the muted heroism open to men and women in a complex world. The novel's most notable failures, Bulstrode and Casaubon, lack all the qualities that allot man a modicum of greatness. Lydgate, a compassionate man with a sense of historical progress, is the novel's great tragic character because his heroic temper is geared to science alone; in other things, like the judgment of women, his mind is common and uncritical. His "spots of commonness" destroy

the aims of his life, which were "to do good small work for Middlemarch" and "great work for the world." The failure of this noble man, understood in its every detail, is the most heartrending drama in all of George Eliot's fiction.

Daniel Deronda is a logical continuation of *Middlemarch*, which constantly emphasizes themes of quest: Dorothea seeks a spiritual ideal, Lydgate scientific discovery and medical reform, Casaubon scholarly recognition, Bulstrode divine instrumentality, Ladislaw a purposeful vocation, and English society seeks Reform. Daniel Deronda seeks his roots in those of his people; he seeks to establish a national center for the Jews so that they may have their own identity as a nation. The far-resonant action which presumed an era of epos in the prelude and which was not apparent to George Eliot as a possibility in *Middlemarch* became apparent to her when she wrote *Daniel Deronda*.

The novel opens in the casino at Leubronn where Gwendolen Harleth is playing roulette. This scene is based on George Eliot's experience in the Kursaal at Homburg where in October 1872 she saw Lord Byron's grandniece "completely in the grasp of this mean, money-raking demon." The germ of Gwendolen's story was here. Mordecai's also had a German origin. Born in Silesia and educated in Berlin, Emanuel Deutsch came into George Eliot's life in 1866. He was a cataloguer of books in the British Museum by profession but a radical Jewish nationalist by preference. He taught George Eliot Hebrew and gave her the idea of a Jewish national homeland. She visited him when he was ill with cancer and mourned his death in May 1873. In June she began thinking about a new book and soon was reading in Jewish sources. Her work on *Daniel Deronda* was delayed by the publication of *The Legend of Jubal and Other Poems* (May 1874) but by June she was again at work on the novel. John Blackwood agreed to publish it in eight parts, the first book appearing on 1 February 1876 and the last on 1 September 1876. The novel was then published in a four-volume edition.

After being reared by Sir Hugo Mallinger, Daniel Deronda finds out that his parents were Jews and that his mother, the daughter of a proto-Zionist, is still alive and wishes to see him before she dies. Having already befriended Ezra Cohen (familiarly called Mordecai) and his sister Mirah, Deronda rejoices in an ancestry that gives him a sense of himself, makes possible his marriage to Mirah, and enables him to fulfill Mordecai's prophecy that he will be a leader of his people. *Daniel Deronda* centers on this quest for self that is at

John Walter Cross, who married George Eliot on 6 May 1880

now they dismiss the Jewish half of *Daniel Deronda*." Deronda is damned as "the Prince of Prigs" for not marrying Gwendolen and for imbibing too deeply the "bottled moonshine of Mordecai's mysteries." In 1948 F. R. Leavis went so far as to retitle the novel "Gwendolen Harleth." George Eliot nevertheless held her ground and insisted that she "meant everything in the book to be related to everything else there." For her, *Daniel Deronda* examines man's need to establish a rule within himself before he can effectively establish himself among other men. It treats this need in the context of a yearning for deliverance from individual and racial bondage so that men and women can live fuller and better lives. At the novel's center is the age-old Hebrew myth of the deliverance of Israel from exile to the promised land. George Eliot finds in this myth a transcendent moral impulse that encompasses Jew and Gentile alike and that leads all men to yearn for spiritual as well as political freedom. Thus the mastery over self that Gwendolen and Deronda seek makes Daniel as integral a part of her life as Mordecai is of Daniel's. For many the ideal ending of such mutual quests would be marriage, but George Eliot denies her readers this easy conclusion. In *Daniel Deronda* the psychological development of Gwendolen and Daniel demands the emergence of moral independence for self-realization. For Gwendolen to marry Daniel would be for her to commit herself to continuous dependence on him, which would be a reversion to her childhood and a denial of maturity. Gwendolen has finally to choose for herself in accordance with the standards she has taken from Deronda and from the experience of sorrow in her awful marriage. George Eliot is finally ruthless with Gwendolen so that she may be truly free.

When Deronda learns of his heritage and accepts it, his life opens out not only beyond any future that Gwendolen could share with him but also beyond the limits of Jewishness itself. Deronda cannot be the kind of intolerant man that his grandfather Daniel Charisi was. He tells his mother that "the Christian sympathies in which my mind was reared can never die out of me." He adds his Jewish heritage to his Christian upbringing and reconciles Jew and Christian within himself; his vocation to a Jewish cause enlarges the scope of his Christian principles. Just as Israel is meant in this novel to figure forth a universal brotherhood—it is to be the "halting-place of enmities"—Daniel Deronda is meant to figure forth a universal man. With him George Eliot's fiction had reached the limit of her moral imagination. She had written her last novel.

If George Eliot's fiction is considered from

the same time a quest for others; but it is anything but a simple romance. It is a story of psychological growth that is achieved by the experience of nearly unbearable pain. It has a counterpoint in another story, that of Gwendolen Harleth, in which Deronda must act as guide for a troubled soul: he must be to Gwendolen what Mordecai is to him. She has made, against her conscience, a hideous marriage to Henleigh Grandcourt—his mistress and the mother of his four children is the woman Gwendolen knows he should have married—and she involves Deronda in her miseries, falling in love with him as well. The story of Gwendolen and Grandcourt—a story of jaded aristocratic England in the 1860s—is far more thoroughly dramatized and consequential than that of Deronda and the Jewish community that surrounds him. The critics, as David Carroll says, were quick to see this: "Just as they had jettisoned the final volume of *The Mill on the Floss*, the historical background of *Romola*, and the tendentious commentary of *Middlemarch*, so

beginning to end, certain broad patterns can be seen in it. From "Amos Barton" to *Silas Marner* she concentrates on the individual in his community, conceived of as a traditional group; from *Romola* to *Daniel Deronda* she concentrates on the individual in his world, conceived of as a polity in a state of change. In *Adam Bede* a new man is created, in *The Mill on the Floss* an old world is destroyed by flood, and in *Silas Marner* a man is redeemed and a new Eden is created and presided over by Unseen Love. In the later novels these patterns of creation, destruction, and redemption are repeated more complexly. In *Romola* a Renaissance civilization is re-created, in *Felix Holt* and *Middlemarch* an old world dies and the world of reform is born, and in *Daniel Deronda* Israel, the halting-place of enmities, is the home of fellow feeling itself. Each of the last four novels reworks themes of the first three and sets them at crucial moments for civilization: Florence in the 1490s wavering between democracy and tyranny; England from 1829 to 1833 wavering between the old corruption and reform; and the people of Israel nearing the end of exile from the New Jerusalem. In all the novels constant patterns of human experience are organized into constant patterns of aesthetic experience. George Eliot moves from tragicomedy (*Adam Bede*) through tragedy (*The Mill on the Floss* and *Romola*) to comedy as "tragedy in the disguise of mirth" (*Silas Marner* and *Felix Holt*) to epic (*Middlemarch* and *Daniel Deronda*). She ends her career as a novelist not with man accepted and assimilated into his community or rejected from it, but with man questing for new values and modes of existence.

Her last book, *Impressions of Theophrastus Such*, a collection of essays, was published in May 1879. It came from the press between the deaths of the two men who knew her best. George Henry Lewes died on 30 November 1878. Lewes had said of George Eliot, "She is a Mediaeval Saint with a grand genius"; she could not but grieve long and deeply over the death of the man who first called that genius out of the depths of her soul and supported it tirelessly all his life. George Eliot understood that no author could have had a better editor and publisher than John Blackwood. When he died on 29 October 1879, she paid him the tribute he deserved: "He has been bound up with what I most cared for in my life for more than twenty years and his good qualities have made many things easy for me that without him would often have been difficult." Bereft of the two men who were her support in life, she turned to John Walter Cross to help her with many of the things that Lewes or Blackwood would

otherwise have done for her. Cross had been an intimate of the Leweses since 1869. A banker, he had handled their investments, and when they sought a country house, it was he who found The Heights at Witley for them. Although the Leweses called him Johnny and referred to him as their nephew, he proposed to George Eliot, who was twenty years his senior, three times. They were married on 6 May 1880 at St. George's Church, Hanover Square. Isaac Evans, who had not written to his sister since 1857, sent his congratulations. George Eliot did not, however, live long enough to enjoy the respectability conferred upon her by a church wedding. She died rather suddenly on 22 December 1880 after an attack of acute laryngitis followed by an attack of kidney stones that together brought on heart failure. She was buried next to Lewes in Highgate Cemetery, a place in Westminster Abbey being denied her as a woman, in Thomas

George Eliot's grave in Highgate Cemetery, London

Henry Huxley's words, "whose life and opinions were in notorious antagonism to Christian practice in regard to marriage, and Christian theory in regard to dogma." In the centenary year of her death, nonetheless, George Eliot made her way to the Poet's Corner of Westminster Abbey when a memorial stone was placed there in her honor.

Translations:

David Friedrich Strauss, *The Life of Jesus, Critically Examined*, translated by Evans from the fourth German edition (3 volumes, London: Chapman, 1846);

Ludwig Feuerbach, *The Essence of Christianity*, translated by Evans from the second edition, Chapman's Quarterly Series VI (London: Chapman, 1854).

Letters:

John W. Cross, ed., *George Eliot's Life as Related in Her Letters and Journals* (3 volumes, Edinburgh & London: Blackwood, 1885);

Gordon S. Haight, ed., *The George Eliot Letters* (9 volumes, New Haven: Yale University Press, 1954-1955; 1978).

Bibliography:

David Leon Higdon, "A Bibliography of George Eliot Criticism, 1971-1977," *Bulletin of Bibliography*, 37: 2 (April-June 1980): 90-103.

Biography:

Gordon S. Haight, *George Eliot: A Biography* (New York: Oxford University Press, 1968).

References:

David R. Carroll, ed., *George Eliot: The Critical Heritage* (New York: Barnes & Noble, 1971; London: Routledge & Kegan Paul, 1971);

Constance M. Fulmer, *George Eliot: A Reference Guide, 1858-1971* (Boston: G. K. Hall, 1977);

Gordon S. Haight, ed., *A Century of George Eliot Criticism* (Boston: Houghton Mifflin, 1965);

Barbara Hardy, *The Novels of George Eliot: A Study in Form* (London: Athlone Press, 1959);

W. J. Harvey, *The Art of George Eliot* (London: Chatto & Windus, 1961);

Harvey, "George Eliot," in *Victorian Fiction: A Guide to Research*, edited by Lionel Stevenson (New York: Modern Language Association, 1964), pp. 294-323;

U. C. Knoepflmacher, "George Eliot," in *Victorian Fiction: A Second Guide to Research*, edited by George H. Ford (New York: Modern Language Association, 1978), pp. 234-273;

Knoepflmacher, *George Eliot's Early Novels: The Limits of Realism* (Berkeley: University of California Press, 1968);

Knoepflmacher and George Levine, eds., "George Eliot, 1880-1980," *Nineteenth-Century Fiction*, 35: 3 (December 1980): 253-455;

Bernard J. Paris, *Experiments in Life: George Eliot's Quest for Values* (Detroit: Wayne State University Press, 1965);

Ruby V. Redinger, *George Eliot: The Emergent Self* (New York: Knopf, 1975);

Joseph Wiesenfarth, *George Eliot's Mythmaking* (Heidelberg: Carl Winter Universitatsverlag, 1977);

Hugh Witemeyer, *George Eliot and the Visual Arts* (New Haven: Yale University Press, 1979).

Papers:

The principal collections of George Eliot's papers are those of the British Museum and the Beinecke Rare Book and Manuscript Library, Yale University; there are also important collections in the New York Public Library, the Pforzheimer Library, the Folger Shakespeare Library, and the Princeton University Library.

Juliana Horatia Ewing
(3 August 1841-13 May 1885)

Margaret Blom
University of British Columbia

BOOKS: *Melchior's Dream and Other Tales*, edited by Mrs. Gatty (London: Bell & Daldy, 1862; Boston: Roberts, 1886);

Mrs. Overtheway's Remembrances (London: Bell & Daldy, 1869; Boston: Roberts, 1881);

The Brownies and Other Tales (London: Bell & Daldy, 1870; New York: Hurst, 1901);

A Flat Iron for a Farthing (London: Bell, 1872; Boston: Roberts, 1886);

Lob Lie-By-The-Fire; or, The Luck of Lingborough and Other Tales (London: Bell, 1874; New York: Young, 1885);

Six to Sixteen (London: Bell, 1875; Boston: Roberts, 1876);

Jan of the Windmill (London: Bell, 1876; Boston: Roberts, 1877);

A Great Emergency and Other Tales (London: Bell, 1877; Boston: Roberts, 1886);

We and the World (London: Bell, 1880; Boston: Roberts, 1880);

Old Fashioned Fairy Tales (London: Society for Promoting Christian Knowledge, 1882);

Brothers of Pity and Other Tales (London: Society for Promoting Christian Knowledge, 1882; New York: Young, 1890);

Blue and Red; or, The Discontented Lobster (London: Society for Promoting Christian Knowledge, 1883);

Jackanapes (London: Society for Promoting Christian Knowledge, 1883; Boston: Roberts, 1884);

Daddy Darwin's Dovecot (London: Society for Promoting Christian Knowledge, 1884; Boston: Roberts, 1885);

The Story of a Short Life (London: Society for Promoting Christian Knowledge, 1885; New York: Young, 1885);

Mary's Meadow (London: Society for Promoting Christian Knowledge, 1886; Boston: Little, Brown, 1900);

Dandelion Clocks, and Other Tales (London: Society for Promoting Christian Knowledge, 1887);

The Peace Egg, and A Christmas Mumming Play (London: Society for Promoting Christian Knowledge, 1887);

Snap-Dragon and Old Father Christmas (London: Society for Promoting Christian Knowledge, 1888);

Verses for Children (3 volumes, London: Society for Promoting Christian Knowledge, 1888).

COLLECTION: *Complete Works* (18 volumes, London: Society for Promoting Christian Knowledge, 1894-1896).

In the field of mid-nineteenth-century children's literature, Juliana Horatia Ewing's work ranks with that of Charles Kingsley, George Mac-

Donald, Charlotte Yonge, Mrs. Molesworth, and Jean Ingelow. Most of her stories and poems first appeared in *Aunt Judy's Magazine* (1866-1885), one of the most important British publications for children, which was edited first by her mother, Margaret Gatty (1809-1873), author of *Parables from Nature* (1855-1871); then by Juliana and her sister, Horatia Katherine; and finally by Horatia Katherine alone. The second of eight children who survived infancy, Juliana was her mother's favorite child, the heiress to her literary ambitions, and, latterly, her confidante and most dependable contributor to *Aunt Judy's Magazine*, which provided a small but necessary addition to the always straitened family finances. From early childhood, Juliana was the mistress of the nursery entertainments: known in the family as Aunt Judy, she was the organizer of private theatricals; the leading spirit in imaginative games; the editor of the family magazine, the "Gunpowder Plot"; and, above all, the never-failing source of original stories. Mrs. Gatty delighted in and fostered her daughter's talent, naming two volumes of stories—*Aunt Judy's Tales* (1859) and *Aunt Judy's Letters* (1862)—after her; encouraging her to write for publication; and exulting when, in 1861, her first story, "A Bit of Green," was published in the *Monthly Packet* edited by Charlotte Mary Yonge.

Mrs. Ewing's close, lifelong ties to home and family were among the most significant influences on her life, and her finest work reflects her happy experience of the bond between brothers and sisters and between children and loving adults. Until her marriage to Alexander Ewing in 1867, Juliana Gatty lived in Ecclesfield, Yorkshire, where for sixty-two years her father, Alfred Gatty, was vicar; and her intimate knowledge of village life is shown in such books as *A Flat Iron for a Farthing* (1872), *Lob Lie-By-The-Fire* (1874), *Six to Sixteen* (1875), *We and the World* (1880), *Jackanapes* (1883), and *Daddy Darwin's Dovecot* (1884), which in their shrewd observation of scene and manners are reminiscent of Mrs. Gaskell's *Cranford* (1853). As the wife of a commissariat officer in the British army, Mrs. Ewing was also familiar with life in the peacetime military. In 1867, she accompanied her husband to Fredericton, New Brunswick, and on their return to England in 1869, they were stationed at Aldershot, where they remained until 1877. Some of her best work—*The Peace Egg* (1887), *Lob Lie-By-The-Fire*, *Jackanapes*, and *The Story of a Short Life* (1885)—celebrates the humanity and heroism of the soldier. After her return from Canada, Mrs. Ewing never again left England. In the late 1870s her always delicate health deteriorated, making it impossible for her to

Frontispiece for Ewing's novel The Peace Egg

accompany her husband when he was sent abroad—first to Malta in 1879 and then to Ceylon in 1881. Until 1883, when Major Ewing returned to England to be stationed at Taunton, she had no settled home, and the stories she wrote during those years of loneliness derive much of their power from nostalgic evocation of the domestic happiness of her childhood.

One of Mrs. Ewing's earliest tales remains one of her most famous. "The Brownies" (first published in 1865 in the *Monthly Packet* and last reprinted in 1954) provided the inspiration for the terminology and ritual of the Brownie division of the Girl Scouts. Using as background the folk tradition of helpful household spirits who perform useful tasks in secret, Juliana Ewing tells a story of two lazy boys who, after searching in vain for a Brownie to do the work of the home, themselves begin secretly to complete these tasks, thus finally proving to their widowed father and grandmother that in truth "bairns are a blessing." The same folk tradition lies behind *Lob Lie-By-The-Fire*, in which an abandoned Gypsy child, after years of casual disobedience that disrupts the lives of the two kindly ladies who have taken him in, runs off from the Hall at Lingborough to become a follower of a Highland regiment. Through his friendship with a soldier whose addiction to drink has placed him in danger of court-martial and execution, the boy is led to see that he should return to his benefactresses. He does so; but—ashamed of his past ungratefulness—instead of revealing his presence, he secretly performs the farmyard tasks, saving the two elderly women from financial disaster. Thus he becomes the embodiment of the long-departed household spirit rumored to be "the Luck of Lingborough."

Like all the finest writers of children's literature, Juliana Ewing speaks to a double audience: the adult who is reading aloud and the listening child, who at a conscious level may be interested only in the story yet is subtly influenced by the value system it illustrates. Witty, gay, gentle, and tenderhearted, Mrs. Ewing wrote stories that teach as they entertain. The conscientious, but therefore unduly apprehensive young mother in "Timothy's Shoes" (1871), who immediately after the birth of her first child falls into a despairing muddle fearing her children may "have bandy legs from walking too soon, or crooked spines from being carried too long," is told by her fairy godmother, "It's too late to talk about that now my dear." In *Lob Lie-By-The-Fire*, the ladies of Lingborough, who live in genteel poverty doing good works in secret by denying themselves such small luxuries as sugar, are "heiresses . . . to a diamond brooch which they wore by turns." When, walking home with the parson from a village whist party, Miss Betty catches "sight of the brooch in Miss Kitty's lace shawl" and notices "where one of the precious stones should have been, there [is] a little black hole," she exclaims, "Sister, you've lost a stone out of your brooch!"—because "the little ladies were well trained, and even in that moment of despair Miss Betty would not hint that her sister's ornaments were not her sole property."

In *Jackanapes*, the antics of a harum-scarum child who grows to manhood and heroically lays down his life for his friend on the battlefield are framed by the voices of the characters from his home village: the neighbors; the postman; his aunt, Miss Jessamine; the Grey Goose, who still waddles on Goose Green, where Jackanapes first learned to ride his red pony, Lollo. But though for the village, "Jackanapes' death was sad news. . . , a sorrow just qualified by honourable pride in his gallantry and devotion," his is not, Mrs. Ewing insists, "a sorrowful story, and ending badly, . . . [of] a life wasted that might have been useful." For "there is a heritage of heroic example and noble obligation, not reckoned in the Wealth of Nations, but essential to a nation's life. . . ; there be things . . . which are beyond all calculation of worldly goods and earthly uses: things such as Love, and Honour, and the Soul

Ewing's grave at Trull, Somerset

of Man, which cannot be bought with a price, and which do not die with death." And the memory of Jackanapes remains to sweeten the lives of those he loved and who loved him. "Lollo, . . . very aged, draws Miss Jessamine's bath-chair slowly up and down the Goose Green"; Captain Tony Johnson—the man for whom Jackanapes died—and his brother officer lovingly bend over the old woman as she speaks of her gay-hearted, valiant nephew. "The sun, setting gently to his rest, embroiders the sombre foliage of the oak tree with threads of gold. The Grey Goose is sensible of an atmosphere of repose, and puts up one leg for the night. The grass glows with a more vivid green, and, in answer to a ringing call from Tony, his sisters, fluttering over the daisies in pale-hued muslins, come out of their ever-open door, like pretty pigeons from a dovecote. And if the good gossips' eyes do not deceive them, all the Miss Johnsons, and both the officers,

go wandering off into the lanes, where bryony wreaths still twine about the brambles."

The quiet emphasis with which Mrs. Ewing speaks to and of the possible best in human nature is the hallmark of her fiction. Though she suffered ill health from childhood and wrote under the constant pressure of pain during her last eight years, her work is remarkable for its gaiety of spirit. Written in a lucid and flowing style, her stories are compassionate and tender, not mawkishly sentimental; deeply Christian, they are never pietistic.

References:

Horatia K. F. Gatty, *Juliana Ewing and Her Books* (London: Society for Promoting Christian Knowledge, 1885);

Christabel Maxwell, *Mrs. Gatty and Mrs. Ewing* (London: Constable, 1949).

Elizabeth Cleghorn Gaskell

Edgar Wright
Laurentian University

BIRTH: London, 29 September 1810, to William and Elizabeth Holland Stevenson.

MARRIAGE: 30 August 1832 to the Reverend William Gaskell; children: Marianne, Margaret Emily ("Meta"), Florence, William, Julia.

DEATH: Holybourne, Hampshire, 12 November 1865.

BOOKS: *Mary Barton: A Tale of Manchester Life*, anonymous (2 volumes, London: Chapman & Hall, 1848; 1 volume, New York: Harper, 1848);

Libbie Marsh's Three Eras: A Lancashire Tale, as Cotton Mather Mills, Esquire (London: Hamilton, Adams, 1850);

Lizzie Leigh: A Domestic Tale, from "Household Words," attributed to Charles Dickens (New York: Dewitt & Davenport, 1850);

The Moorland Cottage, anonymous (London: Chapman & Hall, 1850; New York: Harper, 1851);

Ruth: A Novel, anonymous (3 volumes, London: Chapman & Hall, 1853; 1 volume, Boston:

Ticknor, Reed & Fields, 1853);

Cranford, anonymous (London: Chapman & Hall, 1853; New York: Harper, 1853);

Lizzie Leigh and Other Tales, anonymous (London: Chapman & Hall, 1855; Philadelphia: Hardy, 1869);

Hands and Heart and Bessy's Troubles at Home, anonymous (London: Chapman & Hall, 1855);

North and South, anonymous (2 volumes, London: Chapman & Hall, 1855; 1 volume, New York: Harper, 1855);

The Life of Charlotte Brontë, Author of "Jane Eyre," "Shirley," "Villette" etc., 2 volumes (London: Smith, Elder, 1857; New York: Appleton, 1857);

My Lady Ludlow, A Novel (New York: Harper, 1858); republished as *Round the Sofa* (2 volumes, London: Low, 1858);

Right at Last, and Other Tales (London: Low, 1860; New York: Harper, 1860);

Lois the Witch and Other Tales (Leipzig: Tauchnitz, 1861);

Sylvia's Lovers (3 volumes, London: Smith, Elder,

Elizabeth Cleghorn Gaskell

1863; 1 volume, New York: Dutton, 1863);
A Dark Night's Work (London: Smith, Elder, 1863;
New York: Harper, 1863);
Cousin Phillis: A Tale (New York: Harper, 1864);
republished as *Cousin Phillis and Other Tales*
(London: Smith, Elder, 1865);
The Grey Woman and Other Tales (London: Smith,
Elder, 1865; New York: Harper, 1882);
Wives and Daughters: An Every-Day Story (2 volumes,
London: Smith, Elder, 1866; 1 volume, New
York: Harper, 1866).

COLLECTIONS: *The Works of Mrs. Gaskell*,
Knutsford Edition, edited by A. W. Ward (8
volumes, London: Smith, Elder, 1906-1911);
The Novels and Tales of Mrs. Gaskell, edited by C. K.
Shorter (11 volumes, Oxford: Oxford University Press, 1906-1919).

A recent review of Mrs. Gaskell's critical
reputation divided her critics into three camps. One
group, now fading, still treats her mainly as the

author of *Cranford* (1853). A second emphasizes her
"social-problem" novels but insists that they be regarded as literature and not just as social history.
The third and dominant one regards her as "a
maturing artist, and considers each of her works in
relation to the others and her general views, preferring the late fiction but giving all her writing respectful, and perhaps even admiring attention." To
this summary should be added a recent special focus
on her role and influence as a woman writer, and
studies of her as a provincial novelist, relating her
work to that of George Eliot and Thomas Hardy in
its presentation of life in a regional community. It is
also probably true to say that the reputation of her
late fiction—the "nouvelle" *Cousin Phillis* (1864) and
the novel *Wives and Daughters* (1866)—is still growing.

She won instant recognition with her first
novel, *Mary Barton* (1848), which shocked readers
with its revelations about the grim living conditions
of Manchester factory workers and antagonized
some influential critics because of its open sympathy
for the workers in their relations with the masters;
but the high quality of the writing and the characterization were undeniable. (Its accuracy as social
observation has been compared to the work of
Friedrich Engels and other contemporaries by critics such as John Lucas.) At the same time it presented a new world, the world of Lancashire factory
people, making them the main characters and using their dialect (judiciously modified) for the
dialogue. In so doing Mrs. Gaskell, with the
Brontës, opened a path for George Eliot and later
novelists. Yet her next success was with *Cranford*,
stories that drew on memories of her childhood in
the small Cheshire town of Knutsford to present an
affectionate picture of a class and customs already
becoming anachronisms. *Cranford* has charm,
humor, and pathos without sentimentality, and no
purpose other than to present and regret the passing of a community whose values are worth recalling. The two elements of Mrs. Gaskell's fiction responded to different elements in her nature: as her
Cranford narrator says, "I had vibrated all my life
between Drumble [Manchester] and Cranford
[Knutsford]." After her biography of Charlotte
Brontë (1857), it was the Knutsford side that predominated, providing the setting and the main
themes for her later work.

Although she began by creating controversy
with social-problem novels and by suggesting the
adoption of genuine Christian conduct as a solution, it can be seen now that her real interests always
lay with individuals and the underlying moral stan-

dards by which they act and are to be judged. Along with this went an appreciation of the changes in attitudes being created by the rapid social and industrial changes of the period. Knutsford and Manchester came to symbolize contrasting values and ways of life; she worked toward reconciling tradition and change, depicting traditional values while recognizing the necessity and desirability of new ideas and a new society. As a result, the direct role of religion drops away rapidly even in her social-problem novels; in the Cranford novels it appears rarely, and then only as a natural element of custom or behavior.

Her attention was also focused from her earliest work on the social and emotional problems of her women characters. She was capable of drawing fine and intelligent portraits of men, but it is the women who receive her closest and most sympathetic attention. Along with Charlotte Brontë, she gave a depth and credibility to her women characters that influenced succeeding novelists such as George Eliot.

Mrs. Gaskell achieved popular and critical esteem in her lifetime, with *Cranford* easily her most popular work. Although her reputation suffered along with those of all other Victorian writers dur-

ing the period of critical reaction in the early twentieth century, some of her books were always in print; and A. W. Ward's Knutsford edition of her work (1906-1911), still essential reading for its introductions, was reprinted in 1920. (One can get an idea of the quality of critical estimates at that time by noting that the *Cambridge History of English Literature* gathered George Eliot along with Disraeli, Charles Kingsley, and Mrs. Gaskell into a chapter on the political and social novel.)

Besides novels, Mrs. Gaskell wrote short stories, essays, and articles for periodicals. Some of the essays deserve to be better known (for example, "French Life"), for she was a natural essayist. Her most famous work of nonfiction is *The Life of Charlotte Brontë*, still recognized as among the finest biographies in English. Her letters reveal her alert, intelligent curiosity about people and events matched by an eager eye and ear for describing everyday matters. As she says when concluding an early letter to her sister-in-law "Lizzy" Gaskell, "Now mind you write again, and none of your nimini-pimini notes but a sensible nonsensical crossed letter as *I do. . . .*" ("Crossed" means the double use of space by writing vertically across a section written horizontally.) She is not an "intellectual" writer, though a bright and

Knutsford, the original of Mrs. Gaskell's Cranford and Hollingford, in 1863. The women in the window of the building on the left are Mrs. Gaskell's cousins, Mary and Lucy Holland.

very well-read one; any comparison would relate her to Jane Austen rather than to George Eliot in terms of erudition, though she stands somewhere between them in approach and outlook. There is no longer any question about whether or not she is a major novelist; she qualifies both as an artist and in relation to the development of the English novel. The publication of the letters (1966), of the information in J. G. Sharps's invaluable *Mrs. Gaskell's Observation and Invention* (1970), and of Winifred Gérin's biography *Elizabeth Gaskell* (1976) has provided scholars and critics with the material for further interpretation and reassessment.

Elizabeth Stevenson was born of Unitarian parents in London, where her father, William, was keeper of the treasury records. He was a man of parts who had trained as a minister, tried being a farmer, and developed into a respected writer for the major journals, a career he continued until his death. His marriage to Elizabeth Holland would bring the future novelist into the Holland family of Knutsford in Cheshire, a relationship that was to dominate her life. Mrs. Stevenson died when Elizabeth was only thirteen months old; the child was immediately "adopted" by her mother's sister, Aunt Lumb, and removed to Knutsford, where she grew up in the quiet and tranquil atmosphere of an old-fashioned country town, close to Sandlebridge Farm where her grandfather lived and her other Holland relatives visited. There seems to have been little further contact with her father until she returned to London about a year before he died.

Dissenters, and especially Unitarians, believed in education for girls as well as boys. After lessons at home that included French and dancing instruction from an émigré, she was sent at the age of twelve to the Byerley sisters' school at Barford; the school was moved in 1824 to Stratford-on-Avon. The education was of high quality, broad in range (Latin, French, and Italian were standard in the curriculum), and liberal in outlook. She spent five years in surroundings that admirably suited her tastes, intelligence, and love of the country, leaving the school in 1827 an accomplished and—according to the evidence of friends and artists—a vivacious and attractive young woman. She returned to Knutsford, but the disappearance of her only brother brought her back to London in 1828. John Stevenson sailed for the East India Company; nothing is known of how he disappeared, but the sense of loss can be felt in the account of young Peter in *Cranford* and the Frederick episodes in *North and South* (1855). Her father had married again, and when Elizabeth met her stepmother there was antipathy

rather than sympathy. (The portrait of Molly's stepmother, the incomparable Mrs. Gibson, in *Wives and Daughters*, is said to reflect Mrs. Gaskell's impressions.) She stayed with her father until his death in 1829, when, after visits to a banker uncle, Swinton Holland, and a doctor uncle, Henry Holland (later Sir Henry and physician to Queen Victoria)—visits recollected in the opening of *North and South*—she returned to live in Knutsford until her marriage.

During a visit to Manchester she met the Reverend William Gaskell, newly appointed as assistant minister at the Cross Street Chapel; they were married on 30 August 1832. Manchester's Unitarian community was prominent in both commercial and cultural life; Cross Street Chapel was an important Unitarian center, and her husband became a leading figure in the community. Some early biographers have suggested that tensions developed in the marriage, but the evidence does not support this view. The Gaskells seem to have been two intelligent and sensitive people who respected each other's independence and temperament without denying the basic roles of husband and paterfamilias, wife and mother; the letters show that they cared about

Elizabeth Cleghorn Stevenson shortly before her marriage in 1832 (Manchester University Library)

The Reverend William Gaskell

and supported each other's work and habits throughout the marriage. The obvious loss to Mrs. Gaskell was in exchanging Knutsford for Manchester. Knutsford is only sixteen miles from Manchester and is now a commuter suburb, but in the early nineteenth century it was an old-fashioned, sleepy little country town. Although the Gaskells lived on the country edge of Manchester, she was affected physically and mentally by its atmosphere; at the same time, she admired and respected its people and its leading place in the world. The love-hate attitude to "dear old dull ugly smoky grim grey Manchester" is reflected in the earlier social-problem fiction and in her later emphasis on the world of "Cranford."

Mrs. Gaskell spent the next fifteen years mainly in domestic and humanitarian activity. A particular grief was the death in 1837 of Aunt Lumb, who left her an annuity of £80. There were small signs of creativity: a sonnet to her stillborn child (1836), and a narrative poem (1837) in the style of George Crabbe written in collaboration with

her husband and meant to be the first of a number of *Sketches among the Poor*. A friendship with the well-known writers and editors William and Mary Howitt led to a recollection of her schooldays, "Clopton Hall," appearing in their *Visits to Remarkable Places* (1840). These scattered creative impulses were brought into sharper focus after the death of her nine-month-old son in 1845. Ward states that her husband advised her to turn to writing as a relief from sorrow and encouraged her to begin her first novel, which was completed in 1847 and eventually taken by Chapman and Hall for £100. *Mary Barton: A Tale of Manchester Life* was published anonymously on 25 October 1848. It created a sensation.

The tale is developed around a standard romantic plot. Mary Barton, the motherless daughter of a mill hand, is nearly seduced by young Carson, the mill owner's son. At the same time, a depression hits Manchester, and in the growing labor troubles John Barton, Mary's father, is selected by lot to kill young Carson as an act of union protest. He carries out the murder, but suspicion falls on Jem Wilson, who loves Mary. After complications and difficulties the truth is revealed with the aid of John Barton's outcast sister, Esther. Barton, dying, is reconciled with Carson; Mary and Jem move away. But a summary of the plot gives little hint of the real force of the novel: the presentation of Manchester life and the pressures that turn John Barton into a murderer. A few attempts had been made to portray factory life in fiction, notably Disraeli's *Sybil* (1845), mainly with a reform intent. But *Mary Barton* is the first realistic portrayal of the phenomenon of the new major industrial city and its people, just as it is a new development in the use of regional dialect and detail. Manchester and its social context were to most readers an eye-opening revelation, whether it was to "hear of folk lying down to die i' th' streets, or hiding their want i' some hole o' a cellar till death come to set 'em free"; or to learn about self-taught operatives with scientific reputations such as Job Legh (based on a real person); or to realize how the drive for profit and jobs was creating a type of society based, not on human relationships, but on what Carlyle—an influence on Mrs. Gaskell—called the "Cash Nexus." (Carlyle wrote a letter of praise to the still-anonymous author.) At the heart of the novel is her bitter comment: "Are ye worshippers of Christ? or of Alecto? Oh, Orestes! you would have made a very tolerable Christian of the nineteenth century!"

Yet the novel is not ponderous, though at this stage Mrs. Gaskell's faith in the Christian ethic as a solution is too facilely displayed. Although critics such as W. R. Greg protested that the novel was unfair to the masters, they recognized the high quality of the writing, the humor that laced its observations and episodes, and the genuineness of the sentiment. Within a year—for the anonymity was quickly broken—Mrs. Gaskell was being lionized in literary London and pressed by Dickens to contribute to his new journal, *Household Words*. Her rather Wordsworthian tale of guilt, remorse, and repentance, "Lizzie Leigh" (1850), led off the opening number and was the beginning of a long association, often with exasperation on both sides, between Dickens as editor and Mrs. Gaskell as contributor. Some minor stories had already appeared in other periodicals before *Mary Barton* came out; by the end of 1851 ten more items were published. They included a Christmas book, *The Moorland Cottage* (1850), the first in her long short story or "nouvelle" form. Then came a story that was to become one of her finest novels as well as her most popular: *Cranford*.

"Our Society at Cranford," now the first two chapters of *Cranford*, appeared in *Household Words* on 13 December 1851 and was itself a fictional version of an earlier essay, "The Last Generation in England," first published in America in 1849. Further episodes were written at irregular intervals until 1853, when the book was published. In the process of writing it, Mrs. Gaskell's natural talent developed a rudimentary plot around Miss Matty's problems and the search for her missing brother, but the attractiveness of *Cranford* lies in the way in which she recreates with humor and affection a way of life that was already old-fashioned when she was a young girl growing up among the little group of ladies of good birth but small income who constituted Cranford society and maintained traditions of social behavior and dress by practicing "elegant economy." While their eccentricities are noted, the essential humanity of the characters is never forgotten.

The original episode was created around the formidable Miss Deborah Jenkyns and her softhearted younger sister, Miss Matty. With the Cranford setting established, the story chronicles the arrival of an elderly widower, Captain Brown, and his two daughters as newcomers to Cranford and their reception by the "Amazons," who are won over by his honest frankness even though he is a man. The sickly elder daughter finally dies; as she is dying the captain is killed by a train while rescuing a young child. A faithful admirer returns to marry the younger daughter. Dickens, as editor of *Household Words*, pressed Mrs. Gaskell for more; at ir-

An 1851 portrait of Mrs. Gaskell by George Richmond (National Portrait Gallery)

regular intervals between January 1852 and May 1853 eight more episodes appeared (there was a hiatus in the middle while she concentrated on *Ruth*). In the process there was a shift of interest and a structural change. As Mrs. Gaskell told Ruskin, "The beginning of 'Cranford' was *one* paper in 'Household Words'; and I never meant to write more, so killed Capt. Brown very much against my will." In expanding the episode into a series she quickly "killed off" Deborah, making the gentler Miss Matty the central figure and developing a rudimentary plot around a long-lost brother who finally returns from India. (This recollection of her own lost brother, John, has already been noted.) The novelist in Mrs. Gaskell was taking over. The interest remains fixed, however, on feelings, relationships, and social conduct. As Winifred Gérin says, "It is a tale told without apparent effort in a style of intimate confidence, like gossip exchanged with a friend"—like Mrs. Gaskell's letters, in fact, only with the vital difference that the gossip is being shaped by the imagination and control of a developing novelist. A few months before she died, Mrs. Gaskell confided to Ruskin that "It is the only

Sandlebridge Farm, near Knutsford, the home of Mrs. Gaskell's grandfather, Samuel Holland. It was the model for Hope Farm in Cousin Phillis.

one of my own books that I can read again; but whenever I am ailing or ill, I take 'Cranford' and—I was going to say, *enjoy* it! (but that would not be pretty!) laugh over it. And it is true too, for I have seen the cow that wore the grey flannel jacket. . . ." The freshness of the telling mirrors the fresh delight in recollection. She would return to the Knutsford world to produce greater work, but not again anything so delightful. (In 1863 she did write one further episode, "The Cage at Cranford," now usually published as an "appendix" to the volume.)

During 1851 and 1852 Mrs. Gaskell was also at work on *Ruth*, published in January 1853, for which Chapman paid £500. Charlotte Brontë, to whom Mrs. Gaskell had sent an early sketch of the plot, admired it sufficiently to make her own publishers delay the publication of *Villette* for a few days so that critics could concentrate on *Ruth*. Its subject was again controversial, this time prompted by anger at the moral conventions that condemned a "fallen woman" to ostracism and almost inevitable prostitution. Dickens's work on behalf of such women may have influenced her choice of subject, but she had already touched on it in the character of Esther

in *Mary Barton*. As before, she drew on background and people she knew: the Reverend Mr. Turner, an old family friend, and his home town of Newcastle provided some of the personality and the setting for the unworldly Dissenting minister Thurston Benson, who befriends the abandoned Ruth, helps her to bring up her child, then stands by her when the deception that she is a widow is revealed. The melodramatic ending, with Ruth redeeming herself as a nurse in a cholera epidemic and dying as she cares for her old lover, while grounded in medical realities of the time, still shows a somewhat desperate reliance on the dramatic conclusion for a plot. The strength of the novel lies in its presentation of social conduct within a small Dissenting community when tolerance and rigid morality clash—Mr. Bradshaw is a finely conceived study of self-righteousness that clearly influenced Dickens's caricature of Mr. Bounderby in *Hard Times* a year later. Although some element of the "novel with a purpose" is present, Mrs. Gaskell's sensitivity in portrayal of character and, even more, her feel for relationships within families and small communities, show a developing sense of direction as a novelist. At the same time, the range of character and the naturalness of the dialogue show increasing command of her material. Sally, the blunt and loyal housekeeper to the Thurstons, is the first of a line of domestic portraits that are a notable feature of Mrs. Gaskell's fiction. Mrs. Gaskell knew the Nightingale family; A. W. Ward, in the introduction to his collection of Mrs. Gaskell's works, quotes a report that Florence Nightingale not only thought *Ruth* to be "a beautiful work" but approved of the fact that Mrs. Gaskell "had not made Ruth start at once as a hospital nurse, but arrive at it after much *other* nursing experience." Mrs. Gaskell knew the situations she wrote about; her experience as a minister's wife in Manchester during cholera outbreaks comes through in the novel.

Ruth touched off an immediate reaction from shocked moralists, though many critics and readers praised it for its courage and its quality. But Mrs. Gaskell, though such attacks made her physically ill, stood by her work. " 'An unfit subject for fiction' is *the* thing to say about it; I knew all this before; but I determined notwithstanding to speak my mind out about it. . . ," she said, though she admitted it was a prohibited book to her own daughters.

She now, somewhat unwillingly, gave in to Dickens's request for a full-length novel for *Household Words*. This would be her final "problem-novel," *North and South*; but before getting down to it she traveled and visited friends. A notable visit was to Haworth: she had met Charlotte Brontë in 1850, and a friendship had developed. Another new friend was Mme Mohl, whose Paris home would be a regular base for future visits abroad. But finally, early in 1854, she began work on the as-yet-untitled novel and was soon anxiously inquiring from Dickens, who was publishing *Hard Times*, if he was going to "strike," a reference to the central episode of her own book. This is a scene in which a crowd of angry strikers attempts to storm the cotton mill run by John Thornton, who is employing Irish immigrants as "knobsticks" (strikebreakers). Dickens assured Mrs. Gaskell, who was concerned about apparent plagiarism, that such a detailed strike scene would not appear in *Hard Times*. The basic plot of the novel is straightforward. The setting is once again Manchester (here called Milton). Margaret Hale is a well-bred girl from Helstone in the rural south of England who is suddenly pitchforked with little money or status into the harsh world of the industrialized north. A leading manufacturer, John Thornton, falls in love with her. They finally learn to understand each other's worth, and in the process to appreciate the qualities of social background each had initially despised in the other.

The novel is far from naive in its development, however, or in the complex structure of plot and subplots used to identify various themes and sets of social or personal relationships. *North and South* develops by stages. It begins in the south, where Margaret's father is a country clergyman who resigns his living and moves north after his conscience rejects traditional articles of faith. It is a misleading beginning since it appears to anticipate, in the popular fashion of the period, a novel of religious doubt. Once the shift north is achieved, on the advice of a wealthy friend from Milton, the novel moves with force and purpose. Layers of social tension are revealed as men are opposed to masters, unionists to nonunionists, wealth to poverty, preconceptions to preconceptions. Mr. Hale becomes a private tutor of classics; Mrs. Hale, clinging desperately to gentility, slowly fades and dies. Nicholas Higgins, the workers' leader, is led from atheism to at least a respect for religion through Margaret's friendship with his daughter Bessie, who is dying from consumption brought on by mill conditions. Mrs. Gaskell even uses a subplot that recalls once again her own vanished brother: Margaret's brother is a naval officer forced to live abroad after standing up to a sadistic captain and being accused of mutiny; Frederick returns incognito to see his dying mother and is suspected by Thornton of being Margaret's secret lover. The various levels of the complicated plot move to resolution through reconciliation and understanding, always Mrs. Gaskell's method and point of view. Thornton gives work to the unemployed Higgins after the strike. Margaret inherits a fortune and saves Thornton from ruin which threatens not only his mill but his experiments with Higgins in improved working conditions. Finally Margaret and Thornton marry.

The contrasts and themes are presented with far more power and subtlety than a plot summary can suggest. For example, the beauty of Helstone contrasts with the ugliness of Milton, but the beauty is a surface for ignorance and cruelty, while the ugliness conceals intelligence and vigor. Furthermore, the values of both Helstone and Milton are laid alongside the idleness and luxury of fashionable London. *North and South* upset preconceived ideas to create an understanding of the new industrial power that had emerged, whose reality was little known and less appreciated. At the same time, with some deliberateness, it balanced the one-sided workingman's view of factory life that Mrs. Gaskell had been criticized for after *Mary Barton*.

North and South, for which she received £ 600

in all, marks a major stage in Mrs. Gaskell's development in several ways. She consciously instituted a comparison between the old rural and new industrial societies; when the problems of the rural laborer and those of the industrial hand were compared, the advantage lay with the new society, as Margaret admits: "If the world stood still it would retrograde—I must not think so much of how circumstances affect me myself, but how they affect others, if I wish to have a right judgment." Even more important is the extent to which her most complex and well-motivated plot to date is firmly structured around the detailed and sensitive study of emotional and intellectual growth in the heroine. In *North and South* Mrs. Gaskell achieves maturity as a novelist. A mark of her confidence in herself was her quiet refusal to modify her way of writing to suit Dickens. In truth, *North and South* is not well suited to weekly serialization; one can feel sympathy with Dickens's increasing frustration—though she did compress the ending, which was rewritten for book publication. Not until the easier bondage of the *Cornhill* would she allow another major novel to be serialized.

North and South was completed by January 1855, and as usual Mrs. Gaskell recuperated by going visiting, this time to Paris and London. She was still away when she heard that Charlotte Brontë had died on 31 March. She had already begun to think of a memoir of her friend when, to her surprise, Brontë's father and husband both asked her to write an official biography. On 18 June she wrote to George Smith, Brontë's publisher, agreeing to undertake it. It was to occupy her fully for the next two years; the result was *The Life of Charlotte Brontë*, published on 25 March 1857, for which Smith paid her £800.

The Life of Charlotte Brontë was an immediate success and has established itself as one of the great biographies. Within the conventions of the period (she did not, for example, feel free to deal with Brontë's feelings for Constantin Heger) it is remarkably frank and full in its search for truth. Later biographies have modified but not replaced it; *The Life of Charlotte Brontë* still stands as a portrait of a remarkable family and its background, as well as being a detailed study of the development and motivation of its exceptional heroine.

For Mrs. Gaskell personally, however, the immediate result of the biography was disastrous. An initial wave of praise was quickly followed by angry protests from some of the people dealt with. In a couple of cases legal action was threatened; she had in fact allowed her sympathies in these cases to color her judgment and had accepted a one-sided view. With the help of her husband and George Smith the problems were resolved without recourse to law, although in the case of Lady Scott, where Mrs. Gaskell had accepted Branwell's version of his dismissal from his tutoring job and laid the blame on his refusal to be seduced by his employer's wife, a public retraction in the *Times* was needed. As she wrote ruefully to Ellen Nussey, Charlotte's old friend: "I am in a hornet's nest with a vengeance." A second edition had to be withdrawn and a revised third edition published on 22 August 1857; this became the standard text.

The Life of Charlotte Brontë is successful because Mrs. Gaskell could treat it as she did her novels. There is perceptive self-criticism in a comment she made that same year to George Smith when rejecting a request to do another biography, one with a political background: "I like to write about character, and the manners of a particular period—for the life of a great Yorkshire Squire of the last century I think I could have done pretty well; but I cannot manage politics." Character, manners, a given period, and a specific community constituted her natural territory. The reference to Yorkshire and the last century has, however, a particular interest, for this would be the background of her next novel, *Sylvia's Lovers* (1863), which owes something of its tone and its heightened psychological insight to the work on the biography.

Mrs. Gaskell had left England on 13 February 1857, before *The Life of Charlotte Brontë* was published, to be the guest of the American sculptor William Whetmore Story in Rome, where she arrived while the carnival was in progress. The holiday was ever afterward recalled as a high point in her life, not only for the impression made by Rome itself but also as the start of a lifelong friendship with the young Charles Eliot Norton (later professor of fine arts at Harvard), a friendship well described by Gérin as "half maternal, half platonic." The letters between them are a major source of information about Mrs. Gaskell's later years. She returned refreshed to find the "hornet's nest" and to pick up once again her life in Manchester and her work as a novelist.

During 1858-1859 she wrote rapidly, mainly items for Dickens, of which two are of more than passing interest. *My Lady Ludlow* (1858) is a short novel cut in two by a long digressive tale. But the basic narrative has something of the *Cranford* touch in its setting of a remembered past with its society and characters; it is the first evidence of a shift back to a *Cranford* approach as the vehicle for the

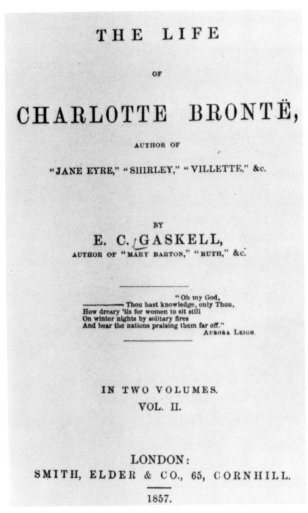

THE LIFE

OF

CHARLOTTE BRONTË,

AUTHOR OF

"JANE EYRE," "SHIRLEY," "VILLETTE," &c.

BY

E. C. GASKELL,

AUTHOR OF "MARY BARTON," "RUTH," &c.

> "Oh my God,
> Thou hast knowledge, only Thou,
> How dreary 'tis for women to sit still
> On winter nights by solitary fires
> And hear the nations praising them far off."
>
> AURORA LEIGH.

IN TWO VOLUMES.

VOL. II.

LONDON:

SMITH, ELDER & CO., 65, CORNHILL.

1857.

Title page for the first edition of Mrs. Gaskell's biography of Charlotte Brontë. The third edition, published the same year and revised under the threat of lawsuits, is now the standard text.

novelist's imagination. On this occasion, however, the basis is not Knutsford, though similar; the setting of the great house and its wide-ranging domain introduces a social breadth that anticipates *Wives and Daughters*, though the period is the late eighteenth century rather than the early nineteenth. The second item, *Lois the Witch* (1861), is a powerfully somber nouvelle about the Salem witch trials whose manner prefigures, by its interest in morbid psychology, her treatment of Philip's relationship with Sylvia in her next novel. This work for Dickens provided money for travel for Mrs. Gaskell and her daughters. Meta, in particular, because of a broken engagement as well as her health in general, was of continuing concern to the anxious mother. Gérin argues that this broken engagement was one of the sources for the central episode of

Sylvia's love for Kincaid in *Sylvia's Lovers*; the plot of the return of a "dead" husband had already been anticipated in a story for Dickens, "The Manchester Marriage" (1858).

Mrs. Gaskell's relationship with George Smith, begun with the biography, had by now developed on friendly as well as business terms. She was already in contact with him over "The Specksioneer" (an early title suggestion for *Sylvia's Lovers*) by the end of 1859. The appearance of his new periodical, the *Cornhill* magazine, in 1860 would provide an outlet for her later work more congenial than *All the Year Round* (Dickens's successor to *Household Words*); the longer sections and monthly publication were better suited to her type of fiction, and she hoped to reserve her better work for it. In a revealing letter to Smith she says of a one-volume-length story (probably "A Dark Night's Work") that it "*is not good enough for the CM*—I am the best judge of that please—but might be good enough for HW." *Sylvia's Lovers* was not, however, for serial publication.

The period between the publication of *My Lady Ludlow* and the completion of *Sylvia's Lovers* was particularly strenuous. At home, on top of the demands on the wife of a busy minister and mother of four daughters whose futures were a source of concern, there were the calls on her time as a hostess and a celebrity. (A good example is the occasion when Manchester was host to the annual meeting of the British Association for the Advancement of Science in 1861, and her house was full of visitors.) Yet the effects of Manchester on her health and spirits made holidays a necessity—even if they were usually working holidays—whether at her favorite seaside at Silverdale, or in Heidelberg or Paris. Her travels frequently supplied her with material for minor stories or articles that she could write quickly and send off, mainly to Dickens, to pay for the trips. A special visit was one to Whitby in November 1859 to research the background for *Sylvia's Lovers*.

The writing moved quickly at first, but by the end of 1860 the novel was only a quarter finished. It progressed fitfully, now provisionally named "Phillip's Idol," through 1861 and 1862, much of it written when Mrs. Gaskell was away from home. Before it was finished, she was caught up in the relief efforts to deal with the depression caused by the cotton shortage in the last month of 1862, when the American Civil War cut off supplies. Her feelings come out in a letter to Smith written during a September visit to the south coast: "I believe we ought to be going back to Manchester (and very hard work, I fear, which exhausts one both bodily and mentally with depressing atmosphere of both kinds)." The

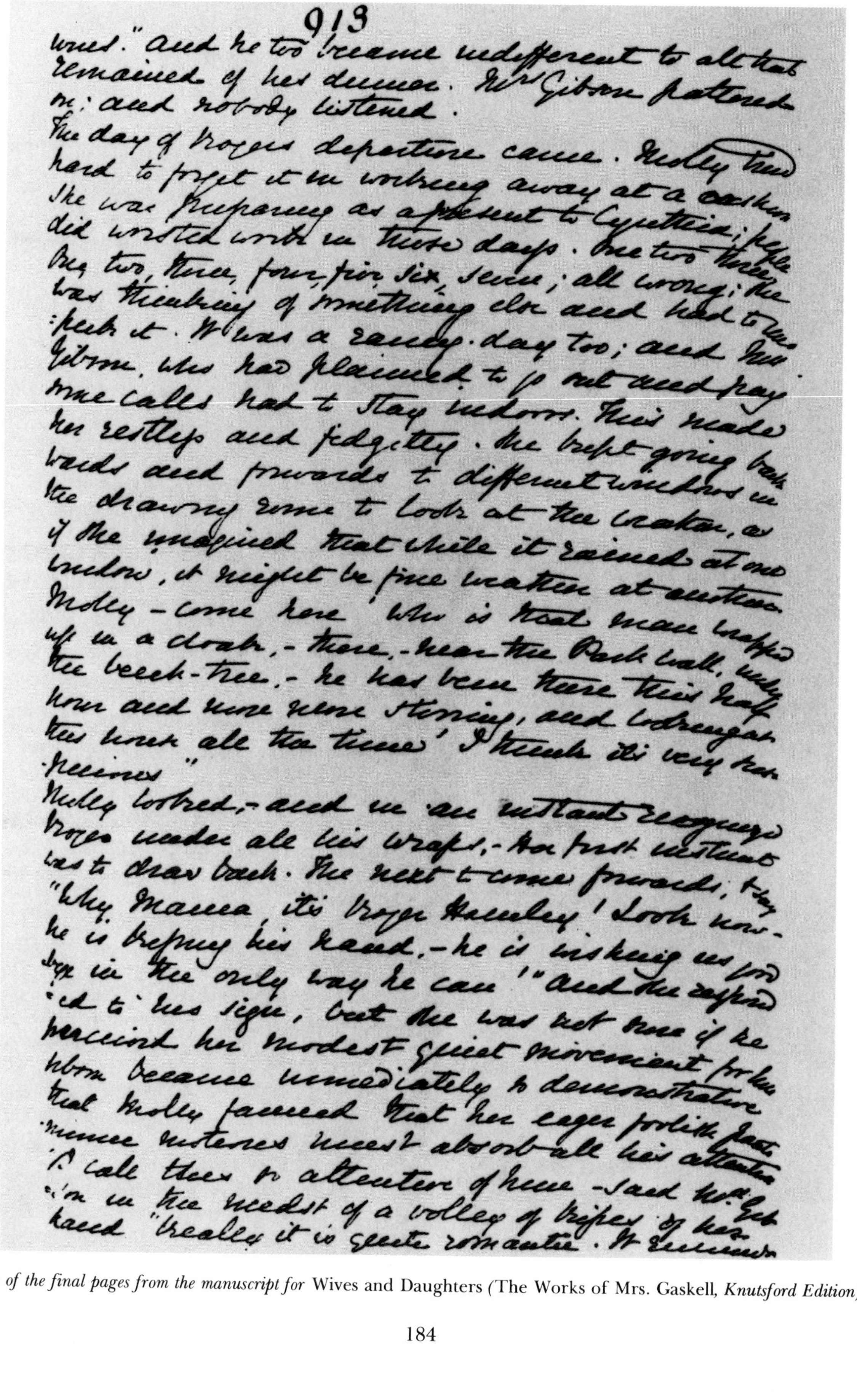
913
[illegible]." and he too became indifferent to all that
remained of her dinner. Mrs Gibson pattered
on; and nobody listened.
The day of Roger's departure came. Molly tried
hard to forget it in working away at a cushion
she was preparing as a present to Cynthia; people
did worsted work in those days. One two three
One, two, three, four, five, six, seven; all wrong; she
was thinking of something else and had to un-
-pick it. It was a rainy day too; and Mrs
Gibson, who had planned to go out and pay
some calls had to stay indoors. This made
her restless and fidgetty. She kept going backwards and forwards to different windows in
the drawing room to look at the weather, as
if she imagined that while it rained at one
window, it might be fine weather at another.
"Molly—come here! Who is that man wrapped
up in a cloak,—there,—near the Park wall, under
the beech-tree,—he has been there this half
hour and more never stirring, and looking at
this house all the time! I think it's very sus-
-picious"
Molly looked,—and in an instant recognized
Roger under all his wraps,—her first instinct
was to draw back. Her next to come forwards, & say
"Why Mamma, it's Roger Hamley! Look now—
he is kissing his hand,—he is wishing us good
bye in the only way he can!" and she respond-
-ed to his sign, but she was not sure if he
perceived her modest quiet movement for Mrs
Gibson became immediately so demonstrative
that Molly fancied that her eager polite panto-
-mime must absorb all his attention.
"I call that so attentive of him—said Mrs Gib-
-son in the midst of a volley of kisses of her
hand "really it is quite romantic. It reminds

One of the final pages from the manuscript for Wives and Daughters *(*The Works of Mrs. Gaskell, *Knutsford Edition)*

depression and exhaustion can be sensed in the final volume of *Sylvia's Lovers*, where both imagination and vitality flag. The novel was finished by the end of the year, and on 31 December she received payment of £ 1000 from Smith. *Sylvia's Lovers* was published in three volumes in February 1863, dedicated to "My Dear Husband, By Her Who Best Knows His Value."

Many of the themes and influences in *Sylvia's Lovers* can be traced in earlier works. The wild countryside and crude habits of its people owe something to the Brontës. Several of Mrs. Gaskell's shorter pieces had used historical episodes as their bases; the background for Whitby ("Monkshaven"), its whaling industry, and the riot against the press-gang were in the sources she had used for these pieces. The story of the return of the "dead" husband, which is the climax of the plot, was taken from Crabbe's poem "Ruth" in *Tales of the Hall* (1819). What is new is the general tone and power of what Easson calls a "tragical history."

Sylvia Robson is the center of a powerful, if somewhat melodramatic, story. Mrs. Gaskell created in Sylvia a portrait of passionate intensity without parallel in her work, which for three quarters of the novel it is difficult to fault. The author had watched her own daughters mature, rejoice, and suffer; she had pondered over the details of Charlotte Brontë's life. All her experience is imaginatively applied to the history of Sylvia. Sylvia's early scorn for her cousin Philip, her love for the harpooner (specksioneer) Kincaid, Kincaid's removal by the press-gang and Philip's false report that presumes his death, her weary acceptance of Philip as husband after her father's execution following the riot—these episodes are welded into a tightly structured narrative that holds the interest. As always, Mrs. Gaskell excels in presenting the setting and community life of the locality. But it is Sylvia's emotional vitality and intensity that give the book its force.

Sylvia's Lovers is a fine work that has been given a tragic ending by a novelist whose temperament and approach are not really tragic. Mrs. Gaskell's view of life accepted the tragic, but was basically melioristic. The first two volumes are full of energy; they sparkle and have humor, as does Sylvia's own character. The ending shows forced invention rather than true tragedy. Philip vanishes, returns unrecognized, and rescues his daughter from drowning before he dies, reconciled with his wife.

The novel's strength lies in the characters and in the insight into relationships between those characters in their setting. Critics vary in their views of it as tragedy but there is wide agreement on the power of the presentation. The tone was not, however, one that was finally congenial to Mrs. Gaskell. In her last works, without losing this new maturity of insight into character, she revisited and reinterpreted the Knutsford world and the changes in attitude that had overtaken society since she was a child there.

By 1863 Mrs. Gaskell seemed to be moving into a calmer, less strenuous way of life, so that when she returned from a Paris holiday to find an appeal from George Smith for a *Cornhill* story, she was able to offer him *Cousin Phillis*, a long short story that she had already started writing. Along with some other pieces, she sold the copyright of the story for £ 250. *Cousin Phillis* ran from November 1863 to February 1864.

The world of the communities created by Mrs. Gaskell in *Cousin Phillis*, and later in *Wives and Daughters*, while based on the *Cranford* world, is experiencing change. The card from the man she secretly loves that shatters Phillis's hope and health is brought by the penny post (created in 1840). The railway, though not physically destructive as it is in Dickens's *Dombey and Son* (1846-1848), brings industrial progress and its new breed of men to the pastoral setting of Hope Farm, an evocation of her grandfather's Sandlebridge Farm (as Minister Holman is based on Samuel Holland himself). This is still a stable world, based on work and sound moral values. The story is an uncomplicated one; its virtues are in the manner of its development and telling. When Paul Manning, an engineer trainee on a railway development nearby, first visits his cousin, his narrative reflects the sense of having stumbled into some idyllic retreat: "I fancied that my Sunday coat was scented for days afterwards by the bushes of sweetbriar and the fraxinella that perfumed the air." Change comes from contact between the two worlds; Phillis's love for Paul's employer, Holdsworth, changes her from quiet girl to suffering woman. Holdsworth himself never quite succumbs to the idyll. His work moves him on beyond Phillis and Hope Farm: his implied failure is a lack of sensitivity, of moral discrimination. Phillis will eventually recover; but the ending has, perhaps, overtones of irony, as she agrees to a change of scene and convalescence. "Only for a short time, Paul! Then—we will go back to the peace of the old days. I know we shall; I can, and I will!"

Most critics would agree with Arthur Pollard's assessment of *Cousin Phillis* as the author's crowning achievement in the short novel; the praise is virtually unanimous. It is also recognized as a fitting prelude to her final novel, *Wives and Daughters*, the idea for which had developed in such detail that she was able to offer it to George Smith with a full synopsis on 3 May 1864. Mrs. Gaskell's wish to carry out a personal plan was also an incentive to writing it. For some time she had been considering the purchase of a house in the country which would be ready for her husband's retirement (he never did retire; he died in Manchester in 1884), and would at the same time be a retreat from Manchester. She had finally found one about fifty miles from London; the £ 2,000 that Smith paid her for the novel enabled her to make the purchase. *Wives and Daughters: An Every-Day Story* ran in the *Cornhill* from August 1864 to January 1866; the final installment was never written, yet the ending was known, and the novel as it exists is virtually complete.

Henry James, "testifying . . . to the fact of her genius" in the year the novel appeared, noted "the gentle skill with which the reader is slowly involved in the tissue of the story" and the way in which its new world presents "this seeming accession of social and moral knowledge." A comparison to Jane Austen for its combination of humor and moral judgment in the observation of character and conduct is often made, not unjustly, though Mrs. Gaskell's canvas is larger than Austen's bit of ivory.

The plot of *Wives and Daughters* is complex, since it relies far more on a series of relationships between family groups in Hollingford than it does on the dramatic structure, which nevertheless is well controlled and integrated with the themes. The novel is set in the same general period as *Cranford* and *Cousin Phillis*, but the Knutsford of Mrs. Gaskell's youth is now reinterpreted as a much wider community. The novelist's matured art and judgments combine with her natural interests, particularly in the portraits of her heroine and what may be called her "anti-heroine." For in Cynthia Kirkpatrick, Mrs. Gaskell created a personality less tragic, yet more intriguing and sophisticated than Sylvia Robson, possessing in W. A. Craik's words "qualities that any novelist before her would find reprehensible." While this perhaps overstates the pioneering element, it does aptly recognize a character of the complexity of Thackeray's Beatrix Esmond within the "every-day story" of Hollingford. Cynthia's less complex but equally well-observed stepsister, Molly Gibson, will marry Roger Hamley, whose career and character draw in part on Mrs. Gaskell's distant relative, Charles Darwin, to present a conjunction

The Gaskells' grave in the Unitarian cemetery, Knutsford

of traditional values and new conceptions. But without doubt the finest creation is the doctor's second wife and Molly's stepmother, Mrs. Gibson. Through speech and conduct she presents, as Margaret Ganz points out, "the humorous and ironical appraisal of a vain and hopelessly petty nature" that is yet "not wholly ill-natured." It may be noted that the world Mrs. Gaskell sees is one without villains in the accepted sense; trouble and suffering are caused by life itself, by selfishness, by a failure of sensitivity to human feelings, by a lack of deeply felt moral standards. The reader is left with the feeling that even Mr. Preston, whose machinations cause the main trouble for Molly, is as much sinned against as sinning.

Hollingford is a community where society, from the great house to the tradespeople, has to grapple with a changing world, whether in technology or conduct or ideas. The length and the leisurely pace of serialization allowed the novelist to move, as James appreciated, with details of daily life and psychology; Gérin points out that Molly Gibson is distinguished from the author's previous heroines not only by her class—"she is a lady—but [by] the gradualness and naturalness of her growth." Throughout *Wives and Daughters* the humorous, ironical, and sometimes satirical view of the Knutsford generation, along with serious undertones, is developed with a heightened sense of artistic self-confidence and maturity.

As already mentioned, the novel was not completed. Mrs. Gaskell's health was poor, and she felt fatigue at the pressure of regular stints of work. She was on a visit to her new house when, on Sunday, 12 November 1865, she suddenly collapsed and died.

Mrs. Gaskell once wrote to a friend about the contradictory elements in her own nature—her "Mes," as she called them. "One of my Mes is, I do believe, a true Christian—(only people call her socialist and communist), another of my mes is a wife and mother. . . . Now that's my 'social self' I suppose. Then again I've another self with a full taste for beauty and convenience which is pleased on its own account. How am I to reconcile all these warring members?" This self-analysis helps to explain the variety as well as the common themes to be found in her work, just as it helps to explain how she earned the respect and friendship of people from all ranks and religions. She was intensely interested in all types of human behavior and activity; it was an interest that provided her with material for essays and short stories as well as for her major fiction. Critical awareness of her as a social historian is now more than balanced by awareness of her innova-

tiveness and artistic development as a novelist. James Donald Barry summed up recent criticism in 1978 with the comment that "she is surely among the best of the second rank of Victorian novelists and perhaps has joined the first." Since that time a number of editions of individual works and collections of shorter pieces, properly edited, have become available; they are helping to consolidate her reputation as undoubtedly major.

Letters:

J. B. V. Chapple and Arthur Pollard, *The Letters of Mrs. Gaskell* (Manchester: Manchester University Press, 1966).

Bibliographies:

R. L. Selig, *Elizabeth Gaskell; A Reference Guide* (Boston: Hall, 1977);

Jeffery Welch, *Elizabeth Gaskell: An Annotated Bibliography, 1929-75* (New York: Garland, 1977).

Biographies:

Annette Brown Hopkins, *Elizabeth Gaskell: Her Life and Work* (London: Lehmann, 1952);

Arthur Pollard, *Mrs. Gaskell: Novelist and Biographer* (Manchester: Manchester University Press, 1966);

Winifred Gérin, *Elizabeth Gaskell: A Biography* (Oxford: Clarendon Press, 1976).

References:

James Donald Barry, "Elizabeth Cleghorn Gaskell," in *Victorian Fiction: A Second Guide to Research*, edited by George H. Ford (New York: MLA, 1978);

P. Beer, *Reader, I Married Him. . . .* (London: Macmillan, 1974);

W. A. Craik, *Elizabeth Gaskell and the English Provincial Novel* (London: Methuen, 1975);

A. Easson, *Elizabeth Gaskell* (London: Routledge & Kegan Paul, 1979);

Margaret Ganz, *Elizabeth Gaskell: The Artist in Conflict* (New York: Twayne, 1969);

C. Lansbury, *Elizabeth Gaskell: The Novel of Social Crisis* (New York: Barnes & Noble, 1975);

J. Lucas, "Mrs. Gaskell and Brotherhood," in *Tradition and Tolerance in Nineteenth Century Fiction*, by D. Howard, J. Lucas, and J. Goode (London: Routledge & Kegan Paul, 1966);

John Geoffrey Sharps, *Mrs. Gaskell's Observation and Invention: A Study of the Non-Biographic Works* (London: Linden, 1970);

Edgar Wright, *Mrs. Gaskell: The Basis for Reassessment* (London: Oxford University Press, 1965).

Papers:
Important collections of Mrs. Gaskell's papers include those at Harvard University, Leeds University, the Manchester Central Reference Library, Manchester University, Princeton University, and the John Rylands Library.

James Hannay
(17 February 1827-9 January 1873)

George J. Worth
University of Kansas

BOOKS: *Biscuits and Grog: Personal Reminiscences and Sketches by Percival Plug RN* (London: Darling, 1848);

A Claret-Cup: Further Reminiscences and Sketches of Percival Plug RN (London: Darling, 1848);

Hearts are Trumps: An Amphibious Story (London: Kent, 1848);

King Dobbs: Sketches in Ultra-Marine (London: Darling, 1849; London & New York: Routledge, 1856);

Singleton Fontenoy RN (3 volumes, London: Colburn, 1850);

Blackwood v. Carlyle by a Carlylian (London: Wilson, 1850);

Sketches in Ultra-Marine (London: Addey, 1853);

Satire and Satirists: Six Lectures (London: Bogue, 1854; New York: Redfield, 1855);

Sand and Shells: Nautical Sketches (London & New York: Routledge, 1854);

Eustace Conyers: A Novel (3 volumes, London: Hurst & Blackett, 1855);

Essays from "The Quarterly Review" (London: Hurst & Blackett, 1861);

A Brief Memoir of The Late Mr. Thackeray (Edinburgh: Oliver & Boyd, 1864);

Characters and Criticisms: A Book of Miscellanies (Edinburgh: Nimmo, 1865);

A Course of English Literature (London: Tinsley, 1866);

Three Hundred Years of a Norman House (London: Tinsley, 1867);

Studies on Thackeray (London: Routledge, 1869).

James Hannay is best remembered today as a critic: for example, his *Studies on Thackeray* (1869) was one of the earliest, and in the judgment of some it remains one of the most perceptive, appreciations of that giant among Victorian novelists. But in the 1850s there were those who regarded Hannay himself as one of the leading novelists of the day. One reviewer compared his *Singleton Fontenoy RN* (1850) to such masterpieces as Dickens's *Pickwick Papers* (1836-1837), Charlotte Brontë's *Jane Eyre* (1847), and Thackeray's *Vanity Fair* (1847-1848); and the 1856 edition of a mid-Victorian reference work, *The Men of the Time*, called *Eustace Conyers* (1855) "one of the cleverest and most charming works of fiction that has appeared in recent years."

Hannay's origins and early life explain much in his writings, both fictional and nonfictional. Descended from two ancient Scottish families, the Hannays and the Afflecks, he joined the Royal Navy in 1840 at the age of thirteen. After five years' duty, principally in the Mediterranean, Hannay was found guilty by a court-martial of serious misconduct and two counts of riotous behavior, and he was "discharged from Her Majesty's Service with disgrace." Though his sentence was ultimately reversed, Hannay retained a profound contempt for the time-serving incompetents who ran not only the navy but all public institutions in an England that, full of pride in his own ancestry and imbued with the teachings of Thomas Carlyle, he scorned as having sunk into abject mediocrity under the twin weights of materialism and democracy.

On leaving the navy, Hannay turned to journalism in London, working for a time on the *Morning Chronicle* and then writing for two short-lived comic magazines, *Pasquin* and the *Puppet-Show*. By 1850 he had become known not only as an irreverent satirist but also as the author of lively accounts of naval life. He soon began contributing to *Punch* and to more serious periodicals such as *Household Words*, the *Leader*, the *Athenaeum*, and the *Quarterly Review* and became chief political writer for the *Illustrated Times* when it was founded in 1855. In the general election of 1857 Hannay indulged his penchant for oratory and expounded his conservative political convictions in an unsuccessful contest for a parliamentary seat in his native town of Dumfries. Three years later he returned to Scotland to assume the editorship of the Edinburgh *Courant*, a post he held until the winter of 1864-1865. After another sojourn in London, where he served on the staff of another new paper, the *Pall Mall Gazette*, he was appointed British consul in Barcelona in 1868, dying there in what he regarded as exile.

However disappointing Hannay's naval experience may have been, it furnished him with the raw material and the predominant theme of all his fiction. Beginning with such brief works as *Biscuits and Grog* (1848), *A Claret-Cup* (1848), and *Hearts are Trumps* (1848), continuing through the considerably longer *King Dobbs* (1849), and culminating in the three-volume novels *Singleton Fontenoy RN* and *Eustace Conyers*, he told over and over again the tale of the idealistic young man—really James Hannay in several not very different and equally transparent disguises—who encounters disillusionment

as well as adventure in shipboard life but who holds fast to and discovers new meaning in the time-honored values of "blood and culture." "Great in what he teaches, great in what he suggests, greater than all in what he *inspires*," Carlyle is the most potent influence not only on Singleton Fontenoy, whose words these are, but on Hannay's other protagonists as well: as Fontenoy says, "that man has called from the depths of my being what good lay buried there, with a voice as 'twere the trump of a resurrection angel!" Two other volumes of fiction, *Sketches in Ultra-Marine* (1853) and *Sand and Shells* (1854), consist of material published earlier in magazine or book form. These naval stories and novels are sprightly good fun, even though their creaky plots, paper-thin characters, and relentless didacticism may tend to induce weariness.

Though Hannay's fiction is largely ignored today, his criticism—largely the outgrowth of his ceaseless activity as a graceful, learned, and witty writer for periodicals and newspapers and as a spellbinding lecturer on literary topics—remains of considerable interest. His best-known piece of criticism is *Studies on Thackeray*, his great idol among novelists; but such books as *Satire and Satirists* (1854), *Essays from "The Quarterly Review"* (1861), and *Characters and Criticisms* (1865) also display a high degree of acuity as well as a remarkable consistency in his conservative ideological and literary allegiances. John Gross, the only recent writer to pay much attention to Hannay's criticism, does him an injustice in calling him "no more than a very minor period curiosity."

References:

Sir Joseph Crowe, *Reminiscences of Thirty-Five Years of My Life* (London: John Murray, 1895), pp. 42-45;

Francis Espinasse, *Literary Recollections and Sketches* (London: Hodder & Stoughton, 1893), pp. 301-337;

John Gross, *The Rise and Fall of the Man of Letters* (London: Weidenfeld & Nicolson, 1969), pp. 93-94;

John Cordy Jeaffreson, *A Book of Recollections*, volume 1 (London: Hurst & Blackett, 1894), pp. 143-162;

Alexander Smith, *Last Leaves* (Edinburgh: Nimmo, 1869), pp. 250-270;

George J. Worth, *James Hannay: His Life and Works* (Lawrence: University of Kansas Press, 1964).

Geraldine Jewsbury
(22 August 1812-23 September 1880)

Roy B. Stokes
University of British Columbia

BOOKS: *Zoe: The History of Two Lives* (3 volumes, London: Chapman & Hall, 1845; 1 volume, New York: Harper, 1845);

The Half-Sisters: A Tale (2 volumes, London: Chapman & Hall, 1848; 1 volume, New York: Graham, 1848);

Marian Withers (3 volumes, London: Colburn, 1851);

The History of an Adopted Child (London: Griffith & Farran, 1853; New York: N.p., 1853);

Constance Herbert (3 volumes, London: Hurst & Blackett, 1855; 1 volume, New York: Harper, 1855);

The Sorrows of Gentility (2 volumes, London: Hurst & Blackett, 1856);

Angelo; or, The Pine Forest in the Alps (London: Grant & Griffith, 1856);

Right or Wrong (London: Hurst & Blackett, 1859).

Geraldine Jewsbury is now, just over a hundred years after her death, almost completely forgotten. She is largely ignored by literary critics and historians and unread by all other than devotees of the nineteenth-century novel. Her importance is for those who wish to trace the development of both ideas and action among the emergent "new women" of the century. She was not one of the great writers of social reform, such as George Eliot or Mrs. Gaskell; she was not of the "fashionable school" with Mrs. Gore and Mrs. Norton; but she was an independent woman who established a niche for herself in the literary and social life of her century. She is not easily put into any pigeonhole; as she wrote to Jane Carlyle, "It is no good your getting up a theory about me. I was born to drive theories and rules to distraction."

It would be difficult to consider Geraldine Endsor Jewsbury in isolation from her older sister Maria Jane (1800-1833), especially when assessing the influences upon her in her early life. The two girls were the daughters of a father in the cotton trade and a mother of artistic skills and interests. They were born in Measham in Derbyshire; the family moved to Manchester in 1818, the year before the Peterloo Massacre in which the military

attacked a working-class crowd assembled in St. Peter's Field, killing eleven and wounding over four hundred. Their father, Thomas, established himself in the city as a merchant and insurance agent, but soon after their transfer Mrs. Jewsbury died. As a result, Maria Jane, at the age of nineteen, became responsible for the upbringing of Geraldine and her four brothers.

Maria Jane's personality and interests had a great effect on her younger sister, who was only seven years old at the time of her mother's death. All the accounts of Maria Jane at this time give the impression of a lively and attractive girl with a gift for making friends. Unformed literary longings were an important part of her makeup: "I was nine

Geraldine Jewsbury

years old when the ambition of writing a book, being praised publicly, and associating with authors, seized me as a vague longing." One of Maria Jane's household tasks was that of reading the newspapers to their father in great detail, with the reports of parliamentary debates being the favorite items; part of these duties devolved upon Geraldine while she was still young and helped to create the rather unusual cultural atmosphere in which she grew up. As Maria Jane sought to improve her literary skills, she wrote to Wordsworth for help and received several long letters of constructive criticism. Through this contact she developed a strong friendship with Wordsworth's sister, Dorothy, who once stayed with the Jewsburys on a journey south. Maria Jane's other close friend was Felicia Hemans, a much more worldly and practical-minded lady than readers of her poetry might suspect. This was a heady environment in which Geraldine grew up. In 1832, when Geraldine was twenty, Maria Jane married a chaplain to the East India Company, went to India with him, and died the following year; but her influence on Geraldine was very real and lasting.

Mr. Jewsbury died in 1840 and shortly afterward Geraldine was ill. It was a time of great political and economic anxiety, and nowhere more so than in Manchester and its surrounding areas. In a state close to desperation, Geraldine wrote to Thomas Carlyle following a reading of his essays. He seemed to be perhaps the one person who could answer the question which she posed to a friend: "My God! I would give the rest of the years of my life to be able to know why life is given us, and I would say it and leave it behind me." This led to a friendship with Carlyle and his wife, Jane, lasting over many years. Jane was a confidante to whom Jewsbury could communicate her most intimate hopes and fears; Carlyle was a stern mentor who was, nevertheless, touched by the earnest, exuberant young woman who sometimes literally lay on the hearthrug at his feet. "Miss Jewsbury, our fair pilgrimess, is coming again tomorrow and then departs for the north. She is one of the most interesting young women I have seen for years; clear, delicate sense and courage looking out of her small sylph-like figure." Jewsbury's life at this period was a round of meetings and discussions with friends drawn from the literary, artistic, and theatrical communities, punctuated from time to time by her ardent friendships and love affairs. Jane Carlyle held the opinion that Geraldine Jewsbury was only happy when she was in the throes of a *grande passion*. The excitement was an essential element in her creative processes.

The combination of her personality and the cultural influences to which she had been subjected since birth dictated the kind of writing which she was likely to attempt in her own career. The publication of her first novel, *Zoe: The History of Two Lives* (1845), created something of a minor sensation. It is set in the eighteenth century but makes no pretense of providing a portrait of that time. Zoe, the beautiful girl with Greek blood in her veins like several of Jewsbury's Manchester friends, talks with such real-life literary figures as Dr. Johnson, Boswell, Fanny Burney, Walpole, and Hannah More with the same ease and zest with which Jewsbury held her own in discussions within her circle. Although some reviewers saw this primarily as a novel of ideas, the reviews in the more popular journals registered a degree of shock at the author's "indelicacy." One of the leading characters, the Catholic priest Everhard Burrows, is undergoing a crisis in his faith which prefigures many a similar character and situation in later nineteenth-century novels with a religious setting. Burrows experiences a strong romantic attraction to Zoe, and when he carries her in his arms to save her from a fire, "he crushed her into his arms with ferocious love,—he pressed burning kisses upon her face, her lips and her bosom; but kisses were too weak to express the passion that was in him. It was a madness like hatred—beads of sweat stood thick on his forehead and his breath came in gasps." When it is remembered that this scene culminates on the altar steps in the chapel to which he has carried Zoe, having "sprinkled her face and hands with water from a vessel that stood near," it can be seen how it could offend the susceptibilities of the period. Everhard resigns his priesthood and, fulfilling other nineteenth-century ideals, moves to South Wales to practice a muscular, social Christianity. The Wesleyan influence is too strong, however, and after further affronting public opinion by writing an extremely unorthodox book, he goes to Germany. Here he wins fame with a great "philosophical history." When eventually he returns to England, he dies before Zoe can reach him. The themes of the book made offense possible to a wide range of readers, but it was timely. It indicated something of the confusion then current in religious affairs. It was a year of difficulties for the Oxford Movement, which had begun in 1833 as a High-Church movement within the Church of England to counteract the decline of standards of worship and the acceptance of an increasingly liberal theology. In 1845 Oxford University condemned William Ward's *Ideal of a Christian Church* (1844), and later in the year John Henry Newman, another of the movement's leaders, joined the Roman Catholic Church. It would be absurd to suggest that *Zoe* is an important nineteenth-century novel, but it is significant in pointing the direction in which Geraldine Jewsbury's thinking and writing were leading.

Her concern with social and political affairs was deepening, to the extent that she traveled to Paris in May 1848 in order to experience firsthand the sensations of the revolution. Just prior to her visit to Paris, she had published her second novel, *The Half-Sisters*. She used the story to unfold her ideas on the feminist situation. As she wrote to Jane Carlyle, "I believe we are touching on better days when women will have a genuine normal life of their own to lead. . . . I regard myself as a mere faint indication, a rudiment of the idea, of certain higher qualities and possibilities that lie in women. . . ." The half sisters of the title exemplify the extremes of two kinds of women. Bianca is the beautiful illegitimate daughter of Philip Helmsby, and Alice is the legitimate daughter. Bianca is an actress determined to devote herself to her art; Alice marries a successful ironmaster. Men view them in different ways, and the interplay of personal relationships is depicted throughout a thoughtful but sometimes lifeless story. Eventually Jewsbury's strong interest in the social and political climate of the time led to her third novel, the one which most adequately represents such powers as a novelist which she possessed and the issues which moved her. *Marian Withers* was first published as a serial in the *Manchester Examiner and Times* and subsequently in book form in 1851. Around the thread of the story Jewsbury depicts Lancashire life in general and the problems of the cotton trade in particular. Into the mouths of mill owners she puts her theories as to the economic problems of the trade and their solution. Recalling her father's experiences, she depicts the problems caused by the development of the canal system and the anxious reliance on harvests. One mill owner reminisces about learning cotton spinning under the old Sir Robert Peel and then establishing his business in a cellar. One reviewer of her first book had pointed out a weakness in her writing: "We observe in our authoress that tendency to fly at every game, which, though courageous, is indiscreet." She never overcame this problem, and *Marian Withers* suffers as a consequence. Nothing is left out of this all-embracing work; the author was concerned that her readers should be as fully aware as possible of the situation in which the cotton trade found itself. Nineteenth-century virtues are revealed in the depiction of the characters. John

Withers, one of the two waifs with whom the book opens, becomes through hard work and integrity a model and successful mill owner. Alice, the second waif, goes into domestic service and, after the death of John's wife, takes over as his housekeeper. She exerts great influence over John's daughter, Marian, and instructs her in "the mysteries that fit a woman to become the queen of that arcanum called Home in which she must have her root and find her place to dwell." Marian experiences many of the personal crises through which Jewsbury had passed, but she emerges to represent the new womanhood whose cause the author always espoused. She takes an intelligent and active interest in her father's mill and seeks to understand his labor problems and his concern with new inventions.

Jewsbury's passages describing the locale of her story are important contributions to the literary landscape of the regional novel; she added an atmospheric quality which gave depth and realism to her narrative. Her description of the weather when John Withers makes his first appearance as a waif displays this quality: "It was a regular Manchester wet day, of more than ordinary discomfort! The rain came down with a steady, heavy determination, aggravated from time to time to an emphatic energy by gusts of wind, which swept down the streets, rippling the puddles which had gathered in the uneven flags, and rendering all attempts to shelter under an umbrella entirely vain. The atmosphere was a murky composition of soot and water, which rendered the daylight only a few shades brighter than night. Nothing could be discerned beyond the distance of a few yards, the sky and the earth being seemingly mixed together in a disorganized fog. Few persons were in the streets, for nearly everyone had sought shelter in the vain hope that the rain was too violent to continue." She could evoke a sense of locality which justifies her being considered among the regional novelists, although she failed to reach the heights of a Brontë or a Hardy. She clearly depicted a concern with the social problems of her day; if this causes her to be considered with George Eliot and Mrs. Gaskell, she is a lesser, but not an unworthy, companion. She wrestled with the moral issues of the time, and it is not difficult to think of her work in relation to that of Mrs. Humphry Ward. She enjoyed considerable popularity in her own day, all of which, a century after her death, has evaporated. If she failed to reach the stature to which her talents might have suggested she would attain, this may be due in part to a less than complete sense of commitment.

Her late novels, those of the late 1850s, clearly

Thomas and Jane Welsh Carlyle, Jewsbury's friends for much of her life

show her limitations as a novelist. They continued to deal with themes of interest, but the creative spark was lacking. Only sporadically is life breathed into rather shallow novels. *Constance Herbert* (1855) is an involuted family story which fails to raise much concern for any character in the minds of the majority of readers. Charles Herbert becomes engaged to Miss Wilmot. He then decides to marry Kate Hatherton; she accepts him and they have a daughter named Constance. Kate becomes insane because she is convinced that Charles has really married Miss Wilmot. Constance, in due course, fears that her mother's insanity may be hereditary and so refuses her true love, Phillip Beaucham. It is a very slender thread for a story, even though Jewsbury pointed out the moral of Constance's having achieved her peace of mind. *The Sorrows of Gentility* (1856) lives up to its title. The heroine, Gertrude Morley, is an innkeeper's daughter who is educated above her station in life. She elopes with a young Irishman, impoverished but of a "good family." When he becomes destitute she returns to her

family, while the husband goes to Africa. He returns home to die and so release her to the honest—and rich—tanner who has always loved her. *Right or Wrong* (1859) boasts an even less credible story. The heroine, Marguerite, is seduced by the Vicomte de Vallambrosa. She has a child by him and lives with him for a year and a half until his death in a duel. Then she falls in love with Paul, but he is a monk. Nevertheless, for a period of twenty years he spends six months of the year with Marguerite and six months in the monastery. This unorthodox arrangement works well until he is elected prior and has to abandon her and their children. This condition he finds insupportable and so leaves the monastery to return to his family.

Geraldine Jewsbury was too perceptive a critic not to realize when her powers as a novelist were fading. It was for this reason that she decided in 1852 to write a novel for children, *The History of an Adopted Child* (1853). It is the story of an adopted girl, Clarisse, at a small school in the country. The pictures of the English countryside and later of

Ireland are more appealing than the characters or the plot. Its value now is in presenting a simple tale which has no overwhelming moral to punch home and which is fresher than many others of the same period. Her second story for children, three years later, was *Angelo* (1856), a shorter and even simpler tale. The hero lives in a small village in the Swiss Alps where he learns wood carving. A stranger takes him away to Rome where he becomes a famous painter.

Jewsbury had always yearned for a career in journalism rather than authorship. Although she failed to achieve that ambition fully, she was able to accomplish something within the field. She joined the staff of the *Athenaeum*, according to that journal's own account, "soon after the merits of her earlier books had given her a position amongst professional writers" and was a regular reviewer of novels for them for thirty years after 1849. She became an influential figure in the literary world, not only through her position with the *Athenaeum* but much more so in her capacity as a publishers' reader. For many years she performed this office for Hurst and Blackett and for Richard Bentley. No other woman held such a position for a major publishing house at this time. Although Bentley did not always accept her advice, he could never have been in any doubt as to the opinions she held of the works which she had read. Rhoda Broughton's *Not Wisely but Too Well* (1867) received short shrift from her. She described it as "absolute and unredeemed nonsense" and added, "I am sorry you have accepted it & I am sorry it is going to be published at all—the interest is of highly coloured & hot blooded passion & the influence is pretended to be quenched by a few drops of lukewarm rose water sentimentality."

It is sad that her reports remain unpublished, but they are at least safe for posterity in the British Library.

Geraldine Jewsbury's health began to deteriorate as early as 1868, and she was badly afflicted with poor eyesight. By around 1878 it was known that she had contracted cancer. She grew gradually weaker, saw fewer and fewer of her friends, and finally died in the fall of 1880. When she wrote to Jane Carlyle that "I was born to drive theories and rules to distraction," she wrote nothing but the truth. She defies pinning to a neatly arranged specimen board. Even though she may never again be regarded as worthy of critical consideration in her own right, no study of the thought of the Victorian period should ignore her. If nothing else, she is a splendid example of that eccentricity which enlivened life and literature in nineteenth-century Britain and one who vigorously claimed, through her own example, the right for a woman's voice to be heard.

Letters:

Mrs. A. Ireland, ed., *A Selection of the Letters of Geraldine Jewsbury to Jane Welsh Carlyle* (London: Longmans, Green, 1892).

Biography:

Susan Howe, *Geraldine Jewsbury: Her Life and Errors* (London: Allen & Unwin, 1935).

Reference:

Virginia Woolf, "Geraldine and Jane," *Times Literary Supplement* (28 February 1929): 149-150; correspondence (7 March): 185; (4 April): 276.

Charles Kingsley

Patrick Scott
University of South Carolina

BIRTH: Holne, Devon, 12 June 1819, to the Reverend Charles Kingsley and Mary Lucas Kingsley.

EDUCATION: Magdalene College, Cambridge, 1838-1842 (scholar, 1839; B.A., 1842; M.A., 1860).

MARRIAGE: 10 January 1844 to Fanny Grenfell; children: Rose, Maurice, Mary, and Grenville Arthur.

DEATH: Eversley, Hampshire, 23 January 1875.

SELECTED BOOKS: *The Saint's Tragedy: or, The True Story of Elizabeth of Hungary* (London: Parker, 1848; New York: International Book Co., 1855);

Twenty-five Village Sermons (London: Parker, 1849; Philadelphia: Hooker, 1855);

Cheap Clothes and Nasty, as Parson Lot (Cambridge: Macmillan, 1850);

Alton Locke, Tailor and Poet: An Autobiography (2 volumes, London: Chapman & Hall, 1850; 1 volume, New York: Harper, 1850);

Yeast: A Problem (London: Parker, 1851; New York: Harper, 1851);

Phaeton; or, Loose Thoughts for Loose Thinkers (Cambridge: Macmillan, 1852; Philadelphia: Hooker, 1854);

Hypatia; or, New Foes with an Old Face (2 volumes, London: Parker, 1853; 1 volume, New York: Lowell, 1853);

Alexandria and Her Schools (Cambridge: Macmillan, 1854);

Brave Words for Brave Soldiers and Sailors, anonymous (Cambridge: Macmillan, 1855);

Westward Ho! or, The Voyages and Adventures of Sir Amyas Leigh, Knight, of Burrough in the County of Devon, in the Reign of Her Most Glorious Majesty Queen Elizabeth (3 volumes, Cambridge: Macmillan, 1855; 1 volume, Boston: Ticknor & Fields, 1855);

Glaucus; or, The Wonders of the Shore (Cambridge: Macmillan, 1855; Boston: Ticknor & Fields, 1855);

The Heroes; or, Greek Fairy Tales for My Children

(Cambridge: Macmillan, 1856; Boston: Ticknor & Fields, 1856);

Two Years Ago: A Novel (3 volumes, Cambridge: Macmillan, 1857; 1 volume, Boston: Ticknor & Fields, 1857);

Andromeda and Other Poems (London: J. W. Parker, 1858; Boston: Ticknor & Fields, 1858);

Miscellanies (2 volumes, London: Parker, 1859);

The Limits of Exact Science as Applied to History: An Inaugural Lecture (Cambridge: Macmillan, 1860);

Speech of Lord Dundreary in Section D on Friday Last. On the Great Hippocampus Question, anonymous (Cambridge & London: Macmillan, 1862);

The Water-Babies: A Fairy Tale for a Land-Baby (London: Macmillan, 1863; Boston: Burnham, 1864);

Mr. Kingsley and Mr. Newman: A Correspondence (London: Longmans, Green, 1864);

"What, Then, Does Dr. Newman Mean?": A Reply (London: Macmillan, 1864);

The Roman and the Teuton (Cambridge & London: Macmillan, 1864);

The Irrationale of Speech, by a Minute Philosopher (London: Longmans, 1864);

Hereward the Wake: "Last of the English" (2 volumes, London: Macmillan, 1866; 1 volume, Boston: Ticknor & Fields, 1866);

The Hermits (London: Macmillan, 1868; Philadelphia: Lippincott, 1868);

Madam How and Lady Why; or, First Lessons in Earth Lore for Children (London: Bell & Daldy, 1870; New York: Macmillan, 1885);

At Last: A Christmas in the West Indies, 2 volumes (London: Macmillan, 1871; New York: Harper, 1871);

Town Geology (London: Strahan, 1872; New York: Appleton, 1873);

Plays and Puritans, and Other Historical Essays (London: Macmillan, 1873);

Prose Idylls, New and Old (London: Macmillan, 1873);

Health and Education (London: Isbister, 1874; New York: Appleton, 1874);

Lectures Delivered in America in 1874 (London: Longmans, 1875; Philadelphia: Coates, 1875);

The Tutor's Story: An Unpublished Novel, revised and completed by Kingsley's daughter, Lucas Malet (Mrs. Mary St. Leger Harrison) (London: Smith, Elder, 1916; New York: Dodd, Mead, 1916).

COLLECTION: *The Works of Charles Kingsley* (28 volumes, London: Macmillan, 1880-1889).

Charles Kingsley is one of those prolific second-rank Victorian writers whose works have in recent years been undergoing marked reappraisal. Kingsley himself is a fascinating, because representative, Victorian figure with wide-ranging interests in religion, philosophy, politics, social reform, urban conditions, poetry, fiction, literary criticism, history, and two different branches of science. His books—over sixty of them in all—reflect this awesome diversity, and his six novels have most com-

monly been read simply as propaganda for his ideas; in Louis Cazamian's revealing phrase, Kingsley "gives a definitive view of the most vital aims and ideals of his time, under the guise of fiction." Kingsley's "social problem" novels, especially *Alton Locke* (1850), still have an academic reputation because they present the Christian Socialist interpretation of the central issues of the 1840s. His later historical novels and his children's books, especially *The Water-Babies* (1863), have often been read as more educationally oriented versions of the same theological beliefs. But even at the low ebb in Kingsley's reputation at the time of his death, no less a critic than Matthew Arnold could refer to his "fine talents and achievements in literature," and recent studies have emphasized the literary qualities of his work. In particular, the modern biographical studies of R. B. Martin and Susan Chitty have pointed the way for a new recognition of the psychological, not just the propagandist, sources of Kingsley's fiction. From the new studies there has emerged a new sense of the imaginative strength behind Kingsley's very diverse writings.

Charles Kingsley was born in 1819, the second son of a rather unworldly and conservative clergyman and a strong-minded, very practical, Evangelical mother from the West Indies. His elder brother, Gerald, entered the navy and died of fever aboard his becalmed ship in 1844; another brother, Herbert, died young of rheumatic fever in 1834; the two youngest, George and Henry, were both travelers and literary men. Only Charles followed his father into the church or attained early respectability.

With the gap of a few years in the Fen country near Peterborough, most of Kingsley's boyhood was spent in Devonshire, at Holne, Ilfracombe, and Clovelly, and two of his novels, *Westward Ho!* (1855) and *Two Years Ago* (1857), are set there. During his early schooldays at Clifton, he saw the 1831 Bristol riots, with a "savage, brutal, hideous mob of inhuman wretches, plundering, destroying, burning," and charred bodies laid out in the streets before the smoldering buildings; some of his later sense of social apocalypse must have originated then. Kingsley was considered too shy as a boy to attend a regular public school, but he got two advantages from the smaller school where he was sent at Helston in Cornwall: he was taught by Derwent Coleridge, the poet's son, who introduced him to the religious idealism of German thought; and he was encouraged by another master to collect botanical and geological specimens. In his last year at Helston, he seems to have had the first in a series of nervous breakdowns. For his final years of schooling, after his father had moved to a parish in Chelsea, London, in 1836, Kingsley went as a day student to the new King's College in the Strand.

It was as an undergraduate at Cambridge from 1838 to 1842 that Kingsley began to develop his own religious views and to discover his vocation. In later life, he referred to his Cambridge days as "wicked," and he certainly enjoyed hunting and drinking, as well as the more respectable pursuits of rowing and studying; certainly, also, he resented the traditional university curriculum, and he had doubts about the orthodox religious creed the university officially endorsed. But in the summer of 1839, when he was twenty, he met the twenty-four-year-old Fanny Grenfell and fell in love. In love he found stability, and Miss Grenfell encouraged him to read Samuel Taylor Coleridge's religious work, *Aids to Reflection* (1825), and the social and philosophical writings of Carlyle, and in these Kingsley discovered a new, more broadly based sense of religion. He abandoned his original career plan, the law, in favor of the church, and he settled down enough to gain a first-class degree in classics and a second-class in mathematics. He became curate, and in 1844 rector, of the small country parish of Eversley in Hampshire. Also in 1844 he married Fanny, over the objections of her aristocratic family. Although he sometimes lived elsewhere for extended periods for health reasons, Eversley remained Kingsley's home for the rest of his life.

As Susan Chitty's recent biography has shown, Fanny's influence was not simply on the externals of Kingsley's career. It went deep into his psychological and philosophical development. His letters to her during and after their courtship are very personal, and seem shockingly un-Victorian in their emphasis on physical love. Kingsley came to believe that marriage was the key to all true philosophy and theology, because in it the body and the soul, the physical and the spiritual worlds, were brought into harmony. He had earlier admired the way a fellow student, the athlete and scientist Charles Mansfield, had—through accepting the material world on its own terms—seemed to achieve inner stability; now he came to believe that traditional religion had been wrong to be so otherworldly and so suspicious of physical pleasure. In the mid-1840s, he found a theological framework for these intuitions in the writings of F. D. Maurice, who argued that just as God became flesh in the Incarnation, so the spiritual Kingdom of God was to be discovered and realized here in the material world. From Kingsley's marriage experience sprang one of the fiercest negatives of his later writings, his prejudice against

anyone (such as the Tractarians or some Roman Catholics) who advocated a celibate or unmarried holiness; but the same experience also underlay many of Kingsley's positive ideas—an awareness of sexuality as central to personal development, a respect for physical or military heroism as a kind of secular saintliness, a concern with the living and working conditions of his parishioners (something he thought a religious duty as important as preaching), a willingness to embrace the findings of modern science as revelations of God, and a belief that the course of this-worldly history showed God's spiritual purposes. Much of the fierceness and emotionality of Kingsley's beliefs stem from their very personal origin.

Even during his engagement, he had attempted to explore the theological significance of married love in a prose life of the married medieval saint, Elizabeth of Hungary; he had intended this manuscript to be his personal wedding present to Fanny, and had illustrated it with rather lurid sketches of the naked saint's tribulations. After his marriage, he reworked the material into a poem published, without the illustrations, as *The Saint's Tragedy* (1848). The poem foreshadows his novels,

Charles and Fanny Kingsley at Eversley

not only in using historical events to debate current issues, but also in its concern with lower social classes and their economic and social conditions. Kingsley continued to write verse intermittently and published a second volume in 1858; throughout his life, there would be a poetic intensity of imagery and language about his prose descriptions.

But by the 1840s, blank-verse poems could hardly find publishers; and Kingsley's ambition as a clerical writer was to influence the expanding Victorian reading public. As he wrote in an early sermon, "This is the age of books. . . . a flood of books, newspapers, writings of all sorts, good and bad, is spreading over the whole land. . . . now, if ever, are we bound to put holy and wise books, both religious and worldly, into the hands of all." Throughout the 1840s, Carlyle and others had been drawing attention to class divisions and the "Condition-of-England" question, and 1848, the year of revolutions in Europe, saw in England the final irruption of the popular political reform movement, Chartism. Kingsley spent a good deal of time in London, and with the theologian F. D. Maurice, the lawyers J. M. Ludlow and Thomas Hughes, and others, he started writing as a "Christian Socialist," arguing that social, economic, and religious-ideological change was more important than mere parliamentary reform. Maurice was the moving spirit in a new venture in women's higher education, Queen's College, at which Kingsley became part-time professor of English literature and composition until his health forced him to resign in 1849. Later, Kingsley would give occasional help with another Christian Socialist venture, the Working Men's College. Hughes's novel *Tom Brown's School Days* (1857) shows Kingsley's influence in its "muscular Christian" ideas. Kingsley's first popular writings were articles and stories about social questions for working-class readers in the Christian Socialist paper *Politics for the People* (May-July 1848).

It was in the same spirit of improvised response to the immediate social crisis that Kingsley began his first novel, *Yeast: A Problem* (1851), which was serialized in the unconventional, Carlylean monthly *Fraser's Magazine* in the second part of 1848. The novel was aimed at young upper-class readers, and its hero, Lancelot Smith, begins as a rather purposeless young country gentleman without any decided religious or political views, riding to hounds and feeling disgruntled, like a character from Thackeray or Surtees. The novel shows Lancelot's development into a committed Christian Socialist, eager to right social conditions for the laboring poor. *Yeast* is unusual among condition-of-England novels in that it deals with rural, not urban, problems; Kingsley used his personal knowledge of rural housing conditions from his parish at Eversley, and he also drew on official government investigations for gruesome details. Carlyle's influence is apparent when Kingsley makes the Game Laws (which forbade the poor to poach on the land of the rich) a major symbol of class conflict; and it is the young gamekeeper, Tredegar, who first enables Lancelot to bridge the class gap and discover for himself how the rural poor live, by taking him to a drunken rural fair.

But social discovery makes up only a part of Lancelot's pilgrimage. The novel also presents a satiric view of the religious debates of the 1840s. Interspersed with Lancelot's initial skepticism and bewildered speculation are the aesthetic hedonism of his artist friend Mellot; the amoral worldliness of Captain Bracebridge; an extended correspondence with a palely Tractarian curate, Luke (a subplot Kingsley expanded when *Yeast* was published in book form in the anti-Catholic year of 1851); a wicked caricature of an Evangelical preacher, the Reverend Dionysius O'Blareaway; and a visit to the fake-medieval estate of the High-Church Lord Vieuxbois, who wants to revive the "good old times" of medieval faith and feudalism. Kingsley's aim in this satire is to show the maelstrom of contradictory religious ideals that surround Lancelot: "Do not young men think, speak, act, just now, in this very incoherent, fragmentary way . . . with the various stereotyped systems which they have received by tradition, breaking up under them like ice in a thaw . . . —a very yeasty state of mind altogether, like a mountain burn in a spring rain, carrying down with it stones, sticks, addled grouse-eggs and drowned kingfishers, fertilizing salts and vegetable poisons."

Lancelot's development from this spiritual incoherence is given direction not by preaching but by love, when he meets the two Lavington sisters, the charitable and practical Honoria and the beautiful but High-Church Argemone. From Honoria's example, he and Argemone both learn their duty toward the poor, and in his love for Argemone Lancelot discovers his own spirituality. Clearly, this section of the novel is autobiographical, and significantly *Yeast* was Fanny Kingsley's favorite among her husband's books. However, Lancelot loses his personal fortune in a bank failure, and Argemone dies of typhus contracted from sick-visiting in local slums. In an extraordinary final scene, St. Paul's Cathedral and its echoing, soot-encrusted emptiness become Kingsley's symbol of

One of Kingsley's illustrations for his unpublished life of Saint Elizabeth of Hungary. Fanny Kingsley was the model for the saint. (Susan Chitty, The Beast and the Monk*)*

traditional religion, in contrast with the teaching of a new character, the mysterious prophet Barnakill. F. D. Maurice had stressed "the necessity of an English theological reformation" to avert "an English political revolution," and Barnakill echoes Maurice's teaching about the humanity of Christ when he points Lancelot to "Jesus Christ—THE MAN."

Early reviewers admired the social commentary in *Yeast,* but criticized Kingsley's extended preaching about religion and his indulgent attitude to Lancelot's "youthful profligacy." Subsequent critics have pointed out the structural weakness of the novel by conventional Victorian realist standards. Some of this structural "problem" may stem from the external circumstances of composition: the novel had provoked some sharp criticism while it was coming out in periodical form; also, Kingsley fell ill and had to finish the novel off very abruptly, in "a state bordering on hysteria." Indeed, Kingsley became so sick that, he wrote, "My poor addle brain feels as if someone had stirred it with a spoon," and

he had to leave Eversley for nearly six months' recuperation in Devon. But some of the narrative disjunction was a deliberate attempt to mirror the disjunctions and difficulties of modern experience. A headnote to the first number had warned readers it was "composed according to no rules of art whatsoever," but followed "a spiritual sequence and method." The epilogue to the book version refers defensively to the novel's "very mythical and mysterious denouement" and its "fragmentary and unconnected form," but argues that these show the way young men were thinking. *Yeast,* as Kingsley's first novel, certainly has flaws of craftsmanship, but it shows how from the start his interest lay not just in external realism but in the underlying psychological development of his central characters. As A. J. Hartley argues, *Yeast* is "seminal" for all Kingsley's later novels.

Alton Locke, Kingsley's second novel, is much better known and takes up political, religious, and psychological concerns similar to those in *Yeast.* It is written in the form of a workingman's autobiography, and some Victorian readers took it for reality, not fiction. Alton Locke, the son of a narrow-minded Baptist widow, is apprenticed in a tailor's sweatshop; there he encounters Chartist politics, loses his religious faith, and finds his only imaginative freedom in romantic poetry. (Kingsley had written several newspaper articles for the *Morning Chronicle* and an 1850 pamphlet, *Cheap Clothes and Nasty,* about the working conditions of London tailors, and the Christian Socialists were to sponsor one of the first cooperative workshops to help tailors escape exploitation.) A very Carlylean Scottish bookseller, Sandy Mackaye, introduces Alton to the tragedy of urban poverty, admonishing him to abandon poetic romanticism, for "Shelley's gran'. . . but fact is grander . . . all around ye, in every gin shop and costermonger's cellar, are God and Satan at death grips; every garret is a haill Paradise Lost or Paradise Regained." So admonished, Alton sets out to be a radical journalist and the "People's Poet." However, he has met in an art gallery a beautiful upper-class clergyman's daughter, Lillian, and deep divisions develop between his political beliefs and his hopes for poetic (and thus social) respectability. Indeed, it is Lillian's father who persuades him to expurgate the political acerbity from his poetry before publication. Among the poems Kingsley writes for Alton is his most famous—but wholly nonpolitical—lyric, "The Sands of Dee." Remorseful at his own political disloyalty, Alton undertakes a mission for the London Chartists into the countryside, where he is unjustly implicated in a riot, is convicted of leading the mob, and spends three years in prison (this part of the novel parallels the real-life story of Thomas Cooper, the Leicester Chartist poet). When he is released, he discovers that Lillian has abandoned him, but he is nursed through the ensuing (emotionally symbolic) typhus fever by her cousin Eleanor, who teaches him more realistic, earnest views of poetry, politics, and religion. Receiving a small legacy from Sandy Mackaye, he resolves, like many workingmen in the 1840s, to leave England behind and emigrate to a new life in America. On the voyage, however, he dies, and the ideal remains unreached.

Alton Locke gives some of the most vivid descriptions of any condition-of-England novel. The lurid account in chapter fourteen of the insanitary Jacob's Island, Bermondsey (where Kingsley and other Christian Socialists had been working for improvement), is often compared to Dickens's earlier version of the same site in *Oliver Twist* (1838). Beside Dickens, Kingsley's picture of a "phosphorescent" ditch, where the "bloated carcases of dogs" floated

The theologian F. D. Maurice, one of the founders of Christian Socialism

on a "stagnant olive-green hell-broth" seems phantasmagoric; of course, the reactions are meant to be those of Alton the poet, but such critics as Raymond Williams and Peter Keating have found Kingsley's picture weakened by unrealistic exaggeration and link this to the book's rather melodramatic political stance. What has not been recognized until recently is the extraordinary psychological power not only of the descriptive passages but of the book's structure. Alton's final religious development comes neither from objective experience nor from Eleanor's preachy and rather one-sided conversation, but in an amazing delirious dream—a mixture of Old Testament story, Hindu myth, and scientific fantasy—in which (several years before Darwin) Alton imagines himself recapitulating the evolution of humanity, moral as well as physical, from soft, shell-less, vulnerable sea creature (like the algae he saw in the backyard rain tub as a child), to jealous, violent, adolescent ape, to primitive man and moral leader. In each metamorphosis, he must meet and be rejected by a Lillian who remains fully human throughout. Even in those pre-Freudian days, the physicality of this dream chapter shocked some of Kingsley's friends, and such a visionary conclusion might seem politically escapist. But Kingsley is trying something none of the more documentary social novelists attempted: he imaginatively creates a psychological subtext to the endless political and religious wranglings of the 1840s.

In 1851, Kingsley's health again broke down, and he left Eversley for a tour down the Rhine valley with his parents; he and his brother Henry hiked part of the way, and in one small town managed to get arrested as foreign revolutionaries.

By the 1850s, the temper of English culture was changing. The dramatic conflicts of the previous decade gave way to the greater social and cultural stability that W. L. Burn has called the "age of equipoise." Kingsley's next novel shows no slackening of his own controversial commitment, but in it he shifts ground from contemporary confusions to the "richer and more picturesque" field of the historical novel. *Hypatia* (1853), which began appearing in *Fraser's Magazine* in January 1852, dramatizes the religious conflicts of fifth-century Alexandria after the Goths had sacked imperial Rome. Hypatia was a beautiful Neoplatonic philosopher, and Kingsley perceived a parallel between her aristocratic mysticism and the transcendentalist philosophers of his own day. He had already satirized Emerson, for example, as "Professor Windrush" in *Alton Locke*, and he published *Phaeton* (1852), a Socratic dialogue against Emerson's "magniloquent unwisdom," while *Hypatia* was appearing. His historical researches into Neoplatonism issued also in a nonfiction volume, *Alexandria and Her Schools* (1854). Hypatia (whom W. D. Howells neatly described as "an Alexandrian Margaret Fuller") represents for Kingsley the inadequacy of abstract Greek (or Emersonian) philosophy in dealing with actual life and history. The central plot of the novel traces the spiritual development of a young monk, Philammon, and of a rich young Alexandrian Jew, Raphael; both are drawn to Hypatia's teaching but eventually discover the superior truth of Incarnational Christianity as preached by Augustine.

Around this main thread are woven a multiplicity of subplots, minor characters, and emotional complexities. Philammon may reembrace Christianity, but in his desert grave he is found embracing also the corpse of his sister, the prostitute Pelagia. The corrupt ambitiousness of the Roman prefect Orestes, Hypatia's supporter, is set against the equally repellent opportunism and anti-Semitism of the Christian bishop Cyril and his subordinate, Peter the Reader, who leads the mob that finally drags Hypatia into a church and tears her, naked, limb from limb. One of the most admirable characters in the novel is Wulf, the Goth leader, who refuses Christian baptism, preferring to join his forefathers in a heathen Valhalla.

Victorian readers were often shocked at the sensuality of Kingsley's descriptions of Alexandrian decadence and were especially aroused by the lurid account of Hypatia's death. The novel's fiercely anti-Catholic interpretation of early church history provoked two rival novels by Catholic leaders, Cardinal Wiseman's *Fabiola* (1854) and John Henry Newman's *Callista* (1856). But *Hypatia* has always been recognized as imaginatively powerful, and Larry Uffelman has recently called it "the best of Kingsley's novels" because it does not present a simple melodrama of good versus evil, the church against pagan decadence, but instead presents the more complex "struggle between ancient intelligence and medieval fanaticism."

In the winter of 1853-1854, the Kingsleys spent several months at Torquay for Fanny's health. There Kingsley met the naturalist P. H. Gosse and gathered the material for his popular book on marine biology, *Glaucus* (1855), first published as a magazine article late in 1854. In the spring, the Kingsleys moved on to Bideford, where they remained for nearly a year and a half. At Bideford, aside from an informal drawing class he gave for local youths, Kingsley was able to devote himself to writing and set to work on a novel with a Devon setting, *Westward Ho!* (1855).

Early in 1854, war had broken out between Russia and Turkey in the Crimean peninsula in the Black Sea, and Britain and France both sent armies in Turkey's support. Kingsley, like many of his contemporaries, was stirred by the war as a new and clear-cut moral crusade, indeed almost as an emotional release from the tame compromises of commercial peacetime. The new novel, though again historical, was his response to the war. *Westward Ho!* was Kingsley's attempt to inspire his own generation with the spirit of the great Elizabethans and, incidentally, to show that their mixture of gallantry, adventure, bloodthirstiness, and antipopery was the proper model of Christian manliness for young Victorians. The darker side of Kingsley's response to the war comes out in his comment to a friend, "Oh for one hour's skirmishing" against the Russians, "and five minutes butt and bayonet . . . to finish with." The same moral ambiguity is exemplified in Kingsley's dedicating the book jointly to Rajah Brooke, a contemporary adventurer whose subjugation of the Dyaks in Sarawak had been criticized for its cruelty, and Bishop Selwyn, the missionary bishop of New Zealand.

At the novel's opening in 1575, the hero, Amyas Leigh, is an impatient Devon schoolboy anxious to join the great voyages of exploration. He accompanies Sir Francis Drake on his voyage around the world and participates in a massacre of Spanish forces invading Ireland in 1580. One of the Spanish prisoners from that battle, Don Guzman, falls in love with the local Devon beauty Rose Salterne, and elopes with her to South America. Amyas and his friends, all admirers of Rose, sail off in an attempt to rescue her, capturing a Spanish galleon and bringing back to England an Indian princess. Kingsley recounts with perhaps too much gusto the cruelty of the Spanish colonizers; it is at the hands of the Catholic Inquisition that both Rose and Amyas's brother Frank die. The climax of the book comes with the English defeat of the invading Spanish Armada in 1588, but Amyas uses the national struggle to pursue his own personal vendetta against Don Guzman, who is with the armada. At the moment he is about to reach his enemy, lightning strikes and Amyas is blinded. (It is worth noting that this rather chastening outcome to a very fierce novel was written when the British army, after early successes, had run into difficulties in its Crimean campaign.) Only years later does Amyas come to accept the blinding as a divine judgment on his pride, and find love with the Indian princess

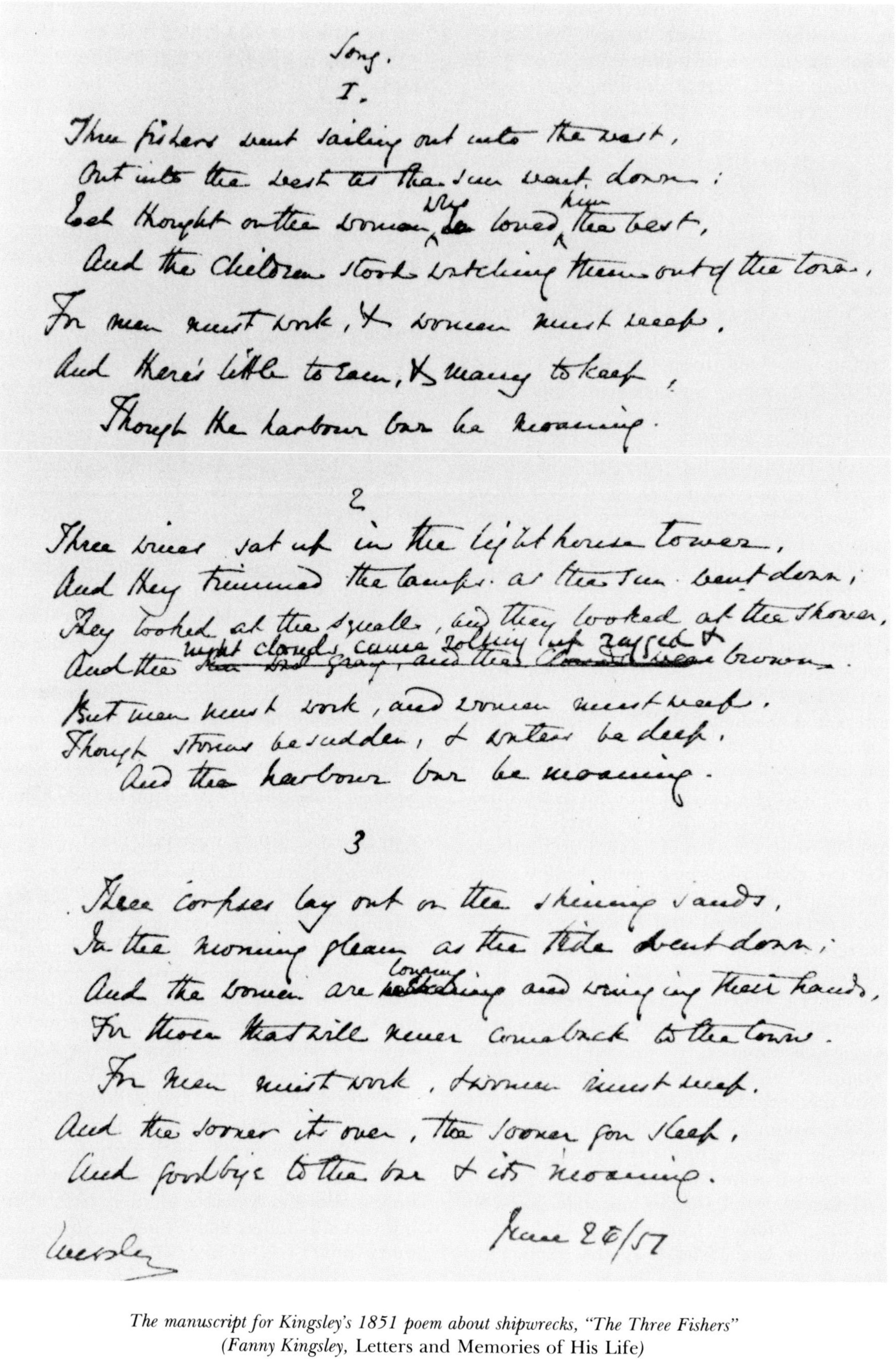

Song.

I.

Three fishers went sailing out into the west,
Out into the west as the sun went down;
Each thought on the woman who loved him best,
And the children stood watching them out of the town.
For men must work, & women must weep,
And there's little to earn, & many to keep,
Though the harbour bar be moaning.

2

Three wives sat up in the lighthouse tower,
And they trimmed the lamps as the sun went down;
They looked at the squall, and they looked at the shower,
And the night clouds came rolling up ragged & brown.
But men must work, and women must weep,
Though storms be sudden, & waters be deep.
And the harbour bar be moaning.

3

Three corpses lay out on the shining sands,
In the morning gleam as the tide went down;
And the women are coming and wringing their hands,
For those that will never come back to the town.
For men must work, & women must weep,
And the sooner it's over, the sooner for sleep,
And goodbye to the bar & its moaning.

June 20/51

Kingsley

The manuscript for Kingsley's 1851 poem about shipwrecks, "The Three Fishers"
(*Fanny Kingsley*, Letters and Memories of His Life)

(who turns out to be the daughter of an earlier English explorer). It makes a vivid adventure story, and Kingsley tells it in a kind of pastiche Elizabethan English; the episodic structure echoes the structure of Kingsley's Elizabethan sources, such as Hakluyt's *Divers Voyages touching the Discovery of America* (1582). Kingsley himself saw the novel as an epic, honoring the "faith and valour" of those to whom England owed not only her Protestant religion but "the foundation of her naval and commercial glory."

Westward Ho! was the first of Kingsley's novels to enjoy substantial sales. As John Sutherland has shown, it established both Kingsley and his new publisher, Macmillan, on the general literary scene. Though George Eliot, in the *Westminster Review*, remarked on the book's "ferocious barbarism," most reviewers were kinder, praising the "manly earnestness"; one even called it "the best historical novel of the day." But *Westward Ho!* represents a turning point in Kingsley's career, not just a success, because in all but its best scenes he has shifted away from the exploratory nature of his earlier works toward a rather philistine conventionality.

Kingsley's next novel, *Two Years Ago* (1857), confirmed this development. In it, he reverts for the first time since *Alton Locke* to contemporary social and cultural issues, yet now, instead of showing the complex development of understanding of a single character, Kingsley takes sides in the debates from the beginning. The novel opens with a rather off-putting discussion of how much social conditions have improved since the 1840s (an ominous difference from the earlier books). It then flashes back to trace two contrasted careers, the manly and the unmanly, and the reader is left in no doubt as to which is which. The hero, Tom Thurnall, is an affectionate portrait of a very self-sufficient, muscular, extroverted physician's son who emigrates to Australia, makes a fortune, is shipwrecked off the Cornish coast, and settles near his rescuers as a practically minded village doctor. (Tom's interest in science allowed Kingsley to reuse material from *Glaucus*.) The other career is a crude caricature: John Briggs, old Dr. Thurnall's apprentice, has Byronic pretensions as a poet. He goes up to London; takes the name Elsley Vavasour; publishes a book, *The Soul's Agonies*; marries for money; and becomes utterly self-absorbed. In 1854, a cholera epidemic strikes the village, and Tom has to fight not just the disease but the religious prejudices of those who believe cholera to be a divine punishment for sin. Through his activity, both the local High-Church parson and the Methodist schoolmistress, Grace, come to learn a kind of Kingsleyan Christian

Socialism. Nonconformist reviewers were particularly offended by Kingsley's hostile treatment of Methodist revival meetings, but what is also significant is Kingsley's changed attitude toward social problems since the 1840s—then he had seen them as symbols of class oppression and moral degradation, while now he presents them as simply the outcome of lower-class ignorance and superstition. Elsley's marriage breaks up, and he dies of laudanum addiction and despair (though not before a kind of revelation in a mountain thunderstorm). Most of the other characters go off to fight in the Crimean War (again presented in simple patriotic terms); even Grace goes off to nurse with Florence Nightingale at Scutari. Tom is taken prisoner by the Russians, has a conversion experience in captivity, and after two years returns to marry Grace. In a subplot, added as an afterthought because Mrs. Harriet Beecher Stowe visited Kingsley at Eversley in 1856, Kingsley propagandizes against American slavery by showing the successful marriage of an American politician to a beautiful quadroon actress. *Two Years Ago* is very loosely plotted; it has a much narrower range of class sympathy than Kingsley's earlier novels; and the caricatures of Kingsley's religious and poetic opponents now seem very overdrawn. But, partly because of *Westward Ho!*, it achieved commercial success, and it was a review of this novel that first gave Kingsley the label "muscular Christian."

As the young radical novelist gave way in the 1850s to a more conventional, if more successful, writer, so Kingsley's clerical and public career gathered a rather surprising momentum also. He was lucky in attracting the support of royalty: Queen Victoria and Prince Albert inclined to Broad Church religious views, and Albert in particular approved of Kingsley's social reformism and scientific interests. Kingsley was appointed successively chaplain to the queen (1859), Regius Professor of Modern History at Cambridge (1860), and tutor to the Prince of Wales (1861): all these were posts he could hold in addition to his parish at Eversley. He published a second volume of poems, *Andromeda and other Poems* (1858), and collected his periodical essays in volume form as *Miscellanies* (1859). He was well known, too, for his popular scientific writings, especially on geology and sea life, and he was one of the earliest churchmen to welcome Darwin's evolutionary theory. His inaugural lecture at Cambridge, *The Limits of Exact Science as Applied to History* (1860), and the broad generalizations of his first lecture series on Romans and Teutons drew criticism from the new professional historians, but he

Eversley rectory in Hampshire, where Kingsley lived from 1844 until the end of his life

was a popular professor with undergraduates and lectured on such up-to-date issues as the American Civil War. By the age of forty, then, Kingsley had become a well-recognized public figure.

As a novelist, however, Kingsley felt himself to be drying up, and he found himself incapable of carrying through a projected novel about the sixteenth-century Pilgrimage of Grace. Quite suddenly, in 1862, he found imaginative release by turning instead to a children's fantasy story, *The Water-Babies*, now his most famous work. Fantasy, in the form of dreams, had been important in his earlier novels, and he had already written for his young sons an inspirational retelling of Greek myths in *The Heroes* (1856). *The Water-Babies* was an original modern fairy tale, an important contribution, with George MacDonald's *Phantastes* (1858) and Lewis Carroll's *Alice's Adventures in Wonderland* (1865), to the mid-Victorian interest in fantasy literature.

Like Kingsley's earlier novels, the book is the symbolic account of one character's moral development. The hero, Tom, begins as a stock character from Victorian pathos, a cruel chimney sweep's mistreated apprentice. Enchanted and ashamed by the contrast between his filthiness and an innocent, white-clad, upper-class girl he comes on while working at a country house, Tom runs away, falls into a river, and becomes a water-baby. Here Kingsley's scientific interests take over, for the strange river and sea creatures Tom meets are explained in moral-Darwinian terms; Tom learns that "your soul makes your body, just as a snail makes its shell." His selfishness and unkindness lead to physical changes (when he steals candy, his body grows prickles, for instance). Two moralistic fairies, Mrs. Doasyouwouldbedoneby and the retributive Old Testament Mrs. Bedonebyasyoudid, govern evolution in the physical world as in the moral, and Tom must learn, with the girl's help, to submit to their teaching before he can return to the human world, go home to tea with the girl, and become a famous scientist. Kingsley wrote to his old mentor F. D. Maurice that he had tried "in all sorts of ways, to make children and grown folks understand that there is a quite miraculous and divine element underlying all physical nature."

The moral preachiness of *The Water-Babies* and Kingsley's constant direct exhortations to his young readers put off some modern critics, and

Colin Manlove has pointed out inconsistencies in the religious position Kingsley preaches. But the very "safeness" of Kingsley's central moral parable seems to have set his imagination free in the details of telling the tale. The looseness of the fantasy form allowed Kingsley to include satirical episodes about schoolteachers, prison, the new examination system, and other contemporary issues, yet he treated them all with a playfulness some of his adult writings lack. The book is full of rich, almost surreal descriptions of underwater creatures, and even language becomes playful in Kingsley's Rabelaisian catalogues of scientific or mock-scientific polysyllables, words the child reader or listener can enjoy for their sound without any real understanding of meaning, rather like Edward Lear's contemporary nonsense poetry. *The Water-Babies* earned good reviews on its first appearance and became, often in shortened versions, a children's classic. It had practical results, too: within a year of publication, Parliament passed the Chimney Sweepers Regulation Act to control the exploitation of child apprentices.

Early in 1864, Kingsley got, almost by accident, into a public controversy that was to severely damage his subsequent public reputation. In a historical review for *Macmillan's Magazine*, he cited in passing as an example of Roman Catholic sophistry the famous Catholic convert John Henry Newman. Kingsley did not have any documentation from Newman's writings to support his comments, and after a bitter exchange of letters and pamphlets between the two men, Newman published a massive defense of his religious sincerity in his moving autobiography, *Apologia pro Vita Sua* (1864), the first section of which (omitted in later editions) was a brilliant and crushing attack on Kingsley's intelligence and good faith. Kingsley had been made to look a prejudiced fool, and educated opinion sided overwhelmingly with Newman in the dispute. Kingsley wrote to a friend soon afterward, "I fear I am a very Esau now with the Press."

Kingsley was to publish only one more novel, *Hereward the Wake* (1866). Again, it is a sign of change in his literary ambitions that the book was serialized in a very safe, religious monthly, *Good Words*, while in the forties *Yeast* had been in the literary and dangerous *Fraser's*. *Hereward the Wake* was another historical novel, this time set in the East Anglian fens at the time of the Norman Conquest. One important refrain in mid-Victorian nationalist historiography argued that all that was best in British political and religious institutions had come from pre-Conquest Saxon England, before the incursion of the aristocratic, Catholic Norman

French. Kingsley's new hero, Hereward, "the Last of the English," is a kind of golden-haired Viking Robin Hood, who leads a band of fenland resistance fighters and holds out against the Norman invaders on the remote Isle of Ely until betrayed by the local monks. Hereward embodies, wrote Kingsley, "the old outlaw spirit, which . . . makes, to this day, the life and marrow of an English public school." In some ways, therefore, it is yet another version of Kingsley's message about the moral value of muscular manliness; but at some level, Kingsley had lost confidence in the sufficiency of such ideals, because Hereward's story turns into a tragedy, and his ultimate downfall and death are caused not just by Norman treachery but by his own apostasy from the chivalric altruism that first led him to defend the English against the Normans. The retreat is symbolized by his unfaithfulness to his wife, the lady Torfrida. (A. J. Hartley has pointed out a parallel between Kingsley's treatment of Hereward and his 1864 series of sermons on the life of King David.) Kingsley put a great deal of effort into historical research for the details of the novel; for most modern commentators, however, *Hereward the Wake* has

The grave of Charles and Fanny Kingsley at Eversley

seemed, by comparison with Kingsley's earlier novels, a rather predictable potboiler.

Kingsley never really achieved the further public advancement one might have expected from his successes at midcareer. He resigned his Cambridge professorship, and soon afterward was appointed to the part-year honorific post of cathedral canon, first at Chester in 1869 and then, from 1873, at Westminster Abbey. He traveled to the West Indies, where his mother's family had come from, and published his reactions in a travel book, *At Last* (1871). He remained active in the sanitary reform movement and initiated a local scientific society in Chester. In 1874, he traveled with his daughter across the United States, from the East to San Francisco and back, on a financially motivated lecture tour. Behind all the rather self-important bustle of this sustained public activity, it is hard not to infer a drawing back from the risky, experimental committedness of his younger self. He died early in 1875, following a bout of pneumonia.

In the years after his death, Kingsley's reputation declined but he remained very widely read. Partly from the publishing canniness of Macmillan, and partly from their sheer readability, his later English historical novels came to be standard reading for late-Victorian schoolboys, just as *The Water-Babies* was standard nursery fare for their younger brothers and sisters. His general reputation as a novelist outside the schoolroom has been linked closely with that of the moral and religious outlook he preached. As "muscular Christianity" and patriotic Protestantism fell into disrepute in the twentieth century, so Kingsley's novels came to seem dated, preachy rather than inspiring. Occasional efforts were made by progressive critics to rehabilitate the earlier Christian Socialist writings, and with renewed attention given to the Victorian social problem novel generally, both *Yeast* and *Alton Locke* have attracted modern comment as documentaries on working-class life. After more than a century, however, it is possible to see, at any rate in his earlier books, a more considerable literary talent behind the propagandist and social commentator. If Kingsley never wrote a great work or an unflawed masterpiece, he can now, in light of the new biographical evidence, be recognized as a writer of considerable psychological complexity, one who produced searching and imaginative responses to some of the central issues of the late 1840s.

Letters:
Charles Kingsley: Letters and Memories of His Life,

edited by Frances Kingsley (2 volumes, London: King, 1877);
American Notes: Letters from a Lecture Tour, 1874, edited by R. B. Martin (Princeton, N. J.: Princeton University Library, 1958).

Bibliographies:
Robert A. Campbell, "Charles Kingsley: A Bibliography of Secondary Studies," *Bulletin of Bibliography*, 33 (1976): 78-91, 104, 127-130;
Styron Harris, *Charles Kingsley: A Reference Guide* (Boston: Hall, 1981).

Biographies:
Stanley E. Baldwin, *Charles Kingsley* (Ithaca, N. Y.: Cornell University Press, 1934; London: Humphry Milford, 1934);
Margaret F. Thorp, *Charles Kingsley, 1819-1875* (Princeton, N. J.: Princeton University Press, 1937; London: Humphry Milford, 1937);
Una Pope-Hennessy, *Canon Charles Kingsley: A Biography* (London: Chatto & Windus, 1948; New York: Macmillan, 1949);
Robert B. Martin, *The Dust of Combat: A Life of Charles Kingsley* (London: Faber & Faber, 1959; New York: Norton, 1960);
Susan Chitty, *The Beast and the Monk: A Life of Charles Kingsley* (London: Hodder & Stoughton, 1975; New York: Mason, Charter, 1975);
Brenda Colloms, *Charles Kingsley* (London: Constable, 1975; New York: Barnes & Noble, 1975).

References:
William J. Baker, "Charles Kingsley and the Crimean War: A Study in Chauvinism," *Southern Humanities Review*, 4 (1970): 247-256;
Gillian Beer, "Charles Kingsley and the Literary Image of the Countryside," *Victorian Studies*, 8 (1965): 243-254;
Louis Cazamian, *Le Roman Social en Angleterre (1830-1850)* (Paris: Didier, 1903); translated by Martin Fido as *The Social Novel in England 1830-1850* (London: Routledge & Kegan Paul, 1973);
Owen Chadwick, "Charles Kingsley at Cambridge," *Historical Journal*, 18 (1975): 303-325;
Susan Chitty, *Charles Kingsley's Landscape* (Newton Abbott & North Pomfret, Vt.: David & Charles, 1976);
Dorothy Coleman, "Rabelais and 'The Water Babies,' " *Modern Language Review*, 66 (1971): 511-521;
David A. Downes, *The Temper of Victorian Belief:*

Religious Novels of Pater, Kingsley, and Newman (New York: Twayne, 1972);

G. R. Dunstan, ed., *Theology*, Charles Kingsley Centenary Number, 78 (1975);

(George Eliot), "Westward Ho!," *Westminster Review*, 64 (July 1855): 288-294;

Bruce A. Haley, *The Healthy Body and Victorian Culture* (Cambridge: Harvard University Press, 1978), pp. 107-119, 180-188;

Henry R. Harrington, "Charles Kingsley's Fallen Athlete," *Victorian Studies*, 21 (1973): 73-86;

Allan J. Hartley, *The Novels of Charles Kingsley: A Christian Social Interpretation* (Folkestone: Hour-Glass Press, 1977);

Walter E. Houghton, "The Issue between Kingsley and Newman," *Theology Today*, 4 (1947): 80-101;

Arthur Johnston, " 'The Water-Babies': Kingsley's Debt to Darwin," *English*, 12 (1959): 215-219;

Peter J. Keating, *The Working Classes in Victorian Fiction* (London: Routledge & Kegan Paul, 1971);

Guy Kendall, *Charles Kingsley and His Ideas* (London & New York: Hutchinson, 1947);

Q. D. Leavis, "The Water-Babies," *Children's Literature in Education*, 23 (Winter 1976): 155-163;

Colin N. Manlove, "Charles Kingsley and 'The Water-Babies,' " *Modern Fantasy: Five Studies* (Cambridge & New York: Cambridge University Press, 1975), pp. 13-54;

Stephen Prickett, "Adults in Allegory Land," *Victorian Fantasy* (Hassocks, Sussex: Harvester Press, 1979; Bloomington: Indiana University Press, 1979), pp. 150-173;

Mark Reboul, *Charles Kingsley, La Formation d'une personnalité et son affirmation litteraire (1819-1850)* (Paris: Presses Universitaires de France, 1973);

Sheila M. Smith, "Blue Books and Victorian Novelists," *Review of English Studies*, n. s. 21 (1970): 23-40;

Smith, *The Other Nation: The Poor in English Novels of the 1840s and 1850s* (Oxford: Clarendon Press, 1980);

John A. Sutherland, " 'Westward Ho!': 'A Popularly Successful Book,' " in his *Victorian Novelists and their Publishers* (London: Athlone Press, 1976; Chicago: University of Chicago Press, 1976), pp. 117-132;

Larry K. Uffelman, *Charles Kingsley* (Boston: Twayne, 1979);

Uffelman and P. G. Scott, "Kingsley's Serial Novels: 'Yeast,' " *Victorian Periodicals Newsletter*, 9 (1976): 111-119;

John O. Waller, "Charles Kingsley and the American Civil War," *Studies in Philology*, 60 (1963): 554-568;

Raymond Williams, *Culture and Society, 1780-1950* (London: Chatto & Windus, 1958; New York: Columbia University Press, 1958);

Robert Lee Wolff, *Gains and Losses: Novels of Faith and Doubt in Victorian England* (New York: Garland, 1977; London: John Murray, 1977).

Papers:

There are substantial collections of Kingsley material in the British Library (in the Kingsley, Gladstone, and Macmillan archives); Cambridge University Library (in the Ludlow papers); the Stapleton and Parrish collections at Princeton; Imperial College, London (in the Huxley papers); the Tennyson Research Centre, Lincoln; the Pierpont Morgan Library, New York; the Berg Collection of the New York Public Library; the Huntington Library, San Marino, California; and the University of Illinois, Champaign-Urbana.

Henry Kingsley
(2 January 1830-24 May 1876)

Tom Winnifrith
University of Warwick

BOOKS: *The Recollections of Geoffrey Hamlyn* (3 volumes, London: Macmillan, 1859; 1 volume, Boston: Ticknor & Fields, 1862);

Ravenshoe (3 volumes, London: Macmillan, 1861; 1 volume, Boston: Ticknor & Fields, 1862);

Austin Elliott (2 volumes, London: Macmillan, 1863; 1 volume, Boston: Ticknor & Fields, 1863);

The Hillyars and the Burtons: A Story of Two Families (3 volumes, London: Macmillan, 1865; 1 volume, Boston: Ticknor & Fields, 1865);

Leighton Court: A Country House Story (2 volumes, London: Macmillan, 1866; 1 volume, Boston: Ticknor & Fields, 1866);

Silcote of Silcotes (3 volumes, London: Macmillan, 1867; 1 volume, Boston: Ticknor & Fields, 1867);

Mademoiselle Mathilde (3 volumes, London: Bradbury & Evans, 1868; 1 volume, New York: Longmans, Green, 1899);

Stretton (3 volumes, London: Tinsley, 1869; 1 volume, New York: Harper, 1869);

Tales of Old Travel Re-narrated (London: Macmillan, 1869);

The Boy in Grey and Other Stories and Sketches (London: Strahan, 1871; New York: Longmans, Green, 1899);

Hetty and Other Stories (London: Bradbury & Evans, 1871);

The Lost Child (London: Macmillan, 1871);

Old Margaret and Other Stories (2 volumes, London: Tinsley, 1871; 1 volume, Chicago: Donnelly, Lloyd, 1876);

Valentin: A French Boy's Story of Sedan (2 volumes, London: Tinsley, 1872; 1 volume, New York: Longmans, Green, 1899);

Hornby Mills and Other Stories (2 volumes, London: Tinsley, 1872);

Oakshott Castle: Being the Memoir of an Eccentric Nobleman, as Granby Dixon (3 volumes, London: Macmillan, 1873; 1 volume, New York: Longmans, Green, 1899);

Reginald Hetherege (3 volumes, London: Bentley, 1874; 1 volume, New York: Longmans, Green, 1899);

Number Seventeen (2 volumes, London: Chatto & Windus, 1875);

Fireside Studies (2 volumes, London: Chatto & Windus, 1876);

The Grange Garden: A Romance (3 volumes, London: Chatto & Windus, 1876);

The Mystery of the Island (London: Mullan, 1877; Philadelphia: Lippincott, 1896).

COLLECTION: *The Novels of Henry Kingsley*, edited

by C. K. Shorter (8 volumes, London: Ward, Lock & Bowden, 1894-1895; 6 volumes, New York: Scribners, 1895).

Henry Kingsley wrote some very bad novels, and his life appears to have been similarly disorganized. There are, however, occasional flashes of good writing in some of his earlier books, written before the scandals of his life caught up with him. The subject matter of his novels has a certain topical interest.

Henry Kingsley was born in the Northamptonshire village of Barnack, where his father was clergyman, although in the same year the family moved to Clovelly, Devonshire. In 1836 Charles Kingsley, Sr., was presented with the living of St. Luke's Church, Chelsea; Devonshire and Chelsea figure prominently in Henry Kingsley's novels. Kingsley's elder brothers, Charles and George, achieved considerable fame in public life, the former as a novelist and political thinker, the latter as a traveler and scientist; but Henry was always considered a bit of a failure, with his novels the one redeeming feature of his life. After going to school at King's College, London, he went to Worcester College, Oxford, in 1850. Here he was popular and athletic, once winning a bet that he could row a mile, ride a mile, and run a mile within fifteen minutes; but he left Oxford without a degree in 1853 and traveled to the Australian goldfields with some fellow students.

In Australia he was unsuccessful and for some time lost contact with his family, returning suddenly in 1858 to discover that his eldest brother, Charles, was a famous clergyman and novelist. Fired by his example, Henry turned his Australian experiences to good account in *The Recollections of Geoffrey Hamlyn* (1859). The novel was well received and is indeed full of vigorous incident as well as original descriptions of Australian scenery; but there are also unnecessary digressions and a surfeit of manly men and plucky women. The villain, George Hawker, a desperate character with some redeeming features, is more interesting than the protagonists.

Kingsley's next novel, *Ravenshoe* (1861), is probably his best, although it is curiously little known. Charles Ravenshoe of Ravenshoe in Devonshire, at the moment of his triumphal rowing for Oxford in the boat race, is informed that his father, Densil, is dying. He reaches home to discover that Densil is dead and was not really his father at all. There had been a substitution at birth between

Charles and his groom, William Horton, who accordingly takes Charles's place as heir to his older brother Cuthbert Ravenshoe; Charles Horton joins the army and takes part in the charge of the Light Brigade. After Cuthbert Ravenshoe dies, it turns out that Charles is the real heir after all since his father, James Horton—supposedly an illegitimate brother of Densil Ravenshoe—is really Densil's legitimate elder brother. Charles is discovered in poor health in an East End slum by his friend John Marston, who is in love with Mary Corby, who, in turn, had long been in love with Charles, whom she eventually marries in spite of his changed appearance. He had previously been recognized by Lord Ascot (previously known as Lord Weller), who had been left the fortune of Lord Saltire, which had been destined for Charles. The final clue, which solves all difficulties—the marriage certificate of James Horton's mother—is supplied by Ellen Ravenshoe, Charles's real sister, who has rather improbably (and in Victorian eyes shockingly) been the mistress of Lord Weller and of Charles's employer before he joined the army, Lieutenant Hanby, but has subsequently become a nun.

This bald summary of the plot of *Ravenshoe* draws attention to its improbabilities but not to its strengths. Kingsley could certainly write a vivid chapter: the boat race, Balaclava, and Derby Day are all convincingly described. Although Charles Ravenshoe is a little too good to be true, the heroism of characters ready to sacrifice themselves for his interest is certainly moving. Except toward the end of the novel there are none of the digressions which mar *The Recollections of Geoffrey Hamlyn* and Kingsley's later works. There is some hostility to Catholicism reminiscent of Charles Kingsley: Charles Ravenshoe's disinheritance is part of a plot by Father Mackworth, a sinister Roman priest, to keep the Ravenshoe estate in the hands of the Catholics, as Charles is a Protestant. Apart from this, the novel has little serious preaching in it.

Austin Elliott (1863) was written in the same year and tells how Austin is sent to prison for taking part in a duel in which his friend Lord Charles Barty was shot by the villainous Captain Hertford, but is eventually released and marries Eleanor Hilton. As in almost all his novels, Kingsley introduces characters who appear to promise much but are never developed. Thus, early on in the work Austin appears to fall in love with a Miss Cecil, but rather tamely she marries a peer and vanishes from the action. Another fault is conspicuous in the novel: dark hints of impending tragedy are given so often

*Kingsley and Sarah Haselwood at the time
of their marriage in 1864*

that the eventual death of Lord Charles Barty comes almost as an anticlimax. The historical background is uninteresting: it is difficult to believe that Lord Charles and Austin are really concerned about the repeal of the Corn Laws. The best bits of the book involve Austin in prison, although one does not believe he will stay there long any more than one believed Charles Ravenshoe would vanish permanently. It may be possible to trace behind both episodes some autobiographical influence arising from Kingsley's period of disgrace in Australia.

In 1864 Kingsley married his second cousin Sarah Haselwood, a governess, and went to live at Wargrave near Henley on Thames. Sarah suffered from poor health with frequent miscarriages. They moved to London, then to Sussex; their financial position was always precarious. Novels followed thick and fast, but it is difficult to be enthusiastic about works which multiply the faults of the earlier novels. *The Hillyars and the Burtons* (1865) is quite interesting for clues to Kingsley's biography, as the two families of aristocratic Hillyars and plebeian Burtons migrate between Chelsea and Australia; but Kingsley is not good at bridging the gap between high and low life, although he seems painfully anxious to do so. *Silcote of Silcotes* (1867) is more incoherent, with less excuse, and was dismissed by critics as a series of rubbishy love stories whose characters are puppets as active as fleas. The plot is, indeed, improbable, involving, among other things, Italian revolutionaries.

In 1869 Kingsley went to Edinburgh to edit the *Daily Review*, a Free Church paper. The venture was not a success: his prolixity as a novelist did not make him a good journalist. When the Franco-Prussian War broke out in 1870, he obtained permission to act as war correspondent; he was present at the battle of Sedan, using the experience to write the children's novel *Valentin* (1872). By this time he was in grave financial difficulties. His later novels are almost unreadable; *Oakshott Castle* (1873) is full of preposterous melodrama and ludicrous characters such as the hero, Lord Oakshott, although it has occasional good scenes (for example, the shipwreck) which are almost as impressive as those in *Ravenshoe*. (The Prince of Wales appears in this novel.) Clement Shorter, in a biographical summary at the beginning of his edition of the collected novels (1894-1895) says unkindly that it is impossible to conceive of a worse novel written by an author of distinction than Kingsley's *The Grange Garden* (1876). By the time this book was published Kingsley was fatally ill with cancer, and he died in May 1876.

In spite of his uncharitable conclusion, Shorter's essay and his edition were essentially works of rehabilitation; and indeed he claimed that when time had softened the memory of the man's unsuccessful life, "The public interest in Henry Kingsley will be stronger than in his now more famous brother." Such has not proved to be the case. A few of the better novels, such as *Ravenshoe*, were reprinted as World Classics or in the Everyman series in the first part of the twentieth century, and there was one attempt in 1931 to vindicate his memory. But in the latter part of this century, while Charles Kingsley has been given a certain amount of attention for his eccentric but modern religious and social views, Henry Kingsley has been totally ignored. A modest revival of interest in *Ravenshoe* and parts of the Australian novels would not be out of place.

References:

S. M. Ellis, *Henry Kingsley, 1830-1876: Towards a Vindication* (London: Richards, 1931);

E. Huxley, ed., *The Kingsleys: A Biographical Anthology* (London: Allen & Unwin, 1973).

Joseph Sheridan Le Fanu
(28 August 1814-7 February 1873)

Roy B. Stokes
University of British Columbia

BOOKS: *The Cock and Anchor: Being a Chronicle of Old Dublin City*, anonymous (3 volumes, Dublin: Curry, 1845; 3 volumes, London: Longman, Brown, Green & Longmans, 1845; 1 volume, New York: Colyer, 1848);

The Fortunes of Colonel Torlogh O'Brien, anonymous (Dublin: McGlashan, 1847; London: Orr, 1847; New York: Colyer, 1847);

Ghost Stories and Tales of Mystery (Dublin: McGlashan, 1851; London: Orr, 1851);

The House by the Churchyard (3 volumes, London: Tinsley, 1863; 1 volume, New York: Carleton, 1866);

Wylder's Hand: A Novel (3 volumes, London: Bentley, 1864; 1 volume, New York: Carleton, 1865);

Uncle Silas: A Tale of Bartram-Haugh (3 volumes, London: Bentley, 1864; 1 volume, New York: Macmillan, 1899);

Guy Deverell (3 volumes, London: Bentley, 1865; 1 volume, New York: Harper, 1866);

All in the Dark (2 volumes, London: Bentley, 1866);

The Tenants of Malory: A Novel (3 volumes, London: Tinsley, 1867; 1 volume, New York: Harper, 1867);

A Lost Name (3 volumes, London: Bentley, 1868);

Haunted Lives: A Novel (3 volumes, London: Tinsley, 1868);

The Wyvern Mystery: A Novel (3 volumes, London: Tinsley, 1869);

Checkmate (3 volumes, London: Hurst & Blackett, 1871; 1 volume, Philadelphia: Evans, Stoddart, 1871);

The Rose and the Key (3 volumes, London: Chapman & Hall, 1871);

Chronicles of Golden Friars (3 volumes, London: Bentley, 1871);

In a Glass Darkly (3 volumes, London: Bentley, 1872);

Willing to Die (3 volumes, London: Hurst & Blackett, 1873);

The Purcell Papers, with a Memoir by Alfred Perceval Graves (3 volumes, London: Bentley, 1880);

The Watcher and Other Weird Stories (London: Downey, 1894);

Joseph Sheridan Le Fanu

The Evil Guest (London: Downey, 1895);

The Poems of Joseph Sheridan Le Fanu, edited by A. P. Graves (London: Downey, 1896);

Madam Crowl's Ghost and Other Tales of Mystery, edited by M. R. James (London: Bell, 1923).

COLLECTION: *The Collected Works of Joseph Sheridan Le Fanu*, Sir Devendra P. Varma, advisory editor (52 volumes, New York: Arno, 1977).

During his lifetime Joseph Sheridan Le Fanu was a moderately successful novelist in terms of both critical acclaim and the sales of his books. After his death his reputation slid into the typical decline, and only two or three of his novels remained in print. For the past decade or so there has been a slight revival of interest in his work, which has included a reprinting of all his writings in 1977.

Many cities have had periods of great cultural flowering: Athens in the fifth century, Florence in the thirteenth, London in the sixteenth, Edinburgh in the eighteenth, Concord in the nineteenth. Dublin in the eighteenth century had borne more than a superficial resemblance to Edinburgh of the same period, but it had undergone some change for the worse since the Act of Union. The dissolution of the Irish parliament in 1800 had robbed it of an indefinable something, and a portion of its greatness had vanished. The Dublin of the great period, however, still lingered in the mind of Le Fanu, as well it might since he lived for many years in Merrion Square, one of the most unspoiled areas in the city. Le Fanu was born into an old and ennobled Huguenot family; his paternal grandmother was the sister of the dramatist Richard Brinsley Sheridan. He passed the early years of his life at the Royal Hibernian Military School in Phoenix Park, Dublin, where his father was chaplain. When Joseph was twelve years old, his father was created dean of Emly, and the family moved to Abington, a house six miles outside Dublin. Here his schooling was in the capable hands of his father until he entered Trinity College in 1833, where he achieved a great reputation as a debater and member of the Historical Society. In 1839 he was called to the Irish bar but never practiced; by this time he had become involved in journalism, and the main course of his life was set.

The *Dublin University Magazine*, whose field was clearly established by its subtitle, *A Literary and Political Journal*, was a periodical with which Le Fanu was very closely associated—as a member of the staff from 1837, then as a very frequent contributor, and finally as editor and proprietor from 1869 until within a year of his death. His journalistic interests also showed when he purchased a Dublin newspaper called the *Warder* in 1839, soon after secured the *Evening Packet*, and finally became part proprietor of the *Dublin Evening Mail*. He amalgamated all three into a daily paper entitled the *Evening Mail*, with a weekly reprint called the *Warder*. He was a young man of strong political interests and distinct literary ambitions. His earliest published writings were the short stories which appeared in the *Dublin University Magazine*. Within a short period he had published short stories, reviews, and poems, and two historical novels broadly in the manner of Sir Walter Scott but with Irish themes. The popular appeal which his writings enjoyed was not paralleled by their critical reception. Although critics were rarely unkind, there was a lack of serious consideration. The novels were summarily noted as melodramatic or sensational, even when allowed to be good examples of these genres. The situation moved Le Fanu to an unusual protest. At the end of the final installment of *Uncle Silas* in the *Dublin University Magazine* in December 1864, he added a postscript, of which the following is one paragraph: "May he be permitted a few words also of remonstrance against the promiscuous application of the term 'sensation' to that large school of fiction which transgresses no one of those canons of construction and morality which, in producing the unapproachable 'Waverley Novels,' their great author imposed upon himself. No one, it is assumed, would describe Sir Walter Scott's romances as 'sensation novels'; yet in that marvellous series there is not a single tale in which death, crime, and in some form, mystery, have not a place."

From 1847 until 1863 there was little from his pen apart from short stories and journalistic pieces. The reason for this hiatus lay much more in his personal life than in the critical reception of his work. In 1843 he had married Susanna Bennett, the daughter of a leading barrister and one of nine children. Their marriage lasted for fourteen years, during which four children were born to them. They were years of domesticity, but not without difficulty. On the death of his father in June 1845, Le Fanu had to assume wider family responsibilities and also had to resort to more journalism in order to secure a sufficient income. Le Fanu appears never to have enjoyed long stretches of good health, and his wife also fell seriously ill in 1851. The death of her father in 1856 added immeasurably to the sorrow of her final years. She died in 1858 at age thirty-four. For Le Fanu her death was, in a very real sense, the end of his world. Until that moment he and his wife had been part of the social and cultural life of Dublin. Then, abruptly and finally, he withdrew: from the time of his wife's death until his own, fifteen years later, he lived the life of a recluse. Stories, true or apocryphal, have grown up around these years. One obituary notice wrote: "He quite forsook general society, in which his fine features, distinguished bearing, and charm of conversation marked him out as the *beau-ideal* of an Irish wit and scholar of the old school. From this society he vanished so entirely that Dublin, always ready with a nickname, dubbed him 'The Invisible Prince'; and indeed he was for long almost invisible, except to his family and most familiar friends, unless at odd hours of the evening, when he might occasionally be seen, stealing, like the ghost of his former self, between his newspaper office and his

Page from an early draft of Le Fanu's historical novel, The Fortunes of Colonel Torlogh O'Brien
(*W. J. McCormack, Sheridan Le Fanu and Victorian Ireland*)

home in Merrion Square; sometimes, too, he was to be encountered in an old out-of-the-way bookshop poring over some rare black letter Astrology or Demonology."

From these years of his seclusion came the novels for which he is chiefly remembered and, above all, those on which rest his chief claims for critical appreciation as distinct from the qualities which secured for him a diverse and general readership. The four novels which are most characteristic of him, and which show his powers at their height, are *The House by the Churchyard* (1863), *Wylder's Hand* (1864), *Uncle Silas* (1864), and *Guy Deverell* (1865). His name and reputation are associated with writings which are distinguished by a sense of mystery, of the supernatural, and of the macabre; by a feeling for place which is revealed in his descriptions; and also by a clear understanding and expression of character. These qualities are in his work from the outset, as can be seen in the early short stories beginning in 1838, when "The Ghost and the Bonesetter" appeared in the *Dublin University Magazine*.

The House by the Churchyard is an episodic novel without one clear story line. The theme, around which are embroidered several subplots, concerns the unraveling of a mystery. Lord Dunoran, an Irish peer, has been executed for murdering a man in London, and his estates are forfeited. His son, assuming the name of Mr. Mervyn, arrives in Dublin eighteen years after Dunoran's death, hoping to prove him innocent, and moves into what is locally regarded as a haunted house. The solution is worked out through scenes depicting late eighteenth-century life which show a firm control of historical detail. There is comedy to offset the mounting violence and murder of the second half of the book, as well as scenes of terror. In Dorothy Sayers's words: "For sheer grimness and power, there is little in the literature of horror to compare with the trepanning scene . . . [which] itself would entitle Le Fanu to be called a master of murder and horror."

Wylder's Hand is a much more straightforward story than its predecessor. It is concerned with the disappearance of Mark Wylder, a young naval officer engaged to a wealthy heiress, Dorcas Brandon. His absence enables his rival, Stanley Lake, to marry the heiress. Letters come from Wylder from abroad, and later he seemingly reappears at Brandon Hall. Shortly afterward Stanley Lake is thrown from his horse and killed, and the accompanying dogs bark at a spot in a bank where Wylder's body is then discovered. He had been murdered by Lake in a dispute over Dorcas, and Lake had arranged to have the letters dispatched; the man seen at the hall turns out to have been a former employee of the Brandons' who resembled Wylder. The story is uncomplicated, and it is regarded by some critics as Le Fanu's masterpiece. The characterization, especially of Wylder, is of Le Fanu's best, and the setting and atmosphere of Brandon Hall and its surroundings are magnificently controlled.

Uncle Silas, undoubtedly his best-known story, also benefits from a clear narrative. Maud Ruthyn, the only child of a wealthy widower and hypochondriac, is on her father's death made the ward of her Uncle Silas. Silas is a man with a dubious past, in all probability a murderer. Maud's father had intended his wishes regarding her to be an indication of his belief in the innocence of his younger brother. Silas attempts to secure Maud's fortune by marrying her to his son Dudley, and when this plan fails, he determines with the help of a terrifying governess, Mme de la Rougierre, to murder her. It is the characterizations of the novel, above all of Uncle Silas and the governess, which give the story its great power.

Guy Deverell is again a story of an attempt to settle old scores within a mysterious environment. One might almost be forgiven for thinking that Marlowe Hall is the chief character in the book; its architectural design plays a considerable part in the development of the plot. The central character, the immensely rich owner of the house, Sir Jekyl Marlowe, is a finely resolved figure. Years before the story opens he had killed a man in a duel. This man was Guy Deverell, the father of the Guy Deverell of the title. Into the comfortably regulated life of Sir Jekyl, Le Fanu introduces the mysterious figure of M. Varbarriere. The strange visitor is in truth Herbert Strangeways, whose sister was married secretly to the original Guy Deverell. Their son, under the name of Guy Strangeways, accompanies Varbarriere, who is seeking to benefit his nephew. Everything is rounded off by the end of the story with Sir Jekyl's deathbed confession and the marriage of his daughter to Guy Deverell. It is apparent from even the barest outlines of the plots that the novels are tales of mystery, adventure, murder, and retribu-

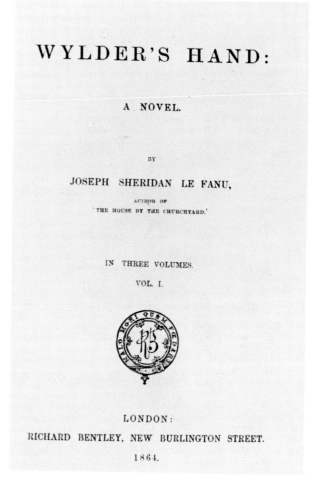

WYLDER'S HAND:

A NOVEL.

BY

JOSEPH SHERIDAN LE FANU,

AUTHOR OF
'THE HOUSE BY THE CHURCHYARD.'

IN THREE VOLUMES.
VOL. I.

LONDON:
RICHARD BENTLEY, NEW BURLINGTON STREET.
1864.

Title page of one of Le Fanu's four most famous horror novels (Cooper Library, University of South Carolina)

tion, but not ghost stories in the usual sense of the phrase. Le Fanu correctly appreciated that it is difficult to maintain the atmospheric tension of a ghost story over the length of a full novel. The medium is better served by the short story, and it is this form which Le Fanu used for his tales of the supernatural.

"Green Tea" first appeared in *All the Year Round* in October 1869, "Carmilla" in the *Dark Blue* from December 1871 to March 1872; both were reprinted in *In a Glass Darkly* (1872). "Green Tea" is the story of the haunting of the Reverend Mr. Jennings by a small monkey which at first followed him along the street; but that was only the beginning. "It was my silent travelling companion, and it remained with me at the vicarage. When I entered on the discharge of my duties, another change took place. The thing exhibited an atrocious determination to thwart me. It was with me in the church—in the reading-desk—in the pulpit—within the communion rails. At last it reached this extremity, that while I was reading to the congregation it would spring upon the open book and squat there, so that I was unable to see the page." "Carmilla" is a vampire story, conceivably the best in the English language. It is less long-drawn-out than many others, and it does not concern itself overmuch with the outward appearances of vampirism—the sharp fangs, the blood. The terror of the tale is in its restraint, its ordinariness, yet it retains all the traditional familiar elements: the lonely castle in Styria, the innocent girl as victim, the nightmares, and the eventual destruction of the evil.

It is common to speak of Le Fanu as writing within the tradition of the Gothic novel. Understandable as this comment is, it creates difficulties because *Gothic* is not a term which can be adequately defined. Le Fanu certainly has common ground with the better exponents of the "Gothic art" in his skill in the creation of atmosphere: landscape and buildings are endowed with an air of menace and of mystery. Yet within this apparatus of suspense there is very little reliance on the mechanics with which he creates his illusions. He rarely—and never in his

Le Fanu's wife, Susanna. After her death at the age of thirty-four, Le Fanu became a recluse.

best work—joins with the lesser luminaries of the art who depended heavily upon sliding panels, descending ceilings, and all the machinery which could occasionally dominate the story. M. R. James, one of the finest writers of ghost stories in the twentieth century and one who greeted Le Fanu as "the master of us all," wrote that an important element in a successful ghost story is that it should not explain itself. The sense of mystery must remain at the end—not be explained away by any logical process. Le Fanu demonstrates this ideally. The footsteps which pursue Captain Barton in "The Watcher" are not in any sense explained, although they can be understood in the context of the apparition of Barton's shipmate. The "small black monkey, pushing its face forward in mimicry to meet mine" which sat on the open Bible from which the Reverend Mr. Jennings was endeavoring to preach in "Green Tea" can only be explained as the embodiment of evil. To see here a connection between this personal apparition and *The Origin of Species*, as has been suggested, is to deny an important element in Le Fanu's work: evil is a reality in his writings, and has as much power to affect human lives as goodness. It is never clear precisely what is the origin of that evil, but there is no doubt that it exists and is an influence which cannot be ignored.

As in the best fantasy, where one is moved to and fro across the narrow line between reality and an imagined world, so in Le Fanu's tales one is conscious of the nearness and the constant presence of the supernatural. As in a dream, the reader passes between the two, and each has its individual substance. Each of the four novels already mentioned has a mystery at the heart of the plot: the mystery of the death of Doctor Sturk, whose skull is found in the churchyard at Chapelizod; the mystery of the disappearance of Mark Wylder; the mystery of the past of Uncle Silas and the suspicion of a murder committed some years earlier; the mystery of the green room in *Guy Deverell*. When the supernatural is introduced in the novels, as in the "narrative of the ghost of a hand" in *The House by the Churchyard*, it is a very brief episode but an important one in the creation of the atmosphere of the work. The novels depend much more upon an element of horror than of the supernatural; even so, it is a horror which is an integral part of the story and not stirred in gratuitously for its own sake. It is the appearance from the rain-soaked soil of murdered Mark Wylder's "hand and arm, disclosed from about the elbow, enveloped in a discoloured coat-sleeve, which fell back from the limb, and the fingers, like it black, . . . extended in the air," which caused the

The Bennett tomb in Dublin's Mount Jerome Cemetery, where Le Fanu is buried with his wife and members of her family. The sandstone monument has eroded so badly that Le Fanu's name has been obliterated.

murderer's horse to rear up and kill its rider.

The hints of the supernatural and the elements of terror are, moreover, displayed within a larger setting. The arrival at the gates of Bartram-Haugh in *Uncle Silas* is more than a mere backdrop to the action. In a style similar to a Renaissance title page it leads into the action and frames the setting in a manner which, as Elizabeth Bowen wrote, "demands a John Piper drawing": "At last the postilions began to draw bridle, and at a slight angle, the moon shining full upon them, we wheeled into a wide semicircle framed by the receding park walls, and halted before a great fantastic iron gate, and a pair of tall fluted piers, of white stone, all grass-grown and ivy-bound, with great cornices, surmounted with shields and supporters, the Ruthyn bearings washed by the rains of Derbyshire for many generations of Ruthyns, almost smooth by this time, and looking bleached and phantasmal, like giant sentinels, with each a hand clasped in his comrade's, to bar our passage to the enchanted castle—the florid tracery of the iron gate showing like the draperies of white robes hanging from their extended arms to the ground."

Le Fanu peopled his world of country houses, in their decayed and desolate splendor, with vivid imagination: young girls who are considerably more realistic and believable than many in Victorian fiction; villains such as Stanley Lake, who humanly exhibit weakness rather than malicious power; or the awe-inspiring, malevolent Uncle Silas. But long after reading *Uncle Silas*, one finds that it is the somber figure of Mme de la Rougierre who returns to disturb the memory: "She was tall, masculine, a little ghostly perhaps, and draped in purple silk, with a lace cap, and great bands of black hair, too thick and black, perhaps, to correspond quite naturally with her bleached and sallow skin, her hollow jaws, and the fine but grim wrinkles traced about her brows and eyelids." Maud is dominated by this large, ugly, graceless, and cruel woman with her "vein of superstitious dread." Evil, which Le Fanu found to be so real, has rarely been so graphically personified.

The last five or so years of Le Fanu's life were spent in almost complete isolation. When he died, at half past six in the morning of 7 February 1873, it was from exhaustion following an attack of bronchitis.

Le Fanu is generally ranked as a minor Victorian novelist, but it would be more just to think of him as a major practitioner of minor form. The mysterious, so-called Gothic novel is commonly regarded as a lesser form of literature, but in this category no writer has surpassed Le Fanu. His corpus of writing makes him an interesting figure in the Anglo-Irish tradition. In the newspapers which he owned or edited he wrote on political issues; his stance was that of an Irish Tory, suspicious of the activities of the distant Parliament at Westminster and, as the son of a Protestant clergyman, anxious about the rising power of Irish Catholicism. They were days of confusion in the political scene, discussion and debate were rife, and Le Fanu was at the center of much of it. His political writings help toward an understanding of a confused period; his poetry is a part of the body of revived balladry of the nineteenth century. "Carmilla" was read by a fellow Dubliner who was also a young newspaper reporter. Twenty-five years later, removed from both Dublin and the newspaper world, Bram Stoker wrote *Dracula* (1897). Literary ancestry is not a negligible achievement.

References:

Nelson Browne, *Sheridan Le Fanu* (London: Arthur Baker, 1951);

S. M. Ellis, *Wilkie Collins, Le Fanu and Others* (London: Constable, 1951);

W. R. Le Fanu, *Seventy Years of Irish Life* (London: Edward Arnold, 1893);

W. J. McCormack, *Sheridan Le Fanu and Victorian Ireland* (Oxford: Clarendon Press, 1980).

Charles Lever
(31 August 1806-1 June 1872)

Robert L. Meredith
and
Philip B. Dematteis

BOOKS: *The Confessions of Harry Lorrequer*, anonymous (12 monthly parts, Dublin: Curry, 1839-1840; 1 volume, New York: Dutton, 1839);

Charles O'Malley, the Irish Dragoon, as Harry Lorrequer (10 monthly parts, Dublin: Curry, 1840-1841; 2 volumes, Philadelphia: Carey & Hart, 1840-1841);

Our Mess; Volume I, Jack Hinton, the Guardsman (13 monthly parts, Dublin: Curry, 1842; 1 volume, Philadelphia: Carey & Hart, 1843);

Our Mess; Volume II, Tom Burke of "Ours" (22 monthly parts, Dublin: Curry, 1843-1844; 2 volumes, Philadelphia: Carey & Hart, 1844);

Arthur O'Leary: His Wanderings and Ponderings in Many Lands (3 volumes, London: Colburn, 1844; 1 volume, Boston: Little, Brown, 1894);

Nuts and Nutcrackers (London: Orr, 1845);

Tales of the Trains, Being Some Chapters of Railroad Romance by Tilbury Tramp, Queen's Messenger (5 monthly parts, London: Orr, 1845);

The O'Donoghue: A Tale of Ireland Fifty Years Ago (11 monthly parts, Dublin: Curry, 1845; 1 volume, New York: Colyer, 1845);

St. Patrick's Eve (London: Chapman & Hall, 1845; New York: Colyer, 1845;

The Knight of Gwynne: A Tale of the Time of the Union (20 monthly parts, London: Chapman & Hall, 1846-1847; 1 volume, New York: Colyer, 1847);

Diary and Notes of Horace Templeton Esq., Late Secretary of Legation at ———, anonymous (2 volumes, London: Chapman & Hall, 1848);

Roland Cashel (20 monthly parts, London: Chapman & Hall, 1848-1849; 1 volume, New York: Harper, 1849);

Confessions of Con Cregan, the Irish Gil Blas, anonymous (19 monthly parts, London: Orr, 1849-1850; 1 volume, New York: Stringer & Townsend, 1850);

The Daltons: or, Three Roads in Life (13 monthly parts, London: Chapman & Hall, 1851-1852; 1 volume, New York: Harper, 1852);

Maurice Tiernay, the Soldier of Fortune, anonymous (New York: Harper, 1852; London: Hodgson, 1855);

The Dodd Family Abroad (20 monthly parts, London: Chapman & Hall, 1852-1854; 1 volume, New York: Harper, 1854);

Sir Jasper Carew: His Life and Experiences, anonymous (New York: Harper, 1854; London: Hodgson, 1855);

The Martins of Cro' Martin (20 monthly parts, London: Chapman & Hall, 1854-1856);

The Fortunes of Glencore (3 volumes, London: Chapman & Hall, 1857; 1 volume, New York: Harper, 1857);

Davenport Dunn: A Man of Our Day (22 monthly parts, London: Chapman & Hall, 1857-1859; 2 volumes, New York: Munro, 1878);

One of Them (15 monthly parts, London: Chapman & Hall, 1859-1861; 1 volume, New York: Harper, 1861);

A Day's Ride: A Life's Romance (New York: Harper, 1861; 2 volumes, London: Chapman & Hall, 1863);

Barrington (12 monthly parts, London: Chapman & Hall, 1862-1863; 1 volume, New York: Routledge, 1876);

Luttrell of Arran (16 monthly parts, London: Chapman & Hall, 1863-1865; 1 volume, New York: Harper, 1865);

Cornelius O'Dowd upon Men and Women and Other Things in General, anonymous (3 volumes, Edinburgh & London: Blackwood, 1864-1865);

Tony Butler, anonymous (3 volumes, Edinburgh & London: Blackwood, 1865; 1 volume, New York: Harper, 1865);

A Rent in a Cloud, anonymous (Edinburgh & London: Blackwood, 1865; New York: Munro, 1877);

Sir Brook Fossbrooke (3 volumes, Edinburgh & London: Blackwood, 1866; 1 volume, Boston: Littell & Gay, 1866);

The Bramleighs of Bishop's Folly (3 volumes, London: Smith, Elder, 1868; 1 volume, New York: Harper, 1868);

Paul Goslett's Confessions in Love, Law, and the Civil Service, anonymous (London: Virtue, 1868; New York: Munro, 1881);

That Boy of Norcott's (London: Smith, Elder, 1869; New York: Harper, 1869);

Lord Kilgobbin: A Tale of Ireland in Our Own Time (3 volumes, London: Smith, Elder, 1872; 1 volume, New York: Harper, 1872);

Gerald Fitzgerald, "the Chevalier" (London: Ward & Downey, 1899; New York: Munro, 1899).

COLLECTIONS: *Works*, Harry Lorrequer Edition (34 volumes, London & New York: Routledge, 1876-1878);

The Novels of Charles Lever, Edited by His Daughter, edited by Julia Kate Neville (37 volumes, Boston: Roberts, 1898).

Now little read or critically studied, Charles Lever was for thirty years one of the most popular novelists in England. His career is a paradigm of Victorian novel publishing, demonstrating the varied problems of magazine serialization, monthly numbers, "three-decker" novels, and "library" editions. Lever is also significant because he dealt with subjects beyond the sphere of interest of other Victorian writers: the military; English expatriates and tourists on the Continent; and, most importantly, Ireland.

Born in Dublin to James Lever, a building contractor from Lancashire, and Julia Candler Lever, Charles James Lever was a member of the Anglo-Irish class, a fact which had great influence on his career. Charles attended various academies in Dublin starting at the age of three, and gained a reputation as a prankster. Pretending to help a slow-witted fellow student learn his lessons, for example, Lever would fill the boy's mind with outrageously altered versions of the material; this caused howls of laughter from the other students and even the teacher when the victim recited the nonsense he had been told. At home, Lever played similar tricks on his own parents, making up plausible but wholly fictitious items which he pretended to read from the newspaper. His imagination and ability to extemporize carried over into his writing career and made him popular socially as a raconteur all his life.

Lever entered Trinity College, Dublin, at the age of sixteen and took five years to earn his degree. It was while he was in college that he published his first writing: an essay on opium, "Recollections of the Night," appeared in a Cork quarterly in 1826.

After receiving his bachelor of arts degree in 1827, Lever went to Canada, where he toured the frontier. He later used his adventures there—including a several-month stay with an Indian tribe—as the basis of incidents in his novels. The following year he went to Germany to study at Göttingen and Heidelberg, returning to Dublin via Vienna, Weimar (where he met Goethe), and Paris. In Dublin, Lever studied medicine at Stevens

Hospital and at Trinity College, where he started a German-type student club; he also contributed pieces to local periodicals. He failed the examination for the Royal College of Surgeons but received his bachelor of medicine degree in 1831; he did not go on for the M.D. When a cholera epidemic broke out in 1832, Lever worked for the Board of Health in County Clare for four months. He was extremely popular with his patients and probably saved many of their lives more by raising their spirits with his humorous anecdotes than by his medical skills.

Soon thereafter, Lever received an appointment to a dispensary at Portstewart, a resort town in County Derry, Ulster; he annoyed his superiors by taking on several other medical jobs in nearby towns in an effort to earn enough money to support his extravagant habits. He married his childhood sweetheart, Kate Butler, on 16 November 1831; the couple eventually had three daughters and a son. Lever's financial problems were eased slightly at the beginning of 1832, when his parents died and he received a legacy of £ 250 a year.

In the summer of 1835, Lever met the Reverend William Hamilton Maxwell in Portstewart. Maxwell was an author who contributed to the *Dublin University Magazine*; his influence inspired Lever to take up writing again. After several rejections, the *Dublin University Magazine* published "The Black Mask," a romance set in eighteenth-century Budapest. Lever's first novel, *The Confessions of Harry Lorrequer* (1839-1840) began as simply a short, humorous "anecdote" contributed to the periodical. As with Dickens's *Pickwick Papers* (1836-1837), popular enthusiasm for this anecdote bred another and then another, until Lever found himself with a novel. *The Confessions of Harry Lorrequer* is a collection of stories told by and to the titular character, tied together with a thin plot. While lacking formal structure, however, its humorous stories and exciting adventures, especially of the "wild" Irish, made it popular. The novel appeared anonymously, but people who knew Lever recognized the anecdotes. The series increased the circulation of the *Dublin University Magazine*, but the publishers concealed this fact from Lever so that he would not demand higher payments.

While *The Confessions of Harry Lorrequer* was appearing, Lever—despairing of medical advancement in Ireland—acquired through political connections a post as physician to the English colony in Brussels. For a while, his practice was quite successful. Meanwhile, his publishers arranged to publish *The Confessions of Harry Lorrequer* in twelve monthly numbers under separate covers, with il-

lustrations by Hablôt K. Browne ("Phiz"), who had illustrated *The Pickwick Papers*. The manuscripts of several installments were lost in the mail to Dublin; some were found, but Lever—who never kept copies and had trouble remembering what he had written—was forced to reconstruct others. The entire project took three years; Lever wanted to stop with the tenth installment, but the publishers insisted on the full twelve.

In his next novel, *Charles O'Malley, the Irish Dragoon* (1840-1841), Lever determined to emphasize the most popular features of *The Confessions of Harry Lorrequer*, namely, Irish scenes and military adventures. The young hero, who grows up in the wild west of Galway, is the English equivalent of the American frontiersman: a hard-drinking, hard-riding, devil-may-care fellow, perfectly reckless of life and limb. He enlists in the army and sees action with Wellington on the Peninsula and at Waterloo. While the novel was appearing in monthly parts, a Dublin lawyer named Charles O'Malley threatened to sue unless the title character's name was changed; but Lever refused to back down, and the matter was dropped. The character of Major Monsoon was based on Commissary-General Mayne, a Falstaffian personality stationed in Brussels, who also supplied many of the funniest anecdotes in the novel in exchange for payments from Lever. During the writing of the novel, Lever's medical practice fell off as many of the English—fearful of a war between Belgium and Holland—left Brussels. Living, as always, beyond his means, Lever found himself with mounting debts. He also suffered the first of the attacks of gout that were to plague him for the rest of his life.

Though not his best novel, *Charles O'Malley, the Irish Dragoon* was Lever's most popular work and the only one still commonly read. (It did receive a negative review in *Graham's Magazine* from Edgar Allan Poe, who called the story "vulgar" and added perceptively that the anecdotes appeared to be remembered rather than invented.) Unfortunately, it stereotyped him as both a comic and a military novelist; for the rest of his career, his audience wanted more tales like *Charles O'Malley*. For the moment, he happily complied with two more novels in the same vein: *Jack Hinton, the Guardsman* (1842) and *Tom Burke of "Ours"* (1843-1844). While superficially similar to *Charles O'Malley*, these works demonstrate that Lever was attempting to move from rollicking adventures to more serious themes. *Tom Burke of "Ours"* deals with "The '98"—the failed Irish rebellion and French invasion—and is told from the rebel viewpoint. The hero leaves Ireland

and enlists under Napoleon.

The relatively serious tone of *Tom Burke of "Ours"* coincided with Lever's increased commitment to literary work. In 1842 he abandoned the medical profession and, turning down the editorship of *Bentley's Miscellany* because he did not want to live in London, he returned to Dublin as editor of the *Dublin University Magazine*. There he found himself caught between two rival camps. The *Dublin University Magazine* had always been an Anglo-Irish (pro-English and pro-Protestant) periodical. William Carleton and other writers of the *Nation* (a pro-Catholic, anti-English paper) attacked Lever and other Anglo-Irish writers. Lever—neither a religious nor a political partisan—attempted to reconcile the two sides and to moderate the bigoted tone of the *Dublin University Magazine*. The sympathetic portrayal of Irish rebels in *Tom Burke of "Ours"* had been an effort to demonstrate his empathy with Irish nationalism. *St. Patrick's Eve* (1845), a short novel, might be mistaken for one of Carleton's own works on the Irish peasantry in its description of a famine in the south of Ireland, an episode that Lever had himself witnessed as a young man. But he continued to be attacked for libeling the Irish character and was also blamed for Phiz's illustrations, which—as Lever himself had objected—tended to caricature the Irish.

Despite his problems, Lever continued to enjoy himself. He moved his family into Templeogue House, a Jacobean mansion four miles southwest of Dublin, where he could live the life of a country squire. He bought a dozen horses, which he named after characters in his books, for the use of his guests, and earned a reputation as an enthusiastic and uninhibited—though unskillful—rider. He had a passion for whist, and frequently hosted all-night card parties. He was visited by Thackeray, who was in Ireland to gather material for a book; Thackeray dedicated the resulting *Irish Sketch Book* (1843) to Lever. Many Irish, however, were annoyed by Thackeray's depiction of them and blamed Lever for supplying the information. Lever also met Anthony Trollope, who had not yet started to write, but was in Ireland on assignment from the post office.

Lever's efforts to bridge the gap between the Irish and the Anglo-Irish factions were unsuccessful; "Irish" writers continued to believe him an enemy, while the Anglo-Irish suspiciously criticized him as a turncoat. In frustration, Lever resigned his editorship in 1845 and moved his family to the Continent, where (except for brief visits to Dublin and London) he remained until his death. For the rest of his life, Lever was plagued by money problems: he had a wife and four children to support solely with his pen; and he still refused to bring his life-style in line with his income, even living for a while in a rented castle in Bregenz, Germany. In addition, his brother-in-law, to whom he had lent hundreds of pounds, ran away in February 1845, and Lever took on the responsibility of helping to support his family.

Lever moved to a villa on Lake Como, Italy, in 1847, and began writing *Diary and Notes of Horace Templeton Esq., Late Secretary of Legation at _____* (1848), a rather formless series of episodes about a man traveling to Italy to die of an incurable illness. In the course of his journey, Templeton comments on politics and reminisces about romantic incidents in his earlier life. While the novel was being serialized, Lever decided Lake Como was too expensive, so he moved his family to Florence. He soon ran out of ideas for the novel, so he had Templeton die suddenly in Florence. *Diary and Notes of Horace Templeton* was one of his least successful novels.

As always, Lever was socially popular among the English community in Florence, acting in amateur theatricals and hosting dinner and whist parties at which he regaled his guests with his endless supply of anecdotes. (One of his guests said it did not matter how often one heard Lever tell the same story; it got better and more elaborate each time.) He was still living beyond his means, and his financial situation was not helped by a dispute with his former publisher over royalties from his earlier novels. In 1848 the publisher, Curry, went bankrupt, and unsold copies and printing plates of Lever's books were sold to pay off the creditors. Lever now began the practice of writing two novels at a time, one for part-issue by Chapman and Hall and one for the *Dublin University Magazine*. All of Lever's works, in fact, were written for serialization of one kind or another; he was constitutionally incapable of writing any other way, saying that he had to see earlier chapters in printed form before he could go on. But he never learned to keep copies, so that when manuscripts or proofs were lost in transit between the Continent and the publisher in London or Dublin, Lever had to reinvent the entire installment, sometimes changing the whole plot in the process.

From 1846 to 1872 Lever published twenty-four novels, plus many articles on European politics and reflections on foreign life for periodicals like *Blackwood's Magazine* and the *Cornhill*. About half of these novels are strictly potboilers. In serious novels

Title page of one of Lever's novels about Irish tourists on the Continent (Cooper Library, University of South Carolina)

like *The Knight of Gwynne* (1846-1847) and *The Martins of Cro' Martin* (1854-1856), Lever continued his exploration of Irish life, while in others, such as *The Daltons* (1851-1852) and *The Dodd Family Abroad* (1852-1854), he described the problems of English or Irish visitors to the Continent. One of his best novels, *Roland Cashel* (1848-1849), concerns an adventurer in South America who becomes a millionaire in Ireland; the novel climaxes with a murder. This work contains satires of a number of real people, including Thackeray ("Elias Howle"), who had parodied Lever's early novels in *Punch* the previous year. Lever traveled at different times to Dublin and London in connection with a pair of aborted projects: a lecture tour of America and the editorship of a Conservative party newspaper. While in London, he also tried to straighten out his son Charley, who was leading a life of idleness and dissipation after leaving the army at the end of the Crimean War—in fact, was leading the life of the heroes of his father's early novels.

After much solicitation, Lever finally received a vice-consular appointment at Spezia, Italy (1858-1867). The position turned out to be a disappointment: the pay was low and the duties boring, and Spezia was uncongenial when the tourist season was over. Consequently, Lever retained his home in Florence and traveled to Spezia only when he was specifically needed. He began corresponding with Dickens, who invited him to contribute a serialized novel to *All the Year Round*, and Lever began writing *A Day's Ride* (1861). Although it was praised by George Bernard Shaw, the novel was not popular with readers; Dickens was forced to start serializing *Great Expectations* (1861) in the magazine to improve circulation, relegating *A Day's Ride* to second place. Nevertheless, Dickens's letters to Lever were always warm and encouraging. Dickens later took it upon himself to become Lever's intermediary with Chapman and Hall, negotiating better financial terms than Lever was able to arrange for himself.

Lever's last years as vice-consul at Spezia were filled with sorrow. Charley returned to the army but continued his extravagant habits, having to be bailed out on numerous occasions by his father, who could little afford the expense. He finally left the army and moved into the family's home at Florence, where he died of a hemorrhage at the age of twenty-six. Lever's wife, Kate, developed an internal inflammation and became an invalid. Lever's own attacks of gout and other maladies became more frequent and severe. His official duties continued to be irksome. Nevertheless, he refused to give in to despair: he maintained his hospitable ways, continued riding, took up boating, and, even though he had grown corpulent, swam extensively each day, usually accompanied by his daughters.

In 1867, a new Conservative government appointed Lever consul at Trieste. He was jubilant until he got his first look at the place, which one of his superiors admitted was "a dreary hole." He also found out that his assistant would be paid out of his salary, leaving him with a lower income than he had had as vice-consul at Spezia. The worst hardship, however, was a lack of suitable companions for conversation and whist. He soon reconciled himself to his fate, however, and continued his writing. In addition to such novels as *The Bramleighs of Bishop's Folly* (1868) and *That Boy of Norcott's* (1869), he went on producing his series of satirical sketches on current events that he had started writing for *Blackwood's Magazine* in 1863. In these, he adopted the persona of an Irishman named Cornelius O'Dowd and allowed his sarcasm free rein;

Blackwood judiciously censored the pieces whenever Lever strayed too close to libel.

Lever's wife died on 23 April 1870, and Lever never recovered from the loss. In addition, his own health continued to deteriorate. Nevertheless, in April 1871 he made a prolonged visit to London and Dublin and was invigorated by the lionizing he received in both cities. But a heart condition had added itself to his other ailments, and after several months of decline, he died on 1 June 1872 at his home in Trieste. Characteristically, his death came a few hours after he had hosted a dinner party.

Lever's reputation has been decisively affected by his special circumstances. Most English critics dismiss him as an "Irish" author, while Irish critics have insisted he was not Irish at all. Unquestionably the great turning point in his career was his move to the Continent. Ireland always remained the central focus of his novels, but increasingly he was working from memory, not firsthand observation. Weak in plotting and details and prone to sentimentality, he was skillful in characterization and narrative description. That, along with his good humor and wit, constitutes his main claim to renewed attention.

Periodical Publications:

"Post-Mortem Recollections of a Medical Lecturer," *Dublin University Magazine*, 7 (June 1836): 623-627;

"A Peep at the Mysteries of the Heidelberg Students," *Dublin University Magazine*, 27 (February 1846): 173-181;

"Italian Brigandage," *Blackwood's Magazine*, 93 (May 1863): 576-585;

"Hero-Worship and its Dangers: A Story," *Blackwood's Magazine*, 97 (June 1865): 696-705;

"The Late King of the Belgians," *Blackwood's Magazine*, 99 (January 1866): 129-134;

"The Greek Massacre, from our Own Commissioner's Report," *Blackwood's Magazine*, 108 (August 1870): 240-256.

Letters:

Edmund Downey, ed., *Charles Lever: His Life in His Letters* (2 volumes, Edinburgh: Blackwood, 1906);

Flora V. Livingston, ed., *Charles Dickens's Letters to Charles Lever* (Cambridge: Harvard University Press, 1933).

Biographies:

William John Fitzpatrick, *The Life of Charles Lever* (2 volumes, London: Chapman & Hall, 1879);

Lionel Stevenson, *Doctor Quicksilver: The Life of Charles Lever* (London: Chapman & Hall, 1939).

References:

Thomas Flanagan, *The Irish Novelists 1800-1850* (New York: Columbia University Press, 1959);

Robert B. Lytton, "The Works of Lever," *Blackwood's Magazine*, 91 (April 1862): 452-472.

Frederick Marryat

(10 July 1792-9 August 1848)

Roy B. Stokes
University of British Columbia

BOOKS: *A Code of Signals for the Use of Vessels Employed in the Merchant Service* (London: Richardson, 1817);

A Suggestion for the Abolition of the Present System of Impressment in the Naval Service (London: Richardson, 1822);

The Naval Officer; or, Scenes and Adventures in the Life of Frank Mildmay (3 volumes, London: Colburn, 1829; 2 volumes, Philadelphia: Carey & Hart, 1833);

The King's Own (3 volumes, London: Colburn, 1830; 2 volumes, Philadelphia: Carey & Hart, 1834);

Newton Forster; or, The Merchant Service (3 volumes, London: Cochrane, 1832; 1 volume, New York: Wallis & Newell, 1836);

Peter Simple, 3 volumes (Philadelphia: Carey & Hart, 1833-1834; London: Saunders & Otley, 1834);

Jacob Faithful, 3 volumes (Philadelphia: Carey & Hart, 1834; London: Saunders & Otley, 1834);

The Pacha of Many Tales (2 volumes, Philadelphia:

Carey & Hart, 1834; 3 volumes, London: Saunders & Otley, 1835);

Japhet in Search of a Father (4 parts, New York: Wallis & Newell, 1835-1836; 3 volumes, London: Saunders & Otley, 1836);

The Floral Telegraph: A New Mode of Communication by Floral Signals, with Plates, anonymous (London: Saunders & Otley, 1836);

The Pirate and the Three Cutters (London: Longman, Rees, Orme, Brown, Green & Longmans, 1836; 2 volumes, Philadelphia: Carey & Hart, 1836);

Mr. Midshipman Easy (3 volumes, London: Saunders & Otley, 1836; 2 volumes, Boston: Marsh, 1836);

Snarleyyow; or, The Dog Fiend (3 volumes, London: Colburn, 1837; 1 volume, New York: Colyer, 1837);

The Phantom Ship (3 volumes, London: Colyer, 1839; 1 volume, Boston: Weeks, Jordan, 1839);

A Diary in America, with Remarks on Its Institutions (6 volumes, London: Longman, Orme, Brown, Green & Longmans, 1839; 1 volume, New York: Appleton, 1839);

Poor Jack (12 monthly parts, London: Longman, Orme, Brown, Green & Longmans, 1840; 1 volume, New York: Nafis, 1840);

Olla Podrida (3 volumes, London: Longman, Orme, Brown, Green & Longmans, 1840; 1 volume, New York: Routledge, 1874);

Masterman Ready; or, The Wreck of the Pacific, Written for Young People (3 volumes, London: Longman, Orme, Brown, Green & Longmans, 1841-1842; 2 volumes, New York: Appleton, 1841-1842);

Joseph Rushbrook; or, The Poacher (3 volumes, London: Longman, Orme, Brown, Green & Longmans, 1841; 2 volumes, Philadelphia: Carey & Hart, 1841);

Percival Keene (3 volumes, London: Colburn, 1842; 1 volume, New York: Wilson, 1842);

Narrative of the Travels and Adventures of Monsieur Violet in California, Sonora, and Western Texas (3 volumes, London: Longman, Brown, Green & Longmans, 1843; 1 volume, New York: Harper, 1843);

The Settlers in Canada, Written for Young People, 2 volumes (London: Longman, Brown, Green & Longmans, 1844; New York: Appleton, 1845);

The Mission; or, Scenes in Africa (2 volumes, London: Longman, Brown, Green & Longmans, 1845; 1 volume, New York: Appleton, 1845);

The Privateer's-Man One Hundred Years Ago (2 volumes, London: Longman, Brown, Green & Longmans, 1846; 1 volume, Boston: Roberts, 1866);

The Children of the New Forest (2 volumes, London: Hurst, 1847; 1 volume, New York: Harper, 1848);

The Little Savage, by Marryat and Frank S. Marryat (2 volumes, London: Hurst, 1848-1849; 1 volume, New York: Harper, 1849);

Valerie: An Autobiography (2 volumes, London: Colburn, 1849; 1 volume, New York: Beadle & Adams, 1881).

COLLECTION: *The Novels of Captain Marryat*, edited by R. B. Johnson (24 volumes, London: Dent, 1895-1896).

It has been the fate of very few British writers to have their effigies burned on the streets of New York; it may well be that Captain Frederick Marryat is the only one to whom this has happened. Marryat had arrived in New York early in May 1837 and stayed for two years in the hope of influencing matters related to international copyright. He went from the United States to Canada at a time when relations between the two countries were strained. The vessel *Caroline* was being fitted out by the Americans for the use of Canadian rebels and was lying under the guns of Fort Schlosser on the American side of the St. Lawrence River. A band of Canadian loyalists captured the vessel, removed the crew, and sent the ship to its destruction over Niagara Falls. Marryat, being honored at a St. George's Day banquet in Toronto, seized the opportunity to praise "Captain Drew and his brave comrades who cut out the *Caroline*." It was an act of political indiscretion, but it bore all the marks of Marryat's impulsive temperament.

Although Marryat's life was threatened after this incident, it was typical of him that he continued with his tour of America and maintained his program of public lectures. Following one such lecture in Cincinnati, a seaman named Pierce paid tribute to an incident in Marryat's career nearly twenty-four years earlier, when Pierce had been captured by the British frigate *Newcastle*. The captain, Lord George Stuart, treated his prisoners with indignity and forbade his men any communication with them. To this account, Pierce added regarding Marryat, who was junior lieutenant of the *Newcastle*: "He, and he alone, meliorated in a degree not only my situation, but that of my fellow prisoners. . . . Lieutenant Marryat was the first man belonging to the frigate who spoke to me. He was the man that took me by the hand as I went over the ship's side, on my way to prison, and said, 'Pierce be of good cheer.' From then to the present time I have never met him. I am proud to take him by the hand, and greet him with feelings not rare among seamen."

Such conflicting emotions at the same time and in virtually the same place are not uncommon in Marryat's life. On casual observation he seems to be the stereotype of the bluff sea captain; in reality he was much more complex. Marryat was born in London; his father, Joseph, was a merchant banker, and his mother, Charlotte von Geyer, was the daughter of an American loyalist. Joseph had married her during a visit to America in 1788; of their fifteen children, ten survived. At Frederick's first school in Ponder's End one of his fellow scholars was Charles Babbage, the youthful genius who was to become one of the fathers of the computer. Marryat entered the Royal Navy in September 1806 on board the frigate *Impérieuse*, commanded by Lord

Cochrane, tenth Earl of Dundonald, whose *Autobiography of a Seaman* (1869) reads somewhat like a Marryat novel. Marryat had made several attempts to run away to sea, and his viewing of Nelson's funeral procession had put the seal upon his youthful intentions. He had a distinguished career in the navy which lasted until his resignation in 1830.

Marryat's long years of service were both adventurous and distinguished. He rescued people from drowning on about a dozen occasions, twice in mid-Atlantic when he was in the water miles astern of his ship before he was recovered. It was an active career, including nine years of war service, and virtually all the events of his novels can be related to his own experiences. Peace brought inactivity which fretted him, although it was enlivened by historical moments such as his attendance at the lying in state of Napoleon on St. Helena immediately after the former emperor's death. Having some skill as an artist, Marryat made several sketches of *le petit Caporal* on his deathbed.

The world onto which Marryat was beached on his retirement was a busy and congenial one for him. He had a wide circle of friends and acquaintances, including Lady Blessington, Dickens, Harrison Ainsworth, and Edwin Landseer. He became gentleman in waiting to the duke of Sussex (sixth son of George III) and later his equerry. He left London to take up life as a country landowner in Norfolk. His two years in America, which, apart from the motives already mentioned, were also encouraged by his mother's Bostonian birth and upbringing and his own service in American waters, resulted in the publication of *A Diary in America* (1839).

All these various elements, but especially his naval career, contributed to the novels which he had begun to write before the cessation of that career. *The Naval Officer* (1829) and *The King's Own* (1830) were written while Marryat was still on active service and were followed closely by *Newton Forster* (1832). None of these is an especially distinguished book in its own right, but they begin to point clearly to his chief works. *Peter Simple* (1833-1834) demonstrated the author's powers fully for the first time. Based on Marryat's own experiences, it recounts the history of a young man of gentle upbringing and his adaptation to a naval career. Stripped of its romantic elements, the novel is a vivid picture of the fleet in Nelson's day and is usually regarded as Marryat's masterpiece, although it is not his most popular novel. The author's naval characters, in particular, grant authenticity to the narrative and evoke memories of their real-life counterparts in all

JACOB FAITHFUL

BY THE AUTHOR OF

"PETER SIMPLE," "THE KING'S OWN," &c.

· IN THREE VOLUMES.

VOL. I.

LONDON:
SAUNDERS AND OTLEY, CONDUIT STREET.
1834.

*Title page of Marryat's favorite among his novels
(Cooper Library, University of South Carolina)*

periods: Mr. Chucks, the bos'n, is one of the most memorable minor characters of nineteenth-century fiction and sticks in the mind with all the insistence of other great seafaring characters, such as Dickens's Captain Cuttle. What is true of Chucks in relation to *Peter Simple* remains true for the rest of Marryat's writing. There is consistently strong characterization, especially when the individuals spring from Marryat's own experience: Stapleton in *Jacob Faithful* (1834), Smallbones in *Snarleyyow* (1837), and Aramathea Judd in *Japhet in Search of a Father* (1835-1836) are living creations.

Marryat's descriptive skills were always apparent and bear witness to his personal involvement in the episodes about which he wrote. The death of Captain Savage, a character founded on Lord Cochrane, and the description of the hurricane off St. Pierre in *Peter Simple* both relate to incidents in Marryat's own life. The battle of Trafalgar in *The Naval Officer* is viewed from the frigate which is

relaying signals, a natural vantage point for an author who had compiled an epoch-making *Code of Signals* (1817). This signal book for the use of vessels in the merchant service was one of Marryat's great contributions during his naval career; now, it is also the rarest of all Marryat titles. It followed the flag code of Admiral Popham which Nelson had used at Trafalgar and discovered that it could not transmit the message which he wanted: "England *confides* that every man will do his duty." (Nelson was forced to substitute "expects.") Marryat's code was adopted by Lloyds and was not officially superseded until 1857. It brought him honors: he was named fellow of the Royal Society on the nomination of his friend and old school colleague Charles Babbage; many years later, he received the Legion of Honour.

His most popular book is one which shows clearly the close relationship between his life and his novels. *Mr. Midshipman Easy* (1836) is the story of Jack Easy, the rather spoiled son of a philosopher who preaches the doctrine of equality. Marryat never suggested that naval discipline was harsh, rather that it allowed all that was best in a man to be developed: so Easy is subjected to a series of adventures which turn him into a typical moral, healthy, loyal young hero. (It may be due to such attitudes that Marryat now suffers from neglect.) Easy has his first adventure near Tarragona, resulting in the boat of which he has command becoming separated from the warship *Harpy*. He finds her again in time to be of help in securing a Spanish vessel as a prize. Easy fights a duel in Malta and, thinking that he has killed his adversary, runs away in a small boat which is wrecked on the coast of Sicily. Here he meets a Sicilian family and falls in love with one of the daughters. Adventures, in which Easy distinguishes himself, follow in other areas of the Mediterranean until at last, having come into a large fortune on the deaths of his parents, Easy is able to marry his beautiful Sicilian and settle in to a gentleman's life in England. As is inevitable, an outline of the story does scant justice to the book. Marryat embodies within the story not only factual pictures of life in the Royal Navy but also a deep understanding of naval ideals and standards. Through the egalitarian ideas of Easy's father, Nicodemus, the author also makes pungent comments on society in general. Interwoven with much of this is a sense of humor which, in contrast to some of Marryat's vigorous and robust fun, can be gentle and appealing. Easy's nurse makes her entrance with memorable and heartwarming humor: " 'Good heavens! Dr. Middleton, what can you mean by bringing this person here,' exclaims

Mrs. Easy to the family physician. 'Not a married woman and she has a child!' 'If you please, Ma'am,' interrupts the young woman, dropping a curtsey, 'it was a very little one.' "

It was not solely the navy which Marryat painted in his books: *Jacob Faithful* is set in freshwater rather than salt and became Marryat's own favorite novel. It is a story of the Thames, the working Thames of barges, wherries, lighters, and the men who manned them; of riverside views and riverside characters, with a broad humanity which makes it difficult not to look forward to another neglected nineteenth-century writer—W. W. Jacobs. When it is sometimes suggested that nineteenth-century novels are slow in their openings, *Jacob Faithful* can be cited in refutation: Jacob loses his parents at the very beginning—his mother blows herself up with gin, and his father, in sorrow, is drowned. Both parents gone, as Jacob says, "one by fire and one by water."

In 1819 Marryat had married Catherine Shairp of Linlithgow; there were eleven children of the marriage. Between the time of his marriage and his retirement Marryat had long spells of service overseas, including the East Indies station, where his wife and second son accompanied him. There is no very clear indication as to what went wrong with the marriage; long absences and Marryat's several affairs may well have played their part. A letter which he sent from America in 1837 gives some indication of the situation: "As for coming to England I have no thought of it not that I like America over much but I like to be away from my wife." Their deed of separation came in 1839; she outlived him by over thirty-four years. His years ashore were filled with activity: travel, especially to the United States; his life as a moderate landowner; public affairs, including an unsuccessful attempt to enter Parliament; but especially his work as editor and part proprietor of the *Metropolitan*, "a monthly journal of Literature, Science and the Fine Arts." He edited the journal from 1832 to 1835, and *Newton Forster*, *Peter Simple*, *Jacob Faithful*, *Mr. Midshipman Easy*, and *Japhet in Search of a Father* made their serialized appearances in these pages. These were valuable sources of income to him, but nothing could keep pace with the extravagance of his lifestyle.

Most of his books for children come from his later years, when something near to a peaceful existence came over Marryat's life. The books lack the exuberant vitality of *Mr. Midshipman Easy* and *Peter Simple*, but there is ample action so that, as John Forster said, "children don't read it once, but a

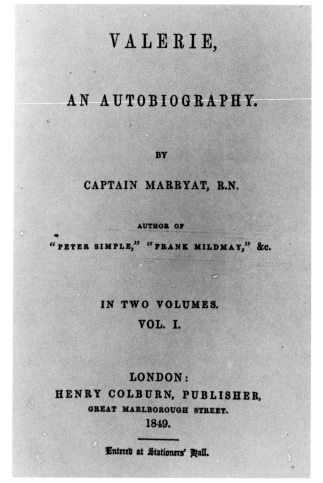

VALERIE,

AN AUTOBIOGRAPHY.

BY

CAPTAIN MARRYAT, R.N.

AUTHOR OF

"PETER SIMPLE," "FRANK MILDMAY," &c.

IN TWO VOLUMES.
VOL. I.

LONDON:
HENRY COLBURN, PUBLISHER,
GREAT MARLBOROUGH STREET.
1849.

Entered at Stationers' Hall.

Title page of Marryat's posthumously published last novel (Cooper Library, University of South Carolina)

dozen times, and that is the true test." Marryat wrote *Masterman Ready* (1841-1842) at the instigation of his children, who had enjoyed Wyss's *Swiss Family Robinson* (1813) but were also disappointed by it. Mr. Seagrave and his family are wrecked on a desert island and lead a life of adventure until they are rescued and continue their journey.

Marryat had always been of a choleric disposition, given to explosive outbursts of both enthusiasm and anger. In July 1847 he felt that he had been slighted by the Admiralty when hoping for a new command, broke a blood vessel in his fit of rage, and was ill for several months. The loss of his son at sea on the following 20 December was the final blow, and he died in August 1848.

Marryat is now a neglected author. Only *Mr. Midshipman Easy* and two of his books for children, *Masterman Ready* and *The Children of the New Forest* (1847), are sufficiently remembered to remain usually in print. Modern critics ignore rather than condemn him. Nevertheless, he has a firm place in the development of the English novel. Michael Sadleir performed a kind of salvage operation for Marryat as he had done so successfully for Trollope. In the case of Marryat, Sadleir wrote: "His fame as a novelist of naval escapade, of risk and makeshift among pirates and barbarians, is fame deserved. The difficulty for one concerned to reappraise his work lies in the fact that there is more to him than is here implied. He is the only writer in the tradition of Fielding and Smollett who can claim consideration on the same plane as these famous authors. That he is overtopped by *Tom Jones* no one will dispute, but that he ranks with and not after Smollett is a contention that permits of argument." As an artist he was admired by Conrad, with whom he also has considerable affinity. As an acute observer and recorder of the naval wars against Napoleon he provided, from firsthand knowledge, an understanding of the world which C. S. Forester created through research. But what triumphs in his work, time and again, is a sense of humor which is an integral part of his characterizations.

> "How long have you been married, Swinburne?" says Peter to him one day.
> "Ever since Christmas '94, I wasn't

going to be hooked carelessly, so I nibbled afore I took the bait. Had four years trial of her first, and, finding that she had plenty of ballast, I sailed her as my own."
> "How do you mean by plenty of ballast?"
> "I don't mean, Mr. Simple, a broad bow and square bulk. You know very well that if a vessel has not ballast, she's bottom up in no time. Now what keeps a woman stiff under her canvas is her modesty."

A writer with such joys to offer should not be left to wilt in obscurity.

Biographies:
Florence Marryat Church, *Life and Letters of Captain Marryat* (London: Bentley, 1872);
David Hannan, *Life of Frederick Marryat* (London: Walter Scott, 1899).

References:
Maurice-Paul Gautier, *Captain Frederick Marryat: L'homme et l'oeuvre* (Montreal: Didier, 1973);
Christopher Lloyd, *Captain Marryat and the Old Navy* (London: Longmans, Green, 1939);
Oliver Warner, *Captain Marryat: A Rediscovery* (London: Constable, 1953).

Harriet Martineau
(12 June 1802-27 June 1876)

Ira B. Nadel
University of British Columbia

BOOKS: *Devotional Exercises for the Use of Young Persons* (London: Norwich, 1823; Boston: Bowles, 1833);
Addresses with Prayers and Original Hymns for the Use of Families and Schools (London: Hunter, 1826);
Principle and Practice; or, The Orphan Family (Wellington, U.K.: Houlston, 1827);
Mary Campbell; or, The Affectionate Granddaughter (Wellington, U.K.: Houlston, 1828);
Traditions of Palestine (London: Longman, Rees, Orme, Brown & Green, 1830; Boston: Crosby, 1839);
The Essential Faith of the Universal Church Deduced from the Sacred Records (London: Hunter, 1831; Boston: Bowles, 1833);

Five Years of Youth; or, Sense and Sentiment (London: Harney & Darton, 1831; Boston: Bowles & Greene, 1832);
Sequel to Principle and Practice (Wellington, U.K.: Houlston, 1831);
Illustrations of Political Economy (25 monthly parts, London: Fox, 1832-1834; 8 volumes, Boston: Bowles, 1832-1835);
Prize Essays (London: British and Foreign Unitarian Association, 1832);
The Faith as Unfolded by Many Prophets: An Essay Addressed to the Disciples of Mohammed (London: Rowland, 1832; Boston: Bowles, 1833);
Providence as Manifested through Israel (London: Rowland, 1832; Boston: Bowles, 1833);

Poor Laws and Paupers Illustrated (4 volumes, London: Fox, 1833-1834; 1 volume, Boston: Bowles, 1833);

Christmas Day; or, The Friends (Wellington, U.K.: Houlston, 1834);

Illustrations of Taxation (5 volumes, London: Fox, 1834);

The Hamlets (Boston: Munroe, 1836);

Miscellanies (2 volumes, Boston: Hilliard, Gray, 1836);

Society in America (3 volumes, London: Saunders & Otley, 1837);

The Guide to Service (London: Knight, 1838);

How to Observe Morals and Manners (London: Knight, 1838; New York: Harper, 1838);

My Servant, Rachel (Wellington, U.K.: Houlston, 1838);

A Retrospect of Western Travel (3 volumes, London: Saunders & Otley, 1838; 2 volumes, New York: Lohman, 1838);

Deerbrook: A Novel (3 volumes, London: Moxon, 1839; 2 volumes, New York: Harper, 1839);

The Martyr Age of the United States of America (London: Hamilton, Adams, 1840);

The Hour and the Man: An Historical Romance (3 volumes, London: Moxon, 1841; 2 volumes, New York: Harper, 1841);

The Playfellow: A Series of Tales (4 volumes, London: Routledge, 1841);

The Rioters (London: Houlston & Stoneman, 1842);

Life in the Sick-Room; or, Essays by an Invalid (London: Moxon, 1844; Boston: Bowles & Crosby, 1844);

Dawn Island: A Tale (Manchester: Gadsby, 1845);

Letters on Mesmerism (London: Moxon, 1845); republished as *Miss Martineau's Letters on Mesmerism* (New York: Harper, 1845);

Forest and Game Law Tales (3 volumes, London: Moxon, 1845-1846);

The Billow and the Rock (London: Knight, 1846);

The Land We Live In, by Martineau and Charles Knight (4 volumes, London: Knight, 1847);

Eastern Life Present and Past (3 volumes, London: Moxon, 1848; 1 volume, Philadelphia: Lea & Blanchard, 1848);

Household Education (London: Moxon, 1849; Philadelphia: Lea & Blanchard, 1849);

History of England during the Thirty Years' Peace 1816-46 (2 volumes, London: Knight, 1849-1850; 4 volumes, Philadelphia: Porter & Coates, 1864);

Two Letters on Cow-Keeping (Edinburgh: Black, 1850);

Letters on the Laws of Man's Nature and Development, by Martineau and H. G. Atkinson (London: Chapman, 1851; Boston: Mendum, 1851);

Introduction to the History of the Peace from 1800 to 1815 (London: Knight, 1851);

Half a Century of the British Empire: A History of the Kingdom and the People from 1800 to 1850, Part I (London: N.p., 1851);

Merdhen, the Manor and the Eyrie, and Old Landmarks and Old Laws (London: Routledge, 1852);

Letters from Ireland (London: Chapman, 1853);

Guide to Windermere, with Tours to the Neighbouring Lakes and Other Interesting Places (Windermere, U.K.: Garnett, 1854);

A Complete Guide to the English Lakes (London: Whittaker, 1855);

The Factory Controversy: A Warning against Meddling Legislation (Manchester: National Association of Factory Occupiers, 1855);

A History of the American Compromises (London: Chapman, 1856);

Sketches from Life (London: Whittaker, 1856);

British Rule in India: A Historical Sketch (London:

Smith, Elder, 1857);

Corporate Traditions and National Rights: Local Dues on Shipping (London: Routledge, 1857);

Guide to Keswick and Its Environs (Windermere: Garnett, 1857);

The "Manifest Destiny" of the American Union (New York: American Anti-Slavery Society, 1857);

Suggestions towards the Future Government of India (London: Smith, Elder, 1858);

Endowed Schools of Ireland (London: Smith, Elder, 1859);

England and Her Soldiers (London: Smith, Elder, 1859);

Health, Husbandry and Handicraft (London: Bradbury & Evans, 1861); republished in part as *Our Farm of Two Acres* (New York: Bunce & Huntingdon, 1865);

Biographical Sketches (London: Macmillan, 1869; New York: Leypoldt & Holt, 1869);

Harriet Martineau's Autobiography, with Memorials by Maria Weston Chapman (3 volumes, London: Smith, Elder, 1877; 2 volumes, Boston: Osgood, 1877);

The Hampdens: An Historiette (London: Routledge, 1880).

A writer of eclectic interests and limitless enthusiasms, Harriet Martineau was a novelist, political economist, journalist, travel writer, essayist, historian, translator, editor, and autobiographer. Her prodigious output resulted in works of uneven quality; but she never restricted her pursuits, which ranged from books for children to studies of the future government of India. Throughout her long, illness-plagued life—she was born without a sense of smell or taste, gradually lost her hearing, and was an invalid for five years until cured by mesmerism—Harriet Martineau was an energetic popularizer of the leading ideas of economics, history, and social thought.

During her career as a writer, Martineau received the attention and praise of Henry Hallam, Sydney Smith, Thomas Malthus, Edward Bulwer-Lytton, and W. C. Macready. Carlyle, among the many to celebrate this early Victorian bluestocking, noted in a letter to Emerson in 1837 that Martineau was "a genuine little Poetess, buckrammed, swathed like a mummy, into Socinian and Political-Economy formulas; and yet verily alive in the inside of that!" George Eliot, however, took a less sympathetic attitude, noting in 1854 that "amongst her good qualities we certainly cannot reckon zeal for other people's reputation. She is sure to caricature any information for the amusement of the next person

to whom she turns her ear-trumpet." Nonetheless, it was none other than the editor of the *Dictionary of National Biography*, Leslie Stephen, who composed her biography for the prestigious reference work. For Martineau, literature was a didactic vehicle to explain to readers the complex workings of society and humanity. For her, no subject was too arcane, no topic too abstruse.

Born in Norwich of a well-to-do Unitarian family, Harriet Martineau was educated at home in languages and the classics, a background which permitted her, she once claimed, even to think in Latin. Between 1813 and 1815 she attended the Reverend Isaac Pervy's school, and for the next two years was taught by masters in Latin and French. Afflicted with hearing problems that led to deafness at the age of eighteen, she led an early life which was the disciplined embodiment of Unitarian behavior, restricting amusements and pleasures. James Martineau, her younger brother, became a well-known theologian. In 1826 their father died, and by 1829 the family's small fortune from wool manufacturing had drastically declined; Harriet did needlework for income, living on £ 50 a year. This early experience with the extremes of financial stability and loss was to be repeated later in her life. Soon, however, she began to contribute reviews to the *Monthly Repository*, published by the Unitarians in Newcastle. By 1831 she conceived her first literary triumph, a set of short stories that illustrated various principles of economics. After difficulty finding a publisher, she convinced Charles Fox of London to attempt the venture. The project began in February 1832 by subscription; two years and twenty-five numbers later, almost 10,000 copies had been sold, and she had become a literary sensation.

Illustrations of Political Economy (1832-1834) followed a general pattern: a dramatic short story supplemented by a list of doctrinal points. Each story focused on a single economic concept. The demand for a free money market, for example, is the subject of "Berkeley the Banker," while an argument for free trade is the theme of "The Loom and the Lugger." *Elements of Political Economy* (1821) by James Mill and the writings of Adam Smith were the principal sources of the economic ideas; Jane Marcet's *Conversations on Political Economy* (1816) provided the literary inspiration. Characteristic of the themes of individualism and capitalism in the stories is this sentence from "Godwin's Thoughts on Man": "When the ends of individual life are duly regarded, the aims of society (which are themselves but means) will be certainly fulfilled." Doctrine and plot often conflicted, but the stories were immensely popular and reprinted frequently. Because of their liberal emphasis, the volumes were banned in Russia, Austria, and Italy, although in England statesmen like Lord Brougham, Cobden, and Bright sought Martineau's advice on Poor Laws, Corn Laws, and Game Laws.

In the 1830s and 1840s Harriet Martineau continued to publish her short fictional tracts dealing with social and political issues such as *Poor Laws and Paupers Illustrated* (1833-1834) and *Forest and Game Law Tales* (1845-1846). During this time she also made a trip to America (1834-1836), where she lectured on abolition in the South and East, often in the face of vocal opposition and occasional threats of personal injury. Upon her return to England, two social histories appeared, the analytical *Society in America* (1837) and the more personal *Retrospect of Western Travel* (1838). In 1841 she published an antislavery novel about the negro leader of Haiti, L'Ouverture, entitled *The Hour and the Man*. But her most important work during this period and her most sustained literary effort is *Deerbrook* (1839).

A didactic novel of English provincial life that suggests certain thematic and stylistic parallels with Jane Austen, *Deerbrook* deals with jealousy between two sisters. Martineau began the novel on her thirty-sixth birthday after hearing an account of an actual situation which satisfied her notion that fictional plots must be grounded in real life. Initially concentrating on the dullness of small-town life, the novel generates interest with the introduction of the Ibbotson sisters, both in their early twenties, who compete with each other for the affection of the village doctor, Mr. Hope. Philip Enderby, another eligible young man, appears but, like Mr. Hope, falls in love with the younger sister, Margaret. Mrs. Grey, a relative of the sisters, plays matchmaker, and Mr. Hope nobly renounces Margaret and proposes to the other sister, Hester. He is accepted and marries her, knowing he does not love her. Margaret soon comes to live with the Hopes, but Hester becomes jealous, recognizing her husband's attraction to her younger sister. As Mr. Hope grows more fond of his sister-in-law, Mr. Enderby proposes to her and she accepts. But gossip spreads that Mr. Hope is unfaithful to his wife, and his medical practice begins to collapse, leading to poverty. Violence follows, as the Hopes' home is robbed and vandalized, while a plague descends on the village. But the birth of a child saves the Hopes' marriage, as Mr. Hope's sacrificial work among the plague-stricken poor restores his practice. By the end, the malicious, gossip-spreading Mrs. Rowlands is exposed and the competitive and jealous sisters are reconciled.

With its attention to middle-class life and theme of a man of science overcoming ignorance in a provincial town, *Deerbrook* achieved critical and popular success. John Sterling, Mrs. Gaskell, and Macready all praised the book, although Carlyle could say no more than that it was "very ligneous, very trivial-didactic, in fact very absurd for the most part." (Carlyle, indeed, was tiring of Harriet Martineau's friendship and once remarked that "one wishes her heartily well—at a distance." This turning against friends, regardless of their assistance to him, frequently characterized Carlyle's behavior. Martineau's help in promoting a one-volume edition of *Sartor Resartus* and aid in organizing a lecture series for Carlyle in 1837 to ease his lack of finances did not prevent the emergence by 1849 of a "feud" between them which has never been properly explained.) Despite its convoluted and at times comical plot, *Deerbrook* anticipates the themes of later Victorian novels, from its analysis of the deceptions and hypocrisies of provincial life to the importance of medicine in the social behavior of a community. The jealous Hester, submissive Margaret, and detached Maria (a lame governess who is an objective observer) all represent character types soon to dominate Victorian fiction. The disillusionment-with-marriage theme in the novel also predates its elaboration in works such as *Vanity Fair* (1847-1848) and *Jude the Obscure* (1896).

The year *Deerbrook* was published, Harriet Martineau took to her bed. She remained there until completely cured by mesmerism in 1844. Her mother's illness at this time compounded her own poor health, a fact she discussed in *Life in The Sickroom; or, Essays by an Invalid* (1844). *Letters on Mesmerism* (1845) narrates her recovery and the remarkable powers of mesmerists; the book went into a second edition during its first year of publication. In 1845, she decided to build a home, "The Knoll," near Ambleside in the Lake District near Windermere. At the two-story, stone residence with its surrounding two acres, Martineau hosted such visitors as the Wordsworths, Charlotte Brontë, and George Eliot. A typical day for a guest, in the words of Charlotte Brontë to her sister Emily, emphasized independence: "I rise at my own hour, breakfast alone . . . I pass the morning in the drawing-room, she in her study. At two o'clock we meet, talk and walk till five, her dinner-hour,—spend the evening together, when she converses fluently and abundantly, and with the most complete frankness. I go to my room soon after ten, and she sits up writing letters." Brontë also noted that Martineau was "both hard and warm-hearted, abrupt and affectionate. I

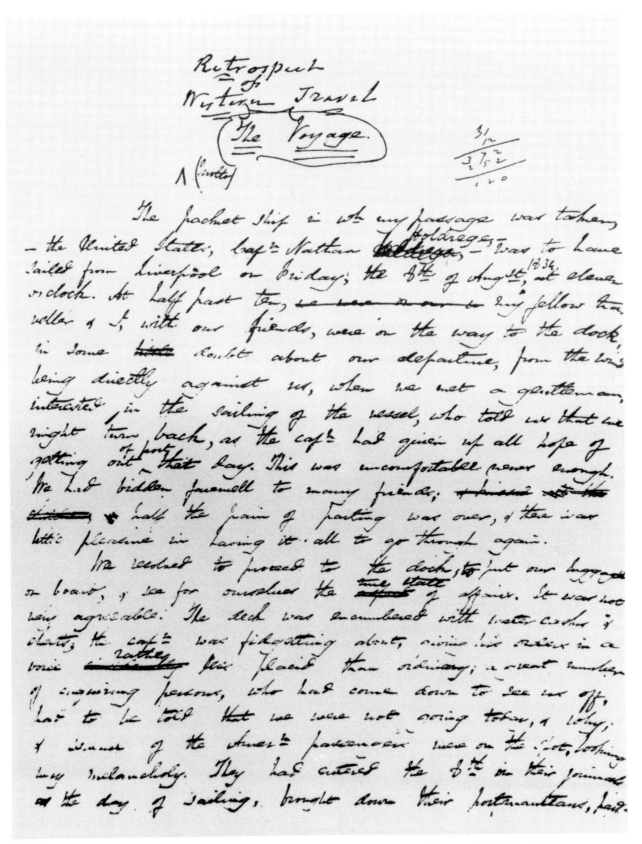

Manuscript page for Martineau's book about her American travels (Parke-Bernet, 17 October 1934)

believe she is not at all conscious of her own absolutism."

Harriet Martineau resumed her writing career after a trip to Egypt and Palestine in 1846-1847 during which she renounced theology. The prophet of Unitarianism became the apostle of Positivism, or, as Douglas Jerrold quipped, "There is no God and Harriet is his Prophet." Martineau herself called her new rationalism "Necessarianism," and in 1851 published *Letters on the Laws of Man's Nature and Development* with the freethinker H. G. Atkinson; the work developed her philosophic ideas but further alienated her from her theologian brother, James.

Martineau's antireligious views led her to the writings of Auguste Comte, whose lengthy *Positive Philosophy* she translated in 1853. The translation was so successful that Comte himself recommended it to his followers. During this period Martineau also began to contribute regularly to journals and newspapers on a variety of topics, including the conditions in Ireland and the census of 1851. Her total contribution of leading articles to the *Daily News* was, in fact, 1,642 stories, including 60 articles against the establishment of licensed brothels in India. She also published (1851) an important study of England's peace between 1800 and 1815, a work Leslie Stephen especially admired.

For Harriet Martineau, almost no activity lacked literary potential. Illness, travel, or history became subjects for a book. A tour of the Lake District resulted in an 1854 travel guide. Heart palpitations and breathlessness led to her conviction that she suffered from an incurable heart disease, a view contradicted by two heart specialists. Anticipating her imminent death in January 1853, Martineau prepared her own obituary for the *Daily News*. The cause of her actual death, twenty-one years later, was an abdominal cyst, not her heart; however, her fear of a sudden demise prompted her to finish her autobiography within three months. She had the sheets printed, corrected, insured, and packed away for immediate publication upon her death, a precaution few writers followed. Indeed, no other nineteenth-century autobiography was so prepared in advance for public reading. In her remaining life, Martineau did not make any alterations to the original text.

Despite the peculiarities of its composition, Martineau's *Autobiography* remains a valuable literary work. Posthumously published in 1877, it is a full, three-volume account of the major events in her life up to 1855, giving boastful summaries and detailed reports of her associations, triumphs, occa-sional failures, and opinions. (Scott, for example, lacked moral earnestness, she writes, while Macaulay was a plagiarist.) Since she demanded her letters be destroyed and made no revisions to the text during the twenty years it was packed away, the *Autobiography* stands as the only testimony to Martineau's attitudes in mid-career. The work also contains accounts of her jealousy of her nearest sister, Rachel, one and a half years older; her deep attachment to her brother, James; and her brief engagement to a neurotic friend of James's. On love and marriage Martineau revealingly writes—in an attempt to dismiss her early engagement to a man who was shortly to go insane and die—"I am in truth very thankful for not having married at all. I have never since been tempted, nor have suffered anything at all in relation to that . . . which is held to be all-important to women,—love and marriage. I can easily conceive how I *might* have been tempted. . . . If I had had a husband dependent on me for his happiness, the responsibility would have made me wretched. . . . If my husband had *not* depended on me for his happiness, I should have been jealous." This honesty of feeling reflects a lively, critical work of prose replete with comments on major artistic and intellectual figures of the age, in addition to an appraisal of the difficulty of maintaining a literary career. The book is one of the most important autobiographies by a woman to appear in the Victorian period. Criticisms of its accuracy (criticisms challenged by James Martineau in a lengthy letter to the *Daily News*, 30 December 1884, in response to a new biography of his sister) continue, but the volume remains a vivid and candid record of mid-Victorian literary life.

In her remaining years, Harriet Martineau turned to social, economic, and governmental issues, publishing books on factory legislation, the schools of Ireland, and the taxes on shipping. In addition, she took up various causes, joining Florence Nightingale and Josephine Butler, for example, in the agitation for the repeal of the Contagious Diseases Acts. These Acts of 1864, 1866, and 1869 placed prostitutes in seaports and garrison towns under police supervision and required medical examinations in order to stop the spread of venereal disease among the armed forces; however, no similar measures existed for men who carried the disease. Pressure to extend the inspections to larger cities increased as the effort to repeal the unjust laws intensified. The reform movement led by Josephine Butler succeeded, however, and the last of the acts was repealed in 1886.

In her final decade, various illnesses in-

Martineau in 1833

capacitated Martineau. As she wrote less and less, her income declined. In 1873 she was offered a Civil List pension by Gladstone; she refused it, as she had earlier refused one from Lord Melbourne. Just after she turned seventy-four, in June 1876, she caught bronchitis and lapsed into a coma, dying on the 27th of the month at The Knoll. Two days later, Florence Nightingale characterized the event in this fashion: "How delightful the surprise to her! How much she must know now, how much she must have enjoyed already! . . . for a long time I have thought how great will be the *surprise* to her."

Of herself Harriet Martineau said she gained intellectual power through "earnestness and intellectual clearness within a certain range." In the tradition of Macaulay and G. H. Lewes, she could, in her words, "popularize, while she could neither discover nor invent." Modern critics, however, have argued for the importance of her efforts at political, social, and legal reform. Her analysis of marriage, coupled with her efforts to revise the understanding of political economy and English history, supplemented her presentation of the frustration of nineteenth-century womanhood in *Deerbrook*. The modern picture of Martineau is of a writer who conscientiously interpreted her age and whose passion for knowledge—vividly recorded in her *Autobiography*—was surpassed only by her desire to disseminate what she understood to her readers.

Other:

Traditions of Palestine, edited by Martineau (London: Longman, Rees, Orme, Brown & Green, 1830; Boston: Crosby, 1839);

The Positive Philosophy of Auguste Comte Freely Translated and Condensed, 2 volumes (London: Chapman, 1853; New York: Appleton, 1853).

Bibliography:

Joseph B. Rivlin, *Harriet Martineau: A Bibliography of Her Separately Printed Books* (New York: New York Public Library, 1947).

Biographies:

R. K. Webb, *Harriet Martineau: A Radical Victorian* (London: Heinemann, 1960);

Valerie Kossew Pichanick, *Harriet Martineau: The Woman and Her Work, 1802-1876* (Ann Arbor: University of Michigan Press, 1980).

References:

Theodora Bosanquet, *Harriet Martineau: An Essay in Comprehension* (London: Etchells & Macdonald, 1927);

Robert Lee Wolff, *Strange Stories and Other Explorations in Victorian Fiction* (Boston: Gambit, 1971).

Caroline Norton
(22 March 1808-15 June 1877)

Lois Josephs Fowler
Carnegie-Mellon University

SELECTED BOOKS: *The Sorrows of Rosalie: A Tale with Other Poems*, anonymous (London: Ebers, 1829);

The Undying One and Other Poems (London: Colburn & Bentley, 1830; Boston: Crosby, Nichols, 1854);

Poems (Boston: Allen & Ticknor, 1833);

Kate Bouverie and Other Tales and Sketches in Prose and Verse (Philadelphia: Carey & Hart, 1835);

The Wife and Woman's Reward, anonymous (3 volumes, London: Saunders & Otley, 1835; 1 volume, New York: Harper, 1835);

A Voice from the Factories (London: Murray, 1836);

The Separation of Mother and Child by the Laws of Custody of Infants (London: Roake & Varty, 1838);

A Plain Letter to the Lord Chancellor on the Infant Custody Bill (London: Ridgway, 1839; New York: Rogers, 1922);

The Dream, and Other Poems (London: Colburn, 1840; Philadelphia: Carey & Hart, 1841);

The Child of the Islands: A Poem (London: Chapman & Hall, 1845);

Aunt Carry's Ballads for Children: Adventures of a Wood Sprite; The Story of Blanche and Brutikin (London: Cundall, 1847);

A Residence at Sierra Leone (London: Murray, 1849);

Stuart of Dunleath: A Story of Modern Times (3 volumes, London: Parlour Library, 1851);

English Laws for Women in the Nineteenth Century (London: Privately printed, 1854);

A Letter to the Queen on Lord Chancellor Cranworth's Marriage and Divorce Bill (London: Longman, Brown, Green & Longmans, 1855);

The Lady of La Garaye (Cambridge & London: Macmillan, 1862; New York: Bradburn, 1864);

Lost and Saved (3 volumes, London: Hurst & Blackett, 1863);

Old Sir Douglas (3 volumes, London: Hurst & Blackett, 1868);

Bingen on the Rhine (Philadelphia: Porter & Coates, 1883; London: Walker, 1888).

Caroline Norton's importance lies mainly in her dramatic demonstration that she, like few other Englishwomen of her time, could surmount convention by living as a public figure estranged from her husband, writing fiction and poetry for money and pamphlets for social reform. Here her talent as a writer and her strong social conscience served her well, but she was also aided considerably by her beauty, wit, and charm, as well as by her status as a member of the lesser aristocracy. She was a noted feminist, but only in her own example and her pleas for amelioration of the inferior position of women; she avoided radical programs and concerted efforts. Her novels and poems, written in the sentimental voice of the time, were read widely by women who responded to her unhappily depen-

234

dent heroines suffering from mistreatment by men and the intolerance of an unjust society. Her pamphlets pleaded for reform of the laws of marriage and child custody and for attention to the plight of child laborers and the poor.

The young Caroline Elizabeth Sarah Sheridan grew up in an atmosphere of literature and politics. Her grandfather was Richard Brinsley Sheridan, the celebrated playwright and member of Parliament. His son, Thomas, socially prominent but not wealthy, married Caroline Henrietta, daughter of Sir James Campbell. Upon Thomas Sheridan's death in 1817, his widow supported her son and three daughters, of whom Caroline was the second, by her writing; her novels are no longer remembered.

Since the girls had no dowries, their mother encouraged them to marry for practical reasons. Thus Caroline accepted the Honorable George Chapple Norton and was married to him on 20 June 1827. She bore three sons and was presented at court in 1831. As time passed, however, the couple's obvious incompatibility produced deep divisions. Norton, though not wealthy, had money but neither wit nor polish; Caroline shone in company and delighted in repartee. His relatives disliked her, and in his suspicion of the flexible sexual code of the aristocratic London circle to which she belonged, he became jealous. He fought with her over her friendships with the king of Belgium and others. William Lamb, Viscount Melbourne, who was twice prime minister, was fascinated by her; Norton, though he owed an appointment as metropolitan police magistrate to Melbourne's interest in his wife, became abusive and violent and sued for divorce by charging her and Melbourne with adultery. After the court rejected his suit on 23 June 1836, Norton angrily threatened Caroline's safety. She took refuge with her family, but was obliged to leave their three children, to whom she had no right under British law, in his custody. Attempts at reconciliation failed, and she never again lived with Norton. He in turn kept her from her children, even when her youngest son was dying. Thus she acquired a powerful motive for her struggle, which went on for years, to gain more rights for women as wives and mothers. Her efforts, in periodical articles, pamphlets, and personal solicitation, helped to influence the adoption of the Divorce Act of 1857 and the Infant Custody Act of 1873.

In the social circle of the Nortons, as well as in the published gossip of the day, sympathy lay with Caroline rather than with her husband. She maintained an active social life as hostess and guest and continued to be sought after by public figures. When in 1846 the *Times* broke the news of the impending repeal of the Corn Laws, gossip attributed the leak to Caroline Norton through her friendship with Sidney Herbert, the current war secretary and a confidant of Prime Minister Robert Peel. This incident served George Meredith as the pivotal episode of his novel *Diana of the Crossways* (1885), whose heroine was also descended from an Anglo-Irish dramatist, engaged in dangerous intimacies with distinguished statesmen, influenced policy behind the scenes, and successfully fought a divorce suit brought by an insensitive, cruel, and jealous husband.

Caroline Norton supported herself largely by means of her poetry and her fiction. Of her verse, *The Sorrows of Rosalie: A Tale with Other Poems* (1829) drew attention from critics, who viewed it, as they did many women's poetry, as appropriate in themes if not great in merit. In it, as in *The Dream, and Other Poems* (1840), she espoused the beauty of nature, of pure love, of dreams for an uncluttered life, of the

William Lamb, Viscount Melbourne, whose alleged affair with Norton led to a sensational divorce trial in 1836

Caroline Norton in 1840. This drawing by Sir Edwin Landseer was used as an illustration for The Dream, and Other Poems

Platonic spirit. But in *A Voice from the Factories* (1836), she graphically describes the cries of a small child forced to work long hours under painful conditions. In *The Child of the Islands* (1845), Norton warns the rich that they will somehow be punished for cruelty to children who work in factories or in homes not their own. The cries from within the walls of work remind the reader of the realistic details of Dickens's poor, of Oliver Twist who asks for just one more bowl of gruel. The exploited child of the islands—the British Isles—leads a tragic existence. The irony of the pictures evoked by the islands, pictures of peace and of beauty, was not lost on contemporary critics, who deplored her venturing into social commentary. These males would have had her keep to the more acceptable feminine flowers in her poetry. She retreated into children's verse, more because of need of money than because of fear of the critics. *Aunt Carry's Ballads for Children* (1847) were read in the nurseries of the rich. But in 1854 she republished *The Undying One and Other Poems* (1830), in which she rebukes the harshness of the educational system, corporal punishment of children, and inhuman conditions in the prisons.

Her fiction, while clearly aimed at sentimental tastes, nevertheless offers enough penetration and subtlety in its depiction of relationships between men and women that George Meredith regarded her as a good, if not great, writer. Though a prolific writer of some hundred books of verse and fiction, Norton's interests pervade her fiction which, though written for popular tastes so as to earn money, transcended those tastes to deal with issues such as the uselessness of a woman's sacrifice of love for the sake of her brother's success in *The Wife and Woman's Reward* (1835). This novel also deals with the political intrigue that Norton understood and deplored; Clavering, the hero, achieves success as a famous statesman at the expense of his wife's happiness.

In *Stuart of Dunleath* (1851), along with the expected Gothic touches one also finds a subtle but strong comment about the importance of friendship between women, from which they receive sustenance in a society where they have so little power. The love between the hero and heroine, though essential to the plot and demanded by the reading public, has little dramatic impact now; however, the supportive relationship between Eleanor and Lady Margaret has substance in the depth of feelings expressed in their conversations. Of even more significance to the modern reader is the marriage of a minor female character to a middle-aged and wise man on whom she becomes sensibly dependent and toward whom she has an attitude of tender but realistic awe very different from her feelings about a younger, impetuous lover who regarded her as a possession. In this novel, especially, Norton uses the Gothic genre but adds to it a deeper psychological level to interest the modern reader. In the relationship between mother and son she anticipates Freud. The reasons she loves her son more than she does her daughter are carefully explored by the sensual Lady Raymond. She explains to her lover that there are women who are incapable of loving their daughters as well as their sons, just as there are men who cannot love their sons as they do their daughters. Perhaps women cannot help being jealous of their daughters' youth and of love just beginning, she reflects.

Similar perceptions in *Old Sir Douglas* (1868) allow Norton to portray a young woman who learns, after her initial attraction to a wild, passionate man—resembling Heathcliff in Emily Brontë's *Wuthering Heights* (1847)—to appreciate the subdued warmth of an older, sensitive, and sensible man, Sir Douglas, and to enjoy with him a mature and tranquil love. Gertrude, the heroine, because of a lonely, fatherless childhood, finds fulfillment in kindness and protectiveness, qualities Norton must have well appreciated. Gertrude, like other Victorian heroines, manifests through her need for a father / lover the playfulness typical of relationships of daughters with seductive fathers. Sir Douglas enjoys her witchery (Norton's word) in a relationship that succeeds for realistic rather than romantic reasons. In this novel, a minor heroine—shy, secretive, and rejected by a father who did not love her mother—falls dependent on a husband who uses her to release his sadistic anger. She resembles the battered wives of today who continue to love regardless of treatment, who believe that the men they love will change. Norton makes it clear to the reader that the men will never change.

Of special interest to modern historians are Norton's powerful pleas for women's rights in her journalistic prose. Her attacks on English marriage laws may have grown out of her own troubles, but they also reflected concern for her less fortunate sisters without money or position. While she could not condone the militant feminists who stormed the House of Commons in search of suffrage, probably because of her allegiance to her class, Norton did not equivocate in her attacks on injustice. Her pamphlet on the custody of infant children (1838) involved her in unpleasant disagreements with her own family, who disliked the publicity; but she held firm, using her own name in publication to argue that young children need a mother's care. In a subsequent pamphlet (1839), she appealed to the lord chancellor to use his forceful eloquence to advocate reform of the divorce laws, which gave all rights to husbands regardless of their character and reputation. She pointed out in an open letter to the queen (1855) that a married woman in England had no legal existence, that her living and her money belonged to her husband. Her most famous pamphlet, *English Laws for Women in the Nineteenth Century* (1854), argues that some marriages are destructive to all parties and that no good can come from having people live simultaneously in marriage and in alienation. This is the pamphlet that has been credited with having influenced the passage of the new Divorce Act in 1857.

Her fiction, of which she produced for a time almost two books a year, depends on melodrama—as in her best-known novel, *Lost and Saved* (1863), where the plot involves a false marriage performed by a fraudulent clergyman. Yet here, too, she adds messages for her favorite causes: men must be held as morally responsible as women; unwed mothers need not be fallen women; arranged marriages are always disastrous; women should not lose control of their money when they marry; divorce laws are unjust to women; political manipulation may be not only dishonest but also a cause of personal tragedy; women can, either by education or by marriage to sensible men, learn to be more independent.

Caroline Norton lived most of her life as one who had all the responsibilities of independence and none of the supports of marriage, since George Norton refused to grant her a divorce. In 1875 he died; and on 1 March 1877 she was married to the historian Sir William Stirling-Maxwell, ten years younger than she, with whom she had lived on intimate terms for years. She, however, died within a year of their marriage; she was then sixty-nine. Given the circumstances of her life, it is not surprising that Norton was what would be called "neurotic" today. Her biographers tell of restless unhappiness and recurrent illnesses. While ill health and fits of depression became more frequent with age, she retained her vitality and sense of humor. She was always able to love, to have friends, to enjoy life, and to fight for what she believed. Yet she always lamented her disabilities as a woman, both the psychological constraints and the legal inequities. In her time, Caroline Norton was known as a witty, provocative, and beautiful woman and as a popular writer of over a hundred books; today, she continues to be of interest because of her dramatic and effective contributions to modifying the ways women see themselves and are seen by men, as well

Norton's sketch of a ruined château, used to illustrate the title page of The Lady of La Garaye

as the ways they are treated by society and state.

Biographies:
Percy Fitzgerald, *The Lives of the Sheridans* (2 volumes, London: Bentley, 1886);
Jane Gray Perkins, *The Life of Mrs. Norton* (London: Privately printed, 1909);
Alice Ackland, *Caroline Norton* (London: Privately printed, 1948).

Reference:
Arthur Arnold, "The Hon. Mrs. Norton and Married Women," *Fraser's Magazine* (April 1878): 492-500.

Papers:
Caroline Norton's letters, private papers, and manuscripts are in the Altschul Collection at Yale University and in the British Museum.

Charles Reade
(8 June 1814-11 April 1884)

Elton E. Smith
University of South Florida

BOOKS: *Peregrine Pickle* (Oxford: Slatter, 1851);
Angelo: A Tragedy in Four Acts (London: Lacy, 1851);
The Ladies' Battle; or, Un Duel en Amour: A Comedy (London: Lacy, 1851; Boston: Spencer, 1855);
The Lost Husband: A Drama in Four Acts (London: Lacy, 1852);
Gold! A Drama in Five Acts (London: Lacy, 1853);
Peg Woffington: A Novel (London: Bentley, 1853; Boston: Dodd, Mead, 1855);
Christie Johnstone: A Novel (London: Bentley, 1853; Boston: Ticknor & Fields, 1855);
The King's Rival: A Drama in Five Acts, by Reade and Tom Taylor (London: Bentley, 1854);
Masks and Faces; or, Before and behind the Curtain: A Comedy in Two Acts, by Reade and Tom Taylor (London: Bentley, 1854);
Two Loves and a Life: A Drama in Four Acts, by Reade and Tom Taylor (London: Bentley, 1854);
Clouds and Sunshine, and Art: A Dramatic Tale (Boston: Ticknor & Fields, 1855);
It Is Never Too Late to Mend: A Matter of Fact Romance (3 volumes, London: Bentley, 1856; 2 volumes, Boston: Ticknor & Fields, 1856);
The Course of True Love Never Did Run Smooth (London: Bentley, 1857);
Propria Quae Maribus: A Jeu d'Esprit; and The Box Tunnel: A Fact (Boston: Ticknor & Fields, 1857);
White Lies: A Story (3 volumes, London: Trübner, 1857; 1 volume, Boston: Ticknor & Fields, 1858);
Cream (London: Trübner, 1858);

A Good Fight and Other Tales (New York: Harper, 1859);
"It is Never Too Late to Mend": Proofs of Its Prison Revelations (London: Bentley, 1859);

Le Faubourg Saint-Germain: Pièce en Deux Actes (Paris: Moris, 1859);

Love Me Little, Love Me Long (2 volumes, London: Trübner, 1859; 1 volume, New York: Harper, 1859);

The Eighth Commandment (London: Trübner, 1860; Boston: Ticknor & Fields, 1860);

Monopoly versus Property (London: Privately printed, 1860);

The Cloister and the Hearth: A Tale of the Middle Ages (4 volumes, London: Trübner, 1861; 1 volume, New York: Rudd & Carleton, 1861);

Hard Cash: A Matter-of-Fact Romance (3 volumes, London: Low & Marston, 1863; 1 volume, New York: Harper, 1864);

It's Never Too Late to Mend: A Drama in Four Acts (London: Williams & Strahan, 1865);

Griffith Gaunt; or, Jealousy (3 volumes, London: Chapman & Hall, 1866; 1 volume, Boston: Ticknor & Fields, 1866);

Dora: A Pastoral Drama in Three Acts, Founded on Mr. Tennyson's Poem (London: Clowes, 1867);

The Double Marriage: A Drama in Five Acts, by Reade and August Maquet (London: Clowes, 1867);

Foul Play, by Reade and Dion Boucicault (3 volumes, London: Bradbury, Evans, 1868; 1 volume, Boston: Ticknor & Fields, 1868);

Put Yourself in His Place (3 volumes, London: Smith, Elder, 1870; 1 volume, New York: Harper, 1870);

Foul Play: A Drama in Four Acts, by Reade and Dion Boucicault (London: N.p., 1871);

Rachel the Reaper: A Rustic Drama in Three Acts (London: Clowes, 1871);

A Terrible Temptation: A Story of the Day (3 volumes, London: Chapman & Hall, 1871; 1 volume, Boston: Osgood, 1871);

To the Editor of the "Daily Globe," Toronto: A Reply to Criticism (London: N.p., 1871);

Kate Peyton; or, Jealousy: A Drama in a Prologue and Four Acts (London: Williams & Strahan, 1872);

The Legal Vocabulary (London: N.p., 1872);

The Wandering Heir: A Matter of Fact Romance (Toronto: Hunter, Rose, 1872; Boston: Osgood, 1873; London: French, 1875);

Cremona Violins: Four Letters Reprinted from the "Pall Mall Gazette" (Gloucester: Bellows, 1873);

A Simpleton: A Story of the Day (3 volumes, London: Chapman & Hall, 1873; 1 volume, New York: Harper, 1873);

A Hero and a Martyr: A True and Accurate Account of the Heroic Feats and Sad Calamity of James Lambert (London: French, 1874; New York: Harper, 1875);

Trade Malice: A Personal Narrative; and The Wandering Heir: A Matter of Fact Romance (London: French, 1875);

The Jilt: A Novel (New York: Harper, 1877);

A Woman-Hater (3 volumes, Edinburgh & London: Blackwood, 1877; 1 volume, New York: Harper, 1877);

Golden Crowns: Sunday Stories (Manchester: Tubbs & Brooke, 1877);

The Coming Man: Letters Contributed to "Harper's Weekly" (New York: Harper, 1877);

Dora; or, The History of a Play (London: Williams & Strahan, 1878);

The Well-Born Workman; or, A Man of the Day (London: Williams & Strahan, 1878);

Singleheart and Doubleface: A Matter-of-Fact Romance (New York: Lovell, 1882; London: Chatto & Windus, 1884);

The Countess and the Dancer; or, High Life in Vienna: A Comedy Drama in Four Acts, based on a comedy by Victorien Sardou (London: N.p., 1883);

Love and Money: An Original Drama in Prologue and Four Acts, by Reade and Henry Pettitt (London: Durant, 1883; New York: Munro, 1884);

Readiana: Comments on Current Events (London: Chatto & Windus, 1883; New York: Munro, 1884);

Good Stories of Man and Other Animals (London: Chatto & Windus, 1884; New York: Harper, 1884);

The White Elephant: A Story (New York: Gibson & King, 1884);

The Jilt and Other Stories (London: Chatto & Windus, 1884);

A Perilous Secret (2 volumes, London: Bentley, 1884; 1 volume, New York: Harper, 1884);

The Picture (New York: Harper, 1884);

Bible Characters (London: Chatto & Windus, 1888; New York: Harper, 1889).

COLLECTION: *Complete Writings of Charles Reade*, Uniform Library Edition (17 volumes, London: Chatto & Windus, 1895-1896).

By the time Charles Reade had reached the age of forty, he had written only two of his fourteen novels, *Peg Woffington* (1853) and *Christie Johnstone* (1853); but he had already written at least fifteen of his forty plays, and he continued to write, translate, and plagiarize plays, and to dramatize novels, as long as he lived.

His dramas tend to fall into three classifications: translations, collaborations, and plays based on or adapted into his own novels. The translations

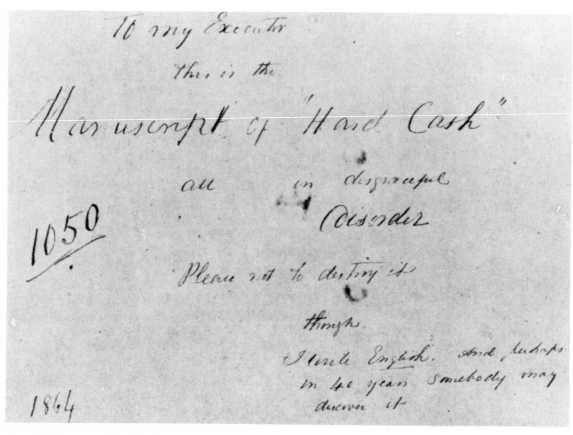

First page for the manuscript of Reade's novel which exposed abuses of patients in private insane asylums (Pierpont Morgan Library)

(usually without permission) were of plays by Augustine Eugène Scribe, Ernest Legouvé, Victor Hugo, George Sand, Eugène Moreau, Paul Siraudin, Alfred Delacour, Edouard Brisbarre, Eugène Nus, Jean Baptiste Molière, August Maquet, Victorien Sardou, and Émile Zola. The most significant of these was probably *Drink*, first performed in 1879, Reade's translation of Zola's novel *L'Assommoir* (already dramatized by Zola in collaboration with William Bertrand Busnach and Octave Gastineau). Conservative critics were shocked and dismayed by French naturalism; critics who followed the theater on the Continent were delighted; William Archer, who usually blasted the bombastic egoism and inordinate length of Reade's sensational spectacles, wrote: "If ever there was a drama which would cause instant conversions from evil ways, 'Drink' was that drama."

The second classification of Reade's drama includes collaborations with Tom Taylor, Dion Boucicault, and Henry Pettitt. The most successful, still occasionally staged, was *Masks and Faces* (1854) with Taylor, although Charles Dickens lamented that Reade "did not stand on his own bottom instead

of getting in with Dion Boucicault, etc." It was at a rehearsal of that play that Reade met the actress Laura Seymour, who advised him to write novels!

The dramas related to novels are: *The Double Marriage* (1867), based on the novel *White Lies* (1857); *Free Labour* (1870), a dramatization of *Put Yourself in His Place* (1870); *Masks and Faces*, a dramatic version of *Peg Woffington*; the unproduced "The Village Tale" (1852), the basis of the novel *Clouds and Sunshine* (1855); *Christie Johnstone* (1852), the basis of the novel by the same name; "Nance Oldfield" (1855), the basis of *Art* (1855); *Gold* (1853), which earned £2,000 in the dramatic version, the basis of the novel *It Is Never Too Late to Mend* (1856), which Reade redramatized as *It's Never Too Late to Mend* (1865); dramatizations of *The Wandering Heir* (1872) and *Singleheart and Doubleface* (1882); *Love and Money* (1883), the basis of the novel *A Perilous Secret* (1884). Reade dramatized (1869) *Griffith Gaunt* (1866) after John Daly had already adapted it for the stage in America. He also dramatized the novels of other authors, such as Smollett's *Peregrine Pickle* (1851), Trollope's *Ralph the Heir* (1871) as *Shilly-Shally* (1872), and Frances

Hodgson Burnett's *That Lass o' Lowrie's* (1877) as *Joan* (1878).

When Charles Reade died on 11 April 1884 at Blomfield Villas, Shepherd's Bush, London, he was buried beside his longtime housekeeper and comrade Laura Seymour, who had preceded him in death by five years. His epitaph, at his own request, was simple: "Dramatist, Novelist, and Journalist"—dramatist first, always first! Yet he earned handsome sums of money from his reluctantly written novels, and lost money on almost all his theatrical ventures.

Both his novels and his plays met contemporary standards of taste with great exactitude: the novels all sensational, the dramas all melodramatic. The standard English drama of the mid-Victorian era was later described as *comédie larmoyante* (tearful comedy) and drew heavily from the plots, characterizations, and set scenes of such elegant and contrived works as the French plays of Scribe, Legouvé, and Sardou; but it was almost always revised with an eye to the British love for violent action and reshaped in climax by the British demand that good should triumph, be it ever so delayed! In a large folio book called "Red Digest," Reade quite frankly noted that he intended to use the scaffolding of French plots, write them out with open spaces between the lines and then insert "interstitial scenes," as well as to anglicize French characterization by attending public trials at the Old Bailey and reading police reports.

But how does a struggling playwright who has not yet become a successful novelist live in the meantime? Born 8 June 1814 at Ipsden House, the youngest child of John Reade of Ipsden and Anna Maria Scott-Waring, from 1822 until 1827 he was painfully educated by the stern disciplinarian the Reverend Mr. Slatter of Rose Hill, Iffley, and more pleasantly and effectively by the Reverend Mr. Hearns at Staines from 1827 to 1829. At seventeen, thanks to a prize essay, he won a demyship at Magdalen College, Oxford, and on 22 July 1835 was elected Vinerian fellow with a living of £600 annually, paid only to celibate dons (thus relegating Mrs. Seymour to housekeeper-comrade status). He enrolled in November 1836 as a law student at Lincoln's Inn and in 1847 received the degree of Doctor of Civil Laws. Never practicing law, he yet became prodigiously litigious; he sued the publisher Richard Bentley over his first two novels and was awarded only £30 damages apiece. At one time he was engaged simultaneously in six lawsuits to protect the rights to his dramatic works, and in 1860 attacked such literary thefts (of which he, himself, was notoriously guilty) in a pamphlet *The Eighth Commandment*. He won an American damage suit of six cents against the publisher of the *Round Table*—whom he attacked as a "Prurient Prude!"

Reade was also engaged for a time in the manufacture and sale of Cremona fiddles, but nothing seemed to work out financially, so in 1851 he accepted the vice-presidency of Magdalen as a sinecure, settled down into his fellowship along with its social restraint, and thereafter used Oxford as a set of quiet rooms to hide in when periodical deadlines loomed and as an easy source of Bodleian Library hacks to dig out the facts for which he had so voracious an appetite.

William Dean Howells described Reade as "a man who stood at the parting of the ways between realism and romanticism," but also accused him of using "the materials of realism to produce the effects of romanticism." Nothing can be clearer than Reade's excessive devotion to the materials of realism. All his dramas exhibit an extraordinary

A clipping in an 1873 notebook of Reade's. He used sensational news items such as this as the bases for incidents in his novels and plays (London Library).

interest in realistic settings and properties. In letters to the editor, he publicly thanked the *Times* for news articles that provided the plots for at least two of his most popular novels. His compendious notebooks, and the enormous notecards which stood like screens in his private library, can still be seen at the London Library and Princeton University Library. Whenever a critic was so foolhardy as to doubt the credibility of a Reade character or plot, the author had only to reach out and produce the clipping: dates, names, places—all the real stuff of journalistic history. One of the reasons he so often pirated other men's plays (just as they were pirating his) may well be that he distrusted his own imagination and adored the authority of something that was already in print. George Orwell commented that the sole interest in three of Reade's best books—*Foul Play* (1868), *Hard Cash* (1863), and *It Is Never Too Late to Mend*—lay in their technical details. Completely in tune with his age of materialism, industrialization, and colonialism, he made exhaustive research into the techniques of mining gold for *It Is Never Too Late to Mend* and the discovery of diamonds for *A Simpleton* (1873). Looking at industry, he was horrified at the mounting abuses of labor unions and wrote *Put Yourself in His Place*. Even when he explained the precise details of forgery in *Foul Play* and *A Woman-Hater* (1877), earnest Victorians had the solid feeling that they were learning something while they read. When he exposed the prison system and the asylums for the insane in *Hard Cash* and *A Terrible Temptation* (1871), he appealed strongly to that marked evangelical tendency to rejoice in one's own righteousness in comparison with the wickedness of others. He constantly satisfied the Victorian passion for inventory, that rising-middle-class need to be bolstered by the sense of ownership. And when his spirits fell momentarily before the onslaught of critics, he adduced in his defense not his writing but the investments—land, stocks, and furnishings—that he had earned by his pen, knowing that this was the very kind of proof that would convince his solid burgher reading audience.

Yet he was a romantic in that all his absorbed interest in the facts of life—statistics, data, techniques—still served essentially romantic ideals. The spate of facts, newspaper clippings, written testimony of seamen (*A Simpleton*), research of university hacks, musty monkish compendia (*The Cloister and the Hearth*, 1861), all had to be reshaped into a simple moral pattern. Good must triumph, evil must be defeated, men must prove their masculinity, and women must be simple farm girls (*Christie*

Johnstone) or silly, tender ladies (*White Lies, Hard Cash, A Terrible Temptation*). Both in his plays and in his novels, the essence was always the formula of sensational melodrama: although evil appears triumphant and good seems so weak, have no fear; the two streams will eventually converge, wrongs will be righted, and all the chaotic pieces of sensation fiction will fall into their rightful places.

Even Reade's most famous historical novel, *The Cloister and the Hearth*, manages to exhibit the perfect Reade plot formula. In 1524, when Erasmus feared he was fatally ill, he wrote in Latin a compendium of his life, which was first published in Leiden in 1607. Reade refers to it as "a musty chronicle, written in tolerable Latin, . . . where every sentence holds a fact." Characteristically, Reade tells not the story of Erasmus but that of the almost unknown parents of the great Dutch Protestant reformer. Whereas his other novels might be considered plays with unusually lengthy stage directions, *The Cloister and the Hearth* may be considered a gallery bringing to the visitor personal experience of the dangers, discomforts, and glories of the Middle Ages. Perhaps this is Reade's masterpiece because a narrative 435 years old exactly fitted his talent: full of event, a picaresque journey, a fraudulent letter, a serious misunderstanding, one of "Reade's Resourceful Heroes," and a frank, honest heroine who might be the daughter of a yeoman farmer in Victorian England. The title of Reade's novel betrays the central dualism: Holland the hearth, where Gerard Eliasson and Margaret Brandt hope to settle into happy married life; Italy the cloister, where Gerard seeks his fortune, receives a forged letter stating his fiancee is dead, and becomes trapped in holy orders. Discovering that Margaret lives, he renounces both Holland and Italy and becomes a hermit. Displaying their son, Gerard, Margaret lures him out of the Gouda cave before she dies of plague. The father dies full of sanctity; the son becomes the great Erasmus, famous writer and theologian of the Protestant Reformation. In their usually discreet *Memoir* (1887), Charles L. and Compton Reade flatly state: "Celibacy also with its cruel claws held Charles Reade prisoner. Had Gerard married, he would have starved. Two-thirds of his [Reade's] life had passed before he could dream of dispensing with what he often termed his prop [financial support only to celibates], viz., his Fellowship at Magdalen." So great was the public acclaim of this novel that Charles Algernon Swinburne declared that "a story better conceived, better constructed, or better related, it would be difficult to find anywhere." Sir Walter

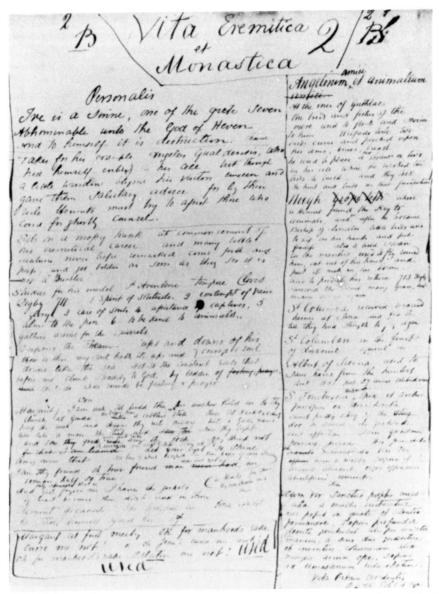

One of Reade's notecards for The Cloister and the Hearth. *The actual size of the card is 22" by 18" (Wayne Burns,* Charles Reade: A Study in Victorian Authorship*).*

Besant rated it as the greatest historical novel in the English language.

For all his successful conformity to the standards of his era, Reade had moments of aberrant curiosity: transvestism titillated some hidden nerve (*Peg Woffington*; *The Wandering Heir*; *The Bloomer*, 1857), and he liked to toy with the idea of women who would be sexual aggressors (*Hard Cash*). He noted strengths in women and weaknesses in men, yet settled for a gallery of stock types: the blonde heroine and the brunette rival (*Griffith Gaunt*); the weak and worthless male strenuously beloved by opposite heroines (*Singleheart and Doubleface*; *A Terrible Temptation*; *Peg Woffington*; *Christie Johnstone*;

Art; *Griffith Gaunt*); a hero of infinite resourcefulness (*A Simpleton*; *Foul Play*; *Love Me Little, Love Me Long*, 1859); the female built upon heroic, classic lines and the ladylike clinging vine (*Peg Woffington*; *A Simpleton*; *Love Me Little, Love Me Long*); the weak upper-class villain who has his dirty work done by a strong working-class villain. His novelistic creations bear a remarkable resemblance to the torrents of ready-made goods to be shipped to the colonies, all stamped Manchester, Birmingham, or Sheffield.

Reade's particular form of the Victorian Compromise was to publicly espouse a realism that he had privately decided to bend to romantic ends. The problem was to some degree intellectual. He could feed the demand of his age for facts, but for plots he had to fall back upon the formulas of melodrama, the trite solution, and the banal morality. He was compared in his own day with the grand triad—Thackeray, Dickens, and George Eliot; yet he could not compete with the artistry of Thackeray, the prodigality of gifts of Dickens, nor the keen analysis and philosophic bent of George Eliot. W. L. Courtney suggests that he had more in common with sensation writers such as Wilkie Collins, Bulwer-Lytton, and Mary Elizabeth Braddon, for all of whom Reade had great admiration although in many ways they were his inferiors. Thus he was estimated to occupy a lonely spot in the pantheon of literary fame between the giants of the first rank and the second-class popular writers of the day.

Recent critics tend to compare his work, in its dependency upon documentary evidence, with that of Daniel Defoe and Émile Zola. The latter is usually considered the father of naturalism, and indeed Reade translated a naturalistic drama by Zola for the London stage. Yet Zola, as reader for the Paris firm of Hachette et Frères, had earlier translated Reade's works of "solid fiction"—the materials of realism—into French. The French and the English authors seem to have collaborated unconsciously in creating a realistic setting for naturalistic characters which was to have a profound effect upon twentieth-century writers.

Translations:
Eugène Moreau, Paul Siraudin, and Alfred Delacourt, *The Courier of Lyons, or The Attack upon the Mail: A Drama in Four Acts*, translated by Reade (London: Lacy, 1854);
Edouard Brisebarre and Eugène Nus, *Les Pauvres de Paris*, translated by Reade as *Poverty and Pride: A Drama in Five Acts* (London: Bentley, 1856);
Jean Baptiste Molière, *Malade Imaginaire*, translated by Reade as *The Hypochondriac* (London: Clowes, 1857).

Bibliography:
Morris L. Parrish, *Wilkie Collins and Charles Reade: First Editions* (London: Constable, 1940).

Biographies:
Charles L. Reade and Compton Reade, *Charles Reade, D. C. L., Dramatist, Novelist, Journalist: A Memoir, Compiled Chiefly from His Literary Remains* (2 volumes, London: Chapman & Hall, 1887);
Malcolm Elwin, *Charles Reade: A Biography* (London: Cape, 1931).

References:
Wayne Burns, *Charles Reade: A Study in Victorian Authorship* (New York: Bookman Associates, 1961);
William Leonard Courtney, "Charles Reade's Novels," in his *Studies, New and Old* (London: Chapman & Hall, 1889), p. 152;
William Dean Howells, *My Literary Passions* (New York: Harper, 1895), p. 193;
Walter C. Phillips, *Dickens, Reade, and Collins: Sensation Novelists: A Study in the Conditions and Theories of Novel Writing in Victorian England* (New York: Columbia University Press, 1917);
Elton Edward Smith, *Charles Reade*, Twayne's English Authors Series (Boston: Hall, 1976; London: Prior, 1976);
Algernon Charles Swinburne, "Charles Reade," in his *Miscellanies* (London: Chatto & Windus, 1886), p. 275;
Albert Morton Turner, *The Making of "The Cloister and the Hearth"* (Chicago: University of Chicago Press, 1938).

Papers:
Many of Reade's notebooks and notecards are in the London Library and the Morris L. Parrish Collection at Princeton University. The Pierpont Morgan Library, New York, has several manuscripts and letters.

Mayne Reid

(4 April 1818-22 October 1883)

Patrick Dunae
British Columbia Provincial Archives

BOOKS: *The Rifle Rangers; or, Adventures of an Officer in Southern Mexico* (2 volumes, London: Schoberl, 1850; 1 volume, New York: Dewitt & Davenport, 1852);

The Scalp Hunters; or, Romantic Adventures in Northern Mexico (3 volumes, London: Skeet, 1851; 1 volume, Philadelphia: Lippincott, Grambo, 1851);

The Desert Home; or, The Adventures of a Lost Family in the Wilderness (London: Bogue, 1852; Boston: Ticknor, Reed & Fields, 1852);

The Boy Hunters; or, Adventures in Search of a White Buffalo (London: Bogue, 1853; Boston: Ticknor, Reed & Fields, 1853);

The Young Voyageurs; or, The Boy Hunters in the North (London: Bogue, 1854; Boston: Ticknor, Reed & Fields, 1854);

The Forest Exiles; or, The Perils of a Peruvian Family amid the Wilds of the Amazon (London: Bogue, 1854; Boston: Ticknor, Reed & Fields, 1855);

The White Chief: A Legend of Northern Mexico (3 volumes, London: Bogue, 1855; New York: Dewitt, 1860);

The Hunter's Feast; or, Conversations around the Camp Fire (London: Hodgson, 1855; New York: Dewitt & Davenport, 1856);

The Quadroon; or, A Lover's Adventures in Louisiana (3 volumes, London: Hyde, 1856; 1 volume, New York: Dewitt, 1856);

The Bush Boys; or, The Adventures of a Cape Farmer and His Family in the Wild Karoos of Southern Africa (London: Bogue, 1856; Boston: Ticknor & Fields, 1857);

The Young Yagers; or, A Narrative of Hunting Adventures in Southern Africa (London: Bogue, 1857; Boston: Ticknor & Fields, 1857);

The Plant Hunters; or, Adventures among the Himalaya Mountains (London: Ward & Lock, 1857; Boston: Ticknor & Fields, 1858);

The War Trail; or, The Hunt of the Wild Horse (London: Brown, 1857; New York: Dewitt, 1857);

Ran Away to Sea (London: Brown, 1858; Boston: Ticknor & Fields, 1858);

Oceola the Seminole (New York: Dewitt, 1858; 3 volumes, London: Hurst & Blackett, 1859);

Mayne Reid

The Boy Tar; or, A Voyage in the Dark (London: Kent, 1859; Boston: Ticknor & Fields, 1860);

Odd People: Being a Popular Description of Singular Races of Men (London: Routledge, 1860; Boston: Ticknor & Fields, 1860);

Quadrupeds, What They Are, and Where Found: A Book of Zoology for Boys (London: Nelson, 1860);

Bruin; or, The Great Bear Hunt (London: Routledge, Warne & Routledge, 1861; Boston: Ticknor & Fields, 1861);

The Wild Huntress (3 volumes, London: Bentley, 1861; 1 volume, New York: Dewitt, 1861);

The Maroon: A Novel (3 volumes, London: Hurst & Blackett, 1862; 1 volume, New York: Dewitt, 1864);

The Tiger Hunter (London: Clarke, 1862; New York: Carleton, 1874);

Croquet (London: Skeet, 1863; New York: Redpath, 1863);

Garibaldi Rebuked by One of His Best Friends: Being a Letter Addressed to Him by Captain Mayne Reid (London: N.p., 1864);

The Cliff Climbers; or, The Lone Home in the Himalayas (London: Ward & Lock, 1864; Boston: Ticknor & Fields, 1866);

Ocean Waifs (London: Boyce, 1864; Boston: Ticknor & Fields, 1865);

The White Gauntlet: A Romance (3 volumes, London: Skeet, 1864; 1 volume, New York: Carleton, 1868);

Lost Lenore, as Charles Beach (3 volumes, London: Skeet, 1864; 1 volume, New York: Dewitt, 1866);

The Boy Slaves (London: Clarke, 1865; Boston: Ticknor & Fields, 1865);

The Headless Horseman: A Strange Tale of Texas (2 volumes, London: Chapman & Hall, 1866; 1 volume, New York: Dewitt, 1867);

Afloat in the Forest (London: Clarke, 1866; Boston: Ticknor & Fields, 1867);

The Bandolero; or, A Marriage among the Mountains (London: Bentley, 1866);

The Guerilla Chief and Other Tales (London: Darton, 1867; New York: Dutton, 1899);

The Giraffe Hunters (3 volumes, London: Hurst & Blackett, 1867; 1 volume, Boston: Ticknor & Fields, 1867);

The Child Wife: A Tale of the Two Worlds (3 volumes, London: Ward, Lock, 1868; 1 volume, New York: Sheldon, 1869);

The Yellow Chief: A Romance of the Rocky Mountains (New York: Beadle & Adams, 1868; London: Brown, 1869);

The Fatal Cord: A Tale of Backwood Retribution (London: Brown, 1869);

The Castaways: A Story of Adventure in the Wilds of Borneo (London: Nelson, 1870; New York: Sheldon, 1870);

The White Squaw and the Yellow Chief (2 volumes, London: Clarke, 1871);

The Lone Ranche: A Tale of the Staked Plain (2 volumes, London: Chapman & Hall, 1871; 1 volume, New York: Carleton, 1884);

The Finger of Fate: A Romance (2 volumes, London: Chapman & Hall, 1872; 1 volume, New York: Munro, 1885);

The Death Shot: A Romance of Forest and Prairie (3 volumes, London: Chapman & Hall, 1873; 1 volume, New York: Hurst, 1874);

The Half Blood (London: Chapman & Hall, 1875);

The Flag of Distress: A Story of the South Sea (3 volumes, London: Tinsley, 1876; 1 volume, New York: Miller, 1876);

Gwen Wynn: A Romance of the Wye (3 volumes, London: Tinsley, 1877; 1 volume, New York: White & Allen, 1877);

Gaspar the Gaucho: A Tale of the Gran Chaco (London: Routledge, 1879; New York: Beadle & Adams, 1883);

The Captain of the Rifles; or, The Queen of the Lakes (New York: Beadle & Adams, 1879); republished as *The Queen of the Lakes: A Romance of the Mexican Valley* (London: Mullan, 1880);

The Free Lances: A Romance of the Mexican Valley (3 volumes, London: Remington, 1881; New York: White & Allen, 188?);

The Ocean Hunters; or, The Chase of Leviathan: A Romance (New York: Beadle & Adams, 1881); republished as *The Chase of Leviathan; or, Adventures in the Ocean* (London: Routledge, 1885);

The Gold Seekers Guide; or, The Lost Mountain (New York: Beadle & Adams, 1882); republished as *The Lost Mountain: A Tale of Sonora* (London: Routledge, 1884);

Love's Martyr: A Tragedy (Perth, Australia: Cowan, 1884);

The Land of Fire: A Tale of Adventure (London: Warnes, 1884);

The Vee Boers: A Tale of Adventure in Southern Africa (London: Routledge, 1885; New York: Dutton, 1904);

The Pierced Heart and Other Stories (London: Maxwell, 1885);

The Star of Empire: A Romance (London: Maxwell, 1886);

No Quarter (3 volumes, London: Sonnenschein, 1888; 1 volume, New York: Hurst, 1899);

The Naturalist in Siluria (London: Sonnenschein, 1889; Philadelphia: Gebbie, 1890).

Regarded today principally as an author of juvenile fiction, Thomas Mayne Reid was in fact one of the most versatile writers of the mid-Victorian period. Besides boys' adventure tales and dime novels, Reid wrote poetry, plays, travelogues, and a treatise on croquet. But he is best known for romantic adventure novels such as *The Rifle Rangers* (1850), *The Scalp Hunters* (1851), and *The Headless Horseman* (1866). Although later appropriated by the juvenile reading public, these and over two dozen other novels were aimed at an adult audience—an audience that delighted in the fast-paced narrative, the exotic settings, and the admixture of sentimentality and sensationalism which characterized Reid's best work.

Reid was born in Ballyroney, County Down,

Northern Ireland. His father was a Presbyterian clergyman, and it was assumed that young Reid would follow suit. But Reid—an impetuous and high-spirited youth—had no inclination toward the church, and in 1839 he abandoned his studies at the Royal Academical Institute, Belfast, and sailed for New Orleans. For the next nine years he led a roving, tumultuous life: he worked as a warehouseman in New Orleans and as a private tutor in Nashville, where he founded a short-lived classical academy; he was a storekeeper in Mississippi and a trader in Santa Fe. From St. Louis he organized hunting trips; the naturalist John James Audubon is said to have accompanied him on one of these. Following stints as an actor in Cincinnati and a playwright in Philadelphia (where he met Edgar Allan Poe), he made his way to New York, where he enlisted in the first New York Volunteer Regiment. He fought with distinction in the Mexican-American War, was severely wounded at the storming of Chapultepec, and in 1847 was invalided out of the army with the rank of captain.

Flushed by his adventures in Mexico and the American West, Captain Reid sailed for Europe in 1849. Arriving too late to take part in the liberal revolutions which had swept the Continent, he changed course for England. There he began courting Elizabeth Hyde, thirteen-year-old daughter of an aristocratic family; he married her in 1853. By that time he had published several novels and for the rest of his life lived entirely by his pen. It was a precarious existence, however, for Reid was notoriously extravagant. He squandered a small fortune building a Mexican hacienda in Buckinghamshire and lost heavily on an evening newspaper he launched in London. He also lost money on a number of ventures during his second sojourn in America from 1867 to 1870. His debts, plus the pain he suffered from his war wound, account for the recurring bouts of melancholia which plagued him during the last years of his life.

Although he was a gifted and deservedly popular writer, Reid's creative powers were limited. His work, consequently, falls into two categories: the stories he wrote prior to about 1870 are fresh and vigorous; his later work—composed largely of dime novels, penny dreadfuls, and other ephemera—is poor. During his latter years he simply repeated old plots, recirculated old characters, and reused old illustrations. In order to maintain a steady literary output and pay off his creditors, he even resorted to plagiarism. But Captain Reid is not remembered for such practices. Rather, his reputation rests on his early frontier tales, such as *The Rifle*

Rangers, *The Scalp Hunters*, *The Quadroon* (1856), and *The Headless Horseman*. Inspired by the author's adventures in America and Mexico, these works are characterized by verve, imagination, and energy. They reflect Reid's abolitionist conscience, his republican fervor, and his dislike of authority—especially authority which derived from monarchies and the Roman Catholic church.

In most of Reid's best romantic tales the hero is autobiographical. Like the young captain, he is an impetuous man of the world. Like Reid, he is interested in geography and natural history. Like Reid (who is said to have taken out American citizenship), the hero is committed to the ideals of liberty and democracy. Villains are usually Spanish colonial officials and Roman Catholic prelates who in some way oppress a pro-American aristocrat and his voluptuous, passionate daughters. Occasionally, the author's discourses on botany and geology, and his diatribes on the evils of slavery, interrupt the narrative. *The Headless Horseman* dramatically illustrates these features. The plot involves the journey of the Poindexter family from Louisiana to southwestern Texas. The villainous Cassius Calhoun pursues their daughter Louise, while the hero, Maurice Gerald (actually Sir Maurice Gerald, a dispossessed Irish lord), is a "mustanger," a cowboy who rounds up wild horses and sells them to settlers. Maurice's fortuitous inheritance prevents Calhoun from foreclosing on the mortgage he holds on the Poindexters' land, but Calhoun seeks to murder Maurice to prevent his intervention. Calhoun kills Louise's brother by mistake, beheading him and propping the body upright on his horse, which wanders the countryside. Maurice is wrongly accused of the crime, but in the end justice triumphs. Set in a carefully rendered western landscape, *The Headless Horseman*, with its attack on slavery, its violent action, and its battle between good and evil, is vintage Reid. It is not surprising, therefore, that his lively and entertaining novels were best-sellers.

Despite the uneven quality of his work, Captain Mayne Reid is an important figure in several respects. He is a pivotal figure in the development of adventure fiction; his tales, reminiscent of James Fenimore Cooper and Frederick Marryat, had a direct influence on Robert Louis Stevenson and H. Rider Haggard. In addition, Reid's early works were important for promoting an alluring image of frontier America; they excited countless mid-Victorian Britons and encouraged immigration and settlement in the West. Finally, Reid, who was a great admirer of Byron, is important for promoting liberal, humanitarian ideals at a time when popular literature—on both sides of the Atlantic—was decidedly conservative in tone. Modern critics have emphasized Reid's attention to detail, accurate representation of the American landscape, and importance as a popular writer. In America as well as in England, his dime novels and adventure tales were immense successes.

Bibliography:

Joan Steele, "Mayne Reid: A Revised Bibliography," *Bulletin of Bibliography*, 29 (July-

September 1972): 95-100.

References:

Maltus Questell Holyoake, "Captain Mayne Reid: Soldier and Novelist," *Strand Magazine*, 2 (July 1891): 93-102;

Roy W. Meyer, "The Western American Fiction of Mayne Reid," *Western American Literature*, 3 (Summer 1968): 115-132;

Joan Steele, *Captain Mayne Reid* (Boston: Twayne, 1978).

G. W. M. Reynolds
(23 July 1814-17 June 1879)

Patrick Kelly
University of Saskatchewan

SELECTED BOOKS: *The Youthful Imposter* (3 volumes, London & Paris: N.p., 1835; 2 volumes, Philadelphia: Carey & Hart, 1836);

Pickwick Abroad; or, The Tour in France (Philadelphia: Carey & Hart, 1838; London: Tegg, 1839);

Grace Darling; or, The Heroine of the Fern Islands: A Tale Founded on Recent Facts (London: Henderson, 1839);

Modern Literature of France (2 volumes, London: Henderson, 1839);

Alfred; or, The Adventures of a French Gentleman (2 volumes, Philadelphia: Carey & Hart, 1839; London: Willoughby, 1840);

Robert Macaire in England, Illustrated by "Phiz" (3 volumes, London: Tegg, 1840);

The Drunkard's Progress: A Tale (London: Henderson, 1841);

Master Timothy's Bookcase (London: Emans, 1842);

Sequel to "Don Juan" (London: Paget, 1843);

The Steam-Packet: A Tale of the River and the Ocean (London: Willoughby, 1844);

The Mysteries of London (4 volumes, London: Vickers, 1845-1848);

The French Self-Instructor (London: N.p., 1846);

Faust: A Romance of the Second Empire (London: Vickers, 1847);

The Parricide; or, the Youth's Career of Crime (London: Dicks, 1847);

The Mysteries of the Court of London (8 volumes, London: Dicks, 1849-1856);

The Bronze Statue; or, The Virgin's Kiss (New York: Burgess, 1850; London: Dicks, 1855);

Rosa Lambert (New York: Long, 1850; London: Dicks, 1854);

Mary Price (2 volumes, London: Dicks, 1852; 1 volume, New York: Long, 1852);

The Soldier's Wife (London: Dicks, 1853);

Joseph Wilmot; or, The Memoirs of a Man Servant (2 volumes, London: Dicks, 1854; 1 volume, Philadelphia: Peterson, 1880);

Ciprina; or, The Secrets of the Picture Gallery (Philadelphia: Peterson, 1855);

Loves of the Harem (London: Dicks, 1855; New York: Long, 1880);

Agnes; or, Beauty and Pleasure (2 volumes, London: Dicks, 1857); republished as *Agnes Evelyn; or, Beauty and Pleasure* (New York: Long, 1860);

Ellen Percy; or, The Memoirs of an Actress (2 volumes, London: Dicks, 1857; 1 volume, New York: Long, 1885);

Wagner the Werewolf (London: Dicks, 1857);

The Empress Eugenie's Boudoir (London: Dicks, 1857);

Canonbury House; or, The Queen's Prophecy (London: Dicks, 1870).

As a writer of penny-weekly novels for the lower classes, G. W. M. Reynolds enjoyed an unparalleled popularity in the 1840s and the 1850s. When the second series of *The Mysteries of London* was appearing in the *London Journal* in 1845, the circulation was about 40,000 copies per week; and in 1854 a contemporary writer estimated the weekly circulation of *Reynolds's Miscellany* (in which most of the author's novels first appeared) at 200,000. Consideration of the ways Reynolds maintained the loyalty of his immense readership, especially through his use of conventions, settings, and themes that are often similar to those found in Dickens's novels, can provide a better understanding of the significance of popular literature in the early Victorian period and of its relationship to some of the major literary works of the time.

George William MacArthur Reynolds was born on 23 July 1814 in Sandwich. Enrolling in the Royal Military College at Sandhurst in February 1828, he seemed destined to pursue the career of his father, a captain in the navy. But he left the school after two and one-half years and financed his way to France with an inheritance from his father. Reynolds's fascination with French literature and his radical political convictions took root during his stay in Paris between 1830 and 1836. Also during this time, probably in 1833, Reynolds married Susanna Frances Pearson. As Mrs. S. F. Reynolds, she was to become a notable popular novelist in her own right with *Greta Green* (1847-1848) and *Wealth and Poverty* (1848).

Although Reynolds squandered his inheri-

tance in Paris, he began his literary career there in 1835, when he was both the editor of the *London and Paris Courier* and the writer of a first novel, *The Youthful Imposter*. When he returned to England and settled in London, he paid tribute to his French influences by his critical study, *Modern Literature of France* (1839), and by his translations of Victor Hugo and Charles Paul de Kock between 1836 and 1840. He also edited the *Monthly Magazine* between 1836 and 1838. It was in this journal that Reynolds published his first truly popular novel, *Pickwick Abroad; or, The Tour in France* (1837-1838). As Louis James points out, Reynolds's work is largely original. The Pickwickians and Sam Weller are all there, and the notion of the tour is copied, but there is little attempt to capture the comic life of Dickens's *Pickwick Papers* (1836-1837). Rather the strong emphasis on French low life looks forward to Reynolds's own *Mysteries* series.

It is not insignificant that Reynolds's first venture into popular fiction was inspired by Dickens, for although he was to imitate almost every fashion of fiction during his amazingly prolific career, his most successful works provided for the readers of the lower classes essentially the same "romance of reality" that Dickens's works gave the middle classes. Thus, in the two long series of tales that appeared as penny weeklies, *The Mysteries of London* (1845-1848) and *The Mysteries of the Court of London* (1849-1856), it is the city's underworld that becomes the setting for the most horrid vice and crime. The main influence in these works is the French writer Eugène Sue, but nevertheless the parallels with Dickens's depiction of London are striking, as in the following passage from *The Mysteries of the Court of London*: "Reader, take the map of the Great Metropolis, and with 'The Mysteries of London' by your side for ready reference, circle with a dark line, either with pen or pencil, each and every loathsome district or neighbourhood which you will find described in the two series of that work or in the one which you are now perusing. Then calculate the proportion which the haunts of crime and the skulking-places of poverty bear to the localities where comfort is found or where opulence and splendour reign. The result will prove that two-thirds of the mighty Babylon are covered with a plague-mist of demoralization, misery, ignorance, wretchedness, squalor, and crime." Although the tone of this passage suggests a bellicose radicalism that is more direct than Dickens's social satire, the emphasis on the chaos and complexity of the city and on the juxtaposition within it of worlds that are strikingly different is also an essential part of the

Frontispiece for the book publication of Reynolds's first popular novel, with characters borrowed from Dickens (Cooper Library, University of South Carolina)

atmosphere of *Oliver Twist* (1837-1839) and *Bleak House* (1852-1853). Yet whereas Dickens raises melodrama and the romance of the city to the level of high art, Reynolds delights throughout his works in crude oppositions of vice and virtue and in an almost voyeuristic delineation of sadism and sensuality.

Complexity of plot and a plethora of characters, both of which one readily associates with Dickens, are a marked feature of the novels that Reynolds sets in the city. In the first series of *The Mysteries of London* the main plot follows the careers of two brothers who, forced to separate, agree to meet exactly twelve years later to compare their fortunes. Richard Markham becomes a victim of forgers in London's underworld, is imprisoned,

and then makes his fortune by becoming a hero in an Italian revolution and marrying a princess. His brother Eugene, on the other hand, becomes a villain and a dishonest member of Parliament, dying in repentance soon after meeting his brother again. The novel also details the innumerable adventures of characters from every rank of society, adventures that have so tenuous a connection with the main plot that they are almost interpolated tales. Reynolds clearly intended them to suggest the inexhaustible variety of London and the multifarious secret connections among those who dwell there; but whereas in Dickens's novels the eventual detection of secrets or mysteries underscores a compelling social vision of interdependence and moral responsibility, in Reynolds's works the mysteries and their detection are merely a conventional way of complicating the plot and intensifying the urban atmosphere in a sensational way.

Many of Reynolds's novels were first printed in *Reynolds's Miscellany*, which the author edited between 1846 and 1869, after having edited the similar *London Journal* briefly between 1845 and 1846. Reynolds's political views, always strongly radical and Chartist, were given a forum in *Reynolds's Political Instructor*, which ran between November 1849 and May 1850, and in *Reynolds's Weekly Newspaper*, which he edited between 1850 and 1879. He first actively expressed his revolutionary sympathies on 6 March 1848. Participating that day in an illegal middle-class protest in Trafalgar Square, he so animated his listeners by a speech in support of the revolution in France that a large part of the crowd followed him to his house. There, speaking from his balcony, he delighted them with more fiery rhetoric. After this incident, as a public speaker at Chartist meetings between 1848 and 1851, Reynolds played an active role during the last years of the working-class movement for parliamentary reform and a more equitable social order. Although Reynolds's novels provided another forum for his radical politics, they are never truly political or thesis novels, since the author's views are subsumed in the conventions of romance.

In 1854 Reynolds moved with his wife to Herne Bay in Kent. After her death he returned to London, where he lived at 41 Woburn Square. Although one sometimes reads that Reynolds continued to write fiction until the end of his life, recent work on his bibliography suggests that many of the novels attributed to him after 1860 were republications of earlier works; for instance, the parts of *The Mysteries of the Court of London* also appeared indi-

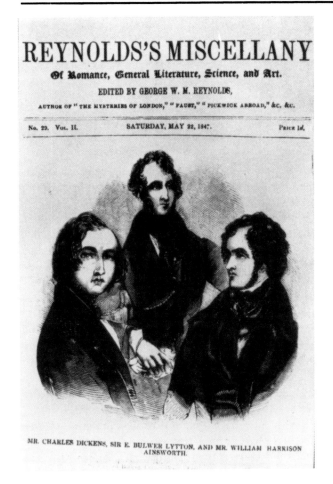

REYNOLDS'S MISCELLANY

Of Romance, General Literature, Science, and Art.

EDITED BY GEORGE W. M. REYNOLDS,

AUTHOR OF "THE MYSTERIES OF LONDON," "FAUST," "PICKWICK ABROAD," &c, &c.

No. 29. Vol. II.   SATURDAY, MAY 22, 1847.   Price 1d.

MR. CHARLES DICKENS, SIR E. BULWER LYTTON, AND MR. WILLIAM HARRISON AINSWORTH.

*Cover of an issue of the magazine Reynolds edited
from 1846 until 1869*

vidually under their separate titles. The bibliography is especially complicated because of the vogue Reynolds enjoyed in the United States, where he was not only plagiarized and pirated but also had his name affixed to the works of other authors. Although Reynolds was not much committed to either the political or the novelistic life in his last twenty years, he continued to be a prodigiously active editor. He died at his residence in Woburn Square on 17 June 1879, leaving two sons and two daughters.

Reynolds's very popularity is to a large extent a sociological rather than a literary matter. Thus, in the most thorough study of Reynolds to date, Mar-

garet Dalziel grants the originality of the author's peculiar mixture of pornography, sadism, and political radicalism, but she implies that these elements correspond to the collective character of Reynolds's readership. Yet Reynolds is of interest to the literary student too, both as a popularizer of French literature and as an effective plagiarist. In the latter capacity, he is a useful barometer of the popular taste of the age, which must influence in some degree even the more serious writer; moreover, in noting the elements of the original work that a plagiarist such as Reynolds chooses to emphasize, the reader can better gauge the qualities in a writer such as Dickens that won him a more limited popularity among the lower classes. More important, since the conventions of romance and melodrama tend to be more baldly exhibited in popular fiction, Reynolds's novels can make the presence of conventions in the work of the sophisticated craftsman more obvious.

Translations:
Victor Hugo, *Songs of Twilight*, translated by Reynolds (Paris: French, English & American Library, 1836);
Hugo, *The Last Day of a Condemned*, translated by Reynolds (London: N.p., 1840);
Paul de Kock, *Sister Anne: A Novel*, translated by Reynolds (London: N.p., 1840).

Bibliographies:
Montague Summers, *A Gothic Bibliography* (New York: Russell & Russell, 1964), pp. 146-159;
Donald Kausch, "George W. M. Reynolds: A Bibliography," *Library*, 5th series, 28 (December 1973): 319-326.

References:
Margaret Dalziel, *Popular Fiction a Hundred Years Ago* (London: Cohen & West, 1957), pp. 35-45;
Louis James, *Fiction for the Working Man: 1830-1850* (London: Oxford University Press, 1963);
Richard C. Maxwell, Jr., "G. M. Reynolds, Dickens, and the Mysteries of London," *Nineteenth-Century Fiction*, 32 (September 1977): 188-213.

Marmion Savage
(? 1803-1 May 1872)

Ira B. Nadel
University of British Columbia

BOOKS: *The Falcon Family; or, Young Ireland*, anonymous (London: Chapman & Hall, 1845; Boston: Wiley, 1846);

The Bachelor of the Albany, anonymous (London: Chapman & Hall, 1847; New York: Harper, 1848);

My Uncle the Curate: A Novel, anonymous (3 volumes, London: Chapman & Hall, 1849; 1 volume, New York: Harper, 1849);

Reuben Medlicott; or, The Coming Man (3 volumes, London: Chapman & Hall, 1852; 1 volume, New York: Appleton, 1852);

Clover Cottage; or, I Can't Get In: A Novelette (London: N.p., 1856);

The Woman of Busness; or, The Lady and the Lawyer: A Novel (London: Chapman & Hall, 1870; New York: Appleton, 1870).

Although now overlooked, Marmion Savage was one of the most popular satirical novelists of the 1840s and 1850s. In witty novels dealing with Irish politics, the Oxford Movement, and the ambitions of young men, Savage obtained a large readership in both England and America. An optimistic writer with a positive sense of human nature, he did not set out to reform society as much as to expose it. Thomas Love Peacock is his precursor, George Meredith his heir. His "wholesome wit and airy vivacity," as the *Athenaeum* phrased it, characterize his novels. Informed about his society but critical of its shortcomings, Savage remains a minor novelist but one worth serious study from the perspectives of Victorian popular fiction and the use of satire.

The son of a clergyman, Marmion Wilmo Savage was born in Ireland and graduated in classics from Trinity College, Dublin, in 1824. Until 1856 he was a civil servant in Ireland, publishing his fiction anonymously until 1852 when, with the appearance of *Reuben Medlicott*, he acknowledged his authorship of three preceding works. In 1856 he left Ireland for England and became editor of the *Examiner*, succeeding John Forster. He resigned three years later because of ill health, although he remained a welcomed and popular member of London society because of his wit and knowledge.

He married twice but left no children. When he died on 1 May 1872 at Torquay, where he retired, he had generally outlived his reputation.

The Falcon Family (1845), Savage's first novel, introduces the satire that characterizes his writing. Focusing on the Physical Force party that seceded from the Repeal Association (which sought to revoke the act of union between Ireland and Great Britain), Savage presents a work called by one reviewer "a caustic and brilliant skit upon the seceders." The *Athenaeum* praised it as "a family picture worthy of Hogarth" in its humorous presentation of three contending groups: Young Ireland, the Anglo-Irish, and the Tractarian Monks.

His second novel, *The Bachelor of the Albany* (1847), is his masterpiece, called by G. H. Lewes "a prodigy of smartness." Ostensibly a satire of the Oxford Movement—the effort to revitalize the established church by arguing that Anglicanism was the via media between Catholicism and Evangelicalism—the novel focuses on the Liverpool family of the Spreads and Mr. Spread's close friend, the cynical London bachelor Mr. Peter Barker, "a man of much worth and more eccentricity." The subjects of church practice, marriage, politics, and money are playfully represented through exact descriptions and comically drawn characters, as in this description of Mr. Barker, the bachelor of the Albany: "Imagine a small, well-made-man, with a smart, compact figure, excessively erect, his action somewhat martial, his eye grey, cold, peevish, critical and contemptuous; a mouth small and sarcastic; a nose long and vulpine; complexion, a pale, dry red; hair stiff and silvery, and evidently under the severest discipline to which brush and comb could subject it, with a view to its impartial distribution." In the novel place is detailed, conversation exact—and the result is an entertaining and well-constructed work. Will the bachelor of the Albany marry? The question, posed by heroes and heroines alike (including the individualistic and witty Laura Smyly), shapes the action of the book, which concludes with a hilarious scene involving a cottage, a fire, and a ladder. The satire of self-indulgence and the irresponsible behavior of bachelors comically ends with

Barker's assumption of political, patriarchal, and familial duties.

Savage's next novel, *My Uncle the Curate* (1849), focuses on the social problems of Ireland in 1831. Set on the coast of Donegal, the novel shows how intelligence and practical strength can unite with love to establish a coherent and workable society through the action of the noble cleric, Hercule Woodward. A whimsical introduction between the narrator and the author opens the novel.

Among the later novels of Savage, only *Reuben Medlicott* (1852) approached the popularity of *The Bachelor of the Albany*. In the manner of Disraeli's treatment of Young England, Savage satirically analyzes the young men of the mid-century and the impractical nature of life devoted to the imagination.

Clover Cottage, Savage's 1856 novelette, was adapted for the stage by the popular playwright Tom Taylor under the title of *Nine Points of the Law*; it premiered on 11 April 1859. *The Woman of Business* (1870), the last novel published by Savage, centers on a legal dispute between the heroine, Mrs. Rowley, and her foe, Mrs. Upjohn. The dedication of the book is to John Forster, the close friend and biographer of Dickens, in recognition of his long association with Savage. Although not a major novelist, Savage remains one of the few mid-Victorian satirists who in his time received both praise and admiration.

Other:

R. L. Sheil, *Sketches, Legal and Political*, edited by Savage (London: Hurst & Blackett, 1855).

References:

Edith C. Batho and Bonamy Dobrée, *The Victorians and After, 1830-1914* (London: Cresset, 1950), pp. 28, 321;

Bonamy Dobrée, "Introduction," *The Bachelor of the Albany* (London: Elkin Mathews & Marrot, 1927), pp. 7-14;

G. H. Lewes, "Recent Novels: French and English," *Fraser's Magazine*, 36 (December 1847): 686-695;

"Marmion Savage," *Athenaeum*, no. 2324 (11 May 1872): 591;

Kathleen Tillotson, *Novels of the Eighteen Forties* (Oxford: Clarendon Press, 1954), pp. 4, 127.

Robert Smith Surtees
(17 May 1803- 16 March 1864)

Norman Page
University of Alberta

BOOKS: *The Horseman's Manual: Being a Treatise on Soundness, the Law of Warranty, and Generally on the Laws Relating to Horses* (London: Miller, 1831; New York: Treadway, 1832);

Jorrocks's Jaunts and Jollities; or, The Hunting, Shooting, Racing, Driving, Sailing, Eating, Eccentric and Extravagant Exploits of that Renowned Sporting Citizen, Mr. John Jorrocks of St. Botolph Lane and Great Coram Street; with Illustrations by Phiz, anonymous (London: Spiers, 1838; Philadelphia: Carey & Hart, 1838);

Handley Cross; or, The Spa Hunt: A Sporting Tale, anonymous (3 volumes, London: Colburn, 1843);

Hillingdon Hall; or, The Cockney Squire: A Tale of Country Life, anonymous (3 volumes, London: Colburn, 1845; 1 volume, New York: Payson, 1933);

The Analysis of the Hunting Field: Being a Series of Sketches of the Principal Characters that Compose One; The Whole Forming a Slight Souvenir of the Season 1845, anonymous (London: Ackerman, 1846; New York: Appleton, 1903);

Hawbuck Grange; or, The Sporting Adventures of Thomas Scott Esq., anonymous (London: Longman, Brown, Green & Longmans, 1847);

Mr. Sponge's Sporting Tour, anonymous (London: Bradbury, Agnew, 1853; New York: Stringer & Townsend, 1856);

Ask Mamma; or, The Richest Commoner in England, anonymous (London: Bradbury, Agnew, 1858; New York: Appleton, 1904);

Robert Smith Surtees

Plain or Ringlets?, anonymous (London: Bradbury, Agnew, 1860; New York: Scribners, 1929);

Mr. Facey Romford's Hounds, anonymous (London: Bradbury & Evans, 1865).

COLLECTION: *The Novels of R. S. Surtees*, 10 volumes (London: Eyre & Spottiswoode, 1929-1930; New York: Scribners, 1929-1930).

Surtees is the best-known example in English of the sporting novelist. His novels offer a detailed picture of a specialized but vividly presented section of early Victorian society: the world of horsemen and huntsmen, sportsmen and farmers representative of English country life. He also records one of the multifarious aspects of social change in his period: the invasion by city dwellers and shopkeepers of the traditional pastimes and established hierarchy of the countryside.

Robert Smith Surtees was born in Durham of a family of landed gentry and educated at Durham Grammar School. His father was a typical country gentleman of the eighteenth century, and the boy acquired a taste for fox hunting early in life. As the second son, however, he was ineligible to inherit his father's estate; he was therefore obliged to take up a profession and was articled to lawyers, first in Newcastle and then (from 1825) in London, eventually qualifying as a Chancery practitioner. During this period he continued to hunt but encountered in the vicinity of London a very different species of huntsman from those he had known in Durham—an urban and socially heterogeneous collection of weekend sportsmen. It was on these experiences that he was to draw when, in the early 1830s, he began to write fiction.

From 1830 Surtees contributed articles to the *Sporting Magazine*. His first book was *The Horseman's Manual* (1831), a guide to "the laws relating to horses." In 1831 he joined with Rudolph Ackermann (1764-1834), a publisher and bookseller famous for his topographical prints, in starting the *New Sporting Magazine*, a periodical with which Surtees maintained a connection for the next five years. It was here that his first novel was published

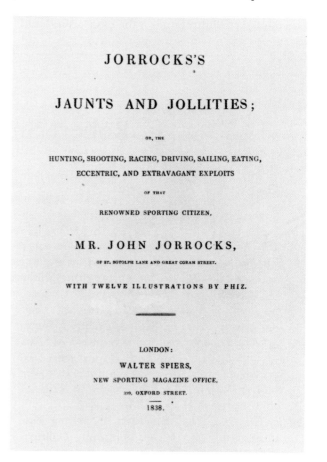

JORROCKS'S

JAUNTS AND JOLLITIES;

OR, THE

HUNTING, SHOOTING, RACING, DRIVING, SAILING, EATING,
ECCENTRIC, AND EXTRAVAGANT EXPLOITS

OF THAT

RENOWNED SPORTING CITIZEN,

MR. JOHN JORROCKS,

OF ST. BOTOLPH LANE AND GREAT CORAM STREET.

WITH TWELVE ILLUSTRATIONS BY PHIZ.

LONDON:
WALTER SPIERS,
NEW SPORTING MAGAZINE OFFICE,
199, OXFORD STREET.
1838.

Title page of the first of Surtees's three "Jorrocks" novels (Cooper Library, University of South Carolina)

in monthly installments (July 1831-September 1834): to give it its full title, *Jorrocks's Jaunts and Jollities; or, The Hunting, Shooting, Racing, Driving, Sailing, Eating, Eccentric and Extravagant Exploits of that Renowned Sporting Citizen, Mr. John Jorrocks of St. Botolph Lane and Great Coram Street.* The work later appeared in volume form (1838) and was reprinted many times. It was illustrated by "Phiz" (H. K. Browne), best known for his association with Dickens.

The protagonist of Surtees's first novel, Mr. John Jorrocks, is a Cockney grocer, energetic, cheerful, vulgar, and fond of sporting life. The book records his pursuit of sporting activities in the neighborhood of London and occasionally farther afield; in its loose construction it resembles the eighteenth-century picaresque novel and enjoys the same opportunities of bringing its hero into contact with a wide variety of places and characters through his frequent travels. The figure of Jorrocks—comic, observant, and exuberant—provides a unifying device and transforms the book into something more than a collection of sketches (though it is, of course, true that Surtees's original readers encountered the various adventures as a series of separate stories published piecemeal over a long period).

Traveling about to Brighton or Margate, London or Paris, the unassuming Jorrocks is continually, comically out of place, whether flirting with a French countess or socializing with the people of the horse-racing town of Newmarket. Jorrocks is himself only when following his great passion, hunting: "My soul's on fire and eager for the chase! By heavens, I declare I've dreamt of nothing else all night, and the worst of it is that in a par-ox-ism of delight, when I thought I saw the darlings running into the warmint, I brought Mrs. J---- such a dig in the side as knocked her out of bed, and she swears she'll go to Jenner and the court for the protection of injured ribs!" Among Jorrocks's most comical jaunts are "Swell and the Surrey," "The Turf: Mr. Jorrocks at Newmarket," and "Mr. Jorrocks in Paris." In his infinite capacity for farcical misadventure, Jorrocks anticipates Dickens's Mr. Pickwick, who was to make his appearance very soon after the serialization of Surtees's book was completed; and in at least one episode (the trial of Mr. Pickwick) Dickens probably borrowed from Surtees.

His elder brother having died unmarried in 1831, Surtees became involved in family affairs; in 1836 he gave up his law practice and his connection with the *New Sporting Magazine* and left London to return to Durham. In 1838, on the death of his father, he succeeded to the family property of Hamsterley Hall Estate; and there for the next quarter of a century he lived the life of a country squire, keeping his own pack of hounds and hunting regularly. He later became a justice of the peace and deputy-lieutenant of the County of Durham. In 1841 he married Elizabeth Fenwick; they eventually had a son and two daughters.

Surtees continued his career of authorship, however, though all his works except the early nonfictional *Horseman's Manual* were published anonymously. Surtees valued the mask of anonymity throughout his career because it gave him the freedom to observe, record, and criticize sporting events and sportsmen. When an editor inadvertently did publish his name, he took quick action to castigate the offender and demand the removal of his identity. In a letter to W. Harrison Ainsworth, the editor of the *New Monthly*, Surtees explained his desire for anonymity: "I find that I can write far better and with far more pleasure to myself when I am freed to deny authorship if I like."

Handley Cross; or, The Spa Hunt: A Sporting Tale was published in three volumes in 1843; it was republished in 1854 with illustrations by the prominent artist John Leech. The subtitle of the later version is *Mr. Jorrocks's Hunt*, and the book forms the second of a trio of novels in which this character appears. Again, the structure is very loose, and indeed the author admits in his preface that it is a "tale" rather that a "novel." Handley Cross is a health resort frequented by a cross section of middle-class society; Jorrocks is appointed Master of Foxhounds to the local hunt. The situation provides Surtees with an opportunity to repeat his earlier success: a combination of minimal plot with a great variety of comic and eccentric characters, the whole being given rough unity by the presence of Jorrocks.

The third of the Jorrocks books is *Hillingdon Hall; or, The Cockney Squire: A Tale of Country Life.* After partial serialization in the *New Sporting Magazine* (1843-1844) it was published in three volumes in 1845. The hero has now quitted London for a country estate where he intends to practice agriculture on new scientific principles (as he observes, "science is the ticket"); his actual ignorance—for example, he confuses pine trees and pineapples—provides material for comedy and satire. In describing the exchange of the life of a city businessman for that of a country squire, Surtees gives expression to the dreams of thousands of Englishmen in the nineteenth century and after in

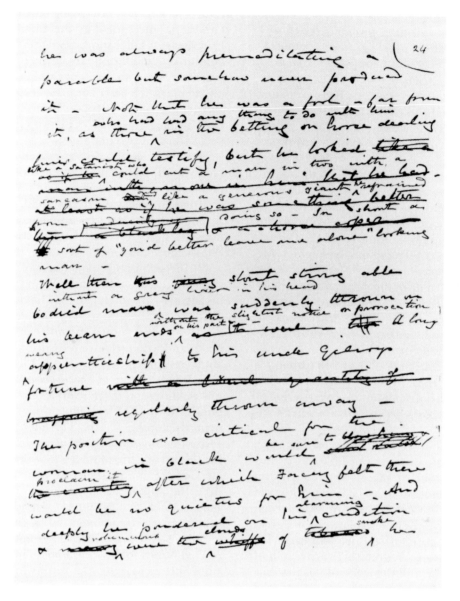

Page from the manuscript for Surtees's final novel (E. D. Cuming, Robert Smith Surtees, Creator of "Jorrocks": 1803-1864)

response to growing urbanization.

Of Surtees's other novels, the best-known is *Mr. Sponge's Sporting Tour*, serialized in the *New Monthly Magazine* (1849-1851) and later published in volume form (1853). Leech was again the illustrator. The central character, "a good-looking, rather vulgar-looking man," is a rogue whose way of life cocks a snook at Victorian earnestness and the work ethic: as his name suggests, he is prepared to sponge on anyone willing to supply him with free board and lodging. His progress from one house to another—and, since he is a sportsman, from one hunting field to another—provides the novel with

its framework. As in all his best work, Surtees offers an abundance of pictures of country life executed with authority and authenticity of detail and a constantly changing cast of characters, many of them comic or eccentric.

Surtees's other novels are *Hawbuck Grange* (1847), which narrates the adventures of a sporting farmer, Tom Scott (illustrated by "Phiz"); *Ask Mamma* (1858), a satire on the pretensions of English society and the problems of the law (illustrated by Leech); *Plain or Ringlets?* (1860), an amusing story of a love triangle between Rosa McDermott, Jasper Goldspink, and Jack Bunting (illustrated by

Surtees toward the end of his life, as depicted by George Denholm Armour. He had lost his nerve for riding across the fields, and would ride along the road parallel to the direction of the hunt.

Leech); and *Mr. Facey Romford's Hounds* (1865), a partial sequel to *Mr. Sponge's Sporting Tour* which traces the comical efforts of Romford in attempting to become Master of the Hounds. The adventures of the picaresque Romford and his heroine, Lucy Glitters, provide some of Surtees's best writing.

Surtees died suddenly while on holiday at Brighton. His literary importance consists of his achieving, in the words of Bonamy Dobrée, "an enlargement of the field of the novel, bringing in a whole new section of society, not only the followers of hounds . . . but the small country dweller, the farmer, people whose interests were entirely local. . . ." His books also furnish a valuable picture of the social background of the period; and thanks to the distinction of the artists who worked for him, they are of some importance in the history of book illustration. Surtees's continuing popularity in the twentieth century is suggested by the appearance of collected editions of his work in 1916, 1926, and 1930; the last of these has recently been reprinted.

References:
Leonard Cooper, *R. S. Surtees* (London: Arthur Baker, 1952);

Bonamy Dobrée, "Robert Smith Surtees," in *Imagined Worlds*, edited by Maynard Mack and Ian Gregor (London: Methuen, 1968), pp. 157-171;

Bonnie Rayford Neumann, *Robert Smith Surtees* (Boston: Twayne, 1978);

W. L. Renwick, "Jorrocks: A Conversation," in *Essays and Studies*, 17 (Oxford: Clarendon Press, 1932), pp. 76-89;

Frederick Watson, *Robert Smith Surtees: A Critical Study* (London: Harrap, 1933);

John Welcome, *The Sporting World of R. S. Surtees* (Oxford: Oxford University Press, 1982).

William Makepeace Thackeray

Edgar F. Harden
Simon Fraser University

BIRTH: Calcutta, India, 18 July 1811, to Richmond Makepeace and Anne Becher Thackeray.

EDUCATION: Trinity College, Cambridge University, 1829-1830.

MARRIAGE: 20 August 1836 to Isabella Gethin Shawe; children: Anne Isabella, Jane, Harriet Marian.

DEATH: London, 24 December 1863.

BOOKS: *Flore et Zéphyr: Ballet Mythologique par Theophile Wagstaffe* (London: Mitchell, 1836);
The Yellowplush Correspondence, as Charles J. Yellowplush (Philadelphia: Carey & Hart, 1838);
Reminiscences of Major Gahagan, as Goliah O'Grady Gahagan (Philadelphia: Carey & Hart, 1839);
An Essay on the Genius of George Cruikshank (London: Hooper, 1840);
The Paris Sketch Book, by Mr. Titmarsh, 2 volumes (London: Macrone, 1840; New York: Appleton, 1852);
Comic Tales and Sketches, Edited and Illustrated by Mr. Michael Angelo Titmarsh (2 volumes, London: Cunningham, 1841);
The Second Funeral of Napoleon, in Three Letters to Miss Smith of London; and The Chronicle of the Drum, by Mr. M. A. Titmarsh (London: Cunningham, 1841); republished as *The Second Funeral of Napoleon, by M. A. Titmarsh and Critical Reviews* (New York: Lovell, 1883);
The Irish Sketch Book, by Mr. M. A. Titmarsh (2 volumes, London: Chapman & Hall, 1843; 1 volume, New York: Winchester, 1843);
Jeames's Diary (New York: Taylor, 1846);
Notes of a Journey from Cornhill to Grand Cairo, by Way of Lisbon, Athens, Constantinople, and Jerusalem, Performed in the Steamers of the Peninsular and Oriental Company, by Mr. M. A. Titmarsh (London: Chapman & Hall, 1846; New York: Wiley & Putnam, 1846);
Mrs. Perkins's Ball, by Mr. M. A. Titmarsh (London: Chapman & Hall, 1847);
Vanity Fair: A Novel without a Hero (19 monthly parts, London: Bradbury & Evans, 1847-

1848; 2 volumes, New York: Harper, 1848);
The Book of Snobs (London: Punch Office, 1848; New York: Appleton, 1852);
Our Street, by Mr. M. A. Titmarsh (London: Chapman & Hall, 1848);
The Great Hoggarty Diamond (New York: Harper, 1848); republished as *The History of Samuel Titmarsh and the Great Hoggarty Diamond* (London: Bradbury & Evans, 1849);
The History of Pendennis. His Fortunes and Misfortunes, His Friends and His Greatest Enemy (23 monthly parts, London: Bradbury & Evans, 1848-1850; 2 volumes, New York: Harper, 1850);
Doctor Birch and His Young Friends, by Mr. M. A. Titmarsh (London: Chapman & Hall, 1849; New York: Appleton, 1853);
Miscellanies: Prose and Verse (8 volumes, Leipzig: Tauchnitz, 1849-1857);
The Kickleburys on the Rhine, by Mr. M. A. Titmarsh

(London: Smith, Elder, 1850; New York: Stringer & Townsend, 1851);

Stubbs's Calendar; or, The Fatal Boots (New York: Stringer & Townsend, 1850);

Rebecca and Rowena: A Romance upon Romance, by Mr. M. A. Titmarsh (London: Chapman & Hall, 1850; New York: Appleton, 1853);

The History of Henry Esmond, Esq., a Colonel in the Service of Her Majesty Q. Anne, Written by Himself (3 volumes, London: Smith, Elder, 1852; 1 volume, New York: Harper, 1852);

The Confessions of Fitz-Boodle; and Some Passages in the Life of Major Gahagan (New York: Appleton, 1852);

A Shabby Genteel Story and Other Tales (New York: Appleton, 1852);

Men's Wives (New York: Appleton, 1852);

The Luck of Barry Lyndon: A Romance of the Last Century (2 volumes, New York: Appleton, 1852-1853);

Jeames's Diary, A Legend of the Rhine, and Rebecca and Rowena (New York: Appleton, 1853);

Mr. Brown's Letters to a Young Man about Town; with The Proser and Other Papers (New York: Appleton, 1853);

Punch's Prize Novelists, The Fat Contributor, and Travels in London (New York: Appleton, 1853);

The English Humourists of the Eighteenth Century: A Series of Lectures Delivered in England, Scotland, and the United States of America (London: Smith, Elder, 1853; New York: Harper, 1853);

The Newcomes. Memoirs of a Most Respectable Family, Edited by Arthur Pendennis Esqre. (23 monthly parts, London: Bradbury & Evans, 1853-1855; 2 volumes, New York: Harper, 1855);

The Rose and the Ring; or, The History of Prince Giglio and Prince Bulbo: A Fireside Pantomime for Great and Small Children (London: Smith, Elder, 1855; New York: Harper, 1855);

Miscellanies: Prose and Verse (4 volumes, London: Bradbury & Evans, 1855-1857);

Ballads (Boston: Ticknor & Fields, 1856);

Christmas Books (London: Chapman & Hall, 1857; Philadelphia: Lippincott, 1872);

The Virginians: A Tale of the Last Century (24 monthly parts, London: Bradbury & Evans, 1857-1859; 1 volume, New York: Harper, 1859);

The Four Georges: Sketches of Manners, Morals, Court and Town Life (New York: Harper, 1860; London: Smith, Elder, 1861);

Lovel the Widower (New York: Harper, 1860; London: Smith, Elder, 1861);

The Adventures of Philip on His Way through the World; Shewing Who Robbed Him, Who Helped Him, and

Who Passed Him By (3 volumes, London: Smith, Elder, 1862; 1 volume, New York: Harper, 1862);

Roundabout Papers (London: Smith, Elder, 1863; New York: Harper, 1863);

Denis Duval (New York: Harper, 1864; London: Smith, Elder, 1867);

Early and Late Papers Hitherto Uncollected, edited by J. T. Fields (Boston: Ticknor & Fields, 1867);

Miscellanies, Volume IV (Boston: Osgood, 1870);

The Orphan of Pimlico; and Other Sketches, Fragments, and Drawings, with notes by A. I. Thackeray (London: Smith, Elder, 1876);

Sultan Stork and Other Stories and Sketches (1829-44), Now First Collected, edited by R. H. Sheppard (London: Redway, 1887);

Loose Sketches, An Eastern Adventure, Etc. (London: Sabin, 1894);

The Hitherto Unidentified Contributions of W. M. Thackeray to Punch, with a Complete Authoritative Bibliography from 1845 to 1848, edited by M. H. Spielmann (London & New York: Harper, 1899);

Mr. Thackeray's Writings in the "National Standard" and the "Constitutional," edited by W. T. Spencer (London: Spencer, 1899);

Stray Papers: Being Stories, Reviews, Verses, and Sketches 1821-47, edited by "Lewis Melville" (Lewis S. Benjamin) (London: Hutchinson, 1901; Philadelphia: Jacobs, 1901);

The New Sketch Book: Being Essays Now First Collected from the "Foreign Quarterly Review," edited by R. S. Garnett (London: Rivers, 1906);

Thackeray's Contributions to the "Morning Chronicle," edited by G. N. Ray (Urbana: University of Illinois Press, 1955).

COLLECTIONS: *The Works of William Makepeace Thackeray*, Library Edition (22 volumes, London: Smith, Elder, 1867-1869);

The Works of William Makepeace Thackeray, Biographical Edition (13 volumes, London: Smith, Elder, 1898-1899);

The Works of William Makepeace Thackeray, edited by "Lewis Melville" (Lewis S. Benjamin) (20 volumes, London: Macmillan, 1901-1907);

The Oxford Thackeray (17 volumes, London: Oxford University Press, 1908);

The Works of William Makepeace Thackeray, Centenary Biographical Edition (26 volumes, London: Smith, Elder, 1910-1911).

Like many of his fellow Victorian novelists, William Makepeace Thackeray is noted for his ability to create memorable characters—like Major Gahagan, Charles Yellowplush, Becky Sharp, Major Pendennis, Henry and Beatrix Esmond, Colonel Newcome, and not least of all the roundabout commentator who addresses the reader in Thackeray's nonfiction as well as in his fiction. In spite of giving such prominence to character delineation, Thackeray also came to develop an important new kind of novel, the "novel without a hero." Such a novel may have a chief figure: one who is neither a romantic hero nor a rogue hero but a flawed, recognizable human being like Arthur Pendennis or Philip Firmin. In the case of several of Thackeray's masterpieces such as *Vanity Fair* (1847-1848) and *The Newcomes* (1853-1855), however, the center of interest is the complex of relationships among the characters—an analogue of society itself.

Thackeray's writing is important for being governed by an intense historical awareness that constantly reveals itself in the precise, concrete detail of an evoked visible world, but also in a persistent consciousness of the flow of time, which ages both things and human experience, diminishing both and calling the value of both into question. Here Thackeray gives eloquent and pronounced articulation to several of the most deeply rooted Victorian, and indeed modern, concerns. In creative tension with this historical awareness, moreover, is Thackeray's satire, which is not limited and local but beyond time and place, radically challenging the reader's most fundamental assumptions about human life, but doing so in a voice that always evokes a personal human presence alongside the reader. He therefore gave a new prominence to the commentary of narrative personae and so offered a permanently valuable counterstance to what later came to be their pronounced opposites in the impressive dramatic novels of Henry James. Finally, one can see the importance of the wit and philosophical irony of Thackeray's fictional voices, with the constant shifting of perspective that alone can mediate to the reader the profound indeterminacy at the heart of his writing—an indeterminacy that finds its counterpart in much subsequent literature.

Service with the British East India Company's Bengal establishment characterized Thackeray's immediate male ancestors on both sides of his family. Thackeray himself was born in Calcutta in 1811 to a well-to-do official of the company. The first major shock of the child's life came not long after his fourth birthday with the death of his father at the age of thirty-three. The second trauma occurred fifteen months later, when he was sent out of the

Thackeray, about three years old, with his parents in India

dangerous Indian climate to England for schooling, his twenty-four-year-old mother remaining behind with the man she was to marry three months later, an officer in the company's military service. In recalling the event years later, Thackeray generalized about this aspect of Anglo-Indian experience: "What a strange pathos seems to me to accompany all our Indian story! Besides that official history . . . should not one remember the tears, too? . . . The lords of the subject province find wives there: but their children cannot live on the soil. . . . The family must be broken up. . . . In America it is from the breast of a poor slave that a child is taken: in India it is from the wife, and from under the palace, of a splendid proconsul."

The pain was intensified at Thackeray's school at Southampton, "which was governed by a horrible little tyrant, who made our young lives so miserable that I remember kneeling by my little bed of a night, and saying, 'Pray God, I may dream of my mother!'" Eventual transfer to a school at Chiswick provided some relief until the separation from his mother ended after three and a half years, when she and her husband arrived in England just before Thackeray's ninth birthday. After only a month of vacation together, however, Thackeray was sent off to Charterhouse, his stepfather's former school in London. Six rather unpleasant years at Charterhouse constituted what Thackeray later called "that strange ordeal" of life in an early nineteenth-century English boarding school, which seemed chiefly notable for the emotional privation and physical brutality a young boy had to endure, together with "the foolish old-world superstitions. . . ; the wretched portion of letters meted out to him . . . —the misery, vice, and folly, which were taught along with the small share of Greek and Latin."

Thackeray managed to find some solace during his last three years at Charterhouse by boarding in a private house nearby and being fortunate enough to associate there with a small group of talented boys of lively interests that ranged from literature and private theatricals to the periodicals of the day and the comical prints of artists such as George Cruikshank. Their companionship, and active private reading of his own, proved more emotionally and intellectually educative than Charterhouse, where the headmaster's increasing indulgence in satire and ridicule of Thackeray made the boy feel "bullied into despair," as he later wrote

to his mother. Weekend excursions into London also proved liberating, especially when Thackeray could attend the theater, imaginatively participate in the romance or boisterous comedy of the stage, and enjoy the fantasy of being in love with a particularly fascinating actress.

Emotionally, however, the chief antithesis to Charterhouse was the home to which he could now go during vacations—especially Larkbeare House, near Ottery St. Mary in Devon, where his mother and stepfather lived between 1824 and 1835. Here he dawdled about the house and grounds, drawing hundreds of caricatures, scribbling verses—partly in the style of Lord Byron and Thomas Moore—and reading widely, his favorite novels being the romances of Scott, Cooper, and other popular writers of the period. His most energetic activity was apparently horseback riding, which allowed him to visit nearby Exeter with its fine cathedral, ruined castle, excellent inns, and its theater. He became a published author in 1828 with the appearance in an Exeter newspaper of a comical poem on an Irish politician, followed by a translation of an amatory ode by Anacreon. Years later he gave some of these experiences imaginative expression in the opening of *Pendennis* (1848-1850), the most emotionally compelling vignette being the engraving "Calm Summer Evenings" and its accompanying prose rendering of "a profusion of . . . embraces" be-

Charterhouse, the boarding school in London where Thackeray was taught a "wretched portion of letters" along with "foolish old-world superstitions" and "misery, vice, and folly"

Larkbeare, the Devonshire home of his mother and stepfather, where Thackeray spent happy vacations away from Charterhouse

tween mother and son alone together on a terrace at sunset.

After entering Trinity College, Cambridge, in early 1829, Thackeray came to find its emphasis upon classical studies and especially mathematics rather stultifying. Intermittent efforts at studies that he found uncongenial turned more and more desultory; his chief pleasures came in reading modern literature, in contributing comical pieces to undergraduate magazines (the *Snob* and the *Gownsman*), in joining a debating society, and in mingling socially with his fellows. The first of what were to be many Continental trips took place during the summer of 1829, which was spent chiefly in Paris, where Thackeray developed a fascination for gambling. After sixteen months' residence at Cambridge, he gave up formal study as a waste of time and left without his degree. Besides expensive habits of personal living, he left Cambridge with gambling debts of £1,500, having been victimized by two professional card players.

Germany attracted him for the next eight months, much of which was spent pleasantly at Weimar, where he studied German, read, trans-

lated, and mingled with the local society (including the aged Goethe) and its foreign visitors—a period he later spoke of as "days of youth the most kindly and delightful." Since Thackeray's gambling days at Paris and his debacle at the university, his mother's reproaches and his own feelings of guilt had made him both defensive and penitent. On the one hand, he could tell his mother that her letters "always make me sorrowful. . . , for there seems some hidden cause of dissatisfaction, some distrust which you do not confess & cannot conceal & for which on looking into myself I can find no grounds or reason," yet on the other hand he could acknowledge still being "too open" to "idleness irresolution & extravagance," and having "*deserved*" her dissatisfaction with his "unworthiness." As part of his effort to win from her "one day . . . something like satisfaction & confidence in me," he agreed to study for the bar, and after his return to London he was admitted to the Middle Temple in June 1831.

At the time, law seemed a much more plausible profession to him than the church, the army, or medicine, but by January 1832 he was calling preparatory legal education "certainly one of the

A sketch by Thackeray of two professional cardsharps, like those who cheated him at Cambridge

November 1832, mainly at Paris. By this time—evidently out of guilt and shame at the repeated failure of his attempts to resist gambling—Thackeray resorted to the practice of shifting from English to German when making diary entries recording his fortunes at play; the foreign language seemed to serve the function of a private cipher. Thus he would laconically note: "spielte und verlierte acht pfund" ("gambled and lost eight pounds"), "spielte und winnte fünf pfund" ("gambled and won five pounds"), and more unhappily, "spielte und wie gewohnlich verlierte" ("gambled and, as usual, lost"). In France, his play continued: "have in these latter days been to Paris wo ich spielte."

Aside from occasional serious reading, he spent much of his time sketching, dining, imbibing, dancing, theatergoing, and dawdling about in idle company. He found himself "growing loving on every pleasant married woman I see," and although "talking of debauchery & [its] consequences" made him "long for a good wife, & a happy home," he also found himself recording a new transgression in his private "cipher": "spielte und fegelte" ("gambled and fornicated"). More lawful pleasures included

A sketch by Daniel Maclise of Thackeray in 1832 (Garrick Club)

most cold blooded prejudiced pieces of invention that ever a man was slave to." As his legal studies became more occasional, they were succeeded by miscellaneous reading, leisurely dining, frequent visits to the opera and the theater, intermittent gambling, and late hours that typically led to ensuing days of "seediness repentance & novel reading." He had become one of that group he was later to term "the Temple Bohemians." Although he dallied with various schemes for producing income—drawing for a print seller, writing for a newspaper, and composing a novel—the only enterprise he actually took up was an electioneering campaign in Devon and Cornwall for a friend during part of June and July 1832. By this time he had told his mother of a formal decision to give up the study of law and briefly mentioned an implausible alternative: "I am thinking of turning Parson & being a useful member of society."

A more characteristic decision took him to France, where he remained from August until

burning a collection of salacious books ("meine schlechte Bucher") and engaging in further musings about writing a novel, which he felt would be witty in nature, though he still had no idea of a possible plot. He also had the more immediately practicable notion of extending his knowledge of modern French writing, so that he could compose an article for one of the English reviews.

Back in London by the end of the year, he engaged for several months in bill discounting, with indeterminate results, and in May 1833 bought a recently founded two-penny weekly newspaper, the *National Standard and Journal of Literature, Science, Music, Theatricals, and the Fine Arts*. The paper served as a natural sequel to his undergraduate involvement with the *Snob* and the *Gownsman*, calling forth from him comic verses and sketches—both verbal and pictorial—of French and English political and theatrical figures. The lightheartedness of Thackeray's efforts also reflected itself in the casualness of his participation: much of the newspaper's copy was edited from other publications with the help of a subeditor. Within a few weeks of buying the paper, he settled in Paris, serving for several months as correspondent for the *National Standard*, before again taking up the study of painting as his main activity. Although the newspaper venture did not draw significantly upon Thackeray's talent, it was an important experience, for it marked the beginning of his involvement with periodical journalism.

But 1833 proved even more crucial to Thackeray's fortunes by being the year in which he lost his patrimony. His payment the previous year of gambling losses and his comfortable style of living had begun the process of dissipating his inheritance, but the resounding failure of Indian financial houses at this time accounted for most of the depletion, so that at the end of October he alluded to the loss of £ 11,000, and by the end of the year he accurately described himself as poor. He reluctantly left Paris for London, where he struggled to keep the *National Standard* alive; but he gave up in February 1834, losing several hundred more pounds. During the fall of 1834 he returned to Paris with his maternal grandmother to resume once again the study of painting, which he had described a year previously as "the only metier I ever liked." Taking advantage of the low cost of living and enjoying the pleasures of being an art student in Paris, the twenty-three-year-old Thackeray experienced what he later recalled as "a very jolly time. I was as poor as Job: and sketched away most abominably, but pretty contented: and we used to meet in each others little

A self-portrait of Thackeray in 1835. The inscription indicates the financial difficulties he was having at the time (Huntington Library).

rooms and talk about Art and smoke pipes and drink bad brandy & water."

His failure to make any significant progress in his studies came to be depressing, but after a year of frustrated, sometimes desultory effort, his spirits were lightened when he fell in love during the summer of 1835 with "a girl without a penny in the world," Isabella Shawe. The daughter of a deceased Irish army officer, Isabella was an uncomplicated seventeen-year-old girl living in a Paris boardinghouse with her domineering mother, who became the prototype for unpleasant mothers-in-law throughout Thackeray's fiction. At first Mrs. Shawe tolerated Thackeray's courtship of Isabella but later tried to disrupt the relationship as Thackeray worked to improve his financial prospects. First he apparently took employment with an English newspaper published in Paris, but this venture seems to have had a quick demise in early 1836. Then, the financial support of a friend helped arrange the appearance in London and Paris during March or (more likely) April 1836 of Thackeray's first separate publication: a series of eight tersely captioned lithographs, together with an illustrated title page, called *Flore et Zéphyr: Ballet Mythologique*. This venture of Thackeray's also seems to have been a failure, however, for it attracted no significant notice. Finally, he became involved in another newspaper enterprise.

Meanwhile, the appearance of *Flore et Zéphyr* under the pseudonym "Theophile Wagstaffe" showed not only Thackeray's interest in ballet and his humble skills as a draftsman but also the fact that his abilities as a graphic artist expressed themselves best in the form of burlesque and caricature. Even more, in retrospect one can see *Flore et Zéphyr* as a quintessential expression of his artistic vision. To begin with, it is a work that Thackeray drew and

Title page of Thackeray's first published book

captioned under one of his many pseudonyms—a self-conscious, waggish role that itself combines various perspectives, psychological and social, generalizing and personal. The work is also quite allusive, adopting the title of a neoclassical ballet choreographed by Charles Didelot that had been given its London premiere in 1796, had been restaged at the Paris Opéra in 1815, and had been revived a number of times thereafter. One of Thackeray's favorite dancers, Marie Taglioni, had used it as a vehicle for her London debut in June 1830; Thackeray may have seen it at that time, especially because his enthusiasm for Taglioni had been aroused eleven months previously when he saw her dance in Aumer's *La Fille mal Gardée* at the Paris Opéra. Since Taglioni repeated her role in the ballet during 1831 in Paris and London, and again in London during 1833, when Thackeray was in residence, his allusions would have been readily understandable to audiences in both cities where his series of caricatures was published.

In *Flore et Zéphyr*, however, Thackeray does more than burlesque Taglioni's aging vehicle, her aging costar, Albert, and Albert's successor, the gymnastic Antoine Paul. The caption of the first lithograph, "La danse fait ses offrandes sur l'autel de l'harmonie" ("The dance makes its offerings at the altar of harmony"), reveals in fact that Thackeray is burlesquing ballet itself. As his art was characteristically to do, *Flore et Zéphyr* focuses upon a series of fundamental ironic discrepancies. For one thing, Thackeray emphasizes the disjunction between the conventions of artistic behavior (here the poses or gestures of the dance) and the actual human emotions meant to be expressed by those conventions, especially grave emotions of sorrow and despair. For another thing, he directs comic attention to the discrepancy between the ethereal costumes, settings, and whole mythological dimension of the ballet on the one hand, and the human reality of the performers, with their unravishing features and unclassical figures, on the other. Similarly, he stresses the disjunction between the ideal beings enacted upon the stage and the crude, everyday human beings who witness them from the theater seats. Finally, Thackeray takes the dancers offstage after the ballet has ended; to modify the language of his final caption, "Les Délassements de Zéphyr," he "declasses" them by showing the discrepancies between the ennobled stage roles of the performers and their own everyday selves amid the mild sordidness of their real lives and those of their unprepossessing admirers. The final resting point of the series, then, is an ironic awareness of the

Thackeray's mother with his stepfather, Major Carmichael-Smyth, who invested in one of Thackeray's ill-fated business ventures

limiting conditions of everyday human life.

Thackeray's third effort to establish a financial basis for marriage to Isabella Shawe was assisted by his stepfather, Major Carmichael-Smyth, who agreed to invest in the revival of a London newspaper that was to be renamed the *Constitutional and Public Ledger* and was to be an organ of political Radicalism. Thackeray, in addition to the yearly income of £100 saved from the wreck of his fortune, was to draw eight guineas a week (£450 a year) as Paris correspondent of the *Constitutional*. With the prospect of such an income, he understandably felt himself not only financially able to marry Isabella but to have a happy prospect of "competence & reputation." He was mistaken, however, for instead of being free of "a doubtful future, a precarious profession, and a long and trying probation," he was to find that those grim phrases described exactly what he would have to endure.

If the art of the mature Thackeray can be discerned in work of these Paris years, so too can his psychic habit of considering himself old before his time. Thus, while still twenty-four, he told Isabella that he was "a sulky grey headed old fellow" and in spite of his comic overstatement conveyed the sense not only of being jaded by experience by also of being especially attracted by Isabella's naive, childlike nature. After a great and protracted struggle with her mother, Thackeray and Isabella were married in August 1836 in Paris; he was twenty-five and she five and a half years younger. Within a month Isabella was pregnant and though Thackeray's contributions to the *Constitutional* now began, the prospect of a family goaded him to make efforts to discover additional outlets for his talents in the fields of journalism and illustration. Earlier that year while plans were still being formulated for the *Constitutional*, he had unsuccessfully applied to Charles Dickens for the job of illustrating *The Pickwick Papers* to replace the recently deceased

Thackeray's portrait of his wife, Isabella

Robert Seymour. Additional schemes as etcher, Paris correspondent for a second English newspaper, contributor to a friend's periodical, and illustrator of W. Harrison Ainsworth's *Crichton* (1837) all came to naught, as did a proposal to minor publisher John Macrone for a two-volume work with illustrations to be called "Rambles & Sketches in old and new Paris"—though the latter project would eventually culminate in *The Paris Sketch Book* (1840).

Meanwhile, as the *Constitutional* remained unable to attract enough subscribers and Major Carmichael-Smyth assumed more and more financial responsibility for the newspaper, whose Radical views he warmly endorsed, Thackeray moved to London in March 1837 to help consolidate their affairs. He brought Isabella with him, and their first child, Anne, was born in June. For all Thackeray's journalistic and entrepreneurial efforts, however, the *Constitutional* ceased publication on 1 July, placing Major Carmichael-Smyth in financial difficulties and leaving Thackeray unemployed once again—indeed, poorer than ever, for he transferred all of the income from the small remainder of his inherited capital to his stepfather. The Carmichael-Smyths in turn migrated to Paris, where living expenses were significantly cheaper and where creditors could not have them imprisoned for debt.

Thackeray's career as an independent writer, free of familial subsidy, now necessarily began. The first of a dozen anonymous reviews for the *Times* appeared in August 1837 with a favorable notice of *The French Revolution* by Thomas Carlyle, who shortly thereafter spoke of Thackeray as "now writing for his life in London." The following month, the first of Thackeray's magazine tales, "The Professor"—a comic extravaganza about Dando, an impostor fond of oysters and ladies—came out pseudonymously in *Bentley's Magazine*. Although no more of Thackeray's stories were published in *Bentley's*, November 1837 marked the beginning of a sustained relationship with *Fraser's Magazine* as Thackeray's first series of tales, "The Yellowplush Correspondence," began to appear. The first paper was occasioned by a recently published book of fashionable etiquette, the vulgarity of which induced Thackeray to invent as an appropriate reviewer an illiterate footman, Charles J. Yellowplush, who mocked the book from the posture of his more "knowing" experience of the fashionable world—thereby not only undermining the book's claims but also exposing his own naiveté.

Thackeray's sense of the possibilities of the

Frontispiece drawn by Thackeray for The Paris Sketch Book

Yellowplush persona was such that he went on to write seven more papers under that name, with occasional illustrations. Most of them were completely fictional, especially the extended accounts of Yellowplush's corrupting service with the Honorable Algernon Percy Deuceace, a disreputable nobleman who was partly modeled upon gamblers and other raffish types whom Thackeray had met in England and on the Continent. Several of the papers, however, reverted to the review format in satirizing Lady Charlotte Bury's gossipy, pretentious *Diary Illustrative of the Times of George the Fourth* and Dionysius Lardner's ponderous *Cabinet Cyclopaedia*, as well as Edward Bulwer's literary pretensions. With an adieu in August 1838, Yellowplush's correspondence broke off, except for the appearance in January 1840 of the final paper, "Epistles to the Literati," which satirized Bulwer's inept drama

The Sea Captain (1839) and its apologetic preface.

After publishing the first two Yellowplush papers in *Fraser's Magazine* during November 1837 and January 1838, Thackeray began what grew into another series, which came out irregularly in the *New Monthly Magazine* between February 1838 and February of the following year. Reviving the pseudonym loosely attached to "The Professor," Thackeray developed the name into a true persona: Major Goliah O'Grady Gahagan, the autobiographical narrator of what came to be known as "The Tremendous Adventures of Major Gahagan," another extravaganza—this time of love and war in British India during the time of Wellesley. Combining amusing Irish braggadocio with the naive self-revelations of the narrator, Thackeray also found a vehicle for burlesquing military narratives; he accomplished this with extensive use of oral and written Anglo-Indian materials that had come to him through relatives, especially his stepfather, and through avid reading about the country where his father had prospered and died.

Thackeray spent March 1838 in France, mostly Paris, where he combined pleasure with business—recounting Yellowplush's adventures abroad, doing an article for the *Times*, and drawing a caricature for *Fraser's*—but also reading and gathering visual impressions for what he described as "the book"—the work about Paris he had proposed to Macrone over a year previously. On his return to London he submitted a long Yellowplush paper to *Fraser's*, "Mr. Deuceace in Paris," which was printed in three installments. He also began planning a short twelve-part rogue's autobiography called *Stubbs's Calendar; or, The Fatal Boots*, relating the multifarious failed schemes of Bob Stubbs; illustrated by his friend George Cruikshank, it appeared shortly before Christmas in the *Comic Annual for 1839*, published by Charles Tilt.

Perhaps Thackeray's most significant nonfictional work of 1838, "Strictures on Pictures," appeared in the June issue of *Fraser's* under what was to become Thackeray's favorite pseudonym, "Michael Angelo Titmarsh," the persona of an artist and critic of art whose chief resemblance to his famous namesake is a broken nose, which Thackeray had himself received during a fight at Charterhouse. As in Thackeray's own case, Titmarsh's appreciation of painting far exceeds his capacity to execute it. As Thackeray's first critical article for *Fraser's* on the annual May exhibition of pictures at the Royal Academy, "Strictures on Pictures" gave him an opportunity to express not only his judgments on the work of contemporary painters but

also some of the central principles of his aesthetic outlook. The first of these he states immediately: the necessity of an artist's "feeling for the beauty of Nature, which is . . . neither more nor less than Art." Hence Thackeray's is a credo of realism limited by the artist's feeling for the beauty of what he observes around him in everyday life. On the one hand, therefore, a heartless verisimilitude is found wanting by Thackeray; on the other hand, certain technical shortcomings in the painter's rendering are overshadowed by an ability to render his sympathetic response to observed beauty. Thus the figures are wooden in the painting *Crusaders Catching a First View of Jerusalem* by Keats's friend Joseph Severn, but the work embodies a "majestic and pious harmony." The religious nature of the subject is important, for Thackeray uses this particular picture to emphasize that there "is a higher ingredient in beauty than mere form; a skilful hand is only the second artistical quality, worthless . . . without the first, which is *a great heart*. This picture is beautiful, in spite of its defects." Citing Severn's picture of Ariel merrily riding through the evening sky on a bat's back, Thackeray argues that Severn "possesses that solemn earnestness and simplicity of mind and purpose which makes a religion of art"—by which Thackeray does not mean that art is an end in itself, but that the spiritual qualities of an artist like Severn make the practice of his calling a religious act by its worship of the Creator. Such beliefs about art were maintained by Thackeray to the end of his career.

The essay is also remarkable for the way in which it reveals Thackeray's imagination responding to a certain picture of William Etty's that evidently deeply stirred memories of his own experience: "the prodigal kneeling down lonely in the stormy evening, and praying to Heaven for pardon." Not only does Thackeray vividly enter the picture and feel the atmospheric and spiritual powers manifesting themselves there—from the howling and chill of the wind, and the oppressive emblematic presence of the goat and boar, to the comforting promises of the star above—but, even more, he compulsively imagines the ongoing life of the prodigal as the promise is fulfilled and he is welcomed home. One can observe in this entire response Thackeray's lifelong tendency, derived especially from his eighteenth-century and classical heritage, to see human life in terms of a few central, ever-repeated patterns—fables, in fact, like that of the prodigal son, which his own life seemed to reflect. Even more, one notices in the narrative of the kneeling figure's subsequent life how closely "home and hope" are linked for Thackeray, and how the terrors of isolation and a sense of personal unworthiness are largely overcome by the figures who greet the wandering son: most immediately, "a good father, who loves you," and "a dear, kind, stout, old mother." (The narrator's direct address to the returning prodigal is also notable.) Realistically, there must also be "an elder brother, who hates you" and a prosperous childhood rival, but more than adequate compensation is imagined in the mother, "who liked you twice as well as the elder," and especially in the figures of the girl left behind but still faithful and the future mother-in-law who is not hostile but welcoming.

As Thackeray continued to write for his livelihood and to hope that better employment might gain him "a little durable reputation," his family grew with the birth in July 1838 of a second daughter, Jane. Following the appearance of "Mr. Yellowplush's Ajew" in August, Thackeray saw evidence that his recent work, at least, had attained an American reputation of sorts, for a Philadelphia publisher pirated some of it, publishing *The Yellowplush Correspondence* before the end of the year; ironically, it was the first separate volume of Thackeray's fiction to be published. Meanwhile, gleanings from the French journey began to appear in the *New Monthly Magazine* and in *Fraser's* during 1838 and in a new magazine for Thackeray, the *London and Westminster Review* of April 1839.

The following month's issue of *Fraser's* then brought out the first installment of a new illustrated serial "Catherine: A Story," which appeared somewhat irregularly in seven installments between May 1839 and February 1840 and marked Thackeray's first use of an eighteenth-century setting, being based upon the life of a famous murderess, Catherine Hayes. Thackeray invented a new persona, "Ikey Solomons, Esq. Junior," the alleged son of a notorious London receiver of stolen goods who had been tried, convicted, and transported earlier in the 1830s. In "Catherine," however, the persona seems largely nominal; because of the educated nature of his language and a certain heaviness of irony in his addresses to the reader, one tends to feel that he gives direct expression to Thackeray's satirical anger. Hence any awareness one may have of the distinction between narrator and author comes to be obliterated.

Another anomaly of "Catherine" is its eagerness to place itself in the context of literary controversy. Critics have often identified "Catherine" as an ironic version of a then-popular genre, Newgate fiction—narratives of the 1830s based upon eighteenth-century criminals and their adventures, which had been starkly reported in the Newgate Calendar but were now being treated in a manner that Thackeray satirically termed a reflection of "the present fashionable style and taste," since these "low" and "disgusting" subjects were made to seem "eminently pleasing and pathetic." In that context, the choice of Ikey Solomons as a narrative persona seems designed to make the ironic point that Newgate novelists of the 1830s are in fact the willing heirs of criminals, whose morally and socially disruptive exploits they emulate with their novelistic adulation and encourage in their audiences.

Indeed, the burgeoning effects of such novels were some of Thackeray's most urgent concerns. He was therefore satirizing not simply Newgate novels but a variety of contemporary fictive creations that had in common their romanticizing of evil, whether it came from the Newgate Calendar and was being "fenced" to willing buyers, or whether it was being freshly invented in analogous works. From the sympathetic use of a rogue hero as well as a highwayman near the beginning of the decade by Bulwer in *Paul Clifford* (1830) and *Eugene Aram* (1832)—to be followed by *Ernest Maltravers* (1837)—had come novels like Ainsworth's *Rookwood: A Romance* (1834), with the highwayman Dick Turpin for a hero, and Dickens's *Oliver Twist* (1837-1839), which encouraged its readers, Thackeray believed, to follow the crimes of Fagin breathlessly, with a morally anesthetized, merely narrative interest; to sympathize with the "errors" of Nancy; to respond with "a kind of pity and admiration" for Sikes; and to feel "an absolute love for the society of the Dodger."

Even more, the success of these novels caused theatrical entrepreneurs to exploit the public admiration still further by offering stage representations of the novels' characters. Inevitable results ensued, the most striking recent example being another highwayman romance of Ainsworth's—*Jack Sheppard*, which began appearing serially in January 1839 (four months before "Catherine") and by the end of the year had been out on the stage, Thackeray emphasized, in "four different representations." As Thackeray wrote to his mother that December, the exploitation was carried so far that a receptive public was being offered "*Shepherd-bags*" [sic] in the lobby of one of these theaters, "a bag containing a few picklocks. . . , [and] one or two gentlemen have already confessed how much they were indebted to Jack Sheppard who gave them ideas of pocketpicking and thieving wh. they never would have had but for the play." Accordingly,

Thackeray intended "Catherine" not as a romance but as a realist "cathartic" which depicted the viciousness of its rogues and concluded with an emphatic account of their gruesome fates. For all his aim to purge the public of its taste for the corrupting aspects of contemporary fiction, however, Thackeray also found himself intermittently engaged by the personages he was creating and came to acknowledge privately that he felt "a sneaking kindness for his heroine" that interfered with a full working out of his satirical intention.

During the late summer of 1839, Thackeray revisited Paris, this time with Isabella and their daughter Anne (Jane having died at the age of eight months in March of that year). One result of the visit was a two-month hiatus in the serial appearance of "Catherine," but another was a renewed impetus to write short articles on Paris that could be sent to *Fraser's Magazine* and later gathered together into his long-planned book. Thackeray also worked on another twelve-part tale illustrated by Cruikshank in the *Comic Annual for 1840*, "Barber Cox and the Cutting of his Comb," which relates the bumbling misadventures of a hero misled by the imperious pretensions of his wife until his happy fall back into his humble calling. France also provided Thackeray with a tale of a minor writer, Charles de Bernard, that Thackeray used as the basis of a three-part tale that appeared during early 1840 in the *New Monthly Magazine*, "The Bedford-Row Conspiracy," an amusing tale of one couple's successful love and marriage amid the social and political maneuvering of others. In its implicit defense of the hero's "idleness, simplicity, enthusiasm, and easy good-nature," and in its endorsement of the heroine's struggle against aggressive female dominance, the tale seems to reflect important aspects of Thackeray's and Isabella's lives, but the future is also anticipated as Thackeray turns away from rogue narrative toward greater dramatization of social behavior generated by the interaction of middle- and upper-class characters.

Between March and September 1840, Thackeray was "in a ceaseless whirl and whizz from morning to night, now with the book, now with the drawings, now with articles for Times, Fraser, here and there." His miscellaneous pieces included a sixty-page essay on George Cruikshank's works for the *London and Westminster Review* (soon published separately as well); his annual review of the May Royal Academy exhibition for *Fraser's*; the beginning of a new serial for *Fraser's* called "A Shabby Genteel Story"; a memorable article on Courvoisier's execution—"Going to See a Man Hanged"—also for *Fraser's*; a review of Fielding's *Works* for the *Times*; and especially the two-volume book on Thackeray's French experiences, published by Cunningham for the recently deceased Macrone, entitled *The Paris Sketch Book* and published under the Titmarsh pseudonym.

The latter work, which appeared in July 1840, more or less equally mixed previously published articles and stories with new material. Of the nineteen pieces, eight were fictional (including adaptations from the French); one was a group of translations of Béranger poems; and the rest were reviews of French art and literature and sketches of French manners and customs. Thackeray also illustrated the book, which he comically dedicated to his French tailor, who had lent him money during its composition. The book had a modest success, though only the *Spectator* and Thackeray seemed to like the illustrations. The most important results of Thackeray's success with *The Paris Sketch Book*, however, seem to have been the encouragement of the author, the growth of his reputation, and the finding of an additional publisher.

Following the birth in May of another daughter, Harriet Marian, Isabella had seemed to recover normally from her confinement. Consequently, at the beginning of August, Thackeray enthusiastically dashed over to Belgium for a two-week stay that was intended both as a holiday and as a preparation for "a little book on Belgium & the Rhine." By the time of his departure he had also made plans for a two-volume work to be called "Titmarsh in Ireland," and he looked forward to being freed from "that odious magazine-work, wh. wd. kill any writer in 6 years." Upon his return to England, he found his wife in "an extraordinary state of languor and depression" that persisted in spite of his efforts to cheer her up and that also resisted medical diagnosis. It diminished somewhat during a recommended holiday at a seaside resort, but resumed on their return to London. Thackeray therefore held in abeyance his plans for the travel book on Belgium and the Rhine, turning instead to his Irish project. He made plans to take Isabella and the children to her mother and sister, who were living at Cork, and on 8 September 1840 he signed a contract for the Irish book with his new publishers, Chapman and Hall, that provided him with a much-needed advance of £120. He also completed the fourth installment of "A Shabby Genteel Story" for *Fraser's*, suspending it in a manner that permitted him to resume at some undetermined future date. (He was never to complete the work but in 1861-1862 wrote a sequel, *The Adventures of Philip*, which summarizes the earlier tale and draws upon the ending he had intended to write for it.)

On the boat to Ireland, Isabella tried to commit suicide by throwing herself into the sea, but she was rescued and prevented from making another attempt. For the remaining fifty-three years of her life, though there were periods of improvement, she remained insane. Eventually, she had to be put away, but not before Thackeray had explored the best means of restoring her that he could discover. An Irish doctor seemed at first to provide assistance, but after a month spent enduring Isabella's ceaselessly aggressive mother, whom Thackeray came to consider somewhat deranged herself, he made for Paris and the help of his own mother; passing through London, he arranged with Cunningham for publication of his "comic miscellanies." In Paris he entrusted his children to his mother and grandmother; placed his wife in the care of Esquirol's, one of the leading mental hospitals in Europe; and set about writing once more, mainly to provide for her upkeep.

A contemporary event furnished a ready subject, so that during a portion of December Thackeray quickly wrote a humorous version of it, *The Second Funeral of Napoleon*, and a poetic epilogue, *The Chronicle of the Drum*. The two works were published together by Cunningham in January 1841, with a cover design by Thackeray, in a small paper-covered format under the pseudonym of M. A. Titmarsh. Sales remained very low, however, and Thackeray soon prepared an article for the March issue of *Fraser's*—his first contribution to that periodical in five months.

By this time, he was completing work for the comic miscellanies that were to be issued by Cunningham during April 1841 in two volumes under the title *Comic Tales and Sketches*, with a number of new illustrations by Thackeray, including a title page showing Yellowplush and Gahagan leading Titmarsh "to the very brink of immortality" (that is, to the edge of a cliff). Besides reprinting Gahagan's adventures and the correspondence of Yellowplush (with the exception of "Fashnable Fax"), Thackeray included in this collection "The Professor," "The Bedford-Row Conspiracy," and "Stubbs's Calendar." Whether for reasons of space or by deliberate choice, *Flore et Zéphyr*, "Barber Cox," and "Catherine" were not included. With *Comic Tales*, however, Thackeray still failed to achieve notable success.

After writing the opening of a never-to-be-finished novel of the fifteenth century, "The Knights of Borsellen," Thackeray put it aside to

Thackeray's title page showing Charles J. Yellowplush and Major Goliah O'Grady Gahagan leading Michael Angelo Titmarsh "to the very brink of immortality"

earn immediate money. An improvement in Isabella's condition caused him suddenly to remove her from the mental hospital in late March and to have renewed hope for her eventual recovery. One result, however, was that he had to devote most of his time to her for the next six weeks. Ultimately, he hired an attendant for Isabella and took up writing again, notably for *Fraser's*, publishing four articles during the summer. Now free to travel, he visited England, the most important experience there being a visit to the country seat of a friend, John Bowes, during the general election of 1841. During this visit Thackeray learned about an ancestor of Bowes's who became the inspiration for Thackeray's novel *The Luck of Barry Lyndon* (1852-1853). Thackeray immediately proposed writing the novel for *Fraser's*, but the project was postponed.

Arrangements had evidently been made already for Thackeray's newest serial, *The History of Samuel Titmarsh and the Great Hoggarty Diamond*, which began to appear in the September *Fraser's*, concluding at the end of the year. Here again, Thackeray used a naive autobiographical persona, though in this case the narrative is not a rogue autobiography but in certain essential details a fable of Thackeray's own life and of his hopes for the future. Samuel Titmarsh, Michael Angelo's cousin, unexpectedly receives a diamond pin that enables him to marry the simple girl he loves, but the pin also leads him into a life of expensive habits and an illusory pursuit of success. Duped and self-deluded, separated from his wife, and faced with ruin, he pawns the diamond pin, escapes from his follies, is reunited with his wife, accepts his humbled existence, and comes to enjoy modest circumstances. As Thackeray looked back ten years later, he characterized himself as "a boy . . . bleating out my simple griefs in the Great Hoggarty Diamond." He also bleated out some of his hopes—hopes that implicitly chastised his past life, for as he wrote in a diary that summer, "there is not one of the sorrows or disappointments of my life, that as I fancy I cannot trace to some error crime or weakness of my disposition."

In early 1842, Thackeray continued his attempts to sell magazine articles and succeeded in placing his first contribution with the *Foreign Quarterly Review* and several with the newly founded *Ainsworth's Magazine*. A series of miscellaneous sketches published under a new pseudonym, "George Fitz-Boodle," began to appear in the *Fraser's* issue for June, the same month in which began a long series of contributions to *Punch*, which he described privately as "a very low paper," but one that offered "good pay, and a great opportunity for unrestrained laughing sneering kicking and gambadoing." Finally, also in June, he set out for Ireland, where he spent four months gathering material for his postponed book and beginning to write it. *The Irish Sketch Book* finally appeared in May of the following year, during which Thackeray continued to write miscellaneous works for the magazines—chiefly *Fraser's* and *Punch*. Thackeray wanted to give *The Irish Sketch Book* the title "Cockney in Ireland," but though his publishers overruled him, the planned title reveals that the London narrator is as central to the book as Ireland itself. Given the unity provided by the book's subject matter—the "manners and the scenery" of Ireland—its narrator, and its generally sober narrative tone, the work has much more coherence than *The Paris Sketch Book*. Thackeray illustrated the

book and attributed it to M. A. Titmarsh, but for the first time in his career he added his own name as well by signing a dedication to Charles Lever, the Irish novelist who had befriended him on his tour. By signing his name, Thackeray acknowledged the transparency of his mask but also implied his opinion of the book's merits. Except for Lever, Irish reviewers generally attacked the book—as Thackeray knew they would, and as he indicated in the dedication—for they resisted the depiction of Irish dirt, dilapidation, rhetoric, superstition, and quarrelsomeness that formed a part of Thackeray's sketch. The English reception was much more favorable, however, both with reviewers and the public. The book represented Thackeray's widest success so far in his career; it even went into a second edition two years later.

During the rest of 1843 Thackeray continued his contributions to *Punch* and wrote additional sketches for *Fraser's* under the name of Fitz-Boodle, a pseudonym he also attributed to the author of his ensuing work of fiction. Toward the end of the year he prepared for a new serial novel, which had been on his mind since the visit to Bowes over two years before, and which began to appear in the January 1844 *Fraser's*: *The Luck of Barry Lyndon: A Romance of the Last Century*. Here Thackeray returned not only to the eighteenth century but to the rogue autobiographer, who naively reveals himself as he unfolds the egotistical narrative of his rapacious adventures on the Continent, in Ireland, and in England. Soldier, gambler, brutal husband and stepfather, prodigal dissipator of his wife's fortune, and finally broken-down prisoner, Barry never falters in his devotion to the fortunes available through luck and cunning and to the values of success. Thackeray not only sustains more coolly than ever the ironic discrepancy between Barry's values and the standards violated by his misdeeds but also permits Barry degrees of "success" sufficient to emphasize increasingly the hollowness of his achievements. Objections from members of Thackeray's audience to the immorality of Barry's views apparently prompted the novelist gradually to expand the almost imperceptible editorial presence of Fitz-Boodle by having him repeatedly point out the viciousness of Barry's principles and behavior and emphasize his disapproval of them. As this expedient may suggest, Thackeray's serial was not popular, and his initial hopes of publishing the novel in "a handsome saleable volume" were not fulfilled at the end of its serial appearance in the December 1844 issue of *Fraser's*. (The novel was brilliantly adapted by Stanley Kubrick for the 1975 film *Barry Lyndon*.)

TO

CHARLES LEVER, Esq.

OF TEMPLEOGUE HOUSE, NEAR DUBLIN

MY DEAR LEVER,

HARRY LORREQUER needs no complimenting in a dedication; and I would not venture to inscribe this volume to the Editor of the *Dublin University Magazine*, who, I fear, must disapprove of a great deal which it contains.

But allow me to dedicate my little book to a good Irishman (the hearty charity of whose visionary red-coats, some substantial personages in black might imitate to advantage), and to a friend from whom I have received a hundred acts of kindness and cordial hospitality.

Laying aside for a moment the travelling-title of Mr. Titmarsh, let me acknowledge these favours in my own name, and subscribe myself, my dear Lever,

Most sincerely and gratefully yours,

W. M. THACKERAY.

London, April 27, 1843.

The dedication of The Irish Sketch Book, *marking the first time Thackeray's name appeared on any of his works*

By that time, Thackeray already had another travel book under way, for when the Peninsular and Oriental Company suddenly in August offered him free passage on one of their ships sailing to Cairo, with many stops along the way throughout the Mediterranean, he accepted forthwith and was at sea four days later. Throughout the cruise and during a stay of several months in Rome on the return journey, Thackeray kept busily at work— finishing *Barry Lyndon*, writing his travel book as well as sketching for it, sending contributions to *Punch*, and beginning a Christmas book. During 1845, his miscellaneous writings for *Punch* supplied most of his income, supplemented by occasional contributions to the *New Monthly Magazine*; several to *Fraser's Magazine*, including his last annual review of the Royal Academy exhibition; and several to *George Cruikshank's Table Book* and the *Morning Chronicle*. In June he grumbled, "I can suit the magazines (but I can't hit the public, be hanged to them)." He continued to try to hit the public, nevertheless, for earlier in the year he had given to Colburn "the commencement of a novel"—which is generally understood to be the beginning of what later became *Vanity Fair*. Colburn, however, failed

to respond, leading Thackeray to recall that manuscript, together with the commencement of another tale, and to busy himself with "scores of little jobs comme à l'ordinaire."

For several years Thackeray had wished to have his children with him in London, but he did not want to separate them from his mother, who was extremely attached to them. Furthermore, Major Carmichael-Smyth did not wish to move to London because of greater expenses and because of writs against him relating to debts from the collapse of the *Constitutional*. Mrs. Carmichael-Smyth's visit to London with the two girls in June 1845 brought matters somewhat closer to a resolution, as did Thackeray's decision to bring his wife to England, where she was placed under what became permanent care in Camberwell in south London. His efforts to persuade the Carmichael-Smyths failed even when he rented a house in June 1846, but his mother finally brought the children to him in the late autumn, afterward returning alone to her husband in France. After an interval of six years, Thackeray had reconstituted his family life, having his daughters permanently under his own roof.

The year 1846 had opened with the appearance of his illustrated Eastern travel book, *Notes of a Journey from Cornhill to Grand Cairo*, published by Chapman and Hall. As in *The Irish Sketch Book*, Thackeray writes in the persona of a London traveler humorously content with his national ignorance but delightedly responding to scenes of natural beauty and human idiosyncrasy. The style, somewhat less sober than in the Irish book, is even more fluent and polished. By this time Thackeray had achieved a prose of notable flexibility and range. His success among critics and the public was also more pronounced. A second edition again followed, this time within eight months of original publication. Later that year, Thackeray published his first Christmas book, *Mrs. Perkins's Ball*, organized essentially as a group of character sketches centering on an evening entertainment, which sold over 1,500 copies by the end of December and led to an immediate second edition.

But 1846 was more important for the appearance of Thackeray's longest and most notable series of contributions to *Punch*: "The Snobs of England. By One of Themselves," which began in February and ran anonymously for fifty-three weeks, with accompanying illustrations. Taking the term "snob," which at that time denoted someone of the lower class, Thackeray extended its meaning to include members of the middle and upper classes—his reading audience—by defining a snob as one *"who meanly admires mean things."* Following the progress of the social year, and ranging from the Snob Royal to the lowest orders but concentrating upon the middle class, Thackeray examines the influence of the aristocracy and "respectability" upon snobs and characterizes "City" snobs together with military, clerical, university, literary, political, country, and club snobs, among others. Through the prose and through illustrations like that of a liveried court footman asking a startled social superior in court dress, "Am I not a man and a brother?" (the appeal made famous by those working for the abolition of slavery), Thackeray emphasizes how much emancipation remains to be undertaken. Although the series was published anonymously, and only a small group of knowing readers could identify the author from the writing or from his artistic "signature" on a number of the illustrations—a pair of spectacles with crossed earpieces—Thackeray's authorship of the series was publicly made known in December 1846, when Bradbury and Evans, the publishers of *Punch*, began to advertise the fact in announcing the appearance of *Vanity Fair*, which they were about to issue in separate monthly installments. The Snob

Cover of the collected edition of the Snob papers, with the "man and brother" illustration

papers thus became an important work in establishing Thackeray's public reputation as a leading satirist of his day—a reputation that increased when the Snob papers were published in 1848 in a single volume, which carried Thackeray's name (as did all his subsequent publications) and the "man and brother" illustration on its paper cover.

Eighteen forty-six was also to have been the year of *Vanity Fair*, for by January Thackeray had reached a publishing agreement with Bradbury and Evans; but like a number of his other projects, this too had to be postponed from its planned appearance in May—presumably because Thackeray was too busy with other matters to reimmerse himself in the novel, which he had evidently begun after his return from his Eastern and Italian journey in February 1845. Toward the end of 1846 he began to take up the novel again and suddenly recalled the phrase *Vanity Fair*, from Bunyan's *The Pilgrim's*

Progress (1678, 1684); it gave him the title for his major work, but can aptly be said to characterize all his narratives, and indeed his view of human life. His own brief summary of his subject, paraphrased from St. Paul (Ephesians 2 : 12), was "a set of people living without God in the world." Though at the last minute he wanted to change its subtitle to *A Novel without a Hero*, the first monthly installment for January 1847 and subsequent installments bore the heading, *Vanity Fair: Pen and Pencil Sketches of English Society*, thereby suggesting the satirical influence of the Snob papers, which still had eight weeks to run in *Punch*. The revised subtitle appeared on the title page when the novel came out in one-volume form during 1848, however, and served to suggest that with *Vanity Fair* Thackeray was offering not a series of sketches, like the Snob papers or *Mrs. Perkins's Ball*, but a carefully planned and well-executed whole. The revised subtitle also emphasized Thackeray's disinterest in creating a

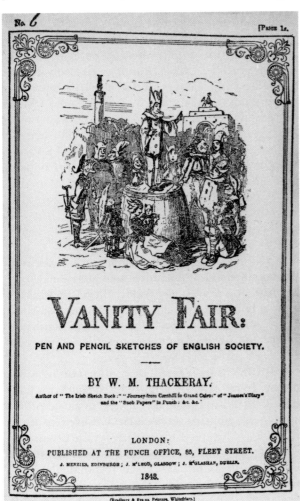

Cover of one of the monthly numbers of Thackeray's major work, showing its original subtitle

romantic hero or in narrating the adventures of a central personage. His subject was a whole society and the unheroic lives of people who lived in it, following for the most part their worldly, illusory aims.

As Thackeray was revising his manuscript of the third installment, he inserted several passages that alluded to his novel's new title of *Vanity Fair*. The first of these insertions deserves special mention, for in it Thackeray now proclaimed the narrator's intention "as a man and a brother" not merely to introduce the characters in his narrative but also at times "to step down from the platform, and talk about them"; the latter constitutes the famous Thackerayan narrative commentary. Here he also reveals a dual function of the narrator that is crucial to an adequate understanding of the novel. On the one hand, as the term "platform" shows, the narrator is what Thackeray elsewhere called "the Manager of the Performance," a stage manager who is also a puppeteer, distinct from his puppets and in a basic sense superior to them. From another perspective, however, as the phrase "a man and a brother" indicates, he is their equal, for he is also a character in the narrative, and like all men is not simply acted upon by others but is also the puppet of his own desires and illusory aims. This interplay of perspectives is the source of *Vanity Fair*'s narrative complexity, one of the sources of its intermittent melancholy, and one of the reasons for doubt as to its efficacy as a morally instructive fiction.

Depending structurally upon a complex series of contrasts and pairings within individual installments and from one installment to another, *Vanity Fair* has five main characters who are also contrasted and paired: Becky Sharp, Amelia Sedley (modeled partly on Isabella), George Osborne, William Dobbin (modeled partly on Thackeray himself), and Rawdon Crawley. From the start, as the gentle, subdued Amelia and the witty, determined Becky emerge from school into the world, it is the latter who especially captures the reader's attention with her rebellious rejection of the school's "diploma"—a copy of Johnson's *Dictionary*. As George and William depart from their school to take up military careers, the girls contemplate marriage—Amelia to George and Becky to anyone she can conquer. Amelia's real education comes only when she can grow sufficiently to emerge from her failed marriage to George, recognize the superior merits of the outwardly unprepossessing William, and find whatever happiness remains to them from their saddening growth. Becky, after failing to ensnare Amelia's wealthy brother but succeeding with Rawdon, who is the younger son of a baronet, appears to have made the more successful marriage. The false expectations in her case, however, are of monetary inheritance, for her husband is impoverished, and Becky's famous attempts "to live well on nothing a-year" by creating and sustaining the illusions of other people lead only to inevitable downfall, followed by exiled wandering and eventually a determined, partial recovery of the appearance of "respectability."

Opening in Regency England, the novel follows the intertwined relationships of these five characters amid a wide range of supplementary characters, from a chimney sweep to the king, and in settings extending from London and Brighton to Belgium, France, and Germany. With the victory of the British and their allies at Waterloo (treated in a few brief paragraphs) comes the death of George and the novel's first climax at the end of part nine; the spatial and especially the temporal scope of the novel widen even further thereafter, as it traces the fortunes of Becky, Rawdon, Amelia, and William in England and post-Napoleonic Europe, concluding in the early 1830s with a typically Thackerayan ending that stabilizes the plot but resolves very little in a conclusive way. The idea of a happy ending to a fiction was unpalatable to Thackeray, except as a joke. His kind of moral realism required that the novelist not flatter the reader's ego, or leave him satisfied with his earthly condition: "I want to leave everybody dissatisfied and unhappy at the end of the story—we ought all to be with our own and all other stories."

The form of the serial novel, issued in separate monthly installments of thirty-two pages at one shilling a copy, with an illustrated paper cover and two full-page etched plates, had been initiated by Dickens with *The Pickwick Papers* (1836-1837). Such works were typically planned as twenty installments in nineteen issues, the last issue being a double number priced at two shillings, with forty or so pages of text and four plates, plus a bound novel's usual preliminaries. A subscriber could thereby have his own set of serial parts bound; at the end of serial publication other readers could buy a bound volume from the publisher or from booksellers. In reaching agreement with Bradbury and Evans, who were also publishing Dickens, Thackeray came to work in the same format. Instead of Dickens's green covers, however, *Vanity Fair* and ensuing novels of Thackeray's appeared in yellow covers—leading to a Thackerayan joke about his more bilious novelistic outlook. Thackeray also supplemented the two etched plates with wood engravings inserted di-

rectly into the text, and he, unlike Dickens, drew his own illustrations. The yellow numbers sold rather slowly for the first twelve months; but during 1848, when the novel became available in a single bound volume, sales more than doubled, though they were still far from spectacular. Favorable critical opinion already began to be published early in the novel's serial run, reviews of the published volume extending this reception. Among fellow novelists, the most notable tribute was offered by Charlotte Brontë, who dedicated the second edition of *Jane Eyre* to Thackeray and praised the intellectual, prophetic, Old Testament power of *Vanity Fair*'s satire, which she ranked above Fielding's. By July 1848, then, Thackeray had emerged into recognition not simply as a clever magazine writer but as one of the best of contemporary novelists—the rival of Dickens in excellence, if not in popularity.

For some time, however, Thackeray continued his magazine work. With an article for the January 1847 issue of *Fraser's*, Thackeray's contributions to that magazine almost entirely halted; but concurrently with the installments of *Vanity Fair* he continued his submissions to *Punch*, notably a series of parodies called "*Punch*'s Prize Novelists." Beginning with "George de Barnwell," a satire on Bulwer's novels (particularly *Eugene Aram*, which had recently been reprinted), Thackeray went on to direct gentler mockery at the fiction of Disraeli, Catherine Gore, and other novelists of fashionable life, G. P. R. James, Lever, James Fenimore Cooper, and French writers on English life. In addition, the "Fat Contributer" now reported not on the pyramids of Egypt, as during 1844, but on Brighton; he was succeeded by "Spec," who made his "Travels in London." In December 1847 Chapman and Hall published Thackeray's second Christmas book, another illustrated series of sketches, *Our Street*. As usual, then, Thackeray found it both congenial and profitable to busy himself with more than one task. His income was still not notable, but he was finally able to settle with the last of Major Carmichael-Smyth's creditors.

By the time *Vanity Fair* appeared in one-volume form during July 1848, Thackeray had agreed with Bradbury and Evans to do another twenty-part monthly serial. First, however, he took advantage of his freedom to make for the Continent and enjoy a month's solitary holiday in Belgium and Germany. One of his favored correspondents while on this trip was Jane Brookfield, the wife of an old college friend William Brookfield, who had become a clergyman in London. Thackeray had first met Jane in early 1842 and a year afterward jokingly

The Reverend William Brookfield and his wife, Jane, with whom Thackeray was in love

told his mother that "pretty Mrs. Brookfield" was the latest woman he had fallen in love with. More soberly in 1846 he wrote his mother that Mrs. Brookfield was his "beau-ideal. I have been in love with her these four years—not so as to endanger peace or appetite but she always seems to me to speak and do and think as a woman should." To his good friend, her husband, he acknowledged in early 1847 that Jane's "innocence, looks, angelical sweetness and kindness charm and ravish me to the highest degree," but called it "a sort of artistical delight (a spiritual sensuality so to speak)." By November the unconcerned Brookfield had proposed that they share Thackeray's house and housekeeping expenses and that Jane supervise care of the children, but Thackeray knew *that* arrangement would be dangerous—for him, at least—and arranged to keep his love within manageable bounds. Thackeray told Jane that he had modeled *Vanity Fair*'s Amelia upon her as well as upon his wife and mother; but Jane, while responding to Amelia's affectionateness, was put off by the character's selfishness and apathy toward her loving admirer, William Dobbin, and thereby failed to realize the degree to which Thackeray was drawing upon her own traits (as well as Isabella's) to a greater extent than upon his mother's.

In early August 1848, while still on the Continent, Thackeray began his next novel, which started its run in November 1848 under the title *The History of Pendennis. His Fortunes and Misfortunes, His Friends and His Greatest Enemy*. He now received £100 per part instead of £60, and the publishers felt confident enough to make the size of the initial printing (9,000 per part) double the figure for *Vanity Fair*. By this time too, Bradbury and Evans had republished the Snob papers in a single paper-covered collection entitled *The Book of Snobs* (1848), and a shrewd entrepreneur offered unsold copies of the old 1841 edition of *Comic Tales and Sketches* with a new title page identifying Titmarsh as the "Author of 'Our Street,' 'Vanity Fair,' etc." Thackeray also wrote a Christmas book for 1848, *Doctor Birch and His Young Friends*; and he continued his contributions to *Punch* during the run of *Pendennis*, his most notable series being the topical "Mr. Brown's Letters to a Young Man about Town." Other signs of his growing success were the republication of *Samuel Titmarsh and the Great Hoggarty Diamond* (1849) from *Fraser's Magazine* by Bradbury and Evans and of *Vanity Fair* in a Continental edition (1849) by Tauchnitz of Leipzig; and the publication of the first volume (1849) of a series called *Miscellanies: Prose and Verse*, also by Tauchnitz, the initial volume containing *The*

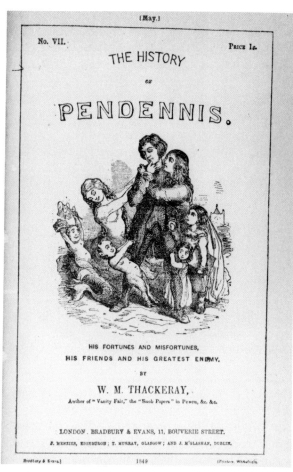

[May.]

No. VII.

PRICE 1s.

THE HISTORY

OF

PENDENNIS.

HIS FORTUNES AND MISFORTUNES,
HIS FRIENDS AND HIS GREATEST ENEMY.

BY

W. M. THACKERAY,

Author of "Vanity Fair," the "Snob Papers" in Punch, &c. &c.

LONDON. BRADBURY & EVANS, 11, BOUVERIE STREET.

J. MENZIES, EDINBURGH; T. MURRAY, GLASGOW; AND J. M'GLASHAN, DUBLIN.

Bradbury & Evans.]

1849

[Printers, Whitefriars.

*Cover of one of the monthly installments of Thackeray's novel
about a young man torn between worldly temptation
and domesticity*

Great Hoggarty Diamond and *The Book of Snobs*.

This surge of publication and republication came to a temporary end following the appearance of the eleventh number of *Pendennis* (September 1849), for Thackeray contracted a serious illness diagnosed as cholera, which dangerously afflicted him between mid-September and mid-October, leaving him to face a slow recovery thereafter. As a result, there was a hiatus of three months in the publication of *Pendennis*, which reappeared at the end of December 1849; shortly afterward, Bradbury and Evans published a volume containing the first twelve parts of the novel, as did Tauchnitz on the Continent. As this publishing decision suggests, Thackeray had decided to extend his serial novel from the Dickensian length of twenty installments to twenty-four. These new dimensions seemed to be congenial, for his next two serials for Bradbury and Evans came to be of a similar length.

Although Thackeray's serious illness and extended recovery delayed his resumption of *Pendennis*, he found it did not prevent the less tiring occupation of composing *Rebecca and Rowena*, which became his Christmas book for 1849, published again by Chapman and Hall (this time, however, with illustrations by Richard Doyle). Long-standing dissatisfaction with the ending of a favorite work, Scott's *Ivanhoe* (1819), prompted Thackeray to resurrect an old piece written in 1846 for *Fraser's*, "Proposals for a Continuation of *Ivanhoe*," and to enact them more fully. Hence Ivanhoe finally manages to get free of the dull, conventional Rowena and to find and marry the attractive Rebecca, who converts to Christianity for his sake, thus defeating Rowena's calculating deathbed exaction of his promise not to marry a Jewess. The ending, however, is a typically Thackerayan anticlimax: "Of some sort of happiness melancholy is a characteristic, and I think these were a solemn pair, and died rather early."

Thackeray's own melancholy, however, diminished as he began to write once more for *Punch* and resumed work again on *Pendennis*, which concluded with the double number for December 1850. Its title figure, Arthur Pendennis, has more prominence than any single character in *Vanity Fair*; and the emblematic illustration on the monthly wrappers identifies the narrative subject as Pen's making of a choice between two female figures, one representing worldly temptation and the other, domesticity. In tracing Pen's progress, Thackeray drew upon his own memories of Larkbeare in Devon; of Cambridge; and of bohemian, Grub Street, and fashionable life in London. People Thackeray had known tended to be models for the main characters—especially Pen's mother, Helen, but also his friend George Warrington and the two girls between whom Pen must choose: Blanche Amory and Laura Bell. After considerable vacillation, and partial yielding to the two main competing influences upon him, represented by his mother and his worldly uncle, Major Pendennis, Pen finally chooses Laura—thereby basically committing himself to a guiding set of moral values. *Pendennis* is Thackeray's version of the great nineteenth-century theme of the young man from the provinces, impoverished, simple, and undereducated but intelligent and full of high hopes, who comes to a disillusioning but also maturing understanding of himself and of his place in the world.

As the latter statement may suggest, therefore, the novel gives as much prominence to Pen's context as to Pen himself. All of the characters live in

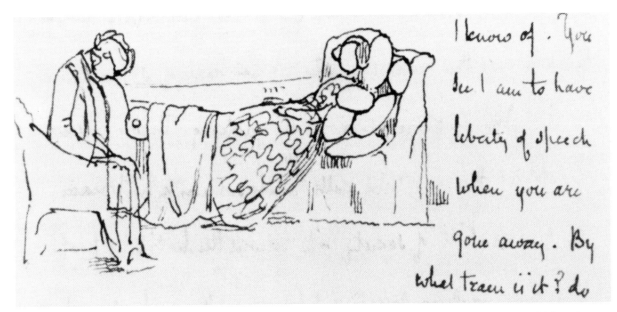

A sketch by Thackeray of himself in chains at the foot of Jane Brookfield's sofa (Rosenbach Museum and Library)

Vanity Fair, have the inevitable limitations of their virtues, require the giving up of enriching possibilities, and, though they may represent desirable values, make possible only a limited happiness. In Thackerayan fashion, Pen is a quite flawed character, a crucial aspect of Thackeray's presentation of him being the ironic relationship between Pen's hopes and enthusiasms and the narrator's more mature perspectives. At the same time, as Thackeray reveals that Laura's love is a partial renewal of Helen Pendennis's love for her son ("and arms as tender as Helen's once more enfold him"), the novelist implies his awareness that he is dramatizing his own repeatedly frustrated need for domestic affection.

Pendennis was in fact written during the closest and most intense period of his relationship with Jane Brookfield. During his younger days, he had used German in confiding to his diary matters about which he felt reluctant to speak; now, in verbalizing his love for Jane, he used French. Thus, when he wrote her a letter during November 1848 confessing his longing to tell someone, anyone, that he loved her, he wrote in French throughout, carrying the letter with him for days, trying to decide whether or not he should send it. Not long afterward, he did tell a friend and again used French, speaking of being "moitié fou" ("half mad"), of suffering from "horribles peines de coeur qui sans cesse me poursuivent" ("horrible anguish of the heart that ceaselessly pursues me"), and of not having his love returned: "Elle ne m'aime pas. Elle me

plaint" ("She does not love me. She complains of me"). Thackeray apparently did finally send Jane the French letter and received an expression of her husband's confidence in him, so that Thackeray began to write her in English of his love—but he placed it in a religious context ("By love I believe and am saved"), and connecting her with his mother, he said that the pair of them kept him "straight and honest." Thackeray and Jane agreed to call each other "friend," "sister," and "brother," but while this distant fondness seems to have been as strong an emotion as Jane Brookfield ever felt toward Thackeray, he was constantly having to restrain the power of his feelings for her and the language with which he gave them utterance.

Some measure of his feelings may be seen in a letter he wrote to a friend in early 1850, when his response to Jane's first pregnancy caused him to allude to his own poetic circumlocution for sexual intercourse: "A comic poet once singing of an [attractive] Irishwoman said 'Children if she bear blest will be their daddy.' " Thackeray then went on to speak of Jane and, in effect, of his own fantasy: "And indeed I can conceive few positions more agreeable than his who is called upon to perform the part of husband to so sweet a creature." Thackeray's relationship with Jane, however, was always one-sided and never even remotely close to being consummated. At the same time, Thackeray found a certain fulfillment as well as frustration and anguish in the relationship—indeed, he even enjoyed sardonic laughter at his predicament and received as well some fresh material for his next novel.

Before writing that novel, however, Thackeray completed what was to be his next-to-last Christmas book, *The Kickleburys on the Rhine*, for which he asked more than Chapman and Hall were willing to pay, and which therefore came out in late 1850 under the imprint of an eager publishing house that was new to Thackeray: Smith, Elder. The book's success immediately led to a second edition. Meanwhile, made anxious by the threat of death a year before, Thackeray determined to endow a suitable legacy for his wife and especially his daughters. Accordingly, he began preparations for a series of lectures on the English humorists of the eighteenth century that he hoped would bring him a good income as he delivered them in England, Scotland, and America. Beginning in May 1851, he read the six lectures to a responsive audience in London that consisted not only of notable literary figures but also of prominent members of fashionable society; Thackeray had been regularly welcomed into the homes of the latter upon the serial appearance of *Vanity Fair*, with which his reputation was prominently established.

In his lectures, Thackeray explained his belief that humor was the response of a moral sensibility, revealing a manly, pious, feeling heart. Making a

Caricature by an unknown artist of Thackeray preparing to give one of his lectures

familiar Victorian distinction between levity and gravity, Thackeray found in humor an underlying sense of weightiness and seriousness. For him humor is rooted in a profound recognition of the human condition and of mankind's immortal destiny, and it reminds the humorist's audience of the moral imperatives implied by that common destiny. Hence humor is separate from mere laughter or wit, for they imply an egoistic sense of superiority, and thereby they separate human beings; while humor, with its deep awareness of human communality, draws people together in sympathetic understanding. As he had written at the end of his previous novel, the claim of Arthur Pendennis upon the reader is the recognition not that he is a hero but that he is "a man and a brother." Correspondingly, Thackeray emphasized in his lectures the humorist's role as "week-day preacher"—not only by his language but by the example of his life. Therefore, of the figures upon whom he lectured—which included Swift, Addison, Congreve, Steele, Pope, Hogarth, Fielding, Sterne, and Goldsmith—Thackeray is hardest upon Swift and Sterne, who were ordained clergymen but seemed to him guilty not only of religious skepticism but of blasphemy. Some members of his audience immediately disagreed with the severity of these judgments, as subsequent readers have increasingly done, but there was a general consensus about the brilliance, grace, and power of his lectures. Thackeray thereby had another notable success, and a quite profitable one as well. The lectures are also significant because in giving them over a period of two years, Thackeray established a direct relationship between himself and his audiences, to whom he spoke no longer through a mask but with repeated, personal testimony.

Immediately after completing the lectures, Thackeray signed an agreement with Smith, Elder for his next novel, which was not to be a serial fiction but—for the only time in his career—was to be completed before publication. For agreeing to provide matter to fill three post octavo volumes, Thackeray was to receive £1,200. He celebrated with a six-week holiday on the Continent, for the first time taking his two daughters with him. A month after his return he quarreled with Brookfield over his friend's frequently insulting treatment of Jane; this allowed Brookfield to terminate Thackeray's association with her, though friends brought about a nominal reconciliation among the three. It was the third in the lifetime series of agonized separations—the first from his mother when he was five; the second from his wife, upon the outbreak of her madness, when he was twenty-nine; and now the third, from Jane Brookfield, when he was forty.

In mid-November 1851, when he could speak somewhat calmly about himself, he acknowledged the sexual desire implicit in his love for Jane but recognized its absurdity: "for say I got my desire, I should despise a woman; and the very day of the sacrifice would be the end of the attachment." He observed: "Very likely it's *a* woman I want more than any particular one. . . . It is written that a man should have a mate above all things[.] The want of this natural outlet plays the deuce with me." Referring to himself by the generic name of Tomkins, he asked, "Why cant I fancy some honest woman to be a titular Mrs. Tomkins?" He was able to do that, however, only in his fiction—especially in his next novel, *The History of Henry Esmond, Esq.* (1852), with the figure of Rachel, Lady Castlewood, who is partly modeled upon Jane.

Thackeray appears to have begun *Henry Esmond* at about the time of his rupture with the Brookfields in September 1851. In October he wrote a "frightfully glum" portion but a month later was getting on "pretty well & gaily" with his novel and finding diversion no longer in writing for *Punch*, which he ceased doing by the end of November, but in delivering his lectures from time to time around the country. Steady advancement with *Henry Esmond* brought it to a conclusion in May 1852, following which he made an unaccompanied tour on the Continent. *The History of Henry Esmond, Esq.*, which marked Thackeray's return to historical fiction, finally appeared in three volumes, handsomely printed in eighteenth-century Caslon type, and with a degree of archaic spelling meant to help give the book the physical appearance of an earlier age.

Cast in the form of Esmond's autobiography, Thackeray's novel takes place amid Jacobite plotting during the reigns of William III and Anne to restore the Stuarts and prevent the Hanoverian succession. It also reflects Thackeray's own life, as would be expected from so autobiographical an author. To his mother he confessed that Esmond was in part "a handsome likeness of an ugly son of yours." Ignorant of his father, separated early from his mother, and mistreated by those looking after him, Esmond feels his early days "cast a shade of melancholy over the child's youth, which will accompany him, no doubt, to the end of his days." Later, after the happily married Lord and Lady Castlewood make him a part of their home, complications develop that mirror aspects of Thackeray's relationship with the Brookfields—including pain-

Portrait by Samuel Laurence which made Thackeray's face almost as well known as his name. Charlotte Brontë hung an engraving of the portrait at Haworth Parsonage.

ful rejection by Lady Castlewood.

Because Esmond is isolated from his parents, and because manipulative people conceal his legitimacy, the question of personal identity becomes the central problem and quest of his life. His attempt to discover himself, moreover, becomes entwined with his efforts to find fulfillment in a truly self-expressive love, a part of Esmond's confusion being an attraction both to Lady Castlewood and to her daughter, Beatrix. Even in this deeply personal novel, however, the historical circumstances of Esmond's searches are inseparable from the searches themselves; for Thackeray fuses Esmond's personal story with the religious, military, and political events of Esmond's day and requires that his growth be seen in the context of those larger historical developments. Hence, as the reader follows Esmond in his military and civilian careers through a thicket of plottings and counterplottings, he becomes aware how questions of personal legitimacy, for example, are illuminated by questions of kingly legitimacy, and vice versa. When Esmond finally gives up his plotting for the Jacobite cause, he also gives up his pursuit of Beatrix and burns the papers that prove his legitimacy and his right to a

Sarah (Sally) Baxter, with whom Thackeray flirted during his visits to New York. She later married into a prominent South Carolina family and died of tuberculosis about a year before Thackeray's death.

title. Having understood that his identity is defined by his own character and actions, he destroys the pretense that anything else can define him— whether a piece of paper, an empty title, a political cause, or a brilliantly fashionable wife. Hence he chooses the widowed Lady Castlewood and moves to family estates in Virginia, where he devotes himself to a love that he sees as offering the best of earthly fulfillments and partaking of religious devotion: "To have such a love is the one blessing, in comparison of which all earthly joy is of no value; and to think of her, is to praise God."

The definiteness of this ending, perhaps motivated in part by the intensity of Thackeray's own need for such a love, gives the appearance of a somewhat uncharacteristic conclusion for a Thackeray novel. Much of the rest of the novel implies, however, that the definiteness comes more from Esmond than from Thackeray, who gives frequent evidence of his distance from his narrator, and who completed his composition of the novel by writing a preface showing the decided imperfections of the love apostrophized by Esmond at the end. The ending of *Henry Esmond*, given its context, is therefore generally consistent with Thackeray's practice of writing deliberately tempered conclusions. As this discussion may suggest, *Henry Esmond* has come to be seen as a work of tantalizing complexity. It has

also been given just praise for its shapely coherence and the grave eloquence of its style.

The History of Henry Esmond, Esq. was published at the end of October 1852, just as Thackeray was leaving for the United States, where he successfully delivered his lectures on the English humorists in the major cities of the east coast from Boston to Savannah. He was also fortunate in receiving payment from American publishers such as Harper, who had been pirating his works, and Appleton. Many invitations kept him socially busy and produced lasting friendships with prominent men of letters and with an especially congenial family in New York, the Baxters, where he found a place always ready for him—which was enlivened by an attractive daughter, Sally, whom he addressed as Beatrix and with whom he played at being in love. After his departure, Sally and her mother came to be among his favorite correspondents—who were, revealingly, all women, for Thackeray told Mrs. Baxter that he never wrote "to any man except on business."

Upon his return to London in May 1853, Thackeray set about correcting errors in proofs of *The English Humourists*, which Smith had prematurely set up in type before Thackeray could make revisions. A faulty text with an incomplete list of errata resulted, which was only partly corrected when a second edition appeared in July. Another Continental holiday followed, again with his daughters, prior to the appearance of a new serial novel for Bradbury and Evans that commenced with the number for October 1853: *The Newcomes. Memoirs of a Most Respectable Family*, illustrated by Richard Doyle and narrated by "Arthur Pendennis"—one of many characters who reappear in Thackeray's works. For *The Newcomes* Thackeray received £ 150 per serial installment, a total of £ 3,600 for the twenty-four numbers, plus £ 500 from Harper and Tauchnitz. Thackeray called 1853 the first "year of putting money away" and, with the prospect of a good income from *The Newcomes* before him, bought his first house.

Thackeray began composing the novel while on his Continental holiday, completing four numbers before the beginning of serial publication. Although he supplied Doyle with ideas for the illustrations, giving the artist most of the responsibility for them left Thackeray free to travel—all the more because he continued to write the text well before it was needed by the printers. Consequently he spent October in Paris and took his daughters to Italy during the winter of 1853-1854. During his travels, however, Thackeray's health became increasingly

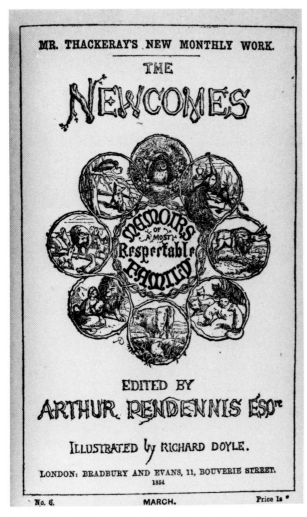

MR. THACKERAY'S NEW MONTHLY WORK.

THE

NEWCOMES

MEMOIRS
OF
A MOST
Respectable
FAMILY

EDITED BY
ARTHUR PENDENNIS ESQ^{re}

ILLUSTRATED by RICHARD DOYLE.

LONDON: BRADBURY AND EVANS, 11, BOUVERIE STREET.
1854

No. 6.   MARCH.   Price 1s *

*Cover of one of the monthly parts of Thackeray's novel about the
Newcome family*

troublesome. From August until December 1853 he
was ill once a month and then was stricken in Rome
with malarial fever, which not only prostrated him
but left him weak for days afterward and completed
the permanent damaging of his health. Emotionally, too, he felt debilitated, telling his mother, "A
man who has been a pleasuring for twenty years
begins to settle down as a sort of domestic
character—. . . [with] a sort of mild melancholy. . . .
By the time I am fifty I shall be a good deal older
than you are." At the time, Thackeray, who had
long been gray-haired, was only forty-two, but his
sense of aging was to grow markedly as the periods
of sickness recurred with increasing regularity.
Though his illnesses significantly reduced his lead
time in completing installments of *The Newcomes*, he
had time to compose a final Christmas book during
1854: *The Rose and the Ring*, a mock fairy tale that

Smith, Elder published at the end of the year, became a long-lasting, popular favorite.

With the final number of *The Newcomes*, for
August 1855, Thackeray completed one of his
largest-scaled works, and his most richly allusive
one. Again, the central dramatized reality is the
selfishness of the human heart—here, as brought to
a focus by the manipulations that characterize the
arranging of marriages, especially fashionable ones.
The Newcomes themselves epitomize the way in
which an upper-middle-class English family seeks to
increase its wealth and satisfy its social ambition by
means of aristocratic marriages and attendent benefits, including political ones. Thus of three
brothers, one marries Lady Ann Kew, eventually
becoming a baronet and member of Parliament.
The second brother marries a woman of his own
station and manages the family bank. The third
brother, however, falls in love and has his love
match broken up; he goes to India, follows a military career, and comes to have a marriage both
undistinguished and empty. The latter brother,
Colonel Newcome, comes back to England to be
with his son, Clive. From this central web of relationships come most of the novel's conflicts, in
their internal as well as external manifestations.
Thus the Colonel's old love is forcibly married to a
French count but still loves the Colonel; Sir Brian's
daughter, Ethel Newcome, is attracted to an aristocratic cousin, Kew, as well as to Clive, and later
seems on the verge of rejecting Clive for a marquis;
and Lady Clara Pulleyn forsakes her impoverished
lover to marry Ethel's brother, Sir Barnes Newcome, but later leaves her unpleasant husband and
her children for an unhappy relationship with her
former lover. Though Clive has the advantage of a
father who denounces marriages of convenience,
he nevertheless marries Rosey Mackenzie to please
his father and is miserable for it. In short, all of the
family relationships are difficult, even with the love
existing between Clive and his fond, upright, eccentric father, who became one of Thackeray's most
noted creations.

Thackeray's own experience can, as usual,
readily be seen in *The Newcomes*—for example, in
Clive's unfashionable and disillusioning attempts to
be a painter. Colonel Newcome was partly taken
from Major Carmichael-Smyth, Rosey from
Isabella, and the terrible Mrs. Mackenzie from Mrs.
Shawe, while aspects of Ethel came from Lucy Baxter, and accounts of the fashionable marriage market came from Thackeray's considerable experience in well-to-do society. His critics praised the
work for its authentic depiction of its contemporary

36

it bent the stiff neck of the younger Pitt. Even his illnesses never conquered that indomitable spirit. As soon as his brain was clear it resumed the scheme only laid aside when his reason left him: as soon as his hands were out of the strait waistcoat, they took up the pen & the plan w.^h had engaged him up to the moment of his malady. Think of that imperious Mother of his who owns that her Son is dull and ill-educated, for ever calling to him George be a King! Stupid you are but command the wisest of your subjects - not capable of understanding much but impose your will on those who do! Govern your people: break their leaders down. To this end Heaven has created you. Defender of the Faith, the oracles testify to you: the Bishops have anointed you: the Divine decrees order that your people should honor & obey you!' This Cæsar only asked that the nation should render to him what was his: but Cæsar demanded that he should send in the account and the people not question it.

I believe, it is by persons believing themselves in the right, that nineteen-twentieths of of the tyranny of this world has been perpetrated. Arguing on

Page from the manuscript for Thackeray's lecture on George III

subject, and they responded warmly to the benevolence of Colonel Newcome—not commenting very extensively, however, on his decided excesses and partial moral collapse. His pathetic ending as transfigured child indeed became one of the most famous death scenes in Victorian fiction. Thackeray, however, continued to resist happy endings and made any marriage between Clive and Ethel the responsibility of readers who wished to create their own fairy land. As in *Vanity Fair*, Thackeray wanted to leave his readers with the instructive dissatisfaction that seemed to him to characterize profound awareness of the human condition.

After a month's holiday abroad, Thackeray returned to London to prepare a new series of lectures intended for delivery in America, and later in England and Scotland, on the lives and times of the first four Hanoverian kings of England. Between August and October he composed the first three lectures, completing the one on George IV just prior to delivering it in November 1855. For the next six months he renewed old friendships and lectured in most of the same cities as before but also extended his itinerary as far west as New Orleans, St. Louis, and Cincinnati. Again he found good income from audiences who receptively responded to his brilliant verbal sketches of the Georges and the society of their times.

As in Thackeray's travel books and in his earlier series of lectures, *he*, as responsive spectator, is the central figure of the discourses, who seeks, affirms, doubts, speculates, welcomes lovable human presence, and passes judgment—upon himself as well as upon others. As in Thackeray's fiction, there are frequent shifts between limited and omniscient narration, especially as specific, individual perspectives alternate with panoramic views. In evoking the past, Thackeray assumed his audiences were knowledgeable about his subject and frequently drew upon this shared knowledge, especially through the use of allusion. Hence the lectures were not as fully successful in some of the American cities as they were in England and Scotland, where Thackeray, after returning to Europe in May 1856, gave them during the winter and spring of 1856-1857.

While he was still in America, however, Bradbury and Evans followed the example of Tauchnitz in Leipzig and Appleton in New York by beginning

Cover of a monthly number of Thackeray's unsuccessful novel about the American Revolution

a collection of Thackeray's previously published shorter prose works, including *The Yellowplush Correspondence*, *Barry Lyndon*, and *The Book of Snobs*, as well as some of his comic verse. These were gathered into four volumes of *Miscellanies: Prose and Verse* that appeared between November 1855 and May 1857. Each individual work within these volumes was also available separately in paper covers, while cheap editions of longer novels like *Pendennis* and *Henry Esmond* (published by Smith, Elder) were also published in a format uniform with that of the *Miscellanies*. Chapman and Hall also participated in this republication, with new editions of the Christmas books and *The Irish Sketch Book*. Hence Thackeray's income from these older works was renewed.

By the end of 1857, moreover, a new, twenty-four-part serial novel was beginning its appearance—*The Virginians*, for which he received his largest sum ever: £250 for each installment, a total of £6,000, with further income from Harper and Tauchnitz. By a cruel irony, however, Thackeray's financial success was accompanied by the beginning of an artistic decline. Although there are plenty of vital characters and incidents in *The Virginians*, there is an overall loss of concreteness and specificity, together with signs of a loss of inventiveness. Intended as a sequel to *Henry Esmond*, the novel was meant to center around Colonel Esmond's two grandsons during the American Revolution, when one served the king and the other fought as a republican soldier, as Thackeray's cover illustration for the serial installments emphasized. On the one hand, however, an overdeveloped beginning helped defer Thackeray's treatment of the war until the novel's very end; on the other hand, he did not manage to intertwine the narratives of Harry and George Warrington so much as he simply divided the novel between them.

Thackeray's greatest successes are with Beatrix, whom he daringly brings back as stout and elderly, but still domineering; and with Harry, a likable young prodigal, like Pendennis, whose misadventures in love and gambling—with his aging English cousin, Lady Maria; with her rascally family; and with veterans of the bottle and the card tables—form the most entertaining part of the novel. In other details where Thackeray draws upon his past, he is less successful—notably as George Warrington (grandfather of the George Warrington in *Pendennis*) finds unexpected poverty and struggles in the profession of authorship to support his young wife and child. As these details suggest, Thackeray continues to explore his own history, but with somewhat failing imaginative pow-

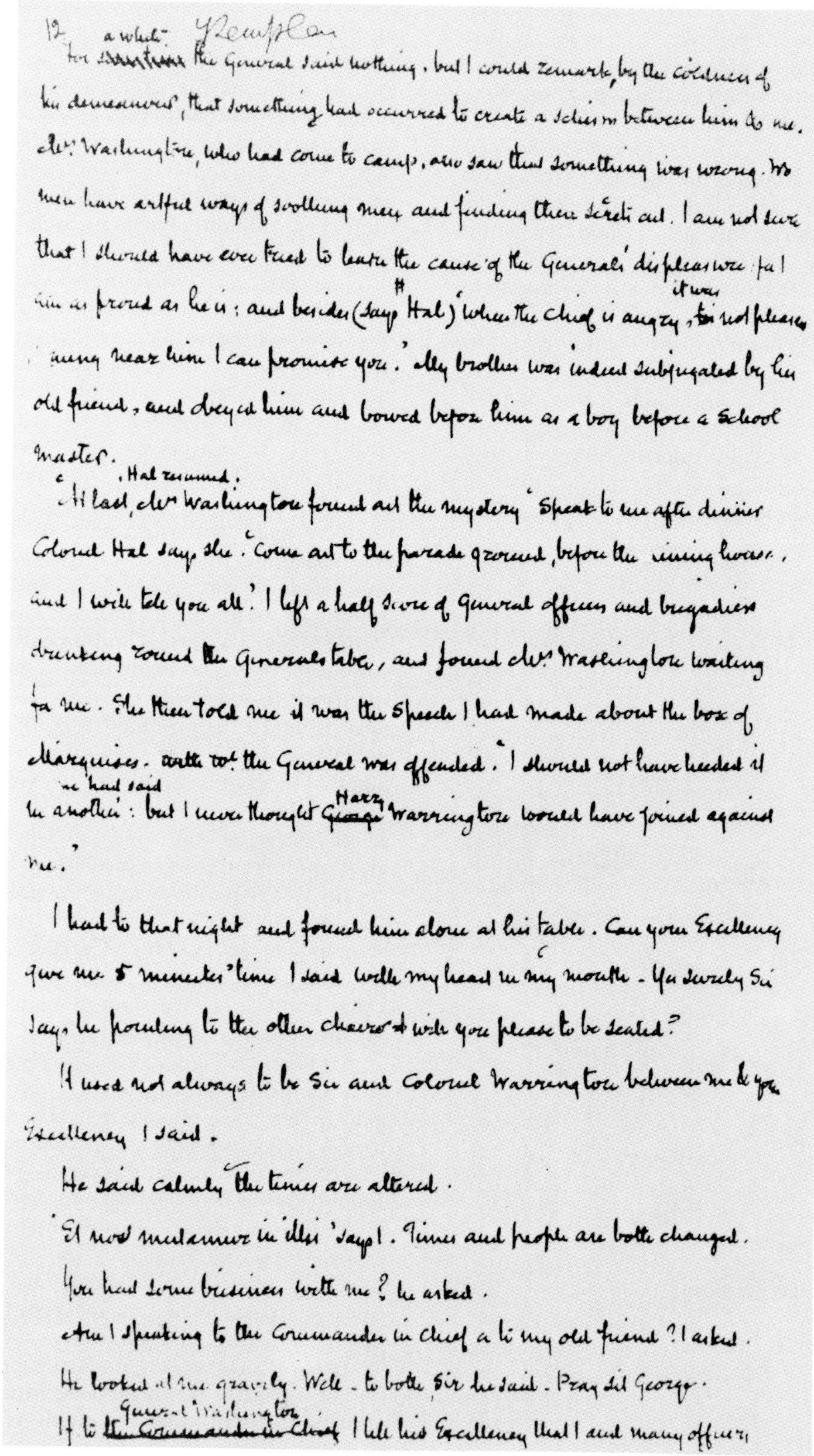

12   a while   Rensselaer

The General said nothing, but I could remark, by the coldness of his demeanour, that something had occurred to create a schism between him & me. Mrs Washington, who had come to camp, also saw that something was wrong. Women have artful ways of soothing men and finding their secrets out. I am not sure that I should have ever tried to learn the cause of the General's displeasure, for him as proud as he is: and besides (says Hal) "when the chief is angry, it was not pleasant being near him I can promise you." My brother was indeed subjugated by his old friend, and obeyed him and bowed before him as a boy before a schoolmaster.

. Hal resumed .

"At last, Mrs Washington found out the mystery. "Speak to me after dinner Colonel Hal says she. "Come out to the parade ground, before the evening lines, and I will tell you all." I left a half score of General officers and brigadiers drinking round the General's table, and found Mrs Washington waiting for me. She then told me it was the speech I had made about the box of Marquises, with which the General was offended." I should not have heeded it he had said in another: but I never thought Harry Warrington would have joined against me."

I went to him that night and found him alone at his table. Can your Excellency give me 5 minutes' time I said with my heart in my mouth - Yes surely Sir says he pointing to the other chairs & will you please to be seated?

It used not always to be Sir and Colonel Warrington between me & you Excellency I said.

He said calmly the times are altered.

"Et nos mutamur in illis "says I. Times and people are both changed.

You had some business with me? he asked.

Am I speaking to the Commander in chief or to my old friend? I asked.

He looked at me gravely. Well - to both, Sir he said - Pray Sir George.

If to the General Washington Commander in Chief I tell his Excellency that I and many officers

Page from the manuscript for The Virginians *(Anderson Galleries, 24 January 1929)*

286

ers. There is a corresponding increase of narrative commentary, but without all of its earlier sparkle and caustic wit. Readers seemed to respond accordingly; the book had large printings but only mediocre sales, and the publishers failed to recover their investments.

While writing *The Virginians*, Thackeray lectured in England and Scotland on the Georges, as he had done on the humorists during the writing of *Henry Esmond*. Some of this income was dissipated when Thackeray took time during July 1857 to stand as an Independent candidate for Parliament from the city of Oxford, for he was defeated by a Liberal and had little to show for his efforts except election expenses of £900. A new source of income opened in 1859, however, when the publisher George Smith made plans to begin a new monthly magazine. Thackeray agreed to write one or two serials for it, receiving £350 per month; and then, as *The Virginians* was moving toward its conclusion in the installment for October 1859, he was named editor of the new periodical, drawing a yearly salary of £1,000. When the *Cornhill Magazine* appeared with the issue for January 1860, it sold a record number of copies for such a periodical: 120,000, with a readership perhaps three or four times larger. Thackeray's success in attracting prominent and knowledgeable contributors held most of that original audience, one immediate result of his success being the doubling of his salary as editor. With the guarantee of such an opulent income, Thackeray began to build himself a new home, which he constructed in the red-brick style of Queen Anne, thereby beginning a revival of that architectural style in London.

For his first serial contribution to the *Cornhill*, Thackeray reworked a play he had written in 1855 called "The Wolves and the Lamb," but for which he had not been able to find a producer. The fictional result was a six-part narrative called *Lovel the Widower* (1860), which rather uneasily mingles a serious narrative tone with farcical events. The circuitous mental processes of the narrator, Batchelor, constitute the main interest of the work—especially as he mingles memories of the past with his current observations of the quietly maneuvering governess, Elizabeth Prior, who shrewdly captures Lovel—but Batchelor tends at times to be displaced by the comical eruptions of minor characters. Thackeray's novelistic contributions to the *Cornhill* began in a low key, for he gave pride of place to Anthony Trollope's novel, *Framley Parsonage*; but Thackeray reserved for himself the final portion of the monthly issues, where he began to publish a series of familiar essays that became known as the *Roundabout Papers* from their characteristic mode of proceeding.

These splendid works represent the culmination not only of the increasing narrative commentary in his fiction but of the discursive persona at the center of his travel books and of his many periodical essays. Whether writing "On a Lazy, Idle Boy," "On Ribbons," on "Thorns in the [Editorial] Cushion," "De Juventute," "On Being Found Out," on "Ogres," "On a Pear-Tree," or "On Some Carp at Sans-Souci," as Thackeray looks "Autour de Mon Chapeau" ("around my hat"), he finds objects, events, and aspects of the human condition that provoke his musing, his laughter, and his irrepressible urge to communicate his processes of thought and feeling. As Thackeray's difficulty in writing novels seemed to increase, and as his health deteriorated so as constantly to threaten his ability to complete his month's installment, he found in the *Roundabout Papers* an especially congenial form of utterance, one in which his humor, his rich allusiveness, and his stylistic ease are especially notable.

After *Lovel the Widower* completed its run, Thackeray published *The Four Georges* in successive installments of the *Cornhill* and then waited two months before opening what was to be his last completed novel, which came out in twenty installments, beginning with the *Cornhill* for January 1861: *The Adventures of Philip on His Way through the World, Shewing Who Robbed Him, Who Helped Him, and Who Passed Him By*. Drawing partly upon material from the unfinished "Shabby Genteel Story" of 1840 and from his struggling days as a writer in the first years of his married life, Thackeray intended *The Adventures of Philip* as a novel of contemporary life that would recapture readers who had been disappointed with *Lovel the Widower*. In spite of protracted efforts, however, Thackeray wrote a dull novel, managing often to repeat himself rather than to render the past in a new imaginative vision. In spite of another horrendous mother-in-law, Mrs. Baynes, who helps provide animation, and Dr. Firmin, who interestingly combines emotional anarchy with polished hypocrisy, the novel generates only an intermittent liveliness. Pendennis is again the narrator, but he is increasingly under the influence of his rigidly moralistic wife. Except for Mrs. Baynes, the female characters tend to be uninteresting, while Philip himself manages to be rebellious and boring at the same time.

Increasingly feeling the pressures focused upon the editorial chair and unhappy with the necessity of reading, evaluating, and often refusing the submissions of other people—duties that of course interfered with the writing of his own works—Thackeray resigned from his editorship of the *Cornhill* in March 1862. A few weeks later, he moved into his new, opulently furnished home in Kensington, in the quiet surroundings of which he enjoyed his remaining months of life accompanied by his two daughters and his recently widowed mother. Following the completion of *The Adventures of Philip* in the August 1862 issue of the *Cornhill* came a visit to Paris and a period of nine months during which he published nothing but a half-dozen Roundabout papers. Then, in May 1863, he began his final novel, *Denis Duval* (1864), set in the late eighteenth century. During the next seven months he completed only four serial installments, but the writing is unusually fresh and accompanies a surprising return to the novel of adventure. The events are recalled by the narrator, Denis, living in contented maturity with his former child-lover, Agnes, now his wife.

Feeling like "an old gentleman sitting in a fine house like the hero at the end of a story," Thackeray had attained ease and comfort, but his ever more

Thackeray's Queen Anne-style house at
2 Palace Green, Kensington

prostrating gastric and urinary attacks had made him pale, drawn, and frequently unable to enjoy what he had won. Yet he was able to make a short Continental trip during part of August, to enjoy a certain amount of nightlife, and to write two final papers for the *Cornhill*. During the latter part of the year, social pleasures and illnesses regularly alternated, his death coming suddenly on 24 December 1863 of a ruptured blood vessel in the brain that followed ten days of gastric upset. He was only fifty-two years of age.

Thackeray's daughter Harriet married Leslie Stephen in 1867, dying eight years later in childbirth. His daughter Anne, who had published a short novel before her father's death, went on to develop a career as a professional writer, producing additional novels as well as critical and biographical works, which included biographical introductions to her father's collected writings. Since Thackeray had asked that no biography of him be written, Anne's introductions to each of the volumes discuss the circumstances in which his individual works were composed and thereby provide biographical commentary on the writings rather than a formal biography of the man himself.

Thackeray left behind a massive body of work—lyric and dramatic as well as narrative and expository—including criticism of art, of travel books, of historical writing, of fiction, of biography, and of memoirs, in addition to his own travel writings, historical and biographical sketches, illustrations, familiar essays, tales, and of course his novels, among which *Vanity Fair*, *Pendennis*, *Henry Esmond*, and *The Newcomes* remain preeminent. In all his work the motive is to increase the reader's moral awareness. Such a task includes the satirical attempt to modify the expectations of his readers, which is accomplished with burlesques of fictional conventions of his day that pretend "to represent scenes of 'life,' " with recurrent instances of mock-heroic deflation, and with a complex, powerful narrative irony. Similarly, by means of frequent structural parallels, of telling metaphorical linkages, and of actions and gestures that are emblematically resonant, he seeks to reveal the observable qualities of actual life. To use his own words, he seeks "to convey as strongly as possible the sentiment of reality," the feel of it, thereby adjuring the sham substitute and evoking instead the consciousness of experienced actuality. Hence his characters, whether recurring in different works or not, all seem to cluster in a single, continuous world thick with solid, palpable objects; and they carry within them an immense power of memory that can instantly evoke their

Thackeray near the end of his life in the library of his home
(National Portrait Gallery)

densely populated past lives. Indeed, Thackeray's deeply felt view of human life as the reflection of the past in the present causes him to be one of the preeminent novelists of memory.

With a man of such wide and diverse reading habits, criticism has tended to keep commenting on the one obvious literary relationship: that between Fielding and Thackeray. Minor English and Continental figures seem to have had as much influence upon him as major ones, but among the latter should be mentioned his favorite classical author, Horace; his nineteenth-century predecessor, Walter Scott; familiar essayists like Montaigne, Addison, and Steele; and the pictorial satirist, William Hogarth, together with Hogarth's followers, Gillray and Cruikshank.

Although Charlotte Brontë praised the author of *Vanity Fair* as a satirist, a number of other Victorian commentators felt that the satirical outlook was too deeply grounded in Thackeray's novels. Even George Eliot was discomfited by the revelation of secret, partly unconscious motives in *Henry Esmond*, though she later judged that for "the majority of people with any intellect" Thackeray was probably "the most powerful of living novelists." The charges

of "cynicism" persisted well into the twentieth century, by which time the sentiment intermittently present in his fiction came to be called "sentimentality," and one formulator termed him a "sentimental cynic." More recent criticism has begun to emphasize by contrast the witty intellectual play of his language and to challenge the often-repeated charge of "carelessness" made by Anthony Trollope and others. One quality, however, has been continuously recognized: the masterfulness of his style.

Periodical Publications:
FICTION:
"The Professor," as Major Goliah O'Grady Gahagan, *Bentley's Miscellany* (September 1837);
"The Yellowplush Correspondence," as Charles J. Yellowplush, *Fraser's Magazine* (November 1837-August 1838; January 1840);
"Some Passages in the Life of Major Gahagan," as Major Goliah O'Grady Gahagan, *New Monthly Magazine* (February 1838-February 1839);
"Catherine: A Story," as Ikey Solomons, *Fraser's Magazine* (May 1839-February 1840);
"The Bedford-Row Conspiracy," anonymous, *New Monthly Magazine* (January-April 1840);
"A Shabby Genteel Story," anonymous, *Fraser's Magazine* (June-October 1840);
"The History of Samuel Titmarsh and the Great Hoggarty Diamond," as Michael Angelo Titmarsh, *Fraser's Magazine* (September-December 1841);
"The Luck of Barry Lyndon: A Romance of the Last Century," as George Fitz-Boodle, *Fraser's Magazine* (January-December 1844);
"Lovel the Widower," as Batchelor, *Cornhill Magazine* (January-June 1860);
"The Adventures of Philip," as Arthur Pendennis, *Cornhill Magazine* (January 1861-August 1862);
"Denis Duval," as Denis Duval, *Cornhill Magazine* (March-June 1864).
NONFICTION:
"Il était un Roi d'Yvetot—Béranger—The King of Brentford," anonymous, *Fraser's Magazine* (May 1834);
"Carlyle's *French Revolution*," anonymous, *Times* (London) (3 August 1837);
"Our Batch of Novels for Christmas 1837," anonymous, *Fraser's Magazine* (January 1838);

"A Diary Relative to George IV and Queen Caroline, by Lady Charlotte Bury," anonymous, *Times* (London) (11 January 1838);

"Strictures on Pictures," as Michael Angelo Titmarsh, *Fraser's Magazine* (June 1838);

"A Second Letter on the Fine Arts," as Michael Angelo Titmarsh, *Fraser's Magazine* (June 1839);

"A Pictorial Rhapsody," as Michael Angelo Titmarsh, *Fraser's Magazine* (June-July 1840);

"George Cruikshank's Works," anonymous, *Westminster Review* (June 1840);

"Going to See a Man Hanged," anonymous, *Fraser's Magazine* (August 1840);

"Fielding's *Works*," anonymous, *Times* (London) (2 September 1840);

"Memorials of Gourmandizing," as Michael Angelo Titmarsh, *Fraser's Magazine* (June 1841);

"Sultan Stork," as Major Goliah O'Grady Gahagan, *Ainsworth's Magazine* (February-March 1842);

"Fitz-Boodle's Confessions," as George Fitz-Boodle, *Fraser's Magazine* (June 1842-November 1843);

"The Legend of Jawbrahim-Heraudee," anonymous, *Punch* (18 June 1842);

"The Last Fifteen Years of the Bourbons," anonymous, *Foreign Quarterly Review* (July 1842);

"Mrs. Tickletoby's Lectures on English History," anonymous, *Punch* (2 July-1 October 1842);

"Bluebeard's Ghost," as Michael Angelo Titmarsh, *Fraser's Magazine* (October 1843);

"The History of the Next French Revolution," anonymous, *Punch* (24 February-20 April 1844);

"Jesse's *Life of George Brummell, Esq.*," anonymous, *Morning Chronicle* (6 May 1844);

"Greenwich—Whitebait," as Lancelot Wagstaff, *New Monthly Magazine* (July 1844);

"Wanderings of our Fat Contributor," as the Fat Contributor, *Punch* (3 August 1844-8 February 1845);

"Picture Gossip," as Michael Angelo Titmarsh, *Fraser's Magazine* (June 1845);

"A Legend of the Rhine," anonymous, *George Cruikshank's Table Book* (June-December 1845);

"Jeames's Diary," as C. Jeames De La Pluche, *Punch* (8 November 1845-7 February 1846);

"The Snobs of England. By One of Themselves," anonymous, *Punch* (23 February 1846-27 February 1847);

"Proposals for a Continuation of *Ivanhoe*," as Michael Angelo Titmarsh, *Fraser's Magazine* (August-September 1846);

"*Punch*'s Prize Novelists," anonymous, *Punch* (3 April-9 October 1847);

"Travels in London," as Spec, *Punch* (20 November 1847-25 March 1848);

"Mr. Brown's Letters to a Young Man about Town," as Mr. Brown, *Punch* (24 March-18 August 1849);

"The Dignity of Literature," *Morning Chronicle* (12 January 1850);

"The Proser," as Dr. Solomon Pacifico, *Punch* (20 April-3 August 1850);

"Roundabout Papers," as Mr. Roundabout, *Cornhill Magazine* (January 1860-November 1863);

"The Four Georges," anonymous, *Cornhill Magazine* (July-October 1860).

Letters:

The Letters and Private Papers of William Makepeace Thackeray, edited by Gordon N. Ray (4 volumes, London: Oxford University Press, 1945-1946).

Bibliographies:

Henry S. Van Duzer, *A Thackeray Library* (Port Washington, N.Y.: Kennikat Press, 1965);

Edward M. White, "Thackeray's Contributions to *Fraser's Magazine*," *Studies in Bibliography*, 19 (1966): 67-84;

Dudley Flamm, *Thackeray's Critics: An Annotated Bibliography of British and American Criticism 1836-1901* (Chapel Hill: University of North Carolina Press, 1967);

John C. Olmsted, *Thackeray and His Twentieth-Century Critics: An Annotated Bibliography, 1900-1975* (New York & London: Garland, 1977).

Biographies:

"Lewis Melville," (Lewis Benjamin), *William Makepeace Thackeray: A Biography* (2 volumes, London: John Lane, 1910);

Lionel Stevenson, *The Showman of Vanity Fair* (New York: Scribners, 1947);

Gordon N. Ray, *William Makepeace Thackeray: The Uses of Adversity* (New York: McGraw-Hill, 1955);

Ray, *William Makepeace Thackeray: The Age of Wisdom* (New York: McGraw-Hill, 1958);

Ann Monsarrat, *An Uneasy Victorian: Thackeray the Man* (New York: Dodd, Mead, 1980).

References:

John Carey, *Thackeray: Prodigal Genius* (London:

Faber & Faber, 1977);

Robert A. Colby, *Fiction with a Purpose* (Blooming-ton: Indiana University Press, 1967);

Colby, *Thackeray's Canvass of Humanity* (Columbus: Ohio State University Press, 1979);

Colby, "William Makepeace Thackeray," in *Victorian Fiction: A Second Guide to Research*, edited by George H. Ford (New York: Modern Language Association of America, 1978), pp. 114-142;

Costerus, special Thackeray issue, N.S. 2 (1974);

G. Armour Craig, "On the Style of *Vanity Fair*," in *Style in Prose Fiction*, edited by Harold C. Martin (New York: Columbia University Press, 1959), pp. 87-113;

John W. Dodds, *Thackeray: A Critical Portrait* (New York: Oxford University Press, 1941);

A. E. Dyson, "*Vanity Fair*: An Irony Against Heroes," *Critical Quarterly*, 6 (1964): 11-31;

Spencer L. Eddy, Jr., *The Founding of "The Cornhill Magazine"* (Muncie, Indiana: Ball State University Press, 1970);

Martin Fido, "*The History of Pendennis*: A Reconsideration," *Essays in Criticism*, 14 (1964): 363-379;

Philip Gaskell, "Thackeray, *Henry Esmond*, 1852," in his *From Writer to Reader: Studies in Editorial Method* (Oxford: Clarendon Press, 1978), pp. 156-182;

John Hagan, "'Bankruptcy of His Heart': The Unfulfilled Life of Henry Esmond," *Nineteenth-Century Fiction*, 27 (1972-1973): 293-316;

Hagan, "*Vanity Fair*: Becky Brought to Book Again," *Studies in the Novel*, 7 (1975): 479-506;

Edgar F. Harden, "The Discipline and Significance of Form in *Vanity Fair*," *PMLA*, 82 (1967): 530-541;

Harden, *The Emergence of Thackeray's Serial Fiction* (Athens: University of Georgia Press, 1979);

Harden, "The Fields of Mars in *Vanity Fair*," *Tennessee Studies in Literature*, 10 (1965): 123-132;

Harden, "A Partial Outline for Thackeray's *The Virginians*," *Journal of English and Germanic Philology*, 75 (1976): 168-187;

Harden, "The Serial Structure of Thackeray's *Pendennis*," *Revue de l'Université d'Ottawa*, 45 (1975): 162-180;

Barbara Hardy, *The Exposure of Luxury: Radical Themes in Thackeray* (London: Owen, 1972);

John Harvey, "'A Voice Concurrent or Prophetical': The Illustrated Novels of W. M. Thackeray," in his *Victorian Novelists and their Illustrators* (London: Sidgwick & Jackson, 1970), pp. 76-102;

Keith Hollingsworth, *The Newgate Novel* (Detroit: Wayne State University Press, 1963);

Wolfgang Iser, "The Reader as a Component Part of the Realistic Novel: Esthetic Effects in Thackeray's *Vanity Fair*," "Self-Reduction: The Self-Communication of Subjectivity in Autobiographical Fiction. Wm. Thackeray: *Henry Esmond*," in his *The Implied Reader* (Baltimore & London: Johns Hopkins University Press, 1974);

John A. Lester, Jr., "Thackeray's Narrative Technique," *PMLA*, 69 (1954): 392-409;

George Levine, "Thackeray: 'The Legitimate High Priest of Truth' and the Problematics of the Real," "Thackeray: Some Elements of Realism," "*Pendennis*: The Virtue of the Dilettante's Unbelief," in his *The Realistic Imagination* (Chicago & London: University of Chicago Press, 1981);

John Loofbourow, *Thackeray and the Form of Fiction* (Princeton: Princeton University Press, 1964);

William H. Marshall, "Dramatic Irony in *Henry Esmond*," *Revue des Langues Vivantes*, 1 (1961): 35-42;

Juliet McMaster, *Thackeray: The Major Novels* (Toronto: University of Toronto Press, 1971);

McMaster, "Thackeray's Things: Time's Local Habitation," *The Victorian Experience*, edited by Richard A. Levine (Athens: Ohio University Press, 1976), pp. 49-86;

Rowland D. McMaster, "'An Honorable Emulation of the Author of *The Newcomes*': James and Thackeray," *Nineteenth-Century Fiction*, 32 (1977-1978): 399-419;

McMaster, "The Pygmalion Motif in *The Newcomes*," *Nineteenth-Century Fiction*, 29 (1974-1975): 22-39;

J. Hillis Miller, *The Form of Victorian Fiction* (Notre Dame & London: University of Notre Dame Press, 1968);

Isadore G. Mudge and M. Earl Sears, *A Thackeray Dictionary* (New York: Dutton, 1910);

Lidmila Pantůčková, "Thackeray as a Reader and Critic of French Literature," *Brno Studies in English*, 9 (1970): 37-126;

Pantůčková, *W. M. Thackeray as a Critic of Literature* (Brno, Czechoslovakia: Purkyne University Press, 1972);

Pantůčková, "W. M. Thackeray's Literary Criticism in the *Morning Chronicle* (1844-1848)," *Brno Studies in English*, 2 (1960): 79-111;

K. C. Phillipps, *The Language of Thackeray* (London: Deutsch, 1978);

Arthur Pollard, ed., *Thackeray. "Vanity Fair." A*

Casebook (London & Basingstoke: Macmillan, 1978);

Jack P. Rawlins, *Thackeray's Novels: A Fiction That Is True* (Berkeley, Los Angeles & London: University of California Press, 1974);

Gordon N. Ray, *The Buried Life: A Study of the Relation between Thackeray's Fiction and His Personal History* (London: Oxford University Press, 1952);

Ray, "*Vanity Fair*: One Version of the Novelist's Responsibility," *Essays by Divers Hands*, N.S. 23 (London: Oxford University Press, 1950);

Winslow Rogers, "Thackeray's Self-Consciousness," in *The Worlds of Victorian Fiction*, edited by Jerome H. Buckley (Cambridge: Harvard University Press, 1975), pp. 149-163;

George Saintsbury, *A Consideration of Thackeray* (London: Oxford University Press, 1931);

M. Corona Sharp, "Sympathetic Mockery: A Study of the Narrator's Character in *Vanity Fair*," *ELH*, 29 (1962): 324-336;

Robin Ann Sheets, "Art and Artistry in *Vanity Fair*," *ELH*, 42 (1975): 420-432;

Peter L. Shillingsburg, "The First Edition of Thackeray's *Pendennis*," *Papers of the Bibliographical Society of America*, 66 (1972): 35-49;

Shillingsburg, "The Printing, Proofreading, and Publishing of Thackeray's *Vanity Fair*," *Studies in Bibliography*, 34 (1981): 118-145;

Shillingsburg, "Textual Problems in Editing Thackeray," *Editing Nineteenth-Century Fiction*, edited by Jane Millgate (New York & London: Garland, 1978), pp. 41-60;

Joan Stevens, "A Roundabout Ride," *Victorian Studies*, 13 (1969-1970): 53-70;

Stevens, "Thackeray's *Vanity Fair*," *Review of English Literature*, 6 (1965): 19-38;

Lionel Stevenson, "William Makepeace Thackeray," in *Victorian Fiction: A Guide to Research*, edited by Stevenson (Cambridge: Harvard University Press, 1964), pp. 154-187;

Studies in the Novel, special Thackeray issue, 13 (1981);

Jean Sudrann, " 'The Philosopher's Property': Thackeray and the Use of Time," *Victorian Studies*, 10 (1966-1967): 359-388;

M. G. Sundell, ed., *Twentieth Century Interpretations of "Vanity Fair"* (Englewood Cliffs: Prentice-Hall, 1969);

John A. Sutherland, "*Henry Esmond*: The Shaping Power of Contract," in his *Victorian Novelists and Publishers* (London: Athlone Press, 1976), pp. 101-116;

Sutherland, *Thackeray at Work* (London: Athlone Press, 1974);

Henri-A. Talon, "Time and Memory in Thackeray's *Henry Esmond*," *Review of English Studies*, 13 (1962): 147-156;

Myron Taube, "Contrast as a Principle of Structure in *Vanity Fair*," *Nineteenth-Century Fiction*, 18 (1963-1964): 119-135;

The Thackeray Newsletter (1975-present);

John Tilford, "The Love Theme of *Henry Esmond*," *PMLA*, 67 (1952): 684-701;

Geoffrey Tillotson and Donald Hawes, eds., *Thackeray: The Critical Heritage* (London: Routledge & Kegan Paul, 1968);

Tillotson, *Thackeray the Novelist* (London: Cambridge University Press, 1954);

Kathleen Tillotson, "Introductory," "*Vanity Fair*," in her *Novels of the Eighteen-Forties* (Oxford: Clarendon Press, 1954), pp. 1-156, 224-256;

Alexander Welsh, ed., *Thackeray: A Collection of Critical Essays* (Englewood Cliffs, N.J.: Prentice-Hall, 1968);

James H. Wheatley, *Patterns in Thackeray's Fiction* (Cambridge & London: M.I.T. Press, 1969);

Ann Y. Wilkinson, "The Tomeavesian Way of Knowing the World: Technique and Meaning in *Vanity Fair*," *ELH*, 32 (1965): 370-387;

Ioan M. Williams, *Thackeray* (London: Evans, 1968);

George A. Worth, "The Unity of *Henry Esmond*," *Nineteenth-Century Fiction*, 15 (1960-1961): 345-353.

Papers:

The British Library has notebook and page proofs for *Denis Duval*, manuscripts for *The Second Funeral of Napoleon* and "The Wolves and the Lamb," diaries, notebooks, and correspondence; the Charterhouse School Library has much of the manuscript for *The Newcomes*; Harvard University has portions of the manuscript for *The Four Georges*, *Pendennis*, *Roundabout Papers*, and *Stubbs's Calendar*, and correspondence; the Huntington Library has parts of the manuscripts for *Adventures of Philip*, *The English Humourists*, *The Four Georges*, *Lovel the Widower*, *Our Street*, and *Roundabout Papers*, fragments of minor unpublished manuscripts, and correspondence; the Pierpont Morgan Library has partial or complete manuscripts for *Denis Duval*, *The Four Georges*, *Lovel the Widower*, *The Rose and the Ring*, *Vanity Fair*, and *The Virginians*, fragments of minor unpublished manuscripts, diaries, notebooks, and correspondence; the National Library of Scotland has a small portion of the manuscript for *Denis*

Duval and correspondence; at the New York Public Library, the Arents Collection has a small amount of page proofs for *The Adventures of Philip*, while the Berg Collection has partial manuscripts for *The English Humourists*, *The Newcomes*, and *Roundabout Papers*, fragmentary portions of other published works, fragments of minor unpublished manuscripts, diaries, notebooks, and correspondence, and the Manuscript Division has a notebook for *Henry Esmond* and fragments of minor unpublished manuscripts; at New York University, the Fales Collection contains fragmentary portions of published works and correspondence; at Princeton University, the Parrish Collection has correspondence, and the Taylor Collection contains fragmentary portions of published and unpublished

works and correspondence; the *Punch* office has correspondence; the Rosenbach Foundation Museum contains a notebook for *The Four Georges* and correspondence; Trinity College, Cambridge University, has almost all of the manuscript for *Henry Esmond*; the Humanities Research Center of the University of Texas at Austin has a small portion of the manuscript for *Our Street*, proof plates for *Doctor Birch*, *The Kickleburys on the Rhine*, and *Mrs. Perkins's Ball*, fragmentary portions of published works, and correspondence; and Yale University has a small portion of the manuscript for *The Adventures of Philip*, galley proofs for *The Four Georges*, *Lovel the Widower*, and *The Adventures of Philip*, a notebook for *The Virginians*, and correspondence.

Anthony Trollope

Juliet McMaster
University of Alberta

BIRTH: London, 24 April 1815, to Thomas Anthony and Frances Milton Trollope.

MARRIAGE: 11 June 1844 to Rose Heseltine; children: Henry Merivale and Frederick Anthony.

DEATH: London, 6 December 1882.

BOOKS: *The Macdermots of Ballycloran* (3 volumes, London: Newby, 1847; 1 volume, Philadelphia: Peterson, 1871);
The Kellys and the O'Kellys; or, Landlords and Tenants: A Tale of Irish Life (3 volumes, London: Colburn, 1848; 1 volume, New York: Munro, 1882);
La Vendée: An Historical Romance (3 volumes, London: Colburn, 1850);
The Warden (London: Longman, Brown, Green & Longmans, 1855; New York: Dick & Fitzgerald, 1862);
Barchester Towers (3 volumes, London: Longman, Brown, Green, Longmans & Roberts, 1857; 1 volume, New York: Dick & Fitzgerald, 1860);
The Three Clerks: A Novel (3 volumes, London: Bentley, 1858; 1 volume, New York: Harper, 1860);

Doctor Thorne: A Novel (3 volumes, London: Chapman & Hall, 1858; 1 volume, New York: Harper, 1858);
The Bertrams: A Novel (3 volumes, London: Chapman & Hall, 1859; 1 volume, New York: Harper, 1859);
The West Indies and the Spanish Main (London: Chapman & Hall, 1859; New York: Harper, 1860);
Castle Richmond: A Novel (3 volumes, London: Chapman & Hall, 1860; 1 volume, New York: Harper, 1860);
Framley Parsonage (3 volumes, London: Smith, Elder, 1861; 1 volume, New York: Harper, 1861);
Tales of All Countries (2 volumes, London: Chapman & Hall, 1861-1863);
Orley Farm (20 monthly parts, London: Chapman & Hall, 1861-1862; 1 volume, New York: Harper, 1862);
The Struggles of Brown, Jones, and Robinson, by One of the Firm (New York: Harper, 1862; London: Smith, Elder, 1870);
North America, 2 volumes (London: Chapman & Hall, 1862; pirated American edition, New York: Harper, 1862; authorized American

(Mansell Collection)

edition, New York: Lippincott, 1862);

Rachel Ray: A Novel (2 volumes, London: Chapman & Hall, 1863; 1 volume, New York: Harper, 1863);

The Small House at Allington (2 volumes, London: Smith, Elder, 1864; 1 volume, New York: Harper, 1864);

Can You Forgive Her? (20 monthly parts, London: Chapman & Hall, 1864-1865; 1 volume, New York: Harper, 1865);

Hunting Sketches (London: Chapman & Hall, 1865; Hartford, Conn.: Mitchell, 1929);

Miss Mackenzie (2 volumes, London: Chapman & Hall, 1865; 1 volume, New York: Harper, 1865);

The Belton Estate (3 volumes, London: Chapman & Hall, 1866; pirated American edition, 1 volume, New York: Harper, 1866; authorized American edition, 1 volume, New York: Lippincott, 1866);

Travelling Sketches (London: Chapman & Hall, 1866);

Clergymen of the Church of England (London: Chapman & Hall, 1866);

The Claverings (New York: Harper, 1867; 2 volumes, London: Smith, Elder, 1867);

Nina Balatka: The Story of a Maiden of Prague, 2 volumes (Edinburgh & London: Blackwood, 1867; London & New York: Oxford University Press, 1951);

The Last Chronicle of Barset (32 weekly parts, London: Smith, Elder, 1867; 1 volume, New York: Harper, 1867);

Lotta Schmidt and Other Stories (London: Strahan, 1867; London & New York: Ward & Lock, 1883);

Linda Tressel (2 volumes, Edinburgh & London: Blackwood, 1868; 1 volume, Boston: Littell & Gay, 1868);

He Knew He Was Right (32 weekly parts, London: Virtue, 1868-1869; 1 volume, New York: Harper, 1870);

Phineas Finn: The Irish Member (2 volumes, London: Virtue, 1869; 1 volume, New York: Harper, 1869);

Did He Steal It? A Comedy in Three Acts (London: Privately printed, 1869);

The Vicar of Bullhampton (11 monthly parts, London: Bradbury & Evans, 1869-1870; pirated American edition, 1 volume, New York: Harper, 1870; authorized American edition, 1 volume, New York: Lippincott, 1870);

An Editor's Tales (London: Strahan, 1870);

The Commentaries of Caesar (Edinburgh & London: Blackwood, 1870; Philadelphia: Lippincott, 1870);

Ralph the Heir (19 monthly parts, London: Hurst & Blackett, 1870-1871; 1 volume, New York: Harper, 1871);

Sir Harry Hotspur of Humblethwaite (London: Hurst & Blackett, 1871; New York: Harper, 1871);

The Golden Lion of Granpère (London: Tinsley, 1872; New York: Harper, 1872);

The Eustace Diamonds (New York: Harper, 1872; 3 volumes, London: Chapman & Hall, 1873);

Australia and New Zealand (2 volumes, London: Chapman & Hall, 1873);

Lady Anna (2 volumes, London: Chapman & Hall, 1874; 1 volume, New York: Harper, 1874);

Phineas Redux (2 volumes, London: Chapman & Hall, 1874; 1 volume, New York: Harper, 1874);

Harry Heathcote of Gangoil: A Tale of Australian Bush Life (London: Low, Marston, Low & Searle, 1874; New York: Harper, 1874);

The Way We Live Now (20 monthly parts, London:

Chapman & Hall, 1874-1875; 1 volume, New York: Harper, 1875);

The Prime Minister (8 monthly parts, London: Chapman & Hall, 1875-1876; 1 volume, New York: Harper, 1876);

The American Senator (3 volumes, London: Chapman & Hall, 1877; 1 volume, New York: Harper, 1877);

Christmas at Thompson Hall (New York: Harper, 1877; London: Low, 1885);

The Lady of Lannay (New York: Harper, 1877);

Is He Popenjoy? A Novel (3 volumes, London: Chapman & Hall, 1878; 1 volume, New York: Harper, 1878);

How the "Mastiffs" Went to Iceland (London: Virtue, 1878);

South Africa (2 volumes, London: Chapman & Hall, 1878);

An Eye for an Eye (2 volumes, London: Chapman & Hall, 1879; 1 volume, New York: Harper, 1879);

John Caldigate (3 volumes, London: Chapman & Hall, 1879; 1 volume, New York: Harper, 1879);

Cousin Henry: A Novel (2 volumes, London: Chapman & Hall, 1879; 1 volume, New York: Munro, 1879);

Thackeray (London: Macmillan, 1879; New York: Harper, 1879);

The Duke's Children: A Novel (3 volumes, London: Chapman & Hall, 1880; 1 volume, New York: Munro, 1880);

The Life of Cicero, 2 volumes (London: Chapman & Hall, 1880; New York: Harper, 1881);

Dr. Wortle's School: A Novel (New York: Harper, 1880; 2 volumes, London: Chapman & Hall, 1881);

Ayala's Angel (3 volumes, London: Chapman & Hall, 1881; 1 volume, New York: Harper, 1881);

Why Frau Frohmann Raised Her Prices, and Other Stories (London: Isbister, 1882; New York: Harper, 1882);

The Fixed Period: A Novel (2 volumes, Edinburgh & London: Blackwood, 1882; 1 volume, New York: Harper, 1882);

Lord Palmerston (London: Isbister, 1882);

Marion Fay: A Novel (3 volumes, London: Chapman & Hall, 1882; 1 volume, New York: Harper, 1882);

Kept in the Dark: A Novel (2 volumes, London: Chatto & Windus, 1882; 1 volume, New York: Harper, 1882);

The Two Heroines of Plumplington (New York: Munro, 1882; London: Deutsch, 1953);

Not if I Know It (New York: Munro, 1883);

Mr. Scarborough's Family (3 volumes, London: Chatto & Windus, 1883; 1 volume, New York: Harper, 1883);

The Landleaguers (3 volumes, London: Chatto & Windus, 1883; 1 volume, New York: Munro, 1883);

An Autobiography (2 volumes, Edinburgh & London: Blackwood, 1883; 1 volume, New York: Harper, 1883);

Alice Dugdale and Other Stories (Leipzig: Tauchnitz, 1883);

La Mère Bauche and Other Stories (Leipzig: Tauchnitz, 1883; New York: Munro, 1884);

The Mistletoe Bough and Other Stories (Leipzig: Tauchnitz, 1883);

An Old Man's Love (2 volumes, Edinburgh & London: Blackwood, 1884; 1 volume, New York: Lovell, 1884);

The Noble Jilt: A Comedy, edited by Michael Sadleir (London: Constable, 1923);

London Tradesmen, edited by Michael Sadleir (London: Mathews & Marrot, 1927; New York: Scribners, 1927);

Four Lectures, edited by M. L. Parrish (London: Constable, 1938);

The Tireless Traveller: Twenty Letters to the "Liverpool Mercury" 1875, edited by Bradford Allen Booth (Berkeley & Los Angeles: University of California Press, 1941);

Novels and Tales, edited by J. Hampden (London: Pilot Press, 1946);

The Parson's Daughter and Other Stories, edited by J. Hampden (London: Folio Society, 1949);

The Spotted Dog and Other Stories (London: Pan, 1950);

Mary Gresley and Other Stories, edited by J. Hampden (London: Folio Society, 1951);

The New Zealander, edited by N. John Hall (London: Oxford University Press, 1972).

COLLECTIONS: *The Oxford Illustrated Trollope*, edited by M. Sadleir and F. Page (15 volumes, Oxford: Oxford University Press, 1948-1954);

Selected Works of Anthony Trollope, edited by N. John Hall (62 volumes, New York: Arno, 1980).

"I do lay claim to whatever merit should be accorded to me for persevering diligence in my profession," Anthony Trollope wrote in one of the concluding paragraphs of his *Autobiography* (1883). No one has ever been able to deny him that claim: as the author of some forty-seven novels, and many further volumes of travels, sketches, criticism, and short fiction, he was fully justified in his pride in the quantity of his production. He was more modest about claiming quality; but the continued sale of his many novels through a century after his death, and the increasing testimony among critics as to the power and subtlety of his work, make it clear that he did indeed achieve "the permanence of success" that he would not himself lay claim to. Among the great nineteenth-century novelists of England, he stands in critical reputation close after Jane Austen, Charles Dickens, and George Eliot; and perhaps level with Charlotte and Emily Brontë, and with Scott and Thackeray, whom he admired and emulated. He certainly wrote more than any of them.

Success was particularly important to him because of a grinding sense of failure in his childhood. The narrative shape that he gives to his life in his *Autobiography* is the story of an ugly duckling who through great trials and great feats came to be recognized as a swan. His childhood was unhappy, by his own account miserable. His father was a down-at-heel gentleman and scholar who failed at the law, failed at scholarship, and then took to farming and failed at that, too. Anthony was sent as a day student to Harrow, where the boarders sneered at him for the muddy boots he incurred by his long walk to school; then as a boarder to Winchester, where he was often beaten; and then back to Harrow. He was insufficiently supplied with money and suffered deep embarrassment among his peers and before the masters. Though coveting popularity, he felt like a pariah, and left school with the conviction that

Frances Trollope's unsuccessful Cincinnati emporium

he had "been flogged oftener than any human being alive."

During his school years the family was in poor circumstances. His father was unable to support them, so his mother, the vigorous Frances Trollope, took matters into her own hands. In 1827 she made an excursion to America, where she set up a bazaar in Cincinnati with the intention of making money by selling gewgaws and objets d'art. This enterprise failed, but her experience prompted her to write; and on her return she sold her book, *The Domestic Manners of the Americans* (1832), which was not the less a success for being highly critical of American mores. Thereafter she supported the family by her pen, even when they had to escape ahead of the bailiffs to Bruges in Belgium. Here she continued to write in the intervals of nursing a tubercular son and daughter and her husband, who had long been subject to bouts of illness. All three died between 1834 and 1835. Fanny Trollope continued to write through a long career, during which she produced more than forty books. She was an inspiration to her children, particularly her surviving sons, Thomas Adolphus and Anthony, who both took to "the family business" of writing in due course.

Anthony seems to have been viewed as a burden in the family, being in Bruges "that most hopeless of human beings, a hobbledehoy of nineteen." In 1834 he became an usher at a school in Brussels, but then returned to England to become a junior clerk in the post office. Although he had now found a career, his life did not immediately improve. From 1835 to 1841 he got into various scrapes over money and women. Some of these are described in the chapters on Charley Tudor, Johnny Eames, and Phineas Finn in his novels *The Three Clerks* (1858), *The Small House at Allington* (1864), and *Phineas Finn* (1869). Aside from these novels and a number of his short stories that are similarly based on his own experience, Trollope's fiction does not in any direct way recreate his life. At a conscious level, at least, he worked on a principle of abstracting himself from his fiction, laying his own identity aside.

In the summer of 1841, when he was twenty-six, he took the chance of changing his unsatisfactory life by successfully applying for the position of a post office surveyor's clerk in Ireland. Ireland was for Trollope what the fairy godmother was for Cinderella; it transformed him and opened out new vistas in his life. "There had clung to me a feeling that I had been looked upon always as an evil, an encumbrance, a useless thing,—as a creature of whom those connected with him had to be ashamed. . . . But from the day on which I set my

Rose Heseltine, Trollope's wife

foot in Ireland all these evils went away from me." In Ireland he became good at his job and valued in it; he married Rose Heseltine, who was his devoted wife and literary assistant for the rest of his life; he began to hunt; and he wrote his first novels.

Trollope did not, like Dickens, find his métier and his public at once. His first three novels were tentative and experimental, and did not sell well. He tells how he conceived the idea for his first novel, *The Macdermots of Ballycloran* (1847), in a preface to it and in the *Autobiography*. Being delayed in the small Irish town of Drumsna, he took a walk with his friend John Merivale and came across "the modern ruins of a country house. It was one of the most melancholy spots I ever visited. . . . We wandered about the place, suggesting to each other causes for the misery we saw there, and while I was still among the ruined walls and decayed beams I fabricated the plot of *The Macdermots of Ballycloran*." (It is characteristic that Trollope should first have his imagination stirred by a place, a country residence which prompted the creation of its residents: the same thing was subsequently to happen with *The Warden*, 1855.) The tumbledown estate led Trollope to envisage a set of characters and a situation that would lead to its desolation; and his first novel is in the

tragic, not the comic mode. Euphemia Macdermot, the daughter of an old Irish family that has seen better days, is seduced by an English police captain, Ussher. Finding the couple together, her outraged brother, Thady, strikes Ussher, who dies as a result. Thady is put on trial and condemned to death, and his sister rather improbably dies in the courtroom from complications of pregnancy. The plot is enlarged by Thady's dealings with a group of Irish nationalist conspirators.

Trollope's publisher was T. C. Newby of Mortimer Street, who also published Emily Brontë's *Wuthering Heights* and Anne Brontë's *Agnes Grey* at about the same time. Such a crop seems to have been due to luck rather than good management on Newby's part, for he did not treat his authors courteously. The Brontë novels were published without benefit of proofreading, and Trollope received no remuneration and no accounting for the sales of his first novel. As Charlotte Brontë said in a letter of 1847, "If Mr. Newby always does business in this way, few authors would like to have him for their publisher a second time." It is not surprising that Trollope went to another publisher, Henry Colburn, with his next novel.

The Kellys and the O'Kellys (1848) is also set in Ireland, and presents high and low Irish life and the relations of landlords and tenants, fortunes and fortune-hunters. This novel also deals sympathetically with the Irish and their problems, but it sold only 140 copies in the first edition, in spite of being briefly noticed in the *Times*. "It is evident that readers do not like novels on Irish subjects as well as on others," his publishers told him. Eager to take advice, Trollope altogether changed his subject matter for his next novel, *La Vendée* (1850), a historical romance set in eighteenth-century France; on this work he made his first £20 by writing, but he still found no substantial readership. *The Macdermots of Ballycloran* and *The Kellys and the O'Kellys* were later discovered and enjoyed by readers who had learned to admire Trollope's subsequent works, but *La Vendée* has never been much read.

In the early 1850s Trollope's post office work absorbed all his energies. He was assigned to work out the routes for rural deliveries, first in a district in Ireland and then in a number of counties in England, particularly in the west. He did his work with zeal, riding over all the routes himself, and determined to make it possible that a letter could be delivered to every remote residence in his district. It was while visiting the close of Salisbury Cathedral that he conceived the story of *The Warden*, the first in the series of novels about his invented county of

Barsetshire that was to make him famous.

The Warden was published in 1855, and its success, and that of its sequel, Barchester Towers (1857), marked the public's recognition of a new major novelist. In The Warden appear many of the characteristics that were to distinguish his work as a whole: his delicacy in the handling of nuances of character, his reservations about moral zeal, his propensity to view his characters in their public and professional capacities as well as in their private and domestic roles, and his qualified conservatism according to which the High Church and landowning classes are portrayed with affectionate sympathy as well as irony. The warden himself, Mr. Harding, a gentle, middle-aged innocent, has accepted a sinecure administering charitable monies for the maintenance of twelve bedesmen. A zealous young man, John Bold, who is in love with the warden's daughter Eleanor, nevertheless brings public attention to the fact that the warden, rather than the bedesmen, is the main beneficiary of the charity. Sides are taken, legal proceedings are instituted, the daily Jupiter (a satirical representation of the Times) and even the attorney-general are drawn into the burgeoning issue. The book is to some extent a mock epic, making fun of the "heroes" John Bold and Tom Towers, who arm themselves in the conflict against doughtily clad ecclesiastics, and humorously dwelling on battles at tea parties and campaigns conducted at whist. In the midst of this war, the warden, whose conscience has been touched even though he is told his side will win, simply resigns his position. As the furor dies down, no new warden is appointed, and the twelve bedesmen are left uncared for. The zeal of the reformers, despite the apparent justice of their cause, has done nobody any good.

In Barchester Towers Trollope reintroduced many of the same characters, including Mr. Harding and his vigorous son-in-law Dr. Grantly, an archdeacon and a pillar of the church establishment. The plot turns on the machinations of the greasy, Low Church Mr. Slope, chaplain to the mild new bishop of Barchester, Dr. Proudie, and favorite of the bishop's domineering wife. Mr. Slope's marital and professional ambitions become amusingly involved as he dangles after two attractive ladies, Eleanor Bold, now a widow, and the siren-like Signora Vesey Neroni, while trying at the same time to stay in the good graces of his exacting patroness. Eleanor, the heroine, similarly has more than one marital prospect: besides the persistent Mr. Slope himself—whom finally she can dismiss only by administering a resounding slap in the face—she has

Bertie Stanhope as a hopeful suitor. He is a good-natured dilettante, brother to the seductive signora, and he too likes the thought of getting Eleanor and her money. The reader is induced to interest himself in this matter of Eleanor's choice among rogues, and at one point the narrator addresses him directly: "But let the gentle-hearted reader be under no apprehension whatsoever. It is not destined that Eleanor shall marry Mr. Slope or Bertie Stanhope. And here, perhaps, it may be allowed to the novelist to explain his views on a very important point in the art of telling tales. He ventures to reprobate that system which goes so far to violate all proper confidence between the author and his readers, by maintaining nearly to the end of the third volume a mystery as to the fate of their favourite personage.... Our doctrine is, that the author and the reader should move along together in full confidence with each other." Such an authorial intrusion was offensive to Henry James, who took Trollope to task for his propensity to give himself away, to admit while telling his story that the story is merely a fiction. More recent critics, however, such as James Kincaid, have found much to praise in Trollope's art of maintaining an intimate relation with his reader.

The other novels in the Barset series, with which Trollope was engaged intermittently over the next decade, were Doctor Thorne (1858), Framley Parsonage (1861), The Small House at Allington (1864), and The Last Chronicle of Barset (1867). Each of these novels is distinct and separable from the rest, with its own plot and new major characters. So far as the series has a unity, it is supplied by the setting, the quiet cathedral city of Barchester with its surrounding town, villages, and ancestral estates of Barsetshire; by its continuing concern with ecclesiastical matters; and by a few recurring characters. Mr. Harding, the perpetual innocent, is in the tradition of Cervantes's Don Quixote, Sterne's Uncle Toby, Dickens's Mr. Pickwick, and Thackeray's Colonel Newcome. His son-in-law the archdeacon, vociferous and bigoted, is nonetheless unable to dominate the gentle old man. The Barsetshire aristocrats are the arrogant De Courcys of Courcy Castle and the duke of Omnium of Omnium Gatherum Castle (Trollope has often been criticized for his facetious names). In the henpecked Bishop Proudie and his outspoken virago of a wife, Trollope first developed a continuing concern with the distribution of power in marriage, and indeed in all human relations. Later in the series, as a result of overhearing at his club an impatient comment on the ever-present Mrs. Proudie, he killed her off—

not without many regrets, as he explained: "It was not only that she was a tyrant, a bully, a would-be priestess, a very vulgar woman, and one who would send headlong to the nethermost pit all who disagreed with her; but that at the same time she was conscientious, by no means a hypocrite, really believing in the brimstone which she threatened, and anxious to save the souls around her from its horrors." The description typifies Trollope's habitually careful weighing of opposites, his exact measurement of the good even in his worst characters and of the shortcomings even in his best.

The plot of *Doctor Thorne* is on a favorite theme of Trollope's: a courtship that is complicated by the unequal social status of the lovers. Mary Thorne, who as a penniless and illegitimate orphan became the ward of her uncle, Dr. Thorne, is loved by Frank Gresham of Greshamsbury Park, but will not marry him because she has not the money he needs to unburden the encumbered family estate. Her maternal uncle, however, is the railway magnate Sir Roger Scatcherd, a capricious alcoholic with an invalid son. He does not know of his relation to Mary, since she was illegitimate and Dr. Thorne was sworn to secrecy. The doctor, who could resolve Mary's love troubles by telling what he knows, is sore beset in his conscience, particularly as he is Sir Roger's medical attendant. Eventually Sir Roger and his rickety son both die, and Mary and Frank can be prosperously married. Trollope records that his brother Thomas Adolphus Trollope, who was also a successful professional writer at this time, supplied him with the plot for *Doctor Thorne*. It is a rare instance of any kind of collaboration in his work. For the most part he was reticent about his writing, never discussing his work in-process except with his wife and never reading it aloud.

Framley Parsonage is similarly concerned with a scrupulous girl, Lucy Robarts, who refuses to marry a lord (even though she loves him) because his mother disapproves of the match. Trollope handles such issues with great delicacy. The scene in which Lucy refuses Lord Lufton's proposal is a fine specimen of Trollope's many courtship scenes:

"It is impossible that I should be your wife."

"Do you mean that you cannot love me?"

"You have no right to press me any further," she said; and sat down upon the sofa, with an angry frown upon her forehead.

"By heavens," he said, "I will take no such answer from you till you put your hand upon your heart, and say that you cannot love me."

"Oh, why should you press me so, Lord Lufton?"

"Why, because my happiness depends upon it; because it behoves me to know the very truth. It has come to this, that I love you with my whole heart, and I must know how your heart stands towards me." She had now again risen from the sofa, and was looking steadily in his face.

"Lord Lufton," she said, "I cannot love you," and as she spoke she did put her hand, as he had desired, upon her heart.

"Then God help me! for I am wretched. Good-bye, Lucy," and he stretched out his hand to her.

"Good-bye, my lord. Do not be angry with me."

"No, no, no!" and without further speech he left the room and the house and hurried home. . . .

And when he was well gone—absolutely out of sight from the window—Lucy walked steadily up to her room, locked the door, and then threw herself on the bed. Why—oh! why had she told such a falsehood?

"There must be love in a novel," Trollope declared; and he became an acknowledged expert in handling a character's intricate vacillations between love and social constraints. It was for such portraits as that of Lucy Robarts that Henry James remembered Trollope as an author who celebrated the "simple maiden in her flower. . . . He is evidently always more or less in love with her." Another such maiden is Grace Crawley in *The Last Chronicle of Barset*, who resists the suit of Major Grantly, the son of the archdeacon, because her father is under suspicion of theft. Perhaps, in the scene where he shows how the archdeacon has all his resistance to the marriage charmed away by Grace's quiet goodness, Trollope was dramatizing his own susceptibility to the simple maiden.

With *Framley Parsonage* Trollope had reached a new stage of success. The novel was solicited for the much-advertised and eagerly awaited new journal, the *Cornhill Magazine*, which was launched as a new venture in 1860 by the enterprising publisher George Smith. The editor was Thackeray, whom Trollope regarded as the greatest living writer and author of the best novel in the English language, *The History of Henry Esmond, Esq.* (1852). Recognition from such a quarter, of which he was very proud, gave him occasion to make some adjustments in his

Lord Lufton and Lucy Robarts of Framley Parsonage,
as depicted by Sir John Everett Millais

post office work. He obtained a transfer from Ireland to England and settled in Waltham House in Hertfordshire, within easy distance of London and the publishers, as well as of good hunting country. *The Small House at Allington* also ran serially in the *Cornhill*. John Everett Millais was engaged as the illustrator for both novels, and a mutually satisfactory relation of novelist and illustrator was established between the two and maintained in *Orley Farm* (1861-1862) and *Phineas Finn*. For subsequent novels Trollope had several other illustrators, including George Thomas, Marcus Stone, Frank Holl, Luke Fildes, and (briefly and abortively) Hablôt Browne, or "Phiz"; but he regarded Millais as his best illustrator.

The Small House at Allington varies the courtship situation by introducing a heroine, Lily Dale, who engages herself to a plausible suitor, Crosbie, and is subsequently jilted by him when he pursues the more fashionable Lady Alexandrina De Courcy. Lily comes to recognize that Crosbie is a scoundrel not worth pining over, but is unable to

cure herself or to accept a more worthy and persistent suitor, Johnny Eames (in whom may be recognized some characteristics of the young Trollope). Trollope prolonged Lily's ultimately unreasonable resistance to Johnny not only through *The Small House at Allington* but to the end of *The Last Chronicle of Barset*, though many of his readers wrote letters begging him to marry her happily to Johnny at last. It is always difficult for Trollope's women—at least for his *good* women—to form a second attachment, but in the case of Lily Dale he suggests that her continuing loyalty to the man who deserted her is an almost morbid condition.

The Last Chronicle of Barset is typical of Trollope's copious, variegated kind of novel. Its concerns unfold amply and progressively, its characters are numerous and diverse, and its world is composed of several plots and different milieux. Although he wrote a number of relatively short novels in which a classic unity of action is clearly preserved, his greatest works are the "big ones"—such as *The Last Chronicle of Barset*, *The Eustace Diamonds* (1872), *The Way We Live Now* (1874-1875), and *Mr. Scarborough's Family* (1883)—in which the main plot is amplified by subplots and the themes are enlarged and qualified. "Though [the novelist's] story should be all one, yet it may have many parts," he explained. "Though the plot itself may require but few characters, it may be so enlarged as to find its full development in many. There may be subsidiary plots, which shall all tend to the elucidation of the main story, and which will take their places as part of one and the same work." Some critics, including several of his original reviewers, have found fault with his subsidiary plots and have wished them away. Recent criticism, however, has shown Trollope's impressive art in the orchestration of plot with subplot. Gordon Ray, in an article entitled "Trollope at Full Length," shows how Trollope "knew exactly how to assign each set of characters its proper part in the story, to time his shifts from one plot to another so as to obtain maximum emphasis, contrast, and change of pace, and to bring the whole to a smooth conclusion within the space allotted. Trollope, in fact, made himself a great master of the contrapuntal novel long before anyone had thought of the term." In *The Last Chronicle of Barset*, for instance, the main story of Josiah Crawley, the proud and poverty-stricken country curate of Hogglestock and a man of intense moral integrity though limited practical acumen, is set off against the shabby, self-interested doings of a number of London characters who dabble in financial and sexual intrigues and constitute a cynical society in

Waltham House in Hertfordshire, Trollope's home from 1859 until 1871

strong counterpoint to Crawley's intense intellectual, moral, and religious commitment. Crawley is suspected on circumstantial evidence of having stolen a check for £20. He is unable to account for his possession of it and is threatened with the loss of his ministry and his living, and attendant shame and degradation. The sufferings of this proud, unaccommodating, intensely sensitive man reach tragic dimensions. It is chiefly for the characterization of Josiah Crawley that *The Last Chronicle of Barset* has been labeled by many—including the author himself—Trollope's best novel.

Trollope's numerous readers and reviewers loudly lamented his decision to make this chronicle of Barset the last. His progressively emerging novels with their familiar characters had firmly lodged themselves in the public's affection. "What am I to do without ever meeting Archdeacon Grantly?," pathetically asked one reader who was quoted in the *Spectator*; "he was one of my best and most intimate friends, and the mere prospect of never hearing his 'Good heavens!' again when any proposition is made touching the dignity of Church or State, is a bewilderment and pain to me."

Trollope wrote several novels besides the Barset ones during these years. In *The Three Clerks* he drew on his experience as a civil servant to delineate the careers of his clerks. The story of the bright and successful Alaric Tudor is one of moral degeneration, while Charley Tudor, the prodigal (recognizable as a self-portrait), is morally redeemed. The novel contains some satire against the newly instituted civil service examinations, which Trollope always hated.

In *Orley Farm* the central character, Lady Mason, is—like Mr. Crawley—a figure of considerable moral rectitude who is suspected of an act of fraud, but—unlike Mr. Crawley—she is guilty. During the infancy of her son, Lucius, she had forged a codicil to her husband's will in order to

Millais's illustration for the title page of the fifth of Trollope's Barset novels (C. P. Snow, Trollope: His Life and Art*)*

provide for the child. As a widow she keeps her secret for years as Lucius grows up, but is at last constrained to confess. Trollope, who believed "a novel should give a picture of common life enlivened by humour and sweetened by pathos," was proud of his handling of the confession scene in which Lady Mason owns her guilt to her elderly fiancé, Sir Peregrine Orme; but to modern taste the pathos is perhaps overwrought.

The publication of *Rachel Ray* (1863) involved Trollope in an unexpected disagreement with his publishers. The book was solicited by Norman Macleod, who was editor of the evangelical publication *Good Words*, as well as being chaplain to Queen Victoria. Macleod invited Trollope to "let out the *best* side of your soul in *Good Words*—better far than ever in *Cornhill*." Trollope set a price of £1,000 for the proposed novel and accordingly wrote *Rachel Ray*. But on reading the manuscript Macleod was dismayed. Trollope had shown clearly enough his

views on Low Church zealots in such figures as Obadiah Slope in *Barchester Towers*; but he was perhaps rather tactless in producing further satire on evangelical self-righteousness in a story commissioned for such a journal as *Good Words*. Here the heroine Rachel is subjected to tyranny by her puritanical relations, who object to her dancing and other social activities; and another unctuous Low Church clergyman, Mr. Prong, is roundly exposed as mercenary and hypocritical. In some embarrassment Macleod backed out of his agreement, more afraid of offending his readership than Trollope. Ruefully amused, Trollope wrote to Millais, who might have illustrated the story, "X (a Sunday magazine) has thrown me over. They write me word that I am too wicked." He let *Good Words* off their full contractual obligation of £1,000 but exacted £500 for his trouble. He subsequently published *Rachel Ray* with his usual publishers, Chapman and Hall.

Cover of the first installment of Trollope's final Barset novel (C. P. Snow, Trollope: His Life and Art*)*

Also concurrently with the Barset novels appeared *Miss Mackenzie* (1865), a muted tale of a spinster on the threshold of middle age who suddenly comes into money and so enters the marriage market. It is a sensitive handling of what its reviewers recognized as an unusual choice of a central character, and Trollope shows himself able to touch even a humdrum story with romance. *The Belton Estate* (1866) tells of Clara Amedroz and her two suitors, the effete member of Parliament Frederick Aylmer and her more virile cousin Will Belton, who inherits her father's estate and finally persuades her to stay on it as his wife. Besides these and other novels, Trollope wrote a number of short stories, tales, sketches, and books of travel during the Barset period. Meanwhile, he still worked full-time with the post office.

Also during his highly successful years of the 1860s he tried a curious experiment. He wanted to test his theory that "a name once earned carried with it too much favour," and so wrote some stories which he insisted on publishing anonymously; this action was to his considerable financial disadvantage, as John Blackwood, who accepted the stories for *Blackwood's Magazine*, would not pay as much for them as he would for work with Trollope's name attached. The experiment certainly proved that an earned name does indeed carry favor, for those who did not recognize the stories as Trollope's scarcely noticed them. But Trollope perhaps had other motives for his experiment: he had begun to discover that his great productivity was sometimes to the detriment of his reputation. "I quite admit that I crowded my wares into the market too quickly," he wrote; but he was inclined to blame the publishers: so long as George Smith kept demanding novels for the *Cornhill*, and Messrs. Chapman and Hall contracted for more, what was a good-humored and energetic novelist to do but oblige them? "Could I have been two separate persons . . . of whom one might have been devoted to Cornhill and the other to the interests of the firm in Piccadilly, it might have been very well; but as I preserved my identity in both places, I myself became aware that my name was too frequent on title-pages." It seems likely that he thought an answer to this dilemma was to remove his name from some title pages, and by publishing anonymously to succeed "in obtaining a second identity." It is yet another testimony to his enormous energy that, while maintaining two distinct and highly demanding professions, he could contemplate subdividing himself yet again to become two novelists.

He made moderate attempts to disguise him-

An illustration by Millais for Orley Farm. *The original for the picture is Julians, the farm near Harrow where Trollope lived as a boy.*

self in his new identity. He was best known as a delineator of English life and English character, but *Nina Balatka* (1867) and *Linda Tressel* (1868), both serialized anonymously in *Blackwood's Magazine* between 1866 and 1868, are set abroad, in Prague and Nuremburg respectively; and Trollope permitted himself more than usual in the way of romance. The first treats of a Christian girl who engages herself to a Jew, and the horrified reactions of the families of both principals. *Linda Tressel* deals with the woes of a girl whose pious aunt tries to force her into marriage with an elderly and repulsive suitor. In spite of Trollope's attempts at disguise, he was discovered by Richard Holt Hutton, the shrewd reviewer for the *Spectator*, so he did not succeed in creating his new literary identity.

"I have long been aware of a certain weakness in my own character," said Trollope, "which I may call a craving for love." His relatively loveless childhood and awkward youth now behind him, and his meed of success achieved, he delighted in the chance to be visible and popular. He joined clubs, becoming one of the pillars of the Garrick Club ("the first assemblage of men at which I felt myself to be popular"), and was elected to the Athenaeum. The ugly duckling had at last become a swan among swans, and he reveled in their company. He joined with others in founding such journals as the *Fortnightly*, the *Pall Mall Gazette*, and *Saint Paul's Magazine*; he gave speeches; he dined out and talked loudly. At social gatherings he was a bluff and blustering presence, and people were often astonished at the contrast between the delicacy of his novels and the aggressive assertiveness of their author: "The books, full of gentleness, grace and refinement; the writer of them, bluff, loud, stormy, and contentious," wrote his friend W. P. Frith. He was likened to Dickens's Mr. Boythorn in *Bleak House* (1852-1853), the good-hearted but litigious neighbor whose bark is worse than his bite. George Augustus Sala characterized him at the end of his life as "crusty, quarrelsome, wrong-headed, prejudiced, obstinate, kind-hearted and thoroughly honest old Tony Trollope." His appearance, bald and bushy-bearded and heavy, was of a piece with his dominating social presence. In commenting on a photograph of himself of 1860, Trollope said, "I think the portrait as it now stands will do very well. It looks uncommon feirce [*sic*], as that of a dog about to bite; but that I fear is the nature of the animal portrayed."

His immense energy found an outlet in fox hunting as well as in his active social life. In the years between 1859 and 1871, when he was at Waltham House, he generally kept four hunting horses and hunted regularly during the season. He could not fully account for his unfailing love of the sport, since he was not a good horseman: he was heavy and shortsighted, and frequently came to grief when in the field. "I am also now old for such work," he confessed when writing the *Autobiography* at sixty-one, "being so stiff that I cannot get on to my horse without the aid of a block or a bank. But I ride still after the same fashion, with a boy's energy." He delighted in incorporating hunting scenes into his novels and frequently made the action turn on some obstacle or accident of the field: as in *Ralph the Heir* (1870-1871), where the hero inherits an estate when his uncle is killed at a ditch. Hunting also provided a fruitful source of metaphor, particularly for courtships; the sadistic Sir Griffin Tewett in *The Eustace Diamonds* pursues Lucinda Roanoke as a vixen: "There are men in whose love a good deal of hatred is mixed;—who love as the huntsman loves the fox, toward the killing of which he intends to use

all his energies and intellects." In *The American Senator* (1877) the woman is the huntress and the man the prey. Arabella Trefoil sees Lord Rufford as a desirable husband and sets out to catch him, doing much of her work of subduing his resistance and engaging his affections in the hunting field. Lord Rufford is a wily quarry and manages to elude her. But when he has escaped he almost regrets it, recognizing her beauty and cleverness and skill at the game. "As for hunting him,—that was a matter of course. He was as much born and bred to be hunted as a fox." Though he escapes Arabella, he is presently captured by another kind of huntress, a patient lady with a baited hook. Trollope saw his own working habits in hunting terms, too, and often wrote in the same way he rode: in beginning a new novel, he confesses, "I have rushed at the work as a rider rushes at a fence which he does not see. Sometimes I have encountered what, in hunting language, we call a cropper."

Another of Trollope's activities that added to the number of his volumes was travel. He traveled as a tourist on holiday all over Europe and frequently set scenes of his novels in foreign cities. He also traveled professionally, on post office business and as a writer. His extensive travels in England and Ireland laying out postal delivery routes occupied what he called two of the happiest years of his life. His gusto was unquenched by a visit to Egypt in 1858 and a long voyage to the West Indies beginning in the winter of the same year, on missions for the post office. The latter journey, however, also gave him the opportunity to contract with Chapman and Hall for a book, which he published in 1859 as *The West Indies and the Spanish Main*. His next trip, for which he obtained a leave of absence from his post office duties, was to the United States in 1861-1862 and was solely for the purpose of writing a book. He regarded the substantial volumes that resulted, *North America* (1862), as in some sense a peace offering to the New World that his mother had so excoriated in *Domestic Manners of the Americans*. His tone in his travel books is engagingly personal: instead of dividing his subject into abstract categories such as politics, commerce, and so on, he typically provides a narrative that follows his own itinerary, so that his general reflections arise from the immediate personal occasion. A late train that caused him a four-hour delay at Crossline, Ohio, for instance, moves him to characteristic impatience and reflection: "There were many others stationed there as I was, but to them had been given a capability for loafing which niggardly Nature had denied to me. . . . Idle men out there in the West we may say there are none. . . . But they all of them had a capacity for a prolonged state of doing nothing, which is to me unintelligible, and which is very much to be envied."

However much he may have envied such a capacity, Trollope did not cultivate it in himself. Before he had written his last chronicle of Barset, he had already launched into the first of a new series of interconnected novels, the Palliser or Political novels. Young Plantagenet Palliser, a dedicated politician and the heir to the duke of Omnium, was first introduced as a minor character in *The Small House at Allington* in the Barset series; he is reintroduced with some eclat, along with his vivacious and headstrong young wife, Lady Glencora, as a major character in *Can You Forgive Her?* (1864-1865). This couple, with their marital problems and their growing power and prestige in the social and political spheres, supply the unity in the next series. Where the clergy are the focus of interest in the Barset novels, politicians and their business are the concern of the Palliser novels; and the major scene of action shifts from the quiet though sufficiently busy rural county of Barsetshire to the more hectic bustle of the metropolis. Trollope had maintained an amused if affectionate distance from his clergymen; but he was more apt to identify with his politicians, and the tone of the novels is by and large more serious. "It is the highest and most legitimate pride of an Englishman to have the letters M.P. written after his name," he wrote without irony in the opening novel of the series. The Palliser novels comprise *Can You Forgive Her?*, *Phineas Finn* (1869), *The Eustace Diamonds* (1872), *Phineas Redux* (1874), *The Prime Minister* (1875-1876), and *The Duke's Children* (1880). Like the Barset novels, they all have separate plots and are complete in themselves, but the characters introduced in one novel are apt to recur in subsequent ones.

The main plot of *Can You Forgive Her?* concerns the complicated love life of Alice Vavasor, who is first engaged to her cousin George, a dangerous and unpredictable man who expects her to pay for his campaign to enter Parliament, then to the safe and respectable John Grey, and then again to George, and finally again to Grey, whom this time she does marry. Her vacillations result partly from her feminist principles, which prompt her to support her cousin and share in his political career, even though she finds him physically repellent. In the subplot the young Lady Glencora, newly married to the rather dull but highly admirable Plantagenet Palliser, is tempted to elope with a romantic ne'er-do-well, Burgo Fitzgerald, whom she had

loved before her marriage. To complete the pattern, a comic third plot shows a widow similarly hesitating between a wild man and a worthy man. It is only the widow, not the girl or the wife, who resolves the conflict by uniting herself with the wild man; Alice and Lady Glencora sensibly realize that they love where they approve and cast off their wild men. Alice's story had been one of continuing interest to Trollope, as he first wrote it in 1850 as a play, "The Noble Jilt," which was rejected and set aside. (It was finally published in 1923.) Although he took considerable trouble over her characterization, his readers found her vacillations exasperating, and she was not popular. Lady Glencora, however, the racy aristocratic wife with a high ambition, a powerful but touchy husband, and a talent for managing other people's lives, was recognizably a character whom his readers would like to meet again, and she and her husband became the major figures whose continuing saga was to occupy Trollope for more than the next decade and almost to the end of his life.

Phineas Finn and its sequel *Phineas Redux* are concerned with the political and marital aspirations of a personable but impecunious young Irishman. Largely by good luck, Phineas manages to enter Parliament early in life; he hopes eventually to make his living by politics, if he can get a salaried position in the Liberal government. Lady Laura Standish, a clever daughter of a cabinet minister, takes him under her wing and introduces him to influential people. He duly falls in love with her and proposes; but she tells him they should both make more financially profitable marriages and engages herself to a rich Scottish landowner, Mr. Kennedy. Her marriage is a disaster, as she comes to hate her dour and exacting husband and finally separates from him. Her uncontrollable love for Phineas and Kennedy's jealousy, violence, and eventual insanity, form a powerful continuing interest in the two books. Phineas, meanwhile, has other ambitions and other women. He succeeds in getting his place in the government but is obliged to resign it when he chooses to vote against his party on the issue of Irish tenant right. At the same time he withdraws from the marriage stakes, rejecting the rich and attractive Mme Max Goesler for a youthful Irish sweetheart.

Phineas Finn's parliamentary career allowed Trollope to pursue certain topics that are of perennial interest in his political novels: the interaction of the private with the public life; the balance between a politician's individual conscience and his allegiance to party policy; and the financing of a political career, which ideally should be open to the best men regardless of their means, yet pursued only from pure and disinterested motives.

Between the writing of *Phineas Finn* and *Phineas Redux* Trollope made an attempt to enter Parliament himself. This had been a lifelong ambition, but before he could pursue it seriously he had to clear the decks and make some decisions about his two existing professions. His career in the post office was inevitably onerous as his literary commitments increased, and he made tentative plans to leave the service when he had saved enough to replace his pension. When he was disappointed of a promotion to under secretary that he had applied for, he had additional reason to "sigh for liberty," as he put it. In 1867, not without many regrets, he wrote his letter of resignation.

New activities quickly took up his new free time. At the invitation of an ambitious printer, James Virtue, he undertook the editorship of a new journal, *Saint Paul's Magazine*, at the salary of £1,000 a year. It was here that *Phineas Finn* had its serial run. (The journal was not a success, and Trollope gave up the editorship in 1870.) Then, despite his recent resignation, he undertook a special mission for the post office that took him in the spring of 1868 on a second visit to the United States. Besides negotiating a postal agreement in Washington, he tried to effect some literary business for himself and his English colleagues: like other English writers he had long been exasperated by the flagrant piracy of his works across the Atlantic, and he tried to arrange an international agreement on copyright. In this he failed.

When he returned to England, he had his chance to pursue his political ambition. "I have always thought that to sit in the British Parliament should be the highest object of ambition to every educated Englishman," he declared. After the dissolution of Parliament in 1868, Trollope stood as a Liberal candidate for Beverley, in Yorkshire; and he swiftly found that the process of getting into Parliament was enough to discourage him. He spent, he said, "the most wretched fortnight of my manhood" in canvassing, found that nobody was interested in his political ideas, and finished at the bottom of the poll. Some of his humiliating experience at Beverley is recalled in *Ralph the Heir* in the campaign of Sir Thomas Underwood at Percycross: "The desire for the seat which had brought him to Percycross had almost died out amidst the misery of his position. Among all the men of his party with whom he was associating, there was not one whom

he did not dislike, and by whom he was not snubbed and contradicted."

It was perhaps now that Trollope may have conceived of his parliamentary novels as a continuing series. He had intended in any case to bring Phineas Finn back into the political arena, but he was now conscious of a new motive for writing his political fictions: "As I was debarred from expressing my opinions in the House of Commons, I took this method of declaring myself. And as I could not take my seat on those benches where I might possibly have been shone upon by the Speaker's eye, I had humbly to crave his permission for a seat in the gallery, so that I might thus become conversant with the ways and doings of the House in which some of my scenes were to be placed." One might expect from such a statement that Trollope would have written novels that strongly advocated certain topical measures and opposed others, but although he does include episodes in which actual issues of the day are introduced and debated in *his* House of Commons—for instance, the ballot, parliamentary reform, Irish tenant right, and the disestablishment of the church—he seldom either advocates or opposes them. His interest is primarily in the *process* of parliamentary government—the manning of committees, the working of personal influence, and the strategy of debate and human management—rather than in advancing his own political opinions. Nevertheless, he occasionally permits himself some onstage electioneering. He describes his own political position, with habitually careful qualification, as that of "an advanced conservative liberal." He advocated a slow and controlled progress toward equality—or rather, "I will not say equality, for the word is offensive, and presents to the imaginations of men ideas of communism, of ruin, and insane democracy,—but a tendency towards equality." So much he says in the *Autobiography*. In *The Prime Minister* he allows his liberal statesman, Plantagenet Palliser, now duke of Omnium and prime minister, to enlarge on the basic principles of liberalism to his friend Phineas Finn as the two stroll in the ample acres of the duke's estate:

> "The Liberal, if he have any fixed idea at all, must I think have conceived the idea of lessening distances,—of bringing the coachman and the Duke nearer together,—nearer and nearer, till a millenium shall be reached by—"
>
> "By equality?" asked Phineas, eagerly interrupting the Prime Minister, and showing his dissent by the tone of his voice.

"I did not use the word, which is open to many objections. In the first place the millenium, which I have perhaps rashly named, is so distant that we need not even think of it as possible. . . . Equality would be a heaven, if we could attain it. How can we to whom so much has been given dare to think otherwise? How can you look at the bowed back and bent legs and abject face of that poor ploughman, who winter and summer has to drag his rheumatic limbs to his work, while you go a-hunting or sit in pride of place among the foremost few of your country, and say that it all is as it ought to be? You are a Liberal because you know that it is not all as it ought to be, and because you would still march on to some nearer approach to equality."

But such statements of principle, clearly carrying the authority of the writer as well as the speaker, are relatively rare in the political novels. The duke himself acknowledges that "when a man has to be on the alert to keep Ireland quiet, or to prevent peculation in the dockyards, or to raise the revenue while he lowers the taxes, he feels himself to be saved from the necessity of investigating principles"; and Trollope, too, usually gets on with his immediate business of activating his characters and managing his incidents.

The Palliser novels were by no means all that Trollope was writing in the second half of his literary career. His novels were appearing constantly and often concurrently as they were serialized in such journals as the *Cornhill*, the *Fortnightly Review*, *Blackwood's Magazine*, *Saint Paul's Magazine*, *Macmillan's Magazine*, the *Graphic*, and *All the Year Round*. Some novels, such as *Can You Forgive Her?* and *He Knew He Was Right*, emerged in separate shilling or monthly parts. The reading public was not likely to forget him.

The Claverings (1867), which had its serial run in the *Cornhill*, occupies an interesting place between the Barset series and the Palliser series in that it presents in its two heroines an example each of the good girl of the early novels and the experienced woman typical of the later ones—here Florence Burton and Julia, Lady Ongar, who are the rival claimants of the hand of Harry Clavering, the vacillating hero. It is a well-constructed tale of English life, with only a little visible manipulation of plot by which two brothers are conveniently drowned in order that Harry may inherit a title and an estate. The marriage of the hard and loveless Sir Hugh Clavering and his feebly dependent wife is a fine

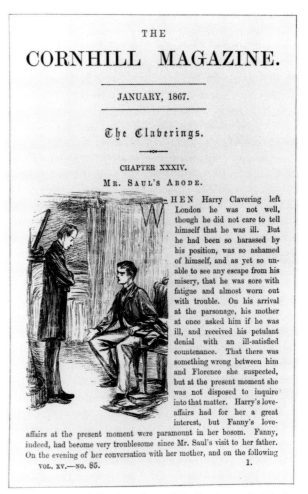

The magazine serialization of one of Trollope's novels. The fact that it begins on page one indicates that it was the most popular novel running in the Cornhill *at the time.*
(Mansell Collection)

study in the deterioration of a relationship.

In *He Knew He Was Right* (1868-1869) Trollope shows a new mastery of morbid psychology. In Kennedy in the *Phineas* novels he also presents a study in the progress toward insanity, but in Louis Trevelyan he is able to examine the process in more detail. Trevelyan is a loving young husband of a rather headstrong woman, Emily. The initial disagreement between them seems trivial enough: a middle-aged man-about-town, Colonel Osborne, tries to engage Emily in a flirtation, and Trevelyan resents his attentions. Emily resents his resentment, they fail to come to a satisfactory explanation, and they separate. As his obsession grows, he convinces himself that she is guilty of adultery and goes to the length of kidnapping their little son and taking him to a remote villa in Italy. The distraught mother is ultimately able to reclaim the child, and Trevelyan, now wasted physically as well as mentally, returns to England under her care; but he does not audibly recant his accusation before he dies. It is for such studies as those of Trevelyan and Kennedy that A. O. J. Cockshut has characterized Trollope as a novelist who became increasingly interested in obsessive and morbid states of mind and followed a "progress to pessimism" in his later novels.

In *The Vicar of Bullhampton* (1869-1870), Trollope based one part of his plot on the story of a fallen woman. He was conscious of dangers in handling such a theme for a Victorian public and showed his nervousness in a preface where he justifies bringing this subject before "our sisters and daughters, . . . the sweet young hearts of those whose delicacy and cleanliness of thought is a matter of pride to so many of us." But his plea was for understanding and compassion: "Cannot women, who are good, pity the sufferings of the vicious, and do something perhaps to mitigate and shorten them, without contamination from the vice?" To the modern ear there is not much that is daring in the presentation of Carry Brattle, the fallen woman, but her condition and its motives and consequences are certainly more deftly handled than those of Dickens's Martha or Little Em'ly in *David Copperfield* (1849-1850).

Trollope quarreled with his publishers over *The Vicar of Bullhampton*, not because of his controversial subject, but because they subordinated his interests to those of Victor Hugo. The novel was completed in 1868 and scheduled to begin its serial run in *Once a Week* in July 1869. Victor Hugo had long delayed the writing of *L'Homme Qui Rit (The Man Who Laughs)*, a translation of which was also booked for *Once a Week*, and the result was that his novel conflicted with Trollope's, and Trollope was asked to publish his in *The Gentleman's Magazine* instead. His reaction is characteristic: "My disgust at this proposition was, I think, chiefly due to my dislike to Victor Hugo's latter novels, which I regard as pretentious and untrue to nature. To this perhaps was added some feeling of indignation that I should be asked to give way to a Frenchman. The Frenchman had broken his engagement. He had failed to have his work finished by the stipulated time. . . . And because of these laches on his part,—on the part of this sententious French Radical,—I was to be thrown over! . . . I would not come out in *The Gentleman's Magazine*, and as the Grinning Man could not be got out of the way, my novel was published in separate numbers." It was not the only occasion on which the punctual Trollope was impa-

tient of the dilatory and unmethodical habits of other writers. He took even his hero Thackeray to task for "that propensity to wandering which came to [him] because of his idleness."

The pattern of Trollope's life seems to have changed in the late 1860s, when he left the post office and had his fling as an editor and in politics. He called the years 1867 and 1868, the years of his resignation, editorship, second trip to America, and political campaign, "the busiest of my life." With the new decade he seemed to slow down a little. He continued to be busy, but he was perhaps less cheerfully ebullient than in the triumphant days of the 1860s. He resigned from the editorship of *Saint Paul's*, he resolved that he would observe parliamentary business only from the Stranger's Gallery, and he even began to think about giving up hunting. The age of fifty-five (Trollope's in 1870) often appears in his novels as a turning point, after which a man is considered old.

His sons were now grown up and needed help in their walks of life. The elder, Henry, who was of a literary turn, studied law and was called to the bar in 1869. Success seemed uncertain, however, and Trollope instead bought him a partnership with his most constant publisher, Frederic Chapman of Chapman and Hall. His younger son, Fred, had early departed to pursue a career as a farmer in Australia, and after a visit home in 1868-1869 decided to return there for good. His parents now contemplated taking the long journey to visit him, and Trollope characteristically determined that he would write a book on Australia while he was about it. The proposed long absence from home led the Trollopes to wonder what to do with their house; and in 1871, before they left, they sold it. Its convenience for Trollope's post office work, which had been the main reason for its purchase, was no longer an issue, and they resolved to settle in London on their return. Trollope speaks of leaving Waltham House as though it were the end of an era: "The work I did during the twelve years that I remained there, from 1859 to 1871, was certainly very great. I feel confident that in amount no other writer contributed so much during that time to English literature. Over and above my novels, I wrote political articles, critical, social, and sporting articles, for periodicals, without number. I did the work of a surveyor of the General Post Office, and so did it as to give the authorities of the department no slightest pretext for fault-finding. I hunted always at least twice a week. I was frequent in the whistroom at the Garrick. I lived much in society in London, and was made happy by the presence of many friends at Waltham Cross. In addition to this we always spent six weeks at least out of England. Few men, I think, ever lived a fuller life."

In May 1871 Trollope and his wife sailed from Liverpool for Melbourne. He had his business well in hand. He had turned his editorship to good account by writing a series called *An Editor's Tales* (1870), and these were just completing their run in *Saint Paul's Magazine*, where *Ralph the Heir* was also coming out. *Sir Harry Hotspur of Humblethwaite* (1871) had just begun in *Macmillan's Magazine*, and *The Eustace Diamonds* was written and already contracted to start its serial run in the *Fortnightly Review*. *Phineas Redux* and *An Eye for an Eye* (1879) were complete and awaiting publishers; and during the voyage to Australia he wrote the whole of *Lady Anna* (1874).

He was away for nineteen months. A few weeks he spent with his son and his new daughter-in-law on their sheep farm, but most of the time he was traveling about the country and beyond it to New Zealand, with his headquarters at Melbourne. He duly produced his book *Australia and New Zealand* (1873), which was published by Chapman and Hall after his return. He arrived home in December 1872 and immediately began to think again about hunting. Although he had intended to give up the sport when he left his country house, he had not in fact disposed of his horses, and he soon settled to hunting three times a week from London. The Trollopes now lived at 39, Montagu Square, and it was here that he wrote many of his novels of the 1870s.

The changes in Trollope's career at the end of the 1860s affected his life in the next decade. He had reached a peak of success, after which some downward trend was inevitable. The visible failures of his editorship of *Saint Paul's Magazine* and the electoral campaign at Beverley perhaps did him bad service with his readership; but in any case, he began to fall off in popularity. For *Phineas Finn* and *He Knew He Was Right* he received the very substantial sums from his publishers of £3,200 each; but sales were disappointing, and he could not again command such prices. His contracts with his publishers maintained for a few years a fairly even price—"£600 for the quantity contained in an ordinary novel volume, or £3,000 for a long tale published in twenty parts, which is equal in length to five such volumes"—but sales were not as good as before, and in the mid-1870s his price likewise sagged. A melancholy footnote to the above passage in the *Autobiography* reads, "Since the date at which this was written I have encountered a diminution in

Kate Field, the American writer and feminist befriended by Trollope

price." It was a hard admission for the old stager to have to make, for he had greatly prized success—and success if possible in a visible, tangible, and quantifiable form. His loss of immediate popularity, however, was not an indication of failing artistic powers: although many of his contemporaries loved him primarily as the chronicler of Barset, and even a reader like Henry James confessed to being unable to wade through the political novels, the criticism of the second half of the twentieth century has by and large found more to admire in Trollope's late novels than in his early ones. But for his last dozen years his name on title pages did not draw readers as it had, and his novels began to be considered rather dated.

He continued to be very prominent on the literary scene, and indeed on many others. He was on intimate terms with a number of writers, including Browning, Alfred Austin, George Eliot and G. H. Lewes, and, since Thackeray's death in 1863, with his daughters, particularly Anne Thackeray,

A self-portrait of Sir John Everett Millais, Trollope's favorite illustrator (Aberdeen Art Gallery and Museum)

who was now a novelist herself. He was over many years a devoted friend of Kate Field, a vivacious American journalist and author, to whom he gave a great deal of advice (which she did not follow) on her literary labors and her feminist activities. He knew many artists, including W. P. Frith, Samuel Laurence, and John Everett Millais, his best illustrator. And of course, as his letters show, he was well known among the publishers, particularly George Smith, John Blackwood, and Frederic Chapman. One memorable anecdote of Trollope in the 1870s is given by Thomas Hardy, who was present at a conference in 1876 on the Eastern question. Trollope, who was by now quite used to "speechifying," as he called it, was on the platform with other prominent men, including Gladstone, Lord Shaftesbury, and the Duke of Westminster: "Trollope outran the five or seven minutes allowed for each speech, and the Duke, who was chairman, after various soundings of the bell, and other hints that he must stop, tugged at Trollope's coat-tails in desperation. Trollope turned round, exclaimed parenthetically, 'Please leave my coat alone,' and went on speaking."

Between the two *Phineas* novels in the Palliser series comes *The Eustace Diamonds*, a lively novel about the machinations of a devious and unscrupulous woman; Lady Glencora and other familiar characters appear as spectators and commentators on the main action. Lizzie Eustace, an attractive young widow who had ensnared a dying baronet into matrimony for the sake of a handsome settlement, lays claim to a diamond necklace which the family lawyers insist belongs, as an heirloom, to the family estate and not to the widow. Even though she is frightened by the marshaling of the lawyers, she cannot bring herself to hand over her plunder, and when the box in which the diamonds are kept is stolen by burglars during a journey, she lets it be known that they have been stolen, thinking to rid herself of trouble by that means. In fact the diamonds were under her pillow, not in the box, at the time of the burglary, and in swearing to their loss she has become guilty of perjury. Lizzie's diamonds are ultimately dispersed and utterly lost, like Pip's great expectations in Dickens's novel; but the wily Lizzie herself escapes punishment, marrying a suitably unpleasant character who is even better than she is at lying. As she clings to diamonds, so she clings to men, and her behavior with her suitors is of a piece with her behavior with other people's property. *The Eustace Diamonds* is a sparkling novel, though it is unusual in the Trollope canon in developing a central character with whom the reader can hardly sympathize. Lizzie is entertaining but so thoroughly sham that she cannot make the devil's party attractive, as does Thackeray's Becky Sharp (whom she somewhat resembles) in *Vanity Fair* (1847-1848). *The Eustace Diamonds* was favorably reviewed and sold well. This was a relief to Trollope, who was aware that he was becoming less popular than he had been.

Phineas Redux, perhaps because it was written after his unfortunate campaign at Beverley, reflects a more somber view of politics than *Phineas Finn*. Phineas, now a widower, who in the first novel had led a charmed life in which beautiful and powerful women favored him and parliamentary seats were always fortunately available, is dogged by misfortune, at odds with his party, denounced by the press, and finally put on trial for a murder he did not commit. He is charged with killing a political opponent, an unpleasant minister named Bonteen, on strong circumstantial evidence. He is acquitted largely due to the heroic efforts of Mme Max Goesler, who bravely collects evidence on his behalf, and he is at last offered the place in the government that he had coveted. But his experience has deeply shaken him, and he refuses the post and so maintains his independence of party. His marriage to the rich and enterprising widow, Mme Max, means that he will still be able to stand for Parliament and serve his country without subservience to party interest.

A powerful recurring antagonist in the two *Phineas* novels and in the Palliser novels at large is Quintus Slide, the editor of the *People's Banner*. In this slimy journalist, who terrorizes public figures in the name of public morality, Trollope continues his attack on the self-righteous pursuit of power: Slide is like Tom Towers in *The Warden*, Slope in *Barchester Towers*, and the squinting evangelical curate Maguire in *Miss Mackenzie*, all of whom use the popular press as their weapon. It is characteristic of Trollope, who was always carefully qualifying his statements and modulating his judgments, that he should have the least patience in his fiction with those whose mode is ruthless overstatement. Yet even to Quintus Slide, as to Mrs. Proudie, Trollope does meticulous justice: he is "not altogether without a conscience, and intensely conscious of such conscience as did constrain him." Trollope was thoroughly at home with such fine distinctions.

The first novel that Trollope wrote from his new home in London was *The Way We Live Now* (1874-1875), his most fully developed satire on modern life. It shows a world of self-seekers busy about their business of getting rich quickly at the expense of others and justifying themselves by the cynical declaration that everybody does it. In the comprehensiveness of its satire it invites comparison with such far-reaching novels as *Vanity Fair* and Dickens's *Little Dorrit* (1855-1857), which similarly anatomize a corrupt society. Through its different plots and subplots, *The Way We Live Now* exposes the moral and spiritual bankruptcy in high and low life, in commerce, politics, religion, and the arts, in the relations of men and women, landlords and tenants, parents and children, English and Americans. In a later estimation of what he had written, Trollope was rather apologetic for his satirist's stance, admitting with the habitual honesty of the convinced realist that "the accusations are exaggerated." But he effectively conveys his vision of a society in which dishonesty has reached high places and so becomes "rampant" and "splendid."

The main plot concerns the meteoric rise to fortune and fashion of a large-scale financier and swindler, Melmotte, a figure who promotes greed in others and a fever of speculation, as Merdle does in *Little Dorrit*. Melmotte entertains on a grand scale, forms fictional companies, acquires a country estate by means of forgery, and is even elected to Parlia-

An illustration by Luke Fildes for
Anthony Trollope's *The Way We Live Now*

An illustration by Sir Luke Fildes for The Way We Live Now

ment before his empire of deceit collapses and he shoots himself. As usual, Trollope manages to create a good deal of interest in and even sympathy for a rogue and his machinations. Other prominent characters through whom Trollope varies and enlarges his theme are Lady Carbury, a writer of potboilers who shamelessly coaxes reviewers for favorable notices of her books; her ne'er-do-well son Sir Felix, who arranges to elope with Melmotte's daughter in order to get her money and then leaves her waiting at the railway station; Mr. Longstaffe, a squire who is ready to sell his family estate to Melmotte; and Paul Montague, who, though honest in intent, maintains compromising relations with two different women and lends his name to one of Melmotte's swindles. The wilder of his two women is a bold American, Mrs. Hurtle, who admits to having shot her boor of a husband. The honest norm of the book is Roger Carbury, a quiet and ineffectual country gentleman who lives appropriately in an outmoded house with a moat, and who loses both his beloved estate and the girl he loves to inferior men. He is one of the few who manage to avoid being drawn into the vortex of Melmotte's spectacular progress: when his relative Hetta Carbury, whom he loves, proposes to visit the Melmottes he remonstrates, and her justification is the usual one:

> "Everybody goes there, Mr. Carbury."
> "Yes,—that is the excuse which everybody makes. Is that sufficient reason for you to go to a man's house? Is there not another place to which we are told that a great many are going, simply because the road has become thronged and fashionable?"

Such is our destination if we continue to live the way we live now.

The reception of the last two of the Palliser novels reflects the decline in Trollope's popularity. *The Prime Minister*, his longest novel and one that was perhaps intended to be a masterpiece, drew a good deal of hostile criticism, and its sales did not recover the sum of £2,500 that Chapman and Hall had paid for the copyright. And *The Duke's Children*, which he had made as long as its predecessor, was declared by Chapman to be too long to be marketable, so that Trollope was obliged with tedious labor to reduce it from four volumes to three.

The penultimate volume of the series, *The Prime Minister*, has a bifurcated plot. The half that Trollope and his readers best liked is devoted to Palliser business. Plantagenet Palliser, now the duke of Omnium, whose political career has taken many turns since he filled the office most dear to his heart, chancellor of the exchequer, is now called upon to be the prime minister of a coalition government. The duchess, who has gained in status though not in prudence since her wild days as the wayward Lady Glencora, is delighted at his promotion and at once resolves to use all the resources of their vast wealth and huge estates to celebrate the new glory. The duke, a dedicated statesman with a taste for parliamentary and domestic tranquility, views his new position as a solemn trust; the duchess sees it as a grand opportunity for social triumph. "I should like to put the Queen down," she says exultantly. "No treason; nothing of that kind. But I should like to make Buckingham Palace second-rate. And I'm not quite sure but I can." The marriage and the ministry are in equally parlous condition. The duke, highly scrupulous and intensely sensitive to criticism, suffers agonies both from adverse publicity in the *People's Banner* and from his wife's social panoply.

Although the power has been painful to him, he nevertheless becomes reluctant to lay it aside, and when the coalition is defeated he is unwilling to submit himself as a subordinate minister in a new government. The second plot concerns the marriage and fortunes of Lopez, an unscrupulous adventurer who marries Emily Wharton for her money but fails to extract her fortune from her tightfisted father. He is ruined, and, in a scene that may well have inspired the denouement of Tolstoy's *Anna Karenina* (1873-1876), he throws himself under an express train at Tenway Junction.

The reviewers were severe with *The Prime Minister*, particularly on the Lopez part of the plot. "*The Prime Minister* represents a decadence in Mr. Trollope's powers," announced the critic for the *Saturday Review*. "The hand begins to falter where it once was cunning, and even as a picture of manners the work is no longer free from reproach. To whatever part of the story he may turn, the reader of *The Prime Minister* is unable to escape the all-pervading sense of artistic vulgarity." By contrast, Geoffrey Harvey in *The Art of Anthony Trollope* (1980) makes a strong case for the same novel as the summit of Trollope's achievement. Trollope's readers have always differed as to the merits of his many novels.

Trollope had not finished with traveling in the 1870s. In 1875 he went via the Mediterranean and Brindisi to Ceylon, sending letters on his travels back for publication in various newspapers, and then on to a second visit with his son in Australia, returning across America to complete his second circuit of the world. In 1877 he went to South Africa and wrote a book on it. The following year he went on an excursion to Iceland, of which he wrote an account in *How the "Mastiffs" Went to Iceland* (1878). Some of these exotic locations were useful in his fiction as well as for travel books. *Harry Heathcote of Gangoil: A Tale of Australian Bush Life* (1874), written in four weeks and published as a Christmas story in the *Graphic*, drew on his experience on Fred's sheep farm, and much of the action of *John Caldigate* (1879) is likewise set in Australia.

Another of his literary activities was scholarship and critical commentary. By his own assertion he had learned little of the classics in all the years of having them drilled into him at Harrow and Winchester; but he had found time to apply himself to them as an adult and began to read Latin and Greek for pleasure. In 1870 he wrote a little book on *The Commentaries of Caesar*; it cost him great pains but went virtually unnoticed by the scholars. His *Thackeray* (1879) is still quoted as an interesting early treatment of Thackeray as man and writer. In 1880

Cover design for a "yellowback" edition of one of Trollope's novels (David Magee Antiquarian Books)

English institutions as fox hunting, church patronage, and class distinctions, the senator comes to the conclusion that "the want of reason among Britishers was so great, that no one ought to treat them as wholly responsible beings."

Trollope's readers continued to wish that he would recover from "the attack of misanthropy from which he was suffering when he wrote *The Way We Live Now*"; but his next novel, *Is He Popenjoy?* (1878) did not satisfy them, and his new worldly churchman, Dean Lovelace, was not as popular as the public's old favorite, Archdeacon Grantly. This is another story of inheritance, turning on the legitimacy of the infant son of the evil marquis of Brotherton. The heroine is the dean's daughter, Mary Germain, who is married to the conscientious but dull younger brother of the marquis. The marquis and his dubious little Lord Popenjoy both die, and the birth of Mary's son, an indubitably legitimate Popenjoy, solves her marital problems and causes great rejoicing to her father and husband. The novel includes some satire on the Women's Rights movement, which is represented by the terrible Baroness Banmann.

In the last of the Palliser series, *The Duke's Children*, the duchess does not appear in person, as she has died suddenly in the interim since *The Prime Minister*. She is present in spirit, however, as the duke, mourning her absence, seeks to make his children reenact in their marriages his own union with Lady Glencora. His daughter, Lady Mary, has fallen in love with Frank Tregear, an impecunious young man who reminds him of his wife's old flame, Burgo Fitzgerald; so he tries to detach her from Tregear and marry her instead to another such tame young aristocrat as he had been himself. At the same time his son, Lord Silverbridge, who had first considered marrying the suitably aristocratic and lively Lady Mabel Grex, falls in love instead with an American girl, Isabel Boncassen. His children are troublesome in other ways: Silverbridge deserts the family party and joins the conservatives, to his father's dismay; besides this, he contracts enormous debts in owning and betting on a racehorse in the Derby. The duke's younger son, Lord Gerald, is sent down from Cambridge for undisciplined behavior. Though he is generous with his children in many ways, the duke clings doggedly to his plans for their marriages and opposes both Silverbridge's and Mary's choices. In this process he even quarrels with Mrs. Finn, Phineas's wife and the cherished friend of Lady Glencora. At last, however, she persuades him to relinquish his plan to reenact his past through his children, and he is reconciled to Isabel

he published *The Life of Cicero*. His *Autobiography*, completed in 1876, contains a good deal of shrewd criticism of his own and others' novels, testifying to wide and careful reading. He had contemplated a book on English prose fiction and even one on the history of English literature, but these ambitious projects are among the few he did not accomplish.

The American Senator (1877) is a lively story that returns in some ways to the Barset mode but is still touched with some satirical bitterness. Set in the country in the invented county of Rufford, it concerns the love and marriage of a young and innocent girl, Mary Masters, who eventually marries the squire; and of a not-so-young and far-from-innocent fortune huntress, Arabella Trefoil, who cunningly hunts the eligible Lord Rufford and his £ 50,000 a year. The novel takes its name from the American senator from Mickewa, Elias Gotobed, who is Trollope's vehicle for social criticism. After a naive but conscientious scrutiny of such hallowed

Boncassen and Frank Tregear as daughter- and son-in-law. The book is a moving study of an old man confronting youth and of the process by which his longing for self-justification makes him insist on imposing his will on others.

There are several comparable features in Trollope's two major series, the Barset and the Palliser novels. The first offers a combination of love and ecclesiastical business, and the second a similar combination of love and political business; both focus on the fascinating interaction of the domestic with the professional life. A major character in each is a dominating woman who competes with her husband for power and then dies suddenly toward the end of the series. A noticeable change is in the presentation of the other female characters. Where in the Barset novels "the simple maiden in her flower" had predominated—such girls as Mary Thorne, Lucy Robarts, and Grace Crawley—in the Palliser novels the interest shifts from innocent girls to experienced women: Lady Laura Kennedy, who deserts her husband and declares her adulterous passion for another man; Mme Max Goesler, who having married once for a settlement pursues a handsome young man for love and actually proposes to him; and Lady Glencora herself, who not only is much more sympathetically handled than Mrs. Proudie but also breaks the standard Trollope code by abandoning her first love and devoting herself to a second. The treatment of the male characters also develops between Trollope's early and late periods. In *Rachel Ray* of 1863 Trollope had expressed a view of character as essentially set and unchanging: "A man cannot change as men change. Individual men are like the separate links of a rotatory chain. The chain goes on with continuous easy motion as though every part of it were capable of adapting itself to a curve, but not the less is each link as stiff and sturdy as any other piece of wrought iron." But in the later novels, and particularly in the long series with a spread of years that allowed for aging, Trollope was deliberately considering "the state of progressive change" in his characters. In writing the two *Phineas* novels, he records, "I had constantly before me the necessity of progression in character,—of marking the changes in men and women which would naturally be produced by the lapse of years." In observing minutely these changes as they occurred in Lady Glencora and Plantagenet Palliser over many years and through several long novels, he created characters who on occasion seem to transcend the limitations of the books in which they belong and assume a life of their own. "I do not think it probable that my name will remain among

Trollope around the year 1880

those who in the next century will be known as the writers of English prose fiction," he admits modestly; "—but if it does, that permanence of success will probably rest on the character of Plantagenet Palliser, Lady Glencora, and the Rev. Mr. Crawley."

The most considerable novel of the end of Trollope's career is *Mr. Scarborough's Family* (1883), which was still running at his death. Mr. Scarborough is old and dying but has a fierce determination to manage his own affairs until the end. His estate is entailed, but his eldest son Mountjoy is so deeply in debt that the estate would go straight into the hands of the creditors at the father's death. The old man, by a series of cunning and unscrupulous maneuvers, is able to prove Mountjoy illegitimate; and then, when the creditors have settled for a song, to prove him legitimate after all. It is a remarkable story of a roguish and power-hungry old man who is determined to beat the system, and, to the dismay of his lawyer, succeeds in doing so.

Trollope, who had so often celebrated the stability of the country estate in his fiction, was himself comparatively nomadic. He moved again before he died, leaving Montagu Square for Harting Grange, a house in the country near Petersfield in Sussex. He was now aging and troubled with asthma, deafness, and other ailments. But the Phoenix Park murders in Dublin in 1882 spurred him to write another Irish novel, and his last journeys out of England were again to Ireland to gather material for *The Landleaguers* (1883). For that winter his wife took him to lodgings in London, so as to be within easy reach of the doctors. During a convivial evening with his old friends the Tilleys, in the midst of laughter at a reading of the new comic novel F. Anstey's *Vice Versa*, Trollope had a stroke. He lingered a few weeks, but died on 6 December 1882.

His prudent habit of keeping a manuscript or two on hand meant that the novels kept coming for a while. *Mr. Scarborough's Family* finished its run in 1883; *The Landleaguers*, which he had not lived to finish, was published incomplete; and *An Old Man's Love*, a moving little story about a man of fifty who releases the girl he loves from her engagement to him so that she can marry a younger man, came out in 1884. Even in this century books have continued to emerge: the two works his publishers rejected—*The Noble Jilt*, a play in blank verse, and *The New Zealander*, a book of social criticism—at last saw the light in 1923 and 1972 respectively.

His major posthumous publication, however, was undoubtedly *An Autobiography*, which he finished in 1876 and consigned to his son Henry to see through the press after his death. This engagingly frank account of his professional life and working habits has continued to shock and delight his readers in almost equal measure. His principal biographer, Michael Sadleir, explained how his blunt alignment of novel writing with shoe making and his undisguised interest in the financial rewards of his trade did much to damage his reputation with the aesthetes of the 1880s and caused a "tempest of reaction against his work." But Sadleir perhaps exaggerated the reaction: many of the reviews were favorable, and Trollope had in any case made no secret during his lifetime of his habits of writing. His practice was methodical, not to say mechanical: the process of literary creation has never been so completely divested of glamour. He rose early and started his labors at 5:30 A.M. "It had at this time become my custom . . . to write with my watch before me, and to require from myself 250 words every quarter of an hour. I have found that the 250 words have been forthcoming as regularly as my

watch went." He would work for three hours before breakfast, producing "ten pages of an ordinary novel volume a day" and "three novels of three volumes each in the year," and still have his days free for post office or other business. He carried his "self-imposed laws" to elaborate lengths. Besides his watch, he had a ruled diary, drawn up in days and weeks, in which he calculated in advance the time a given work should take him and recorded the number of pages written per day. To complete this working calendar exactly became a kind of game with him. "*Finis coronat opus*," he sometimes wrote triumphantly at the end of a calendar; "Finished in 24 weeks to the day" is recorded at the end of the calendar for his longest novel, *The Prime Minister*. On the other hand, where travel or committees or a sore throat prevented his usual stint, he records against the pageless day a melancholy "Ah me!"

Besides writing at home before breakfast, he wrote in clubs, on trains, and on ships—in the latter case occasionally interrupting his labors to throw up. He would frequently begin a new novel the very day after completing the last. And so by observing his self-imposed laws he piled up the novels. He was not unaware of the dangers to his reputation of producing too much, but he claimed that the quality of his work had never suffered for the quantity's being ample. "The work which has been done quickest has been done the best," he insisted.

His enormous energy, gusto, and delight in labor are perhaps the most memorable characteristics of Trollope the man. His lonely childhood and unsatisfactory youth probably had much to do with creating an appetite for success; but work in itself seems to have been as necessary to his well-being as love or nourishment. Until he found a means of directing his energies he was miserable. "I hated the office," he writes of his early days in the London General Post Office. "I hated my work. More than all I hated my idleness." Work, and an orderly manner of going about it, were for him moral necessities. "The first impression which a parent should fix on the mind of a child is I think love of order," he wrote in his commonplace book of the same period. "It is the reins by which all virtues are kept in their proper places—& the vices, with whom the virtues run in one team, are controlled."

He was legendary in his own day for industry, punctuality, and reliability. When Thackeray failed to produce the major novel that was needed for the first issue of the *Cornhill*, Trollope was applied to and stepped in at short notice to fill the breach. The special difficulties of serial publication he completely mastered. He scorned the hand-to-mouth

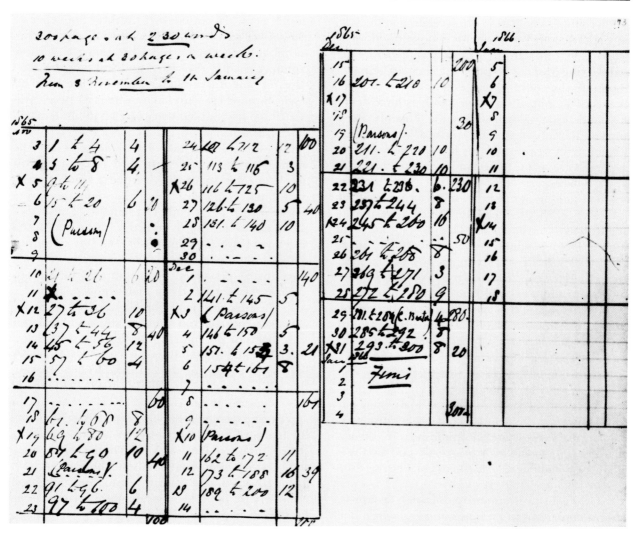

Trollope's working calendar for Nina Balatka, which he completed two and a half weeks ahead
of his self-imposed deadline (Bodleian Library)

methods of Dickens and Thackeray, who completed the month's copy with the printer's devil waiting at the door, and made a rule that every novel of his should be finished before the first number went to press. When Trollope was on his tour of Australia and New Zealand, Arthur Locker, the editor of the *Graphic*, wrote to him in Wellington to engage him for a new novel: "I should not trouble you during your antipodal tour," he apologized, "only that I know you are a man of such unflagging industry that probably you will write a tale on the homeward voyage. If you do, will you give us the offer of it?" Trollope's reply, by return from Wellington, is characteristic: "I have a novel already written called *Phineas Redux*. . . . My price for the copyright would be £2,500." He must frequently have staggered his publishers by his almost superhuman promptitude.

He took the pleasure of a good tradesman in serving his customers well. A quarrel with one of his publishers arose from the latter's shrewd maneuver in stretching a one-volume work, *Lotta Schmidt and Other Stories* (1867), to two volumes and raising the price accordingly. On seeing the proof Trollope indignantly protested: "I cannot allow the tales in your hands to be published in two volumes. . . . I have always endeavoured to give good measure to the public—The pages, as you propose to publish them, are so thin and desolated, and contain such a poor rill of type meandering thro' a desert of margin, as to make me ashamed of the idea of putting my name to the book." He applied his own high standards of honesty to himself.

Notwithstanding his frankly declared interest in the proceeds of his novels, money was not the motive but only the welcome result of his more pressing need to work for work's sake. He wrote to his old friend John Tilley, "You say of me;—that I would not choose to write novels unless I were paid. Most certainly I would;—much rather than not write them at all." The penalty of Adam in having to work in the sweat of his brow he regarded as a blessing rather than a curse. His principal worry about dying was about what he would be able to work at afterward: "My only doubt as to finding a heaven for myself at last arises from the fear that the disembodied and beatified spirits will not want novels." It is to be hoped that in the "Good heavens" so often invoked by Archdeacon Grantly there is still an appetite for good fiction, so that Trollope will not have had to face the hell of enforced leisure.

Trollope's enormous productivity has had much to do with a patronizing dismissal of his work by some critics and a rather apologetic attitude adopted even by his admirers. In a review of *Miss Mackenzie* the young Henry James admitted, "We have long entertained for Mr. Trollope a partiality of which we have yet been somewhat ashamed." It has been a recurring attitude. Even his major biog-

rapher, Sadleir, writing in 1927, and his next major critic, Bradford A. Booth, have been tentative and cautious in their praise and have partly adopted the stance of apologists. Critics have found his elusive but undoubted quality difficult to analyze: "His work resists the kind of formal analysis to which we subject our better fiction," Booth admitted. His pellucid style has not invited critical exegesis. Compared with George Eliot or Meredith he has seemed lowbrow, and compared with Dickens and Hardy his unemphatic social commentary has seemed mild.

If it has taken time for critics to claim a place for Trollope among the greatest novelists, the readers have kept buying and reading his books. He has continued to be "obsessively readable," in C. P. Snow's phrase. He lost some readers during his lifetime and some more after his death; but after the 1890s reprints of his many novels have proved sound investments for many publishers. During the two world wars Trollope and Barset were in enormous demand. In the 1970s his second series was adapted by the BBC as a highly successful television serial, *The Pallisers*. And increasingly in the two de-

Harting Grange, Trollope's country home in Sussex

cades before the centenary of his death, the critics have ceased to be apologists. Trollope has been recognized as a major novelist: a subtle delineator of character and an acute observer of normal and abnormal psychology; a shrewd social commentator; a knowing moralist; a successful humorist who can also on occasion stretch to tragedy; and a master of his art as well as of his craft. "Trollope did not write for posterity," James conceded in his classic essay, written shortly after Trollope's death; "he wrote for the day, the moment; but these are just the writers whom posterity is apt to put into its pocket. . . . Trollope will remain one of the most trustworthy, though not one of the most eloquent, of the writers who have helped the heart of man to know itself."

Letters:

Letters of Anthony Trollope, edited by Bradford A. Booth (London: Oxford University Press, 1951).

Bibliography:

Michael Sadleir, *Trollope: A Bibliography* (London: Constable, 1928).

Biographies:

Michael Sadleir, *Trollope: A Commentary* (London: Constable, 1927);

Lucy Poate Stebbins and Richard Poate Stebbins, *The Trollopes: The Chronicle of a Working Family* (London: Secker & Warburg, 1947);

James Pope Hennessy, *Anthony Trollope* (Boston: Little, Brown, 1971);

C. P. Snow, *Trollope: His Life and Art* (London: Macmillan, 1975).

References:

Ruth apRoberts, *Trollope: Artist and Moralist* (London: Chatto & Windus, 1971); republished as *The Moral Trollope* (Athens: Ohio University Press, 1971);

Bradford A. Booth, *Anthony Trollope: Aspects of His Life and Art* (Bloomington: Indiana University Press, 1958);

A. O. J. Cockshut, *Anthony Trollope: A Critical Study* (London: Collins, 1955; New York: New York University Press, 1968);

P. D. Edwards, *Anthony Trollope: His Art and Scope* (St. Lucia: University of Queensland Press, 1977);

N. John Hall, ed., *The Trollope Critics* (London: Macmillan, 1981);

John Halperin, *Trollope and Politics: A Study of the Pallisers and Others* (London: Macmillan, 1977);

Geoffrey Harvey, *The Art of Anthony Trollope* (New York: St. Martin's Press, 1980);

Henry James, "Anthony Trollope," in his *Partial Portraits* (London: Macmillan, 1888), pp. 97-133;

Walter M. Kendrick, *The Novel-Machine: The Theory and Fiction of Anthony Trollope* (Baltimore: Johns Hopkins University Press, 1980);

James R. Kincaid, *The Novels of Anthony Trollope* (Oxford: Clarendon Press, 1977);

Juliet McMaster, *Trollope's Palliser Novels: Theme and Pattern* (London: Macmillan, 1978);

J. Hillis Miller, *The Form of Victorian Fiction: Thackeray, Dickens, Trollope, George Eliot, Meredith, and Hardy* (Notre Dame, Ind.: University of Notre Dame Press, 1968);

Robert M. Polhemus, *The Changing World of Anthony Trollope* (Berkeley & Los Angeles: University of California Press, 1968);

Gordon N. Ray, "Trollope at Full Length," *Huntington Library Quarterly*, 31 (1968): 313-340;

Donald Smalley, ed., *Trollope: The Critical Heritage* (London: Routledge & Kegan Paul/New York: Barnes & Noble, 1969);

R. C. Terry, *Anthony Trollope: The Artist in Hiding* (London: Macmillan, 1977).

Papers:

Trollope's working papers are collected in the Bodleian Library, Oxford University. Many of the manuscripts of his novels are at the Beinecke Library, Yale University.

Frances Trollope
(10 March 1779-6 October 1863)

Helen Heineman
Framingham State College

BOOKS: *Domestic Manners of the Americans*, 2 volumes (London: Whittaker, Treacher, 1832; New York: Dodd, Mead, 1832);

The Refugee in America: A Novel (3 volumes, London: Whittaker, Treacher, 1832);

The Mother's Manual; or, Illustrations of Matrimonial Economy: An Essay in Verse (London: Truettel & Wurtz & Richter, 1833);

The Abbess: A Romance (3 volumes, London: Whittaker, Treacher, 1833);

Belgium and Western Germany in 1833 (2 volumes, London: Murray, 1834);

Tremordyn Cliff (3 volumes, London: Bentley, 1835);

Paris and the Parisians in 1835 (2 volumes, London: Bentley, 1836);

The Life and Adventures of Jonathan Jefferson Whitlaw; or, Scenes on the Mississippi (3 volumes, London: Bentley, 1836);

The Vicar of Wrexhill (3 volumes, London: Bentley, 1837);

Vienna and the Austrians (2 volumes, London: Bentley, 1838);

A Romance of Vienna (3 volumes, London: Bentley, 1838);

The Widow Barnaby (3 volumes, London: Bentley, 1839);

The Life and Adventures of Michael Armstrong, the Factory Boy (12 monthly parts, London: Colburn, 1839-1840);

The Widow Married: A Sequel to The Widow Barnaby (3 volumes, London: Colburn, 1840);

One Fault: A Novel (3 volumes, London: Bentley, 1840);

Charles Chesterfield; or, The Adventures of a Youth of Genius (3 volumes, London: Colburn, 1841);

The Ward of Thorpe Combe (3 volumes, London: Bentley, 1841);

The Blue Belles of England (3 volumes, London: Saunders & Otley, 1842);

A Visit to Italy (3 volumes, London: Bentley, 1842);

Jessie Phillips: A Tale of the Present Day (11 monthly parts, London: Colburn, 1842-1843);

The Barnabys in America; or, Adventures of the Widow Wedded (3 volumes, London: Colburn, 1843);

Hargrave; or, The Adventures of a Man of Fashion (3

Frances Trollope (National Portrait Gallery)

volumes, London: Colburn, 1843);

The Laurringtons; or, Superior People (3 volumes, London: Longman, Brown, Green & Longmans, 1844);

Young Love: A Novel (3 volumes, London: Colburn, 1844);

The Attractive Man (3 volumes, London: Colburn, 1846);

The Robertses on Their Travels (3 volumes, London: Colburn, 1846);

Travels and Travellers: A Series of Sketches (2 volumes, London: Colburn, 1846);

Father Eustace: A Tale of the Jesuits (3 volumes, London: Colburn, 1847);

The Three Cousins (3 volumes, London: Colburn, 1847);

Town and Country: A Novel (3 volumes, London: Colburn, 1848);

The Young Countess; or, Love and Jealousy (3 volumes, London: Colburn, 1848);

The Lottery of Marriage: A Novel (3 volumes, London: Colburn, 1849);

The Old World and the New: A Novel (3 volumes, London: Colburn, 1849);

Petticoat Government: A Novel (3 volumes, London: Colburn, 1850);

Mrs. Mathews; or, Family Mysteries (3 volumes, London: Colburn, 1851);

Second Love; or, Beauty and Intellect: A Novel (3 volumes, London: Colburn, 1851);

Uncle Walter: A Novel (3 volumes, London: Colburn, 1852);

The Young Heiress: A Novel (3 volumes, London: Hurst & Blackett, 1853);

The Life and Adventures of a Clever Woman. Illustrated with Occasional Extracts from Her Diary (3 volumes, London: Hurst & Blackett, 1854);

Gertrude; or, Family Pride (3 volumes, London: Hurst & Blackett, 1855);

Fashionable Life; or, Paris and London (3 volumes, London: Hurst & Blackett, 1856).

While she was the author of thirty-four novels, Frances Trollope has been more known as the mother of Anthony Trollope and as the author of a best-selling travel book, *Domestic Manners of the Americans* (1832), than for her achievements in fiction. Yet she was a significant pioneer in expanding the art of fiction in the nineteenth century with her controversial social-reform novels and her many works featuring a new, strong kind of heroine. In using fiction to attack social abuses and in developing more complex characterizations of women, Mrs. Trollope was an influence on the major novelists of the time. Like many of her heroines, she was the "triumphant feminine" in both a personal and a literary sense.

Born Frances Milton, she was a Bristol clergyman's daughter who lost her mother early, a pattern shared by many other nineteenth-century female authors. Educated by her father in languages, the classics, and the arts, "Fanny" Milton grew up in considerable freedom and emerged an independent, cultured, sturdy, young woman. When her father remarried, she went up to London with her brother and sister and lived there for five years, not marrying until she was nearly thirty. Her union with Thomas Anthony Trollope, a serious

barrister from a good family, produced seven children in eight years. After eighteen years of a busy domestic life in London and at Harrow, where the family built a stately home, Julians, financial troubles and a lost inheritance brought the Trollopes to the brink of bankruptcy and ruin. Faced with destitution, Mrs. Trollope opted for a scheme in utopian living in the United States with her friend Frances Wright, heiress and reformer, who had founded a colony for the education and emancipation of slaves in southern Tennessee. With her daughters and one son, Mrs. Trollope went there to live and work while her husband remained behind, trying to recoup their losses. Her eldest son, Tom, stayed in college, and Anthony, the youngest, remained at Harrow School. But the venture was a disappointment, and Mrs. Trollope, her family, and their friend, the French artist Auguste Hervieu, went on to Cincinnati, where they tried to find work to support themselves. Here her life alternated between plans for grandiose business and cultural schemes—the famous Cincinnati Bazaar—and devastating failure. At fifty-two years of age, financially destitute once again, she returned to England and published her first book, *Domestic Manners of the Americans*, an instant and highly controversial bestseller. Exposing "the lamentable insignificance of the American woman" and attacking many of America's most prized beliefs about itself, the book generated some of the harshest and most virulent criticism of its time.

Domestic Manners of the Americans is a chronologically arranged account of her experiences during her almost four-year-long stay in the United States. It offers countless particulars—scenes, events, characters, conversations—culled by Mrs. Trollope from the day-to-day domestic life of her American household. The book's lasting appeal lies in her brilliant selection of detail and the way in which she transforms her material into representative and amusing vignettes of nineteenth-century American life. In the opinion of Mark Twain, a shrewd and observant American of those years, her work was accurate enough to be called "photography." Using the accents, inflections, and vagaries of American speech and vocabulary, she described her encounters with servants, with pretentious "literatti" in Cincinnati, with rigorously independent merchants, farmers, and Mississippi river squatters, and with emotional religious revivalists. Always her scenes resonate with the deeper implications of external behavior.

But the work is not all of a piece: the first half, dealing with her life in Cincinnati, is the more origi-

An American caricature of Mrs. Trollope from 1833, showing the hostile reaction provoked by
Domestic Manners of the Americans

nal and lively part. When she left Cincinnati and headed east, she became a traveler like others before her—Basil Hall, for instance—and her material became more conventional.

The most original part of the book is her underlying analysis—that the sins and flaws of America stemmed mainly from the exclusion of women from the mainstream of American life. This situation, she believed, was caused by male preference, not economic necessity. Throughout, she documented a hostility to women lurking beneath the surface of American life. In one way or another, all her famous subjects—spitting, the servant problem, revivals and camp meetings, indecent postures at the theater, boardinghouse existences, the rough egalitarianism of Americans, the lack of gaiety in their national life—although ramblingly treated, had a relationship to "the lamentable insignificance of the American woman." In attacking what some called the "cult of true womanhood," Mrs. Trollope touched upon themes charged with emotion. Reviewers on both sides of the Atlantic attacked the book and indulged in character assas-

sination. Still, the book sold well, assisted by the political atmosphere in England on the verge of the first Reform Bill of 1832, since there was great interest in America and its political democracy. Even today the book is instructive and in recent years has been increasingly referred to by social historians and commentators.

Domestic Manners of the Americans achieved an almost unheard-of success for a first attempt by an unknown author, going through many editions in America and England and across Europe. The money she earned saved the family from certain ruin and returned them to their home at Harrow; at the age of fifty-three, Mrs. Trollope found herself launched on a writing career. But even the earnings from her subsequent travel books on Germany and Paris and several popular novels—one a Gothic potboiler, *The Abbess* (1833)—failed to suffice, and the family was forced to abandon their English home and flee to Belgium, where Mr. Trollope could not be sued by his creditors.

For several years, they lived in rented lodgings in Brussels, while Mrs. Trollope wrote frantically to support the family and at the same time nursed several of her children who were dying of tuberculosis. Often she spent her time alternating between the care of the mortally ill and the grinding out of fiction. During these years were forged her spartan writing habits, which she later passed on to her son Anthony. Every day she rose at 4:00 A.M. to complete her quota of writing before the family awakened and needed her constant assistance. When time was short, she stayed up on alternate nights, dosing herself with strong green tea to stay awake. Her first novels—*The Refugee in America* (1832), *The Abbess, Tremordyn Cliff* (1835)—were melodramatic and conventional, but they were also an apprenticeship in the art of fiction. In them she found her true voice and style and learned the narrative art. During these years, too, she continued to make tours, hoping to repeat the success of *Domestic Manners of the Americans*. She soon realized, however, that much of what she earned was spent in transporting herself and her family to the places she needed to see. Thus, for reasons economic and domestic, she turned then primarily to fiction.

Once Mrs. Trollope set her sights on fiction as more than a time-filling device between journeys, she began to turn out novels at odds with the more dominant trends of the time. One critic soon noted, "Mrs. Trollope had the nature of a pioneer." Her travels had made her an observer of society, and now they led her to write on subjects not usually treated in fiction. Her penchant for satire—so evident in *Domestic Manners of the Americans*—soon focused on characters and situations which her contemporary critics described as "repulsive." Through her concentration on social abuses she became one of the first novelists to bring unpleasant subject matter squarely into what had been aptly called "the fairyland of fiction." The first of her social-reform novels grew out of her strong revulsion for American slavery, also depicted in *Domestic Manners of the Americans*. In *The Life and Adventures of Jonathan Jefferson Whitlaw* (1836) she told the story of a cruel overseer, anticipating by fifteen years the more famous *Uncle Tom's Cabin* by Harriet Beecher Stowe. In Whitlaw Mrs. Trollope established certain themes, plot devices, and character types that would eventually dominate the antislavery novel. The book contains a sadistic overseer, a loving slave couple, and benevolent Europeans. Mrs. Trollope set amid vivid American scenery the tale of Paradise Plantation, where slavery pollutes, degrades, and corrupts all who touch it. A minister and his sister try to help the slaves, but in the end, he is lynched. The debased overseer is finally assassinated by a group of slaves recruited by a black woman. Here Mrs. Trollope reveals that predilection for strong female characters which became so prominent in her later fiction. The book aroused the ire of the critics, but it sold well.

Her next contribution to the area of social-reform fiction was *The Vicar of Wrexhill* (1837), an attack upon evangelical excesses and their unfortunate effects upon women. This subject, too, had already drawn her attention in America, where she had castigated the emotionalism of revival meetings and the way they debilitated young women. In this story, a widowed lady who receives spiritual consolation from the newly appointed vicar of Wrexhill is taken in by his advances, marries him, and nearly loses her estate and possessions in consequence. The novel abounds in scenes which reviewers called "revolting" and "repulsive," as Mrs. Trollope explicitly rendered the vicar's kissing and caressing of his female congregation. Even those reviewers who criticized the book, however, had to admit the truthfulness of the vicar's portrayal. As one critic noted: "His is a fearful character; and some of his later doings are too dark and terrible to have been written down by a woman,—aye, or a man either; but Mrs. Trollope loves debateable ground." While women could write improving tales and romantic stories, most reviewers agreed that they should not enter upon the more heated debates of the period. Thackeray said that Mrs. Trollope, in writing this book, "has only harmed herself and her cause, and had much better have remained at home, pudding-making or stocking-mending, than have meddled with matters which she understands so ill." Despite such controversies, Mrs. Trollope's reputation continued to grow. Before she was finished, she would write two more controversial social-reform novels, one on factory children and the other on the "fallen woman." Having found her material, she was not about to be frightened away from the "repulsive subject."

In 1838, Mrs. Trollope experimented with a long-established and popular genre, the so-called literature of roguery. Again, however, she was innovative. Her rogue was a woman, and, even more unusual, a middle-aged, unattractive one. In this period of the novel, most heroines were, in Thackeray's telling phrase, "pale, pious, pulmonary, crossed in love, of course." Far from wilting or spiritual, the widow Barnaby was the first of Mrs. Trollope's many strong and somewhat outrageous heroines. With her, Mrs. Trollope increased her popularity—even with Thackeray, who now had to admit that despite his aversion to "ladies' novels," he regularly read the productions of Mrs. Trollope; ten years later, he brought out his own version of the female rogue, Becky Sharp, in *Vanity Fair* (1847-1848). But Mrs. Trollope's widow had been first. She is a passionless schemer, whose heart is never engaged by the men she regularly pursues. She lies, cheats, and manipulates the men in her life to gain social status and possessions. Martha Barnaby is Mrs. Trollope's fanciful exploration of the aspirations of women—albeit in a middle-aged, coarse, and somewhat vulgar character. Mrs. Trollope enjoyed her heroine so much that she brought her back in two sequels, a procedure ultimately to be adopted by her son with his favorite literary creations.

In the first book, *The Widow Barnaby* (1839), Martha is married and quickly widowed. The remaining action concerns her humorous attempts to land a rich and fashionable husband by manipulating all the conventional female stances. She openly makes use of the contemporary marriage market, exploiting postures of female delicacy and helplessness in her hunt for a husband. By emphasizing the

Illustration by John Leech for The Barnabys in America

widow's honesty with herself, if not with others, Mrs. Trollope makes the character laudable. In *The Widow Married* (1840), Mrs. Barnaby takes a second husband, and in *The Barnabys in America* (1843), the family departs for the United States, where Mrs. Barnaby succeeds, together with her card-sharking husband, in outwitting the Americans. It seemed proper to send her favorite female character on an expedition to the land which had made her famous. The third book, the best of the three, is a farcical vision of what, in Mrs. Trollope's most mischievous dreams, might and perhaps should have happened to a traveler in America. The central swindle is an ingenious plan that Mrs. Barnaby write a book on America and thus procure access to the best society. In the South she writes in praise of slavery, and in Quaker Philadelphia she becomes an abolitionist author. When Mrs. Trollope published *Domestic Manners of the Americans*, the critics had accused her of telling lies about America to make money; Mrs. Barnaby's deceitful project is Mrs. Trollope's answer to such charges. The widow goes on from triumph to triumph. All the Barnaby books were immensely popular. The reviewers hardly knew how to evaluate the heroine, but they found her "a real kind of woman," a refreshing antidote to those sentimental heroines then so much in vogue. But the widow was a type of the new woman, a female on her own in a male-dominated world, who must struggle for existence, advancing herself by her own wits.

In 1839 Mrs. Trollope reentered the field of social-reform fiction with *The Life and Adventures of Michael Armstrong, the Factory Boy*. To write this novel, she embarked on a fact-finding mission to Manchester, where she reviewed firsthand the dreadful conditions among the industrial poor, especially children, in the northern factories. She interviewed radical reform leaders, visited factories and slums, and heard the preachers and orators advocating parliamentary legislation, especially for a ten-hour day. With her typical enthusiasm, she returned home three weeks later and began her novel, which was published in serial parts—a first for a woman author. She tells the heartrending story of a factory boy who is plucked from his environment for a brief display of benevolence by a hypocritical factory owner and then hidden away in a horrid establishment for orphan apprentices. Her novel recounts the dangerous squalor of the slum where little Michael lives and of Hidden Valley, where he works like a slave and fights with the pigs for slops to eat. The book has a fairy-tale ending when Michael escapes and makes a happy marriage,

Illustration by Auguste Hervieu for The Life and Adventures of Michael Armstrong, the Factory Boy

but the realistic settings and stories of the factory and slum environments were, nonetheless, powerful. Mrs. Trollope's theme was original: she placed no hope in individual benevolence but looked instead to legislation to relieve the poor from the burden of Manchester's industrial hell. Her purpose was to awaken the national conscience on behalf of the factory children by describing factory conditions and the horrors of child labor among the machines. Once again, Mrs. Trollope had treated a subject considered unfit for a woman writer and was castigated by the reviewers for her defiant and unladylike message. Never complacent amid human suffering, Mrs. Trollope followed her story of Michael Armstrong with an equally offensive topic: the sympathetically told *Jessie Phillips: A Tale of the Present Day* (1843), the narrative of a "fallen woman" who is destroyed by her seducer as well as by the society which fails to sympathize with her plight or aid her in her need.

During these years of her great literary successes, Mrs. Trollope remained close to all her surviving family. She had lost her husband and all her children except Tom, Cecilia, and Anthony. So much has been said and written about Mrs. Trollope's relationship with her famous son Anthony that it is perhaps necessary to characterize that relationship. After his miserable years at Harrow, Anthony found his way to an appointment at the London Post Office. While intending to write a novel, he had led a dissipated life, not yet possessed of the self-discipline and power of compartmentalization his mother's life had demonstrated. In 1840, Anthony collapsed with an illness that mystified his doctors. While Mrs. Trollope nursed him, she continued, as had been her habit for many years, to write. In the year that he lay sick and debilitated, she composed two novels, both satires on London life and the desire for literary fame: *Charles Chesterfield; or, The Adventures of a Youth of Genius* (1841) and *The Blue Belles of England* (1842). As Anthony lay ill, watching his mother's work, which went steadily on amid distractions, he gradually extricated himself from his inertia. At sixty-one years of age, she had succeeded in teaching her son—perhaps without saying a word about it—how to become a writer.

While Anthony had been learning from his mother, Mrs. Trollope had also seen clearly the strength of the female character. In the decade of the 1840s, following the completion of her last social-reform fiction and Anthony's return to health, her novels began to change. Increasingly she presented determined, intelligent, and willful girls having difficulty in marital ventures. While her main heroines were largely conventional, she drew sympathetically a series of strong female characters including fortune hunters, villainesses, sirens, and unhappy wives. In these novels women longed for excitement as well as security. Noting Mrs. Trollope's interest in these deviant female types, reviewers concluded that she had gone too far, but once again her reading public disagreed.

Mrs. Trollope's son Thomas Adolphus had now become her companion, and she traveled to Florence with him in 1843 for what was to be a year's residence. Instead, it became their permanent home. Anthony had married, as had Cecilia, who was happily settled in the Lake District. But there was to be one more major trial in Mrs. Trollope's life. In 1848, Cecilia succumbed to the tuberculosis that had claimed three of her family before her. At seventy years of age, Mrs. Trollope journeyed across revolution-torn Europe to nurse her daughter in her last illness and to help care for her five small grandchildren, continuing, even among these tragic scenes, her daily ritual of writing.

After Cecilia's death, Mrs. Trollope returned to her beloved Florence, where she embarked upon her last fictional innovation: a group of novels in which the heroines are truly triumphant females, whose most obvious quality is a sturdy, even aggressive independence, and whose most frequent trials are confronting tyrannical fathers or coping with marriages to weak or evil men. From the comical widow Barnaby, through her series of desperate fortune hunters, Mrs. Trollope had focused on the position of women. These latter-day heroines emerged victorious in ways strikingly disregardful of the proprieties and goals around which most Victorian ladies shaped their lives. In *Second Love* (1851), three women struggle with unhappy unions—one with a man not her intellectual or moral equal, another with a man she pities, a third with an elderly man she does not love. Throughout, the women are strong and dominant, their men stupid pawns. Release comes not through female submission, but through the deaths or disappearances of these inferior spouses.

Mrs. Mathews (1851) perfectly exemplifies Mrs. Trollope's theme of the triumphant feminine. Here, an older single woman marries in deference to her aging father's request, only to find herself saddled with a vicious, oppressive husband. Her struggles against and eventual defeat of this villain demonstrate the power of the independent woman and show clearly that the single state is best, a message rarely heard in Victorian fiction. *Uncle Walter* (1852) assaults the convention of the marriage market and the ritual of arranging marriages. Here again, Mrs. Trollope's heroine sees through the social facade and chooses the man she wants for a husband. Reviewers of these later novels often found them vulgar, written with more than usual of Mrs. Trollope's "coarseness and bad taste." Clearly she had lost none of her ability to shock.

To the end, her plots and situations continued to be subversive. In *The Young Heiress* (1853), a woman revenges herself upon the man who has treated her as a slave by poisoning him, but not before she insures the inheritance for her illegitimate son. *The Life and Adventures of a Clever Woman* (1854) features Mrs. Trollope's most indomitable heroine of all, a motherless seventeen-year-old, who records her triumphs and deceptions in a lively and outrageous journal. Detached and logical, she remains throughout undeceived by the motives of the men who pursue her and marries, finally, only for her own social convenience. As she records in her diary (and the reader agrees), "I have always thought and felt, that I was not quite an ordinary character." Relishing the power struggle with men, she wins in the end. Two more novels followed, and

Frances Trollope in old age (Boston Public Library)

in her last, *Fashionable Life; or, Paris and London* (1856), Mrs. Trollope moved from these dominant ladies to a vision of a community of females living in peace, harmony, and cooperation, happier than they had ever been with the men in their lives.

Mrs. Trollope lived several more years but wrote no more, dying in Florence in her eighty-fourth year.

Although her literary achievements have often been overshadowed by her heroic bread-winning for her family and the fame of her son Anthony, Frances Trollope's work in the field of nineteenth-century fiction deserves serious critical attention. First, she had a truly pioneering nature and broke paths in a number of important fictional areas. In social-reform fiction, she opened up a whole range of new subjects: slavery, evangelical excesses, child labor and the industrial and slum areas of England, and the injustices in the treatment of the "fallen woman." She helped revitalize the travel book, concentrating on people rather than on landscape, and bringing the techniques of fiction to serve that older genre. To this day, *Domestic Manners of the Americans* is the starting point for commentators on the United States. She also was instrumental in breaking down nineteenth-century stereotypes of the heroine with the creation of her strong, independent ladies. She gave women important roles in her social-reform fiction, expanded the female picaresque, and developed a new, more aggressive heroine. Critics of her time were sensitive to her innovations and often bristled at her daring. Still, she became a skillful novelist with a large following, prolific and experimental to the last. Recognition of her contributions must include these considerable literary achievements as well as the inspirational quality of her life.

Biographies:
Frances Eleanor Trollope, *Frances Trollope: Her Life*

and Literary Work from George III to Victoria (London: Bentley, 1895);

Johanna Johnson, *The Life, Manners, and Travels of Fanny Trollope: A Biography* (New York: Hawthorn, 1978);

Helen Heineman, *Mrs. Trollope: The Triumphant Feminine in the Nineteenth Century* (Athens: Ohio University Press, 1979).

References:
Helen Heineman, "Frances Trollope in the New World: Domestic Manners of the Americans," *American Quarterly*, 21 (1969): 544-559;

Heineman, "Frances Trollope's Jessie Phillips: Sexual Politics and the New Poor Law," *International Journal of Women's Studies*, 1 (1978): 60-80;

Heineman, "Starving in that Land of Plenty: New Backgrounds to *Domestic Manners of the Americans*," *American Quarterly*, 24 (1972): 643-660.

Appendices

On Art in Fiction

Edward Bulwer

First Published in the Monthly Chronicle, *1 (March 1838): 42-51; (April 1838): 138-149*.

Art is that process by which we give to natural materials the highest excellence they are capable of receiving.

We estimate the artist, not only in proportion to the success of his labours, but in proportion to the intellectual faculties which are necessary to that success. Thus, a watch by Breguét is a beautiful work of art, and so is a tragedy by Sophocles:—The first is even more perfect of its kind than the last, but the tragedy requires higher intellectual faculties than the watch; and we esteem the tragedian above the watchmaker.

The excellence of art consists in the fitness of the object proposed with the means adopted. Art carried to its perfection would be the union of the most admirable object with the most admirable means; in other words, it would require a greatness in the conception correspondent to the genius in the execution. But as mechanical art is subjected to more definite and rigorous laws than intellectual art, so, in the latter, a comprehensive critic regards the symmetry of the whole with large indulgence towards blemishes in detail. We contemplate mechanical art with reference to its utility—intellectual art with reference to its beauty. A single defect in a watch may suffice to destroy all the value of its construction;—a single blemish in a tragedy may scarcely detract from its effect.

In regarding any work of art, we must first thoroughly acquaint ourselves with the object that the artist had in view. Were an antiquarian to set before us a drawing, illustrative of the costume of the Jews in the time of Tiberius, we should do right to blame him if he presented to our eye goblets in the fashion of the fifteenth century; but when Leonardo da Vinci undertook the sublime and moving representation of the Last Supper, we feel that his object is not that of an antiquary; and we do not regard it as a blemish that the apostles are seated upright instead of being recumbent, and that the loaves of bread are those of an Italian baker. Perhaps, indeed, the picture affected the spectators the more sensibly from their familiarity with the details; and the effect of art on the whole was only heightened by a departure from correctness in minutiae. So, in an anatomical drawing that professed to give the exact proportions of man, we might censure the designer if the length of the limbs were disproportioned to the size of the trunk; but, when the sculptor of the Apollo Belvidere desired to convey to the human eye the ideal of the God of Youth, the length of the limbs contributed to give an additional and super-human lightness and elasticity to the form; and the excellence of the art was evinced and promoted by the sacrifice of mechanical accuracy in detail. It follows, therefore, that intellectual Art and technical Correctness are far from identical;—that one is sometimes proved by the disdain of the other. And, as this makes the distinction between mechanical and intellectual art, so is the distinction remarkable in proportion as that intellectual art is exercised in the highest degree,—in proportion as it realises the Ideal. For the Ideal consists not in the imitation, but the exaltation, of Nature; and we must accordingly inquire, not how far it resembles what we have seen so much as how far it embodies what we can imagine.

It is not till we have had great pictures, that we can lay down the rules of painting;—it is not till we have had great writers in a particular department of intellect, that we can sketch forth a code of laws for those who succeed them: For the theory of art resembles that of science; we must have data to proceed upon, and our inductions must be drawn from a vast store of experiments.

Prose fictions have been cultivated by modern writers of such eminence, and now form so wide and essential a part of the popular literature of Europe, that it may not be an uninteresting or an useless task to examine the laws by which the past may be tested, and the labours of future students simplified and abridged.

PROSE FICTIONS.

The Novelist has three departments for his art: MANNERS, PASSIONS, CHARACTER.

MANNERS.

The delineation of manners embraces both past and present; the Modern and the Historical Romance.

The Historical.

We have a right to demand from the writer who professes to illustrate a former age, a perfect acquaintance with its characteristics and spirit. At the same time, as he intends rather to interest than instruct us, his art will be evinced in the illustrations he selects, and the skill with which they are managed. He will avoid all antiquarian dissertations not essentially necessary to the conduct of his tale. If, for instance, his story should have no connection with the mysteries of the middle ages, he will take care how he weary us with an episodical description that changes his character from that of a narrator into that of a lecturer. In the tale of Notre Dame de Paris, by Victor Hugo, the description of the cathedral of Notre Dame is not only apposite, but of the deepest interest; for the cathedral is, by a high effort of art, made an absolute portion of the machinery of the tale. But the long superfluous description of the spectacle with which the story opens is merely a parade of antiquarian learning, because the Scholars and the Mysteries have no proportionate bearing whatever in the future development of the tale.

The usual fault of the historical novelist is over minuteness in descriptions of dress and feasts, of pageants and processions. Minuteness is not accuracy. On the contrary, the more the novelist is minute, the more likely he is to mar the accurate effect of the whole, either by wearisome tameness or some individual error.

An over-antiquated phraseology is a common and a most inartistical defect: whatever diction the delineator of a distant age employs, can never be faithful to the language of the time, for if so, it would be unintelligible. So, in the German novels that attempt a classical subject, there is the prevalent vice of a cold imitation of a classic epistolary style. It is the very attempt at resemblance that destroys the illusion, as it is by the servility of a copy that we are most powerfully reminded of the difference between the copy and the original. The language of a former time should be presented to us in the freest and most familiar paraphrase we can invent. Thus the mind is relieved at once from the task of forming perpetual comparisons, and surrenders itself to the delusion the more easily, from the very candour with which the author makes demand on its credulity. In selecting a particular epoch for illustration, an artistical author will consider well what is the principal obstacle in the mind of his audience to the reception of his story. For instance, if he select a story of ancient Greece, the public will be predisposed to anticipate a frigid pedantry of style, and

delineations of manners utterly different from those which are familiar to us now. The author will, therefore, agreeably surprise the reader, if he adopt a style as familiar and easy as that which a Greek would have used in common conversation; and show the classical spirit that pervades his diction, by the grace of the poetry, or the lightness of the wit, with which he can adorn his allusions and his dialogue. Thus, the very learning he must evince will only be but incidental and easy ornament. On the other hand, instead of selecting such specimens and modifications of human nature as are most different from, and unfamiliar to, the sympathies of modern times, he will rather prefer to appeal to the eternal sentiments of the heart, by showing how closely the men of one age resemble those of another. His hero, his lover, his epicure, his buffoon, his miser, his boaster, will be as close to the life as if they were drawn from the streets of London. The reader will be interested to see society different, yet men the same; and the Manners will be relieved from the disadvantage of unfamiliarity by an entire sympathy with the humours they mask, or the passions on which they play.

Again, if the author propose to carry his reader to the times of Richard the First or of Elizabeth, he will have to encounter an universal repugnance from the thought of an imitation of Ivanhoe or Kenilworth. An author who was, nevertheless, resolved to select such a period for his narrative would, accordingly, if an artist of sufficient excellence, avoid with care touching upon any of the points which may suggest the recollection of Scott. He would deeply consider all the features of the time, and select those neglected by his predecessor;—would carefully note all the deficiencies of the author of Kenilworth, and seize at once upon the ground which that versatile genius omitted to consecrate to himself.

To take the same epoch, the same characters, even the same narrative, as a distinguished predecessor, is perfectly allowable; and, if successful, a proof at once of originality and skill. But if you find the shadow of the previous work flinging itself over your own—if you have not thoroughly escaped the influence of the first occupant of the soil,—you will only invest your genius to unnecessary disadvantage, and build edifices, however graceful and laboured, upon the freehold of another.

In novels devoted to the delineation of existing manners, the young author will be surprised to find, that exact and unexaggerated fidelity has never been the characteristic of the greatest novelists of their own time. There would be, indeed, something inane and trifling, or mean and vulgar, in Dutch copies of the modern still life. We do not observe any frivolity in Walter Scott, when he describes with elaborate care the set of the ruffle, the fashion of the cloak of Sir Walter Raleigh, nor when he catalogues all the minutiae of the chamber of Rowena. But to introduce your hero of May Fair with an exact portraiture of the colour of his coat, and the length of his pantaloons, to item all the commodes and fauteuils of the boudoir of a lady Caroline or Frances, revolts our taste as an effeminate attention to trifles.

In humbler life, the same rule applies with equal strength. We are willing to know how Gurth was dressed, or Esmeralda lodged; but we do not require the same minuteness in describing the smock-frock of a labourer, or the garret of the girl who is now walking upon stilts for a penny. The greatest masters of the novel of modern life have usually availed themselves of HUMOUR as the illustration of manners; and have, with a deep and true, but, perhaps, unconscious, knowledge of art, pushed the humour almost to the verge of caricature. For as the Serious Ideal requires a certain exaggeration in the proportions of the Natural, so also does the Ludicrous. Thus, Aristophanes, in painting the humours of his time, resorts to the most poetical extravagance of machinery, and calls the Clouds in aid of his ridicule of philosophy, or summons Frogs and Gods to unite in his satire on Euripides. The Don Quixote of Cervantes never lived, nor, despite the vulgar belief, ever could have lived, in Spain; but the art of the portrait is in the admirable exaltation of the Humorous by means of the Exaggerated. With more qualification, the same may be said of Parson Adams, of Sir Roger de Coverley, and even of the Vicar of Wakefield.

Where the author has not adopted the Humorous as the best vehicle for the delineation of manners, he has sometimes artfully removed the scene from the country that he seeks to delineate, so that he might place his portraitures at a certain, and the most advantageous, distance from the eye. Thus, Le Sage obtains his object, of a consummate and masterly picture of the manners of his own land, though he has taken Spain for the theatre of the adventures of Gil Blas; and Swift has transferred all that his experience or his malice could narrate of the intrigues of courts, the chimeras of philosophy, the follies and vices of his nation and his time, to the regions of Lilliput and Laputa.

It may be observed, that the delineation of Manners is usually the secondary object of a novelist of high power. To a penetrating mind, manners are subservient to the illustration of views of life, or the consummation of original character. In a few years the mere portraiture of manners is obsolete. It is the knowledge of what is durable in human nature that alone preserves the work from decay. Lilly and Shakspeare alike painted the prevailing and courtly mannerism of their age. The Euphues rests upon our shelves;—Don Armado will delight us as long as pedantry exists.

CHARACTER.

An author once said, "Give me a character, and I will find the play"; and, if we look to the most popular novels, we shall usually find, that where one reader speaks of the conduct of the story, a hundred readers will speak of the excellence of some particular character.

An author, before resolving on the characters he designs to portray, will do well to consider maturely, first, what part they are destined to play in his performance; and secondly, what is the precise degree of interest which he desires them to create. Having thus considered, and duly determined, he will take care that no other character in the work shall interfere with the effect each is intended to produce. Thus, if his heroine is to be drawn gentle and mild, no second heroine, with the same attributes, should distract the attention of the reader, a rule that may seem obvious, but which is usually overlooked. When the author feels that he has thoroughly succeeded in a principal and predominant character, he will even sacrifice others, nominally more important, to increase the interest of the figure in the foreground. Thus, in the tale of Ivanhoe, Rowena, professedly the heroine, is very properly sacrificed to Rebecca. The more interesting the character of Rowena, the more pathetic the position she had assumed, the more we should have lost our compassion and admiration of the Jewess; and the highest merit of the tale, its pathos, would have been diminished. The same remark will apply to the Clementina and Harriet Byron of Richardson.

The author will take care not to crowd his canvass. He will select as few characters as are compatible with the full agency of his design. Too many plants in a narrow compass destroy each other. He will be careful to individualise each; but, if aspiring to the highest order of art, he will yet tone down their colours by an infinite variety of shades. The most original characters are those most delicately drawn, where the individual peculiarity does not obtrude itself naked and unrelieved. It was a very cheap purchase of laughter in Sir Walter Scott, and a mere trick of farce, which Shakspeare and Cervantes would have disdained, to invest a favourite humorist with some cant phrase, which he cannot open his mouth without disgorging. This was so special a device (because so easy and popular a mode of producing a ludicrous effect) with Sir Walter Scott, that it was almost his invariable resource. The "Prodigious" of Dominie Sampson—the "My Father, the Baillie" of Nichol Jarvie—the "*Provant*" of Major Dalgettie—the "*Dejeuner* at Tillietudlem" of Lady Margaret Bellenden, &c., all belong to one source of humour, and that the shallowest and most hacknied. If your tale spread over a considerable space of time, you will take care that your readers may note the change of character which time has necessarily produced. You will quietly show the difference between the boy of eighteen and the man of forty;—you will connect the change in the character with the influence of the events you have narrated. In the novel of Anastasius, this art of composition is skilfully and delicately mastered; more so than in Gil Blas.

If you bend all your faculties to the developement of some single character, and you make us sensible that such is your object, the conduct of your story becomes but a minor consideration. Shakspeare, probably, cared but little whether the fencing scene in Hamlet was the best catastrophe he could invent: he took the incidents of the story as he found them; and lavished his genius on the workings of the mind, to which all external incidents on this side the grave had become trivial and uninfluential,—weary, unprofitable, stale.

It must rest entirely on the nature of the interest you desire it to effect, whether you seek clearly to place before us, or dimly to shadow out, each particular character. If you connect your hero with supernatural agency, if you introduce incidents not accounted for by purely human means, if you resort to the Legendary and Mysterious, for the interest that you identify with any individual character, it may be most artistical to leave such a character vague, shadowy, and half incompleted. Thus, very skilfully is the Master of Ravenswood, over whose head hang ominous and weird predictions, left a less distinct and palpable creation than the broad-shouldered and much-eating heroes, whom Scott usually conducts through a Labyrinth of adventures to marriage with a wealthy Ariadne.

The formation of characters improbable and grotesque is not very compatible with a high conception of art, unless the work be one that so avowedly deals with beings different from those we mix with, that our imagination is prepared as to the extent of the demand upon its faith. Thus, when Shakspeare introduces us at once to the Enchanted Island, and we see the wand of the magician, and hear the song of Ariel, we are fully prepared to consider Caliban a proper inhabitant of such a soil; or when the Faust opens with the Chorus of the Angels, and the black dog appears in the chamber of the solitary student, the imagination finds little difficulty in yielding assent to the vagaries of the witches, and the grotesque diablerie of the Hartz Mountains; but we are wholly unprepared to find a human Caliban in the bell-ringer of a Parisian cathedral; and we see no reason why Quasimodo should not have been as well shaped as other people. The use of the Grotesque in The Abbot, where Sir Percy Shafto is killed and revived, is an absurdity as gross and gratuitous as can well be conceived.

In the portraiture of evil and criminal characters lies the widest scope for an author profoundly versed in the philosophy of the human heart. In all countries, in all times, the delineation of crime has been consecrated to the highest order of poetry. For as the emotions of terror and of pity are those which it falls to the province of the sublimest genius to arouse, so it is chiefly, though not solely, in the machinations of guilt that may be found the source of the one, and in the misfortunes, sometimes of the victim of the guilt, nay, sometimes of the guilty agent himself, that we arrive at the fountain of the softer passion. Thus, the murder of Duncan rouses our compassion, through our admission to all the guilty doubts and aspirations of Macbeth; and our terror is of far higher and more enthralling order, because it is reflected back upon us from the bared and struggling heart of the murderer, than it would have been if we had seen the physical death of the victim. It may be observed, indeed, that, in a fine tragedy, it is the preparation to the death that is to constitute the catastrophe that usually most sensibly excites the interest of terror, and that the blow of the murderer, and the fall of the victim, is but a release to the suspense of fear, and changes the whole current of our emotions. But the grandest combination is when the artist unites in one person the opposite passions of terror and pity—when we feel at once horror of the crime, yet compassion for the criminal. Thus, in the most stirring of all the ancient dramas, the moment that we discover that Oedipus has committed the crimes from which we most revolt, homicide and incest, is the very moment in which, to the deepest terror of the crimes is united the most intense compassion for the criminal. So, again, before the final catastrophe of the mystic fate of Macbeth, when evil predictions are working to their close, and we feel that his hour is come, Shakspeare has paused, to draw from the dark bosom of the fated murderer those moving reflections, "My way of life," &c. which steal from us insensibly our hatred of his guilt, and awaken a new and softer interest in the approaching consummation of the usurper's doom. Again, in the modern play of Virginius, when the scene opens, and discovers the avenging father upon the body of the murdered Appius, it is in Virginius, at once criminal and childless, that are concentrated our pity and our terror.

In the portraiture of crime, however dark, the artist will take care to throw some redeeming light. The veriest criminal has some touch and remnant of human goodness; and it is according as this sympathy between the outcast and ourselves is indicated or insinuated, that the author profanes or masters the noblest mysteries of his art. Where the criminal be one, so resolute and hardened, so inexorable and preter-human, in his guilt, that he passes the bounds of flesh-and-blood inconsistencies and sympathies, a great artist will bring forth intellectual qualities to balance our disgust at the moral. Thus, in Richard III., it is with a masterly skill that Shakspeare relieves us from the revolting contemplation of unmingled crime by enlisting our involuntary and unconscious admiration on the side of the address, the subtle penetration into character, the affluent wit, the daring energy, the royal will, with which the ruthless usurper moves through the bloody scenes of his treachery. And, at the last, it is, if not by a relic of human virtue, at least by a relic of human weakness, by the working conscience, and the haunted pillow, that we are taught to remember that it is a man who sins and suffers, not a beast that ravages and is slain. Still, despite all the subtle shadings in the character of Richard, we feel that the guilt is overdrawn—that the dark spirit wants a moral as well as intellectual relief. To penetrating critics, it has always, therefore, been the most coarse of all the creations of Shakspeare; and will never bear a comparison, as a dissection of human nature, with the goaded and writhing wickedness of Macbeth.

In the delineation of a criminal, the author will take care to show us the motives of the crimes—the influences beneath which the character has been formed. He will suit the nature of the criminal to the state of society in which he is cast. Thus, he will have occasions for the noblest morality. By concentrating in one focus the vicious influences of any peculiar error in the social system, he will hold up a mirror to nations themselves.

As the bad man will not be painted as thoroughly and unredeemedly bad, so he, whom you represent as good, will have his foibles or infirmities. You will show where even the mainspring of his virtues sometimes calls into play a counter vice. Your just man will be sometimes severe—your generous man will be sometimes careless of the consequences of generosity. It is true that, in both these applications of art, you will be censured by shallow critics and pernicious moralists. It will be said of you in the one case, "He seeks to interest us in a murderer or a robber, an adulterer or a parricide";—it will be said of you in the other, "And this man whom he holds up to us as an example, whom he calls wise and good, is a rascal, who indulges such an error, or commits such an excess." But no man can be an artist who does not prefer experience and human nature to all criticism; and, for the rest, he must be contented to stand on the same ground, or to have filled his urn from the same fountains, as Shakspeare and Boccaccio, as Goethe and Schiller, Fielding and Le Sage. If it be, however, necessary to your design to paint some character as almost faultless, as exempt from our common infirmities and errors, you will act skilfully if you invest it with the attributes of old age. When all the experience of error has been dearly bought, when the passions are laid at rest, and the mind burns clear as the night deepens, virtue does, in fact, become less and less wavering and imperfect. But youth without a fault would be youth without a passion; and such a portrait would make us despair of emulation, and arm against reverence and esteem all the jealousies of self-love.

THE PASSIONS.

Delineation of passions is inseparable from the delineation of character. A novel, admirable in character, may, indeed, be drawn, in which the passions are but coldly and feebly shadowed forth: Gil Blas is an example. But either such novels are intended as representations of external life, not of the metaphysical operations of the inner man, or they deal with the humours and follies, not the grave and deep emotions, of our kind, and belong to the *Comedy* of Romance.

But if a novel of character can be excellent without passion, it would be impossible to create a novel of passion without character. The elementary passions themselves, like the elements, are few: it is the modifications they take in passing through different bodies that give us so inexhaustible a variety of lights and shadows, of loveliness and glory.

The passion of Love is not represented by a series of eloquent rhapsodies, or even of graceful sentiments. It is represented, in fiction, by its effects on some particular character: the same with Jealousy, Avarice, Revenge, &c. Therefore, in a certain sense of the word, all representations of passion in fiction may be considered *typical*. In Juliet, it is not the picture of love solely and abstractedly—it is the picture of love in its fullest effect on *youth*. In Anthony, it is love as wild, and as frantic, and as self-sacrificing; but it is love, not emanating from the enthusiasm of youth, but already touched with something of the blindness and infirmity of dotage.

In Macbeth, it is not the mere passion of ambition that is portrayed,—it is ambition operating on a man physically daring, and morally irresolute; a man whom the darkest agencies alone can compel, and whom the fullest triumphs of success cannot reconcile, to crime. So, if we review all the passionate characters of Shakspeare, we shall find that the passion is individualised and made original by the mould in which the fiery liquid is cast. Nor is the language of that passion declamation upon the passion itself, but the revelation of the effect it produces on a single subject. It is, accordingly, in the perfect harmony that exists between the character and the passion that the abstract and bodiless idea finds human force and corporeal interest. If you would place the passion before us in a new light, the character that represents it must be original. An artistical author, taking advantage of the multiform inconsistencies of human nature, will often give to the most hacknied passion a thoroughly new form, by placing it in a character where it could least be looked for. For instance, should you desire to portray avarice, you will go but on worn-out ground, if you resort to Plautus and to Moliere for your model. But if you find in history the record of a brilliant courtier, a successful general, marked and signalised by the vice of Harpagon, the vice itself takes a new hue, and your portraiture will be a new addition to our knowledge of the mysteries of our kind. Such a representation, startling, untouched, and truthful, might be taken from the character of the Duke of Marlborough, the hero of Blenheim. In portraying the effect of a passion, the rarest art of the novelist is to give it its due weight and no more. Thus, in love novels, we usually find nothing but love; as if, in the busy and complicated life of man,

there were no other spring to desire and action but

"Love, love—eternal love."

Again, if an author portrays a miser, he never draws him otherwise than as a miser. He makes him, not the avaricious miser, but abstract avarice itself. Not so Shakspeare, when he created Shylock. Other things, other motives, occupy the spirit of the Jew besides his gold and his argosies: he is a grasping and relentless miser, yet he can give up avarice to revenge. He has sublime passions, that elevate his mean ones.

If your novel be devoted to love and its effects, you will act more consistently with the truths of life, if you throw the main interest of the passion in the heroine. In the hero, you will increase our sense of the power of the passion, if you show us all the conflicting passions with which in men it usually contends—ambition, or honour, or duty: the more the effect of the love is shown by the obstacles it silently subdues, the more triumphant will be your success. You will recollect that in the novel, as in the drama, it is in the *struggle* of emotions that the science of the heart is best displayed; and, in the delineation of such struggles, there is ground little occupied hitherto by the great masters of English fiction. It was not in the province of Fielding or Smollett; and Scott but rarely indulges, and still more rarely succeeds, in the metaphysical operations of stormy and conflicting feelings. He rather seems to have made it a point of art to imitate the ancient painter, and throw a veil over passions he felt inadequate to express. Thus, after the death and burial of Lucy, it is only by the heavy and unequal tread of Ravenswood, in his solitary chamber, that his agonies are to be conjectured. But this avoidance of the internal man, if constant and systematic, is but a clever trick to hide the want of power.

THE SENTIMENT.

The sentiment that pervades a book is often its most effective moral, and its most universal charm. It is a pervading and indescribable harmony, in which the heart of the author himself seems silently to address our own. Through creations of crime and vice, there may be one pervading sentiment of virtue; through the humblest scenes, a sentiment of power and glory. It is the sentiment of Wordsworth of which his disciples speak, when they enlarge upon attributes of holiness and beauty, which detached passages, however exquisite, do not suffice to justify; for the sentiment of a work is felt, not in its parts, but as a whole: it is undefinable and indefinite—it escapes while you seek to analyse it. Of all the qualities of fiction, the sentiment is that which we can least subject to the inquiries or codes of criticism. It emanates from the moral and predominant quality of the author,—the perfume from his genius; and by it he unconsciously reveals himself. The sentiment of Shakspeare is in the strong sympathies with all that is human. In the sentiment of Swift, we see the reflection of a spirit discontented and malignant. Mackenzie, Goldsmith, Voltaire, Rousseau, betray their several characters as much in the prevalent sentiment of their writings as if they had made themselves the heroes. Of all writers of great genius, Shakspeare has the most sentiment, and, perhaps, Smollett and Defoe the least. The student will distinguish between a work of sentiment and a sentimental work. As the charm of sentiment in a fiction is that it is latent and indefinite, so the charm vanishes the instant it becomes obtruding and importunate. The mistake of Kotzebue and many of the Germans, of Metastasio, and a feeble and ephemeral school of the Italians, was in the confounding sentiment with passion.

Sentiment is capable of many classifications and subdivisions. The first and finest is that touched upon—the sentiment of the whole work: a sentiment of beauty or of grandeur—of patriotism or of benevolence—of veneration, of justice, or of piety. This may be perfectly distinct from the characters or scenes portrayed: it evinces itself insensibly and invisibly; and we do not find its effect till we sum up all the effects that the work has bequeathed. The sentiment is, therefore, often incorporated and identified with the moral tendency of the fiction.

There is also a sentiment that belongs to style, and gives depth and colouring to peculiar passages. For instance, in painting a pastoral life in the heart of lonely forests, or by the side of unpolluted streams, the language and thoughts of the author glide into harmony with the images he creates; and we feel that he has, we scarcely know by what art, penetrated himself and us with the Sentiment of Repose.

A sentiment of this nature will be felt at once by the lovers of Spenser, and of Ariosto and Tasso. In the entrance to the Domains of Death, Milton breathes over the whole description the Sentiment of Awe.

The Sentiments are distinct from the Passions: sometimes they are most eloquent in the utter absence of passion itself; as the sentiment that pervades the poem of The Castle of Indolence;—at other times they are the neighbours, the intervening shades, between one passion and another; as the Sentiment of a Pleasing Melancholy. Regret and Awe are sentiments: Grief and Terror, passions.

As there is a sentiment that belongs to description, so there are characters in which sentiment supplies the place of passion. The character of Jacques, in As You like It, is purely one of sentiment. Usually, sentiment is, in character, most effective when united with humour, as in Uncle Toby and Don Quixote, and, to quote a living writer, some of the masterly creations of Paul de Kock. For the very delicacy of the sentiment will be most apparent by the contrast of what seems to us at first the opposite quality; as the violet we neglect in a flower-bed enchants us in the hollow of a rock.

In a succeeding paper it is proposed to enter upon the construction of the fiction itself—the distinctions between the Drama and the Novel—and the mechanism, conduct, and catastrophe of the different species of Invented Narrative.

THE CONCEPTION.

A story may be well constructed, yet devoid of interest; on the other hand, the construction may be faulty and the interest vivid. This is the case even with the drama. Hamlet is not so well constructed a story as the Don Carlos of Alfieri; but there is no comparison in the degree of interest excited in either tragedy. Still, though we ought not to consider that excellence in the technical arrangement of incidents as a certain proof of the highest order of art, it is a merit capable of the most brilliant effects, when possessed by a master. An exquisite mechanism in the construction of the mere story, not only gives pleasure in itself, but it displays other and loftier beauties to the best advantage. It is the setting of the jewels.

It is common to many novelists to commence a work without any distinct chart of the country which they intend to traverse—to suffer one chapter to grow out of another, and invention to warm as the creation grows. Scott has confessed to this mode of novel-writing[1] but Scott, with all his genius, was rather a great mechanist than a great artist. His execution was infinitely superior to his conception. It may be observed, indeed, that his conceptions are often singularly poor and barren, compared with the vigour with which they are worked out. He conceives a story with the design of telling it as well as he can, but is wholly insensible to the high and true aim of art, which is rather to consider for what objects the story should be told. Scott never appears to say to himself, "Such a tale will throw a new light upon human passions, or add fresh stores to human wisdom: for that reason I select it." He seems rather to consider what picturesque effects it will produce, what striking scenes, what illustrations of mere manners. He regards the story with the eye of the *property man*, though he tells it with the fervour of the poet. It is not thus that the greatest authorities in fiction have composed. It is clear to us that Shakspeare, when he selected the tale which he proposed to render Χτῆμά ἰϛ ἀεἰ ,—the everlasting possession of mankind, made it his first and paramount object to work out certain passions, or affections of the mind, in the most complete and profound form. He did not so much consider how the incidents might be made most striking, as how the truths of the human heart might be made most clear. And it is a remarkable proof of his consummate art, that though in his best plays we may find instances in which the mere incidents might be made more probable, and the theatrical effects more vivid, we can never see one instance in such plays where the passion he desired to represent, could have been placed in a broader light, or the character he designed to investigate, could have been submitted to a minuter analysis. We are quite sure that Othello and Macbeth were not written without the clear and deep and premeditated CONCEPTION of the story to be told us. For with Shakspeare the conception itself is visible and gigantic from the first line to the last. So in the greatest works of Fielding a very obtuse critic may perceive that the author sat down to write in order to embody a design previously formed. The perception of moral truths urged him to the composition of his fictions. In Jonathan Wild, the finest prose satire in the English language, Fielding, before he set pen to paper, had resolved to tear the mask from False Greatness. In his conception of the characters and histories of Blifil and Jones, he was bent on dethroning that popular idol—False Virtue. The scorn of hypocrisy in all grades, all places, was the intellectual passion of Fielding; and his masterpieces are the results of intense convictions. That many incidents never contemplated would suggest themselves as he proceeded—that the technical plan of events might deviate and vary, according as he saw new modes of enforcing his aims, is unquestionable. But still Fielding always commenced *with* a plan—with a conception—with a moral end, to be achieved by definite agencies, and through the medium of certain characters preformed in his mind. If Scott had no preconcerted story when he commenced Chapter the First of one of his delightful tales, it was because he was deficient in the highest attributes of art, viz., its philosophy

and its ethics. He never seems to have imagined that the loftiest merit of a tale rests upon the effect it produces, not on the fancy, but on the intellect and the passions. He had no grandeur of conception, for he had no strong desire to render palpable and immortal some definite and abstract truth.

It is a sign of the low state of criticism in this country that Scott has been compared to Shakspeare. No two writers can be more entirely opposed to each other in the qualities of their genius, or the sources to which they applied. Shakspeare ever aiming at the development of the secret man, and half disdaining the mechanism of external incidents; Scott painting the ruffles and the dress, and the features and the gestures—avoiding the movements of the heart, elaborate in the progress of the incident. Scott never caught the mantle of Shakspeare, but he improved on the dresses of his wardrobe, and threw artificial effects into the scenes of his theatres.

Let us take an example: we will select one of the finest passages in Sir Walter Scott: a passage unsurpassed for its mastery over the PICTURESQUE. It is that chapter in "Kenilworth," where Elizabeth has discovered Amy, and formed her first suspicions of Leicester.

"Leicester was at this moment the centre of a splendid group of lords and ladies, assembled together under an arcade or portico, which closed the alley. The company had drawn together in that place, to attend the commands of her majesty when the hunting party should go forward, and their astonishment may be imagined, when instead of seeing Elizabeth advance towards them with her usual measured dignity of motion, they beheld her walking so rapidly, that she was in the midst of them ere they were aware; and then observed with fear and surprise, that her features were flushed betwixt anger and agitation, that her hair was loosened by her haste of motion, and that her eyes sparkled as they were wont when the spirit of Henry VIII. mounted highest in his daughter. Nor were they less astonished at the appearance of the pale, extenuated, half-dead, yet still lovely female, whom the queen upheld by main strength with one hand, while with the other she waved aside the ladies and nobles, who pressed towards her, under the idea that she was taken suddenly ill. 'Where is my Lord of Leicester?' she said, in a tone that thrilled with astonishment all the courtiers who stood around—'Stand forth, my Lord of Leicester!'

"If, in the midst of the most serene day of summer, when all is light and laughing around, a thunderbolt were to fall from the clear blue vault of heaven, and rend the earth at the very feet of some careless traveller, he could not gaze upon the smouldering chasm which so unexpectedly yawned before him, with half the astonishment and fear which Leicester felt at the sight that so suddenly presented itself. He had that instant been receiving, with a political affectation of disavowing and misunderstanding their meaning, the half-uttered, half-intimated congratulations of the courtiers upon the favour of the queen, carried apparently to its highest pitch during the interview of that morning; from which most of them seemed to augur, that he might soon arise from their equal in rank to become their master. And now, while the subdued yet proud smile with which he disclaimed those inferences was yet curling his cheek, the queen shot into the circle, her passions excited to the uttermost; and, supporting with one hand, and apparently without an effort, the pale and sinking form of his almost expiring wife, and pointing with the finger of the other to her half-dead features, demanded in a voice that sounded to the ears of the astounded statesman like the last dread trumpet-call, that is to summon body and spirit to the judgment seat, 'Knowest thou this woman?' "

The reader will observe that the whole of this splendid passage is devoted to external effects: the loosened hair and sparkling eyes of Elizabeth—the grouping of the courtiers—the proud smile yet on the cheek of Leicester—the pale and sinking form of the wife. Only by external effects do we guess at the emotions of the agents. Scott is thinking of the costume and postures of the actors, not the passions they represent. Let us take a parallel passage in Shakspeare; parallel, for, in each, a mind disturbed with jealousy is the real object placed before the reader. It is thus that Iago describes Othello, after the latter has conceived *his* first suspicions:

> "Look where he comes! Not poppy,
>   nor mandragora,
> Nor all the drowsy syrups of the world,
> Shall ever medicine thee to that sweet sleep
> Which thou ow'dst yesterday.
> *Othello.*   Ha! ha! false to me?"

Here the reader will observe that there is no attempt at the Picturesque—no sketch of the outward man. It is only by a reference to the woe that kills sleep that we can form any notion of the haggard aspect of the Moor. So, if we compare the ensuing dialogue in the romance with that in the tragedy, we shall remark that Elizabeth utters only bursts of shallow passion, which convey none of the deep effects of the philosophy of jealousy; none of the sentiments that "inform us what we are." But every sentence uttered by Othello penetrates to the very root of the passion described: the farewell to fame and pomp, which comes from a heart that, finding falsehood in the prop it leaned on, sees the world itself, and all its quality and circumstance, crumbled away; the burst of vehement incredulity;

the sudden return to doubt; the intense revenge proportioned to the intense love; the human weakness that must seek faith somewhere, and, with the loss of Desdemona, casts itself upon her denouncer; the mighty knowledge of the heart exhibited in those simple words to Iago, "I greet *thy* love";—compare all this with the mere words of Elizabeth, which have no force in themselves, but are made effective by the picturesque grouping of the scene, and you will detect at once the astonishing distinction between Shakspeare and Scott. Shakspeare could have composed the most wonderful plays from the stories in Scott; Scott could have written the most excellent stage directions to the plays of Shakspeare.

If the novelist be contented with the secondary order of Art in Fiction, and satisfied if his incidents be varied, animating, and striking, he may write from chapter to chapter, and grope his way to a catastrophe in the dark; but if he aim at loftier and more permanent effects, he will remember that to execute grandly we must conceive nobly. He will suffer the subject he selects to lie long in his mind, to be revolved, meditated, brooded over, until from the chaos breaks the light, and he sees distinctly the highest end for which his materials can be used, and the best process by which they can be reduced to harmony and order.

If, for instance, he found his tale upon some legend, the author, inspired with a great ambition, will consider what will be, not the most vivid interest, but the loftiest and most durable *order* of interest he can extract from the incidents. Sometimes it will be in a great truth elicited by the catastrophe; sometimes by the delineation of one or more characters; sometimes by the mastery over, and development of, some complicated passion. Having decided what it is that he designs to work out, he will mould his story accordingly; but before he begin to execute, he will have clearly informed his mind of the conception that induces the work itself.

INTEREST.

No fiction can be first-rate if it fail to create INTEREST. But the merit of the fiction is not, by any means, proportioned to the *degree* of excitement it produces, but to the *quality* of the excitement. It is certainly some merit to make us weep; but the great artist will consider from what sources our tears are to be drawn. We may weep as much at the sufferings of a beggar as at the agonies of Lear; but from what sublime sympathies arise our tears for the last! what commonplace pity will produce the first! We may have our interest much more acutely excited by the

"Castle of Udolpho" than by "Anastasius"; but in the one, it is a melo-dramatic arrangement of hair-breadth escapes and a technical skill in the arrangement of vulgar mysteries—in the other, it is the consummate knowledge of actual life, that fascinates the eye to the page. It is necessary, then, that every novel should excite interest; but one novel may produce a much more gradual, gentle, and subdued interest than another, and yet have infinitely more merit in the *quality* of the interest it excites.

TERROR AND HORROR.

True art never disgusts. If, in descriptions intended to harrow us, we feel sickened and revolted by the very power with which the description is drawn, the author has passed the boundary of his province; he does not appal—he shocks. Thus, nothing is more easy than to produce a feeling of intense pain by a portrait of great bodily suffering. The vulgarest mind can do this, and the mistaken populace of readers will cry, "See the power of this author!" But all sympathy with bodily torture is drawn from our basest infirmities; all sympathy with mental torture from our deepest passions and our most spiritual nature. HORROR is generally produced by the one, TERROR by the other. If you describe a man hanging by a breaking bough over a precipice—if you paint his starting eyeballs, his erect hair, the death-sweat on his brow, the cracking of the bough, the depth of the abyss, the sharpness of the rock, the roar of the cataract below, you may make us dizzy and sick with sympathy; but you operate on the physical nerves, and our sensation is that of coarse and revolting pain. But take a *moral* abyss: Oedipus, for instance, on the brink of learning the awful secret which proclaims him an incestuous parricide. Show the splendour of his power, the depth of his wisdom, the loftiness of his pride, and then gradually, step by step, reveal the precipice on which he stands—and you work not on the body but the mind; you produce the true tragic emotion, *terror*. Even in this, you must stop short of all that could make terror revolt while it thrills us. This, Sophocles has done by one of those fine perceptions of nature which open the sublimest mysteries of art; we are not allowed time to suffer our thoughts to dwell upon the incest and self-assault of Oedipus, or upon the suicide of Jocasta, before, by the introduction of the Children, terror melts into pity, and the parricide son assumes the new aspect of the broken-hearted father. A modern French writer, if he had taken this subject, would have disgusted us by details of the incest itself, or forced us from the riven heart to gaze on the bloody and eyeless sockets of the blind king; and the more he disgusted us the more he would have thought that he excelled the tragedian of Colonos. Such of the Germans, on the contrary, as follow the School of Schiller, will often stop as far short of the true boundaries of Terror as the French romanticists would go beyond it. Schiller held it a principle of art never to leave the complete and entire effects of a work of art one of pain. According to him, the pleasure of the art should exceed the sympathy with the suffering. He sought to vindicate this principle by a reference to the Greek drama, but in this he confounded the sentiments with which we, moderns, read the works of Aeschylus and Sophocles, with the sentiments with which *a Greek* would have read them. No doubt, to a Greek religiously impressed with the truth and reality of the woes or the terror depicted, the "Agamemnon" of Aeschylus, the "Oedipus Tyrannus" of Sophocles, and the "Medea" of Euripides, would have left a far more unqualified and overpowering sentiment of awe and painful sympathy than we now can entertain for victims, whom we believe to be shadows, to deities and destinies that we know to be chimeras. Were Schiller's rule universally adopted, we should condemn Othello and Lear.

Terror may then be carried up to its full extent, provided that it work upon us through the mind, not the body, and stop short of the reaction of recoil and disgust.

DESCRIPTION.

One of the greatest and most peculiar arts of the Novelist is DESCRIPTION. It is in this that he has a manifest advantage over the dramatic poet. The latter will rarely describe scenery, costume, *personals*, for they ought to be placed before the eyes of the audience by the theatre and the actors. When he does do so, it is generally understood by an intelligent critic, to be an episode introduced for the sake of some poetical beauty, which, without absolutely carrying on the plot, increases the agreeable and artistical effect of the whole performance. This is the case with the description of Dover cliff, in "Lear," or with that of the chasm which adorns, by so splendid a passage, the monstrous tragedy of "The Cenci." In the classical French theatre, as in the Greek, Description, it is true, becomes an essential part of the play itself, since the catastrophe is thrown into description. Hence the celebrated picture of the death of Hippolyte, in the "Phedre" of Racine—of the suicide of Haemon in the "Antigone" of Sophocles. But it may be doubted whether both Sophocles and his French imitator did not, in this transfer of action to words, strike at the very core of dramatic art, whether ancient or modern; for it may be remarked—and we are surprised that it has not been remarked before, that Aeschylus preferred placing the catastrophe before the eyes of the reader; and he who remembers the sublime close of the Prometheus, the storm, the lightning, the bolt, the shivered rock, and the mingled groans and threats of the Titan himself, must acknowledge that the effect is infinitely more purely tragical than it would have been if we had been told how it all happened by the Aggelos or Messenger. So in the "Agamemnon" of the same sublime poet, though we do not see the blow given, the scene itself, opening, places before us the murderess and the corpse. No messenger intervenes—no description is required for the action. "I stand where I struck him," says Clytaemnestra. "The deed is done!"[2]

But without recurring farther to the Drama of other nations, we may admit at once that in our own it is the received and approved rule that Action, as much as possible, should dispense with Description. With Narrative Fiction it is otherwise: the novel writer is his own scene painter; description is as essential to him as canvass is to the actor— description of the most various character.

In this art, none ever equalled Scott. In the comparison we made between him and Shakspeare, we meant not to censure the former for indulging in what the latter shunned; each did that which his art required. We only lament that Scott did not combine with external description an equal, or, at least, not very inferior, skill in metaphysical analysis. Had he done so, he would have achieved all of which the novelist is capable.

In the description of natural scenery, the author will devote the greatest care to such landscapes as are meant for the localities of his principal events. There is nothing, for instance, very attractive in the general features of a common; but if the author lead us through a common, on which, in a later portion of his work, a deed of murder is to be done, he will strive to fix deeply in our remembrance the character of the landscape, the stunted tree, or the mantling pool, which he means to associate in our minds with an act of terror.

If the duration of time in a fiction be limited to a year, the author may be enabled artfully to show us the progress of time by minute descriptions of the gradual change in the seasons. This is attempted to be done in the tale of "Eugene Aram": instead of telling us when it is July, and when it is October, the author of that fiction describes the signs and characteristics of the month, and seeks to identify our interest in the natural phenomena, with the approaching fate of the hero, himself an observer and an artist of the "clouds that pass to and fro," and the "herbs that wither and are renewed." Again, in description, if there be any natural objects that will bear upon the catastrophe, if, for instance, the earthquake or the inundation be intended as an agent in the fate of those whose history the narrative relates, incidental descriptions of the state of the soil, frequent references to the river or the sea, will serve to make the elements themselves minister to the interest of the plot; and the final catastrophe will be made at once more familiar, yet more sublime, if we have been prepared and led to believe that you have from the first designed to invoke to your aid the awful agencies of Nature herself. Thus, in the Oedipus at Colonos, the Poet, at the very opening of the tragedy, indulges in the celebrated description of the seats of the Dread Goddesses, because the place, and the deities themselves, though invisible, belong yet more essentially to the crowning doom of the wanderer than any of the characters introduced.

The description of *feelings* is also the property of the novelist. The dramatist throws the feelings into dialogue,—the novelist goes at once to the human heart, and calmly scrutinises, assorts, and dissects them. Few, indeed, are the writers who have hitherto attempted this—the master mystery of the hierophant! Godwin has done so the most elaborately; Goethe the most skilfully. The first writer is, indeed, so minute, that he is often frivolous—so lengthened, that he is generally tedious; but the cultivator of the art, and not the art itself, is to be blamed for such defects. A few words will often paint the precise state of emotion as faithfully as the most voluminous essay; and in this department condensation and brevity are to be carefully studied. Conduct us to the cavern, light the torch, and startle and awe us by what you reveal; but if you keep us all day in the cavern, the effect is lost, and our only feeling is that of impatience and desire to get away.

ARRANGEMENT OF INCIDENTS.
Distinctions between the Novel and the Drama.

In the arrangement of incidents, the reader will carefully study the distinctions between the novel and the drama—distinctions the more important, because they are not, at the first glance, very perceptible.

In the first place, the incidents of a play must grow, progressively, out of each other. Each scene should appear the necessary consequence of the one that precedes it. This is far from being the case with the novel; in the last, it is often desirable to go back instead of forward—to wind, to vary, to shift the interest from person to person—to keep even your principal hero, your principal actor, in the background. In the novel, you see more of Frank Osbaldistone than you do of Rob Roy; but bring Rob Roy on the stage, and Frank Osbaldistone must recede at once into a fifth-rate personage.

In our closets we should be fatigued with the incessant rush of events that we desire when we make one of a multitude. Oratory and the drama in this resemble each other—that the things best to hear are not always the best to read. In the novel, we address ourselves to the one person—on the stage we address ourselves to a crowd: more rapid effects, broader and more popular sentiments, more condensed grasp of the universal passions are required for the last. The calm advice which persuades our friend would only tire out the patience of the crowd. The man who writes a play for Covent Garden ought to remember that the Theatre is but a few paces distant from the Hustings: success at either place, the Hustings or the Theatre, will depend upon a mastery over feelings, not perhaps the most commonplace, but the most commonly felt. If with his strong effects on the stage, the dramatic poet can, like Shakspeare, unite the most delicate and subtle refinement, like Shakspeare he will be a consummate artist. But the refinement will not do without the effects. In the novel it is different: the most enchanting and permanent kind of interest, in the latter, is often gentle, tranquillising, and subdued. The novelist can appeal to those delicate and subtle emotions, which are easily awakened when we are alone, but which are torpid and unfelt in the electric contagion of popular sympathies. The most refining amongst us will cease to refine when placed in the midst of a multitude.

There is a great distinction between the plot of a novel and that of a play; a distinction which has been indicated by Goethe in the "Wilhelm Meister." The novel allows *accident*, the drama never. In the former, your principal character may be thrown from his horse, and break his neck; in the latter, this would be a gross burlesque on the first laws of the drama; for in the drama the incidents must bring about the catastrophe; in the novel, there is no such necessity. Don Quixote at the last falls ill and dies in his bed; but in order that he should fall ill and die in his bed, there was no necessity that he should fight windmills, or mistake an inn for a castle. If a novelist had taken for his theme the conspiracy of Fiesco, he

might have adhered to history with the most perfect consistency to his art. In the history, as Fiesco, after realising his ambitious projects, is about to step into the ship, he slips from the plank, and the weight of his armour drowns him. This is accident, and this catastrophe would not only have been admissible in the novel, but would have conveyed, perhaps, a sublimer moral than any that fiction could invent. But when Schiller adapted Fiesco for the stage, he felt that accident was not admissible[3], and his Fiesco falls by the hand of the patriot Verrina. The whole dialogue preceding the fatal blow is one of the most masterly adaptations of moral truth to the necessity of historical infidelity, in European literature.

In the "Bride of Lammermoor," Ravenswood is swallowed up by a quicksand. This catastrophe is singularly grand in romance; it could not be allowable on the stage; for this again is *accident*, and not *result*.

The distinctions, then, between the novel and the drama, so far as the management of incidents is concerned, are principally these: that in the one the interest must always progress—that in the other, it must often go back and often halt; that dealing with human nature in a much larger scale in the novel, you will often introduce events and incidents, not necessarily growing one out of the other, though all conducing to the completeness of the whole; that in the drama you have more impatience to guard against—you are addressing men in numbers, not the individual man; your effects must be more rapid and more startling; that in the novel you may artistically have recourse to accident for the working out of your design—in the drama, never.

The ordinary faults of a play by the novelist[4], and of a novel by the play-writer, will serve as an illustration of the principles which have insensibly regulated each. The novelist will be too diffuse, too narrative, and too refined in his effects for the stage; the play-writer will be too condensed, abrupt, and, above all, too exaggerated, for our notions of the Natural when we are in the closet. Stage effect is a vice in the novel; but, how can we expect a man trained to write for the stage to avoid what on the stage is a merit? A certain exaggeration of sentiment is natural, and necessary, for sublime and truthful effects when we address numbers; it would be ludicrous uttered to our friend in his easy chair. If Demosthenes, urging a young Athenian to conduct himself properly, had thundered out[5] that sublime appeal to the shades of Marathon, Platea, and Salamis, which thrilled the popular assembly, the young Athenian would have laughed in his face. If the dialogue of "Macbeth" were the dialogue of a romance on the same subject, it would be equally good in itself, but it would seem detestable bombast. If the dialogue in "Ivanhoe," which is matchless of its kind for spirit and fire, were shaped into blank verse, and cut up into a five-act play, it would be bald and pointless. As the difference between the effective oration and the eloquent essay—between Pitt so great to hear, and Burke so great to read, so is the difference between the writing for the eye of one man, and the writing for the ears of three thousand.

MECHANISM AND CONDUCT.

THE MECHANISM AND CONDUCT OF THE STORY ought to depend upon the nature of the preconceived design. Do you desire to work out some definite end, through the passions or through the characters you employ? Do you desire to carry on the interest less through character and passion than through incident? Or, do you rather desire to entertain and instruct by a general and wide knowledge of living manners or human nature? or, lastly, would you seek to incorporate all these objects? As you are faithful to your conception, will you be attentive to, and precise in, the machinery you use. In other words, your *progress* must depend upon the order of interest you mean to be predominant. It is by not considering this rule that critics have often called that episodical or extraneous, which is in fact a part of the design. Thus, in "Gil Blas," the object is to convey to the reader a complete picture of the surface of society; the manners, foibles, and peculiarities of the time; elevated by a general, though not very profound, knowledge of the more durable and universal elements of human nature in the abstract. Hence, the numerous tales and nouvelletes scattered throughout the work, though episodical to the adventures of Gil Blas, are not episodical to the design of Le Sage. They all serve to complete and furnish out the conception, and the whole would be less rich and consummate in its effect without them. They are not passages which lead to nothing, but conduce to many purposes we can never comprehend, unless we consider well for what end the building was planned. So if you wish to bring out all the peculiarities of a certain character, you will often seem to digress into adventures which have no palpable bearing on the external plot of incident and catastrophe. This is constantly the case with Cervantes and Fielding; and the critic who blames you for it, is committing the gross blunder of judging the novel by the laws of the drama.

But as an ordinary rule, it may be observed that, since, both in the novel and the play, human life is represented by an epitome, so in both it is desirable that all your characters should more or less be brought to bear on the conclusions you have in view. It is not necessary in the novel that they should bear on the physical events; they may sometimes bear on the mental and interior changes in the minds and characters of the persons you introduce. For instance, if you design in the life of your hero to illustrate the Passion of Jealousy upon a peculiar conformation of mind, you may introduce several characters and several incidents, which will serve to ripen his tendencies, but not have the least bearing on the actual catastrophe in which those tendencies are confirmed into deeds. This is but fidelity to real life, in which it seldom happens that they who foster the passion are the witnesses or sufferers of the effects. This distinction between interior and external agencies will be made apparent by a close study of the admirable novel of Zeluco.

In the mechanism of external incidents, Scott is the greatest model that fiction possesses; and if we select from his works that in which this mechanism is most artistical, we instance not one of his most brilliant and popular, but one in which he combined all the advantages of his multiform and matured experience in the craft: we mean the "Fair Maid of Perth." By noting well the manner in which, in this tale, the scene is ever varied at the right moment, and the exact medium preserved between abruptness and *longueur*; how all the incidents are complicated, so as to appear inextricable, yet the solution obtained by the simplest and shortest process, the reader will learn more of the art of *mechanical* construction, than by all the rules that Aristotle himself, were he living, could lay down.

DIVISIONS OF THE WORK.

In the Drama, the DIVISIONS of the plot into *Acts* are of infinite service in condensing and simplifying the design of the author. The novelist will find it convenient to himself to establish analogous divisions in the conduct of his story. The division into volumes is but the affair of the printer, and affords little help to the intellectual purposes of the author. Hence, most of our greatest novelists have had recourse to the more definite sub-partition of the work into *Books*; and if the student use this mode of division, not from capricious or arbitrary pleasure, but with the same purposes of art, for which, in the drama, recourse is had to the division into Acts, he will find it of the greatest service. Properly speaking, each Book should be complete in itself, working out the exact and whole purpose that the author meditates in that portion of his work. It is clear, therefore, that the number of his Books will vary according to the nature of his design. Where you have shaped your story after a dramatic fashion, you will often be surprised to find how greatly you serve to keep your construction faithful to your design by the mere arrangement of the work into the same number of subdivisions as are adopted in the drama, viz., five books instead of five acts. Where, on the other hand, you avoid the dramatic construction, and lead the reader through great varieties of life and action, meaning, in each portion of the history of your hero, to illustrate separate views of society or human nature, you will probably find a much greater number of subdivisions requisite. This must depend upon your design. Another advantage in these divisions consists in the rules that your own common sense will suggest to you with respect to the introduction of Characters. It is seldom advisable to admit any new character of importance, after the interest has arrived at a certain point of maturity. As you would not introduce a new character of consequence to the catastrophe, in the fifth act of a play, so, though with more qualification and reserve, it will be inartistical to make a similar introduction in the corresponding portion of a novel. The most illustrious exception to this general rule is in "Clarissa," in which the Avenger, the brother of the heroine, and the executioner of Lovelace, only appears at the close of the story, and for the single purpose of revenge; and here the effect is heightened by the lateness and suddenness of the introduction of the very person to whom the catastrophe is confided.

THE CATASTROPHE.

The distinction between the novel and the drama is usually very visible in the Catastrophe. The stage effect of bringing all the characters together in the closing chapter, to be married or stabbed as the thing may require, is, to a fine taste, eminently displeasing in a novel. It introduces into the very place where we most desire verisimilitude, a clap-trap and theatrical effect. For it must be always remembered, that in prose fiction we require more of the Real than we do in the drama (which belongs, of right, to the regions of pure poetry), and if the very last effect bequeathed to us be that of palpable delusion and trick, the charm of the whole work is greatly impaired. Some of Scott's romances may be justly charged with this defect.

Usually, the author is so far aware of the inartist-like effect of a final grouping of all the characters before the fall of the curtain, that he brings but few of the agents he has employed to be *present* at the catastrophe, and follows what may be called the wind-up of the main interest, by one or more epilogical chapters, in which we are told how Sir Thomas married and settled at his country seat, how Miss Lucy died an old maid, and how the miser Grub was found dead on his money chest; disposing in a few sentences of the lives and deaths of all to whom we have been presented—a custom that we think might now give place to less hacknied inventions.

The drama will bear but one catastrophe; the novel will admit of more. Thus, in "Ivanhoe," the more vehement and apparent catastrophe is the death of Bois Guilbert; but the marriage of Ivanhoe, the visit of Rebecca to Rowena, and the solemn and touching farewell of the Jewess, constitute, properly speaking, a catastrophe no less capital in itself, and no less essential to the completion of the incidents. So also there is often a moral catastrophe, as well as a physical one, sometimes identified each with the other, sometimes distinct. If you have been desirous to work out some conception of a principle or a truth, the design may not be completed till after the more violent effects which form the physical catastrophe. In the recent novel of "Alice, or the Mysteries," the external catastrophe is in the vengeance of Caesarini and the death of Vargrave, but the complete *denouement* and completion of the more typical meanings and ethical results of the fiction are reserved to the moment when Maltravers recognises the Natural to be the true Ideal, and is brought, by the faith and beauty of simple goodness, to affection and respect for mankind itself. In the drama, it would be necessary to incorporate in one scene all the crowning results of the preceding events. We could not bear a new interest after the death of Bois Guilbert; and a new act of mere dialogue between Alice and Maltravers, after the death of Vargrave, would be insufferably tame and frigid. The perfection of a catastrophe is not so much in the power with which it is told, as in the feeling of completeness which it should leave on the mind. On closing the work, we ought to feel that we have read a *whole*—that there is an harmonious unity in all its parts—that its close, whether it be pleasing or painful, is that which is essentially appropriate to all that has gone before; and not only the mere isolated thoughts in the work, but the unity of the work itself, ought to leave its single and deep impression on the mind. The book itself should be a thought.

There is another distinction between the catastrophe of a novel and that of a play. In the last, it ought to be the most permanent and striking events that lead to the catastrophe; in the former, it will often be highly artistical to revive for the consummating effect, many slight details—incidents the author had but dimly shadowed out—mysteries, that you had judged, till then, he had forgotten to clear up; and to bring a thousand rivulets, that had seemed merely introduced to relieve or adorn the way, into the rapid gulf which closes over all. The effect of this has a charm not derived from mere trick, but from its fidelity to the natural and lifelike order of events. What more common in the actual world than that the great crises of our fate are influenced and coloured, not so much by the incidents and persons we have deemed most important, but by many things of remote date, or of seeming insignificance. The feather the eagle carelessly sheds by the way-side plumes the shaft that transfixes him. In this management and combination of incidents towards the grand end, knowledge of Human Nature can alone lead the student to the knowledge of Ideal Art.

These remarks form the summary of the hints and suggestions that, after a careful study of books, we submit to the consideration of the student in a class of literature now so widely cultivated, and hitherto almost wholly unexamined by the critic. We presume not to say that they form an entire code of laws for the art. Even Aristotle's immortal treatise on Poetry, were it bequeathed to us complete, would still be but a skeleton; and though no poet could read that treatise without advantage, the most glorious poetry might be, and has been, written in defiance of nearly all its laws. Genius will arrive at fame by the light of its own star; but Criticism can often serve as a sign-post to save many an unnecessary winding, and indicate many a short way. He who aspires to excel in that fiction which is the glass of truth, may learn much from books and rules, from the lecturer and the critic; but he must be also the Imaginer, the Observer. He will be ever examining human life in its most catholic and comprehensive aspects. Nor is it enough to observe,—it is necessary to feel. We must let the heart be a student as well as the head. No man who is a passionless and cold spectator, will ever be an accurate analyst, of all the motives and springs of action. Perhaps, if we were to search for the true secret of CREATIVE GENIUS, we should find that secret in the intenseness of its SYMPATHIES.

[1]See Mr. Lockhart's Life of Scott, vol. vi. p. 232. "In writing I never could lay down a plan," &c. Scott, however, has the candour to add, "I would not have young writers imitate my carelessness."

[2]Even Sophocles, in one of his finest tragedies, has not scrupled to suffer the audience to witness the last moments of Ajax.

[3]"The nature of the Drama," observes Schiller, in his preface to Fiesco, and in excuse for his corruption of history, "does not admit the hand of Chance."

[4]"Why is it that a successful novelist never has been a successful play-writer?" This is a question that has been so often put, that we have been frightened out of considering whether the premises involved in the question are true or not. It is something like the schoolboy question, "Why is a pound of feathers heavier than a pound of lead?" It is long before Tom or Jack ask, "Is it heavier?" *Is it true* that a successful novelist never has been a successful play-writer? We will not insist on Goldsmith, whose comedy of "She Stoops to Conquer," and whose novel of the "Vicar of Wakefield," are alike among the greatest ornaments of our language. But was not Goethe a great play-writer and a great novelist? Who will decide whether the palm in genius should be given to the "Tasso" or the "Wilhelm Meister" of that all-sided genius? Is not the "Ghost-seer" a successful novel? Does it not afford the highest and most certain testimony of what Schiller could have done as a writer of narrative fiction, and are not "Wallenstein," and "Fiesco," and "Don Carlos," great plays by the same author? Are not "Candide" and "Zadig" imperishable masterpieces in the art of the novelist? And are not "Zaire" and "Mahomet" equally immortal? The three greatest geniuses that, in modern times, the Continent has produced, were both novelists and dramatists—equally great in each department. In France, at this day, Victor Hugo, who, with all his faults, is immeasurably the first writer in the school he has sought to found, is both the best novelist and the most powerful dramatist. That it has not happened *oftener* that the same man has achieved equal honour in the novel and the play is another question. But we might just as well ask why it has not happened oftener that the same man has been equally successful in tragedy and epic—in the ode and the didactic—why he who is sublime as a poet is often tame as a prose writer, and *vice versa*—why the same artist who painted the "Transfiguration" did not paint the "Last Day." Nature, circumstance, and education have not fitted many men to be great, except in one line. And least of all are they commonly great in two lines which, though seemingly close to each other, run in parallel directions. The more subtle the distinctions between the novel and the play, the more likely are they to be overlooked by him who attempts both. It is the same with all departments of art; the closer the approximation of the boundaries, the more difficult the blending.

[5]Dem. de Cor.

Modern Novelists—Great and Small

Margaret Oliphant

First published in Blackwood's Magazine, 77 (May 1855): 554-562.

Greatness is always comparative: there are few things so hard to adjust as the sliding-scale of fame. We remember once looking over a book of autographs, which impressed us with an acute perception of this principle. As we turned over the fair and precious leaves, we lighted upon name after name, unknown to us as to a savage. What were these? They were famous names—scraps of notes and hoarded signatures from the great Professor this, and the great Mr that, gentlemen who wrote F. R. S., and a score of other initial letters against their names, and were ranked among the remarkable people of their generation. Yet we—we say it with humiliation—knew them not, and we flatter ourselves that we were not inferior in this particular to the mass of the literature-loving public. They were great, but only in their own sphere. How many spheres are there entertaining each its own company of magnates? How few who attain the universal recognition, and are great in the sight of all men! There is not a parish or a county in the three kingdoms without its eminent person—not an art or a science but has its established oligarchy; and the great philosopher, who maps the sky like any familiar ocean, is not more emphatically distinguished among his fellows than is some individual workman in the manufactory from which came his great telescope—so true is it, in spite of the infinite diversity of individual constitution, that we have but a series of endless repetitions in the social economy of human nature. Nor is it much easier to define greatness than to limit the number of those for whom it is claimed. In the generation which has just passed, are there not two or three grand names of unquestionable magnitude and influence, the secret of whose power we cannot discover in anything they have left behind them? In fact, all that we can do when we descend from that highest platform whose occupants are visible to the whole world, and universally acknowledged, is to reconcile the claims of the lesser and narrower eminences, by permitting every individual of them to be great "in his way."

And there is no sphere in which it is so necessary to exercise this toleration as among the great army of novelists who minister to our pleasures. In no other department of literature is the field so crowded; in few others do success and failure depend so entirely upon the gifts of the artist. A biography, however indifferently executed, must always have something real in it. History may be intolerably heavy—may be partial, or disingenuous, or flippant, but still it is impossible to remove fact and significance altogether from its pages. Fiction, on the other hand, has no such foundation to build upon, and it depends entirely upon the individual powers of its professors, whether it is merely a lying legend of impossible people, or a broad and noble picture of real things and real men. To balance this, it is also true that few people are without their bit of insight, of whatever kind it may be, and that the greater portion of those who have the power of speech, the trick of composition, have really seen or known something which their neighbours would be the better for hearing. So far as it professes to represent this great crowded world, and the broad lights and shadows of universal life, with all its depths and heights, its wonders and mysteries, there are but few successful artists in fiction, and these few are of universal fame; but there remains many a byway and corner, many a nook of secret seclusion, and homes of kindly charity, which genius which is not the highest, and minds of a lower range and scantier experience, may well be content to embellish and illustrate. Nor does it seldom happen that a storyteller of this second rank finds a straight road and a speedy entrance to the natural heart which has but admired and wondered at the master minstrel's loftier tale.

Place aux dames! how does it happen that the cowardice of womankind is a fact so clearly established, and that so little notice is ever taken of the desperate temerity of this half of the creation? It is in vain that we call to the amazon, as the lookers-on at that famous tourney at Ashby-de-la-Zouch called to the disinherited knight, "Strike the Hospitaller's shield—he is weak in his saddle." While we are speaking, the feminine knight-errant rushes past us to thunder upon the buckler of Bois Guilbert, the champion of champions. Where philosophic magnates fear to tread, and bodies of divinity approach with trembling, the fair novelist flies at a gallop. Her warfare, it is true, is after the manner of women: there is a rush, a flash, a shriek, and the combatant comes forth from the melée trembling with delight and terror; but the sudden daring of her attack puts bravery to shame. This, which is the age of so many things—of enlightenment, of science, of progress—is quite as distinctly the age of female novelists; and women, who rarely or never find their way to the loftiest class, have a natural right and claim to rank foremost in the second. The vexed questions of social morality, the grand problems of human experience, are seldom so summarily discussed and settled as in the novels of this day which are written by women; and, though we have little reason to complain of the first group of experienced novelists who lead our lists, we tremble to encounter the sweeping judgments and wonderful theories of the very strange world revealed to us in the books of many of the younger sisterhood.

No; Mrs Gore with her shining, chilly sketches—Mrs Trollope with her rough wit and intense cleverness—Mrs Marsh with her exemplary and most didactic narratives—are orthodox and proper beyond criticism. To have remained so long in possession of the popular ear is no small tribute to their powers; and we must join, to these long-established and well-known names, the name of a writer more genial and kindly than any of them, and one who has wisely rested long upon her modest laurels, without entering into competitions with the young and restless powers of to-day—Mrs S. C. Hall. The *Irish Sketches* of this lady resemble considerably Miss Mitford's beautiful *English* sketches in *Our Village*; but they are more vigorous and picturesque, and bright with an animated and warm nationality, apologetic and defensive, which Miss Mitford, writing of one class of English to another, had no occasion to use.

The novel of conventional and artificial life belongs to no one as much as to Mrs Gore. Who does not know the ring of her regular sentences?—the dialogue which chimes in exactly the same measure, whether the speakers speak in a club, or in the dowager duchess's sombre and pious boudoir? *Mammon* is a good representation of her average productions; and so is *Transmutation*, an anonymous novel recently published, in which, if it is not Mrs Gore's, we are wonderfully deceived. Even in works of the highest genius it is seldom difficult to trace a family resemblance between the different creations of the same hand; and it is impossible to imagine that any mortal fancy could retain originality through the long period which this lady has spent in

the composition of novels; so it is not wonderful that we need to pay especial attention to the names, to make ourselves quite sure that it is a new and not an old novel of Mrs Gore's which we have in our hand. There is the same country house—the same meek lady and morose gentleman—the same "nice young man" for hero—and the same young ladies, good and naughty, in the same white muslin and blue ribbons. There is the same chorus kept up through the book, of conversation at clubs upon other people's business, which the parties interested either overhear or do not overhear, as is best for the story. And so the tale glides on smoothly and easily, its sorrows disturbing our placidity as little as its joys, and everybody concerned having the most composed and tranquil certainty as to how it is to end. Nevertheless, Mrs Gore's novels have a host of readers, and Mrs Gore's readers are interested. People will be interested, we suspect, till the end of the world, in the old, old story, how Edwin and Angelina fell in love with each other; how they were separated, persecuted, and tempted; and how their virtue and constancy triumphed over all their misfortunes. And there is much vivacity and liveliness, and a good deal of shrewd observation in these books. They are amusing, pleasant beguilers of a stray hour; and, after all our grand pretensions, how valuable a property is this in the genus novel, which proclaims itself an ephemeron in its very name!

Mrs Trollope is a different person. It pleases this lady to put her fortune to the touch, whether she will delight or disgust us, and according to her auditors is her success. The bold, buxom, daring, yet very foolish Mrs Barnaby, seems to have been a work entirely after this author's heart, and at which she laboured *con amore*; but we cannot profess to have the smallest scrap of admiration for Mrs Barnaby, though there is no doubt that the coarse tricks, the coarse rouge, the transparent devices, which were too barefaced to deceive anybody, are perfectly kept up throughout the book. We are afraid it is a fundamental error in a book to seek, not our admiration and interest, but our disgust and reprobation for its principal character. We do not choose to leave the hero or the heroine, whose fate we have followed through three volumes, in the hands of Nemesis; we would much rather that it could be possible for her to "take a thought and mend"; and though we can resign to poetic justice a secondary villain, we revolt against entering upon a history which is only to end in confusion and overthrow to its principal actor. That Mrs Barnaby is a real kind of woman, it is impossible to deny; and the success of her representation is but another proof of how strangely people are attracted in fiction by characters from which they cannot keep themselves sufficiently far away in real life; but we do not think the creation of this redoubtable adventurer, nor of her companion portrait, the Vicar of Wrexhill, are things which bring the author nearer to any heart. Mrs Trollope has the same broad coarse humour, which, with such an odd, unlooked-for contrast, breaks into those mincing genteel histories of *Cecilia and Evelina*, which Johnson and Burke sat up all night to read; and though she deals lovingly with Mrs Barnaby, there is a venom and bitterness in her picture of the Low Church Vicar, which is not very edifying. She is perhaps a cleverer woman, but we miss the silken rustle and ladylike pace of her contemporary, and find Mrs Trollope a less agreeable companion than Mrs Gore.

The author of *Emilia Wyndham* is of an entirely distinct character. This lady, whatever else she is, must always be exemplary. We have a distinct impression of a little circle of young ladies, emancipated from the schoolroom, but scarcely entered upon the world, sitting in one of her own pretty orderly morning rooms, clustered about the kind but precise storyteller, when we open one of her novels. *They* dare never be so much engrossed in the tale as to forget the "deportment" which their instructress is so careful of; and she has leisure to pause now and then to bid some forgetful little one hold up her head or throw back her shoulders. Yet there is real goodness, some dramatic power, and the natural instinct of telling a story in Mrs Marsh. Her first and most ambitious work is not addressed to her audience of young ladies, nor would it be very suitable for them; but we prefer the good Emilia to the high-souled and sinful Lucy, and feel that the author is more in her element with one of her own pleasant groups of girls—the good one with her innocent wisdoms, and the other who is not quite good, with her almost equally innocent naughtiness—or with her two lovers, the wild, gay, handsome, young gallant, and the grave, quiet, passionate man—than with those mysteries of sin and misery, which in very abhorrence and pity a good woman is sometimes fascinated to look into, wondering whether something may not be found there to account for the tremendous fall. But the author of *Emilia Wyndham* has lost some ground during these last few years. She has taken to making books rather than to telling stories, and has perceptibly had the printing-press and certain editorial censors before her, instead of the dove's eye of her sweet young audience. Yet there is something pleasant

always in her anxious care to point an example;—"My dear children, here is the good and here is the evil, and you see what they lead to; and here again you perceive how the evil is overcome by the good," is the burden of her tale; and the world has not been slow to acknowledge the goodness that lies in her old-fashioned moral, nor the many indications of power and purpose which her works contain.

When we leave these respectable elder sisters of the literary corporation, we immediately find ourselves on very ticklish ground. Ten years ago we professed an orthodox system of novel-making. Our lovers were humble and devoted—our ladies were beautiful, and might be capricious if it pleased them; and we held it a very proper and laudable arrangement that Jacob should serve seven years for Rachel, and recorded it as one of the articles of our creed; and that the only true-love worth having was that reverent, knightly, chivalrous true-love which consecrated all woman-kind, and served one with fervour and enthusiasm. Such was our ideal, and such our system, in the old halcyon days of novel-writing; when suddenly there stole upon the scene, without either flourish of trumpets or public proclamation, a little fierce incendiary, doomed to turn the world of fancy upside down. She stole upon the scene—pale, small, by no means beautiful— something of a genius, something of a vixen—a dangerous little person, inimical to the peace of society. After we became acquainted with herself, we were introduced to her lover. Such a lover!—a vast, burly, sensual Englishman, one of those Hogarth men, whose power consists in some singular animal force of life and character, which it is impossible to describe or analyse. Such a wooing!—the lover is rude, brutal, cruel. The little woman fights against him with courage and spirit—begins to find the excitement and relish of a new life in this struggle—begins to think of her antagonist all day long—falls into fierce love and jealousy—betrays herself—is tantalised and slighted, to prove her devotion—and then suddenly seized upon and taken possession of, with love several degrees fiercer than her own. Then comes the catastrophe which prevents this extraordinary love from running smooth. Our heroine runs away to save herself—falls in with another man almost as singular as her first love—and very nearly suffers herself to be reduced to marry this unloved and unloving wooer; but, escaping that risk, finally discovers that the obstacle is removed which stood between her and her former tyrant, and rushes back straightway to be graciously accepted by the blind and weakened Rochester. Such was the impetuous little spirit which dashed into our well-ordered world, broke its boundaries, and defied its principles—and the most alarming revolution of modern times has followed the invasion of *Jane Eyre*.

It is not to be wondered at that speculation should run wild about this remarkable production. Sober people, with a sober respect for womankind, and not sufficient penetration to perceive that the grossness of the book was such grossness as only could be perpetrated by a woman, contested indignantly the sex of the writer. The established authorities brought forth proofs in the form of incorrect costume, and errors in dress. Nobody perceived that it was the new generation nailing its colours to its mast. No one would understand that this furious love-making was but a wild declaration of the "Rights of Woman" in a new aspect. The old-fashioned deference and respect—the old-fashioned wooing—what were they but so many proofs of the inferior position of the woman, to whom the man condescended with the gracious courtliness of his loftier elevation! The honours paid to her in society—the pretty fictions of politeness, they were all degrading tokens of her subjection, if she were but sufficiently enlightened to see their true meaning. The man who presumed to treat her with reverence was one who insulted her pretensions; while the lover who struggled with her, as he would have struggled with another man, only adding a certain amount of contemptuous brutality, which no man would tolerate, was the only one who truly recognised her claims of equality. "A fair field and no favour," screams the representative of womanhood. "Let him take me captive, seize upon me, overpower me if he is the better man—let us fight it out, my weapons against his weapons, and see which is the strongest. You poor fellow, do you not see how you are insulting and humiliating that Rachel, for whom you serve seven years? Let her feel she is your equal—make her your lawful spoil by your bow and by your spear. The cause of the strong hand for ever—and let us fight it out!" Whereupon our heroine rushes into the field, makes desperate sorties out of her Sebastopol, blazes abroad her ammunition into the skies, commits herself beyond redemption, and finally permits herself to be ignominiously captured, and seized upon with a ferocious appropriation which is very much unlike the noble and grand sentiment which we used to call love.

Yes, it is but a mere vulgar boiling over of the political cauldron, which tosses your French monarch into chaos, and makes a new one in his stead. Here is your true revolution. France is but one of the Western Powers; woman is the half of the world. Talk of a balance of power which may be adjusted by taking a Crimea, or fighting a dozen battles—here is a battle which must always be going forward—a balance of power only to be decided by single combat, deadly and uncompromising, where combatants, so far from being guided by the old punctilios of duello, make no secret of their ferocity, but throw sly javelins at each other, instead of shaking hands before they begin. Do you think that young lady is an angelic being, young gentleman? Do you compare her to roses and lilies, and stars and sunbeams, in your deluded imagination? Do you think you would like to "deck and crown your head with bays," like Moutron, all for the greater glory to her, when she found you "serve her evermore"? Unhappy youth! She is a fair gladiator—she is not an angel. In her secret heart she longs to rush upon you, and try a grapple with you, to prove her strength and her equality. She has no patience with your flowery emblems. Why should *she* be like a rose or a lily any more than yourself? Are these beautiful weaklings the only types you can find of *her*? And this new Bellona steps forth in armour, throws down her glove, and defies you—to conquer her if you can. Do you like it, gentle lover?—would you rather break her head and win, or leave her alone and love her? The alternative is quite distinct and unmistakable—only do not insult her with your respect and humility, for this is something more than she can bear.

These are the doctrines, startling and original, propounded by Jane Eyre; and they are not Jane Eyre's opinions only, as we may guess from the host of followers or imitators who have copied them. There is a degree of refined indelicacy possible to a woman, which no man can reach. Her very ignorance of evil seems to give a certain piquancy and relish to her attempts to realise it. She gives a runaway, far-off glimpse—a strange improper situation, and whenever she has succeeded in raising a sufficient amount of excitement to make it possible that something very wrong might follow, she prevents the wrong by a bold *coup*, and runs off in delight. There are some conversations between Rochester and Jane Eyre which no *man* could have dared to give—which only could have been given by the overboldness of innocence and ignorance trying to imagine what it never could understand, and which are as womanish as they are unwomanly.

When all this is said, *Jane Eyre* remains one of the most remarkable works of modern times—as remarkable as *Villette*, and more perfect. We know no one else who has such a grasp of persons and places, and a perfect command of the changes of the atmosphere, and the looks of a country under rain or wind. There is no fiction in these wonderful scenes of hers. The Yorkshire dales, the north-country moor, the streets of Brussels, are illusions equally complete. Who does not know Madame Beck's house, white and square and lofty, with its level rows of windows, its green shutters, and the sun that beams upon its blinds, and on the sultry pavement before the door? How French is Paul Emmanuel and all his accessories! How English is Lucy Snowe! We feel no art in these remarkable books. What we feel is a force which makes everything real—a motion which is irresistible. We are swept on in the current, and never draw breath till the tale is ended. Afterwards we may disapprove at our leisure, but it is certain that we have not a moment's pause to be critical till we come to the end.

The effect of a great literary success, especially in fiction, is a strange thing to observe,—the direct influence it has on some one or two similar minds, and the indirect bias which it gives to a great many others. There is at least one other writer of considerable gifts, whose books are all so many reflections of *Jane Eyre*. We mean no disparagement to Miss Kavanagh; but, from *Nathalie* to *Grace Lee*, she has done little else than repeat the attractive story of this conflict and combat of love or war—for either name will do. *Nathalie*, which is very sunny and very French, is, for these its characteristic features, to be endured and forgiven, closely though it approaches to its model; but *Daisy Barns*, which is not French, has much less claim on our forbearance, and the last novel of this author exaggerates the repetition beyond all toleration. The story of *Grace Lee* is a story of mutual "aggravation," in which the lady first persecutes the gentleman with attentions, kindnesses, scorn, and love; and the gentleman afterwards persecutes the lady in the self-same way. When John Owen is worried into falling in love with her, it becomes Grace Lee's turn to exasperate and tantalise, which she does with devotion; and it is not till after a separation of many years, and when they are at least middle-aged people, that this perverse couple are fairly settled at last. The lady is a pure heroine of romance throughout, and has no probability in her; but that is a lesser matter; and the hero, without a single amiable quality, so far as appears in the story, has only to recommend him this same bitter *strength*, which we must conclude to be the sole heroic attribute worth mentioning, in the judgment of the author. We might perhaps trace the origin of

this passion for *strength* further back than *Jane Eyre*; as far back, perhaps, as Mr Carlyle's idolatry of the "Canning"—the king, man, and hero. But it is a sad thing, with all our cultivation and refinement, to be thrown back upon sheer blind force as our universal conqueror. Mr Carlyle's Thor, too, is a sweet-hearted giant, and bears no comparison to Mr Rochester and Mr John Owen. We suspect, indeed, that Thor would be even sheepish in love, and worship the very footsteps of his princess; whereas it is principally in love, and in vanquishing a woman, that the strength of the other gentlemen seems to lie. No, it is no Thor, no Berserker, no mighty Goth or Northman. One could fancy how such a genuine and real personage might eclipse the "manly beauty" of the bland Greek Apollo, to certain forms and moods of mind. These ladies, however, are not so solicitous to have some one who can conquer war or fortune, as to find someone who can subdue, and rule with a hand of iron—themselves. Nor is the *indirect* influence of this new light in literature less remarkable.

Mrs Gaskell, a sensible and considerate woman, and herself ranking high in her sphere, has just fallen subject to the same delusion. *North and South* is extremely clever, as a story; and, without taking any secondary qualification to build its merits upon, it is perhaps better and livelier than any of Mrs Gaskell's previous works; yet here are still the wide circles in the water, showing that not far off is the identical spot where Jane Eyre and Lucy Snowe, in their wild sport, have been casting stones; here is again the desperate, bitter quarrel out of which love is to come; here is love itself, always in a fury, often looking exceedingly like hatred, and by no means distinguished for its good manners, or its graces of speech. Mrs Gaskell is perfect in all the "properties" of her scene, and all her secondary people are well drawn; but though her superb and stately Margaret is by no means a perfect character, she does not seem to us a likely person to fall in love with the churlish and ill-natured Thornton, whose "strong" qualities are not more amiable than are the dispositions of the other members of his class whom we have before mentioned. Mrs Gaskell lingers much upon the personal gifts of her grand beauty. Margaret has glorious black hair, in which the pomegranite blossoms glow like a flame; she has exquisite full lips, pouted with the breath of wonder, or disdain, or resentment, as the case may be; she has beautiful rounded arms, hanging with languid grace; she is altogether a splendid and princely personage; and when, in addition to all this, Margaret becomes an heiress, it is somewhat hard to see her delivered over to the impoverished Manchester man, who is as ready to devour her as ever was an ogre in a fairy tale. The sober-minded who are readers of novels will feel Mrs Gaskell's desertion a serious blow. Shall all our love stories be squabbles after this? Shall we have nothing but encounters of arms between the knight and lady—bitter personal altercations, and mutual defiance? It is a doleful prospect; and not one of these imperilled heroines has the good gift of an irate brother to exchange civilities with the love-making monster. There is one consolation: Have we not in these favored realms a Peace Society? And where could these most respectable and influential brethren find a fairer field?

There is one feature of resemblance between Mrs Gaskell's last work and Mr. Dickens' *Hard Times*. We are prepared in both for the discussion of an important social question; and in both, the story gradually slides off the public topic to pursue a course of its own. *North and South* has, of necessity, some good sketches of the "hands" and their homes; but it is Mr. Thornton's fierce and rugged course of true love to which the author is most anxious to direct our attention; and we have little time to think of Higgins or his trades-union, in presence of this intermitting, but always lively, warfare going on beside them. Mrs Gaskell has made herself an important reputation. The popular mind seems to have accepted *Mary Barton* as a true and worthy picture of the class it aims to represent; and *Ruth*, though a great blunder in art, does not seem to have lessened the estimation in which her audience hold her. *Ruth* is the story of a young girl betrayed and fallen while little more than a child—innocent in heart, but with her life shipwrecked at the earliest outset; and Ruth is the sole heroine and subject of the book. The vain attempts of her friends to conceal the irrevocable downfall of this poor child— the discovery that comes after many years—her humility and devotion and death—are, of course, the only circumstances in which the author can place her unfortunate heroine; the mistake lies in choosing such a heroine at all. Every pure feminine mind, we suppose, holds the faith of Desdemona—"I do not believe there is any such woman"; and the strong revulsion of dismay and horror with which they find themselves compelled to admit, in some individual case, that their rule is not infallible, produces at once the intense resentment with which every other woman regards the one who has stained her name and fame; and that pitying, wondering fascination which so often

seems to impel female writers to dwell upon these wretched stories, by way of finding out what strange chain of causes there was, and what excuse there might be.

We will only instance one other young writer touched by the spirit of Jane Eyre, the author of the *Head of the Family*; but the long and most tantalising courtship of Ninian Graeme, the hero of this book, with its "many a slip between the cup and the lip," is redeemed by the fact that it is the lover here who is humble, patient, and devoted, and not the lady. There is a great deal of talent in this lady's works, and a great deal of love. Alas! for this hard world, with all its rubs and pinches! how soon it teaches us the secret of harder struggles than those of love-making. In the last work of this writer, *Agatha's Husband*, we have plenty of quarreling; but these are legitimate quarrels between married people, lawful sport with which we have no right to interfere, and which the author describes with genuine relish, and with no small truth.

We suppose it is a natural consequence of the immense increase of novels that the old material should begin to fail. It is hard to be original in either plot or character when there are such myriads of "examples" treading in the same path as yourself, and prior to you; and many a shift is the unfortunate fictionist compelled to, if he would put some novelty into his novel. We have before us at this moment two different books which we are constrained to class together as novels of disease. *The House of Raby* is a tale of a family afflicted with insanity. We have first some legendary information about a "wicked earl," whose madness is furious and vicious, but scarcely known as madness to the world. Then comes his son, an amiable and worthy gentleman, who falls in love, and is refused by a virtuous Margaret Hastings, who is deeply attached to him but thinks it a sin that he should marry. In this view the gentleman coincides for a while; but ultimately gets rid of his conscientious scruples, and marries his cousin. Then comes a second generation, the twin sons of this couple, of whom one inherits the family malady in periodical fits, but in his sane intervals shows the greatest genius, takes an important place in society, and has no *weakness* about him. This is the hero; and *he* falls in love with a second Margaret Hastings, the niece of the former one, whom, however, more self-denying than his father, he never wishes to marry, but is content to have a very fervid and loving friendship with. Margaret is a clergyman's daughter, and, being left with no great provision, accepts an appointment as housekeeper at Carleton Castle, the ancestral house of the family, where she has always been a friend and favourite, and lives there, taking care of her lover in his dark hours, and enjoying his society when he is in his proper mind,—all with the fullest sanction of his elder brother the earl, and Margaret's friend the countess; and so the story ends. With less incident, and also with less interest, Miss Jewsbury follows in the train of the anonymous author of *The House of Raby*. The hereditary malady is the most shadowy possibility in the world in the family of *Constance Herbert*; but her mother, in whose blood there is no such disease by descent, becomes suddenly mad, and settles into a hopeless idiot. Constance, too, has an Aunt Margaret—Aunt Margarets are fashionable in novels—and when she is in all the joyful excitement produced by her young lover's first declaration, she is carried away for the first time to see her mother, and is told how the case stands with her, and how she is bound not to marry, lest she should transmit to others this dreadful inheritance. Such is the argument of these books; and they form one of the many modern instances of super-refinement and improvement upon the infallible laws of nature and revelation. That there could be anything which possibly might make up to the unfortunate supposed children— for whose sake Arundel Raby will not marry Margaret, nor Constance Philip—for the great calamity of being born, our authors do not seem to suppose; but Miss Jewsbury's heroine, when she feels herself very miserable, takes refuge in abusing Providence and God for her dreadful privations, and for the cruel injustice of creating her under such circumstances. Indeed, Miss Jewsbury's opinion seems to be, that the only business which God has to do with at all is to make His creatures happy, and prevent those discourteous ills and misfortunes from laying hands upon them; and when grief does come, the unfortunate afflicted person has full permission to upbraid the great Author of his misery, who ought to have paid attention to it, and taken means to stay the evil; nay, is quite justified in refusing altogether to believe in the existence of the careless Deity, who will not exert himself to keep troubles away. This, indeed, seems a very fashionable doctrine in these days, when we have all become so very much kinder and more charitable than the God who preserves the life in these ungrateful hearts. Now, we cannot help thinking it a great error to make any affliction, like that of hereditary insanity, the main subject of a story. It is permissible as a secondary theme; but a thing out of which no

satisfactory result (according to our carnal and mundane ideas of happiness) *can* come—is not a fit central point for fiction. The position of the lady housekeeper and her lover patient, alternately a madman and a genius, is in the highest degree uncomfortable, and we cannot reconcile ourselves to it in any shape; and we have seen few books so perfectly unsatisfactory as *Constance Herbert*. The anonymous author has the advantage of Miss Jewsbury—there is always interest, at least, in the *House of Raby*.

There is one other class of books, written "on principle," and in which some very pleasant results have been attained—books which we will not call "religious," but rather "Church" novels. The *Heir of Redclyffe* and *Heartsease* are important individuals in this family. There is no accounting for the wonderful rise of the "bubble reputation" in many instances; but though we cannot admit that these books deserve *all* the applause they have got, they are still very good books, and worthy of a high place. The best thing in the *Heir of Redclyffe*, to our judgment—though not the pleasantest—is the wonderful impersonation of a "prig" in Philip Morville. This intolerable coxcomb, solemn and faultless, does—with the best intentions—the villain's work in the book; and we have no patience with the cruel murder of the good young Guy, to make room for this disagreeable cousin. *Heartsease*, too, is very clever and lively, and has a great deal of character in it. And there are other unobtrusive books of the class, which, putting aside their High-Churchisms, and all the little martyrdoms their heroines suffer in the cause of district-visiting and Dorcas societies, have much shrewd appreciation of common life, and a quiet eye for a piece of oddity. Such books as *Katherine Ashton*, in spite of their occasional tedium, are by no means bad fare for the young ladies of the party they represent; and any little bit of fanciful harm that may be in their mild Puseyism is more than counterbalanced, in our opinion, by a great deal of substantial merit.

We cannot deny that, in this second rank of eminence, the magnitude and variety of the female professors of our art do somewhat pale the glory of our literary craftsmen of the nobler sex, though it seems true that the Broad Church, in the stalwart person of the Rev. Charles Kingsley, is rather more than a match even for the *Heir of Redclyffe*, the most notable of the High Church novelists. Yet Mr Kingsley himself will scarcely hold his own by the side of some of the lady-writers whom we have already mentioned. We do not intend to discuss the merits, as a novelist, of this stout and boisterous champion of popular rights, and of the unspeakable latitudes of doctrine to which a man may reach, while still he sits under the shadow of the Prayer-book and the Thirty-nine Articles, as under his own vine and his own fig-tree. Mr Kingsley is a speculatist, and not a born story-teller, and we leave him for the present.

Criticism In Relation To Novels

G. H. Lewes

First published in Fortnightly Review, *3 (April 1863): 352-361.*

Although the fame of a great novelist is only something less than the fame of a great poet, and the reputation of a clever novelist is far superior to that of a respectable poet, the general estimation of prose fiction as a branch of Literature has something contemptuous in it. This is shown not only in the condescending tone in which critics speak, and the carelessness with which they praise, but also in the half-apologetic phrases in which very shallow readers confess that they have employed their leisured ignorance on such light literature. It is shown, moreover, in the rashness with which writers, confessedly incapable of success in far inferior efforts, will confidently attempt fiction, as if it were the easiest of literary tasks; and in the insolent assumption that "anything will do for a novel."

The reason of this fame, and the reason of this contempt, are not difficult to find. The fame is great because the influence of a fine novel is both extensive and subtle, and because the combination of high powers necessary for the production of a fine novel is excessively rare. The contempt is general, because the combination of powers necessary for the production of three volumes of Circulating Library reminiscences is very common; and because there is a large demand for the amusement which such reminiscences afford. The intellectual feebleness of readers in general prevents their forming a discriminating estimate of the worth of such works; and most of those who are capable of discrimination have had their standard of expectation so lowered by the profusion of mediocrity, that they languidly acquiesce in the implied assumption that novels are removed from the canons of common-sense criticism. Hence the activity of this commerce of trash. The sterile abundance casts a sort of opprobrium on the art itself. The lowered standard invites the incapable. Men and women who have shown no special aptitudes for this difficult art flatter themselves, and not unreasonably, that they may succeed as well as others whom they openly despise. And their friends are ready to urge them on this path. No one looking over the sketchbook of an amateur turns to him with the question—"Why not try your hand at a fresco?" But many men, on no better warrant, say to a writer—"Why not try your hand at a novel?" And there is great alacrity in trying the hand.

There is thus action and reaction: acquiescence in mediocrity increases the production of mediocrity and lowers the standard, which thus in turn admits of inferior production. We critics are greatly to blame. Instead of compensating for the inevitable evils of periodical criticism by doing our utmost to keep up the standard of public taste, too many of us help to debase it by taking a standard from the Circulating Library, and by a half-contemptuous, half-languid patronage of what we do not seriously admire. The lavish eulogies which welcome very trivial works as if they were masterpieces, are sometimes the genuine expression of very ignorant writers (for easy as it is to write a poor novel, to review it is easier still; and the very language of the reviews often betrays the intellectual condition of the writers); but sometimes they are judgments formed solely in reference to the degraded standard which the multitude of poor works has introduced. Thus although the same terms of commendation are applied to the last new novel which are applied to "Vanity Fair," or "Pride and Prejudice," the standard is nevertheless insensibly changed, and the critic who uses the same language respecting both never really thinks of placing both in the same class.

The general public knows nothing of this change of standards; and thus a foreigner, casting his eye over our advertisements, would suppose, from the "opinions of the press," that England boasted of two or three score writers of exquisite genius; but if, seduced by this supposition, he familiarized himself with the masterpieces thus extolled, he would perhaps conclude that England was suffering from a softened brain. One thing would certainly arouse his curiosity, and that would be to meet with a sample of what are everywhere called "the ordinary run of novels." He would hear that Mr. A's work was far superior to this ordinary run; that Mrs. B's exquisite story was carefully separated from the ordinary run; that Miss C's tale displayed a delicacy of conception, a depth of insight into character and passion, and a purity of moral tone sought for in vain in the ordinary run of novels. But he would appeal to Mudie in vain for a novel which was acknowledged as one of the ordinary run.

Although I have a very high opinion of Fiction as a form of Literature, and read no kind of Literature with more delight and gratitude, I cannot pretend to an extensive acquaintance with recent novels; indeed there are writers of considerable reputation whose works I have never opened, either because they have not fallen in my way in hours of leisure, or because those whose judgment I respect have not by their praises induced me to make a trial. Nevertheless, living in a great literary centre, and naturally inclined to seek the immense gratification which a good novel always gives, I have become tolerably acquainted with the typical specimens, and come to the conclusion that if many of the novels of to-day are considerably better than those of twenty or thirty years ago, because they partake of the general advance in culture, and its wider diffusion; the vast increase of novels, mostly worthless, is a serious danger to public culture, a danger which tends to become more and more imminent, and can only be arrested by an energetic resolution on the part of the critics to do their duty with conscientious rigour. At present this duty is evaded, or performed fitfully. There is plenty of sarcasm and ill-nature; too much of it; there is little serious criticism which weighs considerately its praise and its blame. Even in the best journals poor novels are often praised in terms strictly applicable to works of genius alone. If a thoughtful reader opens one of these novels, he sees such violations of common sense and common knowledge, such style and such twaddle, as would never gain admission into the critical journals themselves, for these journals recommend to readers what they would refuse to print. The reason generally is that critics have ceased to regard novels as Literature, and do not think of applying to the style and sentiments of a fiction those ordinary canons which would be applied to a history, an article, or a pamphlet.

And there is sometimes a certain justification for this exception; only it should be always brought prominently forward. The distinctive element in Fiction is that of plot-interest. The rest is vehicle. If critics would carefully specify the qualities which distinguish the work they praise, and not confound plot-interest with other sources of interest, above all not confound together the various kinds of plot-interest, readers would be guided in their choice, and have their taste educated. For example, it is quite fair to praise Miss Braddon for the skill she undoubtedly displays in plot-interest of a certain kind—in selecting situations of crime and mystery which have a singular fascination for a large number of readers; and the success she has obtained is due to the skill with which she has prepared and presented these situations so as to excite the curiosity and sympathy of idle people. It is a special talent she possesses; and the critic is wrong who fails to recognise in it the source of her success. But he would be equally wrong, I think, if he confounded this merit with other merits, which her novels do not display. I have only read two of her works—"Lady Audley's Secret," and "Sir Jasper's Tenant"—but from those I have no hesitation in concluding that her grasp of character, her vision of realities, her regard for probabilities, and her theoretical views of human life, are very far from being on a level with her power over plot-interest. In praising stories there should be some discrimination of the kind of interest aimed at, and the means by which the aim is reached. A criminal trial will agitate all England, when another involving similar degrees of crime, but without certain adjuncts of interest, will be read only by the seekers of the very vulgarest stimulants. It is not the crime, but the attendant circumstances of horror and mystery, of pathetic interest, and of social suggestions, which give importance to a trial. In like manner the skill of the story-teller is displayed in selecting the attendant circumstances of horror, mystery, pathos, and social suggestion, bringing the events home to our experience and sympathy. And the critic should fix his attention on this mode of presentation, not demanding from the writer qualities incompatible with, or obviously disregarded by his method. In a story of wild and startling incidents, such as "Monte Christo," it is absurd to demand a minute attention to probabilities; provided the improbabilities are not glaringly obtrusive, that is, provided our imaginative sympathy is not checked by a sense of the incongruous, we grant the author a large licence. But in proportion as the story lies among scenes and characters of familiar experience, in proportion as the writer endeavors to engage our sympathy by pictures of concrete realities, and not by *abstractions* of passion and incident, the critic demands a closer adherence to truth and experience. Monte Christo may talk a language never heard off the stage, but Major Pendennis must speak as they speak in Pall Mall. It is obviously a much easier task to tell a story involving only the abstractions of life, than to tell one which moves amidst its realities. It is easier to disregard all those probabilities which would interfere with the symmetrical arrangement of incidents in a culminating progression, and all those truths of human character which in real life would complicate and thwart any scheme of prearranged events, than to tell a story which carries with it in every phase of its evolution a justification of what is felt, said, and done, so that the reader seems, as it were, to be the spectator of an actual drama. Nevertheless, both are legitimate forms of art; and although the latter is incomparably the more difficult, and the more valuable in its results, the former is and always will be popular with the mass of readers. A picture made up of improbable combinations and unreal elements may interest us once; but unless it be a pure play of fancy avowedly soaring away into regions beyond or beside this life of ours, it cannot sustain its interest, for it cannot withstand the inevitable scrutiny of deliberation. It will not bear re-reading. It cannot be thought of without misgiving. A picture made up of nature's sequences will interest for all time.

Plot-interest is, as I said, the distinctive element in Fiction; and the critic ought to mark plainly what the nature of the interest is no less than the skill with which it is presented. Having done this, if he speaks of the historical, pictorial, moral, religious, or literary details, he should speak of them as amenable to the ordinary canons. Nonsense is not excusable because it forms part of the padding of a story. People ought to be ashamed of having written, or of having praised trash, wherever it may have appeared. And a little critical rigour exercised with respect to the descriptions, dialogues, and reflections which accompany a story, would act beneficially in two ways: first, in affording a test whereby the writer's pretensions might be estimated; secondly, by making writers more vigilant against avoidable mistakes.

As a test: You may have a very lively sense of the unreality with which a writer has conceived a character, or presented a situation, but it is by no means easy to make him see this, or to make his admirers see it. In vain would you refer to certain details as inaccurate; he cannot recognise their inaccuracy. In vain would you point to the general air of unreality, the conventional tone of the language, the absence of those subtle, individual traits which give verisimilitude to a conception; he cannot see it; to him the conception does seem lifelike; he may perhaps assure you that it is taken from the life. But failing on this ground, you may succeed by an indirect route. In cases so complex as those of human character and human affairs, the possibilities of misapprehension are numerous; and if we find a man liable to mistake sound for sense, to misapprehend the familiar relations of daily life, to describe vaguely or inaccurately the objects of common experience, or to write *insincerely* in the belief that he is writing eloquently, then we may *à fortiori* conclude that he will be still more liable to misapprehend the complexities of character, to misrepresent psychological subtleties, to put language into people's mouths which is not the language of real feeling, and to modify the course of events according to some conventional prejudice. In a word, if he is feeble and inaccurate in ordinary matters, he may be believed to be feeble and inaccurate in higher matters. If he writes nonsense, or extravagant sentimentality, in uttering his own comments, we may suspect his sense and truthfulness when his personages speak and act.

Before proceeding to the second result of critical rigour it will be desirable to apply the test in a specific instance, and I select "Maxwell Drewitt" for this purpose, rather than "Sir Jasper's Tenant," because the author has been specially lauded for powers of portraiture which I have been unable to recognise. It is but right to add that I have read none of this author's previous works; and to add further that there is much even in this work which I shall presently have to praise. If any of my remarks seem severe, let them be understood as at least implying the compliment of serious criticism. It is because I wish to treat her novel as Literature, and because she has an earnestness of purpose and a literary ability which challenge respect, that I make choice of her work for illustration; though at first sight any selection must seem invidious where so many examples abound.

"Maxwell Drewitt" is not a novel of incident, but a picture of life and character. Its interest is not meant to lie in the skilful combination of the abstractions of passion and situation, irrespective of concrete probabilities, irrespective of real human motives in the common transactions of life; in other words, it is not a romance, it is not a sensation story, trusting solely to the power of ideal presentation of abstractions, or to the appeal to our sympathies with mystery and crime. The obvious aim of the writer is to paint a picture of Irish life, and to inculcate a moral lesson. The aim is high; and being high, it challenges criticism as to its means. The aim is one which tasks a writer's powers; and success can only be proportionate to the verisimilitude with which the picture is painted. I do not think the degree of verisimilitude attained is such as to justify the praises which have been awarded it. There are excellent intentions; but the execution is approximative, inaccurate, wanting in the sharp individuality which comes from clear vision and dramatic insight. The first hazy conception of the characters is not condensed into distinctness. The careless, good-natured, indolent Irish landlord—always in difficulties, always cheery and improvident—is described but not depicted. His energetic, clever, scheming, hard-hearted nephew is drawn with more detail, but nevertheless falls very short of a recognisable portrait. The rascally Irish lawyer, and the virtuous English lawyer, are pale lifeless conventionalities. The reckless Harold and the vindictive but virtuous Brian, are shadows. The coquettish Lady Emeline, the loving Jenny Bourke, and the patient Mrs. Drewitt, are lay figures. The language has never that nice dramatic propriety which seems as if it could only come from the persons. None of the characters have the impress of creative genius. The same haziness and conventionality may be noted of the attempts to represent the fluctuations of feeling, and the combinations of motive, in the actors. We are informed at great length of what the people felt, we listen to their conversation and soliloquies, but we never seem to hear a real human voice, we never see a soul laid bare.

Such briefly is the impression produced on my mind by this novel as a picture of life and character. I do not really *see* the election riot, I do not feel myself ideally present at those scenes; I do not seem to know Archibald Drewitt's improvidence; nor does Maxwell's patient prosecution of his plans for improving the estate and making his fortune, although told at some length, come home to me like an experience. Both are described, neither is vividly painted. The scenes in Dublin and London are weak and shadowy. In fact, the execution is wanting in the sharpness of distinct vision, where it is not absolutely inaccurate. At the best it is but approximative, never lifelike.

But having said thus much, I should leave a false impression if I did not add that I have been judging "Maxwell Drewitt" by a higher standard than that of the novels which are produced by the score. There is a certain gloomy earnestness in the writer, and a rhetorical power which carry you unwearied, though not unoffended, through the volumes. There is, moreover, a certain distinctiveness in the mode of treatment, and in the selection of the subjects. Without knowing anything of Ireland, I am quite sure that life at Connemara was not like what it appears in these pages; but then the fact that we are taken to unfamiliar scenes lightens our sense of the imperfect verisimilitude. The *suggestions* of the novel are interesting. The obvious effort of the writer to depict the improvidence and ignorance of the Irish and the ready means by which the land may be immensely improved, gives it a more serious aim than if it were a mere love story, or story of incident. What I consider its gravest defects, are the absence of sufficient clearness of Vision, and of sufficient attention to the principle of Sincerity (as these have formerly been explained in this Review); which defects might to a great extent be remedied by a resolute determination on her part not to write until her vision became clear, and only to write what she had distinctly in her mind.

Let us see what the application of our Test will do towards justifying such an impression. We find the hero, a young man of our own day, talking thus to himself:—

"'Yes, yes,' he cried at last, halting suddenly, and looking away towards the hills that rose to heaven—'yes, yes, Kincorth, you shall yet be mine—you and many a fair property beside; but you in especial, because I have sworn that neither man nor devil shall keep you from me. And shall a woman? No, before God!' And the veins came swelling up in his forehead as he stretched out one clenched hand towards Kincorth, and registered his oath."

It is difficult to suppose the author hearing her characters talk in this style, or believing it to be a representation of modern life, which could be accepted by a reflecting reader. Still worse is this rhapsody—

"'I love the wind,' she thought; 'it is fresh and pure, and it comes from travelling over the great sea, instead of bringing the taint of large cities on its breath'; and she turned, even while she was thinking this, round Eversbeg Head, and the wide Atlantic and the full force of the western breeze burst upon her at once.

"Thousands of miles! Millions upon millions of tossing billows! Oh! thou great God Almighty! who can look across the restless ocean and not think of Thee? Who can forget, while standing by the sea and watching the great waters come thundering upon the shore, that Thou hast set bounds to the waters and said, 'Here shall thy proud waves be stayed'—who, looking over the trackless expanse of ocean, but must feel that all unseen the feet of the Most High have traversed it?

"When we see this work of the Lord, His wonders in the deep; when we perceive how at His command the floods arise, and how at His word the storm ceases; when we remember that though the waves of the sea are mighty and rage horribly, still that the Lord God who dwelleth on high is mightier; when we think that He holds the waters in the hollow of His hand, do we not seem for a moment, amid raging tempests and foaming billows, to catch a glimpse of the Infinite? Looking over the waste of waters, does not our weak mortality appear able to grasp for an instant the idea of immortality? Can we not imagine that no material horizon bounds our view—that we are gazing away and away across the ocean into eternity?

"Thousands of miles, friends! Which of us has not at one time or other let his heart go free over the waters? Who has not stood by the shore silent, while his inner self—his self that never talks save to his God, and his own soul—has gone out from his body and tossed with the billows, and answered the sullen roar of the waters, and risen and sunk with the waters as they rose and fell, rose and fell, and felt the breaking of the foam, the sobbing plash of the great ocean, as it rolls up on the sands and over the rocks and stones and shells of earth, while depth calleth unto depth, and the giant floods clap their hands together?

"And oh! with what terrible sadness does that second self come back to us! It has been out listening to strange voices, hearing strange sounds, learning solemn truths. It has been out on the billows, on the foam, among the spray and the clouds and the tempest—out and away to the very confines of the invisible world. It has been restless like the ocean, and it comes back to be set within the bounds of flesh; it has been free, and behold it must return to chains and fetters; it has been telling of its troubles to the ocean, and the ocean has lift up its mighty arms and mourned out its sorrowful reply.

"Mourning—mourning—never silent, never still—now lashing itself up into fury—now tossing hither and thither as it seems to us without plan or purpose; now wave following after wave, as man follows after man in the ranks of a vast army; now flinging its waters on the shore—now striving to climb the steep sides of some rugged rock; fretting itself as we fret ourselves—moaning as we moan—toiling as we toil—restless as we are; now receding—now advancing—but never at peace; in its strong moods wild and tumultuous—in its calmest moments stirred by the ground swell, ruffled by the lightest breeze! Well may man love this deep, inexplicable, unfathomable ocean, for as it through the ages has gone on sobbing and mourning and struggling, so man through the years of his life goes mourning and struggling too.

"Some thoughts like these passed through Mrs.

Drewitt's mind as she stood at the base of Eversbeg Head, and looked out over the Atlantic."

This ambitious, but most injudicious passage is given as a representation of the thoughts which passed through the mind of a gentle, unhysterical, matter-of-fact woman! On reading it, every one will be able to form an estimate of the probability of a writer, who could present such a picture with a belief in its truthfulness being able to delineate truly the complexities of character under exceptional conditions. It is quite clear that she was led away by the temptation of "fine writing" to substitute what she considered an eloquent passage about the sea, for what Mrs. Drewitt was likely to have felt by the sea-shore. This is what I have named insincerity; and it is one of the common vices of literature.

There is an unpleasant redundance of "fine writing" and emphatic platitudes in these volumes. The desire to be eloquent, and the desire to sermonise, lead to pages upon pages which offend the taste, and which, if found out of a novel or a sermon, would provoke the critic's ridicule; but on the assumption that novels are not to be criticised as Literature, they pass without rebuke. Imagine any one of ordinary cleverness called upon to meditate on a truism thus ambitiously worded:—

"Within a week Ryan took a house in Duranmore next door to his office, and moved his furniture and himself and his sister away from the pretty cottage by the shore. *But the waves came rolling up the bay for all that:* though there was no human ear to listen to their music, they still rippled over the stones and sand—the shutters of the cottage windows were closed and fastened, *but the fuchsias bloomed the same as ever*—no Jenny now stood by the stream, singing her love songs, dreaming her love fantasies, *but the* stream went dancing over the stones to the sea none the less joyously—there were none to look up at the everlasting hills, *but the summer's sun shone on them*, and the winter's snows lay on them, as the sun had shone and the snow had lain since the beginning of time."

For whose instruction is this wisdom proffered? Was it a *possible* supposition that the removal of Jenny should cause the disappearance of the mountains and the cessation of the tides, or that fuchsias would cease to bloom because the window shutters were closed? Surely common sense ought not to be thus disregarded in the search for eloquence?

The truth seems to be that writing hastily, and unchecked by any sense of her responsibilities, never pausing to ask herself whether what she was setting down had truth or value, and would bear reflection, she indulged a propensity to vague moralising, feeling that anything was good enough for a novel. Thus, having killed her hero, she preaches a sermon on his career, in which we have remarks like this:—

"Pitiful! most pitiful! In his prime this man was taken away from among his treasures—from the place he had longed to possess—from the country of his birth—from the scenes he had loved to gaze over. What did it matter, then, whether he had been rich or poor, wealthy or indigent, lofty or lowly, peer or peasant?—what did it matter? what even in life had the lands and the houses, had the silver and the gold, profited him?"

And this—

"Never more may he walk by the sea shore, or stand under the arching trees that shade the avenue, or ride by lake or river, past mountains and through the valleys—never more for ever. . . . The great mountains rear their blue summits to heaven, the lakes ripple and ripple, the rivers flow onward to the sea, and the boulders and the blocks of granite lie scattered about on the hill sides—the great Atlantic beats against the iron-bound coast, and up the thousand bays the waves steal gently as ever—on that strange country through which Maxwell rode when he was still young, when he had life all before him, the moon looks down with as cold a light, playing as many fantastic tricks, creeping up the hills, and lying in the waters just as she did then."

There are several other passages I had marked for comment,[1] but those already given will suffice to confirm both my opinion of the quality of "Maxwell Drewitt," and my position respecting the advantage of testing a writer's quality by a consideration of the way in which he handles minor points. If we find him wanting in truthfulness, insight, and good sense in these minor points, we may be prepared to find him inaccurate, inadequate, and conventional in the more difficult representation of life and character. He may make foolish remarks, and yet tell a story well; but if his remarks are deviations from common sense, his story will be a deviation from human experience; and the critic who detects this may avoid the appearance of arbitrariness in his judgment on higher matters less easily brought within the scope of ordinary recognition, by showing that a writer who is not to be trusted in the one case cannot be trusted in the other.

This leads me to the second benefit which would accrue from a more stringent criticism, especially applied to minor points. It would soon greatly purge novels of their insincerities and nonsense. If critics were vigilant and rigorous, they would somewhat check the presumptuous facility and *facundia* of indolent novelists, by impressing on them a sense of danger in allowing the pen to wander at random. It would warn them that rhetoric without ideas would lead them into ridicule. It would teach them that what they wrote would not only be read, but reflected on; and if their glittering diction proved on inspection to be tinsel, they would suffer from the exposure. This would lead to a more serious conception of the art, and a more earnest effort to make their works in all respects conformable to sense and artistic truth. The man who begins to be vigilant as to the meaning of his phrases is already halfway towards becoming a good writer. The man who before passing on to his next sentence has already assured himself that the one just written expresses the thought actually in his mind, as well as he can express it, and declines to believe that insincere expressions or careless approximative phrases are good enough for a novel, will soon learn to apply the same vigilance to his conception of character and incident, and will strive to attain clearness of vision and sincerity of expression. Let criticism only exact from novels the same respect for truth and common sense which it exacts from other literary works; let it stringently mark where the approbation of a novel is given to it as Literature, and where it is given to plot-interest of a more or less attractive nature, and some good may be effected both on writers and readers.

[1]Among the slight but significant indications of imperfect attention to accuracy, may be mentioned the inadvertency with which the French language is treated on the two occasions when French phrases are used: *bête noir* might be charitably accepted as a misprint, but *au discrétion* tasks even charity.

Sensation Novels

H. L. Manse

First published in Quarterly Review, *113 (April 1863): 482-495, 501-506, 512-514.*

"I don't like preaching to the nerves instead of the judgment," was the remark of a shrewd observer of human nature, in relation to a certain class of popular sermons. The remark need not be limited to sermons alone. A class of literature has grown up around us, usurping in many respects, intentionally or unintentionally, a portion of the preacher's office, playing no inconsiderable part in moulding the minds and forming the habits and tastes of its generation; and doing so principally, we had almost said exclusively, by "preaching to the nerves." It would almost seem as if the paradox of Cabanis, *les nerfs, voilà tout l'homme*, had been banished from the realm of philosophy only to claim a wider empire in the domain of fiction—at least if we may judge by the very large class of writers who seem to acknowledge no other element in human nature to which they can appeal. Excitement, and excitement alone, seems to be the great end at which they aim—an end which must be accomplished at any cost by some means or other, "si possis, recte; si non, quocunque modo." And as excitement, even when harmless in kind, cannot be continually produced without becoming morbid in degree, works of this class manifest themselves as belonging, some more, some less, but all to some extent, to the morbid phenomena of literature—indications of a wide-spread corruption, of which they are in part both the effect and the cause; called into existence to supply the cravings of a diseased appetite, and contributing themselves to foster the disease, and to stimulate the want which they supply.

The sensation novel is the counterpart of the spasmodic poem. They represent "the selfsame interest with a different leaning." The one leans outward, the other leans inward; the one aims at convulsing the soul of the reader, the other professes to owe its birth to convulsive throes in the soul of the writer. But with this agreement there is also a difference. There is not a poet or poetaster of the spasmodic school but is fully persuaded of his own inspiration and the immortality of his work. He writes to satisfy the unconquerable yearnings of his soul; and if some prosaic friend were to hint at such earthly considerations as readers and purchasers, he would be ready to exclaim, with a forgotten brother of the craft (alas, that we should have to say *forgotten* after such a *hiatus!*):—

"Go, dotard, go, and if it suits thy mind,
Range yonder rocks and reason
                                        with the wind,
Or if its motions own another's will,
Walk to the beach and bid the sea be still;
In newer orbits let the planets run,
Or throw a cloud of darkness o'er the sun;
A measured movement bid the comets keep,
Or lull the music of the spheres to sleep:
These may obey thee; but the fiery soul
Of Genius owns not, brooks not,
                                        thy control."

Not so the sensation novelist. No divine influence can be imagined as presiding over the birth of his work, beyond the market-law of demand and supply; no more immortality is dreamed of for it than for the fashions of the current season. A commercial atmosphere floats around works of this class, redolent of the manufactory and the shop. The public want novels, and novels must be made—so many yards of printed stuff, sensation-pattern, to be ready by the beginning of the season. And if the demands of the novel-reading public were to increase to the amount of a thousand per season, no difficulty would be found in producing a thousand works of the average merit. They rank with the verses of which "Lord Fanny spins a thousand such a day"; and spinning-machines of the Lord Fanny kind may be multiplied without limit.

Various causes have been at work to produce this phenomenon of our literature. Three principal ones may be named as having had a large share in it—periodicals, circulating libraries, and railway bookstalls. A periodical, from its very nature, must contain many articles of an ephemeral interest, and of the character of goods made to order. The material part of it is a fixed quantity, determined by rigid boundaries of space and time; and on this Procrustean bed the spiritual part must needs be stretched to fit. A given number sheets of print, containing so many lines per sheet, must be produced weekly or monthly, and the diviner element must accommodate itself to these conditions. A periodical, moreover, belongs to the class of works which most men borrow and do not buy, and in which, therefore, they take only a transitory interest. Few men will burden their shelves with a series of volumes which have no coherence in their parts, and no limit in their number, whose articles of personal interest may be as one halfpennyworth of bread to an intolerable quantity of sack, and which have no other termination to their issue than the point at which they cease to be profitable. Under these circumstances, no small stimulus is given to the production of tales of the marketable stamp, which, after appearing piecemeal in weekly or monthly instalments, generally enter upon a second stage of their insect-life in the form of a handsome reprint under the auspices of the circulating library.

This last-named institution is the oldest offender of the three; but age has neither diminished the energy nor subdued the faults of its youth. It is more active now than at any former period of its existence, and its activity is much of the same kind as it was described in the pages of this Review more than fifty years ago.* The manner of its action is indeed inseparable from the nature of the institution, varying only in the production of larger quantities to meet the demand of a more reading generation. From the days of the "Minerva Press" (that synonym for the dullest specimens of the light reading of our grandmothers) to those of the thousand and one tales of the current season, the circulating library has been the chief hot-bed for forcing a crop of writers without talent and readers without discrimination. It is to literature what a *magasin de modes* is to dress, giving us the latest fashion, and little more. Its staple commodities are "books of the present season," many of them destined to run their round for the season only,—

> "Sons of a day, just buoyant on the flood,
> Then numbered with the puppies
>   in the mud."

Subscription, as compared with purchase, produces no doubt a great increase in the quantity of books procurable, but with a corresponding deterioration in the quality. The buyer of books is generally careful to select what for his own purposes is worth buying; the subscriber is often content to take the good the gods provide him, glancing lazily down the library catalogue, and picking out some title which promises amusement or excitement. The catalogue

of a circulating library is the legitimate modern successor to that portion of Curll's stock in trade which consisted of "several taking title-pages, that only wanted treatises to be wrote to them."

The railway stall, like the circulating library, consists partly of books written expressly for its use, partly of reprints in a new phase of their existence—a phase internally that of the grub, with small print and cheap paper, externally that of the butterfly, with a tawdry cover, ornamented with a highly-coloured picture, hung out like a signboard, to give promise of the entertainment to be had within. The picture, like the book, is generally of the sensation kind, announcing some exciting scene to follow. A pale young lady in a white dress, with a dagger in her hand, evidently prepared for some desperate deed; or a couple of ruffians engaged in a deadly struggle; or a Red Indian in his war-paint; or, if the plot turns on smooth instead of violent villany, a priest persuading a dying man to sign a paper; or a disappointed heir burning a will; or a treacherous lover telling his flattering tale to some deluded maid or wife. The exigencies of railway travelling do not allow much time for examining the merits of a book before purchasing it; and keepers of bookstalls, as well as of refreshment-rooms, find an advantage in offering their customers something hot and strong, something that may catch the eye of the hurried passenger, and promise temporary excitement to relieve the dulness of a journey.

These circumstances of production naturally have their effect on the quality of the articles produced. Written to meet an ephemeral demand, aspiring only to an ephemeral existence, it is natural that they should have recourse to rapid and ephemeral methods of awakening the interest of their readers, striving to act as the dram or the dose, rather than as the solid food, because the effect is more immediately perceptible. And as the perpetual cravings of the dram-drinker or the valetudinarian for spirits or physic are hardly intelligible to the man of sound health and regular appetites, so, to one called from more wholesome studies to survey the wide field of sensational literature, it is difficult to realise the idea which its multifarious contents necessarily suggest, that these books must form the staple mental food of a very large class of readers. On first turning over a few pages of the average productions of this school, he is tempted to exclaim "Quis leget haec?" but the doubt is checked as it rises by the evidently commercial character of the whole affair. These books would certainly not be written if they did not sell; and they would not sell if they were not read; *ergo*, they must have readers, and numerous readers too. The long list of works standing at the head of this article is, with a few exceptions, but a scanty gleaning from the abundant harvests of the last two seasons. Great is the power of fiction in attracting readers by its name alone. We have heard of a lady who was persuaded into reading "Plutarch's Lives" by being told that the book was a delightful novel, and who was indignant at the trick, when she discovered that history had won her approbation under the guise of fiction. If the name of a novel can carry down, with readers of this class, the bitter pill of solid merit, it may easily have its influence in seasoning the less unpalatable morsel of trash. It would be well, indeed, if this were all. Unhappily there is too much evidence that the public appetite can occasionally descend from trash to garbage. We have ourselves seen an English translation of one of the worst of those French novels devoted to the worship of Baal-Peor and the recommendation of adultery, lying for sale at a London railway-stall, and offered as a respectable book to unsuspecting ladies; and the list now before us furnishes sufficient proof that poison of the same kind is sometimes concealed under the taking title of the circulating library.

A sensation novel, as a matter of course, abounds in incident. Indeed, as a general rule, it consists of nothing else. Deep knowledge of human nature, graphic delineations of individual character, vivid representations of the aspects of Nature or the workings of the soul—all the higher features of the creative art—would be a hindrance rather than a help to a work of this kind. The unchanging principles of philosophy, the "thing of beauty" that "is a joy for ever," would be out of place in a work whose aim is to produce temporary excitement. "Action, action, action!" though in a different sense from that intended by the great orator, is the first thing needful, and the second, and the third. The human actors in the piece are, for the most part, but so many lay-figures on which to exhibit a drapery of incident. Allowing for the necessary division of all characters of a tale into male and female, old and young, virtuous and vicious, there is hardly anything said or done by any one specimen of a class which might not with equal fitness be said or done by any other specimen of the same class. Each game is played with the same pieces, differing only in the moves. We watch them advancing through the intricacies of the plot, as we trace the course of an x or a y through the combinations of an algebraic equation, with a similar curiosity to know what becomes

of them at the end, and with about as much consciousness of individuality in the ciphers.

Yet even the dullest uniformity admits of a certain kind of variety. As a shepherd can trace individual distinctions in the general air of sheepishness which marks the countenances of his fleecy charge; as the five sons of Sir Hildebrand Osbaldistone exhibited an agreeable variety in the mixture of the ingredients of sot, gamekeeper, bully, horse-jockey, and fool; so in the general type of character which marks a novel as belonging to the sensational genus, there may be traced certain minor differences constituting a distinction of species. A great philosopher has enumerated in a list of sensations "the feelings from heat, electricity, galvanism, &c.," together with "titillation, sneezing, horripilation, shuddering, the feeling of setting the teeth on edge, &c."; and our novels might be classified in like manner, according to the kind of sensation they are calculated to produce. There are novels of the warming-pan, and others of the galvanic-battery type—some which gently stimulate a particular feeling, and others which carry the whole nervous system by steam. There are some which tickle the vanity of the reader, and some which aspire to set his hair on end or his teeth on edge; while others, with or without the intention of the writer, are strongly provocative of that sensation in the palate and throat which is a premonitory symptom of nausea. To go through the details of any minute division would be impossible with such a voluminous list as we have before us: they may, however, all be classified under two general heads—those that are written merely for amusement, and those that are written with a didactic purpose.

Of the two, we confess that we very much prefer the former. As a fly, though a more idle, is a less offensive insect than a bug; as it is more pleasant that the exhilaration of a noisy evening should be forgotten in the morning than that it should leave its remembrance in the form of a headache; so it is better that the excitement of a sensation novel should evaporate in froth and foam, than that it should leave a residuum behind of shallow dogmatism and flippant conceit. For what other results can be expected from the popular novelist's method of prejudice teaching by caricature? There is nothing under the sun, divine or human, to which this method cannot be applied; reversing the power of Goldsmith in Johnson's epitaph, it leaves nothing untouched, and touches nothing which it does not deface. As universal as the oracles of the Athenian sausage-seller, it is ready on the shortest notice to discourse on all subjects—

> "About the Athenians,
> About pease-pudding and porridge,
>   about the Spartans,
> About the war, about the pilchard-fishery,
> About the state of things in general,
> About short weights and measures
>   in the market,
> About all things and persons whatsoever."

Let a writer have a prejudice against the religion of his neighbour, against the government of his country, against the administration of the law, against the peerage, against the prohibition that hinders a man from marrying his grandmother, against plucking in examinations, against fermented liquors, against the social position of women who have lapsed from virtue, against capital punishments, against the prevailing fashion in dress, against any institution, custom, or fact of the day—forthwith comes out a tale to exhibit in glowing colours the evil which might be produced by the obnoxious object in an imaginary case, tragic or comic, as suits the nature of the theme or the genius of the writer, and heightened by every kind of exaggeration. The offensive doctrines are fathered on some clerical Tartuffe; the governmental department is exhibited as a "Circumlocution Office"; the law ruins the fortunes of some blameless client, or corrupts the conscience of some generous young practitioner; the nobleman of the tale is a monster in depravity, or an idiot in folly; the table of prohibited degrees breaks two loving hearts who cannot live without each other; the promising youth is plucked for his little-go, and plunges into reckless dissipation in consequence; the single glass of port or sherry leads by sure stages to brandy and *delirium tremens*, and the medical virtues of pure water work cures in defiance of the faculty; &c. &c. The method is so far perfectly impartial that it may be applied with equal facility to the best things and the worst; but an argument that proves everything is of precisely the same value as an argument that proves nothing. Mr. Dickens, we regret to say, is a grievous offender in this line; and, by a just retribution, the passages that are written in this spirit are generally the worst in his works. He never sinks so nearly to the level of the ordinary sensation-novelist as when he is writing "with a purpose." Unfortunately, *decipit exemplar vitiis imitabile*; the vice of a great writer has been copied by a hundred small ones, who, without a tithe of his genius, make up for the defi-

ciency by an extra quantity of extravagance.

The sensation novel, be it mere trash or something worse, is usually a tale of our own times. Proximity is, indeed, one great element of sensation. It is necessary to be near a mine to be blown up by its explosion; and a tale which aims at electrifying the nerves of the reader is never thoroughly effective unless the scene be laid in our own days and among the people we are in the habit of meeting. We read with little emotion, though it comes in the form of history, Livy's narrative of the secret poisonings carried on by nearly two hundred Roman ladies; we feel but a feeble interest in an authentic record of the crimes of a Borgia or a Brinvilliers; but we are thrilled with horror, even in fiction, by the thought that such things may be going on around us and among us. The man who shook our hand with a hearty English grasp half an hour ago—the woman whose beauty and grace were the charm of last night, and whose gentle words sent us home better pleased with the world and with ourselves—how exciting to think that under these pleasing outsides may be concealed some demon in human shape, a Count Fosco or a Lady Audley! He may have assumed all that heartiness to conceal some dark plot against our life or honour, or against the life or honour of one yet dearer: she may have left that gay scene to muffle herself in a thick veil and steal to a midnight meeting with some villanous accomplice. He may have a mysterious female, immured in a solitary tower or a private lunatic asylum, destined to come forth hereafter to menace the name and position of the excellent lady whom the world acknowledges as his wife: she may have a husband lying dead at the bottom of a well, and a fatherless child nobody knows where. All this is no doubt very exciting; but even excitement may be purchased too dearly; and we may be permitted to doubt whether the pleasure of a nervous shock is worth the cost of so much morbid anatomy if the picture be true, or so much slanderous misrepresentation if it be false.

Akin to proximity is personality, and its effect is similar in creating a spurious interest. Personality, moreover, has an additional advantage, resembling that which Aristotle attributes to the use of metaphors in rhetoric. It gives rise to a kind of syllogism, whereby, without too great an exertion of thought, the mind of the reader is enabled to conclude that this is that. Of these advantages our novelists are not slow to avail themselves. If a scandal of more than usual piquancy occurs in high life, or a crime of extraordinary horror figures among our *causes célèbres*, the sensationist is immediately at hand to weave the incident into a thrilling tale, with names and circumstances slightly disguised, so as at once to exercise the ingenuity of the reader in guessing at the riddle, and to gratify his love of scandal in discovering the answer. Sometimes the incident of real life is made the main plot of the story, sometimes it figures as an episode in the history of two imaginary lovers, with whom the flesh-and-blood criminal comes in contact, like the substantial Aeneas on board the shadowy bark of Charon, nearly making shipwreck of the frail vessel of their fortunes. The end and moral of the narrative, in the one case and in the other, is much the same; namely, to elicit from the gratified reader the important exclamation, "I know who is meant by So-and-so."

Of particular offences, which are almost always contemporary and sometimes personal, undoubtedly the first place must be given to Bigamy. Indeed, so popular has this crime become, as to give rise to an entire sub-class in this branch of literature, which may be distinguished as that of Bigamy Novels. It is astonishing how many of our modern writers have selected this interesting breach of morality and law as the peg on which to hang a mystery and a dénouement. Of the tales on our list, no less than eight are bigamy stories:—"Lady Audley's Secret," "Aurora Floyd," "Clinton Maynyard," "Recommended to Mercy," "The Law of Divorce," "The Daily Governess," "Only a Woman," "The Woman of Spirit," all hang their narrative, wholly or in part, on bigamy in act, or bigamy in intention, on the existence or supposed existence of two wives to the same husband, or two husbands to the same wife. Much of this popularity is, no doubt, due to the peculiar aptitude of bigamy, at least in monogamous countries, to serve as a vehicle of mysterious interest or poetic justice. If some vulgar ruffian is to be depicted as having a strange influence over a lady of rank and fashion, it is a ready expedient to make him conscious of the existence of another husband, or the child of another husband, supposed to be long dead. If lowly virtue is to be exalted, or high-born pride humiliated, the means are instantly at hand, in the discovery of a secret marriage, unsuspected till the third volume, which makes the child of poverty the heir to rank and wealth, or degrades the proud patrician by stripping him of his illegal honours. It is really painful to think how many an interesting mystery and moral lesson will be lost, if Sir Cresswell Cresswell's Court continues in active work for another generation. Bigamy will become as clumsy and obsolete an expedient for the relief of discontented partners as the axe was in Juvenal's

day, compared with the superior facilities of poison. With such an easy legal provision of being "off wi' the auld love," it will be worse than a crime, it will be a blunder, to have recourse to illegitimate means of being "on wi'the new."

Of our list of Bigamy Novels, some will be noticed under other characters, and some are not worth noticing at all. The two first-named claim a notice as bigamy novels *par excellence*, the whole interest of the story turning on this circumstance. Though both exaggerated specimens of the sensational type, they are the works of an author of real power, who is capable of better things than drawing highly-coloured portraits of beautiful fiends and fast young ladies burdened with superfluous husbands. Lady Audley, *alias* Mrs. George Talboys, is a Vittoria Corombona transferred to the nineteenth century and to an English drawing-room. But the romantic wickedness of the "White Devil of Italy" suffers by being transplanted to home scenes and modern associations. The English White Devil, however, if not quite so romantic and interesting, is more than the rival of her prototype in boldness and guilt. She does with her own hand what Vittoria does by means of others. She has married a second husband, knowing or suspecting her first one to be still living; and the desperate means to which she has recourse to avoid discovery furnish an abundance of incidents of various degrees of ingenuity and villainy. She advertises her own death in the newspapers, having previously procured a young woman who resembles her in person to die and be buried in her stead; she throws her first husband down a well, whence he finally emerges, we are not told how, with a broken arm; she breaks into a lawyer's chambers during his absence, and destroys his papers; she burns down a house to get rid of a dangerous witness, having locked the door of his room to prevent his escape. Yet, notwithstanding all the horrors of the story—and there are enough of them to furnish a full supper for a Macbeth— notwithstanding the glaring improbability of the incidents, the superhuman wickedness of the principal character and the incongruities of others; notwithstanding the transparent nature of the "secret" from the very beginning; the author has succeeded in constructing a narrative the interest of which is sustained to the end. The skill of the builder deserves to be employed on better materials.

It is difficult to do justice by extracts to a work whose chief merit consists in the cleverness with which an interesting whole is made out of faulty parts. The following description is not, perhaps, the best specimen of the author's powers; but it is worth quoting, not only in itself, but as exhibiting in strong contrast the personal fascinations of the lady whose character and actions have been described above. Here is a portrait of the heroine under her supposed maiden name of Lucy Graham:—

"Wherever she went she seemed to take joy and brightness with her. In the cottages of the poor her fair face shone like a sunbeam. She would sit for a quarter of an hour talking to some old woman, and apparently as pleased with the admiration of a toothless crone as if she had been listening to the compliments of a marquis; and when she tripped away, leaving nothing behind her (for her poor salary gave no scope to her benevolence), the old woman would burst out into senile raptures with her grace, her beauty, and her kindliness, such as she never bestowed upon the vicar's wife, who half fed and clothed her. For you see Miss Lucy Graham was blessed with that magic power of fascination by which a woman can charm with a word or intoxicate with a smile. Every one loved, admired, and praised her. The boy who opened the five-barred gate that stood in her pathway ran home to his mother to tell of her pretty looks and the sweet voice in which she thanked him for the little service. The verger at the church who ushered her into the surgeon's pew; the vicar who saw the soft blue eyes uplifted to his face as he preached his simple sermon; the porter from the railway-station who brought her sometimes a letter or a parcel, and who never looked for reward from her; her employer; his visitors; her pupils; the servants; everybody, high and low, united in declaring that Lucy Graham was the sweetest girl that ever lived."

Aurora Floyd, as a character, is tame after Lady Audley. The "beautiful fiend," intensely wicked, but romantic from the very intensity of her wickedness, has degenerated into a fast young lady, full of stable talk, deep in the mysteries of the turf, and familiar with "Bell's Life,"—a young lady with large beautiful eyes, and with very little else to command any feeling either of love or the reverse. She runs away from school to contract a secret marriage with a consummate blackguard of a groom—

"A bridegroom, say you? 'tis a groom
indeed."

She separates herself from him after a short and bitter experience of his character, comes home, and deceives her father by assuring him that "that person" is dead when she knows him to be alive; afterwards, on the report of his death, deceives two worthy men by accepting one and marrying the other without breathing a word of her previous escapade (we are informed that "her natural dis-

position is all truth and candour"); and finally deceives her husband again, when she discovers that the man she had supposed dead is alive, by making arrangements for sending the obnoxious individual to Australia and retaining the second and illegal spouse as the more agreeable personage of the two. She is inferior to Lady Audley, as a pickpocket is inferior to a thug; but there is this important difference,—that Lady Audley is meant to be detested, while Aurora Floyd is meant to be admired. The one ends her days in a madhouse; the other becomes the wife of an honest man, and the curtain falls upon her "bending over the cradle of her first-born." By a fortunate arrangement of nature, which is always at the command of novelists, the birth of the infant is delayed beyond the usual time, till the groom is really dead and a re-marriage has repaired the irregularity of the bigamy. Fortunately also, there is no little pledge of affection born to the Damasippus of her first vows.

Though the moral teaching of the story is more questionable than that of its predecessor, and the interest, on the whole, less sustained, the individual characters are drawn with greater skill. Aurora, with all her faults, is a woman and not a fiend; and John Mellish, the honest, genial, tender-hearted, somewhat henpecked husband, is a portrait superior to any in the more romantic volume. As a companion to the picture of Lucy Graham in a calm may be exhibited the following description of Aurora Floyd in a storm. The "stable-man" of the piece is not the one whom she has acquired a conjugal right to chastise, but another of the same profession, by no means so good-looking, but as great a scoundrel:—

"Aurora sprang upon him like a beautiful tigress, and catching the collar of his fustian jacket in her slight hands, rooted him to the spot upon which he stood. The grasp of those slender hands, convulsed by passion, was not to be easily shaken off; and Steeve Hargraves, taken completely off his guard, stared aghast at his assailant. Taller than the stable-man by a foot and a half, she towered above him, her cheeks white with rage, her eyes flashing fury, her hat fallen off, and her black hair tumbling about her shoulders, sublime in her passion. . . . She disengaged her right hand from his collar, and rained a shower of blows upon his clumsy shoulders with her slender whip; a mere toy, with emeralds set in its golden head, but stinging like a rod of flexible steel in that little hand."

In direct opposition to the bigamy-novels are those which, instead of multiplying the holy ceremony, betray an inclination to dispense with it altogether. There is a school of fiction the practical lesson of which seems to be to reduce marriage to a temporary connexion *durante bene placito*, and to exalt the character of the mistress at the expense of that of the wife. This is a favourite theme with French novelists of a certain class; and the tale entitled "Recommended to Mercy" may claim to be considered as an English exponent of the same doctrine. It has, indeed, an episode of bigamy, to show the inconveniences of matrimony; but the chief interest centres in a heroine whose ideas on this subject are rather on the side of a defect than of excess. Helen Langton, *alias* Mrs. Vaughan, is a young lady whose opinions on the conjugal relation are borrowed from Eloisa, filtered through the dregs of Mary Wollstonecraft:—

"Not Caesar's empress would I deign
                                        to prove;
No, make me mistress to the man I love"—

reappears from the mouth of this strong-minded young lady in the form of the following declaration volunteered to a male cousin:—

"I consider the ceremony of marriage as one of the most absurd inventions ever inflicted on human beings by mortal men. . . . In the first place, do we not swear to *love* always and to the end, when to do so is too often clearly and simply out of our power? Is human love the growth of human will? Certainly not; and as certainly is it only as words of course, that we vow to 'honour and to obey' the man who may turn out a dishonourable wretch, or a monster of tyranny and oppression."

The practice of this fair philosopher is in accordance with her theory. She lives for some years as the mistress of the man she loves; is discarded, as a matter of course, on his marriage; leads a life of virtuous and ill-used poverty for a time; returns to her lover again when he has separated from his wife on suspicion of her infidelity; becomes the legatee of his whole property on certain peculiar conditions of trust; and is thus enabled to become a model of virtue in wealth, as formerly of virtue in poverty (her charities furnishing some graphic illustrations of the manners and customs of the "social evil"); and finally makes a magnanimous surrender of her riches to the rightful heir, on making a discovery which enables her to do so according to the conditions of the will.

Such is the outline of the story. The moral that would be drawn by the author may be conjectured from the title of the book; that which will be drawn by many of its readers may be summed up in the comfortable doctrine of Hans Carvel's wife,—

"That if weak women went astray,
Their stars were more in fault than they."

In truth, we much doubt the wisdom or the morality of drawing fictitious portraits of noble-minded and interesting sinners, by way of teaching us to feel for the sinner while we condemn the sin. We do not deny that the feeling is a right one, nor that such characters may actually exist; but it makes all the difference in the world to the moral whether we meet with the persons in real life or in a novel. The real person is a human being, with human qualities, good or bad, to which the particular sin in question attaches itself as one feature out of many. The fictitious character is but the sin personified and made attractive as the source and substance of many virtues. In the one, the person is the principal figure, the sin is accessory; in the other, the sin is the primary idea, to embellish which the rest of the character is made to order. And when, as a foil to this diamond with but a single flaw, is drawn the "respectable" woman whose chastity is beyond the breath of scandal, but who sullies that one virtue by a thousand faults—cold, selfish, pharisaical, hollow-hearted, ill-tempered, &c.—to what does such a story naturally lead, but to the conclusion that, whatever a censorious world may say to the contrary, female virtue has really very little to do with the Seventh Commandment? Novelists of this school do their best to inculcate as a duty the first two of the three stages towards vice—"we first endure, then pity, then embrace"; and, in so doing, they have assisted in no small degree to prepare the way for the third.

* * *

From vice to crime, from the divorce-court to the police-court, is but a single step. When fashionable immorality becomes insipid, the materials for sensation may still be found hot and strong in the "Newgate Calendar"; especially if the crime is of recent date, having the merits of personality and proximity to give it a nervous as well as a moral effect. Unhappily, the materials for such excitement are not scanty, and an author who condescends to make use of them need have little difficulty in selecting the most available. Let him only keep an eye on the criminal reports of the daily newspapers, marking the cases which are honoured with the especial notice of a leading article, and become a nine-days' wonder in the mouths of quidnuncs and gossips; and he has the outline of his story not only ready-made, but approved beforehand as of the true sensation cast. Then, before the public interest has had time to cool, let him serve up the exciting viands in a réchauffé with a proper amount of fictitious seasoning; and there emerges the criminal variety of the Newspaper Novel, a class of fiction having about the same relation to the genuine historical novel that the police reports of the "Times" have to the pages of Thucydides or Clarendon. More than one of the books on our list belong to this class. The very dull tale called "Wait and Hope," consisting for the most part of insufferably tedious conversations, aims at enlivening its general torpor by exciting a momentary shudder at the carpet-bag mystery of Waterloo Bridge; while the author of "Recommended to Mercy" deals out the same wares on a larger scale, under the appropriate title of "Such Things Are." The latter author "ventures to remind the reader of the fact that all which trenches on either the mysterious or the horrible has for the present generation an apparently irresistible attraction"; and by way of feeding this depraved taste, has "brought again to the light of recollection a shadowy vision of two past, but as yet undiscovered crimes,"—in other words—the Road murder and the Glasgow poisoning. These two crimes are taken out of their original associations, and, with some change of circumstances, are fastened upon two "fast young ladies," bosom friends to each other, and who, by a most marvellous coincidence, become the wives of two brothers. The one, some time after her marriage, is discovered by her horrified husband to be the person principally suspected of "the famous Bogden murder"; the other, on the eve of her marriage, being threatened with an exposure of some passages in her earlier life, quietly gets rid of the obnoxious witness by a dose of strychnine, and, on the day but one following, figures as a bride in a "quiet and unostentatious wedding at St. George's, Hanover Square."

There is something unspeakably disgusting in this ravenous appetite for carrion, this vulture-like instinct which smells out the newest mass of social corruption, and hurries to devour the loathsome dainty before the scent has evaporated. When some memorable crime of bygone days presents features which have enabled it to survive the crowd of contemporary horrors, and, by passing into the knowledge of a new generation, has in some degree attained to the dignity of history, there is much to be said in defence of a writer of fiction who sees in the same features something of a romantic interest which makes them available for the purposes of his art; but it is difficult to extend the same excuse to the gatherer of fresh stimulants from the last assizes. The poet or the philosopher may be allowed to moralise over the dry skeleton turned up to view in the graveyard or the battlefield, but we doubt whether the strongest-stomached medical student would find a theme equally poetical or equally instructive in the subject laid out in the dissecting-room.

But all this is done, as the author tells us, "with a purpose," to warn fast young ladies, forsooth, of the fatal consequences to which fastness may lead them! As if any moral end could be served by a real crime tacked on to an imaginary criminal, without even a *callida junctura* to disguise the clumsy patchwork! Crimes of this horrible individuality are the very last from which any one will draw a general moral: they are the crimes of their perpetrators, and of no one else. Even the plain lesson that might be drawn from the real dying speech and confession of the actual criminal is lost in this diluted mixture of fact and fiction. Everybody knows that the crimes as described were not really committed by the persons to whom they are attributed in the story, but by very different persons and under very different circumstances; and the whole moral is at once destroyed by the glaring untruthfulness and incongruity of the story. A book of this sort is simply a chamber of horrors without even the merit of giving a correct likeness of the criminals exhibited. To think of pointing a moral by stimulants of this kind is like holding a religious service in a gin-palace.

Where the excitement of a real police-report is wanting, the novelist of criminal life may supply its place by variety and strangeness of imaginary adventure. Of all heroes of the felonious class, commend us to George Messenger, *alias* Scarisbrick, *alias* Dandy Dangerfield, the prominent figure in the group of blackguards of both sexes who form the principal *dramatis personae* of the "Old Roman Well." This marvellous personage, within the compass of two volumes, goes through adventures enough to furnish half a dozen Turpins or Jack Sheppards. He begins life, where George Talboys is supposed to end it, at the bottom of a well—scarcely in this case the habitation of truth—though his biographer, more communicative than the narrator of "Lady Audley's Secret," is kind enough to explain the circumstances under which he got out unhurt, after falling a depth of a hundred and fifty feet. "I expex, ye know, it's owin' to its bein' so light—all gristle instead of bones—and p'raps its clothes spread out as it wint down, and so sunk its fall like." Thus marvellously preserved, the child is doubtless destined to be a great man; but unfortunately his greatness is of the wrong kind—that of a scoundrel, not of a hero. He first figures as a juvenile poacher in the country; then runs away to London, and falls into the meshes of a beautiful fiend, a sort of Lady Audley of low life (these female fiends are a stock article with sensation novelists), and passes through various stages of town rascality, under the tutorage of a gentleman who has graduated in the successive honours of a "shiverer," a "cadger," a "duffer," an "area-sneak," a "shop-bouncer," a "fogle-buzzer," a "swell-mobbite," a "rampsman," and a "cracksman." Under this hopeful instructor, he ascends from theft to robbery, and from robbery to murder, with interludes of softer vice as a lady-killer; is hanged, very justly, in the middle of his course; is brought to life again through a wonderful elixir administered by an old ferryman, who turns out to be the husband of the beautiful fiend; is sent by the said ferryman to America, furnished with medical secrets by which he makes his fortune as a doctor; comes back to England in ten years, rolling in wealth, and with a "supernatural paleness" (the remains of the *sus. per coll.*) which disguises his identity from all his former friends; spends untold thousands in all kinds of charitable works; succeeds to the estates of his ancestors, whom he discovers to be of an old family in his native county; becomes a husband and a father; and dies at last in the odour of sanctity, under the influence of which "his face glowed with a heavenly light." The reader closes the book impressed with a conviction (not in the judicial sense) of the beneficial effects of hanging as a moral restorative, if the patient is only fortunate enough to survive the operation, and of the author's profound acquaintance with thieves' Latin, which he coins *ad libitum* by the simple process of spelling words backwards.

A very brief notice will be sufficient to dispose of some of the smaller fry on our multifarious list.

"Miriam May," "Crispin Ken," and "Philip Paternoster" are specimens of the theological novel, which employs the nerves as a vehicle for preaching in the literal sense of the term. The object of these tales is to inculcate certain doctrines, or rather a hatred of certain opposite doctrines, by painting offensive portraits of persons professing the obnoxious opinions. The two former preach on the High-Church side, by exhibiting villainous specimens of Low-Churchmen and Dissenters; the third preaches on the Low-Church side, by drawing ludicrous caricatures of Tractarians, and by the original and ingenious witticism of calling St. Barnabas St. Barabbas. "The Weird of the Went-

worths" (a sensation title) teaches a lesson the very opposite of theological, being chiefly remarkable as showing the agreeable varieties which it is possible to introduce into the art of profane swearing. "Passages in the Life of a Fast Young Lady" (another sensation title) is one of those tales of personal scandal of which we have already spoken. "Only a Woman," a tale of feminine passion and masculine weakness, is chiefly remarkable for the author's high estimate of the female sex—the heroine being a young woman whose animal charms are dwelt upon with unnecessary minuteness; but who is described as having "no troublesome moral principles to keep her in check"; while at the same time she is "as far above" another young woman "as Cotopaxi is above Primrose Hill." "Harold Overdon" and "Liberty Hall, Oxon," are offenders of another and a far worse kind—coarse tales of unblushing profligacy, which would be mischievous were not their immorality counteracted by their stupidity. "Ashcombe Churchyard" is an attempt to combine the sensational with the domestic. The double purpose extends the story to a tedious length, and the glowing tints of the former ingredient harmonise badly with the sober background of the latter. In connexion with the quiet history of an impoverished family, and commonplace moral reflections coloured to match, we are dazzled by fitful flashes of the pathetic and the horrible, comprising a cruel father and a victim daughter; a seduction transacted in a *more ferarum* style, which it is to be hoped is not often to be met with in fact or in fiction; a murder, or something very like one, through medical breach of trust; a mysterious legend and a family doom; a second murder—this time by a pistol—and three broken hearts, leading respectively to immediate death, imbecility, and lunacy. The hero or villain of the piece (in tales of this kind the two terms are nearly synonymous) is a certain fascinating dispensary doctor, whose charms beguile his female patients into a forgetfulness, sometimes of prudence, sometimes of duty, sometimes of common decency; who is attached, rather beyond Platonic bounds, to another man's wife; is assailed with fierce love by an earl's daughter on one side, and an heiress of vast wealth on the other; and is finally married, sorely against his will, and shot on his wedding-day; after which we are confidently told that his spirit waited at the gates of Paradise till it was joined by that of a married lady (not his own wife), with the following celestial results:—

"They had found the star that had shone a moment

on their early youth and then disappeared, leaving them to grope to the end of their pilgrimage in darkness. They had found the harp that they had strongly swept in life's morning, but which, as soon as it was touched, 'passed in music out of sight,' leaving them in a howling wilderness of discord. They had found the solution of that dark enigma which had been propounded to them when they began their rugged march through earth, and the meaning of which seemed till now hidden from them by a thousand mystical wrappings. They had found the missing verity."

The above samples may be considered as belonging to the aristocratic branch of sensational literature, so far at least as high prices and hotpressed paper can make them so. But the craving for sensation extends to all classes of society—

"Plebeium in circo positum est et in aggere
                                            fatum";

and our task would be incomplete without some notice of the cheap publications which supply sensation for the million in penny and halfpenny numbers. These publications are not directly included in the list of works contemplated in our previous observations, and to examine them in detail would require a separate article, and a somewhat different method of treatment; but, indirectly, they belong to our subject, as the anatomy of the skeleton frame belongs to the surgical treatment of the living body. In a rigidly scientific study of the subject they would perhaps claim the principal place, so far as science aims at studying effects in their causes, at analysing compounds and exhibiting their simplest elements. These tales are to the full-grown sensation novel what the bud is to the flower, what the fountain is to the river, what the typical form is to the organised body. They are the original germ, the primitive monad, to which all the varieties of sensational literature may be referred, as to their source, by a law of generation at least as worthy of the attention of the scientific student as that by which Mr. Darwin's bear may be supposed to have developed into a whale. Fortunately in this case the rudimental forms have been continued down to the epoch of the mature development. In them we have sensationism pure and undisguised, exhibited in its naked simplicity, stripped of the rich dress which conceals while it adorns the figure of the more ambitious varieties of the species.

* * *

It is unnecessary to multiply our examples,

whether of the higher or the lower order. Evidence enough has been adduced to show that sensation novels must be recognised as a great fact in the literature of the day, and a fact whose significance is by no means of an agreeable kind. Regarding these works merely as an efflorescence, as an eruption indicative of the state of health of the body in which they appear, the existence of an impure or a silly crop of novels, and the fact that they are eagerly read, are by no means favourable symptoms of the conditions of the body of society. But it is easier to detect the disease than to suggest the remedy. The praiseworthy attempts of individual proprietors of circulating libraries, to weed their collections of silly or mischievous works, have been too partial and isolated to produce any perceptible result, and have even acted as an advertisement of the rejected books. A more general and combined attempt in this direction is a thing rather to be wished than expected. Could a taste for the best class of fictions be cultivated in the minds of the rising generation, it might, perhaps, have its effect in lessening the craving for this kind of unnatural excitement; and could any check be imposed on the rapidity of production, it might improve the quality of the article produced. It is difficult to believe that the habitual devourers of sensation novels have ever read Scott; indeed, we have known young persons, familiar with the latest products of the circulating library, who not only had never read Scott, but who had no idea that he was worth reading. It is as easy to imagine that the blessed sun of heaven should prove a micher and eat blackberries, as that one capable of appreciating the creations of the great magician should relish the sort of stuff of which three-fourths of the books on our present list are made. But, alas! Scott himself has well-nigh shared the fate which he lamented as having befallen Richardson, Mackenzie, and Burney.—A new generation of readers has sprung up, who have reversed the fault of which Horace complains, and gone back to that for which Homer apologises. We have no need of the subtlety of "the rule that laid the horsetail bare" to argue against readers who admire no authors of less than a hundred years old: we have rather to echo the comment of Telemachus on the taste of his day:—

"For novel lays attract our ravished ears,
But old, the mind with inattention hears."

By way of experiment, and to give the old at least a fair chance of competing with the new, we should like to see a lending library established somewhat on the principle of the "Retrospective

Review," which should circulate no books but those which have received the stamp of time in testimony of their merits. No book should be admitted under twenty years old, a very liberal allowance for the life of a modern novel, and which is long enough to give rise to a new generation who could not have read the book on its first coming out. Such an establishment, if the public mind could be persuaded to tolerate it, would have at least one commercial advantage which is denied to some of its present rivals. It would be relieved from the necessity, which is often imposed upon them, of buying up nearly the whole impression of the last work of some popular author, which, having been already published for a very trifling sum in the pages of some magazine, is forthwith reprinted at five or six times the price, as a separate work. A real competition between old favourites and new would have a good effect, not in destroying, which is not to be wished, but in weeding the luxuriant produce of the present day. The appetite, even of a novel-reader, has its limits; and if the best of the old books could be brought in, the worst of the new must drop out to make way for them. There would be an increased struggle for existence, under the pressure of which the weaker writers would give way, and the stronger would be improved by the stimulus of effective competition.

Even if no remedy can be found, it is something to know the disease. There is a satisfaction in exposing an impostor, even when we feel sure that the world will continue to believe in him. The idol may still be worshipped, yet it is right to tell its worshippers that it is an idol; grotesque, it may be, or horrible in its features, but mere wood or stone, brass or clay, in its substance. The current folly may be destined to run its course, as other follies have done before it; and it must be confessed that there are as yet but few signs of its abating. But the duty of the preacher is the same, whether he succeed or fail. Though we cannot flatter ourselves with the hope that our protest will have the disenchanting influence of "Dian's bud o'er Cupid's flower," we are not the less bound to place on record the grounds of our belief, that, when the reading public wakes up from its present delusion, it will discover, with regard to some at least of the favourites of the day, that its affections have been bestowed upon an object not very different in kind from the animal of which Titania was enamoured.

*"Quarterly Review," vol. iii., pp. 340, 341.

Novels with a Purpose

Justin M'Carthy

First published in Westminster Review, *82 (July 1864): 24-29, 40-49.*

The novelist ought to be the happiest of all authors. He enjoys the most perfect freedom known to literature. Any ray of genius, any special faculty whatever which he may happen to possess, is at full liberty to develope itself in the direction which best suits it. The novelist almost alone among his brethren of letters may "walk his own wild way whither that leads him." He is allowed an almost complete immunity from the trammels, and prescriptions, and pedantries of criticism. No one thinks of ordaining for him that he must tread in one particular path and no other; that he must beat round and round for ever in one prescribed circle. For him there is no dignity of history. For him there are no dramatic unities. For him there are no laws of rhythm, no dactyles and spondees, no Alexandrine and *ottava rima*, or Spenserian or English heroic. There are no codes of critical laws to ordain that a romancist must follow this or that pattern, must not deal with this or that topic, must only introduce this character or situation on these given conditions. There are no contending schools of romance-critics; there is no mutual persecution among romancists; there is no wrangling of classic and romantic known among the free races who write novels. Innumerable are the poets who have been blighted because of Virgil; the dramatists who had to waste all their life's energies trying to dance in the Sophoclean fetters, or to jump in the Terentian sack; the historians cursed to everlasting stupidity and oblivion, because critical custom prescribed that they must write in a dead language which was the living tongue of Sallust and Tacitus. Corneille might have moved the whole world and all generations if he had not been condemned to observe some supposed adherence to imaginary laws of Greek tragedy. The imbecile pedantry of the rules of epical poetry finally killed the epic poem altogether, and now the age of the epic seems almost as extinct an era as that of the mastodon. Dante was only saved by a happy venture of reckless audacity from becoming a petrifaction in the Latin tongue; and there was a point in the career of Molière when he seemed likely to fall a victim to the memory of Plautus. Indeed in poetry and the drama, and we might perhaps even add in history, hardly any man has ever become great except by braving in the first instance the literary dangers and penalties of rebellion. The motto of Danton was almost always the watchword of him who desired for his epic, his tragedy, or his history a better fate than the critical approval of to-day, and the contempt or neglect of all succeeding generations.

All this the novelist escaped. Le Sage was not condemned *in limine* and out of hand because the first volume of "Gil Blas" failed to follow in the track of Cervantes. No one insisted that "Tom Jones" ought to have talked in the style of the "Grand Cyrus," or for ever held his peace. The existence of "Tom Jones" did not necessitate sentence of death upon "Waverley"; nor did "Waverley" interfere with "Oliver Twist," nor "Oliver Twist" darken the rising prospects of "Pendennis." If a man or woman attempt to be a novelist and fail, the blame cannot be laid to the account of pedantic critical legislation. Perhaps this happy freedom was greatly owing in the first instance to the fact that criticism deliberately ignored the novelist altogether, and regarded him as a creature outside the pale of art, no more responsible to rule and law of critical courts than Richardson's show is expected to conform to the dramatic unities. It is only of recent days that critics have begun seriously to occupy themselves in the consideration of prose fiction. It forced itself on them by its popularity and its influence. When it became utterly impossible to ignore it any longer, when criticism must either condescend to recognise the new and growing power or submit to abdicate its own special functions altogether, then only did it acknowledge the novelist as a man having a distinct and important place in literature. It was then, however, too late to set about laying down laws, and forming schools, and prescribing this and proscribing that, and attempting all the freaks of pedantic power in which criticism delighted to indulge from the days of Zoilus to those of Rymer, and from the age of Rymer to the age of Schlegel. In our more liberal generation, we seem to have got rid almost entirely of the canonical laws and ecclesiastical courts of literature. Our poets do as they like, and so long as they do it well remain unwhipt of justice. Our dramatists, if we had any, might develope their genius with the freedom even of eccentricity, and no critic would venture to hint of unities neglected or Elizabethan models ignored. We have all come at last to recognise the great truth, which if perceived earlier would have saved authorship much suffering and criticism much blundering—the truth that genius, like the strong man and the waterfall of Goethe's axiom, makes its own channel. The novelist, therefore, now obtains that leave and licence by right of matured public opinion which he formerly obtained only by virtue of his outlawed social position. He was always free, but at one time his was only the freedom of Bohemia and the *demi-monde*—a liberty to do as he liked, because society regarded him as beneath its dignified notice, and outside the pale of its virtuous laws. He may now write for a purpose or for no purpose, he may be a politician, a satirist, or a mere teller of stories; he may be a realist or an idealist; he may be mirthful or melancholy; may find his subjects anywhere, and conduct his readers whither he will; he is sure to be criticized and judged on the ground which he has spontaneously assumed. He will be valued for what he is, and not simply condemned because he is not something else. He will be estimated for what he has done and for his manner of doing it, and is not likely to hear a word of complaint urged because he has not done something which he never professed or desired to accomplish.

One result of all this is that the novelist's art is by far the most fresh, vigorous, and flourishing of all the literary professions of the day. We have, or we had until within a few months, two great, supreme novelists; two men who would have been justly accounted great at any period or in any country; than whom, indeed, no age ever produced a contemporaneous pair more distinguished in their art. But besides these, the present generation of English literature reckons many novelists and romancists who are entitled to high and honourable distinction in the field of letters. Mr. Disraeli's political novels still remain, in their own peculiar range, unequalled, and we venture to think not to be surpassed. Mr. Trollope has brought easy realism in the painting of a certain section or two of English life to a degree of perfection such as nobody, not even Thackeray himself, had attained before. As a novelist and a man of genius he is indeed not to be compared with the author of

"Vanity Fair," but within the narrow range which he prescribes for himself, he has realized something which assuredly no English novelist had done before. Charlotte Brontë was a woman endowed with a power which, in any literary age, would fairly have been regarded as extraordinary, and a longer life might have enabled her to reconcile that power with an equal degree of artistic refinement and matured self-command. The career of the authoress of "Adam Bede" and "Romola" is yet, we trust, only in its opening, and no other woman ever contributed to English fiction with anything like the same promise of capacity to attain a supreme place. We could mention many others endowed with remarkable gifts, even if we were to leave out of our consideration that much-admired and much-abused class—that class whom nearly all critics condemn, and nearly all readers now run after—the Sensation Novelists. But there is something to be said in defence of that most popular section of our romancists too. In the first place they are an inevitable reaction against the realism of far greater authors; and in the next place, with all their grievous sins against art and taste, and perhaps even in one sense against morals, they are, on the whole, much superior to the sensation novelists whose tales lifted the hair and curdled the blood of a preceding generation. Even Miss Braddon's poisonings, and stranglings, and conflagrations, and plunges into wells, are but modest and inoffensive incidents when compared with some of the sensational events wherewith Maturin was wont to delight his horrified readers. Considering the facility with which novels are written, published, and read in our day, considering that a certain public is to be found for anything which issues in three volumes and calls itself a romance, it is really much to the credit of the age, and testifies highly to the progress of public education, that so many books of this class are produced which deserve to be read, and that so small a number, comparatively, are worthy only of utter contempt or positive condemnation.

The novelist is now our most influential writer. If he be a man of genius his power over the community he addresses is far beyond that of any other author. Macaulay's influence over the average English mind was narrow compared with that of Dickens; even Carlyle's was not on the whole so great as that of Thackeray. The readers of "The Idylls of the King" were but a limited number when compared with the readers of "Jane Eyre"; nor could Mr. Browning's finest poem pretend to attract as many admirers, even among people of taste and education, as were suddenly won by "Adam Bede." Yet our English novelists are not by any means the most cosmopolitan in the public they address. No British authors are read in France as George Sand, and Victor Hugo, and Sue, and Dumas have been read in England. It may be doubted whether any contemporary English work of fiction was read so extensively even in England as "The Mysteries of Paris," or "The Wandering Jew," or the "Count of Monte Christo." All this shows how decisively the current of public feeling at present sets in favour of prose fiction. The influence of the novelist is beginning, too, to be publicly acknowledged of late more frankly than was once the fashion. For a long time his power over society, except as a mere teller of stories and provider of easy pastime, was ignored or disputed. It was, indeed, something like the power of women in politics; an influence almost all-pervading, almost irresistible, but silent, secret, and not to be openly acknowledged. Anybody in politics who suddenly throws down the screen is sure to find Lady Teazle behind it. But it is generally thought better not to throw the screen down, and not to acknowledge that we hear the rustle of the petticoat. So it used to be with regard to the novelist. We all felt his influence, but were rather ashamed to acknowledge it. Only of late years have cabinet ministers ventured to quote from popular stories, and princes paid tribute to the genius of departed novelists.

Can this influence be turned to any direct and deliberate account? Is it given to the novelist to accomplish any definite social object, to solve, or even help towards the solution of any vexed social question? Is his mission, to use the conventional phrase, merely that which Lessing assigned to art—to delight? We are not undervaluing that mission. Taken in Lessing's sense it involves all that art needs to attempt or to accomplish. It contains a distinct social purpose; having an independent, important, elevated influence; an essential part of education, civilization, and progress. We do not ask therefore in any depreciating tone, but merely as a question interesting and appropriate, whether this is all the novelist can do? Can he without detriment to his artistic faculty set himself to solve some difficult social question, or to preach down some evil social influence? Is there any real use in producing that class of books which our readers can easily and distinctly identify if we call them, for lack of a better generic title, Novels with a Purpose? The temptation to use the novel as a political or social pamphlet, satire or sermon, is so irresistible that earnest and clever, as well as flippant and shallow men and women, are continually making efforts, more or less unsuccessful, towards this end. There is always the chance that some successful hand may yet reconcile imagination with social philosophy, and so produce a work which shall be great as a story, and likewise great as a sermon, or a social science essay, or a political pamphlet, or a tract. The books which we have named at the head of this article are grouped together for our present object, because they are all of the class which we venture to call Novels with a Purpose. In each case the author seems to have written, not because he or she felt inspired to tell a story, but because certain meditations, or convictions, or doubts, on some subject connected with human society, seemed to find convenient and emphatic expression through the medium of a work of fiction. In each of these books the philosophical critic of humanity, the social reformer, or the social accuser, stands behind the storyteller and inspires and guides his utterance. In some instances the author has a direct and distinct purpose to accomplish; in others he only expresses, vaguely perhaps, the general result of his meditations upon human life as seen in modern sociey. But in all alike the story is not the end, but only the means; and this is the general characteristic which distinguishes the class of books we now desire to notice.

* * *

. . . The greatest social difficulty in the England of to-day is not that which is created by the relations between wealth and poverty. These, however painful, still are hardly any longer perplexed. They seem at least to be brought as directly in the way towards a gradual adjustment as human enlightenment and benevolence can place them for the present. The object cannot be attained by any rapid process; but we seem to be in the right way for a gradual approach towards it. A much more complicated difficulty is found in the relations between man and woman. If we are to believe the teachings and the revelations of newspapers, sermons, pamphlets, speeches, and stories, the social life of England to-day shows scarcely any improvement in this direction. The principal difference between ourselves and our ancestors is, that they took society as they found it, and never troubled themselves on the subject; while we are self-conscious and perplexed. We see the difficulties and dangers, but we do not see the way out of them. The institution of marriage might almost seem to be, as was said, on a remarkable occasion, of constitutional government, just now upon its trial. What English people used to think Madame George Sand very wicked years ago for saying, newspapers, and books, and even sermons, not uncommonly say now. It is discovered

that throughout English social life immorality is a much more general institution than successful and satisfactory marriage. Leading newspapers have admitted grave and earnest argument to prove that the mistress is a far cheaper, more convenient, and agreeable companion than the wife. Fashionable young ladies in London are reputed to make no secret that they dress and get themselves generally up after the pattern of certain more successful sisters, whom once it was accounted a vice to know. Anonyma's portrait hangs in almost every photographer's window. Anonyma's biography is bought by thousands, and elaborately reviewed in fashionable weekly journals. Anonyma is to a certain extent the pet of the age, and is openly pleaded for by many practical moralists as a present necessity to the convenience and harmony of the world. But as no one has the courage to say that he thinks Anonyma is in herself a desirable institution, and as even her warmest admirers only profess to stand up for her as a temporary arrangement, a passing convenience, a sort of living bridge over which humanity is to cross from absolute vice into final and roseate virtue, it is but natural that we should all incline much to the consideration how the transit may be most rapidly and easily effected, and how Anonyma may be most promptly got rid of, and having served her ignoble but convenient purpose, may be pushed from her place and allowed to drop once for all into the depths of the gulf which lies between the two conditions.

Now to this theme, or at least to some topic bearing on and connected with it, some novelists who write with a purpose to-day are boldly addressing themselves. We readily admit its great importance, and quite as readily acknowledge the utter folly of ignoring it. That sense of propriety which is satisfied by simply pretending that we do not see and hear things which no human precaution can shut out from our eyes and ears, is worthy of nothing but contempt. The innocence which is ignorance becomes impossible after a certain age, and if it were not impossible it would be merely despicable. When Mrs. Norton published her "Lost and Saved" she was criticized rather sharply because of the peculiar nature of her subject. She was reminded by one reviewer that such reading was not good for the young. Her defence of herself was, we think, unassailable. It might, indeed, have been summed up in a sentence. The book was not intended to be read by the young. Its peculiar nature was to be sought for in the fact that it was not meant to be reading for the young. It was meant to teach something which cannot be taught by "Goody Two

Shoes." It was designed to expose certain social dangers which are not described in the "Seven Champions of Christendom." To condemn such a book out of hand because it was not pretty reading for school-girls, is like condemning Mill's "Political Economy" because it cannot be converted into nursery rhymes. This much is fairly to be said for the principle of Mrs. Norton's novel. Strangely enough, however, the authoress was assailed for her purpose, which deserved all praise; and generally praised for the manner in which she accomplished the purpose, wherein she seems to us to have merited but very doubtful panegyric. We admit that "Lost and Saved" is a decidedly clever book; we were about to add "for a woman," but when we remember what some women have done in our day, we feel that the qualification would be entirely out of place. It is full of vivacious writing; it has two or three characters admirably drawn; it is enriched with the most varied illustrations and experiences drawn from social life, and it has some passages which occasionally rise almost to the simple dignity of the pathetic. But although clever, it has scarcely any originality; it exhibits a common-place cleverness from beginning to end. There is no real thought in it, but only a clever imitation of thought. It differs from any ordinary young lady's story only inasmuch as the authoress has had a real and lengthened experience of the fashionable life she describes, and has the talent to turn her knowledge to effective and showy account. But the story is the old, old story over again. A beautiful young girl is ensnared by a handsome, selfish young aristocrat: she is deceived by a pretended marriage, and finally abandoned with her child. Then she suffers all the neglect, misconstruction, and harshness of a cold and cruel world, and is reduced to terrible exigencies—selling her drawings, and offering herself as a model, and the like; until at last the time comes for bringing the tale to a genial close, and she is saved by the love of a charming Italian nobleman, who marries her, and makes her wealthy and happy. There is a great deal of fashionable selfishness touched off vigorously enough in the novel; and there are some smiling, delightful, and very wicked ladies of Belgravia; and there is a tolerably vigorous use of strong poison here and there, when an inconvenient personage has to be killed-off. But while all these incidents are certainly so skilfully put together as to make an entertaining and sometimes even a brilliant story, one cannot help wondering here and there what new light on life the authoress supposed herself to be shedding, what original and valuable moral lesson she believed herself to be

expounding? For there is scarcely a page of the book which does not indicate to us that the writer feels conscious of a high purpose. What is it? That it is wrong to seduce young women by means of a pretended marriage all the world, including even the criminals themselves, will readily admit. That the man who so deceives poor Beatrice in the novel was justly punished when he swallowed a dose of poison intended for somebody else and expired in agonies, we for ourselves are quite ready to concede. That fashionable ladies do sometimes deceive their husbands, correspond with their lovers through cyphers in the *Times*, and make assignations through the medium of "that political pretence, the Ladies' Gallery in the House of Commons"; all this is possible enough. And all this—as a mere illustration of certain lives, and characters, and ways—may be read with interest. But the book is evidently designed to expound some moral, and we fail to understand what the moral is. The authoress is sometimes very hard upon that impersonal scapegoat of individual wrong-doing— Society. She seems to think that society treated Beatrice Brooke very cruelly, and that society somehow was responsible for the greater part of her misfortunes. Now, we have long been of opinion that romance has rather overdone the complaints against society. At least, it seems futile to pour out sentimental complaints, if no one will or can help society to mend its ways, or even suggest how an approach towards amendment may be essayed. Was society to be blamed because it declined to receive into its house, as governess for its children or companion for its wife, a young unmarried lady with a baby? For we fear the complaint against society in "Lost and Saved" narrows itself to this somewhat practical and homely issue. Or was society much to blame because it hesitated to believe the marvellous story about the marriage which was not a marriage after all? As a mere matter of fact, society was right in this case, and Beatrice Brooke was wrong: for society refused to believe her married, and the event proved that she was not married. A stern attorney declines to give Miss Brooke a "character" that she may become a governess or companion, and the authoress seems to think this was very cruel of the attorney; but was it not a simple act of honesty and truth? Supposing even that the attorney did not himself condemn Beatrice, would he have had any right to give her a character which omitted all notice of her "misfortune"? True, the attorney's own wife was not a spotless personage, and besides a little taste for intrigue had a taste for poisoning as well; but the attorney was not aware of these proclivities:

and even if he had been, he was not about to send his wife out as governess or companion. True, several fashionable ladies in the book are far worse than Beatrice, who, poor girl! is indeed innocent of all but amazing simplicity; but society does not and cannot stop to scrutinize everybody's private life. If it finds a palpable offender in its way, it pronounces condemnation, harshly and hastily, no doubt, in too many cases; but we do not see how the justice or injustice of the particular sentence is affected by the fact that there may be other offenders just as bad, whom society has not taken the trouble to find out. The authoress of "Lost and Saved" does not take up George Sand's early views of life, and argue boldly that love is all—marriage and proprieties nothing. Right or wrong, that view of the question would be intelligible. Society and its code might justly be assailed from this stand-point. Society does at present deliberately, theoretically, and practically regard the one error of a too loving and perhaps unselfish woman as a crime infinitely greater than a whole life passed in selfishness and meanness, in the seeking of petty, ignoble objects, in the ignoring of all the better aims of human existence, in a condition which is but legalized prostitution. An author who chooses boldly to assail society on that ground has a fair, distinct, and noble cause of quarrel. All that can be said against his pleadings is that in the present condition of English social ethics, he merely wastes his time and calls aloud to solitude. But the authoress of "Lost and Saved" by no means accepts that issue. Her complaint against society seems to be that society believed a young woman guilty of sin who really was not guilty; while society did not discover or overlooked the errors of some who were genuine sinners. We confess that we think there is a good deal to be said for society in this quarrel, and that what is fairly to be urged against it is hardly worth the saying. Nor do we think very highly of the value of that moral tendency which runs through so many modern books, and which would almost entirely relieve of responsibility the tangible individual, in order to shift the burden to the impalpable shoulders of the abstraction, Society. It is quite open to question whether much more evil than good is not done by the stern and implacable sentence with which society visits certain offences in women. It can hardly ensure any really good purpose to create a pariah class from which there is to be no redemption. Of course, the evil effect is much aggravated if the sentence is necessarily uncertain and capricious; if the scarlet letter be affixed to the bosom of the poor victim of an error, while half a dozen dexterous and callous offenders escape unbranded. But while the punishment may be far too severe, we yet would not diminish the individual responsibility. We would not teach women that they are mere puppets of man's passion, soulless creatures for whom, as for children, an absence of all individual responsibility may be claimed. It is a great pity that novelists in general delight to make their heroines such hopeless idiots, and demand for them only the kind of reverence which the Oriental acknowledges towards idiotcy. The author of a recent novel entitled "Recommended to Mercy" has had the courage to strike out something of a new path. This book (for which an apologetic preface pleads that it is a "not wholly imaginary, but somewhat hastily written tale") has the sense not to lay upon society's shoulders any of the original sin of his heroine's fall. The Helen of this novel frankly despises marriage, and is, like Dryden's Antony, all for love. She braves society, lives with the man she loves, is abandoned by him, and redeems her error of principle or judgment by a life devoted to active and unwearying benevolence. The book does not possess any sustained merit. It opens with a thrilling scene which at first leads the reader to believe that he has met with a new intellect of fresh and uncommon power; but the little burst of inspiration soon collapses and is gone, and the story degenerates into an ordinary tale of complicated mystery and extravagant sensation. Its general purport, however, seems to be a healthful insistance that a life shall be judged in its whole, and not by this or that chapter cut out and printed in letters of gold, or burned by the hands of the common hangman. It introduces us to a good many scenes whereon propriety must look astounded and shocked, and where the life of the *demi-monde*, naked and not ashamed, confronts us at almost every turn. Artistically there is not much to be said for the book. It has chiefly commended itself to our notice because here at least is one woman for whose fall beneath society's surface of smooth propriety none of the conventional excuses of romance is pityingly urged. The heroine sees and understands her risk, accepts it, suffers for her venture, and pays the penalty with a brave heart. The error was committed by herself, and her fate is redeemed by herself. We own to a much greater sympathy with this description of heroine, than with the forlorn creatures of the ordinary British novel, who are always crying "I didn't mean to do it" when the evil is done, and for whose individual errors the pitying author makes society a whipping-boy. If any real good can come of treating such social questions through the medium of fiction, the good, it seems to us, must be attained rather by endeavouring to increase than to lessen the sense of individual responsibility. The best justification for the adoption of such topics as the groundwork of novels destined for general reading assuredly is that women may perhaps be thus redeemed from the possibility of remaining in that imbecile and ignorant condition which the romancist commonly regards as innocence, and which woman is so generally encouraged to cherish as her special virtue, even by those who are so earnest in describing it as the principal cause of her ruin.

Are, then, such topics suited for fiction? Are novels with a purpose likely ever to prove successful works of art? "That," the critic may fairly say to the author, in the words of Hamlet, "you must teach me." It is yet for some man or woman of great genius to solve the problem. Experience thus far is discouraging. The novels which we have just glanced over do not warrant us in saying that the question is yet any nearer to a satisfactory solution than it was in the last generation of romance. No doubt efforts will always be made, and rightly, towards this end. Any real success thus obtained ought to be a triumph well worthy of a life's struggle. Yet nothing can be more certain than the fact that the greatest novelists have not made any such effort, or having made it, had to confess themselves defeated. We do not recollect even one great novel with a purpose. Cervantes certainly did not produce "Don Quixote" in order to smile Spain's chivalry away. Le Sage had no great moral object in view while developing the life and character of "Gil Blas." Fielding wrote with no deliberate purpose, and "Tom Jones" is immortal. Smollett had no grand social reform in his mind when he plunged into the adventures of "Peregrine Pickle"; and the world will always read of Peregrine, and Trunnion, and Pipes. Richardson, on the other hand, had a great moral purpose, and where is poor Pamela now, and who cares about her queer virtue—her "anatomical chastity," as Heine would have called it—which found such an appropriate coronal in the hardly-won marriage-ring? "Robinson Crusoe" is not a book with a moral purpose; neither is "The Vicar of Wakefield." Scott is a splendid story-teller, but his novels are not tracts. The didactic portions of "Wilhelm Meister" are insufferably tedious. Dickens has always failed where he has set out to write a book expressly for some specially philanthropic object; and the great fault which a certain class of practical persons find with Thackeray is, that he had no purpose whatever, and that his books illustrate no moral. The greatest book with a purpose produced for many years is Victor Hugo's

"Misérables"; and of that we cannot help thinking that the story was nearly crushed by the weight of the moral, while the moral went astray because it had to entrust itself to the guidance of the story. In the books which we have just been reviewing, all the old difficulties and objections revive. It is very hard indeed to serve two masters; it is especially hard to serve them both at once. Mrs. Norton's story makes sad work of her moral purpose, and reduces it indeed to inanity. Mr. Meredith's philosophic temperament interferes in every chapter with his artistic success. If the latter would really win a lasting name, he will have to choose his path more decisively. He must resolve to do justice to his own genius, and let the world go its own way, as it is very likely to do no matter how the philosopher lectures it.

We have already alluded to a peculiarity in the books just noticed, which may in many eyes seem a serious objection. To us it does not thus present itself. It is worthy of notice, because it raises a somewhat important question relating to the morale of the novelist's art. Each of the four books we have noticed is a practical protest, more or less direct and bold, against the tacit arrangement by which fiction in our day is expected to ignore all the perplexities, dangers, and sufferings springing from the relations between man and woman. We think the protest was needed. We can see no reason whatever why the novelist should be expected to shrink from taking into account one of the greatest sources of human trial, difficulty, and fall. We sympathize with the author who feels impelled to infuse more reality into his work than is necessary to make a pretty prose idyll or humorous caricature. There is no need to allow into our literature any taint of the prevailing vice of the French novel and the French drama. Nine out of every ten French novels of today, and nearly all French dramas, turn upon what is called in polite English prose illicit love. Life, indeed, as depicted by the French novelist, is occupied in an unceasing pursuit of our humble neighbour's daughter or our wealthy neighbour's wife. Now we should be sorry indeed to see this style of art imported into English fiction. If there were no other reason for objecting to it, it would be enough to say that it presents an entirely false view even of French social life. It would be as absurd to judge of the domestic life of France by the pictures which Feydeau, and Dumas *fils*, and Edmond About, and the author of "Madame Bovary," and dramatists of the Sardou school, have drawn, as it would be to conclude that every English family circle must include at least one murderer or murderess, and one maniac, because Wilkie Collins and Miss Braddon have found it convenient thus to represent the social existence of English people. Besides, the whole tone and temper of French fiction at present is corrupt and degrading. There is an absence of earnestness and of heart about it which in itself is an evil. Vice is either painted in alluring, fascinating, and sensuous colours, or it is touched off with a dash of gay and pleasant cynicism as something which sensible men and women do not think it worth their while to avoid, or to lament, or to condemn. But between this style and that of most English authors, there surely might be a middle place conveniently and effectively found. The world of most of our British novelists of the present day is really no more like the real world which we all see around us, than the pastoral life of the opera is like the actual condition of the Swiss mountain peasantry. The author of "Pendennis" complained that since the days of "Tom Jones," no great English novelist had ventured to draw a faithful picture of an ordinary young man. The complaint had sufficient justification. In Dickens's books, for instance, if a man is not simply wicked he is simply good. The heroes, and still more the heroines, walk through the world absolutely without passion of any kind that leads to temptation. Common-place young men, if they are only meant to be the heroes of the stories, pass through the worst dangers of life as unscathed as a virgin martyr of old over her red-hot ploughshares. Nay, the most extraordinary part of the matter is, that we are not even allowed to acknowledge the existence of the ploughshares, although we know well enough, every one of us, that there they are, red and glowing, and that even very good fellows who turn out decent members of society have not escaped without burnt skin from the contact. The world of fiction is still, for the most part, a nursery and bread-and-butter world. Terrible dangers no doubt are described as therein to be met; dragons, and ogres, and giants, and strangely wicked people waiting to devour the good little boys and girls. But the familiar, homely, real, seductive dangers of grown-up human life are not to be talked of there. The heroine of the modern novel seems always as if she still ought to wear short-clothes and trousers with frills round them. Even the downright bad people in most novels are not bad as in the ordinary world. They are so hopelessly bad that we feel no claim of kindred with them at all. Their wrong-doing affects us not in the least; it carries no more warning or moral to ordinary living human beings than would a diatribe against the cruelty of a tiger or the unbridled excesses of a shark. The great source of human temptation, and discord, and unhappi-

ness affects the romance people not in the least. The hero has but one desire in his life—to marry the heroine; and as he never felt any movement of passion before his eyes fell upon her, so having married her, all human weakness, all anger, envy, jealousy, selfishness, impatience, are purged thoroughly out of him, and he and his wife are rapt away in a roseate cloud from the ken of common-place mortality. The women of course have no passions at all. Even the wicked women—the harsh stepmothers, and jealous sisters, and heartless coquettes—have no pulse whatever in their frames which could throb for one moment to an improper emotion. When a girl in a modern English novel is seduced, it is always an example of the old conventional tale of the tempter and his hapless, guiltless, too confiding victim. The victim never, except in some instances of rare audacity on the part of the novelist, conduces in the slightest towards her own wrong. She is passionless, guileless, only to be wept over. Even Charles Dickens's Nancy, who, one would think, must have sounded the lowest depths, talks delightful sentiment, and melts away into refreshing Sunday-school piety and pathos. We scarcely remember in a modern English novel of note any single instance, except that of Hetty in "Adam Bede," where a seduced girl is acknowledged to have advanced one willing step, and with her eyes even half open, towards the ruin which awaited her. We feel convinced that the conventional mode of dealing with such subjects, if it has any effect whatever, has an influence for evil. There is no good end attained by trying to persuade ourselves that women are all incorporeal, angelic, colourless, passionless, helpless creatures, who are never to suspect anything, never to doubt anyone, who regard the whole end of passion of human life as ethereal, Platonic love, and orderly, parent-sanctioned wedlock. Women have especial need, as the world goes, to be shrewd, self-reliant, and strong; and we do all we can in our literature to render them helpless, imbecile, and idiotic. When Charlotte Brontë endeavoured to do otherwise, we can all recollect that a prudish scream was raised against her, and genteel virtue affected to be horrified with the authoress who drew women and girls endowed with human passion. Something of the same kind has been said against the authoress of "Adam Bede"; and there was a time when a discreet Englishwoman would have blushed to acknowledge acquaintance even with a chapter of George Sand. We are so thoroughly impressed with the conviction that art and morals alike suffer by the prudish conventionalites of our present English style, that we are inclined to welcome rebellion against it merely because it is rebellion. We are disposed to give a friendly reception to George Meredith and Mrs. Norton, were it for nothing but the mere fact that conventionality might be inclined to shriek out against them. A Parisian critic lately, when noticing some objections urged against the numerous undraped Graces, and Bacchantes, and Nymphs, and Ledas in the season's Exhibition, drily remarked that so long as vast skirts and hoops and spoon-bonnets endured, it was a relief to get a glimpse of the true outlines of womanhood under any circumstances. We own to something of a kindred feeling in regard to our English fiction. While it is coldly, stiffly, prudishly agreed to paint for us as a rule only such life as might be lectured on in a young ladies' boarding-school, we feel thankful to the novelist who has the courage to approach some of the great problems of existence, and to show us human creatures as we know them around us, tried by the old passions and quivering with the old pains.

From *The Gay Science*

E. S. Dallas

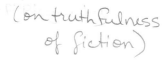

(on truthfulness of fiction)

(London: Chapman & Hall, 1866). The following excerpt is taken from chapter 17.

In speaking of the prominence of biography in current literature, I had some occasion to refer to a kindred fact, the similar prominence of prose fiction. That, however, is an incident of modern times which is important enough to demand separate notice.

It is said that within the space of thirty-five days, not long ago, no less than forty-six novels were offered for subscription in Paternoster Row—that is, nine every week for five successive weeks. The number seems to be prodigious, but in truth it gives no adequate idea of the quantity of fiction which is written and printed, published and read, year by year in this country. Not only are there heaps of stories, great and small, produced in single, in double, and in treble volumes, each one by itself, but let it be remembered that there are an infinity of periodicals, weekly and monthly, varying in price from a halfpenny to half-a-crown, which have, with scarcely an exception, each a story on foot, and some of them two. Now, making every allowance for the fact that nearly all the important novels are first published in the periodical form, and then separately, so that they figure twice in any calculation which we may make of the number of novels, it will still appear to any one who will sit still and think calmly of our fictitious literature that its bulk is enormous. There has never been anything like it before. To the literary historian it is an unparalleled phaenomenon, and brings to mind the remark of Lord Lytton, that the literature of Greece began to exist in poetical fiction and expired in prose fiction. That, however, is a gloomy view of the subject which may suggest in reply an argument parallel to that which accounts for the production of a Plutarch in the decadence of Greek authorship.

A novel is but a fictitious biography, and in the popularity of the novel we have to deal with precisely the same movement and sign of the times as we find in biography. Our interest in the private life of our fellow-men has been developed into a system, and there is nothing in the way of study which people seem now to desire so much as to peep into the house of a neighbour, to watch his ways, and to calculate the ups and downs of fortune. All the efforts of all the moralists cannot restrain the love of gossip or quench the enjoyment of scandal. There is nothing half so interesting to the great mass of mankind as a mysterious murder in a street cab, or a full-blown adultery made patent in court. Many men who care only for ideas and their practical development are apt to scorn these things, and to speak of them as Johnson spoke of green fields. Crimes are wonderfully like, and when you have seen one you have seen all. The passions are monotonous in their action, and are not to be compared for variety with our more intellectual activities. About these matters we may argue as we please; we cannot argue away the fact that it is in passions and the work of passions, not in ideas and the results of ideas, that the majority of men are interested. From year to year, and from month to month, eternally, we are interested in knowing that

John is going to marry Jane, that Smith has quarrelled with Smythe, and that Bluebeard has left all the keys with his wife. Here is a gossiping propensity in human nature which any man of sense can keep within bounds, but which none of us can eradicate. To this gossiping sense the novelist appeals. A novel may be described as gossip etherealized, family talk generalized. In the pages of a novel we can pry without shame into the secrets of our neighbour's soul, we can rifle his desk, we can read his love letters, we are present when he first kisses the maiden of his heart, we see that little maiden at her toilet preparing for the interview, we go with her to buy her simple ribands and to choose her bonnet. To transport us into new villages which we have never known, to lodge us in strange houses which we have never dreamt of, to make us at home among new circles of our fellow-creatures, to teach us to sympathize in all their little pursuits, to love their trifling gauds, to partake of their flimsy hopes and fears, to be one of them and to join in the petty fluctuations of contracted lives—this may not be a lofty occupation, nor need great genius for its perfect exercise; nevertheless, it is good healthy work, and I know not who in this generation is better employed than he who—even if he cannot boast of genius, yet with tact and clearness—widens through fiction the range of our sympathies, and teaches us not less to care for the narrow aims of small people than for the vast schemes of the great and mighty. We read the village gossip with as much concern as if the fate of the nation depended on it, and we take as much interest in a lawyer's poor daughter as if she were a peeress in her own right. Oh, happy art of fiction which can thus adjust the balance of fortune, raising the humble and weak to an equality in our hearts with the proud and the great!

While thus through all fiction the position of the private individual is in the public regard invested with a new importance, there are two especial forms of fiction in which we may note more closely the withering of the individual as an exceptional hero, and his growth as a multiplicand unit.

on Thackeray

The story by which Mr. Thackeray first became famous was entitled A Novel Without a Hero; and throughout all his works, the idea which is most constantly urged upon the reader is that we are all alike, that the differences between the extremes of humankind are very trifling, and are due rather to the force of circumstances than to force of character. He was always insisting that black is not so very black and that white is not so very white. He thus imposed upon himself as an artist Herculean toil.

When a novelist takes two characters that seem to be very nearly alike, and by the skilful laying on of touch after touch proves them to be essentially dissimilar, his method naturally tends to variety of result; each individual is different from every other; within the limits of a village he finds all the elements of a kingdom, and in the end he might realize the scholastic dream and show us legions of existences dancing on the point of a needle. But when a novelist goes upon the opposite tack, surveys each new comer, and passes him on, saying, You are like the rest of us; there is nothing new about you; how are you better than I am? I don't think that you are worse; you are very like the man I painted last—nose, eyes, and mouth; we are all medals, in fact, struck from the same die, and if on some of the medals time makes a few marks, it does not affect the resemblance—he is evidently working after a method which tends to monotony of result. And so it happened that of Thackeray, who, apart from all question as to his truth or as to his power, most certainly possessed one of the richest minds with which a novelist has ever been gifted, it was said more frequently than of men who can boast not one tithe of his genius, that he lacked variety. So it happened, also, that compelled in the last resort to reduce his characters to something like unity—compelled to return always upon one central idea, he was obliged, for the sake of variety, to go further afield in search of his materials than he otherwise would. If he had to prove the identity of personages apparently dissimilar, then to give strength to his argument not less than variety to his narrative, he ought to select these personages from as wide a range as possible, and, every man's range of personal observation being limited, he was forced back upon history. When he set out with the statement: Let any two characters be as dissimilar as possible; let the circumstances in which they are placed be as opposite as the poles, I will prove that their natures are the same, and I do not doubt that, spite of our censures, we in their places would have acted precisely as they did—he was bound to choose a goodly number of his examples from situations in life which are very different from ours, and he found that difference most easily by going back a century or two. Thus, without any special aptitude for it beyond his love of reality, he was in the exercise of his vocation driven to history, which from his point of view was but a study of the present.

* * *

Not only does Thackeray thus insist upon a

theory of character which implies in the sense of the poet the withering of the individual; we see precisely the same tendency in the school of fiction, which is the right opposite of his—what is called the sensation school. In that school the first consideration is given to the plot; and the characters must succumb to the exigencies of the plot. This is so clearly necessary that at length it has become a matter of course to find in a sensation novel a fine display of idiocy. There is always, in a sensation novel, one, or it may be two, half-witted creatures. The utility of these crazy beings is beyond belief. The things they see which nobody thought they would see, and remember which nobody thought they would remember, are even more remarkable than the things which, do what their friends will, they cannot be made to comprehend, and cannot be counted upon to repeat. Now, this species of novel is very much sneered at by persons of supposed enlightenment, and certainly it is more satisfactory to the pride of human nature to write and to read a novel of character. But I am not sure that, viewed in the abstract, such a work is either more true or more philosophical than the species of fiction in which the plot is of most importance. Suppose we attempt to state in abstract terms the difference between the two kinds of fiction.

Both profess to give us pictures of life, and both have to do with certain characters going through certain actions. The difference between the two lies solely in the relation of the characters pourtrayed to the actions described. In the novel of character man appears moulding circumstances to his will, directing the action for himself, supreme over incident and plot. In the opposite class of novel man is represented as made and ruled by circumstance; he is the victim of change and the puppet of intrigue. Is either of these views of life wholly true or wholly false? We may like the one better than the other. We may like to see men generally represented as possessed of decided character, masters of their destiny, and superior to circumstance; but is this view of life a whit more true than that which pictures the mass of men as endowed with faint characters, and as tossed hither and thither by the accidents of life, which we sometimes call fate and sometimes fortune? The art of fiction, which makes character succumb to the exigencies of plot, is just as defensible as that which breaks down incident before the weight of character. In point of fact, however, most novelists attempt to mix up the two extreme views of life, though they cannot help leaning to the one side or to the other; and the chief weakness of the plotting novels, as they are now written, is, that while they represent circumstances and incident as all-important, and characters amid the current of events as corks upon the waves, they generally introduce one character who, in violent contrast to all the others, is superior to the plot, plans the events, guides the storm, and holds the winds in the hollow of his hand. It is quite wonderful to see what one picked character can do in these stories in comparison with the others, who can do nothing. He predominates over the plot, and the plot predominates over all else. The violence of this contrast is an artistic error; but the views themselves which are thus contrasted are not necessarily false. To show man as the sport of circumstance may be a depressing view of human nature; but it is not fair to regard it as immoral nor to denounce it as utterly untrue. And whether it be true or false, still, as a popular view of life, it is one of the facts which we have to regard, when we consider either the Laureate's view, that the individual withers, or Archdeacon Hare's view, that this is an age of superficial character.

Novel-Reading

The Works of Charles Dickens
The Works of W. Makepeace Thackeray

Anthony Trollope

First published in Nineteenth Century, 5 (1879): 24-43.

In putting at the head of this paper the names of two distinguished English novelists whose tales have been collected and republished since their death, it is my object to review rather the general nature of the work done by English novelists of latter times than the contributions specially made by these two to our literature. Criticism has dealt with them, and public opinion has awarded to each his own position in the world of letters. But it may be worth while to inquire what is and what will be the result of a branch of reading which is at present more extended than any other, and to which they have contributed so much. We used to regard novels as ephemeral; and a quarter of a century since were accustomed to consider those by Scott, with a few others which, from *Robinson Crusoe* downwards, had made permanent names to themselves, as exceptions to this rule. Now we have collected editions of one modern master of fiction after another brought out with all circumstances of editorial luxury and editorial cheapness. The works of Dickens are to be bought in penny numbers; and those of Thackeray are being at the present moment reissued to the public with every glory of paper, print, and illustration, at a proposed cost to the purchaser of 33*l.* 12*s.*, for the set. I do not in the least doubt that the enterprising publishers will find themselves justified in their different adventures. The popular British novel is now so popular that it can be neither too cheap nor too dear for the market.

> Aequo pulsat pede pauperum tabernas
> Regumque turres.

I believe it to be a fact that of no English author has the sale of the works been at the same time so large and so profitable for the first half-dozen years after his death as of Dickens; and I cannot at the moment remember any edition so costly as that which is now being brought out of Thackeray's novels, in proportion to the amount and nature of the work. I have seen it asserted that the three English authors whose works are most to be found in the far-off homes of our colonists—in Australia, Canada, and South Africa—are Shakespeare, Macaulay, and Dickens. Shakespeare no doubt is there, as he is in the houses of so many of us not so far off, for the sake of national glory. Macaulay and Dickens, perhaps, share between them the thumbs of the family, but the marks of affection bestowed on the novelist will be found to be the darker.

With such evidence before us of the widespread and enduring popularity of popular novels, it would become us to make up our minds whether this coveted amusement is of its nature prone to do good or evil. There cannot be a doubt that the characters of those around us are formed very much on the lessons which are thus taught. Our girls become wives, and our wives mothers, and then old women, very much under those inspirations. Our boys grow into manhood, either nobly or ignobly partly as they may teach, and in accordance with such teaching will continue to bear their burdens gallantly or to repudiate them with cowardly sloth.

Sermons have been invented, coming down to us from the Greek Chorus, and probably from times much antecedent to the Greek dramatists, in order that the violence of the active may be controlled by the prudence of the inactive, and the thoughtlessness of the young by the thoughtfulness of the old. And sermons have been very efficacious for these purposes. There are now among us preachers influencing the conduct of many, and probably delighting the intellectual faculties of more. But it is, we think, felt that the sermon which is listened to with more or less of patience once or twice a week does not catch a hold of the imagination as it used to do, so as to enable us to say that those who are growing up among us are formed as to their character by the discourses which they hear from the pulpit. Teaching to be efficacious must be popular. The birch has, no doubt, saved many from the uttermost depth of darkness, but it never yet made a scholar. I am inclined to think that the lessons inculcated by the novelists at present go deeper than most others. To ascertain whether they be good or bad, we should look not only to the teaching but to that which has been taught,—not to the masters only but the scholars. To effect this thoroughly, an essay on the morals of the people would be necessary,—of such at least of the people as read sufficiently for the enjoyment of a novel. We should have to compare the conduct of the present day with that of past years, and our own conduct with that of other people. So much would be beyond our mark. But something may be done to show whether fathers and mothers may consider themselves safe in allowing to their children the latitude in reading which is now the order of the day, and also in giving similar freedom to themselves. It is not the daughter only who now reads her *Lord Aimworth* without thrusting him under the sofa when a strange visitor comes, or feels it necessary to have Fordyce's sermons open on the table. There it is, unconcealed, whether for good or bad, patent to all and established, the recognised amusement of our lighter hours, too often our mainstay in literature, the former of our morals, the code by which we rule ourselves, the mirror in which we dress ourselves, the *index expurgatorius* of things held to be allowable in the ordinary affairs of life. No man actually turns to a novel for a definition of honour, nor a woman for that of modesty; but it is from the pages of many novels that men and women obtain guidance both as to honour and modesty. As the writer of the leading article picks up his ideas of politics among those which he finds floating about the world, thinking out but little for himself and creating but little, so does the novelist find his ideas of conduct, and then create a picture of that excellence which he has appreciated. Nor does he do the reverse with reference to the ignoble or the immodest. He collects the floating ideas of the world around him as to what is right and wrong in conduct, and reproduces them with his own colouring. At different periods in our history, the preacher, the dramatist, the essayist, and the poet have been efficacious over others;—at one time the preacher, and at one the poet. Now it is the novelist. There are reasons why we would wish it were otherwise. The reading of novels can hardly strengthen the intelligence. But we have to deal with the fact as it exists, deprecating the evil as far as it is

an evil, but acknowledging the good if there be good.

Fond as most of us are of novels, it has to be confessed that they have had a bad name among us. Sheridan, in the scene from which we have quoted, has put into Lydia's mouth a true picture of the time as it then existed. Young ladies, if they read novels, read them on the sly, and married ladies were not more free in acknowledging their acquaintance with those in English than they are now as to those in French. That freedom was growing then as is the other now. There were those who could read unblushingly; those who read and blushed; and those who sternly would not read at all. At a much later date than Sheridan's it was the ordinary practice in well-conducted families to limit the reading of novels. In many houses such books were not permitted at all. In others Scott was allowed, with those probably of Miss Edgeworth and Miss Austen. And the amusement, though permitted, was not encouraged. It was considered to be idleness and a wasting of time. At the period of which we are speaking,—say forty years ago,—it was hardly recognised by any that much beyond amusement not only might be, but must be, the consequence of such reading. Novels were ephemeral, trivial,—of no great importance except in so far as they might perhaps be injurious. As a girl who is, as a rule, duly industrious, may be allowed now and then to sit idle over the fire, thinking as nearly as possible of nothing,—thus refreshing herself for her daily toils; as a man may, without reproach, devote a small portion of his day to loafing and lounging about his club; so in those perhaps healthier days did a small modicum of novel-reading begin to be permitted. Where now is the reading individual for whom a small modicum suffices?

And very evil things have been said of the writers of novels by their brethren in literature; as though these workers, whose work has gradually become so efficacious for good or evil, had done nothing but harm in the world. It would be useless, or even ungenerous now, to quote essayists, divines, and historians who have written of novelists as though the mere providing of a little fleeting amusement,—generally of pernicious amusement,—had been the only object in their view. But our readers will be aware that if such criticism does not now exist, it has not ceased so long but that they remember its face. The ordinary old homily against the novel, inveighing against the frivolities, the falsehood, and perhaps the licentiousness, of a fictitious narrative, is still familiar to our ears. Though we may reckon among our dearest literary possessions the pathos of this story, the humour of another, the unerring truth to nature of a third; though we may be aware of the absolute national importance to us of a *Robinson Crusoe* or *Tom Jones*, of an *Ivanhoe* or an *Esmond*; though each of us in his own heart may know all that a good novel has done for him,—still there remains something of the bad character which for years has been attached to the art.

> Quo semel est imbuta recens,
> > servabit odorem
> Testa diu.

Even though it be true that the novels of the present day have in great measure taken the place of sermons, and that they feed the imagination too often in lieu of poetry, still they are admitted to their high functions not without forebodings, not without remonstrances, not without a certain sense that we are giving up our young people into the hands of an Apollyon. Is this teacher an Apollyon; or is he better because stronger, and as moral—as an archbishop?

It is certainly the case that novels deal mainly with one subject,—that, namely, of love; and equally certain that love is a matter in handling which for the instruction or delectation of the young there is much danger. This is what the novelist does daily, and, whatever may be the danger, he is accepted. We quite agree with the young lady in the *Hunchback* who declared that Ovid was a fool. "To call that thing an art which art is none."

> No art but taketh time and pains to learn.
> Love comes with neither.

So much the novelist knows as well as Sheridan Knowles's young lady, and therefore sets about his work with descriptive rather than didactic lessons. His pupils would not accept them were he to tell them that he came into the house as a tutor in such an art. But still as a tutor he is accepted. What can be of more importance to us than to know whether we who all of us encourage such tutors in our houses, are subjecting those we love to good teaching or ill? We do not dare to say openly to those dear ones, but we confess it to ourselves, that the one thing of most importance to them is whether they shall love rightly or wrongly. The sweet, innocent, bashful girl, who never to her dearest bosom friend dares to talk upon the matter, knows that it must be so for herself. Will it be her happy future to be joined to some man who, together with the energy necessary

for maintaining her and her children, shall also have a loving heart and a sweet temper?—or shall she, through dire mistake, in this great affair of her life fall into some unutterable abyss of negligence, poverty, and heartless indifference? All this is vague, though still certain, to the girl herself. But to the mother it is in no way vague. Night and morning it must be her dearest prayer that the man who shall take her girl from her shall be worthy of her girl. And the importance to the man, though not so strongly felt, is equal. As it is not his lot to rise and fall in the world as his partner may succeed or the reverse, the image of a wife does not force itself upon his thoughts so vividly as does that of a husband on the female mind; but, as she is dependent on him for all honour, so he is on her for all happiness. It suits us to speak of love as a soft, sweet, flowery pastime, with many roses and some thorns, in which youth is apt to disport itself; but there is no father, no mother, no daughter, and should be no son, blind to the fact that, of all matters concerning life, it is the most important. That Ovid's *Art of Love* was nothing, much worse than nothing, we admit. But nevertheless the art is taught. Before the moment comes in which heart is given to heart, the imagination has been instructed as to what should accompany the gift, and what should be expected in accompaniment; in what way the gift should be made, and after what assurance; for how long a period silence should be held, and then how far speech should be unguarded.

By those who do not habitually read at all, the work is done somewhat roughly,—we will not say thoughtlessly, but with little of those precautions which education demands. With those who do read, all that literature gives them helps them somewhat in the operation of which we are speaking. History tells us much of love's efficacy, and much of the evil that comes from the want of it. Biography is of course full of it. Philosophy deals with it. Poetry is hardly poetry without it. The drama is built on it almost as exclusively as are the novels. But it is from novels that the crowd of expectant and ready pupils obtain that constant flow of easy teaching which fills the mind of all readers with continual thoughts of love. The importance of the teaching is mainly to the young, but the existence of the teaching is almost equally present to the old. Why is it that the judge when he escapes from the bench, the bishop even,—as we are told,—when he comes from his confirmation, the politician as he sits in the library of the House, the Cabinet Minister when he has a half-hour to himself, the old dowager in almost all the hours which she has to herself,—seek for distraction and reaction in the pages of a novel? It is because there is an ever-recurring delight in going back to the very rudiments of those lessons in love.

"My dear," says the loving but only half-careful mother to her daughter. "I wish you wouldn't devote so many of your hours to novel-reading. How far have you got with your Gibbon?" Whereupon the young lady reads a page or two of Gibbon, and then goes back to her novels. The mother knows that the girl is good, and does not make herself unhappy. Is she justified in her security by the goodness of the teaching? There is good and bad, no doubt. In speaking of good and bad we are not alluding to virtue and vice themselves, but to representations made of them. If virtue be made ridiculous, no description of it will be serviceable. If vice be made alluring, the picture will certainly be injurious. Sydney Smith, as far as it went, did an injury to morality at large when he declared in one of his letters that the Prime Minister of the day was "faithful to Mrs. Percival." Desiring to make the Prime Minister ridiculous, he endeavoured to throw a stone at that domesticity which the Prime Minister was supposed to cherish, and doing so he taught evil. Gay did injury to morality when he persuaded all the town to sympathise with a thief. The good teaching of a novel may be evinced as much in displaying the base as the noble, if the base be made to look base as the noble is made to look noble.

If we look back to the earlier efforts of English novel writing, the lessons taught were too often bad. Though there was a wide world of British fiction before the time of Charles the Second, it generally took the shape of the drama, and of that, whether good or bad, in its results we have at present nothing to say. The prose romances were few in number, and entertained so limited an audience that they were not efficacious for good or evil. The people would flock to see plays, where plays could be produced for them, as in London,—but did not as yet care to feed their imaginations by reading. Then came the novelists of Charles the Second, who, though they are less profligate and also more stupid than is generally supposed of them, could certainly do no good to the mind of any reader. Of our novelists, the first really known is Defoe, who, though he was born almost within the Commonwealth, did not produce his *Robinson Crusoe* till the time of George the First. *Robinson Crusoe* did not deal with love. Defoe's other stories, which are happily forgotten, are bad in their very essence. *Roxana* is an accurate sample of what a bad book may be. It relates the adventures of a woman thoroughly de-praved, and yet for the most part successful,—is intended to attract by its licentiousness, and puts off till the end the stale scrap of morality which is brought in as a salve to the conscience of the writer. Putting aside *Robinson Crusoe*, which has been truly described as an accident, Defoe's teaching as a novelist has been altogether bad. Then, mentioning only the names which are well known to us, we come first to Richardson, who has been called the inventor of the modern English novel. It certainly was his object to write of love, so that young women might be profited by what he wrote,—and we may say that he succeeded. It cannot be doubted that he had a strong conscience in his work,—that he did not write only to please, or only for money, or only for reputation, nor for those three causes combined; but that he might do good to those for whom he was writing. In this respect he certainly was the inventor of the modern English novel. That his works will ever become popular again we doubt. Macaulay expressed an exaggerated praise for *Clarissa*, which brought forth new editions,—even an abridgment of the novel; but the tone is too melancholy, and is played too exclusively on a single string for the taste of a less patient age. Nor would his teaching, though it was good a hundred and thirty years ago, be good now. Against the horrors to which his heroine was subjected, it is not necessary to warn our girls in this safer age,—or to speak of them.

Of Fielding and Smollett,—whom, however, it is unfair to bracket,—it can hardly be said that their conscience was as clear in the matter of what they wrote as was that of Richardson, though probably each of them felt that the aim he had in view was to satirise vice. Defoe might have said the same. But when the satirist lingers lovingly over the vice which he castigates so as to allure by his descriptions, it may be doubted whether he does much service to morality. Juvenal was perhaps the sternest moral censor whom the world of letters has produced; but he was, and even in his own age must have been felt to be, a most lascivious writer. Fielding, who in the construction of a story and the development of a character is supreme among novelists, is, we think, open to the same reproach. That Smollett was so the readers of *Roderick Random* and his other stories are well aware; and in him the fault was more conspicuous than in Fielding,—without the redeeming gifts. Novelists followed, one after another, whose tales were good enough to remain in our memories, though we cannot say that their work was effective for any special purpose. Among those Goldsmith was the first and the greatest. His *Vicar of Wakefield* has taken a hold on our national literature equalled perhaps by no other novel.

It is not my purpose to give a history of English ficiton. Its next conspicuous phase was that of the awe-striking mysterious romances, such as the *Mysteries of Udolpho* and the *Italian*, by which we may say no such lessons were taught as those of which we are speaking, either for good or bad. The perusal of them left little behind beyond a slightly morbid tone of the imagination. They excited no passions, and created no beliefs. There was Godwin, a man whose mind was prone to revel in the injuries which an unfortunate might be subjected to by the injustice of the world; and Mrs. Inchbald, who longed to be passionate, though in the *Simple Story*, by which we know her, she hardly rose to the height of passion; and Miss Burney, who was a Richardson in petticoats, but with a woman's closer appreciation of the little details of life. After them, or together with them, and together also with the names which will follow them, flourished the Rosa Matilda school of fiction, than which the desire to have something to read has produced nothing in literature more vapid or more mean. Up to this time there was probably no recognised attempt on the part of the novelist himself, except by Richardson, and perhaps by Miss Burney, to teach any lesson, to give out any code of morals, to preach as it were a sermon from his pulpit, as the parson preaches his sermon. The business was chance business,—the tendency being good if the tendency of the mind of the worker was good;—or bad if that was bad. Then came Miss Edgeworth and Miss Austen, who, the one in Ireland and the other in England, determined to write tales which should have a wholesome bearing. In this they were thoroughly successful, and were the first to convince the British matron that her darling girl might be amused by light literature without injury to her purity. For there had been about Miss Burney, in spite of her morality, a smell of the torchlights of iniquity which had been offensive to the nose of the ordinary British matron. Miss Edgeworth, indeed, did fall away a little towards the end of her long career; but, as we all know, a well-established character may bear a considerable strain. Miss Austen from first to last was the same,—with no touch of rampant fashion. Her young ladies indeed are very prone to look for husbands; but when this is done with proper reticence, with no flavour of gaslight, the British matron can excuse a little evil in that direction for the sake of the good.

Then Scott arose, who still towers among us as the first of novelists. He himself tells us that he was prompted to write Scotch novels by the success of Miss Edgeworth's Irish tales. "Without being so presumptuous as to hope to emulate the rich humour, pathetic tenderness, and admirable tact of my accomplished friend, I felt that something might be done for my own country of the same kind with that which Miss Edgeworth achieved for Ireland." It no doubt was the case that the success of Miss Edgeworth stimulated him to prose fiction; but we cannot but feel that there must have been present to him from first to last, through his long career of unprecedented success, a conviction of his duty as a teacher. In all those pages, in the telling of those incidents between men and women, in all those narratives of love, there is not a passage which a mother would feel herself constrained to keep from the eye of her daughter. It has been said that Scott is passionless in his descriptions of love. He moves us to our heart's core by his Meg Merrilies, his Edie Ochiltree, his Balfour of Burley, and a hundred other such characters; but no one sheds a tear over the sorrows of Flora Mac Ivor, Edith Bellenden, or Julia Mannering. When we weep for Lucy Ashton, it is because she is to be married to one she does not love, not because of her love. But in admitting this we ought to acknowledge at the same time the strain which Scott put upon himself so that he should not be carried away into the seducing language of ill-regulated passion. When he came to tell the story of unfortunate love, to describe the lot in life of a girl who had fallen,—when he created Effie Deans,—then he could be passionate. But together with this he possessed the greater power of so telling even that story, that the lesson from beginning to end should be salutary.

From Scott downwards I will mention no names till we come to those which I have prefixed to this paper. There have been English novelists by the score,—by the hundred we may say. Some of them have been very weak; some utterly inefficacious for good or evil; some undoubtedly mischievous in their tendencies. But there has accompanied their growth a general conviction that it behoves the English novelist to be pure. As on the English stage and with the English periodical press, both scurrility and lasciviousness may now and again snatch a temporary success; so it is with English fiction. We all know the writers who endeavour to be so nearly lascivious that they may find an audience among those whose taste lies in that direction. But such is not the taste of the nation at large; and these attempts at impropriety, these longings to be as bold and wicked as some of our neighbours, do not pay in the long run. While a true story of genuine love, well told, will win the heart of the nation and raise the author to a high position among the worthies of his country, the prurient dabbler in lust hardly becomes known beyond a special class. The number of those who read novels have become millions in England during the last twenty-five years. In our factories, with our artisans, behind our counters, in third-class railway carriages, in our kitchens and stables, novels are now read unceasingly. Much reaches those readers that is poor. Much that is false in sentiment and faulty in art no doubt finds its way with them. But indecency does not thrive with them, and when there comes to them a choice of good or bad, they choose the better. There has grown up a custom of late, especially among tea dealers, to give away a certain number of books among their poorer customers. When so much tea has been consumed, then shall be a book given. It came to my ears the other day that eighteen thousand volumes of Dickens's works had just been ordered for this purpose. The bookseller suggested that a little novelty might be expedient. Would the benevolent tea-dealer like to vary his presents? But no! The tradesman, knowing his businesss, and being anxious above all things to attract, declared that Dickens was what he wanted. He had found that the tea-consuming world preferred their Dickens.

In wide-spread popularity the novels of Charles Dickens have, I believe, exceeded those of any other British novelist, though they have not yet reached that open market of unrestricted competition which a book reaches only when its copyright has run out. Up to this present time over 800,000 copies of *Pickwick* have been sold in this country, and the book is still copyright property. In saying this I make no invidious comparison between Scott and Dickens. I may, indeed, be in error in supposing the circulation of *Waverly* to have been less. As it is open to any bookseller to issue Scott's novels, it would be difficult to arrive at a correct number. Our object is simply to show what has been the circulation of a popular novel in Great Britian. The circulation outside the home market has been probably as great,—perhaps greater, as American readers are more numerous than the English. Among the millions of those into whose hands these hundreds of thousands of volumes have fallen, there can hardly be one who has not received some lesson from what he has read. It may be that many dissent from the mode of telling which Dickens adopted in his stories, that they are indifferent to the stories themselves, that they question the taste, and fail to interest themselves in the melodramatic incidents and unnatural characters which it was his delight to portray. All that has no bearing on the issue which we now attempt to raise. The teaching of which we are speaking is not instruction as to taste, or art,—is not instruction as to style or literary excellence. By such lessons as Dickens taught will the young man learn to be honest or dishonest, noble or ignoble? Will the girl learn to be modest or brazen-faced? Will greed be engendered and self-indulgence? Will a taste for vicious pleasure be created? Will the young of either sex be taught to think it is a grand thing to throw off the conventional rules which the wisdom of the world has established for its guidance; or will they unconsciously learn from the author's pages to recognise the fact that happiness is to be obtained by obeying, and not by running counter to the principles of morality? Let memory run back for a few moments over those stories, and it will fail to find an immodest girl who has been made alluring to female readers, or an ill-conditioned youth whose career a lad would be tempted to envy. No ridicule is thrown on marriage constancy; no gilding is given to fictitious pleasure; no charm is added to idleness; no alluring colour is lent to debauchery. Pickwick may be softer, and Ralph Nickleby harder than the old men whom we know in the world; but the lessons which they teach are all in favour of a soft heart, all strongly opposed to hardness of heart. "What an impossible dear old duffer that Pickwick is!" a lady said to me the other day, criticising the character as I thought very correctly. Quite impossible, and certainly a duffer,—if I understand the latter phrase,—but so dear! That an old man, as he grows old, should go on loving everybody around him, loving the more the older he grows, running over with philanthropy, and happy through it all in spite of the susceptibility of Mrs. Bardell and the fallings off of Mr. Winkle! That has been the lesson taught by *Pickwick*; and though probably but few readers have so believed in Pickwick as to think that nature would produce such a man, still they have been unconsciously taught the sweetness of human love.

Such characters as those of Lord Frederick Veresopht and Sir Mulberry Hawk have often been drawn by dramatists and novelists,—too frequently with a dash of attractive fashion,—in a manner qualified to conceal in the mind of the unappreciating reader the vices of the men under the brightness of their trappings. Has any young man been made to wish that he should be such as Lord Frederick Veresopht, or should become such as Sir Mulberry Hawk? Kate Nickleby is not to us an entirely natural young woman. She lacks human life. But the girls who have read her adventures have all learnt to acknowledge the beauty and the value of modesty. It is not your daughter, my reader, who has need of such a lesson;—but think of the eight hundred thousands!

Of all Dickens's novels *Oliver Twist* is perhaps artistically the best, as in it the author adheres most tenaciously to one story, and interests us most thoroughly by his plot. But the characters are less efficacious for the teaching of lessons than in his other tales. Neither can Bill Sikes nor Nancy, nor can even the great Bumble, be credited with having been of much service by deterring readers from vice;—but then neither have they allured readers, as has been done by so many writers of fiction who have ventured to deal with the world's reprobates.

In *Martin Chuzzlewit*, in *David Copperfield*, in *Bleak House*, and *Little Dorrit*, the tendency of which I speak will be found to be the same. It is indeed carried through every work that he wrote. To whom has not kindness of heart been made beautiful by Tom Pinch, and hypocrisy odious by Pecksniff? The peculiar abominations of Pecksniff's daughters are made to be abominable to the least attentive reader. Unconsciously the girl-reader declares to herself that she will not at any rate be like that. This is the mode of teaching which is in truth serviceable. Let the mind be induced to sympathise warmly with that which is good and true, or be moved to hatred against that which is vile, and then an impression will have been made, certainly serviceable, and probably ineradicable. It may be admitted in regard to Dickens's young ladies that they lack nature. Dora, Nelly, Little Dorrit, Florence Dombey, and a host of others crowd upon our memory, not as shadows of people we have really known,—as do Jeanie Deans, for instance, and Jane Eyre;—but they have affected us as personifications of tenderness and gentle feminine gifts. We have felt each character to contain, not a woman, but something which will help to make many women. The Boythorns, Tulkinghorns, Cheerybles and Pickwicks, may be as unlike nature as they will. They are unlike nature. But they nevertheless charm the reader, and leave behind on the palate of his mind a sweet savour of humanity. Our author's heroes, down to Smike, are often outrageous in their virtues. But their virtues are virtues. Truth, gratitude, courage, and manly self-respect are qualities which a young man will be made not only to admire, but to like, by his many hours spent over these novels. And so it will be with young women as to modesty, reticence, and unselfish devotion.

The popularity of Thackeray has been very much less extended than that of Dickens, and the lessons which he has taught have not, therefore, been scattered afield so widely. Dickens, to use a now common phrase, has tapped a stratum lower in education and wealth, and therefore much wider, than that reached by his rival. The genius of Thackeray was of a nature altogether different. Dickens delighted much in depicting with very broad lines very well-known vices under impossible characters, but was, perhaps, still more thoroughly at home in representing equally well-known virtues after the same fashion. His Pinches and Cheerybles were nearer to him than his Ralph Nicklebys and his Pecksniffs. It seems specially to have been the work of Thackeray to cover with scorn the vices which in his hands were displayed in personages who were only too realistic. With him there is no touch of melodrama. From first to last you are as much at home with Barry Lyndon, the most complete rascal, perhaps, that ever was drawn, as with your wife or your private secretary, if you have one, or the servant who waits upon you daily. And when he turns from the strength of his rascals to the weaker idiosyncracies of those whom you are to love for their virtues, he is equally efficacious. Barry Lyndon was a man of infinite intellectual capacity, which is more than we can say for Colonel Newcome. But was there ever a gentleman more sweet, more lovable, more thoroughly a gentleman at all points, than the Colonel? How many a young lad has been taught to know how a gentleman should think, and how a gentleman should act and speak, by the thoughts and words and doings of the Colonel! I will not say that Barry Lyndon's career has deterred many from rascaldom, as such a career can only be exceptional; but it has certainly enticed no lad to follow it.

Vanity Fair, though not in my opinion the best, is the best known of Thackeray's works. Readers, though they are delighted, are not satisfied with it, because Amelia Sedley is silly, because Osborne is selfish, because Dobbin is ridiculous, and because Becky Sharp alone is clever and successful,—while at the same time she is as abominable as the genius of a satirist can make her. But let him or her who has read the book think of the lessons which have been left behind by it. Amelia is a true loving woman, who can love her husband even though he be selfish—loving, as a woman should love, with enduring devotion. Whatever is charming in her attracts; what is silly repels. The character of Osborne is necessary to that of Dobbin, who is one of the finest heroes ever drawn. Unselfish, brave, modest, forgiving, affectionate, manly all over,—his is just the character to teach a lesson. Tell a young man that he ought to be modest, that he ought to think more of the heart of the girl he loves than of his own, that even in the pursuit of fame he should sacrifice himself to others, and he will ridicule your advice and you too. But if you can touch his sentiment, get at him in his closet,—or perhaps rather his smoking-room,—without his knowing it, bring a tear to his eye and perhaps a throb to his throat, and then he will have learned something of that which your less impressive lecture was incapable of teaching. As for Becky Sharp, it is not only that she was false, unfeminine, and heartless. Such attributes are in themselves unattractive. But there is not a turn in the telling of the story which, in spite of her success, does not show the reader how little is gained, how much is lost, by the exercise of that depraved ingenuity.

Pendennis is an unsteady, ambitious, clever but idle young man, with excellent aspirations and purposes, but hardly trustworthy. He is by no means such a one as an anxious father would wish to put before his son as an example. But he is lifelike. Clever young men, ambitious but idle and vacillating, are met every day, whereas the gift of persistency in a young man is uncommon. The Pendennis phase of life is one into which clever young men are apt to run. The character if alluring would be dangerous. If reckless idle conceit had carried everything before it in the story,—if Pendennis had been made to be noble in the midst of his foibles,—the lesson taught would have been bad. But the picture which becomes gradually visible to the eyes of the reader is the reverse of this. Though Pendennis is, as it were, saved at last by the enduring affection of two women, the idleness and the conceit and the vanity, the littleness of the *soi-disant* great young man, are treated with so much disdain as to make the idlest and vainest of male readers altogether for the time out of love with idleness and vanity. And as for Laura, the younger of the two women by whom he is saved, she who becomes his wife,—surely no female character ever drawn was better adapted than hers to teach that mixture of self-negation, modesty and affection which is needed for the composition of the ideal woman whom we love to contemplate.

Of Colonel Newcome we have already spoken. Of all the characters drawn by Thackeray it is the most attractive, and it is so because he is a man *sans peur* and *sans reproche*. He is not a clever old man,—not half so amusing as that worldly old gentleman, Major Pendennis, with whom the reader of the former novel will have become acquainted,—but he is one who cannot lie, who cannot do a mean thing, who can wear his gown as a bedesman in the Grey Friars Hospital,—for to that he comes,—with all the honour that can hang about a judge's ermine.

Esmond is undoubtedly Thackeray's greatest work,—not only because in it his story is told with the directest purpose, with less of vague wandering than in the others,—but by reason also of the force of the characters portrayed. The one to which we will specially call attention is that of Beatrix, the young heroine of the story. Her mother, Lady Castlewood, is an elder heroine. The term as applied to the personages of a modern novel,—as may be said also of hero,—is not very appropriate; but it is the word which will best convey the intended meaning to the reader. Nothing sadder than the story of Beatrix can be imagined,—nothing sadder though it falls so infinitely short of tragedy. But we speak specially of it here, because we believe its effect on the minds of girls who read it to be thoroughly salutary. Beatrix is a girl endowed with great gifts. She has birth, rank, fortune, intellect and beauty. She is blessed with that special combination of feminine loveliness and feminine wit which men delight to encounter. The novelist has not merely said that it is so, but has succeeded in bringing the girl before us with such vivid power of portraiture that we know her, what she is, down to her shoe-ties,—know her, first to the loving of her, and then to the hating of her. She becomes as she goes on the object of Esmond's love,—and could she permit her heart to act in this matter, she too would love him. She knows well that he is a man worthy to be loved. She is encouraged to love him by outward circumstances. Indeed, she does love him. But she has decided within her own bosom that the world is her oyster, which has to be opened by her, being a woman, not by her sword but by her beauty. Higher rank than her own, greater fortune, a bigger place in the world's eyes, grander jewels, have to be won. Harry Esmond, oh, how good he is; how fit to be the lord of any girl,—if only he were a duke, or such like! This is her feeling, and this is her resolve. Then she sets her cap at a duke, a real duke, and almost gets him,—would have got him only her duke is killed in a duel before she has been made a duchess. After that terrible blow she sinks lower still in her low ambition. A scion of banished royalty comes dangling after her, and she, thinking that the scion may be restored to his royal grandeur, would fain become the mistress of a king.

It is a foul career, the reader will say; and there may be some who would ask whether such is the picture which should be presented to the eyes of a young girl by those who are anxious, not only for the amusement of her leisure hours, but also for her purity and worth. It might be asked, also, whether the Commandments should be read in her ears, lest she should be taught to steal and to murder. Beautiful as Beatrix is, attractive, clever, charming,—prone as the reader is to sympathise with Esmond in his love for this winning creature,—yet by degrees the vileness becomes so vile, the ulcered sores are so revolting, the whited sepulchre is seen to be so foul within, that the girl who reads the book is driven to say, "Not like that; not like that! Whatever fate may have in store for me, let it not be like that." And this conviction will not come from any outward suffering,—not from poverty, ill-usage, from loss of beauty or youth. No condign punishment of that easy kind is inflicted. But the vice is made to be so ugly, so heartbreaking to the wretched victim who has encouraged it, that it strikes the beholder with horror. Vice is heartbreaking to its victim. The difficulty is to teach the lesson,—to bring the truth home. Sermons too often fail to do it. The little story in which Tom the naughty boy breaks his leg, while Jack the good boy gets apples, does not do it. The broken leg and the apples do not find credence. Beatrix in her misery is believed to be miserable.

I will not appeal to further instances of good teaching among later British novelists, having endeavoured to exemplify my meaning by the novels of two masters who have appeared among us in latter days, whose works are known to all of us, and who have both departed from among us; but I think that I am entitled to vindicate the character of the British novelist generally from aspersions often thrown upon it by quoting the works of those to whom I have referred. And I am anxious also to vindicate that public taste in literature which has created and nourished the novelist's work. There still exists the judgment,—prejudice, I think I may call it,—which condemns it. It is not operative against the reading of novels, as is proved by their general acceptance. But it exists strongly in reference to the appreciation in which they are professed to be held, and it robs them of much of that high character which they may claim to have earned by their grace, their honesty, and good teaching.

By the consent of all mankind who read, poetry takes the highest place in literature. That nobility of expression, and all but divine grace of words, which she is bound to attain before she can make her footing good, is not compatible with prose. Indeed, it is that which turns prose into poetry. When that has been in truth achieved, the reader knows that the writer has soared above the earth, and can teach his lessons somewhat as a god

might teach. He who sits down to write his tale in prose makes no such attempt, nor does he dream that the poet's honour is within his reach. But his teaching is of the same nature, and his lessons tend to the same end. By either, false sentiment may be fostered, false notions of humanity may be engendered, false honour, false love, false worship may be created; by either, vice instead of virtue may be taught. But by each equally may true honour, true love, true worship, and true humanity be inculcated; and that will be the greatest teacher who will spread such truth the widest. At present, much as novels, as novels, are sought and read, there still exists an idea,—a feeling which is very prevalent,—that novels at their best are but innocent. Young men and women,—and old men and women too,—read more of them than they read of poetry because such reading is easier; but they read them as men eat pastry after dinner,—not without some inward conviction that the taste is vain if not vicious. We think that it is not vicious or vain,—unless indeed the employment be allowed to interfere with the graver duties of life.

A greater proportion of the teaching of the day than any of us have as yet acknowledged comes, no doubt, from the reading of these books. Whether the teaching be good or bad, that is the case. It is from them that girls learn what is expected from them, and what they are to expect when lovers come; and also from them that young men unconsciously learn what are, or should be, or may be, the charms of love. Other lessons also are taught. In these days, when the desire to be honest is pressed so hard on the heel by the ambition to be great, in which riches are the easiest road to greatness; when the temptations to which men are subjected dull their eyes to the perfected iniquities of others; when it is so hard for a man to decide vigorously that the pitch which so many are handling will defile him if it be touched,—men's conduct will be actuated much by that which is from day to day depicted to them as leading to glorious or inglorious results. The woman who is described as having obtained all that the world holds to be precious by lavishing her charms and caresses unworthily and heartlessly, will induce other women to do the same with theirs; as will she who is made interesting by exhibition of bold passion teach others to be spuriously passionate. The young man who in a novel becomes a hero,—perhaps a member of Parliament or almost a Prime Minister,—by trickery, falsehood, and flash cleverness, will have as many followers in his line as Jack Sheppard or Macheath will have in theirs; and will do, if not as wide, a deeper mischief.

To the novelist, thinking of all this, it must surely become a matter of deep conscience how he shall handle those characters by whose words and doings he hopes to interest his readers. It may frequently be the case that he will be tempted to sacrifice something for effect; to say a word or two here, or to draw a picture there, for which he feels that he has the power, and which, when spoken or drawn, would be alluring. The regions of absolute vice are foul and odious. The savour of them, till custom has hardened the palate and the nose, is disgusting. In these he will hardly tread. But there are outskirts on these regions in which sweet-smelling flowers seem to grow and grass to be green. It is in these border-lands that the danger lies. The novelist may not be dull. If he commit that fault, he can do neither harm nor good. He must please; and the flowers and the soft grass in those neutral territories sometimes seem to give too easy an opportunity of pleasing!

The writer of stories must please, or he will be nothing. And he must teach, whether he wish to teach or not. How shall he teach lessons of virtue, and at the same time make himself a delight to his readers? Sermons in themselves are not thought to be agreeable; nor are disquisitions on moral philosophy supposed to be pleasant reading for our idle hours. But the novelist, if he have a conscience, must preach his sermons with the same purpose as the clergyman, and must have his own system of ethics. If he can do this efficiently, if he can make virtue alluring and vice ugly, while he charms his reader instead of wearying him, then we think that he should not be spoken of generally as being among those workers of iniquity who do evil in their generation. So many have done so, that the English novelist as a class may, we think, boast that such has been the result of their work. Can any one, by search through the works of the fine writers whose names we have specially mentioned,—Miss Edgeworth, Miss Austen, Scott, Dickens, and Thackeray,—find a scene, a passage, or a word that could teach a girl to be immodest or a man to be dishonest? When men in their pages have been described as dishonest, or women as immodest, has not the reader in every instance been deterred by the example and its results? It is not for the novelist to say simply and baldly: "Because you lied here, or were heartless there; because you, Lydia Bennet, forgot the lessons of your honest home, or you, Earl Leicester, were false through your ambition, or you, Beatrix, loved too well the glitter of the world, therefore you shall be scourged with scourges either here or hereafter"; but it is for him to show, as he carries on his tale, that his Lydia, or his Leicester, or his Beatrix, will be dishonoured in the estimation of all by his or her vices. Let a woman be drawn clever, beautiful, attractive, so as to make men love her and women almost envy her; and let her be made also heartless, unfeminine, ambitious of evil grandeur, as was Beatrix,—what danger is there not in such a character! To the novelist who shall handle it, what peril of doing harm! But if at last it has been so handled that every girl who reads of Beatrix shall say, "Oh, not like that! let me not be like that!" and that every youth shall say: "Let me not have such a one as that to press to my bosom,—anything rather than that!" Then will not the novelist have preached his sermon as perhaps no other preacher can preach it?

Very much of a novelist's work, as we have said above, must appertain to the intercourse between young men and young women. It is admitted that a novel can hardly be made interesting or successful without love. Some few might be named in which the attempt has been made, but even in them it fails. *Pickwick* has been given as an exception to the rule, but even in *Pickwick* there are three or four sets of lovers whose amatory flutterings give a softness to the work. In this frequent allusion to the passion which most strongly stirs the imagination of the young, there must be danger, as the novelist is necessarily aware. Then the question has to be asked, whether the danger may not be so handled that good shall be the result, and to be answered. The subject is necessary to the novelist, because it is interesting to all; but as it is interesting to all, so will the lessons taught respecting it be widely received. Every one feels it, has felt it, or expects to feel it,—or else regrets it with an eagerness which still perpetuates the interest. If the novelist, therefore, can so treat his subject as to do good by his treatment of it, the good done will be very wide. If a writer can teach politicians and statesmen that they can do their work better by truth than by falsehood, he does a great service; but it is done in the first instance to a limited number of persons. But if he can make young men and women believe that truth in love will make them happy, then, if his writings be popular, he will have a very large class of pupils. No doubt that fear which did exist as to novels came from the idea that this matter of love would be treated in an inflammatory and unwholesome manner. "Madam," says Sir Anthony in the play, "a circulating library in a town is an evergreen tree of diabolical knowledge. It blossoms through the year; and, depend upon it, Mrs. Malaprop, they who are so fond of handling the leaves, will long for the fruit at last." Sir Anthony, no doubt, was right. But he takes it for granted that longing for the fruit is an evil. The novelist thinks differently, and believes that the honest love of an honest man is a treasure which a good girl may fairly hope to win, and that, if she can be taught to wish only for that, she will have been taught to entertain only wholesome wishes.

There used to be many who thought, and probably there are some who still think, that a girl should hear nothing of love till the time comes in which she is to be married. That was the opinion of Sir Anthony Absolute and of Mrs. Malaprop. But we doubt whether the old system was more favourable to purity of manners than that which we have adopted of late. Lydia Languish, though she was constrained by fear of her aunt to hide the book, yet had *Peregrine Pickle* in her collection. While human nature talks of love so forcibly, it can hardly serve our turn to be silent on the subject. "Naturam expelles furca, tamen usque recurret." There are countries in which it has been in accordance with the manners of the upper classes that the girl should be brought to marry the man almost out of the nursery,—or rather, perhaps, out of the convent,—without having enjoyed any of that freedom of thought which the reading of novels and poetry will certainly produce; but we do not know that the marriages so made have been thought to be happier than our own.

Among English novels of the present day, and among English novelists, a great division is made. There are sensational novels, and anti-sensational; sensational novelists, and anti-sensational; sensational readers, and anti-sensational. The novelists who are considered to be anti-sensational are generally called realistic. The readers who prefer the one are supposed to take delight in the elucidation of character. They who hold by the other are charmed by the construction and gradual development of a plot. All this we think to be a mistake,— which mistake arises from the inability of the inferior artist to be at the same time realistic and sensational. A good novel should be both,—and both in the highest degree. If a novel fail in either, there is a failure in art. Let those readers who fancy that they do not like sensational scenes, think of some of those passages from our great novelists which have charmed them most,—of Rebecca in the castle with Ivanhoe; of Burley in the cave with Morton; of the mad lady tearing the veil of the expectant bride in *Jane Eyre*; of Lady Castlewood as, in her indignation, she explains to the Duke of Hamilton Harry Esmond's right to be present at the marriage of his Grace with Beatrix. Will any one say that the authors of these passages have sinned in being over-sensational? No doubt a string of horrible incidents, bound together without truth in details, and told as affecting personages without character,—wooden blocks who cannot make themselves known to readers as men or women,— does not instruct, or amuse, or even fill the mind with awe. Horrors heaped upon horrors, which are horrors only in themselves, and not as touching any recognised and known person, are not tragic, and soon cease even to horrify. Such would-be tragic elements of a story may be increased without end and without difficulty. The narrator may tell of a woman murdered, murdered in the same street with you, in the next house; may say that she was a wife murdered by her husband, a bride not yet a week a wife. He may add to it for ever. He may say that the murderer burnt her alive. There is no end to it. He may declare that a former wife was treated with equal barbarity, and that the murderer when led away to execution declared his sole regret to be that he could not live to treat a third after the same fashion. There is nothing so easy as the creation and cumulation of fearful incidents after this fashion. If such creation and cumulation be the beginning and the end of the novelist's work,—and novels have been written which seem to be without other attraction,—nothing can be more dull and nothing more useless. But not on that account are we averse to tragedy in prose fiction. As in poetry, so in prose, he who can deal adequately with tragic elements is a greater artist, and reaches a higher aim, than the writer whose efforts never carry him above the mild walks of everyday life. The *Bride of Lammermoor* is a tragedy throughout in spite of its comic elements. The life of Lady Castlewood is a tragedy. Rochester's wretched thraldom to his mad wife in *Jane Eyre* is a tragedy. But these stories charm us, not simply because they are tragic, but because we feel that men and women with flesh and blood, creatures with whom we can sympathise, are struggling amidst their woes. It all lies in that. No novel is anything, for purposes either of comedy or tragedy, unless the reader can sympathise with the characters whose names he finds upon the page. Let the author so tell his tale as to touch his reader's heart and draw his reader's tears, and he has so far done his work well. Truth let there be,—truth of description, truth of character, human truth as to men and women. If there be such truth, I do not know that a novel can be too sensational.

Contributors

Margaret Blom...*University of British Columbia*
Allan C. Christensen...*Rome, Italy*
Michael Collie...*York University*
Philip B. Dematteis ....*Columbia, South Carolina*
Patrick Dunae...*British Columbia Provincial Archives*
George H. Ford ....*University of Rochester*
Lois Josephs Fowler ....*Carnegie-Mellon University*
William E. Fredeman.....................................*University of British Columbia*
Edgar F. Harden...*Simon Fraser University*
Helen Heineman ....*Framingham State College*
Patrick Kelly...*University of Saskatchewan*
Juliet McMaster ....*University of Alberta*
Robert L. Meredith ....*Atlanta, Georgia*
John Merritt.......................................*West Vancouver, British Columbia*
Ira B. Nadel ....*University of British Columbia*
Norman Page ....*University of Alberta*
Herbert J. Rosengarten ....*University of British Columbia*
Daniel R. Schwarz...*Cornell University*
Patrick Scott...*University of South Carolina*
Elton E. Smith ....*University of South Florida*
Roy B. Stokes.......................................*University of British Columbia*
Joseph Wiesenfarth...*University of Wisconsin*
Tom Winnifrith ....*University of Warwick*
George J. Worth...*University of Kansas*
Edgar Wright ....*Laurentian University*

Cumulative Index

Dictionary of Literary Biography, Volumes 1-21
Dictionary of Literary Biography Yearbook, 1980, 1981, 1982
Dictionary of Literary Biography Documentary Series, Volumes 1-3

Cumulative Index

DLB before number: *Dictionary of Literary Biography*, Volumes 1-21
Y before number: *Dictionary of Literary Biography Yearbook*, 1980, 1981, 1982
DS before number: *Dictionary of Literary Biography Documentary Series*, Volumes 1-3

C

E

G

H

Cumulative Index

T

U

V

W

Y

Z